INVESTMENTS

INVESTMENTS
INTRODUCTION TO ANALYSIS AND PLANNING

BERNARD J. WINGER
RALPH R. FRASCA

University of Dayton

Merrill, an imprint of
Macmillan Publishing Company
New York

Collier Macmillan Canada, Inc.
Toronto

Maxwell Macmillan International Publishing Group
New York   Oxford   Singapore   Sydney

Editor: Caroline Carney

Production Editor: Ben Ko

Art Coordinator: Raydelle M. Clement

Production Buyer: Janice E. Wagner

Text Designer: Anne Daly

Cover Designer: Russ Maselli

This book was set in Serifa Light.

Macmillan Publishing Company
886 Third Avenue, New York, NY 10022

Collier Macmillan Canada, Inc.

Library of Congress Catalog Card Number: 90-53481
International Standard Book Number: 0-675-21279-0

Printing: 1 2 3 4 5 6 7 8 9   Year: 1 2 3 4

To our families

Preface

Our purpose in writing *Investments: Introduction to Analysis and Planning* is to help readers make intelligent and practical investment decisions. The text can be used successfully in the first investments course offered at four-year colleges or two-year institutions and in professional certification and continuing education programs. Our conversational tone and the publisher's excellent use of graphics and other visual presentations make the book lively and readable.

IMPORTANT CHARACTERISTICS OF THE TEXT

The text has certain features that most potential adopters like to consider before making a selection. The important characteristics are explained briefly.

Decision-Making Perspective

The text focuses on individual investment decisions. Within this framework, the text has a greater analytical—rather than descriptive—tone. However, the analytical methods are designed for the capabilities of intended users. Both the math and statistics are elementary and fit the first courses in practically all college curricula. (The text does not contain theorems or proofs, which are more appropriate in advanced classes.) Actually, an analytical approach works well in so-called lower-level courses because it is lively and maintains student interest.

Applications Orientation

The text features numerous applications of investment theory and strategies. These are contained in boxed features and chapter-end items, which the authors selected for timeliness and connection to topics discussed. This latter category includes *Review Questions, Problems and Projects,* and *Case Analyses.* Each chapter has two cases designed to illustrate the practical problems in investing. In addition, the cases and problems offer data manipulation exercises and analytical practice. The review questions help students identify important topics and test their comprehension, while the projects (at least two to a chapter) indicate certain activities that bring students in contact with members of the investment community, or direct them towards helpful library references.

A Planning Approach

Investment planning focuses upon goal setting, vehicle selection, performance evaluation with respect to stated goals, and portfolio modifications. Most successful investors follow this path, rather than one of periodic efforts to achieve a super return. While speculative activities are often illustrated, their potential risks are also clearly indicated along with their potential returns.

Focus on Globalization, Ethical Issues, and Technology

In common with other business subjects, investments must recognize the growing importance of globalization, ethical issues, and technology. The text achieves this goal in various ways. Globalization arises in international investing, a topic treated at considerable length in Chapter 20. Political risks of foreign investing are discussed in Chapter 4, and the use of currency futures to hedge exchange-rate risk is explained in Chapter 14. Also, the increasing influence of organized exchanges abroad is noted in Chapter 2.

Ethical issues related to investments often have dominated the news in recent years. In the main, we feature issues and events within the context of boxed essays, such as one on binding arbitration. However, direct in-text discussion occurs throughout. Instructors will find numerous opportunities to raise ethical issues for class discussion.

Clearly, investing has felt the impact of changes in information technology. Investors can utilize their personal computers to gather financial data, perform sophisticated analyses, and even execute trades. Chapter 2 presents this technology in detail.

CHANGES IN THE SECOND EDITION

A good investments text must change because its subject matter is in a constant state of flux. We have responded to market changes by revising both topical coverage and relative emphasis. Our concern in the first edition with the importance of goal setting seems to have been timely in light of the increasing use of asset allocation models, which require a clear specification of goals. In the aftermath of the crash of October 19, 1987, investors have turned in growing numbers to asset allocation strategies, and we retain and, indeed, reinforce our emphasis upon setting and prioritizing goals. This is noted clearly in Chapter 1 and referred to at numerous points throughout the text.

Changes in the second edition are overall in nature and specific-item directed. Each is explained in the following sections.

Overall Changes

There are three major overall changes designed to increase the text's effectiveness.

Enhanced Integration of Risk-Return Analysis.   This edition continues our attempt to integrate risk-return analysis with topical coverage throughout the text. Concepts introduced in the chapters in Part I are utilized constantly in later chapters. This treatment results in a higher level of analytical analysis and avoids the tedium of excessive descriptive material.

Increased Emphasis Upon Investment Strategies.   Investment strategies—such as market timing, dollar-cost averaging, and portfolio weighting—are given greater emphasis. Moreover, Chapter 19, dealing with portfolio management, has been designed for use early in the course. If instructors prefer an expanded treatment of strategies before they discuss investment vehicles, they can easily assign the chapter to follow Chapter 4.

Expanded Chapter-End Items.   The number of chapter-end items has been doubled, going from approximately 230 items in the first edition to 466 items in this edition. This substantial increase is designed to augment the above two changes and also to increase the real-world character of the text.

Specific Changes

Specific changes are detailed below.

1. Chapter 1 notes and discusses the increased importance of private placements.
2. Chapter 1 has been reduced in length and the box on IPOs has been deleted.
3. Chapter 2 has been expanded substantially with broadened coverage of organized exchanges, sources of information (including computer sources), and dividend reinvestment plans.
4. The discussion of return correlations is increased and a brief appendix is added to Chapter 4 to illustrate a beta calculation using historical data.
5. The discussion of risk sources is broadened: there is more material on reinvestment and rollover risks, economic performance risk, and event risk (new to this edition).
6. Chapter 6 discusses recent changes in borrowing on life insurance policies in relation to liquidity management.
7. New material on PIK bonds and PIK preferred appears in Chapters 7 and 11 and is featured in chapter-end case analyses.
8. Chapters 3 and 9 broaden the topic of equity valuation. Multiple growth rates are considered in the dividend model and different methods of valuation (asset-based approaches) are presented.

9. Ratio analysis is expanded, including a discussion of screening with filters.
10. Technical analysis in Chapter 10 includes a new topic—price momentum—and added discussion on the use of moving averages.
11. The growing popularity of convertible issues is noted in Chapter 12, with expanded coverage of convertibles dealing with their price volatility and the problem of early calls.
12. Arbitrage strategies receive considerably greater coverage, both in relation to the use of index options (Chapter 13) and index futures (Chapter 14). Arbitrage is also considered in a chapter-end case.
13. There is expanded discussion of hedging strategies utilizing futures, which includes a presentation of hedge ratios.
14. New material on CMO REITS is added, and the recent problems with limited partnerships are noted and discussed.
15. Chapter 17, real estate analysis, has been broadened considerably by including a discussion of property valuation methods. These also appear in a chapter-end case.
16. Returns on tangibles are now discussed in Chapter 18, rather than Chapter 3, which makes for a more compact treatment.
17. Chapter 19 updates portfolio management to include current asset-allocation techniques and portfolio insurance.

PEDAGOGICAL FEATURES

We and the professionals at Macmillan have designed the text to be very teachable. Along with an informal writing style and the important characteristics noted above, adopters should find that the following items also enrich the teaching-learning environment.

Relevant and Interesting Boxed Items

Boxed items both heighten student interest and show investment activities in a practical setting. For example, a box in Chapter 2 focuses on the activities of a specialist on the floor of the New York Stock Exchange providing useful information in a way most enjoy. However, we have avoided the sensationalism that one often finds in certain popular magazines. In fact, the boxes focus more on the conservative side of investing.

Strong Chapter-End Materials

As noted above, each chapter contains two cases, at least two student projects, and numerous review questions and problems. This comprehensive coverage gives instructors a wide range of assignment material.

Key Term Matching Quiz

The key terms in each chapter are presented in the form of a matching quiz, allowing students an opportunity to self test their comprehension. A number of first edition adopters noted particular enthusiasm for this feature.

A Flexible Organization

Part I presents an overview of the investment setting and covers return and risk analysis. Its four chapters serve as a preparation for the rest of the text. While we cover debt instruments next (Chapter 5, 6, and 7), users could just as easily follow with common stock investing (Chapter 8, 9, and 10). The presentation choice for the remaining ten chapters is entirely flexible. As noted earlier, portfolio analysis in Chapter 19 can be covered after Chapter 4. Of course, any chapter can be either deleted or assigned as supplemental reading.

Learning Objectives and Chapter Outline

Each chapter begins with an outline and a set of learning objectives. The outline helps students visualize a chapter as a whole entity and the objectives focus his or her attention on critical topics.

High-Impact Graphics

The text contains numerous graphics, making student comprehension easier and more interesting. There are both tables and figures (all are called exhibits, for ease of discussion). Many of the exhibits contain brief descriptions or highlight points, making them self-contained learning tools.

Helpful Appendixes

There is an appendix to Chapter 4 that illustrates a beta calculation from historical data. Also, Chapter 19 has an appendix that provides an expanded discussion of the capital asset pricing model. The appendix at the end of the text provides future and present values of single payments and annuities.

ANCILLIARY MATERIALS

Instructors can use a number of ancilliary materials as course aids.

Instructor's Manual

An instructor's manual, prepared by the authors, is available. It contains a detailed topical outline keyed to the text's exhibits, which helps instructors in planning lectures. The IM also contains comprehensive solutions to all chapter-end items, particularly the cases where additional insights are offered.

Test Bank

The authors have also prepared a comprehensive test bank that contains over 600 multiple-choice questions and over 700 true-false questions. The questions have been written to test analytical and interpretative skills as well as material comprehension. Many questions are problem oriented, requiring calculations and analysis. The test bank is also available on disks, which are very easy to use. Tests can be prepared in minutes with virtually no computer background or previous experience.

ACKNOWLEDGMENTS

The dedication and efforts of many people are needed to complete a major textbook, and it is our pleasure to acknowledge those contributions. We are grateful to Macmillan Publishing for engaging the services of many excellent reviewers for this edition: Edward J. Pyatt, Hampton University; Cheryl A. McGaughy, Angelo State University; David J. Crockett, Metropolitan State College; Howard R. Whitney, Franklin University; Joseph Brandt, Incarnate World College; James R. Marchand, Radford University; and Joe B. Copeland, University of North Alabama.

We also wish to thank again those reviewers who contributed to the success of the first edition: Donald Sorenson, University of Wisconsin — Whitewater; Cecil Bigelow, Mankato State University; A. Frederic Banda, University of Akron; Jim Boyd, Louisiana State University; Ray Fernandez, Miami-Dade Community College; and Davis Upton, Texas Tech University.

We also wish to thank our colleagues at the University of Dayton and in the Dayton-Cincinnati area for their help and support. Special thanks are due Carl Chen, Chairman of the Department of Economics and Finance at the University of Dayton, George Euskirchen (Thomas More College), Thomas E. Davidson (Thomas E. Davidson and Associates), and Patricia Decker (Fairleigh Dickinson).

Finally, we are deeply indebted to the staff at Macmillan Publishing for their efforts in helping us produce a successful text. Ben Ko (production editor) and Rebecca Money Bobb (copyeditor) are not only very skilled professionals but personable individuals who create an enjoyable work environment. Finally, we wish to thank Caroline Carney (editor), who assisted considerably in the final stages of the text's development.

Contents

PART ONE
Understanding the Investment Process 1

CHAPTER ONE
Investors and Investments: An Overview 3

INVESTOR PROFILES AND GOALS 4

Investor Attitudes 4
Goals: The Reasons for Investing 6
Investment Professionals 7

THE CONCEPT OF INVESTMENT 10

Debt Instruments 10
Common Stocks 12
Preferred Stocks 12
Leverage-Inherent Securities 13
Pooling Arrangements 14
Real Estate and Other Tangibles 14
Portfolio Management 14
Steps in Investment Planning 14

HOW INVESTMENTS ARE CREATED 15

Financial Facilitation Versus Financial Intermediation 16
Market Participants 20

BASIC INCOME TAX CONSIDERATIONS 21

A Progressive Rate Structure 21
Tax Strategies 23

BOXES

How About a Career in Investments? 8
Five Common Mistakes of Beginning Investors 16

CHAPTER TWO
The Investment Environment 31

PRIMARY AND SECONDARY MARKETS 32

Organized Exchanges 32
Order Execution on the NYSE 34
The Over-the-Counter Market 35

SELECTING A STOCKBROKER 38

Types of Stockbrokerage Firms 38
Factors to Consider in Selecting a Broker 40
Regulation of Securities Markets 41

OPENING AN ACCOUNT AND MAKING TRANSACTIONS 44

Kinds of Accounts 44
Initiating a Position 46
Placing Orders 48

FINDING INVESTMENT INFORMATION 49

Company Sources 49
Government Sources 50
Investment Advisory Services 51
Newspapers and Magazines 51
Computer Data Sources 56
Academic Journals 56

APPENDIX A: UNDERSTANDING MARKET INDEXES 63

APPENDIX B: POPULAR INVESTMENT INFORMATION SOURCES 66

BOXES

A Day in the Life of a Specialist on the NYSE 36
What is Binding Aribitration? 43
Using the Personal Computer in Investing 54

CHAPTER THREE
Investment Return: Measurement and Strategies 71

THE HOLDING PERIOD RETURN 72

Current Return 72
Future Return 74
Measuring the HPR Over Time 75

TIME VALUE OF MONEY 77

Determining Future Values 77
Determining Present Values 81
Finding Rates of Return or Annuity Amounts 83
The Power of Compounding 84

HISTORICAL INVESTMENT RETURNS 86

Returns from Key Financial Assets 86
The Accumulation of Wealth 90
Risk Premiums 92

BASIC INVESTMENT STRATEGIES 93

Long-Term Investing 93
Short-Term Trading 94
Exploiting Economic Cycles 94
Defending Against Potential Losses 95

BOXES

How Important Are Dividends to Investors? 73
Isn't It Time for a Truth in Giving and Wagering Act? 85
October 19, 1987: A Day of Financial Infamy 88

CHAPTER FOUR
Measuring Investment Risk 101

INDIVIDUAL ASSET RISK 102

The Expected Return 102
Dispersion of Returns 103
Historical Risk Statistics on Key Financial Assets 104

PORTFOLIO RISK 105

Return Correlations 107

Random Diversification 108
Purposive Diversification 110
Using the Beta Concept 112

SOURCES OF RISK 115

Changes in the Economic Environment 115
Characteristics of the Security Issuer 119
Other Sources of Risk 120

APPENDIX: ANALYSIS OF HISTORICAL RETURNS 127

BOXES

Do Investors Make Adequate Risk-Return Assessments? 106
Risk and Time: Are They Related? 117

PART TWO
Investing in Bonds and Other Debt Instruments 130

CHAPTER FIVE
Risk and Return with Debt Instruments 133

RETURN WITH DEBT INSTRUMENTS 134

Cash Flows 134
Calculating Yields 137
What Investors Expect in an Interest Rate 142

RISKS WITH DEBT INSTRUMENTS 144

Bond Prices and Changing Interest Rates 144
Determining Interest-Rate Risk 148
The Reinvestment Problem 152
Default Risk 153

HISTORICAL INTEREST-RATE VOLATILITY 154

Short- and Long-Term Rates 156
Forecasting Interest Rates 160

BOXES

Why Have Real Rates of Interest Been So High? 146
Is There a Message in the Yield Curve? 158

CHAPTER SIX
Investing in Debt Instruments to Meet Liquidity Needs 167

LIQUIDITY MANAGEMENT 168

Why Hold Liquid Assets? 168
Financial Institutions 171

ALTERNATIVE TYPES OF LIQUID ASSETS 174

Accounts at Financial Institutions 174
U.S. Treasury Securities 178
Non-Treasury-Issued Securities 181
Money Market Mutual Funds 181

BORROWING AND LIQUIDITY MANAGEMENT 183

Avoiding Future Borrowing 183
Frequently Used Sources of Investment Credit 184

BOXES

Where to Put Your Short-Term Funds 173
Pitfalls in Liquidity Management 186

CHAPTER SEVEN
Investing in Debt Instruments for the Long Term 193

CORPORATE BONDS 194

Bondholders' Rights   194
Special Bond Features   201
The Mechanics of Buying Corporate
   Bonds   204

**U.S. TREASURY AND AGENCY
   ISSUES   206**

Treasury Debt   207
Collateralized Treasury Receipts
   208
Federal Agency Bonds   211

MUNICIPAL BONDS   215

The Income Tax Advantage   215
Kinds of Municipal Bonds   216
Default Risk in Municipal Bonds
   217

BOXES

Pity the Poor Bondholder, Or a
   Lesson in Applied Financial
   Theory   204
If You See a Liability—Securitize It!
   213

**PART THREE
Investing in Equities
226**

CHAPTER EIGHT
Return and Risk in
Common Stocks   229

**COMMON STOCK
   CHARACTERISTICS   230**

Stockholders' Rights   230
Opportunities in Common Stocks
   234
Reading Stock Quotations   236

**RISKS IN COMMON STOCKS
   238**

Liquidity and Inflation Risks   238
Firm-Specific and Industry Risks
   238

Market Risk   241

**ESTIMATING A STOCK'S
   REQUIRED RETURN   242**

The CAPM and the SML   242
Using the SML   247

**DETERMINING EXPECTED
   RETURNS   248**

The Earnings Approach   248
The Dividend Approach   251
Valuation with Multiple Growth
   Rates   252
Other Valuation Methods   253

BOXES

Some Information About Dividends
   235
Where to Look for Value   240

CHAPTER NINE
Fundamental Analysis of
Common Stocks   261

**FINANCIAL STATEMENTS
   262**

The Balance Sheet   262
The Income Statement   265

**EVALUATING FINANCIAL
   PERFORMANCE   268**

Measuring Balance Sheet Strength
   268
Measuring Earnings Strength   271
Was NCR an Undervalued Security?
   274
Using Ratio Analysis   277

**EVALUATING THE ECONOMY
   AND THE INDUSTRY   279**

Brief History of U.S. Cycles   279
Forecasting Economic Cycles   280
Industry Analysis   284

BOXES

Should PSRs Replace P/E Ratios?
   276

If You Think Economic Forecasting
   Is Chaotic, You Could Be Right
   282

CHAPTER TEN
Technical Analysis, Market
Timing, and Efficient
Markets   295

**USING PRESSURE INDICATORS
   296**

Who is Buying or Selling?   296
Interpreting Market Activity   300
Investor Psychology   302
Evaluating Pressure Indicators
   305

**USING CHARTS AND GRAPHS
   309**

Constructing Graphs   309
Interpreting Graphs   309
Evaluating the Use of Graphs   313

EFFICIENT MARKETS   314

What Are Efficient Markets?   315
Implications of the EMH   318

BOXES

Watch the Super Bowl and Be a
   Super Forecaster   308
Do Insiders Really Beat the Market?
   And, Can Outsiders Following
   Insiders Do As Well?   316
Screening for Big Winners   319

CHAPTER ELEVEN
Investing in Preferred
Stocks   329

**PREFERRED STOCK
   CHARACTERISTICS   330**

Basic Stockholder Rights   331
Other Features of Preferred Stock
   334

**PREFERRED STOCK RETURNS
   335**

Straight Preferreds   336
Adjustable Rate Preferred Stock
    339

RISKS IN PREFERRED STOCKS 342

Interest Rate Risk   342
Default Risk   344

BOXES

Hungry for Some Dividend Sweets?
    How About a Preferred Dividend
    Roll?   335
Buying Preferred Stock at Dutch
    Auction   340

PART FOUR
Leverage-Inherent Investments   352

CHAPTER TWELVE
Warrants, Rights, and Convertibles   355

OPTION VALUE 356

Option Features   357
Options and Leverage   358
Determinants of Market Value   359
Predicting Market Values   360

WARRANTS AND RIGHTS 361

Characteristics of Warrants   363
Characteristics of Rights   366

CONVERTIBLES 367

Characteristics of Convertibles
    368
Investment Opportunities in
    Convertibles   369
A Sample of Convertibles   374

BOXES

Why Get Excited? It's Only an
    Academic Formula   362

Convertible Securities: Look Closely
    Before Investing   371

CHAPTER THIRTEEN
Put and Call Options   383

PUT AND CALL CHARACTERISTICS 384

Trading Puts and Calls   384
Reading Put and Call Quotations
    385
Buyers and Sellers   386
Contract Settlement   387
Brokerage Commissions   388

PUT AND CALL TRADING STRATEGIES 388

Naked Positions   389
Hedge Positions   390
Spreads   392
Arbitrage Opportunities   395

OTHER PUT AND CALL USES 397

Covered Option Writing   397
An Option-Bills Portfolio   399
Hedging Market Risk   400

BOXES

Synthetic Fibers, Synthetic Fuels,
    and Now, Synthetic Stocks   392
Arbitrageurs, Program Trading, and
    Ivan Boesky   396

CHAPTER FOURTEEN
Commodity and Financial Futures   407

CHARACTERISTICS OF FUTURES 408

The Futures Contract   408
Trading Futures   410
Organized Exchanges and the
    Clearinghouse   413

COMMODITY FUTURES 414

Speculative Trading   415

Hedging   416
Investing in Commodity Futures
    417

FINANCIAL FUTURES 419

Currency Futures   419
Interest Rate Futures   420
Index Futures   427

BOXES

The Changing Structure of the
    Chicago Board of Trade   422
Are Spreads a Low-Risk Way to Play
    the Market?   426

PART FIVE
Pooling Arrangements 436

CHAPTER FIFTEEN
Investment Companies 439

TYPES OF INVESTMENT COMPANIES 440

Closed-End Funds   441
Open-End (Mutual) Funds   444

FUND OBJECTIVES AND SERVICES 446

Fund Objectives   446
Mutual Fund Services   450

EVALUATING FUND PERFORMANCE 452

Understanding Returns   452
Measuring Risk   456
How Good Are Fund Managers?
    459
Popular Press Fund Evaluations
    460

BOXES

Are Discounts on Closed-End Funds
    Worth Anything?   442

Is the Load on the Load Fund Worth It? 446

CHAPTER SIXTEEN
Other Pooling Arrangements 467

INVESTMENT TRUSTS 468

Unit Investment Trusts 468
Real Estate Investment Trusts 474

LIMITED PARTNERSHIPS 478

Business Activities 478
Investment Potential 481

SELF-DIRECTED POOLING ARRANGEMENTS 481

Investment Clubs 482
Money Manager Limited Partnerships 484

BOXES

Unit Investment Trusts—What You See May Not Be What You Get 471
Investment Clubs Are for Real 483

PART SIX
Investing in Tangibles 492

CHAPTER SEVENTEEN
Real Estate 495

THE PERSONAL RESIDENCE 496

Investment Appeal 496
Housing Affordability 500
Kinds of Properties 501
Rent-Versus-Buy Decision 502

THE RENTAL PROPERTY 505

Residential Properties 505

Commercial and Industrial Properties 510
The Vacation Home 512
Property Valuation 514

FINANCING PROPERTY INVESTMENT 515

Fixed-Rate Mortgage 516
Fixed Rate-Fixed Payment Loans 517
Adjustable-Rate Mortgage 520
Sources of Mortgage Loans 521

BOXES

Risk Perspectives in Real Estate 511
Don't Forget: You Also Invest in the Mortgage 516

CHAPTER EIGHTEEN
Gold and Other Tangibles 529

WHY TANGIBLES? 530

Tangibles' Advantages 530
Tangibles' Disadvantages 533

INVESTING IN GOLD 535

Gold's Price Volatility 536
Supply and Demand Factors 536
Ways to Own Gold 537

OTHER TANGIBLES 539

Silver and Other Precious Metals 539
Diamonds and Other Precious Gems 541
Artworks and Antiques 543
Collectibles and Hobbies 544

BOXES

What's in the Sotheby? 542
Trouble in Numismatics 544

PART SEVEN
The Overall Investment Plan 550

CHAPTER NINETEEN
Portfolio Management 553

CONSTRUCTING THE PORTFOLIO 554

Setting Goals 555
Forecasting the Investment Environment 558
Selecting Specific Assets 559

MONITORING THE PORTFOLIO 560

Estimating Performance 560
Measuring Performance 562
Evaluating Performance 564

MODIFYING THE PORTFOLIO 566

Buy-and-Hold 566
Market Timing 567
Asset Allocation Models 569
Mechanical (Formula) Allocation Plans 570
Defensive Techniques 572

BOXES

Asset Allocations of the Median Household 561
If You Want Portfolio Insurance, Be Your Own Underwriter 573

APPENDIX: MODERN PORTFOLIO THEORY AND THE CAPITAL ASSET PRICING MODEL 581

The Efficient Frontier 581
Selecting a Portfolio 584
The Capital Asset Pricing Model 584

CHAPTER TWENTY
Extending the Portfolio:
International Investing, Life
Insurance, and Retirement
Planning   587

INTERNATIONALIZING THE
    PORTFOLIO   588

Advantages   588
Disadvantages   589
Ways to Internationalize   591

LIFE INSURANCE IN THE
    PORTFOLIO   594

Life Insurance and Your Estate
    594
Popular Forms of Life Insurance
    595

DESIGNING THE PORTFOLIO
    FOR RETIREMENT   600

Planning for Retirement   600
Using Self-Directed Investment
    Plans   602
Planning in Retirement   604

BOXES

Retirement Planning: How Much
    Will You Need and When Should
    You Start Saving?   599
Is There a Replacement for the IRA?
    605

APPENDIX
Time Value of Money
Tables   613

INDEX   619

INVESTMENTS

PART ONE

Understanding the Investment Process

Success in investing usually does not happen by chance, nor does it come quickly. All too often, beginners rush into an investment program without considering its risks in relation to its potential returns and without an understanding of the overall investment environment. The disappointments that often result can be avoided by taking the preliminary steps discussed in Part One.

Chapter 1 highlights the importance of having concrete investment goals and of trading off return and risk in selecting specific investments. It discusses investment planning, introduces specific investment vehicles, and indicates how investments are created. Finally, it explains basic income tax considerations that investors should know.

Chapter 2 highlights the functions of securities markets, explaining organized exchanges and the over-the-counter market. It also defines different types of stockbrokerage firms and the services they provide. The regulation of securities markets is explained within the context of legislation that has been enacted since 1933. Finally, the important task of finding investment information is discussed.

Chapter 3 deals primarily with time-value-of-money concepts that investors must understand if they are to evaluate returns of most investment alternatives. In addition, historical returns on key financial assets are shown.

Chapter 4 explains the nature of investment risk and shows how it is measured. The chapter highlights the importance of diversification and indicates how return correlations affect risk. It also presents risk statistics on key financial assets.

CHAPTER ONE

Investors and Investments:
An Overview

INVESTOR PROFILES AND GOALS

Investor Attitudes

Goals: The Reasons for Investing

Investment Professionals

THE CONCEPT OF INVESTMENT

Debt Instruments

Common Stocks

Preferred Stocks

Leverage-Inherent Securities

Pooling Arrangements

Real Estate and Other Tangibles

Portfolio Management

Steps in Investment Planning

HOW INVESTMENTS ARE CREATED

Financial Facilitation Versus Financial Intermediation

Market Participants

BASIC INCOME TAX CONSIDERATIONS

A Progressive Rate Structure

Tax Strategies

BOXES

How About a Career in Investments?

Five Common Mistakes of Beginning Investors

After you finish this chapter, you will be able to:

- recognize that investors have different attitudes and try to achieve different investment goals.

- understand the concept of investment and identify specific investment alternatives.

- understand what is meant by portfolio management and identify key steps in the investment process.

- distinguish between financial intermediation and financial facilitation and recognize other important characteristics of the securities markets.

- understand the rate structure of the federal income tax and strategies to avoid taxes or to defer them to later years.

I nvesting is very serious business. Indeed, the standard of living many people will enjoy (or tolerate) in the future may well depend upon their investment success (or failure) today. If historical trends continue, we will probably rely less upon the government or our employers to take care of our needs and more upon our own initiative and planning. Successful investing is difficult, however. Prospective investors must first understand their investment personalities and be able to express their investment goals in specific, concrete terms. They also should become familiar with various investment alternatives and understand how securities markets work. Finally, investors must know their marginal tax rates and recognize certain tax avoidance and deferral techniques.

INVESTOR PROFILES AND GOALS

Perhaps the best way for someone to start studying investing is to first study himself or herself. Do you want to be an active investor? Do you like taking risks? Are you looking for a current return, or are you willing to wait for price appreciation? After addressing these questions, you can concentrate on framing specific investment goals. And, you might consider seeking a career in the investments industry.

Investor Attitudes

Not everyone is alike in his or her investment personality or goals. Some people like to be actively involved in the investment process, while others prefer to sit on the sidelines. Some investors are willing to take high risks to achieve ambitious goals, while others are more conservative in outlook and prefer a more cautious approach. Finally, some invest to earn an immediate return, while others are content to defer their returns to later years.

Active Versus Passive Management   Individuals who prefer an active management approach select their own investments and decide when to buy and sell them. They also assume responsibility for reinvesting any cash returns the investments might generate. If you choose this approach, you should be prepared to devote a reasonable amount of time to do it properly. If you are unwilling to make such a commitment, then consider letting others manage most of your investments. A passive strategy can be as simple as limiting investments to mutual funds, or as involved as using a personal investment advisor. Actually, even passive strategies require some effort on the part of investors, because they must choose *which* mutual fund or *what* investment advisory firm. Furthermore, after a choice is made, prudence dictates that they should review the fund's or advisor's performance on a fairly regular basis to determine if it is adequate and in line with investment goals. In reality, there is probably no such thing as a purely passive approach.

Managing your own investments requires some work and a reasonable amount of time.

Disposition Towards Risk   Do you like to take risks? In hypothetical investment situations, many people say they do, but when they confront actual risky choices with their own money at stake, they become very cautious. In studying investors, we identify three broad types—the **risk averter,** the **risk seeker,** and the **risk-indifferent investor**—based on their behavior.

Investors can be risk-averting, risk-seeking, or risk-indifferent.

A risk averter is not one who never takes risks. He or she will take risks but only when the return for doing so is sufficiently high. Line A in Exhibit 1.1 illustrates this point. It is called a **risk-return line**. The vertical axis shows returns from various investments; the horizontal axis shows increasing investment risk. The lines represent minimum returns each investor must receive on an investment, given the degrees of risk indicated. Point *a*, for example, shows the investor needs at least a 20% return to undertake an investment with a risk level of R_1, while point *b* shows that a 40% return is required for risk level R_2. Although the required return doubled, the risk level shown at *b* is obviously not twice that at *a*. This line illustrates risk aversion: the investor requires ever-increasing returns to undertake increasingly risky investments.

Line S in Exhibit 1.1 shows a risk-return line for a risk seeker. At risk level R_1, this investor is content with a 12% return; at level R_2, the required return

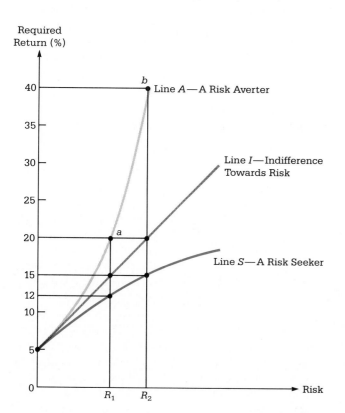

EXHIBIT 1.1
Investor attitudes towards risk

increases to only 15%. For a risk seeker, the increase in required return is always proportionately less than the increase in risk.

Line *I* shows a risk-indifferent investor's risk-return line. As you see, it lies between those of the risk averter and risk seeker. For this person, the increase in required return is always proportional to the increase in risk.

You may not be able to place yourself into any one of the three attitude categories on a consistent basis, and it isn't really necessary to do so. In fact, many of us seem to be a bit of each, acting as risk averters when we buy insurance, and acting as avid risk seekers when we buy state lottery tickets. The important point to learn is that every investor seeks some higher return as risk increases. Consequently, you as an investor must find a level of risk and return you feel comfortable with. If you are satisfied with nothing less than a sure thing, for example, you generally must be content with the lowest possible return, such as the 5% shown in Exhibit 1.1.

Consider both risk and return in making investment decisions.

Preference for Income Versus Price Appreciation   Income refers to interest, dividends, or other types of payment an investment might provide on a regular basis. Most bonds and many common stocks offer such returns. Other investments offer no income. The only way to profit from them is through price appreciation, which comes in the future. Investors may have to decide: Do they want investments with good income and not-so-good chances for price appreciation, or do they want those with little or no income but good chances for growth? Of course, different investors answer this question differently. Retirees, for example, usually favor income, while young people often look for growth opportunities.

Goals: The Reasons for Investing

If you are asked why you want to invest, you might say, "To make money, of course." Actually, it's not quite that simple. As we shall see throughout this text, there are numerous investment alternatives, all designed to make money. But how much money do you want to make, how fast, and with how much risk? If time isn't taken to answer these questions and pinpoint investment objectives, the odds are high that investment performance will be poor. Setting concrete, realistic investment goals is considered by many investment advisors to be the single most important step in the investment process. It sets the stage for many other investment decisions that eventually must be made. Below are some of the more important investment objectives.

We all invest to make money, but how much, how fast, and with what risk?

Meeting Liquidity Needs   An asset is described as liquid when it can be converted to cash quickly with no loss in value. A savings account at a bank is extremely liquid; an acre of raw land held for future development is probably very illiquid. Practically everyone needs some degree of liquidity. We need it to even out irregular receipts of income and payment of expenses. We also like to have it in case of an emergency. So, some investments must be those that provide adequate liquidity. While high yields are sought in these investments, yield is less important than accessibility to funds. Most investors will accept a lower yield for higher liquidity.

Saving for a Large Expenditure   In many cases, we save and invest in order to accumulate sufficient funds for a future expenditure, such as a car or a house. Liquidity plays a less important role in these situations, particularly if the expenditure will not take place for a long time. Thus, an investor can take greater risks to earn higher returns, even though this might invite some inconveniences and lead to possible investment losses.

Retirement Planning   Retirement planning is in many cases the most critical investment objective. It is important because it influences the style and quality of our lives. Few people wish to retire to an existence substantially inferior to the one they enjoyed during their working years. On the contrary, longer life expectancies and improved health have made many retirees seek a lifestyle that is better than what they had when they worked.

Retirement planning is often the most critical investment objective.

The very long investment period that is usually involved in retirement planning permits greater flexibility in choosing investments for a retirement fund. In addition, certain income tax advantages can increase after-tax returns by a considerable amount. (These considerations are discussed in Chapter 20.) Retirement planning is done best when it is begun early in your career. If you are a recent college graduate, probably the last thing you want to hear is that you should begin investing for a retirement that takes place decades from now. However, the sooner and the more carefully you invest, the greater the retirement accumulation for a given dollar of savings. A dollar invested intelligently (using appropriate tax shelters) when you are 25 is worth ten or twenty dollars invested carelessly when you are 45.

Speculating   Those investors fortunate enough to have satisfied tangible investment goals can then invest in more speculative ventures—if they wish. Investors at this stage have adequate funds to afford losses if investments perform poorly; they can also take considerably greater investment risks. Speculate in an oil exploration program if you wish, or start trading options or futures contracts. But don't invest in ignorance. Meeting speculation objectives often demands the greatest investment knowledge because of the wide array of investment alternatives.

Speculative investing involves considerable risk; doing it properly requires extensive investment knowledge.

Investment Professionals

Many people assist others in making investment decisions. They are considered investment professionals, or professional money managers. They might be employed as trust officers at commercial banks, registered representatives at stockbrokerage firms, chartered financial analysts (CFAs), mutual fund or pension

How About a Career in Investments?

Students often enjoy the first course in investments. Many enjoy it so much, they wonder if a career in the field might be for them. What are the opportunities in investments? In a word, excellent. The financial services industry, of which investments is a part, is expected to grow at a rate above that of the overall economy well into the next century. Many more jobs will be created and the demand for qualified people to fill them will be strong. However, to be successful you will need good training and ambition.

What kinds of jobs are available? Here are the more familiar job listings:

Stockbroker. A stockbroker (more appropriately called a registered representative of a stockbrokerage firm) deals with both individual and institutional investors, earning commissions for orders executed. As a stockbroker, you deal with the public, so selling skills are just as valuable as knowledge of investments. Most importantly, clients must have confidence in your ability to suggest appropriate investment alternatives and to help

them manage their investment funds. Building a client base takes time, so don't expect a large income immediately. Successful brokers, however, often earn six-figure incomes. Indeed, according to the Securities Industry Association, the average retail broker earned $97,000 in 1986. So, if financial success is an important career objective, few professions offer potential monetary rewards as great as stockbrokering. The business has its risks, though; the average retail broker's earnings fell sharply to $71,300 in 1988.

Security Analyst. A security analyst is essentially a researcher who tries to determine which industries are attractive for investing and which securities are likely to do well in the future. Security analysts are employed by brokerage houses, mutual funds, insurance companies, and other financial institutions. Salaries are excellent, particularly for those who become CFAs (explained below), although they do not match the figures of successful stockbrokers.

Portfolio Manager. A portfolio manager is typically employed by a mutual fund, insurance company, or commercial bank. He or she is responsible for investing large sums of money to achieve client goals. For example, you might work in the trust department of a commercial bank, managing a number of trust accounts. Compensation levels vary considerably among portfolio managers, depending primarily upon the size of portfolios managed and the type of investing undertaken. A successful manager of a large mutual fund will also earn a six-figure income (or more).

Financial Planner. While financial planners advise clients in a number of areas, investments is often an important one. The financial planner might have his or her own practice, but is more likely to be employed by a financial institution. Financial planners often sell a wide array of securities, but many specialize in limited partnerships or insurance-related financial products. Because of their activities in selling investments or offering investment advice, many planners now must register with the Securities and Exchange Commission, as do stockbrokers. They also must obtain a license with the National Association of Securities Dealers. Financial planners enjoy high incomes, which depend upon both fees and commissions on financial products they sell.

Investment Banker. Investment bankers are involved in the distribution of securities from issuers to buyers. They also serve as consultants in acquisitions and mergers. With often fascinating work and extraordinary compensation, investment banking can be the epitome of success in investments. It is not unusual for someone to start at $60,000 a year immediately upon graduation from a top MBA program, and he or she might be earning well over $100,000 two years later. Unfortunately, such positions are few and they usually go to those with credentials or connections. If you are intelligent and ambitious, though, don't think that landing one is beyond hope.

What background do you need for a career in investments? The following accomplishments will help you to be a success.

College Degrees. A college degree seems a prerequisite for many positions today, including those in the investment field. Any undergraduate degree is appropriate for becoming a stockbroker or financial planner, but a major in finance—or at least some courses in accounting, finance, and business—is best. If your sights are set on becoming a financial analyst, portfolio manager, or investment banker, then you will need more training in finance and business. An MBA or other appropriate master's degree is very helpful.

Certificates. The most appropriate certification is the Chartered Financial Analyst (CFA). You earn this designation by successfully completing a series of tests extending over a three-year period and by meeting other requirements. For more information, write to the Institute

of Chartered Financial Analysts, PO Box 3668, Charlottesville, VA 22903 (telephone 804-977-6600). Earning the CFA will enhance your career success if you wish to become a financial analyst or portfolio manager. The testing is not easy but the rewards are worth the effort.

Many stockbrokers and financial planners are attempting to become Certified Financial Planners (CFPs). This certificate is awarded by The International Board of Certified Financial Planners, 5445 DTC Parkway, Englewood, CO 80111 (telephone 303-850-0333). A similar certificate—the Chartered Financial Consultant (ChFC)—is offered by the American College, 270 Bryn Mawr Avenue, Bryn Mawr, PA 19010. Financial planning is a rapidly growing area and one that is working hard to enhance its professionalism. The CFP and ChFC help considerably in this effort. They too are not easily earned, but having a certificate helps in demonstrating to clients your competence and integrity in the investments profession. As mentioned above, this may be crucial in developing a clientele.

fund managers, or in a number of other positions. Anyone seeking a career in investments can find many opportunities. Compensation is usually good to excellent, and the nature of the work is often interesting.

Do professional investment managers make investment decisions differently than do individuals? The answer is no. Although the professionals should possibly be more sophisticated, their perspective should be the same. We expect the professional to operate on the client's behalf and to attempt to achieve his or her investment goals as if the client were making the investment decisions. Whether you are studying investments to become a better investor or to become a professional investment manager isn't important. You need the same tools of analysis in each case. If a professional career interests you, though, it will be necessary to undertake advanced work for certain types of positions, such as that of CFA.

Whether you study investments to become a better investor or a professional investment manager, the tools of analysis are the same.

THE CONCEPT OF INVESTMENT

Many people think of investments in a narrow sense. They consider stocks and bonds as investments but may not view their homes or savings accounts as such. Actually, an **investment** is any asset—tangible or intangible—that has the potential to provide a periodic return and/or to increase in value. This definition includes homes, savings accounts, and many other assets. You might buy a home for reasons other than profit, but the rent you save by owning and the potential for price appreciation clearly make it an investment. Exhibit 1.2 provides a summary of many important investment alternatives. These, along with portfolio management and steps in investment planning, are discussed below.

Any asset that provides a periodic return or has the potential to increase in value is an investment.

Debt Instruments

Many of our investments represent others' debt obligations. Businesses and governmental units borrow funds by selling debt instruments to the general public. If you own a debt instrument, you are a lender to the organization that issued it. This position gives you certain rights, an important one being that your claim to interest and repayment of principal come before any payments to stockholders. Debt instruments are considered safer than many other investments, although it is dangerous to generalize; surely, the obligation of a weak or bankrupt issuer may not be worth very much. You can categorize debt instruments in several ways, but perhaps the most useful is by maturity. We have short-, intermediate-, and long-term debt obligations. Most investors hold a wide array of debt instruments, and they are explained in Chapters 5, 6, and 7.

Debt instruments are considered safer than many other investments.

Short-Term Debt Instruments Short-term means less than a year, so a short-term debt instrument will mature and be redeemed by its issuer within twelve months. Exhibit 1.2 shows a variety of often-held short-term debt instruments. It also shows the most common reason for holding them is to meet

EXHIBIT 1.2
Investment alternatives

Investment Vehicle	Examples	Reasons for Holding
I. *Debt Instruments:*		
A. Short-term	Treasury bills, savings accounts, Series EE savings bonds, NOW accounts, money market accounts	liquidity, temporary "parking place"
B. Intermediate-term	Treasury notes, nonnegotiable CDs, some government agency issues	Some liquidity, mostly earnings
C. Long-term	Treasury and corporate bonds, municipal bonds, agency bonds	Earnings with safety of principal
II. *Common Stocks:*		
A. Blue chips	IBM, AT&T, Exxon, K-mart	Moderate growth, safety of principal
B. High-risk	Apple Computer, Genentech	Rapid growth
III. *Preferred Stock:*	Con Ed 11% series, Sallie Mae adjustable rate	Income, safety of principal
IV. *Leverage-Inherent Securities:*		
A. Convertibles	Pfizer 8¾%, USX 5¾%	Moderate income, growth with the common stock
B. Warrants	MGM, Federal National Mortgage	Quick capital appreciation
C. Put and call options	Individual stocks, market indexes, bonds, commodities	Quick capital appreciation, hedging
D. Commodity futures contracts	Gold, corn, pork bellies, bonds, foreign currencies	Quick capital appreciation, hedging
V. *Pooling Arrangements*	Mutual funds, investment trusts, limited partnerships	Vary
VI. *Tangibles*	Real estate, collectibles, gold, precious gems	Hedge inflation

liquidity needs, although they are often held as temporary investments whenever the long-term investment environment is uncertain and there is a strong feeling that interest rates might increase in the future. When held for this reason, the investor is described as looking for a "temporary parking place" for his or her cash.

Intermediate-Term Debt Instruments An intermediate term is usually understood to be a period of time between one and ten years. Someone holding securities at the short end of this time span is probably doing so to satisfy liquidity needs, while an investor at the long end is usually seeking income and sacrificing liquidity. Popular intermediate-term instruments are listed in Exhibit 1.2.

Long-Term Debt Instruments   Any debt instrument with a maturity greater than ten years is called long-term. As we shall see in Chapter 5, these instruments can be very risky if they must be sold on short notice. Investors clearly give up liquidity when they purchase these debt instruments. The investment target is to earn a rate of return higher than that available with instruments of shorter maturities. Long-term debt alternatives are shown in Exhibit 1.2.

Common Stocks

A share of common stock represents an ownership interest in the corporation that issued it. As indicated above, a share of common stock is riskier than a debt instrument in the sense that its claims on assets or earnings are inferior. But, on the positive side, common stock has a residual claim on all assets or earnings that are left after creditors' interests have been satisfied. When you buy common stock, you are hoping this residual interest will grow over time as the corporation grows. Needless to say, that doesn't always happen, yet common stock can still be classified as low- or medium-risk and high-risk. Common stock is an important investment vehicle. It is explained thoroughly in Chapters 8, 9, and 10.

Low- and Medium-Risk Common Stock   It should be understood that all common stock is inherently risky; thus, this classification has to do with degree of risk. A low-risk common stock can be thought of as one involving a minimal chance that the issuing corporation might go bankrupt in the foreseeable future. Exhibit 1.2 shows shares of IBM and AT&T as examples. Stocks such as these are often called "blue chips." Even though bankruptcy risk is small, shares of these companies are still very price-volatile and, hence, risky. Still, an adequate portfolio of such stocks held for a sufficiently long period of time can minimize this price risk and produce substantial investment return.

An adequate portfolio of stocks can produce substantial investment return.

High-Risk Common Stocks   High-risk common stocks have a higher bankruptcy risk than the blue chips. They indeed may be the IBMs and AT&Ts of the future, but be prepared for the worst if you buy them, because many will not survive along the way. Again, an adequately diversified portfolio held long enough can lead to substantial investment return, and that is the only way these securities should ever be held.

Preferred Stocks

A preferred stock is a hybrid security; it has characteristics of both common stock and debt. It is like common stock in that it is equity and not debt. So, its claims on assets and earnings come after those of all debtholders (but before common stockholders). It is like debt in that it receives a fixed payment each year. In comparison to debt and common stock, preferred stock plays a much smaller role in most investors' portfolios. The reasons for this situation will be explained in Chapter 11.

Leverage-Inherent Securities

A leverage-inherent security is one that has a "built-in" capacity to increase investment return or loss. By itself, leverage means increasing your investment holdings by borrowing. It's not hard to see that borrowed money invested in securities surely increases investment risk beyond what you have when you limit your investments to those for which you have adequate funds. The risk with a leverage-inherent security is not so clear but is no less real. Popular leverage-inherent securities are described below.

A leverage-inherent security has a built-in capacity to increase your investment return or loss.

Convertibles   A convertible bond or preferred stock allows the holder to exchange it for a given number of shares of common stock. The idea is to have a security that pays a high rate of return while at the same time giving the investor a stake in the common stock through the conversion privilege. However, you pay a premium for such a privilege, which—all other factors being equal—increases your investment risk. Convertibles are covered in Chapter 12.

Warrants   A warrant is issued by a corporation. It gives the holder a right to buy a given number of shares of the corporation's common stock at a set price for a given period of time. The investment appeal with warrants is they generally sell at prices below the price of the common stock. By buying them instead of the common stock, you then increase your ownership potential. However, if the price of the common stock is below the exercise price of a warrant at its maturity, the warrant will expire worthless, leading to a total loss for the investor. Warrants are explained in more detail in Chapter 12.

Put and Call Options   A call option is almost identical to a warrant except it is not necessarily issued by a corporation and it has a much shorter life. A put option differs from a call option in that it gives the holder the right to sell, rather than buy, a given number of shares of stock. There are many investment strategies involving options, and the important ones are explained in Chapter 13.

Commodity Futures Contracts   A commodity futures contract is similar to an option but differs in one important respect: it is an obligation to buy or sell in the future at a price fixed today. Basically, these contracts are wagers on the future price of a commodity with the loser paying the winner the difference between the contract price and the actual price at maturity. Unlike options, which are rights, futures contracts are obligations, so your losses can be virtually unlimited. A commodity futures contract may well be the riskiest investment you ever make. Be sure to read Chapter 14 before you even consider investing in them.

Pooling Arrangements

In a pooling arrangement, your investment dollar buys a diversified portfolio of securities or other assets. These arrangements are excellent whenever you lack adequate capital to achieve diversification on your own. In addition, many offer professional portfolio management. The most popular pooling arrangement is the mutual fund. Mutual funds and unit investment trusts are explained in Chapter 15. Other pooling arrangements—real estate investment trusts, limited partnerships, and self-directed plans—are discussed in Chapter 16.

Real Estate and Other Tangibles

During periods of inflation, many investors look towards tangible assets as a means of hedging inflation's ill effects. Certain assets, such as gold or silver, collectibles, raw land, and income-producing real estate, are believed to be good hedging assets because their price increases are expected to match the inflation rate. Tangible assets are no less risky than the intangibles; in some respects they are far riskier and require considerably more knowledge and expertise. Before considering an investment in any of them, you should read Chapters 17 and 18.

Portfolio Management

A **portfolio** is simply any collection of assets. If you own a home and household furnishings, jewelry, vested benefits in a retirement plan, and checking and savings accounts, you already have a portfolio. It may be bigger than you initially think. As you begin a program of investing, you should think of adding to this portfolio, and how these additions will help you attain your investment objectives. For example, an important aspect of portfolio management is achieving adequate

diversification. So, you may wish not to increase your holdings of tangible assets if you already have a house and other tangibles; or, you might not want to own more long-term bonds if your employer's retirement plan is invested exclusively in such securities. In either of these cases a common stock investment might be more suitable.

Another important aspect of portfolio management is determining when assets should be sold. Should you do this frequently, in an attempt to maximize your return over an investment cycle, or should you follow a more cautious buy-and-hold approach, changing the portfolio only when your investment goals change? Aspects of portfolio management are discussed at various points throughout the text, but the topic is covered in detail in Chapters 19 and 20.

Steps in Investment Planning

In a broad sense, investment planning is concerned with an investor's wealth. As such, it must consider both preserving and increasing wealth. Successful planning follows a series of steps, as indicated in Exhibit 1.3. First, investors must

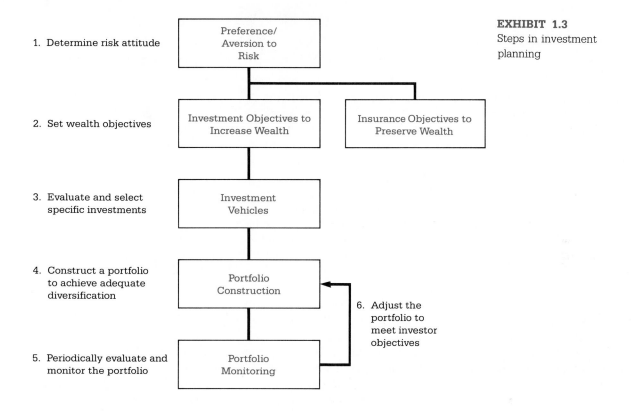

1. Determine risk attitude

2. Set wealth objectives

3. Evaluate and select specific investments

4. Construct a portfolio to achieve adequate diversification

5. Periodically evaluate and monitor the portfolio

6. Adjust the portfolio to meet investor objectives

EXHIBIT 1.3
Steps in investment planning

determine their attitudes towards risk. Next, wealth objectives should be set. To protect existing wealth, adequate insurance coverage is usually necessary. Such coverage should protect against potential losses due to accidents, illnesses, liability suits, and death. Indeed, investing without adequate insurance could be a very costly mistake.

To increase wealth, though, it is necessary to invest. After investment objectives are specified, the task of evaluating and then selecting specific investments begins. The need for adequate diversification must be considered when assets are selected. The resulting portfolio is periodically evaluated and monitored to determine if it is achieving investor objectives. If it is not, the portfolio must be adjusted, which might dictate selling some assets and purchasing others.

HOW INVESTMENTS ARE CREATED

On an average working day, business corporations and government units raise over $2 billion of new funds by issuing debt and equity instruments. As Exhibit 1.4 shows, in 1988, a total of $659.3 billion was raised, most of it through the sale

Securities are created when businesses and government units raise funds.

Five Common Mistakes of Beginning Investors

Mistake 1: *No clear comprehension of return and risk.*   How much return can I expect? Over what period of time? Subject to what risk? Know the answers to these crucial questions before you make any investment. Too many people have vague ideas about risk and return. Surveys consistently show a large number think you should double your money with stocks in a year or two, which is virtually impossible to do consistently and very difficult to do even occasionally. Others believe a doubling in ten years is excellent, even though many investments have done this well. Some people believe that if you hold any stock long enough, it will eventually show a profit. (To dispel this foolish idea, you should see how many companies go bankrupt each year.) Others think stocks are so risky

you might lose everything invested in them. (Such a loss is almost impossible, if the portfolio is reasonably diversified.) With hazy thinking like this, it's no wonder some investors lose heavily in the market and then view it as the world's largest organized crap game, while others are too timid to put their money anywhere that is not federally insured.

Mistake 2: Using a friend or relative as an investment advisor.   If you are about to be graduated from college, you will be amazed at the number of friends you have in the securities or insurance businesses. (Some sell both.) Unfortunately, a good percentage of these friends are former classmates who are learning their trade—on you. Select your broker or other advisor with the

same care you exercise in finding a physician or attorney. If your choice is a friend or relative, make it clear that when it comes to investing, the relationship is strictly professional. And don't rely upon any so-called "inside information" or "hot tips" for investments. If your broker has any, he or she is likely in violation of the securities laws—and if you act on them, so are you.

Mistake 3: Trading too frequently.   Beginning investors are often impatient. They buy a security, expecting an immediate price increase, and then hit the panic button if it doesn't materialize. Their anxiety is heightened by reading price quotations every day (or calling their broker every hour) and finding out that prices of other stocks—ones they wanted to

of debt instruments, and most of it by government units. While this is a huge number, keep in mind it is only one year's production, and it is but a small increment added to the trillions of dollars' worth of all securities that have been previously issued. Moreover, this method of transferring funds involved only financial facilitation, not financial intermediation. While our interest in investments is primarily with the former, it is important to distinguish between the two processes.

Financial Facilitation Versus Financial Intermediation

The term *financial intermediary* is used loosely to describe any institution that assists in transferring funds from those who have them (providers) to those who

buy in the first place—are setting new highs. The solution? Sell the losers and buy the winners—right? Wrong! Over the long run, this investment approach enriches the broker and impoverishes you. As a rule of thumb, allow about 2% for commissions on the value of securities purchased *and* sold. If you buy and sell only twice a year, you dissipate 8% of your capital. Very few investors can overcome a burden this huge and still show a respectable return. If your broker constantly calls with dumb slogans like, ''Maybe it's time to take profits,'' or ''Let's cut your losses short and let the profits run,'' you should look for a new broker.

Mistake 4: Not enough diversification.   Much investment

risk can be eliminated, without sacrificing return, through proper diversification. Yet surveys tell us that most investors hold fewer than five securities, with many holding only one or two. These investors are courting danger, since even the bluest of the blue chips can go for years without showing a decent return. For that matter, so can a whole portfolio of blues. (From 1966 through 1981, you were better off in Treasury bills than in the 30 stocks that make up the Dow Jones Industrial Average.) To be adequately protected, you need a well-diversified portfolio, balanced across a wide array of different investments.

Mistake 5: No clearly formulated investment goals.   This mistake is perhaps the most se-

rious of all because it creates the environment that allows the others to flourish. If you know *why* you are investing, you will know better *how* to invest. Clearly established goals not only pinpoint investments likely to achieve them, they also allow you to measure and evaluate performance. The question *"Am I achieving my goals?"* is concrete and measurable; the question *"Am I getting rich by investing?"* is surprisingly elusive. Until all securities you buy are eventually sold, you never really know how you are doing. Sure, you paid $160 for IBM and now it's only $100 a share, but you haven't lost anything since you haven't sold, and it will go back up. Logic like this makes every investor a winner—but don't try taking your winnings to a bank, or living off of them.

wish to use them (users). An intermediary institution accepts funds from savers and, in turn, invests them elsewhere. Commercial banks, savings and loans, insurance companies, and mutual funds are examples of such institutions. As Exhibit 1.5 indicates, when you deposit your money in such an institution, you receive some evidence of ownership, such as a savings passbook (or a monthly statement), or an insurance policy, which also indicates the institution's liability to you. (Call it an IOU.) It is important to understand that your deposit in the bank is not merely loaned to someone else with the bank acting as an agent; rather, the bank actually creates an entirely new asset with your funds—its loans to customers—and receives customers' IOUs as evidence of the loans. This process is **financial intermediation**.

A financial intermediary helps maintain a flow of funds from providers to users.

EXHIBIT 1.4

Net funds raised in credit and equity markets in 1988 by nonfinancial organizations, in billions of dollars. (Source: *Federal Reserve Bulletin,* August 1989.)

U.S. Treasury debt		$252.7
U.S. Agencies' debt		33.6
Total federal debt		$286.3
Local government (tax-exempt) debt		108.1
Total government debt		$394.4
Corporate debt: bonds, commercial paper, others		222.5
Total debt		$616.9
Corporate Equities:		
Common stock	$ 35.9	
Preferred stock	6.5	
Total equities		42.4
Total funds raised		$659.3
Government raised	$394.4	
Corporate raised	264.9	
Total	$659.3	

In **financial facilitation,** the third party—in this case, an underwriter—assists in the distribution of specific securities issued by users of funds. For example, if IBM sells shares of its common stock, it might do so through an underwriter who buys the shares from IBM and resells them to investors who wish to own IBM. To distinguish between the two, look at it this way: in financial intermediation, your asset (the deposit) creates another asset (the bank loan) and an offsetting IOU on the bank's part to return your money whenever you wish; in financial facilitation, only one asset changes hands—from

EXHIBIT 1.5

Flow of funds

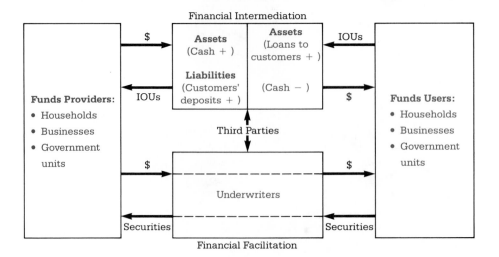

the issuer (IBM) to the underwriter and eventually to you (the investor). Moreover, this asset is typically a negotiable instrument, which means you can sell it easily, if you care to, and if someone wants to buy it. A deposit at a financial institution is not a negotiable instrument.

Underwriting an Issue **Underwriting** a new issue of common or preferred stocks or bonds is a process whereby an investment banker guarantees the issuing organization the sale of its securities at an agreed-upon price. Basically, underwriting is a marketing problem, involving the distribution of thousands or millions of shares from the issuer to the final buyers. For large issues, the lead underwriter will involve other underwriting firms to form an underwriting syndicate (see Exhibit 1.6). Then, each underwriter forms selling groups that consist of individual brokerage firms whose registered representatives attempt to sell shares of the issue to their clients. If the issue is in demand, selling is easy; indeed, if demand exceeds a broker's supply, he or she must find some means for allocating shares among customers. Demand is frequently strong for shares of exciting new companies that are "going public" (making their shares available to the public for the first time), such as Apple Computer and Genentech in the late 1970s. Underwriters earn their compensation through the so-called "spread," which is the difference between the price guaranteed the issuing organization (say, $25 a share) and the selling price to investors (say, $26 a share). This means if you buy a new issue, you do not pay a commission to your broker. This feature appeals to many investors.

Selling on a Best-Effort Basis If demand for an issue is weak, the representatives may have to exert considerable selling effort to move it. Keep in mind that underwriters are at risk from the time they guarantee a price to the issuer until the shares are finally sold. If they fail to sell the shares, or sell them below the guaranteed price, the underwriting will lead to losses. With some issues, these

> Underwriting involves an investment banker who guarantees the sale of securities at a set price.

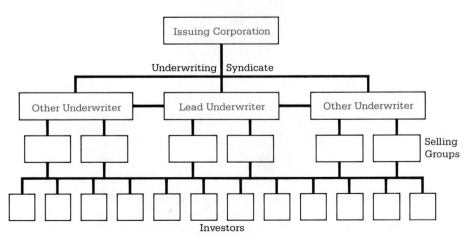

EXHIBIT 1.6
Underwriting a new security issue

A best-effort basis does not guarantee a price or security sales.

risks are so high that the investment banker will refuse to underwrite, agreeing to handle an issue only on a **best-effort basis**. This term means the underwriter will attempt to sell the issue and will receive a commission if he or she is successful. Companies with little public recognition might find this form of share distribution the only type available to them.

Private Placements   A **private placement** is a sale of securities (most often bonds) to a single buyer or a limited number of buyers (usually insurance companies). The private placement market formerly was used by small or risky companies that could not market a public issue. However, in recent years large and very successful companies have been turning to private placements. As a result, the dollar volume has increased from less than $50 billion in 1984 to about $150 billion in 1988. Moreover, the Securities and Exchange Commission is considering easing the registration requirements for securities sales to large institutions. Many observers believe such an easing will increase even more sharply the number of private placements. How small individual investors will be affected by the changes remains to be seen.

Market Participants

Exhibit 1.5 indicated the market participants: households, businesses, and government units. Their roles in financial markets are explained below.

Ultimately, all funds are provided by households.

Households   Households are individuals or families. Ultimately all funds are provided by households because they are the owners of businesses and government units. However, for practical purposes each of the three can provide investment funds during any given period of time. For example, a new bond issue by the U.S. Treasury last year might have been purchased by households (you), businesses (IBM), and government units (the Tennessee Valley Authority).

Businesses   Businesses are both providers and users of funds. In the latter capacity, they issue both debt and equity securities. Debt securities—bonds, notes, commercial paper, and others—are issued in the process of borrowing. Equity securities—common and preferred stock—are issued to provide investors fractional ownership interests in the business. If you buy IBM's bonds, you are its creditor; if you buy its stock, you are a part owner of the company.

Businesses also provide funds to other businesses and to government units, particularly the U.S. Treasury. Many businesses often have temporary excess funds they wish to invest on a very safe and liquid basis. Treasury securities with short maturities are often the most favored vehicles for this purpose.

Government Units   Many government units, ranging from the huge U.S. Treasury to the small local water authority, issue debt instruments to finance their operations. These instruments appeal to investors for various reasons. Treasury issues, as indicated above, are considered the safest of all investments, and local government debt issues are free of federal income tax—an advantage that is highlighted in the next section.

BASIC INCOME TAX CONSIDERATIONS

The federal income tax is a critical factor in investment decisions. The tax law is complex and, what is often worse, it is constantly changing. Few of us can become tax experts, but we can become familiar with the basic elements of the tax law that are important to investing.

A Progressive Rate Structure

The amount of income tax you pay depends upon two factors: taxable income—which is called the tax base—and the tax rates applied to taxable income. In addition to knowing how to calculate your tax liability, you should be aware of your marginal tax rate.

Calculating Tax Liability Federal income tax liability is determined by tax rates and taxable income. Taxable income is defined by the tax code, which is voluminous, complex, and constantly changing. The following discussion centers on tax rates; taxable income is discussed in the section on tax strategies. Exhibit 1.7 shows the 1989 rate structure for both individual and jointly filed tax returns. Exhibit 1.8 illustrates tax liability calculations for various levels of taxable income for Carol Clay, a single filer. As you see, there are three rates to consider in determining tax liability. Ironically, the highest tax rate does not apply to the highest income levels. Applying the 5% surtax (explained in Exhibit 1.7) causes

EXHIBIT 1.7

Federal income tax brackets based on taxable income[1]

Tax Rates	Married, Filing Jointly	Single Filer
15%	$ 0 –$ 29,750	$ 0 –$17,850
28%	$29,751–$ 71,900	$17,851–$43,150
33%[2]	$71,901–$149,250	$43,151–$89,560
28%	over $149,250	over $89,560

[1]Taxable income is gross income minus allowable exemptions and deductions. Investors must review their tax situations to determine deductible items and amounts.

[2]This higher bracket reflects a 5% surtax, which applies until the advantage of the lower 15% bracket is eliminated. For example, a single filer saves $2,320.50 [(0.28 − 0.15) × $17,850] on the first $17,850 of income; in effect, this savings is then gradually taken away with the surtax when income exceeds $43,150. At $89,560, it is eliminated and the 28% rate applies once again. (Actually, another 5% surtax then comes into play to take away exemption allowances; we do not pursue this feature since it works in the same fashion.)

EXHIBIT 1.8

Tax calculations for sample taxable incomes, assuming a single filer

(1) Taxable Income	(2) Tax Calculation		(3) Marginal Tax Rate
$15,000	0.15 × $15,000	= $ 2,250	15%
$30,000	0.15 × $17,850	= $ 2,678	
	+0.28 × ($30,000 − $17,850) =	3,402	
	Total	= $ 6,080	28%
$60,000	0.15 × $17,850	= $ 2,678	
	+0.28 × ($43,150 − $17,850) =	7,084	
	+0.33 × ($60,000 − $43,150) =	5,561	
	Total	= $15,323	33%
$90,000	0.28 × $90,000	= $25,200	28%

this unusual situation. In effect, it creates a third marginal rate that investors must recognize.

The Marginal Tax Rate   A **marginal tax rate** is defined as the additional tax liability that results from additional income. As explained, the current tax law has three marginal rates: 15%, 28%, and 33%. The importance of the marginal rate is that it shows the amount of income that will be available to you out of any increase or decrease in taxable income. For example, suppose Carol Clay's taxable income is $60,000. Suppose further that she is considering investing $50,000 in corporate bonds with a 10% annual pre-tax rate of return, or $5,000 of interest a year. Since this added interest income is still in the $43,150 to $89,560 bracket, her marginal rate is 33% and she will pay an additional $1,650 in taxes. Her after-tax return is $3,350 ($5,000 − $1,650) and her after-tax rate of return on the investment is 0.067 ($3,350/$50,000), or 6.7%.

> The marginal tax rate determines the amount of income available to you out of any increase or decrease in taxable income.

A simpler method for calculating the after-tax return is shown below:

$$r' = (1.0 - MTR)r$$

where r' = the after-tax rate of return,

MTR = the marginal tax rate, and

r = the investment's pre-tax rate of return.

In Carol's case, we have: $0.067 = [(1.0 - 0.33) \times 0.10]$.

You should see that the after-tax return to Carol will increase if her taxable income is in a different tax bracket. For example, at $90,000 of taxable income, r' increases to 7.2% $[(1.0 - 0.28) \times 0.10 = 0.072]$.

Capital Gains and Capital Losses   Prior to the 1986 Tax Reform Act, gains or losses on sales of securities received special tax treatment. Gains no longer receive special treatment, but a limit still exists on the amount of capital losses that can be deducted from other taxable income: it is $3,000 a year. If your losses in a year exceed this figure, you can carry unused portions forward to offset taxable income in future years.

Only $3,000 of capital losses can be taken in a tax year.

The $3,000 deduction is important in investment planning and should be considered before the end of a tax year. For example, suppose Carol Clay's corporate bonds declined by $3,000 from the time she purchased them. She is thinking of selling them and immediately reinvesting the funds—$47,000—in similar bonds. Is this a smart strategy? Yes, because she can deduct the $3,000 loss and, assuming she has a 33% marginal rate, save $990 ($3,000 × 0.33) in taxes. Selling securities to take advantage of tax losses is a common practice.

Several proposals were being considered by Congress in 1990 that would restore some tax advantages to capital gains. Whether any of these proposals, or others, would be enacted into law remained to be seen as of this writing. However, some observers feel the chances of passage are good, so you should be alert to possible changes.

Tax Strategies

Although marginal tax rates were reduced substantially by the 1986 Tax Reform Act, they are still sufficiently high to encourage taxpayers to find ways to reduce their tax liabilities. Two broad strategies are used in this effort. The first is to avoid (not evade) paying taxes altogether, while the second is to defer paying them to a later time.

Tax strategies involve avoiding and/or deferring taxes.

Tax Avoidance   Avoiding taxes is often the better approach since it means you eliminate ever paying the tax. Unfortunately, avoidance techniques aren't always that easy to find. Three methods in investing, though, are widely used. The first is to invest in securities that pay nontaxable income—municipal bonds. Under the federal Constitution, any investment instrument of a state or local government cannot be taxed by the federal government. This provision establishes the tax-exempt status of state or locally issued bonds. It should be easy to see why people with high marginal tax rates prefer such bonds.

Investing in municipal bonds is one way to avoid income taxes.

Suppose Carol Clay could invest in municipal bonds and earn a pre-tax rate of return of 8%. Should she do it, or should she invest in the corporate bonds? All other things held constant, and assuming a 33% marginal tax rate, the municipals are the better investment. The pre-tax and after-tax rates on the municipals are the same, and this rate is higher than the after- tax rate of 6.7% on the corporate bonds of the previous example.

A second avoidance technique is to invest in a personal residence. If you meet certain conditions of age and residency, you are allowed a $125,000 exclusion of any gains on the sale of a personal residence. Moreover, you are free

A popular investment that both avoids and defers income taxes is the personal residence.

to defer any gains from sales until the $125,000 is reached. For example, suppose you buy a house for $20,000 and sell it ten years later for $80,000. The $60,000 gain can be deferred *if* you purchase another home worth at least $80,000 within two years of the time the previous home is sold. Suppose you buy another for $100,000, which you sell for $200,000 twenty years later when you are over 55 years of age. Now, your total gains are $160,000 ($60,000 + $100,000), but $125,000 is excluded, leaving only $35,000 as taxable income. Put simply, it is hard to beat this tax advantage with other investments.

Splitting income among family members avoids taxes.

A third popular avoidance technique is to split income among family members, adding income to those members with low marginal rates and taking it away from those with high marginal rates. Frequently, this reallocation of income is accomplished by giving to children, in the form of outright gifts or through trusts. Unfortunately, only $1,000 of income from such transfers can receive favorable tax treatment. Income over this base amount is taxed at the parents' rate until the dependent reaches age 14; then it is taxed at his or her own rates. While $1,000 of income is not considerable, it still is sufficiently large to make income splitting reasonably attractive. It is used often to accumulate funds for a child's college education.

Deferring Income Taxes   Deferring income taxes means using various strategies that allow you to pay tax at a later time on income that you currently earn and that otherwise would be taxable. On the surface, deferral doesn't appear that attractive because you eventually must pay the tax. But don't underestimate the power of investing on a tax-deferred basis over long periods of time. We will examine this point in more detail in Chapter 20. If retirement income is one of your investment goals, it would probably be foolish not to use a deferral shelter, despite its possible shortcomings. Look upon tax deferral as an interest-free loan from the government. Common sense tells us not to turn down interest-free loans unless the strings attached are particularly onerous.

Tax deferral can be viewed as an interest-free loan from the government.

SUMMARY

Investors have different attitudes and attempt to achieve different investment goals. Some investors are risk averters, others are risk seekers, and still others are risk-indifferent. Investment is undertaken for current liquidity, for a future expenditure, for retirement, or for speculation. Professional investors make investment decisions for others. They are employed in a number of positions in the investments industry.

Investments include short-, intermediate-, and long-term debt instruments, low-, medium-, and high-risk common stocks, preferred stocks, leverage-inherent securities, pooling arrangements, and real estate and other tangibles. Portfolio management considers adequate diversification and when securities should be bought or sold.

Both financial facilitation and financial intermediation are involved in transferring funds from providers to users. Market participants are households, businesses, and government units. Each can be a provider or user.

The federal income tax has a progressive rate structure with three possible rates: 15, 28, and 33 percent. Investors should know their marginal tax rates in making investment decisions. They also should be familiar with strategies for avoiding and deferring taxes.

KEY TERMS

Select the alternative that best identifies the key term.

1. risk averter
2. risk seeker
3. risk-indifferent investor
4. risk-return line
5. investment
6. portfolio
7. financial intermediation
8. financial facilitation
9. underwriting
10. best-effort basis
11. private placement
12. marginal tax rate

a. any asset with the potential to offer a return or increase in value
b. any collection of assets
c. simply transferring securities from issuers to investors
d. guaranteeing sale of securities at an agreed-upon price
e. transferring funds by creating new assets and new liabilities
f. one who takes risks only when expected return is high
g. function showing risk-return points
h. additional tax liability resulting from additional taxable income
i. investor who needs smaller marginal return as risk increases
j. one whose increase in required return is proportional to increase in risk
k. sale of securities to a single buyer
l. underwriting firm receives a commission rather than a "spread"

REVIEW QUESTIONS

1. Distinguish between active and passive investment management approaches.
2. John, Tom, and Judy are three different investors. Each currently owns an investment that yields 10% a year. They are thinking of investing in another asset that has twice the risk of the one they currently own. If John is a risk averter, Tom a risk seeker, and Judy is risk-indifferent, explain whether each might select the second investment if its expected return is 15%.
3. Explain a current return and a future return. Who might be interested primarily in the former? Who might choose the latter?
4. Identify four investment goals. Should you try to achieve all four goals at the same time, or should one or several come later? Explain.

5. Who are investment professionals? Discuss whether you think a career in invest-ments appeals to you.
6. Define *investment* and then briefly identify the investment alternatives indicated in this chapter. How does a common stock differ from a corporate bond? What is meant by a leverage-inherent security?
7. What is a portfolio and what is portfolio management? Also, identify the key steps in investment planning.
8. Explain how financial facilitation differs from financial intermediation. Which involves an underwriter? Explain the underwriting function, contrasting it to sales on a best-effort basis.
9. Who are the market participants and what roles do they play in transferring funds?
10. Explain the following terms: *(a)* progressive rate structure, *(b)* marginal tax rate, *(c)* after-tax rate of return, *(d)* tax avoidance, and *(e)* tax deferral.
11. Explain and discuss income tax advantages associated with a personal residence.
12. Explain and discuss income splitting as a tax avoidance technique.
13. Why is tax deferral referred to as an "interest-free loan" from the federal government?

PROBLEMS AND PROJECTS

1. Complete the following table, which indicates the relationships between required return and risk levels for three investor profiles: risk seeking *(RS)*, risk averting *(RA)*, and risk-indifferent *(RI)*. Your entries should reflect estimated logical amounts.

	Required Return		
Risk Level	RS	RA	RI
0	6%	6%	6%
1	8	9	?
2	9	?	10
3	?	24	12

2. Maria Kelly has recently inherited $25,000 from her grandfather's will. Maria earns $30,000 a year from her job, is not married, and has virtually no debt obligations. She would like to receive some current income from her investments, but she also is interested in accumulating a nest egg for the future. Maria will tolerate a very small portion of her portfolio invested speculatively, although she describes herself generally as a risk averter. Recommend specific investment types for Maria, indicating the amount you believe should be invested in each.
3. You anticipate having a 28% marginal tax rate in the upcoming year. Which investment do you prefer: a municipal bond yielding 9% or a corporate bond yielding 11%? Show your work and assume other characteristics of the bonds are not important.
4. John and Elaine Reston bought a home in 1968 for $40,000. In 1981, they sold this home for $110,000 and purchased another for $150,000. In 1991, the Restons sold this home for $300,000 and retired to an apartment in Florida. Determine the amount of taxable income, if any, from these transactions in 1968, 1981, and 1991. (Assume age and residency requirements are met.)

5. Determine the tax liability for a single filer, given the following taxable incomes: *(a)* $12,000, *(b)* $25,000, *(c)* $70,000, and *(d)* $110,000.
6. Determine the tax liability for a couple filing a joint return, given the following taxable incomes: *(a)* $22,000, *(b)* $50,000, *(c)* $120,000, and *(d)* $200,000.
7. *(Student Project)* Contact a local stockbrokerage firm and ask if they have been involved in a stock underwriting recently. If so, request a prospectus. (This is a document required by law in an underwriting.)
8. *(Student Project)* Think carefully of your major financial goals in life. Then, list them along with their monetary requirements. Finally, indicate the year you expect to achieve each goal. Save this information until you have studied Chapter 3; then you can work out a financial plan involving the time value of money.

CASE ANALYSES

Karen and Frank Schiller are a married couple with a joint income of over $100,000. Karen is 36 and Frank is 35, and they have three children: Mark (8), Cindy (6), and Bryan (2). The Schillers have saved about $28,000 in a savings account at their local bank, where they earn about 6% annually. Frank thinks they should invest the money in a relatively safe investment, such as long-term corporate bonds. Karen disagrees, arguing that they should invest in a few growth stocks that might double in value over several years. Karen believes they need high returns for two reasons: She is concerned that sufficient funds will not be available to help the kids go to college, and she thinks their employer retirement plans are very inadequate. While Frank likes the idea of doubling their money, he is skeptical and cautious because they know so little about stocks. He thinks that if they want greater risk, they should invest in real estate. He has seen a small place in their neighborhood that could be fixed up and rented.

Karen and Frank have asked your advice to help them invest. They heard you are taking a course on the subject and thought you might have some good tips. The Schillers will probably have a 33% marginal tax rate in the future.

a. What type of disposition towards risk do you think Karen and Frank have? Would it be useful if they could describe their risk tolerance to you—and to themselves? Discuss.
b. Do the Schillers have general ideas on why they are investing? Would it help if they made their objectives more concrete? Discuss.
c. The following table indicates potential returns and risks from various investment alternatives. Suppose the Schillers plan to save $10,000 a year. Indicate how you think they should invest the funds in each of the next five years. Also, indicate how the $28,000 currently on hand should be invested.

**1.1
An Investment Approach for the Schillers**

Questions

Investment Alternative	Potential Return	Risk Index (10 = Highest)
1. Common stocks (broad portfolio)	12%	5
2. Corporate bonds	9	4
3. Residential real estate	8	3
4. Municipal bonds	8	4
5. Common stocks (growth)	15	7
6. Savings account	6	1

1.2
Tax Planning for Shirley Moreno's Investments

Shirley Moreno, a recent college graduate, has accepted a position as a chemist with a plastics manufacturer and will be moving to the Washington, D.C., area in the near future. Shirley has about $14,000 accumulated from previous summer jobs and gifts from her grandparents, and she wants to invest these funds along with monthly savings that should total $100. Unfortunately, Shirley has virtually no understanding of investments.

Shirley's father has advised her to buy a condominium in order to save apartment rentals. While this would take her entire $14,000 for a down payment on a $50,000 condo, she still could save the $100 a month. A real estate agent said that housing has been a good investment in the area, with prices increasing about 6% annually. A colleague at work thinks housing is an O.K. investment but he believes Shirley will do much better in corporate bonds. He anticipates a 10% return here, and he urges Shirley to use their employer's tax deferral plan, called a 401(k) plan.

Shirley is considering investing in both the condo and the bonds. However, she thinks she also should have some kind of investment that provides immediate access to her funds in case of an emergency. Along this line, she is considering a money market savings account with a current yield of about 7%; however, she has read a magazine ad for a tax-free money market mutual fund offering 6%. Shirley most likely will have a 28% marginal tax rate in the foreseeable future.

Questions

a. From a tax perspective, how does the condo investment differ from the bond investment? Suppose that Shirley retires after 30 years. Assume her condo is now worth $285,000 and the bond fund is worth $245,000 (through monthly investments and reinvested interest). If Shirley sells the condo and withdraws completely from the bond fund, determine how much income tax she will owe from each event.
b. Which short-term investment seems more appropriate for Shirley? Explain.
c. Overall, how do you evaluate Shirley's investment approach? Discuss.

Ellis, Junius. "Why Initial Public Offerings Are Bad Bets." *Money,* April 1986, pp. 175–88.

"Investment Banks: The New Meccas for Super-Sharp Young Grads Who Want to Make It Big in a Hurry." *Forbes,* April 21, 1986, p. 138.

Jasen, Georgette. "Stock Market Turns Students Into Paper Millionaires." *The Wall Street Journal,* March 10, 1989, p. C1.

"1989 Money Guide." *Forbes,* June 26, 1989, pp. 176–270.

Putka, Gary. "People Invest Little Faith in Wall Street." *The Wall Street Journal,* September 25, 1989, p. B1.

Steptoe, Sonja. "SEC Action Against Firm Shows Pitfalls for Penny-Stock Investors." *The Wall Street Journal,* July 11, 1989, p. C1.

White, James A. "Private Placement Market Attracts More Business Than It Can Handle." *The Wall Street Journal,* February 10, 1989, p. C1.

Winkler, Matthew. "SEC May Shift Plan to Boost Private Issues." *The Wall Street Journal,* March 16, 1989, p. C1.

Wong, Jan. "SEC Files Show How Easily People Take Dubious Investment Advice." *The Wall Street Journal,* November 18, 1986, p. 39.

HELPFUL
READING

CHAPTER TWO

The Investment Environment

PRIMARY AND SECONDARY
MARKETS

Organized Exchanges

Order Execution on the NYSE

The Over-the-Counter Market

SELECTING A STOCKBROKER

Types of Stockbrokerage Firms

Factors to Consider in Selecting a
Broker

Regulation of Securities Markets

OPENING AN ACCOUNT AND
MAKING TRANSACTIONS

Kinds of Accounts

Initiating a Position

Placing Orders

FINDING INVESTMENT
INFORMATION

Company Sources

Government Sources

Investment Advisory Services

Newspapers and Magazines

Computer Data Sources

Academic Journals

APPENDIX A: UNDER-
STANDING MARKET INDEXES

APPENDIX B: POPULAR
INVESTMENT INFORMATION
SOURCES

BOXES

A Day in the Life of a Specialist on
the NYSE

What is Binding Arbitration?

Using the Personal Computer in
Investing

After you finish this chapter, you
will be able to:

- distinguish between primary and
  secondary markets and see how
  trading is conducted on organized
  exchanges and in the OTC market.

- identify and evaluate factors important in selecting a stockbroker.

- recognize how legislation affects
  the securities markets.

- understand the mechanics of
  opening an account and making
  transactions, including the use of
  a margin account and the execution of short sales.

- identify sources of investment information.

- understand how various stock indexes are calculated and how
  these calculation methods are
  used to construct the Dow-Jones
  averages and the Standard and
  Poor's indexes.

P eople who are considering investing for the first time often find the process confusing and intimidating. They lack sufficient understanding of investment vehicles to construct their own portfolios, and many stockbrokers seem to speak a language they don't understand. Moreover, very few investors are aware of their rights and protections provided by law. Experience being the best teacher, you probably will not gain a thorough understanding of the investment process until you actually invest. Nevertheless, much can be learned before you put your funds at risk. This chapter deals with many pre-investment procedures. It explains how primary and secondary markets work, what types of stockbrokerage firms are available, how to open an account and make transactions, and where to find investment information.

PRIMARY AND SECONDARY MARKETS

A **primary market** refers to the initial distribution of securities. It is most often represented by the underwriting process described in Chapter 1. Some securities, however, are sold directly from issuers to buyers in a process called a private placement. In a primary market, funds flow from providers (investors) to users. A **secondary market** comes into existence when investors want to sell the securities they acquired in the primary market. In this case, they sell to other investors, so funds flow from one investor to another. You should understand that transactions in secondary markets have nothing to do with the organization that issued the security initially. You might have purchased 100 shares of IBM at $100 a share through a public offering. At that time IBM would have received $10,000. However, if you later sell the shares for $150 each, you do so in the secondary market, and the buyer pays $15,000 to you, not to IBM.

> Secondary markets are essential for the smooth functioning of primary markets.

Practically all the trading activity that you read and hear about occurs in the secondary market. Expressions such as "the market closed higher" describe prices in the secondary market. The existence of secondary markets is essential for the smooth functioning of primary markets. Being able to sell securities quickly and easily in the secondary market provides considerably greater demand for new issues than would otherwise be the case. Transactions in the secondary markets take place on organized exchanges or in the over-the-counter market.

Organized Exchanges

An **organized exchange** is most appropriately thought of as a place where buyers and sellers of securities physically meet to conduct trading activity. The primary advantage an organized exchange offers investors is that it creates a **continuous market,** which means you can always buy or sell a security at a competitively determined price that varies only slightly from one transaction to the next. Another advantage is that transactions can take place at minimum cost. If you had to hire someone to buy or sell securities for you, and if an organized exchange didn't exist, your commission would be exorbitant and it would be

> An organized exchange creates a continuous market, where securities are traded at competitively determined prices.

difficult to know whether you paid or received a fair price for the securities. In contrast, all trades on certain organized exchanges are recorded almost the instant they are made. The trade price and number of shares traded are then displayed throughout the world via a computerized transmission network. If you visit a stockbroker's office, you will see the so-called "tape," referring to ticker tape, which was used to transmit information in the past. The tape moves continuously, showing each transaction taking place on the trading floor.

Stock exchanges   The largest organized exchange is the New York Stock Exchange (NYSE). There are also the American Stock Exchange (the Amex) and 14 regional stock exchanges, the most important being the Pacific, Midwest, and Philadelphia exchanges. Companies choose to have their securities listed on an exchange, and must meet minimum listing requirements to do so. The most stringent are those of the NYSE. To be listed there, a company must have:

1. at least 1,100,000 shares held by the general public,
2. at least 2,000 shareholders who own 100 shares or more,
3. pretax incomes of at least $2,500,000 in the fiscal year prior to applying for a listing and no less than $2,000,000 in the two preceding years,
4. a total market value of shares held by the public of at least $18,000,000, and
5. net tangible assets of at least $16,000,000.

Organized exchanges account for about two-thirds of all equity shares traded (the other one-third are traded over the counter, which will be explained shortly), and of this total, about 82% are traded on the NYSE, 5% on the Amex, and 13% on regional exchanges. As you see, the NYSE dominates trading of listed securities and so earns its nickname—"the Big Board."

The New York Stock Exchange is the largest exchange in the world; it is truly the "big board."

Other Securities and Other Exchanges   Other countries have national exchanges similar to the NYSE and the Amex in the United States. Canada, for example, has the Montreal Stock Exchange, the Toronto Stock Exchange, and the Canadian Stock Exchange. Important exchanges abroad include the Tokyo Stock Exchange (second in world dollar volume, behind the NYSE) and the London Stock Exchange (third in world dollar volume). Other major stock exchanges are located in Frankfurt, Zurich, Paris, Sydney, and Hong Kong.

Important exchanges also exist abroad. The Tokyo Stock Exchange is second to the NYSE in dollar volume.

The major stock exchanges also trade other equity instruments (such as warrants and rights), bonds, and options. For example, the NYSE and the Amex list approximately 2,500 and 350 corporate bond issues, respectively. Options are traded on the American Stock Exchange, the Pacific Stock Exchange, and the Philadelphia Stock Exchange. It should also be noted that the most important options exchange is the Chicago Board Options Exchange (CBOE).

Futures contracts are traded on a number of exchanges, both in the United States and in other countries. Dominant exchanges in the U.S. include the Chicago Board of Trade (CBOT); the Chicago Mercantile Exchange (CME) and its important division, the International Monetary Market (IMM); the Kansas City

Options and futures are also traded on organized exchanges, such as the CBOE, CBOT, and IMM.

Board of Trade; and the New York Futures Exchange (NYFE), which is a subsidiary of the NYSE.

Order Execution on the NYSE

Organized exchanges are fascinating places to visit. What appears to be utter chaos is actually a very efficient system for transferring billions of dollars worth of securities each trading day. Exhibit 2.1 illustrates order execution on the NYSE and introduces its members who may be involved in the process. To be a member, you must buy a "seat." There are 1,366 seats in total, owned mostly by stockbrokerage firms. (For example, Merrill Lynch has 20.) Seat prices are determined by the demand for them, and they have varied considerably over time; for example, they hit a high of $515,000 in 1969, fell to $35,000 in 1977, and then rebounded to $1.1 million in 1987, right before the big crash on October 19, 1987. However, the price slumped to $390,000 in a sale in mid-January 1990.

Commission brokers are employed by stockbrokerage firms.

Commission Brokers **Commission brokers** are employed by stockbrokerage firms. Assuming you deal with Merrill Lynch and have placed a market order to buy 100 shares of Xerox, your representative will transmit the order to one of

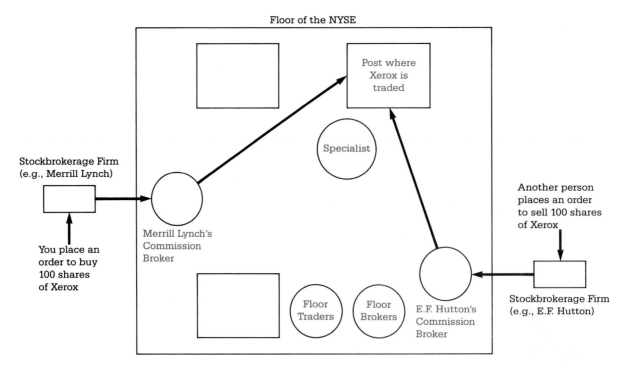

EXHIBIT 2.1
Illustration of a trade on the NYSE

Merrill Lynch's commission brokers on the floor of the exchange. Suppose that at the same time someone else places an order to sell 100 shares of Xerox through her broker, E. F. Hutton. Both commission brokers would then go to the post where Xerox is traded. For an actively traded issue, such as Xerox, there will be a number of brokers and traders bidding to buy or sell shares. All of them will try to get the best possible price, either for their customers or for themselves. In effect, shares are auctioned to the highest bidders. (The NYSE and similar markets are thus called *auction markets*.) Perhaps the Merrill Lynch and E. F. Hutton brokers settle a trade at $50 a share. The entire transaction may be completed in less than two minutes.

Specialists **Specialists** play a number of critical roles in the trading process. They are expected to maintain an orderly and continuous market in the six or seven stocks assigned to them. To keep wide swings in price from occurring, they must buy or sell for their own accounts. For example, assume that when your commission broker arrives at Xerox's trading post, no other broker or trader is there to trade Xerox. Then it is the specialist's responsibility to trade. Another responsibility for the specialist is to maintain the limit books, which contain all limit orders clients have placed with their brokers. (Limit orders will be explained shortly.) Because of the inside information specialists have, it is possible for them to profit handsomely at the expense of outside investors. However, the NYSE insists that customers' interests come first, and specialists' second. This rule is monitored constantly for compliance and enforced rigorously because the integrity of the specialist is critical to maintaining customer confidence in the system.

Specialists play a key role on an organized exchange by maintaining an orderly and continuous market for their assigned securities.

Floor Brokers and Floor Traders **Floor brokers** are not associated with any particular stockbrokerage firm, but serve as independent operators. They assist commission brokers by executing orders on their behalf, for a fee. They also serve stockbrokerage firms who do not own seats on the floor. **Floor traders** operate strictly for themselves, hoping their position on the floor will help them trade stocks profitably.

The Over-the-Counter Market

The **over-the-counter (OTC) market** refers to all security trading not conducted on organized exchanges. In most instances, it is a market that exists by virtue of telecommunications among stockbrokers. For example, suppose you wish to buy shares of Apple Computer, an unlisted company. To do so, your broker uses his or her information terminal to determine if another brokerage house is "making a market" in Apple. (This means a broker holds an inventory of shares that are available for purchase by potential buyers.) Perhaps six such brokers are found, each offering to sell Apple at an ask price and buy it at a bid price. Since you are buying Apple, your broker is interested only in ask prices, and will select the broker offering the lowest one, if there are differences.

The over-the-counter market exists by virtue of telecommunications among stockbrokers.

A Day in the Life of a Specialist on the NYSE

New York—Peter Mauer, a stock-exchange specialist, speeds to Wall Street by boat each morning from his home by the sea in New Jersey. It's an hour's trip each way, but Mauer enjoys it, good weather or bad.

The converted PT boat beats the crowded trains and clogged streets. Besides, he can afford it. Mauer works in the noisy, jostling pit that is the floor of the New York Stock Exchange.

Arriving about an hour before the exchange opens at 9:30 a.m., Mauer dons a dark blue work jacket. Except for his badge and breast pocket filled with papers and pens, he might be mistaken for a waiter or clerk.

But Mauer, a mild-mannered math whiz, is anything but ordinary. With a soft-spoken voice that can suddenly cut like a razor through the clamor all about

him, he handles millions of dollars in stock trading each day. The roughly three-foot-square space he paces is enormously valuable. [The price for a seat on the exchange has ranged from $400,000 to $1.2 million in recent years.]

Mauer and his firm, Benton & Co., are specialists in 20 companies that Benton represents on the floor of the exchange.

He and a handful of colleagues at Benton make the market for such well-known firms as Raytheon, Joy Manufacturing, a recent takeover target, and New York City's Irving Trust Co.

If you buy one share, 100 shares, or 10,000 shares of Nord, Raytheon, or Joy Manufacturing, Mauer puts together the trade. He matches your buy order, placed through your broker, with someone's sell order. If no one is

selling, he gets you the stock from Benton's inventory. If he doesn't have the shares, he'll sell short, if necessary, to supply them. In selling short, he sells shares he doesn't own with the intent of buying them later.

Shorthand of Specialists

Like many specialists, Mauer can pause in mid-sentence during a conversation and bark out a price to a passing trader from a firm such as Merrill Lynch, Shearson Lehman Brothers or E. F. Hutton. He'll then turn and continue his thought.

Specialists use a shorthand, talking in eighths, quarters and halves—meaning $31.13 for an eighth, $31.25 for a quarter and $31.50 for a half.

"Two thousand Raytheon to buy, two thousand to buy," a trader yells walking up to Ben-

The OTC market accounts for about 35% of equity shares traded, but dominates organized exchanges in two respects: it handles a far greater majority of individual stocks (about 30,000 versus about 3,000 on all the exchanges) and trades far more bonds. All government bonds and many corporate bonds (about 90%) trade OTC.

NASDAQ **NASDAQ** stands for National Association of Securities Dealers Automated Quotation System. It is a communication system that applies to about 3,500 actively traded OTC stocks. To be included, a company must meet certain requirements, similar to those imposed by organized exchanges but less

ton's post. His call is swallowed in the mounting din of shouts and counter shouts.

Specialists keep a book for each stock they handle. One part of the book lists "buy" orders. The other half lists "sell" orders. The specialist's job is to bring the two together. The book keeps track of buyers and sellers who want to exercise their trade when the stock reaches a certain price.

"But the customer always comes first, ahead of the interests of the specialists," Mauer and others at the exchange emphasized throughout the day. That means the customer will get the stock he wants, even if the specialist has to take a loss.

When a trade is made, a stock exchange reporter standing nearby, pencil poised, notes the transaction on a card and swiftly puts it into a card reader. The trade then quickly goes into the stock exchange computer and reads out on the familiar electric stock quote board.

Benton's own clerks in the kiosk also note the trade for the company's books.

Mauer is one of 1,366 individuals or companies with seats on the New York Stock Exchange. His firm is one of 55 that handle the stocks of 1,563 corporations. As of September, those companies had 57.9 billion shares worth more than $2.1 trillion.

What Mauer does for Nord Resources, Richard Burke of Henderson Brothers, Inc., does for Ponderosa, Inc., and Jim McMullan of M. J. Meehan & Co. does for NCR Corp.

The specialists like to emphasize their claim that the New York Stock Exchange is superior to the more electronically controlled over-the-counter market.

"This is an auction market. The best bid and the best offer always prevail," McMullan explained as he stood by his NCR post. "There's never any collusion here because all buyers and sellers come to this floor to trade."

In between shouts of quotes and trades, he continued:

"What I do is keep a fair and orderly market. I'm always the willing buyer and the willing seller. I don't necessarily want to sell 50,000 shares up (only) a quarter (25 cents a share). But I'll bring the stock from one price level up to the next price level as smooth and as orderly as I can possibly do it."

SOURCE: Excerpted from Jim Bohman, "Stock Exchange Specialist Works in A Noisy Jungle of Buy and Sell," *The Dayton Daily News and Journal Herald,* January 4, 1987, p.1-E.

stringent. The NASDAQ system allows buyers and sellers to locate each other very quickly, as described above for Apple Computer. Without it, brokers must search for potential buying or selling dealers. In addition to the basic NASDAQ requirements, additional requirements are imposed for firms to be part of the National Market System (NMS). NASDAQ/NMS firms have the benefit of up-to-the minute price and volume quotations, along with end-of-day price and volume data.

NASDAQ connects buyers and sellers quickly. It also has listing requirements, which are more stringent for the National Market System (NMS).

Market Segments   The OTC market is extremely diverse and actually consists of three distinct segments. The first includes firms that meet the basic and NMS requirements; the second includes firms that meet the basic, but not the NMS, requirements; and the third consists of very small firms, which meet neither set of requirements. Price quotations for these firms are available only through the so-called "pink sheets," published by the National Quotation Bureau.

The Third Market   The **third market** refers to OTC trading of securities listed on an exchange. Large institutions frequently conduct such trades in an effort to avoid high commissions set by the exchanges. Participating brokerage houses are willing to reduce their fees because of the large volume of business transacted. Since regulated commissions (commission rates set by the exchanges) no longer exist, third market activity has decreased considerably.

The Fourth Market   The **fourth market** refers to trading activity conducted directly between buyer and seller without the assistance of a broker. Such trades involve a large number of shares of a large company with many millions of shares outstanding, such as General Motors. Suppose an investor owns 40,000 shares of GM. At $80 a share, the total market value is $3.2 million, and even a commission rate as small as 1% means a total commission of $64,000—$32,000 each for buyer and seller. Thus, it might pay investors to try to find each other without using a broker. Since buyers and sellers are usually large institutional investors, such as insurance companies, mutual funds, or retirement funds, it might be possible for a potential seller to locate a potential buyer through telephone inquiry or other means. Because of limited information, the size of the fourth market is not known, but many observers believe it is growing.

SELECTING A STOCKBROKER

Once you decide to invest, the next step is to choose a stockbroker. This step is important because the person you select may influence your investment decisions and certainly will charge you for services provided. This section will explain services and charges; it also will explain protections available to you under various laws, and it offers points to consider when choosing a broker.

Types of Stockbrokerage Firms

Stockbrokerage houses can be classified as full-service or limited-service firms. Services consist of two basic kinds: those related to order execution, and those that are advisory in nature.

Full-Service Firms   A **full-service firm** offers both order execution and a full range of advisory services. You probably can identify these firms by their slogans: "A Breed Apart" (Merrill Lynch), "Rock Solid—Market Wise" (Prudential-Bache), "When E. F. Hutton Talks. . ." (E. F. Hutton). Full-service brokers spend a considerable amount of money on research, which they provide to their clients to help them make investment choices. Very often, this research leads to recommendations to buy, hold, or sell specific securities; for example, a stock might be rated a "buy" for aggressive investors.

Full-service firms typically charge the highest commissions, but they may be lower if the transaction is very small, as Exhibit 2.2 indicates. The high commissions are considered necessary to cover the expenses of research and other services provided, such as the extra advisory time representatives spend with clients. While Exhibit 2.2 indicates commissions on stocks only, you should be aware that full-service brokers usually charge higher commissions for trading other securities, such as options, futures, warrants, and bonds. The rate structure is reasonably competitive within each brokerage class, although there are differences, as Exhibit 2.2 shows, and it makes sense to obtain commission information before selecting a broker.

Full-service brokers generally charge higher commissions but also provided investment research.

Exhibit 2.2 also indicates that commissions are quite low in relation to the amount invested, unless the order is fairly small. However, keep in mind that commissions are shown for only one transaction. If you trade stocks actively, turning over your holdings a number of times a year, your commissions can erode any trading profit you might earn. For example, suppose you use a full-service broker and buy and sell 100 shares at $35 on four occasions during the year. Total commissions will be $664 (8 × $83), or almost 19% of the funds invested. Very few investors can overcome this commission burden, yet many beginning investors trade even more frequently—until they learn better or run out of funds.

Limited-Service Firms A **limited-service firm,** as its name implies, offers a limited range of investor services. Many such firms, called discounters, will only execute orders. They make it very clear that you are to make your own investment decisions; they do not provide any investment advice. More often than not, the discounter you deal with is not located in your community, so all transactions are undertaken by telephone, using a toll-free number.

Discounters generally provide only order execution.

Within the past decade a number of financial institutions, such as commercial banks and savings and loans, have entered the stockbrokerage business. Some offer limited investment advice, others have chosen to be strictly

EXHIBIT 2.2
Illustrative stockbrokerage commissions on common stock transactions

Transaction	Value of the Transaction	Commissions: $ and % of Value					
		Full-Service Broker		Well-Known Discounter		Smaller Discounter	
10 shares @ $35	$ 350	$ 18	5.1%	$ 35	10.0%	$25	7.1%
100 shares @ $35	3,500	$ 83	2.4%	$ 49	1.4%	$34	1.0%
500 shares @ $35	17,500	$263	1.5%	$114	0.7%	$68	0.4%

discounters. They appeal to investors who are reluctant to deal with an outside firm they have never seen; in effect, they are capitalizing on the trust and confidence people have in their local bankers. (That trust has grown thin in some instances in recent years in the wake of many failures and other financial problems.) Their commissions tend to be higher than other discounters and lower than full-service brokerage firms.

Factors to Consider in Selecting a Broker

Since there are many brokerage firms from which to choose, how do you select one? Of course, there is no pat answer appropriate for every investor. You should consider the following factors in making a decision.

How Important is Research?   Do you intend to use the recommendations a full-service broker provides, or do you plan to make your own investment decisions? If the latter situation is true, why do you want a full-service broker? Many investors start with one but find they become more independent over time. If that is the case, there is little reason to pay the higher commissions.

How Good Is Order Execution?   There is no evidence to show that discount brokers have poorer order execution than full-service firms. Each uses the organized exchanges and OTC markets in identical fashion and executes orders at the same prices and within the same lengths of time.

How Important Is the Representative's Advice?   A salesperson of a full-service firm (the person you deal with and probably call "your broker") usually holds the title of registered representative or account executive. He or she has probably passed an examination and has met other requirements to become licensed to sell securities, and is qualified to explain investments to you and to consider their importance in relation to your stated investment objectives. If you are seeking investments offering high income, you can—and should—expect the representative to ·recommend appropriate securities to achieve the goal: bonds, for example, and not growth stocks. If this type of service is important, then a full-service broker should be selected.

A registered representative is generally qualified to explain investments and to relate them to your objectives.

How Frequently Will You Trade?   Clearly, whether a full-service firm or a discounter is used, total commissions paid over a period of time depends upon the number of transactions. As noted above, frequent trading may be prohibitively expensive. However, you should be aware that commissions can be negotiated with many brokers. Active traders often receive discounts based on volume, but you might have to ask to receive them. Before selecting a broker, you should ask for commission information based upon your estimate of activity. By all means, let the representative know that you are doing comparative shopping and that you expect to receive all available concessions. And keep in mind that discount firms also offer concessions.

To avoid high commissions associated with small transactions, and as a means of gaining good diversification, you should consider **monthly investment plans** offered by some brokers. These plans allow you to select securities in which you wish to invest, and then each month (or other period) you pay a set amount to the firm. In turn, the firm buys shares in your designated companies in the proportions you select. Commissions are relatively low, around 2% or so. (Also be aware that many individual companies, such as IBM, offer dividend reinvestment plans that allow investors to receive additional shares of stock in lieu of cash dividends. There is a very small service charge with these plans, which makes them attractive vehicles for accumulating shares over time.)

Regulation of Securities Markets

As you might suspect, the nature of the securities industry has offered disreputable people considerable opportunities to defraud investors. Since 1933, important laws have been passed to protect investors; in addition, the industry has initiated reform through self-policing efforts. You have much greater protection now than in the past, but it would be a mistake to think fraud no longer exists, or to believe any losses you might suffer are the fault of your broker. It is important to know your rights and your obligations before you invest.

The Securities Act of 1933   The Securities Act of 1933 calls for full disclosure of new securities to be traded in interstate commerce. Such securities must be registered with the Securities and Exchange Commission (SEC), which approves their sale. To receive approval, the applicant must provide the SEC with economic and financial data relevant to the firm and the new offering. It does so in the form of a **prospectus**. After the SEC has determined that the prospectus represents adequate disclosure of all material information affecting the company's value, and after the SEC has approved the registration, the company must provide the prospectus to any potential investor. Misrepresentation or fraud in preparing the prospectus can be the basis for lawsuits by investors and the SEC against the issuing corporation, its directors, stockbrokers handling the issue, and even public accountants who assisted in its preparation.

Stiff penalties and possible jail sentences have done much to provide investors with reliable and relevant prospectuses. However, SEC approval in no way assures the issue will be successful. Many new firms have prepared impeccably clean prospectuses, and then have gone into bankruptcy. The message is very clear if you are considering investing: obtain a prospectus, read it thoroughly, particularly the section explaining risk factors, and believe what it says. Some investors seem to think a prospectus is a mere formality; it isn't. It is a helpful document and should be regarded as such.

The Securities Exchange Act of 1934   The Securities Exchange Act of 1934 extended regulation to securities that had already been issued. With this provision, it brought under government regulation almost all aspects of the

> Monthly investment plans and dividend reinvestment plans are effective low-cost methods of investing.

> Pay particular attention to risk factors when reading a prospectus, and do not assume SEC approval assures an issue's success.

security markets. It required all securities traded on organized exchanges and the exchanges themselves to be registered with the SEC (which it established). It outlawed fraud and misrepresentation by anyone engaged in the sale of securities, including stockbrokers and their representatives. It forbade price manipulation, and it required registered firms to file with the SEC both a detailed annual report (called a 10-K report) and quarterly financial statements. It also stipulated that annual reports be provided to shareholders.

The Act also established guidelines for security trading by insiders, the intent being to prevent them from taking advantage of their privileged information. Initially, insiders were considered a firm's officers, employees, directors, or relatives of each. In recent years, the SEC has broadened its definition of *insider* to include practically anyone with information not available to the general public. In a noted case, a newspaper reporter was convicted under the law for providing advance information about news items subsequently printed in the paper.

An insider can be anyone with privileged information; trading on such information is illegal.

The Maloney Act of 1938   The Maloney Act of 1938 required any trade association in the securities industry to register with the SEC. Only one—the National Association of Securities Dealers (NASD)—has been formed and registered. The NASD is the self-regulating arm of the securities industry. It establishes and enforces a professional code of ethics and is responsible for testing and licensing dealers (noted earlier).

The Investment Company Act of 1940   The Investment Company Act of 1940 brought regulation to investment companies, which we more frequently call mutual funds. Such companies are required to register with the SEC and to provide shareholders with adequate information about the company's activities. A subsequent amendment to the act forbade paying excessive fees to fund advisors.

Investment advisors must register with the SEC, but such registration does not mean their advice is particularly useful.

The Investment Advisors Act of 1940   The Investment Advisors Act of 1940 requires anyone providing advice to investors (for a fee or for other compensation) to register with the SEC and to indicate his or her methods of investment analysis. The determination of who is an investment advisor has come under scrutiny in recent years as many products and services not usually thought of as investment-related are now being tailored more in that direction. Two good cases in point deal with financial advisors and insurance agents. The former advise clients on a wide range of financial activities, including investments, while the latter sell policies that look like and pay out like investments. Should these professionals register as advisors? The current trend in court cases seems to answer *yes*. As an investor, keep in mind that registration does not improve the quality of advice offered or in some other fashion guarantee its usefulness. Some advisors advertise their registration, perhaps with the intent of impressing potential clients. Do not be impressed—virtually anyone with about $250 to pay the fee can register.

What is Binding Arbitration?

On the advice of a registered representative of a large brokerage company, an elderly couple invests most of their life savings—about $30,000—in bonds issued by a now-defunct energy company. They lose everything and appeal to the broker for compensation on the grounds the representative put them in an unsuitable investment. The company declines to make restitution—now what? In a growing number of cases, the answer is binding arbitration.

Investors with gripes such as the elderly couple's, or those involving excessive trading (called "churning"), or unauthorized transactions, or any other misconduct, can file a claim to have the dispute settled through binding arbitration. Claims are filed either with the National Association of Securities Dealers or with the New York Stock Exchange or American Stock Exchange. The process is quite simple and relatively inexpensive, with filing fees ranging from $15 to $1,000 (for disputes in excess of $500,000).

If a claim is less than $5,000, it is settled by one arbitrator who rules on the evidence provided by each side. Larger claims are heard by 3-person panels in a formal hearing that is similar to a trial. Each side can be represented by an attorney, issue subpoenas, and cross-examine witnesses. If your claim goes to a hearing, expect to be on the "hot seat" with the opposing attorney trying to show that you were an intelligent investor, making your own investment decisions drawn from alternatives suggested by the representative. You, of course, must show that your losses were caused by the representative.

Establishing such evidence might be difficult if you do not keep accurate records of your communications with the rep. As usual, the best evidence is in written form; but you should keep a careful diary of verbal communications, such as tips or other forms of advice. Note the time and date and carefully record the nature of the conversation.

The alternative to arbitration is litigation. This route is very expensive, and it is usually not advised if a claim is less than $200,000 or so. The big advantage with litigation is that you can also go after punitive damages, which are not allowed in arbitration. Actually, you might not have a choice in the matter. Most brokerage houses insist that you sign a customer's agreement form when you open an account. If you read it closely, you probably will find a clause that states that all disputes must be settled by binding arbitration. And, once you agree to arbitration you cannot later seek litigation if the arbitrators bring in a judgment to your disliking. So, if you don't care for that arrangement, read the agreement carefully and insist the binding arbitration clause be deleted before you sign. (The SEC has issued rule changes that make deleting the clause easier.) You can get more information on arbitration from the NASD (Two World Trade Center, New York, NY 10048) or the New York Stock Exchange (11 Wall Street, New York, NY 10006).

The Securities Investor Protection Act of 1970   The Securities Investor Protection Act protects investors from financial losses that might result from the failure of their broker. It created the Securities Investor Protection Corporation (SIPC), which insures an investor's account up to $500,000 for securities held and up to $100,000 in cash holdings. Most brokerage firms are members of the SIPC and contribute to its funding. It has been particularly helpful to discounters in their efforts to overcome investor reluctance to deal with out-of-town brokers.

Some investors believe the SIPC protection extends to any losses on securities they hold while a broker is in financial difficulty. This is not true. SIPC guarantees only that your securities will be delivered eventually to you or to another broker. Any losses or gains during the time the failing firm's arrangements are being sorted out are the investor's. For example, SIPC only guarantees delivery of 100 shares of GM, if that is what you held with a failing broker; it does not guarantee a price for those shares. GM might have been worth $80 a share when your broker ceased to operate, but be worth only $50 a share when you eventually have access to the shares.

> The SIPC is a form of investor insurance. It guarantees eventual delivery of shares if your broker fails financially.

OPENING AN ACCOUNT AND MAKING TRANSACTIONS

After you select a broker, the next step is to open an account. With it, you then can begin buying or selling securities.

Kinds of Accounts

Opening an account takes very little time. If you are married, you should consider a joint account, with each spouse having authority to initiate orders. You can choose a cash account, a margin account, or a discretionary account. Each is explained below.

Cash Account   A **cash account** is similar to a charge account you might have with a retail establishment: you purchase securities and must pay for them within five working days after the day of purchase. (Holidays provide an extra day.) The same time frame applies when you sell: you then have five days to deliver the securities sold. Some brokers request an initial deposit before executing orders, others do not. Also, you can choose to have securities delivered to you or you can leave them with the broker in what is called a *street account*. This means the securities are registered in the broker's name.

Margin Account   A **margin account** allows the broker, at your request, to borrow funds for you, pledging your securities as collateral for the loan. Each brokerage firm establishes a minimum amount (usually $2,000 to $3,000) to open a margin account, and the Board of Governors of the Federal Reserve System (the Fed) imposes an initial margin requirement based on the market value of securities purchased. This requirement varies depending upon the type of

> A margin account allows investors to borrow from their brokers.

security purchased: for common and preferred stocks it is 50% (many OTC stocks, however, cannot be margined because they supposedly lack collateral value); it is 25% for warrants and high-quality bonds; and 5% of face value for Treasury and agency bonds. In addition to the initial margin requirement, the Fed also imposes a maintenance margin requirement. This means you must keep sufficient equity in your account so that it is at least 25% (for stocks) of the securities' market value. If your equity falls below this minimum, your broker is authorized to sell enough shares to restore the account to the initial margin requirement.

Most brokers impose a maintenance margin requirement slightly higher than the legal minimum. When this figure is touched, you get a margin call, which means you either must deposit additional funds to increase your equity or sell some of your shares. The mechanics of margin trading are illustrated in Exhibit 2.3. In this example, the investor received a margin call when the price of her

Activity	Calculation
1. Investor deposits $2,000 and borrows $2,000 to purchase $4,000 of securities; she owns 100 shares of KLM at $40 a share.	Initial margin (M) can be used to leverage purchases (P). At a margin requirement (r) of 0.5: $$P = M/r = \$2000/0.5 = \$4000$$
2. Unfortunately, KLM's price falls. As it does, the investor's equity also falls. At $35 a share, her equity is down to $1500. The broker's loan, of course, is still $2000.	The investor's equity (E) is equal to the market value of securities (V) minus the broker's loan (B); $$E = V - B = \$3,500 - \$2,000 = \$1,500$$
3. Finally, the price hits a point that triggers a margin call; this price is $28.57 a share	The trigger point occurs when the investor's equity is equal to the maintenance margin requirement (r') times the market value of the securities: $E = r'(V)$. If $r' = 0.3$, then $$E = 0.3V; \quad \text{but} \quad E = (V - \$2,000)$$ $$\text{So,} \quad (V - \$2,000) = 0.3V$$ $$0.7V = \$2,000$$ $$V = \$2,857$$
4. The broker requires additional margin to restore the initial margin requirement of 0.5; the amount needed is $571.50	A 0.5 requirement means E must equal $0.5V$. Since V is $2,857, then $$E = 0.5V$$ $$E = 0.5(\$2,857)$$ $$E = \$1,428.50$$ Additional M = required E minus actual E. Additional M = $1,428.50 - $857.00 = $571.50
5. The broker charges interest for the month. (Note: interest is deducted automatically from your equity; however, it is ignored in step 4 above for simplicity.)	Assuming the prime rate is 7%, and the broker charges prime plus 2%: Interest = (.09 × $2,000)/12 = $180/12 = $15

EXHIBIT 2.3
The mechanics of a margin account

shares declined to $28.57; she then deposited $571.50 with the broker, reducing his loan to $1,428.50 (which is the same amount as her equity).

You often are told that margin accounts are risky and should be avoided. Actually, they are no riskier than any other lending arrangement. However, any loan increases risk. This is so because it allows you to magnify the amount of money invested, which is described as *leverage*. Naturally, a greater investment means greater profits—or losses. Moreover, the broker charges interest on the loan, usually at the prime rate (the rate banks charge their most credit-worthy customers) plus one or two percentage points. Finally, you cannot take delivery to your shares with a margin account since they must remain in the broker's street name.

Discretionary Account   A discretionary account gives the broker powers of attorney, enabling him or her to conduct trades without seeking your prior approval. Such accounts are used generally by wealthy clients who wish to turn over to the broker all investing activities. Obviously, you should have the highest confidence in both the broker's investment ability and integrity before considering such an account. Because of possible liability for misconduct, some stockbrokerage firms do not offer discretionary accounts.

Initiating a Position

After an account is opened, you can begin trading. Your first decision is whether you wish to buy or sell securities. When you buy, you take a **long position;** when you sell securities that you do not already own, you take a **short position;** and when you sell securities you originally bought, or buy securities you originally sold, you are **reversing a position**. Long positions seem natural to us because we associate investing with buying and holding securities. However, short positions, also called *short sales,* are very common and no different from a long purchase as far as a broker is concerned.

A long position is taken if we think a security's price will increase (or, if it provides us with income) and, equally obvious, a short position is appropriate if we believe its price will decrease. Buyers are often called "bulls," while sellers are referred to as "bears." Suppose you think IBM is overvalued at $150 a share and is likely to decrease in the future. You could place an order to short 100 shares of the stock at $150, hoping to reverse your position in the future after the price has fallen. The mechanics of the short sale are explained in Exhibit 2.4. Since sellers must use a margin account, margin is included in the illustration.

The SEC requires that all short sales be identified as such. Because of this requirement, the volume of short sales is compiled and reported in the financial press, such as the monthly report in *The Wall Street Journal*. Also, the SEC imposes the so-called *up tick* rule, which means a short sale must be made either on an up tick or a zero tick (a "tick" refers to a price change). Consider the following string of prices for a stock:

25   24   24⅛   24⅛   24¼   23⅞

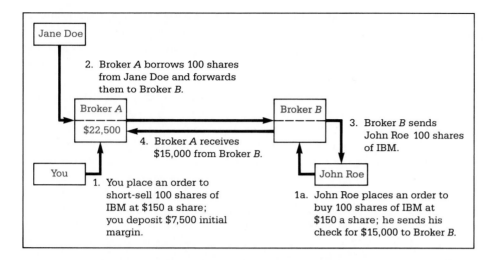

QUESTIONS AND ANSWERS ON SHORT SALES

Q Can you withdraw the $15,000 from the short sale?
A No, your account is credited for the amount, but the funds are restricted.

Q Do you earn interest on the sale proceeds or any margin you put up?
A That depends. Some brokers share interest with active traders; it is earned by investors willing to lend their shares (Jane Doe), and by other brokers if they are the lenders. Most often it is kept by the broker. (Usually the borrowed shares come from the firm's street account).

Q What if IBM pays a dividend while you are short? Who gets it—Jane Doe or John Roe?
A Each receives a dividend. Obviously, IBM pays only one, so you must pay the other.

Q Suppose IBM's price increases to $170 a share; what happens?
A You lose, since you bet on a price decrease. In this case, your loss is $2,000 [($170 − $150) × 100].

Q Since you margined the short sale, can you get a margin call?
A Yes. In fact, with short sales your account is updated for current prices each day. (This is called *marking to market*). At a price of $170, your equity percentage is only 32%. This figure is calculated as shown below:

$$\text{equity \%} = \left(\frac{\text{Initial Sales Amount} + \text{Initial Margin}}{\text{Current Market Value of Securities}} \right) - 1.0$$

$$\text{equity \%} = \left(\frac{\$15,000 + \$7,500}{\$170(100)} \right) - 1.0$$

$$\text{equity \%} = \left(\frac{\$22,500}{\$17,000} \right) - 1.0 = 1.32 - 1.0 = 0.32 \text{ or } 32\%$$

If the maintenance margin requirement is, say, 30% you will get a margin call if IBM increases about another $3 a share.

Q Suppose IBM's price falls to $120 a share?
A You make a profit of $3,000 [($150 − $120) × 100].

Q Is there a time limit on a short sale?
A No, you can keep it forever—as long as you have enough margin.

EXHIBIT 2.4

Mechanics of a short sale

Short sales could have taken place at 24⅛ and 24¼ (the two up ticks) but not 24 or 23⅞ (the two down ticks). The SEC created the up tick rule to reduce the possibility that short sellers could initiate a selling spree that might encompass the general public. After prices had fallen, the short sellers could step in and cover their positions at depressed prices.

Some people believe the broker imposes risks on the shareholders whose shares have been borrowed to complete the short sale. This is not so because of the margin protection. Actually, the broker's cash position is enhanced by both the short seller's margin deposit and the proceeds received from selling the securities. The disposition of interest earned on these amounts is left to the broker; some keep it, while some share it with clients who are active traders or who agree to lend their shares for short-sale purposes. (These latter investors would have cash accounts, which require shareholder approval. However, the broker can lend all shares held in the street account without any prior approval.)

Finally, it should be noted the short seller must pay any dividends declared by the company that issued the stock. At first glance this seems a harsh penalty to pay for short selling. Actually, it isn't, because the price of the stock in the market is automatically reduced by the amount of the dividend on the ex-dividend date. So the short seller breaks even: what is lost through the dividend payment is recouped by a gain on the short sale.

Placing Orders

With an account opened and a position taken, you can place a market order, a limit order, or a stop order. An order for 100 shares is called a *round lot,* while one for less than 100 shares is called an *odd lot*. You are charged a slightly higher commission for an odd-lot order.

A market order attempts to get the best price; however, the actual price may be different from the quoted price when a trade is entered.

Market Order   A **market order** instructs your broker to buy or sell securities at the best possible price. At the time you make a transaction, the broker will give you the last price at which the security traded. For example, you might call wishing to sell 100 shares of Quaker Oats. The broker at a computer terminal will push the letters OAT (Quaker's trading symbol on the NYSE) and see a number, say, 49⅛ ($49.125). This information is given to you, and if you then give the instruction to sell at the market, your sell order will be placed. Within a minute or so, it will reach the floor of the NYSE and be executed at the best possible price for you. However, this price may not be 49⅛. It could be a bit higher or lower because of buying or selling pressure while your order is being processed. However, in a continuous market you can expect any change to be minimal; for example, you might sell at 49¼ ($49.25).

A limit order sets the price of a trade.

Limit Order   A **limit order** sets the price at which a transaction can take place. You could instruct the broker to buy Quaker at 49 ($49.00). This means your order will not be executed unless the price is less than or equal to $49.00. Limit orders remain in effect until they are either cancelled or executed. A day order, for example, terminates at the end of the day, while a good-till-cancelled order remains alive until cancelled. You might consider using limit orders when dealing in OTC securities with low trading activity. Their price swings during the order-processing period could be more dramatic than those of actively traded stocks.

Stop Order   A **stop order** (often referred to as a *stop-loss order*) is a market order that is triggered by the market price of a security. It is used to protect profits or limit losses. Suppose you bought OAT at $20 a share and are quite pleased with the existing profit, since it now sells for $50. Rather than selling and "cashing in," you wish to hold it because there is a chance its price could increase to $60. As a trade-off, you decide to place a stop order at $45 a share. If OAT increases in price, you simply place another stop order at a higher price and cancel the one at the lower price. If OAT's price falls and touches $45, your stop order becomes a market order. You will sell at the best possible price, which again may not be exactly $45.

> A stop order is used to protect profits or limit losses.

Investors often use stop orders to relieve them of the task of watching their securities closely and making frequent buying and selling decisions. (You also can use a stop order to buy a security. The procedure is the same: when the trigger price is reached, a market order to buy is initiated. Short sellers often use stop orders in this fashion to protect their profits.) Moreover, some investors believe they lack adequate discipline to initiate appropriate orders when a security's price is falling rapidly. The stop order makes the process mechanical—once the order is placed.

FINDING INVESTMENT INFORMATION

Most investment decisions require some research. Even if you decide to limit your investing to mutual funds or other pooling arrangements, you still must evaluate the alternative funds available. And if you make your own investment decisions, your research must be quite ambitious. Information is the key to good research, and the sections to follow provide an overview of available sources. Additional sources are highlighted throughout the text with specific topics under discussion. For a summary of popular sources of investment information, see Appendix B at the end of this chapter.

Company Sources

As noted earlier, companies are required by the SEC to provide shareholders with annual and quarterly financial reports. Companies must also provide 10-K reports if they are requested. A 10-K report is a detailed compilation of a company's financial performance for the previous year. It presents the same data found in a company's annual financial report, but may include other information not found there, such as asset depreciation methods or officer compensation levels.

> Individual companies can provide considerable financial data.

Considerable information can be found in company reports. In addition to financial data, these documents contain discussions of past results and plans for the future. Of course, the corporate officers who provide these statements generally wish to present their company in its most favorable light. Thus, caution is necessary.

To gain information more quickly, you might ask that your name be placed on a company's mailing list for press releases to financial analysts and other interested parties. Moreover, some investors call or write companies, requesting information or clarification of certain topics that appear in financial reports. The success of this approach depends upon the nature of your request and willingness of management to respond to it. Naturally, you cannot expect that management will release privileged or sensitive information.

Government Sources

The federal government is a rich source of information about the overall economy and its component industries. Exhibit 2.5 indicates some of the more popular government publications. Most of these are available at university libraries, or you can purchase them through the Superintendent of Documents at rather nominal costs. Moreover, some of their economic series and analyses are now available on floppy discs. This is exceptionally convenient if you are using a personal computer in your research.

Monetary statistics and other useful information can be found in the *Federal Reserve Bulletin,* a monthly publication of the Federal Reserve System. It too is

EXHIBIT 2.5
Government publications

Federal Government
To order, write: Superintendent of Documents
                   U.S. Government Printing Office
                   Washington, DC   20402

Business Conditions Digest	monthly
Business Statistics	biennial
Economic Indicators	monthly
Long Term Economic Growth	book
Statistical Abstract of the U.S.	annually
Survey of Current Business	monthly
U.S. Industrial Outlook	annually

Federal Reserve System
To order, write: Federal Reserve System
                   Board of Governors
                   Division of Administrative Services
                   Washington, DC 20551

Federal Reserve Bulletin	monthly
Annual Chart Book	annually

available at most libraries. Also, each of the twelve Federal Reserve banks offers free publications. You can write to them, asking to be placed on their mailing lists. Their addresses can be found in any issue of the *Bulletin*.

Investment Advisory Services

The three major investment advisory services are Standard and Poor's, Moody's, and Value Line. You should have no trouble finding most of them at your university and local libraries. They are extremely popular research sources and widely used by many investors. Exhibit 2.6 shows a research report for NCR Corporation from the Value Line *Survey*. As you see, it contains a considerable amount of data, which will be more meaningful to you after you have read Chapters 8 and 9. Another useful advisory service is the Weisenberger *Survey of Investment Companies*. It reports information, including historical performances, on many mutual funds.

So-called investment newsletters form a different type of investment advisory service. Such newsletters are published by individuals who tout their skills at forecasting future security prices. They are expensive and their forecasting acumen is questionable. You can read the advertisements of some of these forecasters in each issue of *Barron's*. Read Chapter 10, though, before you decide to subscribe to one.

Investment newsletters are expensive and their forecasts are questionable.

Newspapers and Magazines

Many investors find a considerable amount of information in newspapers and magazines. This information includes investment stories and articles that might stimulate your interest, as well as financial data. Most of the newspapers and magazines mentioned below are available at libraries.

The Wall Street Journal   *The Wall Street Journal* is published each work day. Many investors subscribe to the *Journal* or read it at their offices or libraries. It is not exclusively investment-oriented, but, rather, covers a wide range of business and economic topics. Practically every issue has at least one story of relevance to most investors along with extensive price and trading information on a wide range of securities. It would be fruitless to attempt to describe this publication in detail; you simply must read an issue to appreciate its comprehensive coverage of investments. An interesting part of the *Journal* is its daily report on a variety of market indicators, such as the Dow Jones Industrial Average, illustrated in Exhibit 2.7. The DJIA is perhaps the most widely watched market index in the United States because of its historical significance. Because it covers only 30 individual stocks, however, it is not considered a comprehensive market index. The Standard and Poor 500 Stock Index also has wide appeal and is far more representative of the overall market. It also differs in its method of computation; Appendix A at the end of this chapter illustrates these differences.

The Wall Street Journal and Barron's are popular investment publications.

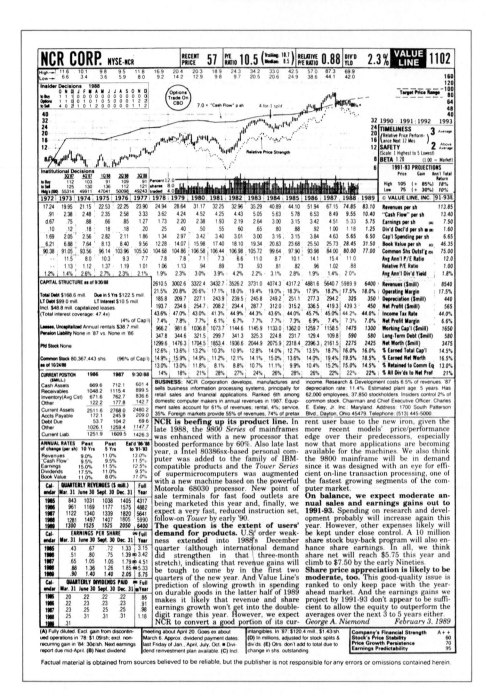

EXHIBIT 2.6

Value Line report on NCR. (Source: *Value Line Investment Survey*, February 3, 1989, p. 1112. © Value Line, Inc. Reprinted by permission.)

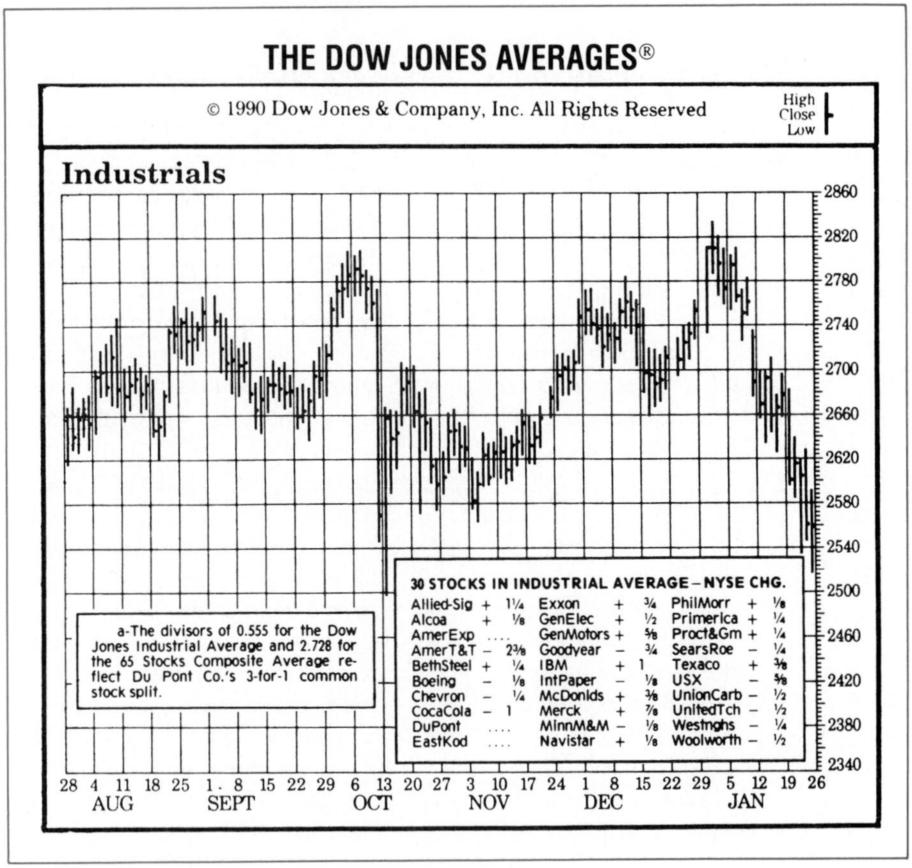
THE DOW JONES AVERAGES®
© 1990 Dow Jones & Company, Inc. All Rights Reserved
High
Close
Low
Industrials
2860
2820
2780
2740
2700
2660
2620
2580
2540
2500
2460
2420
2380
2340
a-The divisors of 0.555 for the Dow Jones Industrial Average and 2.728 for the 65 Stocks Composite Average reflect Du Pont Co.'s 3-for-1 common stock split.
30 STOCKS IN INDUSTRIAL AVERAGE – NYSE CHG.
Allied-Sig + 1¼ Exxon + ¾ PhilMorr + ⅛
Alcoa + ⅛ GenElec + ½ Primerica + ¼
AmerExp .... GenMotors + ⅝ Proct&Gm + ¼
AmerT&T – 2⅜ Goodyear – ¾ SearsRoe – ¼
BethSteel + ¼ IBM + 1 Texaco + ⅜
Boeing – ⅛ IntPaper – ⅛ USX – ⅝
Chevron – ¼ McDonlds + ⅜ UnionCarb – ½
CocaCola – 1 Merck + ⅞ UnitedTch – ½
DuPont .... MinnM&M – ⅛ Westnghs – ¼
EastKod .... Navistar + ⅛ Woolworth – ½
28 4 11 18 25 1 8 15 22 29 6 13 20 27 3 10 17 24 1 8 15 22 29 5 12 19 26
AUG SEPT OCT NOV DEC JAN

EXHIBIT 2.7
The DJIA. (Reprinted by permission of *The Wall Street Journal.* © Dow Jones & Company, Inc., 1990. All rights reserved.)

Barron's *Barron's* is a sister publication to the *Journal*. It is published weekly and is exclusively investment-oriented. It has regular columns dealing with different aspects of investing and a market laboratory section in each issue. Additionally, it features stories on different companies, reports interviews with security analysts and other investment advisors, and offers refresher articles on different aspects of investing. If *Barron's* has a flaw, it would be its advertisements and some of its stories, which often lean to the sensational side of investing.

The Wall Street Transcript A weekly publication, *The Wall Street Transcript* is devoted exclusively to investments. It reports on speeches company executives make to security analysts, and on other important corporate announcements. It also features research reports issued by security analysts and covers topics of interest to market technicians. It is quite expensive and may not be available at your university library. It has limited uses to the beginning investor and so is probably not worth its cost.

Using the Personal Computer in Investing

The personal computer (PC) is rapidly gaining acceptance in both the home and the office, and for good reasons: it not only eliminates much of the drudgery in certain jobs, but it also expands our analytical and creative abilities. Nowhere is that more true than in investing. With some training and rather modest outlays, you now can access data and do investment analyses that previously were the exclusive domain of professionals with virtually unlimited budgets.

However, it is foolish to believe a PC will improve investment performance automatically. Indeed, if it leads us to trade frequently, using all sorts of trading or timing strategies, it might easily have an opposite effect, as brokerage commissions soar. Computational power is no substitute for knowledge and understanding of securities markets and investment techniques. With that warning given, let us review how a PC-based investment system works.

Hardware

Hardware consists of a unit called the computer—NCR's Decision Mate 6, for example—and peripheral equipment, such as a monitor, printer, and modem. The monitor, which is standard with most PCs now, displays output (called *soft copy*) on a screen, while a printer provides printed material (called *hard copy*). A modem links the computer to a telephone line, giving the system access to available sources of data. You should have all three if you intend to use the PC in your investment activities. Before purchasing, do comparative shopping, because prices vary considerably; but be careful not to sacrifice capability. At a minimum, you should have a unit with a double disk drive, a hard disk, and 640K of memory.

Software

Software refers to programs used with hardware to perform the specific tasks you wish to do. In many respects, software is the more important of the two, because without it, the machines are useless. Fortunately, many excellent programs that specialize in most facets of investing are now available on floppy disks. Broadly, these programs can be classified as portfolio management or analytical.

Portfolio Management Programs

Portfolio management programs allow users to maintain records of their investment portfolios. They record and show activities on securities purchased, sold, and currently held. Portfolio returns are calculated easily, and some programs have routines that evaluate portfolio performance in relation to the overall market or other indicators. The Dow Jones *Market Analyzer Plus* is an example of a fairly extensive and sophisticated portfolio program. For the investor who trades often or has a large portfolio, these programs are well worth their costs (about $250 to $500); for those with modest

Forbes often provides a skeptic's view of investment schemes.

Magazines   A number of good magazines provide investment information and ideas. *Forbes* is exclusively investment-oriented. Its stories and regular features are usually realistic in outlook, often forewarning investors of potential problems with various investments. Its annual survey of mutual funds is well worth the price of that issue.

portfolios and less activity, their value is questionable.

Analytical Programs

Analytical programs allow investors to perform many analytical functions that might otherwise be difficult or impossible to do. Programs are available to analyze stocks, bonds, options, futures, convertibles, real estate, and practically any other specific investment or aggregate market index. Moreover, there are different types of analytical models based on different approaches for evaluating investments. These programs can be expensive (over $2,000) if you want a deluxe version that performs many functions. Simpler programs, though, are more reasonable.

You can create your own portfolio management or analytical programs fairly easily if you are familiar with Lotus, Super-Calc, or some other spreadsheet program. Of course, a prerequisite here is having conceptually sound and workable approaches.

(It could be argued that that prerequisite holds for the canned programs as well. If we don't understand what a program is doing, it's hard to see how better investment decisions can be made from it.) Routines created with a spreadsheet can be saved and stored on a disk. These programs are called templates, and you can use them to evaluate new data or new situations.

Getting and Using Data

An important advantage of a PC system is the access it provides to data bases. You can subscribe to various news retrieval services, such as Dow Jones, Warner Computer Services, and Media General. These services report security prices and volume along with much other financial information. The real time-saver is to obtain data from a source and store it on a disk—a process called *downloading*. For example, suppose you are analyzing 20 stocks or so, using daily price data.

Rather than recording all prices by hand and then putting the information into your PC's memory, you can use the news retrieval and have the prices entered automatically. After they are in memory, you can analyze or store for later use as you wish.

Using the PC to Undertake Transactions

Some brokerage houses now allow you to conduct trading activities by linking your PC to their computer systems. This saves time by eliminating the need to call and deal with a sales person. In addition, you can conduct business when it is convenient for you—3:00 A.M., for example, if that is your choice. It is expected that in the future many brokerage houses and other financial institutions will provide computer linkages of this type, although demand for such services has not grown as rapidly as many once thought it would.

Financial World is similar to *Forbes*, but less extensive and, perhaps, less conservative in outlook. Although not a "get-rich-quick" magazine, it takes a more positive view than does *Forbes*.

Fortune magazine usually features in-depth articles on different companies or industries. These articles provide excellent background material but are not geared directly towards investing. Nevertheless, the articles are timely, as are the regular monthly columns.

Money magazine covers a wide range of financial-planning topics, including investing. Its investment articles often provide personal investment stories—almost always of success—that are interesting and thought-provoking. However, after reading *Money* you get the impression that becoming wealthy through investing is a simple task, involving very little risk. More articles on investment failures would help temper that impression.

Computer Data Sources

Many investors are using personal computers (PCs) to assist them in making investment decisions or managing and evaluating their portfolios. There are a number of data sources. First and foremost is the Dow Jones News/Retrieval system. This is a vast source of information, ranging from 10-K extracts to transcripts of "Wall Street Week," the popular PBS weekly investment program.

Another comprehensive source is Standard and Poor's Marketscope, which provides data on approximately 4,800 companies, along with special series focusing on market movers, takeover candidates, and investment ideas. Vickers On-Line is an advisory service that concentrates on insider activity and activities of institutional investors. Argus Research covers 64 industries and 400 stocks; in addition, it allows investors to use various screening devices to detect securities that appear suitable for their investment goals.

These services, and others not mentioned, generally have a set-up charge, a monthly service fee, and user fees related to the amount of time used. Since charges vary widely, it is best to research each, asking for a fee schedule. Of course, the critical question is whether so much readily available data can improve your investment performance, after allowing for its costs. If you already have suitable hardware, the annual cost might be around $500 a year; double that amount if you must first buy a computer, printer, and modem. (Costs will vary depending upon depreciation, obsolescence, and other factors.) Investors should weigh these costs against the amount of money to be invested. If this amount is rather small—say, less than $20,000—computerized investing may not be worthwhile.

A computer is very helpful for investing, but it may not be cost-effective for small investors.

Academic Journals

A number of academic journals cover research related to both investment theory and applications. Readers without a strong mathematical background will not thoroughly understand many of the articles. However, even if you limit your reading to the introduction and summary-and-conclusions sections of some articles, you may still find useful investment insights. The following journals are most appropriate: *Journal of Finance, Journal of Financial and Quantitative Analysis, Financial Analysts Journal, Journal of Portfolio Management, Financial*

Most university libraries receive the important investment journals.

Management, The Financial Review, Journal of Financial Research, and *The C.F.A. Digest.*

Most of the above publications should be available at university libraries. A last journal worth mentioning is the *AAII Journal,* published by the American Association of Individual Investors. While not strictly an academic journal, it contains articles that are professionally prepared and useful to investors who plan to make their own investment decisions.

SUMMARY

A primary market refers to the initial distribution of securities, while a secondary market deals with trading of previously issued securities. Trading takes place on organized exchanges, such as the New York Stock Exchange, and in the over-the-counter market.

Stockbrokerage firms are often classified as full-service or limited-service firms. Factors to consider in selecting a broker include the importance of research, the quality of order execution, and the value of a representative's advice. Securities markets are regulated extensively. Key pieces of legislation are: the Securities Act of 1933, the Securities Exchange Act of 1934, the Maloney Act of 1938, the Investment Company Act of 1940, the Investment Advisors Act of 1940, and the Securities Investor Protection Act of 1970.

In dealing with a stockbroker, investors use cash accounts, margin accounts, and discretionary accounts. Long and short positions are taken, and orders used frequently are market orders, limit orders, and stop orders.

Important investment information is available from individual companies and federal government and Federal Reserve Bank sources. In the private sector, important sources are investment advisory services, newspapers (in particular, *The Wall Street Journal*) and magazines, computer data services, and academic journals.

KEY TERMS

Select the alternative that best identifies the key term.

1. primary market
2. secondary market
3. organized exchange
4. continuous market
5. commission brokers
6. specialists
7. floor brokers
8. floor traders
9. over-the-counter (OTC) market
10. NASDAQ
11. third market
12. fourth market
13. full-service firm
14. limited-service firm
15. monthly investment plan
16. prospectus
17. cash account
18. margin account
19. long position
20. short position
21. reversing a position
22. market order
23. limit order
24. stop order

a. a market featuring slight price changes from one transaction to another
b. work on a trading floor, but employed by brokerage firms
c. sell securities not owned
d. becomes a market order when triggered by a price
e. trading activity without a broker
f. on an exchange floor, they execute orders for other brokers
g. initial distribution of securities
h. physical place where securities are traded
i. involves a broker's loan to leverage security trading
j. order to buy at a specific price
k. operate for themselves on an exchange floor
l. execute orders and provide advice
m. buy securities
n. trades securities via telecommunications networks
o. trades securities acquired in the primary market
p. required to keep markets on assigned securities
q. sometimes called "discounters"
r. a communications system for trading OTC stocks
s. an order to buy or sell at the best price
t. a document describing a public offering
u. with this, you can have securities delivered to you
v. for example, selling after you have been long
w. OTC trading of securities listed on exchanges
x. offered by brokerage houses to assist small investors in building portfolios

1. Distinguish between a primary market and a secondary market. Is the first dependent upon the second? Explain.
2. Explain an organized exchange, including a definition of a continuous market in your answer. Why is the NYSE called "the Big Board"? Also, identify key organized exchanges in the United States and abroad.
3. What requirements must a company meet to have its stock listed on the NYSE?
4. What is a "seat" on an organized exchange and how do you get one? Can a seat be looked upon as an investment? Explain.
5. Provide a brief narrative describing the execution of an order on the NYSE, including descriptions of commission brokers, specialists, floor brokers, and floor traders.
6. Explain the OTC market and then identify the following: NASDAQ, NASDAQ/NMS, the third market, and the fourth market. What are the "pink sheets?"
7. Indicate some reasons for dealing with a full-service broker; why would an investor deal with a limited-service firm?
8. Explain a monthly investment plan and a dividend reinvestment plan. Do they seem suitable for small investors? Discuss.
9. Provide a brief discussion of the following legislation: *(a)* the Securities Act of 1933, *(b)* the Securities Exchange Act of 1934, *(c)* the Maloney Act of 1938, *(d)* the Investment Company Act of 1940, *(e)* the Investment Advisors Act of 1940, and *(f)* the Securities Investor Protection Act of 1970.
10. Explain how a cash account, margin account, and discretionary account differ. Which would you prefer having? Why?
11. In what sense does a margin account provide leverage? Is this "good" or "bad" for investors? Explain.
12. What does it mean to be "long" or "short," and what is "reversing a position?" Identify a "bull" and a "bear."
13. Do stockbrokers impose risks on investors whose shares they have borrowed to complete short sales? Explain.
14. Agree or disagree: Short positions are not advised for dividend-paying stocks since short sellers must pay dividends on all shorted stocks, thereby reducing trading profit.
15. Explain the differences among market orders, limit orders, and stop orders. Give one reason why you might use each.

1. The stockbrokerage firm of W.F. Wallace, Inc. utilizes the following commission schedule:

Value of the Transaction	Commission
A. Under $500	Minimum commission of $25
B. $500–$1,000	$10 plus 3% of the transaction value
C. $1,000–$10,000	$40 plus 1.5% of the transaction value
D. Over $10,000	$190 plus 1.0% of the transaction value

a. Calculate the commission and express it as a percentage of the transaction in each of the following cases: (1) 100 shares @ $15, (2) 500 shares @ $60, (3) 100 shares @ $4, kand (4) 300 shares @ $3.

b. Compare the above commissions to those of other brokerage firms indicated in this chapter. Does Wallace appear to be a full service broker or a discounter? Explain.

2. Brian Wade has $5,000 to invest. He intends to use his margin account to buy 100 shares of General Electric at $100 a share. Answer the following questions: *(a)* What is the initial margin requirement? *(b)* Assuming the broker has a 25% maintenance margin requirement, at what price of GE will Brian get a margin call? *(c)* How much additional margin must Brian deposit if the broker insists the account be brought up to the initial margin requirement? *(d)* How much interest will Brian pay during the first month if the broker charges 0.75% for the month (9% annual rate)?

3. Shirley Han is thinking of short-selling 100 shares of Exxon at $50 a share. She will deposit 50% margin to initiate her position. Answer the following questions about this transaction: *(a)* What will Shirley's profit or loss be if Exxon increases to $60 a share? What if it decreases to $30 a share? *(b)* Exxon will pay a dividend of $2 a share; how does this affect Shirley? *(c)* How much equity will Shirley have in the account if Exxon increases to $60 a share? Will she get a margin call if the maintenance margin requirement is 30%? Explain. *(d)* How long can Shirley maintain the short position?

4. You have placed a limit order to buy 100 shares of Delta Airlines at $60 a share. Your broker indicated Delta was trading at 60⅛ when the order was taken, but you noticed that Delta never traded higher than 59¾ after the order was placed. What price did you pay for the stock? Explain.

5. *(Student Project)*   Call a local company and request a quarterly report, an annual report, and a copy of its 10-K report. Also see if a notice of the annual shareholders' meeting is available.

6. *(Student Project)*   Using your school library, find and review at least one publication in each of the following categories: a federal government publication, a Federal Reserve publication, an investment advisory service, a financial newspaper, an investment-oriented magazine, and an academic journal.

7. *(Student Project)*   Inquire if your school uses a computer data source. If it does, try to obtain fee information. Then determine the annual cost of using a system based upon your estimate of usage. Also, you can inquire if a stockbrokerage firm provides computer services and, perhaps, allows a portion of commissions as a credit against the system's cost.

CASE ANALYSES

**2.1
Dustin Hall
Selects a
Stockbroker**

Dustin Hall is a successful civil engineer, earning about $60,000 a year. His hobby is the stock market, although he has not studied investments formally. In fact, most of his readings are from *Money* magazine and various "how-to-get-rich" books. Dustin often works 60 hours a week or more and travels extensively. Figuring he will save $1,000 a month, he wants to start investing, primarily in common stocks. His investment objective is long-term growth over time, and he has a high tolerance for risk.

Dustin has been contacted recently by a college friend who has just made a career change from chemical sales to retail stock brokering. She is employed by a full-service firm and is working on her licenses. She also is studying in preparation for examinations qualifying her as a certified financial planner. Her firm is highly respected and has excellent research facilities. Dustin is ready to establish an account but first has asked some questions of you. Answer them, indicating your reasons, as they apply in his specific case.

Questions

a. Do you feel a full-service broker is more appropriate than a discounter?
b. Does a margin account seem appropriate? Would you recommend a discretionary account with his friend?
c. Should Dustin be an active short seller?
d. Do you recommend a monthly investment plan? Explain.

**2.2
Fran LaBelle's
Active Trading**

Fran LaBelle has inherited $24,000 from her grandfather, and hopes to parlay this sum into a small fortune. To do so, Fran will "play" the stock market. Fran opened a margin account with a full-service brokerage firm that charges a commission of 1.5% of the value of a transaction. While her broker has recommended a number of stocks to Fran, she generally ignores his advice and makes her own selections, taking a position in only one stock at a time and utilizing margin almost to the fullest extent possible.

She started her trading as soon as she received the $24,000 by taking a long position in 400 shares of IBM at $120 a share. A month later she sold IBM at $125 a share. She then took a long position in 1,000 shares of GM at $48 a share. She sold these shares three months later at $60 a share and immediately shorted 1,000 shares of Eastman Kodak at $69 a share. She has held this position for two months basically because she doesn't want to take a loss, since Kodak has increased to $75 a share. Fran is fairly sure her strategy on Kodak will work out, given enough time. But she is vexed with her trading now that IBM is at $130 a share. She is contemplating closing her Kodak position and buying IBM again.

Questions

a. Calculate Fran's commissions to date. Then, calculate her gain or loss on each trade and her total gain or loss after considering all commissions. Assume also that Eastman Kodak paid a dividend of $1.40 a share while Fran was short.
b. Assume that Fran's margin account had an average monthly loan amount of $24,000 on the IBM trade, $25,000 on the GM trade, and $35,000 on the Eastman Kodak trade. Assuming an interest rate of 1% a month, calculate Fran's interest on the margin account.
c. Evaluate Fran's trading success using the following benchmarks: (1) she simply bought and held IBM, and (2) she invested her funds in a 6-month certificate of deposit with a guaranteed 8% annual rate.

d. Suppose Fran holds her current short position. Assuming her initial margin was $34,500, at what price of Eastman Kodak will she receive a margin call, assuming a 30% maintenance margin requirement?

e. What is your opinion of Fran's investment approach? What specific recommendations do you suggest?

HELPFUL READING

Angrist, Stanley W. "The Account That Couldn't Die: A Tale of Never-Ending Losses." *The Wall Street Journal,* August 10, 1989, p. C1.

Bierman, Harold, Jr. "The Dow Jones Industrials: Do You Get What You See?" *The Journal of Portfolio Management,* Fall 1988, pp. 58–63.

Coyle, Joseph S. "A Day in the Life of the Stock Market." *Money,* June 1986, pp. 106–48.

Giese, William. "Stockbrokers: When Discounts Don't Count." *Changing Times,* February 1989, pp. 50–56.

Gottschalk, Earl C., Jr. "Investors Turn To Stop and Limit Orders to Guard Against Stock Market Swings." *The Wall Street Journal,* February 24, 1988, p. 25.

Miller, Michael. "Wiring Up: Computerized Trading Starts to Make Inroads at Financial Exchanges." *The Wall Street Journal,* April 24, 1989, p. A1.

Salwen, Kevin G. "Investors Swamp Securities Arbitration System." *The Wall Street Journal,* March 15, 1988, p. 35.

Sofianos, Gordon. "Margin Requirements on Equity Instruments." *Quarterly Review,* Federal Reserve Board of New York, Summer 1988, pp. 47–60.

Stern, Richard L., and Michael Fritz. "Where Were the Cops? The Small Investor Is Still Prey to Stock Cheaters." *Forbes,* April 6, 1987, pp. 60–62.

Stoll, Hans R. *The Stock Exchange Specialist System — An Economic Analysis.* New York: Salomon Brothers Center for the Study of Financial Institutions, New York University Graduate School of Business Administration, 1985.

APPENDIX A: UNDERSTANDING MARKET INDEXES

Ask someone how the market did yesterday and the answer will probably refer to one of the more popular market indexes, most likely the Dow Jones Industrial Average. But does the DJIA represent the overall market? And how is it calculated? The answers are provided below, both for the DJIA and the Standard and Poor 500 Stock Index (the S&P 500).

The DJIA

The DJIA is a price-weighted time series; in other words, its value is an average of stock prices. Specifically, it is an average of the prices of 30 industrial stocks. The series has been in existence since 1884; however, it has included 30 stocks only since 1928. And it hasn't consisted of the same 30; some companies have been eliminated and others added. An interesting case is IBM: it was added to the list in 1932 but then replaced in 1939 by American Telephone and Telegraph. It reappeared in 1979 as it and Merck & Co. replaced Chrysler and Esmark.

Computing the DJIA would be a simple task if it were not for the fact that companies often have stock splits or declare stock dividends, each of which increases the number of shares outstanding. This in turn leads to price decreases that bias the average unless they are taken into account. Consider the simple example below that deals with only three stocks.

	Day 1		Day 2	
Stock	Price	No. Shares	Price	No. Shares
A	$10	1,000	$10	1,000
B	20	1,000	10	2,000
C	30	2,000	30	2,000

Total = $60   Total = $50
Divisor = 3   Divisor = ?
Average price = $20   Average price = $20
? = $50/$20 = 2.5

Stocks A, B, and C have prices of $10, $20, and $30, respectively, on Day 1. On Day 2, Stock B splits 2 for 1, increasing its total shares outstanding to 2,000 and reducing its price to $10 a share. In effect, then, its price was unchanged from Day 1, as were Stocks A and B. However, the aggregate value of the three stocks is only $50. Clearly, if we divided by three we would get an average price of $16.67, indicating a drop in the index. But the drop is due solely to the stock split. A new divisor is needed—one that would give an average price equal to what it would have been had the split not taken place. You must solve for this divisor, and in the example it is 2.5.

Over the years, the DJIA has been adjusted often for stock splits and stock dividends. This is reflected in the current low value of its divisor. In mid-1990, this value was 0.505, which is substantially less than 30 (the beginning number).

Problems with the DJIA   Although the DJIA is the most often watched barometer of the overall market, it does have limitations. First, it is heavily influenced by stocks with high prices. In the above example, if each stock increased by the same percentage amount, stock C's influence on the index would be three times greater than stock A's or B's (after the split). Second, since it consists of only 30 issues, you might question whether this is a large enough sample to be representative of the entire stock market. From a statistical point of view, it probably is not. Third, apart from the small size, the sample is clearly biased in favor of large, blue-chip stocks, since the thirty companies are among the largest in the world. The DJIA is considered a fair indicator of this market segment but not necessarily of the entire market.

Other Dow Jones Averages   In addition to the DJIA, Dow Jones also compiles a transportation average consisting of 20 stocks, and a utility average that consists of 15 stocks. The averages are calculated in identical fashion to the DJIA, so the same criticisms apply to them. Surely, though, one very big advantage with all three is they are reported, both graphically and numerically, in each issue of *The Wall Street Journal.* This high visibility makes them very convenient.

The S&P 500 Stock Index

The S&P 500 differs from the DJIA in several important ways. First, it is a value-weighted, rather than price-weighted, index. This means the index considers not only the price of a stock but the number of shares outstanding as well. Consider the example below.

	Day 1			Day 2		
Stock	No. Shares	Price	Market Value	No. Shares	Price	Market Value
A	1,000	$10	$10,000	1,000	$ 9	$ 9,000
B	1,000	20	20,000	2,000	10	20,000
C	2,000	30	60,000	2,000	33	66,000
Totals			$90,000			$95,000

Day 1 = base period = $90,000/$90,000 = 1.000
Day 2 index value = $95,000/$90,000 = 1.056

As you see, a value-weighted index is based on the aggregate market value of the stock; i.e., price times number of shares. An obvious advantage to this index is that stock splits and stock dividends do not affect the index value. Stock B's split had no influence on the Day 2 value of the index since the larger number of shares were multiplied by the lower price. (Price was assumed to be unchanged to simplify the example.) Perhaps a disadvantage to this index is that large capitalization stocks—those with a large number of shares outstanding—heavily influence the index value. In the above example, the index is up 5.6% on the strength of the 10% increase in stock C's price. A's price decline and B's unchanged price exert less influence on the index value because of their fewer shares outstanding.

The Standard and Poor 500 Stock Index actually consists of four separate indexes: the 400 industrials, the 40 utilities, the 20 transportation, and the 40 financial. Each index is value-weighted, as illustrated above. The base period is 1941–1943, and the base number was arbitrarily set at 10. As of late February 1990, the value of the S&P 500 was about 330, which means the index has increased 33-fold since the base period.

Although the S&P 500 is a more comprehensive index than the Dow Jones averages, it is heavily influenced by the large companies it includes. As a result, it too does not reasonably measure changes in smaller capitalization stocks.

Other Indexes

A number of other indexes are computed and reported regularly. The Wilshire 5000 Equity Index is published by Wilshire Associates, Inc. in Santa Monica, California. It includes all stocks on the NYSE and the Amex, plus active OTC issues—some 5000 stocks in all. It is a value-weighted series and is reported each week in *Barron's* and in each issue of *Forbes*.

Both the New York Stock Exchange Index and the American Stock Exchange have value-weighted indexes that include all issues traded on their respective boards. Finally, the NASDAQ Series consists of six separate indexes (all value-weighted) covering industrials, banks, insurance, other financial firms, transportation, and utilities, and a composite index of the six categories. In total, about 2,400 OTC stocks are reported daily. Each issue of *The Wall Street Journal* reports the NYSE, Amex, and OTC (industrials, insurance, banks, and composite) indexes.

APPENDIX B: POPULAR INVESTMENT INFORMATION SOURCES

The sources listed below are used frequently by investors. Information is provided for subscribing to magazines or newspapers. Subscription rates change, so you should check current rates before subscribing. Moreover, some publications have special introductory rates or lower rates for students. Category II and III sources are likely to be found in school or public libraries.

I. Newspapers and Magazines			
Publication (Primary Topics)	Frequency	Annual Cost	Publisher
Barron's (investments)	Weekly	$96	Dow Jones & Co., Inc. 200 Liberty Street New York, NY 10281
Better Investing (investments)	Monthly	$17	National Association of Investment Clubs 1515 E. Eleven Mile Rd. Royal Oak, MI 48067
Changing Times (investments and personal finance)	Monthly	$30	Kiplinger Washington Editors, Inc. 1729 H Street, N.W. Washington, DC 20006
Financial World (investments)	Biweekly	$39	Financial World Partners 1328 Broadway New York, NY 10001
Forbes (investments)	Biweekly	$48	Forbes, Inc. 60 5th Avenue New York, NY 10011
Fortune (company backgrounds, investments)	Biweekly	$50	Time, Inc. Time & Life Bldg. New York, NY 10020–1393
Inc. (small company backgrounds)	Monthly	$36	Inc. Publishing, Inc. 38 Commercial Wharf Boston, MA 02110
Venture (small company backgrounds)	Monthly	$36	Venture Magazine, Inc. 801 Second Avenue New York, NY 10017
The Wall Street Journal (economic and financial markets)	Daily	$130	Dow Jones & Co., Inc. 200 Liberty Street New York, NY 10281

II. Information Services		
Name of Service	Frequency	Information
A. Standard and Poor's		
1. Corporation Records	Daily	Comprehensive reference material on numerous companies.
2. NYSE Stock Reports	Periodic revisions	Current data and recent developments on NYSE stocks.
3. ASE Stock Reports	Periodic revisions	Current data and recent developments on Amex stocks.
4. OTC Stock Reports	Periodic revisions	Current data and recent developments on OTC stocks.
5. Dividend Record	Daily Weekly Quarterly	Dividend information on common and preferred stocks.
6. Daily Stock Price Record	Quarterly	Daily prices on over 7,000 issues; 3 volumes—NYSE, Amex, and OTC stocks.
7. Creditweek	Weekly	Reviews credit conditions and evaluates outlook for fixed-income securities.
8. The Outlook	Weekly	Analyzes common stocks and the outlook for equities.
9. Bond Guide	Monthly	Statistical data on numerous bonds (corporates and governments) and preferred stocks.
10. Stock Guide	Monthly	Statistical data on over 5,000 common and preferred stocks.
B. Moody's		
1. Bond Survey	Twice weekly	Analyses and recommendations on various bond issues.
2. Bond Record	Weekly	Prices, ratings, other data on various bond issues.
3. Industrial Manual	Yearly (supplement twice weekly)	Data on earnings, operations, and management activities for industrial firms.
4. Public Utility Manual	same as 3	Same as 3 for public utilities.
5. Transportation Manual	same as 3	Same as 3, for transportation companies.
6. OTC Industrial Manual	same as 3	Same as 3, for OTC companies.

II. Information Services		
Name of Service	Frequency	Information
7. Unlisted Manual	same as 3	Same as 3, for small, emerging companies.
8. Bank and Finance News Reports	same as 3	Data on financial companies.
9. Municipal and Governments Manual	same as 3	Data and ratings on municipal and foreign bonds.
10. Handbook of Common Stocks	Quarterly	Statistical data on numerous companies.
C. Value Line		
1. Investment Survey	Weekly	Comprehensive data and evaluation of about 1,700 firms.
2. Options and Convertibles	Weekly	Comprehensive data and evaluation of numerous convertible issues, warrants, and options.
D. Wiesenberger's		
1. Investment Companies	Annual	Authoritative statistical review of numerous investment companies.
2. Current Performance	Monthly	A supplement to 1.
E. Dun and Bradstreet Key Business Ratios	Annual	Provides financial ratios for numerous industries.
F. Robert Morris Associates Annual Statement Studies	Annual	Similar to E. Each is an excellent reference for industry analyses.

III. Academic and Professional Publications		
Publication	Frequency	Information
A. *AAII Journal*	Monthly	Articles related to all forms of investing.
B. *C.F.A. Digest*	Quarterly	Abstracts of investment articles.
C. *Financial Analysts Journal*	Bimonthly	Excellent articles covering new developments in investments.
D. *Financial Management*	Quarterly	Deals primarily with financial management applications.
E. *Financial Planning*	Monthly	Covers all aspects of financial planning, including investments.
F. *Institutional Investor*	Monthly	Current-trend articles of interest to professional investors.
G. *Journal of the American Society of CLU and ChFC*	Bimonthly	Articles on insurance and financial planning.
H. *Journal of Business*	Quarterly	Theoretical and research-oriented articles on business topics.
I. *Journal of Finance*	5 a year	Theoretical and research-oriented articles on finance topics.
J. *Journal of Financial and Quantitative Analysis*	Quarterly	Similar to H.
K. *Journal of Financial Economics*	Quarterly	Similar to H; considerable economic theory orientation.
L. *Journal of Financial Planning*	Quarterly	Covers all aspects of financial planning, including investments.
M. *Journal of Portfolio Management*	Quarterly	Articles deal with both investment vehicles and portfolio management.
N. *National Real Estate Investor*	Monthly	Covers real estate investing, finance, management.
O. *Real Estate Review*	Quarterly	Articles cover all aspects of real estate investing.
P. *REIT Fact Book*	Annual	Statistical data and other information on the REIT industry.

CHAPTER THREE

Investment Return: Measurement and Strategies

THE HOLDING PERIOD RETURN

Current Return

Future Return

Measuring the HPR Over Time

TIME VALUE OF MONEY

Determining Future Values

Determining Present Values

Finding Rates of Return or Annuity Amounts

The Power of Compounding

HISTORICAL INVESTMENT RETURNS

Returns from Key Financial Assets

The Accumulation of Wealth

Risk Premiums

BASIC INVESTMENT STRATEGIES

Long-Term Investing

Short-Term Trading

Exploiting Economic Cycles

Defending Against Potential Losses

BOXES

How Important Are Dividends to Investors?

Isn't It Time for a Truth in Giving and Wagering Act?

October 19, 1987: A Day of Financial Infamy

After you finish this chapter, you will be able to:

- understand the concept of a holding period return and why it is important to measure the average of such returns correctly.

- compute the future value of a single payment and an annuity.

- compute the present value of a single payment and an annuity.

- calculate approximate rates of return on investments.

- see historical rates of return on key financial assets, and how these returns have varied over time.

- identify certain risk premiums, which are additional returns for undertaking riskier investments.

- understand basic investment strategies, which include long-term investing, short-term trading, exploiting economic cycles, and defending against potential losses.

Investments differ widely in their return and risk characteristics. Some, such as a savings account, offer returns immediately and have little risk, while others—a zero coupon bond, for example—defer your return for many years and have substantial risk. Selecting investments on the basis of their return and risk characteristics is a difficult task, and much of the difficulty arises in simply measuring each. A discussion of investment risk is presented in the next chapter, while investment return is the topic of this one. We'll look first at measuring investment return with a holding period return and then we'll discuss important concepts dealing with time value of money. The chapter continues by looking at historical returns on common stocks and selected debt instruments, and it concludes with a discussion of basic investment strategies.

THE HOLDING PERIOD RETURN

A **holding period return** is the total return of an investment for a given period of time. It has three cash flow elements to consider: an amount initially invested (P_0); any periodic distribution received while the investment is held (R); and the amount received when the investment is sold (P_1). The dollar holding period return ($\$HPR$) is calculated as follows:

$$\$HPR = R + (P_1 - P_0) \tag{3.1}$$

If P_1 is greater than P_0, there is a capital gain; if it is negative, there is a capital loss.

A holding period return is most often expressed as a ratio in relation to the initial investment, P_0. This relationship is shown below:

$$HPR = \frac{[R + (P_1 - P_0)]}{P_0} \tag{3.2}$$

As an example, suppose $P_0 = \$50$, $P_1 = \$60$, and $R = \$4$; then,

$$HPR = \frac{[\$4 + (\$60 - \$50)]}{\$50}$$

$$= \frac{[\$4 + \$10]}{\$50}$$

$$= \frac{\$14}{\$50} = 0.28, \text{ or } 28.0\%$$

Frequently in discussion, an HPR is presented as a percentage; however, you should see the calculation always gives the decimal.

An HPR considers current return and price changes and is often expressed as a percentage of initial investment.

Current Return

The R term above represents an investment's **current return**. In many investments, it is what you expect to receive on a regular basis: each quarter, or

How Important Are Dividends to Investors?

This is a strange question: why wouldn't dividends be important? Actually, a deeper issue is involved here. Paying a dividend is expensive for several reasons. First, the shareholders give up an opportunity to invest the funds within the business, where investment rates might be higher than elsewhere. Second, the tax law doesn't allow a corporation to deduct dividends in figuring its income tax liability. In effect, this means each dollar of corporate income paid out as a dividend is taxed twice—once at the corporate level and again at the individual investor's level—before it can be reinvested. True, you eventually want to receive funds from the corporation (or to sell your shares at a profit), and taxes must be paid on those funds; but if a dividend is not paid, taxes at least can be deferred, which by itself is a big advantage. Considering the drawbacks, it's a wonder any corporation ever pays a dividend, and some financial theorists have argued that they shouldn't.

But most corporations do, and many have very specific policies about how much to pay and how often. Their officers point out that shareholders want and expect dividends with the same intensity that employees want to be paid. Are shareholders nearsighted or ignorant of the tax law? Perhaps, but risk and uncertainty might explain better their behavior. After all, a dividend is the bird in hand while price appreciation might be the two in the bush. In a risky and uncertain world, this behavior is definitely not irrational.

But can you as an investor profit from it? All things considered, wouldn't companies that pay low or no dividends be better picks than the more generous ones? Probably not, because each dividend-paying policy will attract investors who favor that approach, which is called the "clientele" effect. As investors seek out their preferences, they will bid stock prices up to a point where any extraordinary gain is eliminated. So, your selection should be guided by your investment objectives for current or future return and not by believing one approach is better than others.

each month, for example. The most common types of current return are interest and dividends, but there are others.

Interest   Many debt instruments pay interest on a routine basis. Bonds, for example, pay interest every six months. A savings account, on the other hand, may pay interest quarterly, monthly, or even daily. Some debt instruments, such as mortgage-backed passthroughs (explained in Chapter 7), make payments that include both interest and return of the initial investment. However, the total received can be treated as current return because the security's ending value will be lower by the amount of principal repayments.

Dividends and interest generally are received on a routine basis, such as quarterly or semiannually.

Dividends   Many common stocks and practically all preferred stocks pay dividends (unless the preferred dividends are in arrears), usually on a quarterly basis. Keep in mind, though, we are considering only cash dividends, and not stock dividends. Stock dividends are distributions of additional shares of the issuing company's common stock and do not involve cash.

Other Cash Distribution   Some investments offer cash distribution other than interest or dividends. A partnership, for example, might simply distribute available cash to the partners. As another example, a corporation may have a share repurchase plan that periodically allows you to sell some of your shares back to the corporation. As an investor, you might look upon such redemptions more as a cash distribution rather than as a reduction in the size of your holdings in the company.

Income Tax Savings   If you are a part owner of a partnership, or if you are a sole proprietor, the business operations may result in a tax loss. This loss is reported by you on your individual tax return and, in effect, reduces other taxable income you might have. Under current tax law, if you are active in managing the business, and if you have other income not in excess of $100,000, you can deduct up to $25,000 of losses from such income. (For each $1 of income above $100,000, you lose $0.50 of the deduction until the entire $25,000 is eliminated. Also, the deduction limitation does not apply to losses in oil and gas ventures.) This tax loss has value, the amount depending upon your marginal tax rate: the higher your rate, the greater the value of the tax loss.

Income tax savings are generated by business losses; however, not all losses can offset other income.

Commissions and the HPR   Most investors incur costs in their investing activities and view such costs as a reduction of their return. Any commissions you pay should be deducted from the sales proceeds when you sell securities and added to the purchase outlay when you buy them; that is, P_0 and P_1 should be adjusted for commissions. (Other kinds of costs, such as interest on a margin account or dividends paid on stock sold short, should also be considered in certain situations.)

Returning to the previous example, suppose that a commission of $1 applied at both the purchase and the sale of the asset. Then, the new HPR can be determined.

$$\text{HPR} = \frac{[\$4.00 + (\$59.00 - \$51.00)]}{\$51.00} = \frac{\$12.00}{\$51.00} = 0.235$$

As you see, considering these additional outlays reduces the HPR substantially, from 28.0 to 23.5%.

Future Return

Future return is an investment's price appreciation.

An investment's appreciation in value is referred to as its **future return**. Keep in mind that a security's historical price appreciation is always known with certainty and measured with little difficulty. However, securities are purchased on the basis of expected future appreciation, which is generally very difficult to estimate and never known with certainty. Two estimating techniques discussed in later chapters are the earnings approach and the dividends approach.

An earnings approach assumes a security's future price will be some known multiple of its future earnings per share. For example, if a stock is expected to sell at ten times next year's earnings, and if earnings are estimated at $3 a share, next year's stock price will be $30 a share. As you probably guess, the trick is to estimate next year's earnings and then hope the earnings multiplier doesn't change.

A dividend approach takes the view that a security's price appreciation—in percentage terms—will be the same as its percentage increase in dividends, again on a per-share basis. Thus, if dividends grow 10% next year, the stock's price will also increase by ten percent. For example, ABC, Inc., pays $2 a share in dividends this year and its stock sells for $25 a share. Its dividend next year is expected to increase to $2.20 a share—a 10% increase. So, the stock's price should increase to $27.50 (1.10 × $25.00). If you follow this method, your task is to make a good estimate of dividend growth and then hope the relationship of price growth to dividend growth stays the same.

Measuring the HPR Over Time

An HPR is a simple, easily understood calculation if the holding period in question is exactly one year. When the holding period is less or longer than a year, confusion can—and often does—result. As an example, suppose a friend of yours boasts of an investment he made, claiming he earned an "average" annual rate of return of 26.1% over a three-year period. You are impressed but ask to see his actual investment results, which are shown in Exhibit 3.1. Are you still impressed? Let us look at his "average" a bit more closely.

Calculating Average Returns   We see now how he got the 26.1 figure: it's the arithmetic average of each year's HPR. But does that give us a clear idea of his investment performance? If you look closely, you can see that he invested $100 and three years later received $100 when he sold. Meanwhile, he received $10 in dividends each year. You and I might be more inclined to think that his return was exactly 10% each year and, so, "averaged" 10% for the three years.

The problem with the arithmetic average is it has a built-in bias favoring gains over losses. For example: if you invest $100 and it's worth $200 a year later, you have a 100% gain; but if it falls back to $100 by the end of the second year, you have only a 50% loss. Clearly, if the base period for calculating percentage gains and losses is the first period, gains always have an edge over losses. However, this problem can be avoided by using the geometric average ($\overline{X}_g$). Its calculation is more lengthy but worth the effort. The appropriate formula is shown below:

An investment's arithmetic average and geometric average returns can be quite different.

$$\overline{X}_g = [(HPR_1 + 1.0)(HPR_2 + 1.0) \ . \ . \ . \ (HPR_n + 1.0)]^{\frac{1}{n}} - 1.0 \qquad (3.3)$$

Applying the formula to the data in Exhibit 3.1 indicates a geometric average of 11.6%, quite a bit less than the arithmetic average of 26.1%. The difference between the two average values is always larger when periodic returns are more volatile; and in the current example, returns vary considerably over the three years.

EXHIBIT 3.1

Calculating the arithmetic and geometric average rates of return

(1) Time	(2) Security's Price	(3) Dividend Received	(4) Each Period's Total Return	(5) Each Period's HPR (ratio)	(6) Column (5) Plus 1.0
zero	$100	$—	$—	—	—
1 year later	60	10	−30	−0.300[a]	0.700
2 years later	120	10	+70	+1.167[b]	2.167
3 years later	100	10	−10	−0.083[c]	0.917
Sum				0.784	—
Arithmetic average (divide sum by 3) =				0.261	—
Geometric average ($\overline{X}_g$) =				—	0.116[d]

NOTES:

$$^a\left[\frac{10 + (60 - 100)}{100}\right] = -0.300$$

$$^b\left[\frac{10 + (120 - 60)}{60}\right] = +1.167$$

$$^c\left[\frac{10 + (100 - 120)}{120}\right] = -0.083$$

$$^d[(0.700)(2.167)(0.917)]^{1/3} - 1.0 = 1.11629 - 1.0 = 0.1163$$

The geometric average is considered a better measurement than the arithmetic average, but it differs from an investment's internal rate of return.

Using Average Returns   An important lesson should be learned here: if you are examining the performance of an investment over time (such as a mutual fund), and if the annual returns vary considerably, don't rely upon the arithmetic average (what the fund may brag about) to measure performance. You will get a biased view. Of course, a more fundamental question to ask is whether or not any average should be used in the first place. Returning to our example, we can see that even the geometric average gives a different answer than our "common-sense" feel of the 10% annual return over the three years. Which of these two is correct?

There is no mathematical answer to this question, since it depends upon your perspective. If you feel year-by-year performance measurement is important, then the geometric average is preferred. On the other hand, if your concern is only with return over the entire period, then the common-sense figure is appropriate. Actually, we shouldn't rely too heavily upon intuitive feelings. The above example is a simple one, insofar as the ending value is the same as the beginning value. However, if these differed, common sense may not tell us how to handle the gain or loss. In this situation, we need the investment's rate of return—a concept to be developed shortly.

TIME VALUE OF MONEY

All things considered, we prefer investments that offer returns sooner rather than later. If you have a choice between receiving $100 today or $100 a year from today, you would be foolish not to take the current payment. The reason for your choice is simple: $100 invested at any positive rate of interest will grow to an amount greater than $100 in a year. If you could invest at, say, 10%, the $100 would grow to $110. Similar reasoning tells us that with a 10% inflation rate, $110 received one year from today is actually no better than $100 today. When we think in these terms, we are considering the time value of money.

> Money received or expended at different points in time must be adjusted for the time value of money.

A time-value-of-money problem can be viewed in one of two ways: a future-value application or a present-value application. Each is discussed below.

Determining Future Values

A **future value** is the amount an investment made today will grow to at the end of a given period of time, assuming it is invested at a given rate of interest *and* further assuming that all periodic interest earned on the investment is also invested at the *same rate* of interest. You can find the future value of a single payment or of a series of equal payments, which is called an **annuity**.

Future Value of a Single Payment Suppose you could buy a three-year certificate of deposit (CD) at a bank that is advertising a 10% rate on such CDs. How much would you get back at the end of three years if you invested $1,000 today? Before jumping to a solution, consider the time-line diagram in Exhibit 3.2. It is helpful in setting up time-value-of-money problems. As you move along the line away from the point t_0, assume you are moving forward in time. Each of the

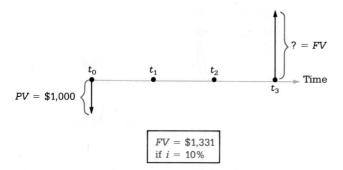

EXHIBIT 3.2
A time-line diagram: Finding the future value of a single payment

points—t_1, t_2, and t_3—represent separate periods of time, usually a year, although other periods can be represented. Any line pointing below the time line indicates an outflow (payment) of cash; any line pointing above the time line indicates an inflow (receipt) of cash. You see, then, the CD involves a $1,000 outflow at t_0 and leads to an unknown inflow three years later. (A problem this simple doesn't require a diagram to help solve it, but diagrams can be useful when more complex investments are evaluated.)

An easy way to find a future value (FV) is to use the formula below:

$$FV = (1.0 + i)^n \times PV \qquad (3.4)$$

where
$$\begin{aligned} PV &= \text{present value, or amount invested today,} \\ i &= \text{interest rate earned on the investment, and} \\ n &= \text{number of periods the investment is held.} \end{aligned}$$

A future value shows how much money is available at a future point, given an investment amount and a rate during the accumulation period.

We then can solve:

$$\begin{aligned} FV &= (1.0 + 0.10)^3 \times \$1,000 \\ &= (1.10)^3 \times \$1,000 \\ &= (1.331) \times \$1,000 \\ &= \$1,331 \end{aligned}$$

The above solution is aided considerably by a calculator. Moreover, many investors now use calculators with financial keys, which makes problem solving even quicker. We will use such a calculator throughout the text to solve problems and will illustrate the applications when appropriate. We use a Hewlett-Packard 12C, but the procedures are similar on other calculators. Exhibit 3.3 indicates the steps to solve the above problem. As you see, we get the same answer as above.

Another solution approach is to use a future value of $1 table, a portion of which is shown in Exhibit 3.4. The entire table (and tables for all other future and present values) can be found in Appendix A at the end of the text. Going down the table to the third period row and then over to the 10% column gives the value

EXHIBIT 3.3
Using a financial calculator* to find the future value of an investment

Step	Enter	Depress Keys	Function
1	—	[f] [CLX]	Clears registers.
2	1000	[CHS] [PV]	Enters present value as a negative number.
3	3	[n]	Enters number of periods.
4	10	[i]	Enters interest rate.
5	—	[FV]	Provides answer: 1,331.00.

*The Hewlett-Packard 12C. Other calculators operate on a similar basis. You should review the owner's manual for instructions on clearing registers and setting up a financial mode.

EXHIBIT 3.4

Portion of a future value of $1 table $(1.0 + i)^n$ (Note: See Appendix A.1 for the complete table.) The number boxed is the one illustrated in the text.

Periods (n)	8%	9%	10%	(i) 12%	14%	15%
1	1.0800	1.0900	1.1000	1.1200	1.1400	1.1500
2	1.1664	1.1881	1.2100	1.2544	1.2996	1.3225
3	1.2597	1.2950	1.3310	1.4049	1.4815	1.5209
4	1.3605	1.4116	1.4641	1.5735	1.6890	1.7490
5	1.4693	1.5386	1.6105	1.7623	1.9254	2.0114
6	1.5869	1.6771	1.7716	1.9738	2.1950	2.3131
7	1.7138	1.8280	1.9487	2.2107	2.5023	2.6600
8	1.8509	1.9926	2.1436	2.4760	2.8526	3.0590
9	1.9990	2.1719	2.3579	2.7731	3.2519	3.5179
10	2.1589	2.3674	2.5937	3.1058	3.7072	4.0456

Illustrated in text example of finding a future value

1.3310. Multiply this by the initial investment to arrive at the future value of $1,331.00.

Whatever method is used, it is important to understand the process. It should be seen, for example, that the above calculation does indeed assume that periodic interest earned is reinvested at 10%. We can show this more concretely by determining the amounts on hand at the end of each period:

$$
\begin{array}{lll}
\text{Period 1} & \$1,100 = \$1,000 + 0.10(\$1,000) \\
\text{Period 2} & \$1,210 = \$1,100 + 0.10(\$1,100) \\
\text{Period 3} & \$1,331 = \$1,210 + 0.10(\$1,210)
\end{array}
$$

A future value is also called a *compound value,* and the process of finding a compound value is called *compounding,* which involves *compound interest.* These terms are often used by financial institutions in describing their financial products.

A future value is also called a compound value.

Future Value of an Annuity   Rather than investing a single amount at the beginning of the investment period, suppose you are considering an investment that calls for an even payment each period. Exhibit 3.5 shows a time-line diagram for an investment requiring a payment of $1,000 a year for a three-year period, the payments being made at the end of each year and the interest rate being 10%. What is the future value of this annuity, called an ordinary annuity (OA)? The formula below finds a future value of an ordinary annuity (FVOA):

$$
\text{FVOA} = \left\{ \frac{[(1.0 + i)^n - 1.0]}{i} \right\} \times A \tag{3.5}
$$

where A = the periodic annuity

EXHIBIT 3.5
A time-line diagram:
Finding the future value
of an ordinary annuity
(FVOA)

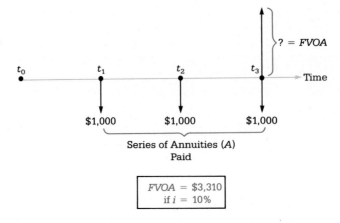

$$\boxed{\begin{array}{c} FVOA = \$3,310 \\ \text{if } i = 10\% \end{array}}$$

Applying the formula to our problem gives an answer of $3,310.

$$FVOA = \left\{\frac{[(1.10)^3 - 1.0]}{0.10}\right\} \times \$1,000 = \left\{\frac{[1.331 - 1.0]}{0.10}\right\} \times \$1,000$$

$$= \left\{\frac{0.331}{0.10}\right\} \times \$1,000 = 3.31 \times \$1,000 = \$3,310$$

Exhibit 3.6 shows a solution using a financial calculator. You can also find the answer with a future value of a $1 annuity table (Appendix A.2).

Some annuities call for annuity payments to be made at the beginning of each period, rather than at the end. This type of annuity is called an *annuity due* (AD). Exhibit 3.7 shows the time-line diagram for an annuity due, illustrating the same problem discussed for the ordinary annuity. You can solve an AD with a financial calculator by simply indicating that payments take place at the beginning of periods. Referring to Exhibit 3.6, change step 2 to [g] [BEG] and follow the other steps as indicated. The answer will be 3,641.00.

An ordinary annuity
calls for end-of-period
payments while an an-
nuity due has beginning-
of-period payments.

EXHIBIT 3.6
Using a financial
calculator to find the
future value of an
annuity

Step	Enter	Depress Keys	Function
1	—	[f] [CLX]	Clears registers.
2	—	[g] [END]	Indicates payments occur at end of periods.
3	1000	[CHS] [PMT]	Changes sign and enters annuity.
4	3	[n]	Enters number of periods.
5	10	[i]	Enters interest rate.
6	—	[FV]	Provides answer: 3,310.00

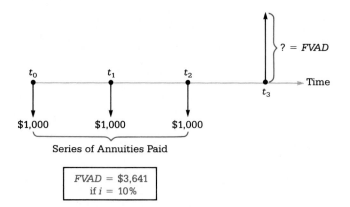

EXHIBIT 3.7
A time-line diagram:
Finding the future value
of an annuity due
(FVAD)

The larger value comes about because of one extra compounding period, which is shown in the following equation:

$$FVAD = (1.0 + i)FVOA \qquad (3.6)$$

Applying this to the current problem confirms the calculator solution:

$$FVAD = (1.0 + 0.10) \$3{,}310 = (1.10) \$3{,}310 = \$3{,}641$$

Determining Present Values

In finding a future value, we are moving forward in time to determine the accumulation of an investment, or series of investments. In finding a **present value,** we reverse the process by asking, how much are amounts received in the future worth today? The arithmetic of finding an answer is called *discounting*.

How much is an amount received in the future worth today? The answer involves finding a present value.

Present Value of a Single Payment   We can rearrange equation 3.4 to find a present value of a single payment. Now, the unknown is PV, while FV is known. For example, how much must you invest today to receive $500 three years from now, assuming an interest rate of 10%? Exhibit 3.8 shows a time-line diagram, and a solution appears below.

$$PV = \frac{FV}{(1.0 + i)^n} = \frac{\$500}{(1.10)^3} = \frac{\$500}{1.331} = \$375.66 \qquad (3.7)$$

You can also find the present value of a single payment by using the financial calculator. Referring to Exhibit 3.3, after entering 500, depress [FV] at step 2 instead of [PV] and do not depress [CHS]; then, depress [PV] at step 5 instead of [FV]. Read the answer: −375.66. The minus sign indicates an outlay. You can also use a present value of $1 table (Appendix A.3) to solve problems.

Present Value of an Annuity   Just as we have a future value of an annuity, we also have a present value of an annuity. A time-line diagram illustrating an

EXHIBIT 3.8
A time-line diagram:
Finding the present
value of a single
payment

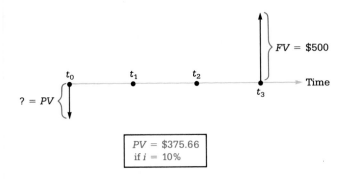

example is shown in Exhibit 3.9. As you see, the problem is to calculate the present value of $1,000 received at the end of each year for the next five years, assuming an interest rate of 10%. Since the receipt takes place at end of the year, this is an ordinary annuity. You can use equation 3.8 below to solve the problem.

$$\text{PVOA} = \left[\frac{1.0 - \dfrac{1.0}{(1.0 + i)^n}}{i}\right] \times A = \left[\frac{1.0 - \dfrac{1.0}{(1.0 + 0.10)^5}}{0.10}\right] \times \$1{,}000$$

$$= \left[\frac{1.0 - \dfrac{1.0}{1.6105}}{0.10}\right] \times \$1{,}000 = \left[\frac{1.0 - 0.6209}{0.10}\right] \times \$1{,}000 \qquad (3.8)$$

$$= \frac{0.3791}{0.10} \times \$1{,}000 = 3{,}791 \times \$1{,}000 = \$3{,}791$$

If you use a financial calculator, refer to Exhibit 3.6 and make the following changes:

at step 3, do not depress [CHS],
at step 4, enter 5 instead of 3,
at step 6, depress [PV] instead of [FV] and read −3,790.79.

EXHIBIT 3.9
A time-line diagram:
Finding the present
value of an ordinary
annuity (PVOA)

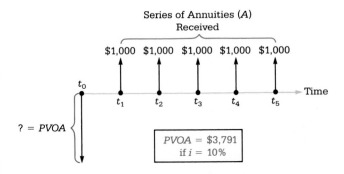

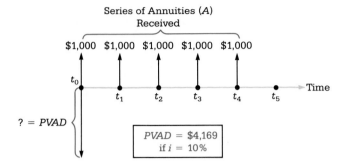

EXHIBIT 3.10
A time-line diagram:
Finding the present
value of an annuity due
(PVAD)

The negative sign indicates an outflow. A present value annuity table (Appendix A.4) can also be used to find the solution.

If the cash inflows took place at the beginning—rather than the end—of each year, we would have an annuity due, as illustrated in Exhibit 3.10. To find the present value of an annuity due (PVAD) using the financial calculator, go through the same steps for finding a PVOA except at step 2, indicate payments take place at the beginning of periods by depressing [g] [BEG]. Making this change, you will read the answer, $-4,169.87$. Also,

$$\text{PVAD} = (1.0 + i)\,\text{PVOA} \qquad (3.9)$$

And,

$$\text{PVAD} = (1.0 + 0.10)3{,}790.79 = (1.10)3{,}790.79 = 4{,}169.87$$

Finding Rates of Return or Annuity Amounts

All the above illustrations assume a known interest rate and number of periods. The problem is to find a future or present value. However, the financial calculator makes it easy to solve for any unknown variable. You merely enter what is known and in the last step depress the key for the unknown variable. For example, assume you wish to know the rate of return of a $2,000 investment that matures in five years and pays $3,000. After clearing the registers, then:

enter 2000	depress [CHS] and [PV],
enter 3000	depress [FV],
enter 5	depress [n],
—	depress [i] and read 8.447177.

A financial calculator is an invaluable tool for finding an investment's rate of return.

The investment has an 8.45% return. Finding rates of return this quickly is an invaluable asset of the financial calculator.

Consider another example: How much must be invested at the beginning of each of the next ten years to accumulate $10,000 at the end of the tenth year, assuming a rate of return of 12%? After registers are cleared and [g] [BEG] are depressed to indicate this is an annuity due, then:

enter	10000	depress [FV],
enter	10	depress [n],
enter	12	depress [i],
—		depress [PMT] and read −508.78718.

The annual payments are $508.79.

The Power of Compounding

During periods of high interest rates, many financial institutions attempt to lure investors with a dramatic promotional tool: values compounded over a long period of time. For example, how much will just $1,000 grow to if you invest it today at 10% and hold the investment 40 years? Answer: $45,259, which isn't exactly petty cash. Even a 10% return was considered rather paltry when some investments were yielding 16% and more. It wasn't hard to find newspaper and magazine ads showing how you could become a millionaire by investing very little each year until your retirement.

High rates of return often are accompanied by high inflation rates.

Were the ads true? Of course they were; they simply failed to tell the whole story, which was that if you are earning high rates of return on your investments you can bet that inflation is also high (which it was) and your real rate of return (an inflation-adjusted return) won't be much higher than its long-term historical average. In other words, your $1,000 will grow to $45,259, but you might pay $20 for a can of Coke and $450,000 for a new car. So, we should avoid drawing unrealistic conclusions from the power of long-term compounding. On the other hand, it isn't unrealistic to see other aspects of the compounding process that might influence our investment decisions.

Do not underestimate the accumulation power of an extra one or two percentage points over a long period of time.

The Power of Small Additional Yield   Very often you might not worry about getting an extra one or two percentage points on your investments, thinking the small extra yield is not worth the aggravation or, perhaps, slightly higher risk. But consider this: how much would your $1,000 grow to over 40 years if it were invested at 12% rather than 10%? Answer: $93,050. You more than double—$93,050 versus $45,259—the accumulation. (See Exhibit 3.11 for a graphic presentation.) You might want to keep this in mind if you are young and starting an investment program. Getting the extra one, two, or three percent consistently over 40 years *does* make a difference.

The Power of a Few Extra Years   Another factor to consider is when to start investing. Let's say your choices are today or ten years from today. How much difference would it make in your accumulation if you held an investment 30 years instead of 40? You can see the answer in Exhibit 3.11. If your investment earns 10%, the 30-year accumulation is only $17,449, which is $27,810 less than the

Isn't it Time for a Truth in Giving and Wagering Act?

Back in the 1960s, lenders were so abusive with interest-rate gimmicks, Congress passed a law—The Truth in Lending Act—to protect borrowers. Today, if you buy something and finance it, the lender is required to tell you the true annual percentage rate (APR) of interest on the loan. Unfortunately, if you buy a lottery ticket from your home state, lottery officials are free to lie through their teeth in telling you how much you might win.

The trouble arises from ignoring the time value of money. For example, suppose you buy a lottery ticket on a $1,000,000 jackpot. Somewhere in the fine print on the ticket, you might read that the winner collects the $1,000,000 with 20 annual payments of $50,000 each. Is that a million? Sure. Would you trade it for, say, $700,000 right now? You would be foolish if you didn't. Even at an investment rate as low as 5%, the $700,000 in hand is far better than the annual payments. Actually, the payments are worth about

$654,266 at the 5% rate. If you take a more realistic rate of about 9% that could actually be earned in mid-1989 on, say, a 20-year Treasury bond, the present value is only $456,427. So, the $1,000,000 lottery turns out to be the $456,427 lottery.

Not to be outdone by public bureaucrats, some private enterprisers know a good gyp when they see one. When interest rates were higher some years ago, all sorts of giveaway schemes were hatched. A particularly imaginative one in our area was a realtor who offered to pay you (eventually) the purchase price of certain homes in his listings—if you bought one now. That's right, folks, he'll pay for your home. (More correctly, the home seller paid for it with the realtor acting as an agent.) What's the gimmick? Well, if you buy a home, you get a zero coupon municipal bond that matures in 30 years. Suppose you buy a $100,000 home; you get a $100,000 bond. Naturally, the bond isn't worth $100,000 until its maturity in 30 years. At the

time the realtor was so generous, a bond like this was priced to yield about 10%, which means the realtor paid about $5,700 for it. This also means the $100,000 home cost $94,300, not zero.

Should the government try to legislate more honesty in reporting future monetary amounts when buyers or gamblers rely upon them in buying or betting? Surprisingly, there isn't much enthusiasm for change. Some people have little sympathy for gamblers, even though many are from low socioeconomic groups who could use a little help. Other people argue that time-value-of-money concepts are just too hard for the average person to understand, so why bother? (That's a curious argument, too. You would think consumer ignorance is a reason to provide protection, not to deny it.) Down deep, maybe the reason support runs low is that all of us like to dream. It's more fun to think of becoming a millionaire than a half-millionaire.

40-year accumulation. The last ten years increases your accumulation 2.6 ($45,259/$17,449) times! The investment moral here is simple to see: the sooner you start investing, the better off you will be. That is why even a small investment, particularly through a tax-deferring arrangement, when you are 25 will be as effective as a much larger investment when you are 45.

Holding an investment a few years longer substantially increases its total accumulation.

EXHIBIT 3.11
Compounding $1,000 at
10% and 12%

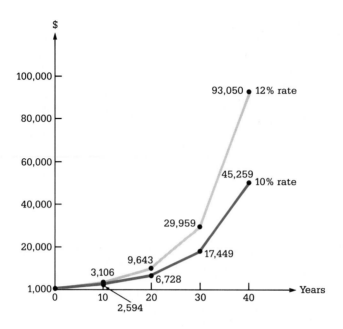

HISTORICAL INVESTMENT RETURNS

The return measurements developed above will be used throughout the text to evaluate investment alternatives. To begin, we can use them to examine the historical returns of broad investment categories. We do so not simply out of curiosity, but, rather, because the past can provide valuable insights about realistic potential returns in the future. Many first-time investors have grossly exaggerated notions and expectations of investment returns. Some feel that doubling your money in two or three years is what you should get with, say, a common stock investment. Anything less than that is considered a bad investment—one to sell and move into something else. The discussion below is intended to temper that unrealistic view.

Understanding historical returns is important in framing reasonable expectations of future returns.

Returns from Key Financial Assets

A number of excellent studies have measured historical returns from key financial assets. One of these is published each year by R. G. Ibbotson Associates, Inc., in their *Annual Yearbook*. This book is a valuable source of information on return and risk measurements for common stocks, long-term bonds, U.S. Treasury bills, and the Consumer Price Index (CPI).

The Return on Common Stocks   Exhibit 3.12 shows year-by-year returns on common stocks of both large and small companies. The large companies are represented by the S&P 500 Stock Index discussed in the previous chapter. The small company index is composed of stocks that make up the fifth (smallest)

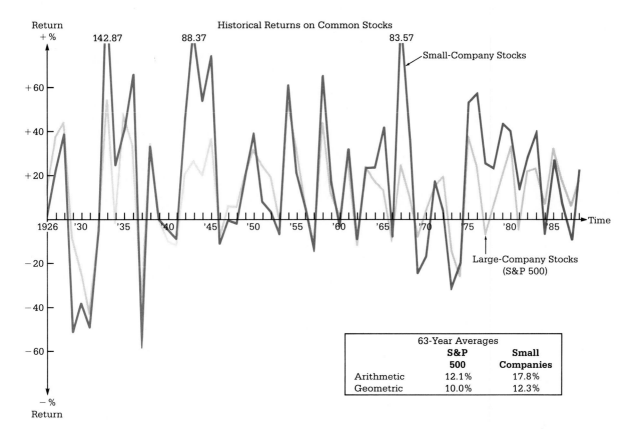

EXHIBIT 3.12
Historical returns on common stocks. (Source: Roger G. Ibbotson and Rex A. Sinquefield, *Stocks, Bonds, Bills, and Inflation,* 1982 edition [Charlottesville, VA: Institute for Chartered Financial Analysts]. Updated in *Stocks, Bonds, Bills, and Inflation,* 1989 Yearbook [Chicago: Ibbotson Associates].)

quintile of stocks listed on the New York Stock Exchange. This grouping is adjusted each five-year period to maintain the small size characteristic, and size is measured by total market capitalization; that is, number of shares outstanding times market price per share. While Exhibit 3.12 speaks for itself, some observations seem particularly warranted.

Small company stocks have offered higher returns than large company stocks, but they are riskier.

To start, notice the big difference between the arithmetic and geometric average returns and how this difference is larger for the small company stocks. This observation confirms our earlier comments that the arithmetic average overstates returns and that the bias increases as the variation in returns increases. Second, the positive returns in both series are occasionally remarkable: you more than doubled your money in small stocks in 1933; and their annual returns exceeded 50% in nine of the 63 years. The big company stocks did well, too: their returns were over 50% in 1933 and 1954, and were in excess of 30% in

October 19, 1987: A Day of Financial Infamy

If you look at any stock market index, 1987 doesn't stand out as a particularly noteworthy year. The Dow Jones Industrials began it at 1,900 and ended at 1,935—a gain of about 2%—and the S&P 500 showed the same percentage increase. Look more closely at 1987, though, and you will find one of the most tumultuous years since indexes have been kept.

To begin with, the Dow was up to 2,740 by late August, a gain of 44%. Had the year ended then, it would have been one of the best years on record. Euphoria was everywhere, and while some analysts were warning of excesses, many were optimistic the bull market would continue. It didn't. Prices began softening in September but rallied towards the end of the month to close the Dow at around 2,650. But the slide continued in October, and at the close on Friday, October 16, the Dow stood at 2,246.

Then came Black Monday—October 19th. When the day was over, the Dow's reading of 1,738 was almost unbelievable. It had lost 508 points! To put this in perspective, the supposedly great crash of October 29, 1929, saw the Dow lose 12.82% of its value, but the loss on Black Monday was 22.67%, almost twice as much. And the volume of shares traded—about 600 million on the New York Stock Exchange—was as remarkable as the price drop. On a normal day volume is 150 million shares or so. Of course, you don't generally buy indexes; you buy specific stocks. Here is how a few fared: IBM, down $33 to $102; USX, down $13 to $21 a share; and GM, down $13.13 to $53.87 a share. Imagine your nausea if your retirement nest egg was tied up in those three.

Do we know what caused the great crash? Not really. A government report (called the Brady Report) cited the heavy influence of two innovations: program trading and portfolio insurance. The evidence is hardly conclusive, though, and other researchers doubt these two practices were the primary causes. We may never know, just as we still do not know what caused the 1929 crash and the terrible depression that followed it.

thirteen different years. But poor performances were also present: you lost almost 60% of your investment in small company stocks in 1937, and lost more than 30% with them on five different occasions. Meanwhile, big company stocks showed their largest loss (−43%) in 1931 and had yearly losses in excess of 20% four times.

What picture emerges from the data? Unless you knew in advance what each year would bring, the most you could expect to earn were the long-term averages—10.0% in big company stocks each year and 12.3% in small company stocks—and be prepared for a roller coaster ride while earning them. These two percentage returns may seem small to you, but you will see shortly that over a long period of time, such as 63 years, they produce enormous accumulations of wealth.

The Return on Long-Term Bonds   Each bond series assumes a long maturity (20 years) and, as you see in Exhibit 3.13, the average returns on government

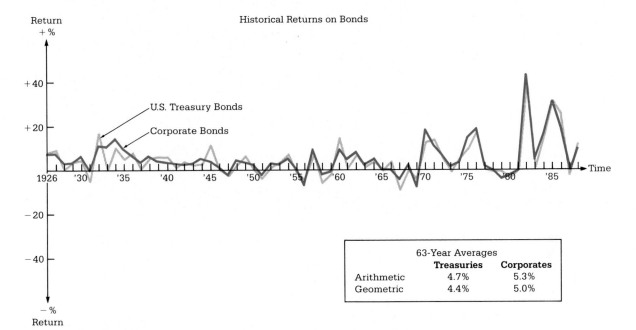

EXHIBIT 3.13

Historical returns on bonds. (Source: Roger G. Ibbotson and Rex A. Sinquefield, *Stocks, Bonds, Bills, and Inflation*, 1982 edition [Charlottesville, VA: Institute for Chartered Financial Analysts]. Updated in *Stocks, Bonds, Bills, and Inflation*, 1989 Yearbook [Chicago: Ibbotson Associates].)

bonds (4.4%) and corporate bonds (5.0%) are much less than the returns on common stocks, but so are their year-to-year variations in returns. Perhaps the most noteworthy observation about bond returns is their increasing volatility in recent years. High inflation in the 1970s and early 1980s ushered in high interest rates, and the constantly changing outlook for future inflation led to the wide year-to-year swings in bond returns. By the mid-1980s, the situation seemed to have stabilized somewhat, although large positive returns were then earned as the inflation rate abated.

Long-term bond prices have been volatile in recent years.

U.S. Treasury Bills and the CPI   Exhibit 3.14 shows returns on U.S. Treasury bills and the CPI. The Treasury bills series is an index based on the shortest term bills, but with no maturity less than one month. The CPI assumes monthly rates of return. As you would expect, the average return on bills (3.5%) is the lowest of all the investments, but so are the variations in return. You would not have had a negative return in any year, but your highest return was only about 15% (1981). The return on bills also increased substantially during the recent inflationary years.

The average inflation rate for the 63-year period is 3.1%, which is a bit less than the average return on bills. Comparing these two rates leads to the

The Treasury bill yield has been close to the inflation rate until recently, when the bill rate has been higher.

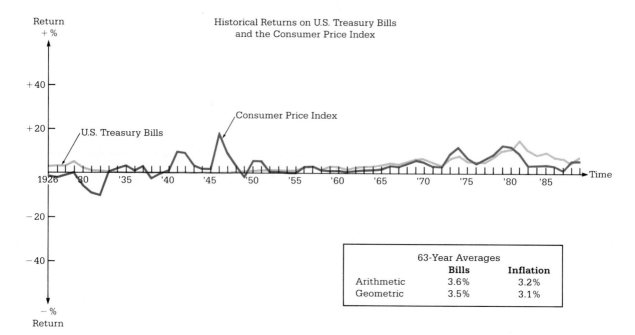

EXHIBIT 3.14

Historical returns on U.S. Treasury bills and the CPI. (Source: Roger G. Ibbotson and Rex A. Sinquefield, *Stocks, Bonds, Bills, and Inflation*, 1982 edition [Charlottesville, VA: Institute for Chartered Financial Analysts]. Updated in *Stocks, Bonds, Bills, and Inflation*, 1989 Yearbook [Chicago: Ibbotson Associates].)

conclusion that the real rate of return on bills was about 0.4%, which is quite low in comparison to real rates available in recent years. These have been in the 2% to 4% range.

The Accumulation of Wealth

Given the rates of return indicated in Exhibits 3.12, 3.13, and 3.14, how much would you have accumulated from a given investment, say $1,000, made in each alternative at the beginning of 1926? The answers to this question appear in Exhibit 3.15. As you see, if you had put $1,000 into the small company stocks, you would now be a millionaire; but if you had played it perfectly safe and chosen U.S. Treasury bills, your $1,000 was worth only $8,900. Such are the rewards for the stout-hearted. Before you rush out and start buying small company stocks, though, keep several things in mind.

Indices of wealth show impressive numbers; actually earning those returns is more complicated.

First, the above return is based on the performance of an index, not an actual portfolio of stocks. As such, it omits commissions and other investing costs. If these costs were considered, your rate of return each period would have been less, and so would the total accumulation. Second, this index consisted of

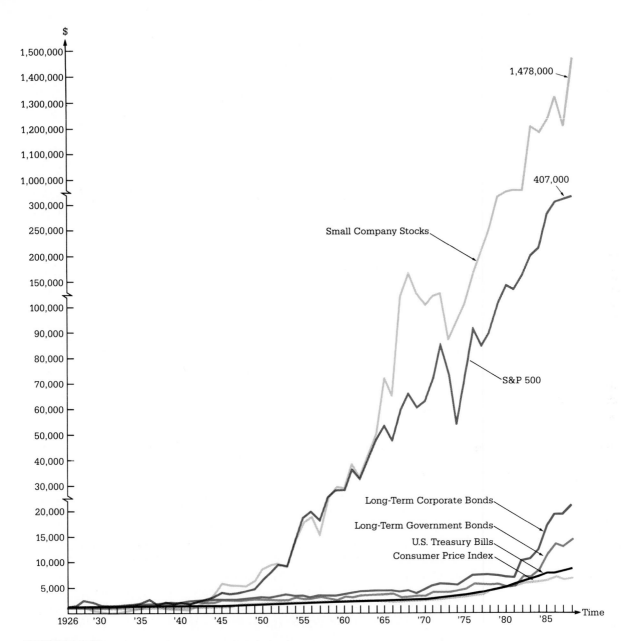

EXHIBIT 3.15

Accumulated wealth from a $1,000 investment made at January 1, 1926, and held through December 31, 1988. (Source: Roger G. Ibbotson and Rex A. Sinquefield, *Stocks, Bonds, Bills, and Inflation,* 1982 edition [Charlottesville, VA: Institute for Chartered Financial Analysts]. Updated in *Stocks, Bonds, Bills, and Inflation,* 1989 Yearbook [Chicago: Ibbotson Associates].)

a fairly large number of securities, enough to achieve a high degree of diversification. If you had purchased only a few small company stocks, your return might have been considerably worse and your variation in return surely would have been much greater. Despite these warnings, though, the fact remains that investors who were willing to take risks were, over the long run, compensated for doing so. And, the greater the risk assumed, the greater was their reward.

Risk Premiums

The idea that investors receive extra return for taking extra risk is expressed by the concept of a risk premium. Essentially, a risk premium is simply the difference between the return on a lower-risk investment and the return on one with higher risk. While risk premiums can be calculated for any pair of investments, the three discussed here are used often and are particularly important.

The Market Risk Premium   The **market risk premium** is defined as the difference in returns between a broad market index, such as the S&P 500, and U.S. Treasury bills. For the total period in question (63 years), this premium is 6.5%, based on geometric averages (10.0% − 3.5%). The investment implication of this premium is extremely important in framing a realistic expectation of a future return in a portfolio of common stocks. For example, if you expect the T-bill rate will average ten percent in the future, you could logically expect a 16.5% return on your stock investment. Are you guaranteed to get it? Of course not—that's the essence of risk; but your expectation is not unrealistic.

Investors taking greater risks can expect to earn risk premiums over time.

Bond Maturity Premium   Another important risk premium is the **bond maturity premium**. It is defined as the difference in returns between long-term U.S. Treasury bonds and U.S. Treasury bills. Over the same 63 years, this premium is 0.9%, based on geometric averages (4.4% − 3.5%). This means investors received a premium for investing in long-term bonds with their greater risks. (The nature of this risk—called interest-rate risk—will be explained in the next chapter.)

Bond Default Risk Premium   The **bond default risk premium** is defined as the difference in returns between corporate bonds and U.S. Treasury bonds. It measures the extra yield bond investors receive by investing in bonds that have default potential. U.S. Treasury bonds are assumed to be free of default risk; that is, you don't have to worry about the Treasury meeting its interest and redemption obligations. However, corporate issuers present a different situation. Here, exceptionally difficult economic times could lead to possible bankruptcies and substantial defaults. Anticipating this, investors demand—and usually get—a default risk premium. For the period in question, this premium was 0.6% (5.0% − 4.4%), again using the geometric averages. This premium will be discussed in greater depth in Chapter 5.

BASIC INVESTMENT STRATEGIES

Our examination of historical return data clearly shows the benefits of investing over long periods of time. Some investors, though, attempt to earn higher returns by frequent trading or by exploiting economic cycles. Still other investors seek to protect the value of their portfolios, giving up some return to achieve greater safety. The sections below present an overview of basic investment approaches.

Long-Term Investing

Long-term investing is often goal-directed in nature—saving for retirement, for example. However, even if the goal is simply wealth accumulation, many investors prefer to hold their investments for relatively long periods of time. Long-term investing works best when a well-conceived portfolio plan is established. This plan considers the investor's risk tolerance and investment objectives. Portfolio planning is discussed at length in chapters 19 and 20.

> Long-term investing is often goal-directed and works best within a well-conceived portfolio plan.

Long-term investing is often thought of as a buy-and-hold approach. We buy securities and hold them until there is some reason to sell, such as a need for cash. While you might follow a buy-and-hold strategy in long-term investing, it is not necessary or even desirable that you do. Indeed, there may be instances when your portfolio should be adjusted by selling some securities and purchasing others. For example, suppose you are a cautious investor who wants a portfolio balanced equally among common stocks, bonds, and short-term securities. So, you construct a portfolio accordingly. As time passes, though, your common stocks might increase substantially in value while the other two portfolio components show little change. The portfolio grows riskier as the common stock component increases in importance. Thus, to rebalance the portfolio, some stocks must be sold and the proceeds invested in the other components.

In addition to rebalancing to restore a risk level, portfolios also are often adjusted to take advantage of the tax law. For example, selling securities with losses allows investors to write off the losses (up to $3,000 a year) against other taxable income; or, larger losses might be taken to offset gains realized on other asset sales, such as personal residences.

> While a buy-and-hold approach often is associated with long-term investing, there are instances when portfolio changes are necessary.

Also, changes may seem warranted within a portfolio component. Certain stocks that you purchased might not perform as you anticipated, leading you to sell them and acquire others. Or, your portfolio of bonds might take on different risk characteristics as time passes, again calling for action to restore a desired risk level. Finally, a long-term investment strategy must consider how current earnings of dividends and interest will be handled. Will they be withdrawn and used for purposes other than investing, or will they be reinvested? As portfolios grow over time, current earnings also grow, and the reinvestment problem increases in importance.

Short-Term Trading

As the name implies, short-term trading is a strategy that attempts to profit from short-term market volatility. Traders change positions frequently, often trading between long positions and cash, or between long and short positions with an occasional stopover in cash. This approach is often called market timing. Obviously, short-term traders believe they can forecast market movements because that is a prerequisite for success. However, even if you are reasonably good at making such forecasts, you may not profit from frequent trading because transactions costs are usually very high. As we saw earlier in this chapter, holding period returns can decline sharply when related commission costs are considered. Several studies have indicated that you must forecast future market directions with over 70% accuracy to benefit from trading on a year-to-year basis. Frankly, very few investors achieve such accuracy levels.

Short-term trading attempts to profit from market volatility; its potential for success is limited by the difficulty of forecasting and high cost of transactions.

It is unfortunate that many beginning investors believe they can forecast that well or that they can follow the advice of someone who supposedly can. While there are numerous studies you might read to the contrary, the best advice is simply to try your approach on paper before you commit hard-earned savings. Allow sufficient time for the experiment and distinguish between luck and skill, particularly if you show extraordinary gains. For most of us, good luck usually ends sooner or later.

Exploiting Economic Cycles

Short-term trading is usually associated with market forecasting: you think the market will go up or down and you trade accordingly. A variant of this approach is designing an investment program to achieve maximum return over an economic—not a market—cycle. An economic cycle is rather long-term in nature (3 to 7 years, for example) and consists of four distinct phases: expansion, peak, contraction, and trough. As the economy goes, so go specific investments. Common stocks tend to do well through the expansion stage, perhaps peaking six months or so before the economic cycle peaks. Bonds are the security of choice in the trough, while short-term securities are favored during the contraction. By going from one to the other, investors supposedly will show better returns than they would by holding a portfolio equally weighted with the three and held throughout the entire economic cycle.

A strategy of exploiting economic cycles involves rotating investments in tune with the four phases of an economic cycle. To be successful, investors must be able to forecast the cycle.

The success of this approach rests squarely on your ability to forecast the four cycle phases. Unfortunately, virtually no one does this with consistent accuracy. A classic example is the economic cycle that began its expansion phase in mid-1982. The peak for this cycle was forecasted by many "experts" in each year beginning in 1985. As of early 1990, the peak has still not occurred, although again there are numerous forecasts indicating this might be *the year*. If you followed the cycle-exploitation approach, you probably sold your common stock holdings in 1985; and as a result, you missed a substantial gain that took place between 1985 and 1990.

Defending Against Potential Losses

Some investment strategies are primarily defensive in nature; that is, they are designed to protect investor wealth. Life insurance is a good example, particularly so-called whole life policies that provide an investment return while simultaneously offering a large payout in the event of the insured's death. While insuring is one way to protect wealth, hedging is another. A hedge arises when an investor establishes two offsetting positions at the same time. For example, suppose you are concerned that the value of a retirement nest egg might decrease substantially in a short period before your retirement. Assuming you will not sell the securities, an alternative would be to buy an option or a futures contract whose value moves in the opposite direction from your nest egg. If a loss does occur on your investments, an offsetting gain will be realized on the hedge instrument.

The stock market crash on October 19, 1987, increased investor awareness of the importance of defensive strategies. It certainly increased the popularity of a technique called portfolio insurance, which is explained in detail in Chapter 19. This method adjusts a portfolio between stocks and short-term securities in an effort not to exceed a predetermined maximum portfolio loss. Many investment firms offer portfolio insurance plans, and you also can invest in several mutual funds specializing in the approach. Defensive strategies vary considerably in terms of potential returns and costs of implementation. They often are very complex and require a thorough understanding of the techniques and instruments involved.

Defending against losses is a conservative strategy with various approaches, the most popular being portfolio insurance.

SUMMARY

Investment profitability often is measured with a holding period return (HPR), which takes into consideration current return items (interest, dividends, and others) and price appreciation (or depreciation). If HPRs are calculated for a number of periods, an average HPR value can be determined using an arithmetic average or a geometric average. The latter measurement is the more accurate, because the arithmetic average can be biased to favor more volatile investments.

Most investment analysis requires understanding of time-value-of-money concepts. The future value of a single payment and the future value of an ordinary annuity or an annuity due can be calculated using appropriate formulas, financial calculators, or tables. The present value of a single payment and the present value of an ordinary annuity or an annuity due can be calculated in similar fashion. Compounding over long periods of time produces substantial future values.

Historical returns on key financial assets show higher returns for stock investments than for bond investments or U.S. Treasury bills. Various risk premiums can be determined and used in selecting or evaluating investments. The market risk premium is the difference in returns between stocks and Treasury bills; the bond maturity premium is the difference in returns between Treasury bonds and Treasury bills; the bond default premium is the difference in returns between Treasury bonds and corporate bonds.

Investors follow various investment strategies. Long-term investing considers a long time horizon and often is associated with an attempt to achieve specific goals. Short-term trading involves frequent trading activity and assumes investors can forecast market directions. It involves substantial transactions costs and there is little evidence indicating investors achieve sufficient forecasting accuracy to make this strategy profitable. Exploiting economic cycles is a variant of short-term trading. It differs in that investors attempt to time their investments in tune with economic cycles. The strategy presumes investors can forecast economic cycles; however, there is little evidence supporting this premise.

KEY TERMS

Select the alternative that best identifies the key term.

1. holding period return
2. current return
3. future return
4. future value
5. annuity
6. present value
7. market risk premium
8. bond maturity premium
9. bond default risk premium

a. additional return of a long-term Treasury bond versus a Treasury bill
b. a return for a period of time; consists of current return and future return
c. additional return of a broad market index versus Treasury bills
d. future worth of an amount invested today
e. return you expect to receive regularly
f. return that results from appreciation in value
g. the present worth of an amount received in the future
h. even payment each period
i. additional return of corporate bonds versus Treasury bonds

REVIEW QUESTIONS

1. Explain a holding period return and show how it is calculated. Also, indicate how commissions should be treated.
2. Identify and explain sources of current return. Explain future return.
3. What is the difference between an arithmetic mean and a geometric mean? Use the following data on XYZ stock in discussing your answer: 1989 price = $25; 1990 price = $50; 1991 price = $25. (Calculate each mean return for the years 1990 and 1991.)
4. Indicate what is meant by a future value of a single payment and indicate how one is determined.
5. Define an annuity. Explain the difference between an ordinary annuity and an annuity due.
6. Explain how the future value of an ordinary annuity can be determined.
7. Explain the concept of a present value and indicate how a present value of a single payment is determined.

8. Explain how the present value of an ordinary annuity can be determined.
9. Indicate how the process of compounding differs from that of discounting.
10. At least four factors are involved in every time-value-of-money problem, and there may be a fifth. Indicate the five factors.
11. Explain the "power" of a small additional yield and a few extra years. Consider 8% and 10%, and 30 and 40 years.
12. Discuss historical returns on key financial assets and the accumulation of wealth with each.
13. Explain the following terms and provide amounts for each based upon historical return data: (a) the market risk premium, (b) the bond maturity premium, and (c) the bond default risk premium.
14. Describe a long-term investment strategy. Does it necessarily mean a buy-and-hold approach is followed? Discuss at least three situations that might require portfolio changes.
15. Describe short-term trading. What basic assumption underlies the use of this strategy? Will the approach be successful if you can predict with just slightly better than 50% accuracy? Explain.
16. How does exploiting economic cycles differ from short-term trading? What basic assumption underlies the use of the former approach?
17. What is a defensive strategy? Discuss a situation where a defensive strategy might be appropriate.

PROBLEMS AND PROJECTS

1. Ed Mason bought 100 shares of Wendy's at 5½ a year ago. Over the year he received a dividend $0.20 a share and the stock closed recently at 7¼.
   a. Calculate Ed's HPR for the year.
   b. Suppose Ed paid commissions of $20 to buy the stock and would pay $25 if he were to sell it now. Calculate the new HPR, assuming Ed sells the 100 shares.
   c. Ed leveraged the purchase by using his margin account and depositing 50% of the purchase outlay (commissions were paid separately). During the year, interest on the account averaged 12%. Considering this information, along with the data of part b, calculate Ed's HPR based on his *actual* investment.

2. Juanita Perez is trying to evaluate an investment she made. She paid $20 for a share of stock two years ago. Today its price is $24, but it has varied considerably while Juanita held it. At the end of the first year, for example, it was $16. It also paid a $1.00 dividend each year and Juanita has just received the second year's dividend.

   Calculate Juanita's average rate of return in the stock, using both the arithmetic and geometric averages. Discuss your results with Juanita.

3. You recently have reviewed the performance of one of your stocks since you purchased 200 shares of it four years ago at $50 a share. Here is your information:

Year	Price One Year Later	Dividends Per Share
1	$45.00	$2.00
2	70.00	3.00
3	53.00	1.00
4	60.00	1.00

Calculate the arithmetic and geometric average returns on your investment.

4. Determine the following future values:
   a. $100 invested at 15% for 20 years.
   b. $200 invested at the end of each of the next 10 years at 9%.
   c. $450 invested at the beginning of each of the next 5 years at 8%.

5. Determine the following present values:
   a. $10,000 received at the end of 13 years; $i = 10\%$.
   b. $800 received at the end of each of the next 11 years; $i = 14\%$.
   c. $300 received at the beginning of each of the next 4 years; $i = 12\%$.

6. Josey Wells is considering making an investment in a tax shelter. The investment requires a cash payment of $5,000 today, and the shelter promoter is sure Josey will double her money in about five years. What is Josey's rate of return on the investment? Construct a time-line diagram to help you solve this problem.

7. (*Student Project*)   You have been hired recently as a marketing specialist of a major commercial bank. The bank is attempting to increase deposits in its tax sheltering devices, such as IRAs. It also wants to gain better penetration in the young-depositor market segment. Prepare a promotional piece that might appeal in this situation. Be sure to include an example, or examples.

   As a side task, management wants you to consider how it might promote a new certificate of deposit it is introducing, called the "Super CD." It guarantees a rate two percentage points higher than the bank's rate on savings accounts for as long as the depositor holds the CD. Management is concerned that potential customers will not get excited about only two percentage points. They want you to write a promotional piece that really "sells" the product.

8. (*Student Project*)   Call or visit a commercial bank or savings and loan and ask if they have any literature on IRAs, Keoghs, or other tax sheltering devices. See if time-value-of-money concepts are covered. If they are, analyze them.

CASE ANALYSES

**3.1
The Hineses
Evaluate Life
Insurance
Policies**

Phil and Janet Hines have married recently and are awaiting the birth of their first child. Neither Phil nor Janet carries life insurance, but they are concerned now that an untimely death of either or both of them would create economic hardships in supporting the child. Consequently, they are considering buying two whole life insurance policies (one for each) that pay $200,000 to a beneficiary in the event of Phil's or Janet's death ($400,000 if both die). Combined premiums will be $5,000 annually, beginning when the policies are signed.

While the Hineses recognize the need for life insurance, they are concerned over its relatively high cost. An insurance agent has told them the policies they are considering are whole life policies, which accumulate cash value. This means the Hineses could cash in the policies in the future if they no longer wanted insurance. The agent further explained that rather than cashing in, the Hineses could choose to convert the policies to annuity contracts that would provide them with retirement income. Moreover, he indicated life insurance investment has an edge over other investments insofar as cash value accumulates on a tax-deferred basis. To illustrate his points, the agent provides the following information, which is based upon an assumption that both policies would be carried for 30 years and then either cashed in or converted to annuity contracts.

1. Guaranteed cash value—$332,194 (lump sum).
2. Annuity contracts with guaranteed payments for 10 years—$47,297 (annually) with payments beginning immediately upon the policy conversion.

a. Determine the implicit rate of return on the policies.
b. Determine the implicit rate of return on the annuity contracts.
c. Suppose the Hineses feel inflation will average 4% annually over the next 30 years. Do you regard the policies as attractive investments? Discuss, indicating the real rate of return on the policies.
d. Would you recommend the insurance policies? Explain.

Questions

Amy Burke is an ambitious young lady. Although she just turned 10 years of age, she has a paper route and works at other odd jobs. She plans to save from the income she earns to help pay her college costs in the future, but she may need help from her parents. Amy's dad has explained that one year in college at the present time costs about $8,000 at the university Amy is considering, but he expects this cost to increase 7% a year indefinitely in the future. He also explained that he and Amy's mom invested $5,000 in a "College-Bound Savings Program" at Amy's birth. This program guarantees an 8% annual rate for 18 years. While Amy expects to earn $3,000 a year for the next 8 years, she wonders if that will be sufficient to meet 4 years of college costs.

**3.2
Amy Burke
Plans for
College**

a. Determine each year's college cost, assuming Amy's dad's inflation estimate is correct and that Amy starts college in 8 years.
b. Determine how much will be available from her parents' savings program when Amy starts college.
c. Regardless of your answer to question a, assume that Amy wants to accumulate $54,980 by the beginning of the first year. After paying first-year costs, she will invest the remainder to earn 7%, thereby assuring adequate funds for the 3 remaining years. Now, considering your response to question b, how much must Amy save each year, assuming the savings are invested at the end of each year in a vehicle that earns 10%? Will her annual earnings of $3,000 be sufficient? Explain.
d. Do you believe Amy can earn a rate as high as 10% on her savings? Explain.

Questions

HELPFUL
READING

Bildersee, J. "U.S. Government and Agency Securities: An Analysis of Yield Spreads and Performance." *Journal of Business,* July 1978.

Clayton, Gary E., and Christopher B. Spivey. *The Time Value of Money*. Philadelphia: W. B. Saunders and Company, 1978.

Grauer, R., and N. Hakansson. "Higher Return, Lower Risk: Historical Returns on Long-Run, Actively-Managed Portfolios of Stocks, Bonds, and Bills." *Financial Analysts Journal,* March-April 1982.

Ibbotson Associates. *Stocks, Bonds, Bills, and Inflation: 1989 Yearbook*. Chicago: Ibbotson Associates, 1989.

Willis, Clint. "Mastering the Math Behind Your Money." *Money,* May 1989, pp. 129–38.

CHAPTER FOUR

Measuring Investment Risk

INDIVIDUAL ASSET RISK

The Expected Return

Dispersion of Returns

Historical Risk Statistics on Key
Financial Assets

PORTFOLIO RISK

Return Correlations

Random Diversification

Purposive Diversification

Using the Beta Concept

SOURCES OF RISK

Changes in the Economic
Environment

Characteristics of the Security
Issuer

Other Sources of Risk

APPENDIX: ANALYSIS OF
HISTORICAL RETURNS

BOXES

Do Investors Make Adequate Risk-
Return Assessments?

Risk and Time: Are They Related?

After you finish this chapter, you
will be able to:

- calculate and understand risk statistics: the variance, standard deviation, and coefficient of variation.

- see historical risk statistics on key
financial assets.

- understand the nature of diversification and how it reduces investment risk.

- recognize that asset correlations
affect portfolio risk, and you will
see historical correlations among
key financial assets.

- calculate a beta value and understand its use in designing a portfolio.

- identify the major sources of investment risk.

M ost people have a general idea of risk but usually find the concept difficult to explain in concrete terms. We often tend to think of risk as a possibility of something bad happening to us. Taking a difficult course, such as investments, is risky because your grade may not be as high as you could earn in an easier course. Betting on a sporting event is obviously risky since there is a good chance of picking a loser. But risk must have a bright side along with the gloomy one, or we would always take Basket Weaving 101 and never place a bet. As we will see in this chapter, investment risk is most properly understood when it is expressed in statistical terms that consider the entire range of an investment's possible returns. Moreover, risk often depends upon the number of individual assets held. In general, you can reduce it by holding a reasonably diversified portfolio of individual assets. To understand how a portfolio reduces risk, we must begin by looking at the risk of individual assets.

INDIVIDUAL ASSET RISK

You can measure an investment's risk with several commonly used statistics: the *variance,* the *standard deviation,* and the *coefficient of variation.* To determine these statistics, you must first calculate an investment's *expected return.* If your investment is limited to a single asset, your consideration of risk does not have to extend beyond that asset's risk statistics. This is the simplest case and a good place to begin our discussion.

The Expected Return

Probability estimates are needed to determine an investment's expected return.

An investment's **expected return** $(\bar{R})$ is a weighted average return determined by multiplying each of its possible returns by the probability of each return occurring. Let's consider an example. Suppose you are planning a relatively safe investment in a bank savings account currently paying 8%. You plan to hold the investment one year, but you aren't sure that your annual return will actually be 8%, because market interest rates could increase or decrease during the year, and your account is the kind that adjusts its interest to market rates. To keep things simple, if rates increase you believe your rate for the year will average 10%; if rates decrease, it will average 6%. As an alternative to this investment, you are also considering investing in a long-term bond. It currently yields 10%, but if interest rates change, so will its market price and so will your holding period return for the year. If rates rise, the bond's price will fall, and your return will fall to zero; if rates fall, the bond's price will rise, and your return jumps to 20%. (Bond prices and market interest rates are inversely related. We'll discuss this relationship in greater depth in the next chapter.)

Before you can choose between the two investments, you must have some idea about market rates of interest in the upcoming year. Suppose your strongest feeling is that rates will be unchanged, but you believe there is a slightly better chance they will fall rather than rise. You could express these feelings in terms of probability estimates, such as: you think there is a 50% chance for unchanged rates, a 30% chance for a fall, and a 20% chance for a rise. With this information, along with the possible returns indicated above, we can calculate each investment's expected return. This is done in Exhibit 4.1, which indicates an expected return of 7.8% for the savings account and 11.0% for the bond.

Dispersion of Returns

In statistics, an average is a measurement of central tendency; that is, how values of the observed events cluster together. Along with averages, we often calculate dispersion statistics—the variance, standard deviation, and coefficient of variation—which measure how the observed values are spread out. These statistics indicate investment risk.

The Variance Exhibit 4.2 shows how each dispersion statistic is calculated. You start with the **variance (σ^2)**. To calculate it, first subtract the expected return from each possible return (column 2); square the answer (column 3); then multiply this number by the probability of the actual return (in column 1) occurring; finally, add the numbers in column 4 and the sum is the variance. As Exhibit 4.2 shows, the wider the range of possible returns and/or the greater the spread of probability estimates, the larger will be the value of the variance. In the reverse case, the variance is smaller. An investment with a zero variance, for example, has only one possible return. It's a sure thing, and there is no risk. Any number other than zero (they all will be positive) means some degree of risk, with larger values meaning greater risk. In this example, the bond is clearly the riskier investment, since its variance is 49.0 versus 1.96 for the savings account.

Large variance and standard deviation values indicate a wide range of possible returns and high risk.

EXHIBIT 4.1
Calculating an expected return ($\bar{R}$)

	Percentage Returns If Market Interest Rates:			
	Rise	Stay the Same	Fall	Expected Returns ($\bar{R}$)*
Probability of Event Occurring	.2	.5	.3	
Investment Alternatives:				
Savings Account	10	8	6	$(.2 \times 10) + (.5 \times 8) + (.3 \times 6) = 7.8$
Long-Term Bond	0	10	20	$(.2 \times 0) + (.5 \times 10) + (.3 \times 20) = 11.0$

*Letting R_i = a possible return and Pr_i = the probability of the return occurring, then the expected return ($\bar{R}$) is calculated:
$$\bar{R} = (R_1 \cdot Pr_1) + (R_2 \cdot Pr_2) + \ldots + (R_n \cdot Pr_n)$$

EXHIBIT 4.2
Calculating risk
measurements: The
variance (σ^2), standard
deviation (σ), and
coefficient of variation
(C)

(1) Possible Returns R_i	(2) $(R_i - \bar{R})$	(3) $(R_i - \bar{R})^2$	(4) $(R_i - \bar{R})^2 \times Pr$
Savings Account:			
10	$10 - 7.8 = \quad 2.2$	4.84	$4.84 \times .2 = 0.968$
8	$8 - 7.8 = \quad 0.2$	0.04	$0.04 \times .5 = 0.020$
6	$6 - 7.8 = -1.8$	3.24	$3.24 \times .3 = \underline{0.972}$
			$\sigma^2 = 1.960$
			$\sigma = \sqrt{\sigma^2} = 1.400$
			$C = 1.400/7.8 = 0.180$
Bond:			
0	$0 - 11.0 = -11.0$	121.0	$121.0 \times .2 = 24.200$
10	$10 - 11.0 = -\ 1.0$	1.0	$1.0 \times .5 = \quad 0.500$
20	$20 - 11.0 = \quad 9.0$	81.0	$81.0 \times .3 = \underline{24.300}$
			$\sigma^2 = 49.000$
			$\sigma = \sqrt{\sigma^2} = \quad 7.000$
			$C = 7.0/11.0 = \quad 0.640$

The Standard Deviation   An often-used statistic is the **standard deviation** (σ), which is simply the square root of the variance. The bond's standard deviation is 7.0 and the savings account's is 1.4. By itself, the standard deviation obviously gives no greater information than does the variance. However, it is used in analytical statistics to form probability estimates about future events occurring. The standard deviation is important to us, because we need it to find the coefficient of variation.

The coefficient of variation compares risk to expected return.

The Coefficient of Variation   The **coefficient of variation (C)** is simply the ratio of the standard deviation to the expected return ($\sigma/\bar{R}$). It is called a risk-to-reward ratio since it shows the amount of risk per unit of return. The savings account, for example, has 0.18% risk per 1.0% of return; while the bond has 0.64% risk per 1.0% of return. Clearly, the bond is riskier not only in absolute terms but also in relative terms; that is, risk relative to return.

The coefficient of variation is generally the better risk statistic to use when you compare investments with different expected returns. The investment with the higher expected return might also show a higher variance and standard deviation. Does this mean it is riskier? Not necessarily—at least not in relation to expected return.

Historical Risk Statistics on Key Financial Assets

In the previous chapter we saw rates of return on important financial assets: common stocks, long-term bonds, and U.S. Treasury bills. Using the risk statistics we have just learned, we can turn our attention to the degree of risk an investor faced in holding these assets. Exhibit 4.3 shows the standard deviation and coefficient of variation for each asset and the CPI. The overall results are not surprising: the high-yielding common stocks have the most risk and the low-yielding Treasury bills have the least. We expect return and risk to go together; that is, the higher the asset's return, the greater its risk.

Somewhat surprising, perhaps, is the poor performance of Treasury bonds relative to corporate bonds. As you see, Treasuries were slightly more risky than corporates, based on their standard deviation values, and they had a somewhat larger coefficient of variation. In retrospect, most investors probably would have preferred the corporates with their extra return.

PORTFOLIO RISK

Suppose you could hold only one asset: would you select the investment with the highest return, or the one with the least risk? You must choose one or the other. In the previous example, you must pick either the bond with its expected return of 11% and high risk, or the savings account with its expected 7.8% return and low risk. However, often other investment alternatives present different return and risk characteristics. Some may represent better alternatives than the two being considered; that is, they might offer a higher return with the same, or less, risk. If such a situation exists, we say the one asset *dominates* the other and, so, we would drop the inferior asset and consider only the better one. But even after we make these eliminations, we are still left with individual assets and their unique risk characteristics.

Fortunately, we are free to hold as many specific assets as we choose. When we combine assets, we create a portfolio with its own return and risk characteristics. The important quality of a portfolio is that it can reduce

Asset	Arithmetic Mean Return	Standard Deviation of Returns	Coefficient of Variation
Common Stocks;			
S&P 500	12.1%	20.9%	1.73
Small company	17.8	35.6	2.00
Long-Term Bonds:			
Corporates	5.3	8.4	1.58
U.S. Treasuries	4.7	8.5	1.81
Short-Term:			
Treasury bills	3.6	3.3	0.92
CPI	3.2	4.8	1.50

EXHIBIT 4.3
Risk measurements on key financial assets: 1926–1988

SOURCE: Roger G. Ibbotson and Rex A. Sinquefield, *Stocks, Bonds, Bills, and Inflation*, 1982 edition [Charlottesville, VA. Institute for Chartered Financial Analysts]. Updated in *Stocks, Bonds, Bills, and Inflation*, 1989 Yearbook [Chicago: Ibbotson Associates].

Do Investors Make Adequate Risk-Return Assessments?

Do you make investment decisions as most people do? And do you and other investors deal with risk and return adequately in selecting investments? How about a short quiz before we tackle these questions? Respond to them as you would *actually* make choices, not as you think you *ought* to make them.

1. You have just won $3,000 in a contest and you are given two choices. Which will you take?
   a. Keep the $3,000.
   b. Exchange the $3,000 for an 80% chance to win $4,000.
2. You are invited to participate in a game of chance involving the flip of a fair coin. You must play heads and each time a head appears, you win $150; if a tail appears, you must pay $100. You will:
   a. not play the game.
   b. play the game
3. Which lottery ticket would you rather have:
   a. one with a 2% chance of winning $3,000?
   b. one with a 1% chance of winning $6,000?
4. Given a choice, which do you prefer:

   a. a sure loss of $3,000?
   b. an 80% chance of losing $4,000 and a 20% chance of losing nothing?

If you chose response a to questions 1 and 2, you are in the company of most respondents. You realize your choices are not the better ones, mathematically speaking; nevertheless, you are unwilling to take the risk alternatives for the compensations indicated. Also, did you take alternative b to question 4? Most people do, which is indeed interesting because it doesn't fit with their answers to questions 1 and 2. In question 4, they take the risk alternative even though it is likely to be the more costly one. Finally, if you picked b to question 3, you are with the majority. About 2 out of 3 respondents choose b even though the expected reward ($60) is the same each way.

Now that you know if you are in the majority or not, you might ask what any of this has to do with investing; surprisingly, some people feel a lot is involved. All types of foolish investing behavior stem from our psychological quirks. Our risk aversion pushes us to accept mediocre, fairly safe returns, rather than taking some risks for much better ones (questions 1

and 2). For example, we prefer IBM to a lesser-known company that might be just as safe and more profitable. Our abhorrence of losses often forces us to take bad risks when we do take them (question 4). We hold on to a disaster, hoping to recoup losses when the better choice would be to cut them by dumping it. Moreover, most of us have difficulty assessing risk and return situations unfamiliar to us (question 3), and so tend to overestimate benefits and underestimate costs. We buy stocks like Genentech because we think they will make us rich with some esoteric technology, and because we have no way of reasonably assessing their potential rewards.

Now that we know what's the matter with us—psychologically—how do we break loose? The answer is simple: go against the majority. Avoid big-name companies and technology all-stars, and buy the lesser-knowns and the out-of-favor stocks. Bucking the trend could cause us emotional stress, so a better alternative might be to let computers make our investment choices. This strategy is not so far-fetched: artificial intelligence systems are already being used precisely for that purpose.

investment risk without necessarily reducing expected return. It is perhaps
the only "sure thing" investors will ever find. Portfolios can be constructed
randomly or in an effort to achieve a purpose, and each will be discussed. First,
though, is a review of correlation statistics that help us understand important
concepts.

Return Correlations

The returns between two assets may be correlated, either positively or negatively.
If they move in the same direction, positive correlation exists; negative
correlation occurs if they move in opposite directions; and, if there is no pattern,
there is no correlation. Statistics measuring correlation are the coefficient of
covariance and the correlation coefficient.

The Coefficient of Covariance In investment analysis, the **coefficient of
covariance (Cov)** is based upon the interaction of one asset's deviations from its
expected return with similar deviations of another asset. These deviations have
already been calculated for the savings account (SA) and the bond (B) and are
shown in Exhibit 4.2. Calculation of the coefficient of covariance between the two
($Cov: SA, B$) is shown in the following table:

(1) $(R_i - \bar{R})$	(2) $(R_i - \bar{R})$	(3) $(1) \times (2)$	(4) Pr	(5) $(4) \times (3)$
2.2	−11.0	−24.2	0.2	−4.84
0.2	− 1.0	− 0.2	0.5	−0.10
−1.8	9.0	−16.2	0.3	−4.86
			$Cov: SA, B$ =	−9.80

While useful in statistical work, this number has little practical meaning to us,
making it necessary to calculate the correlation coefficient.

The Correlation Coefficient The **correlation coefficient** (r) indicates the
strength of the correlation and whether it is positive or negative. It is easily
calculated once the coefficient of covariance is available, along with the standard
deviation of each asset. The correlation between the savings account return and
the bond's return ($r: SA, B$) is calculated as follows:

$$r: SA, B = \frac{Cov: SA, B}{\sigma_{SA} \times \sigma_B} = \frac{-9.8}{1.4 \times 7.0} = \frac{-9.8}{9.8} = -1.0$$

This number tells us the returns are perfectly negatively correlated. Values for r
can range from −1.0 to +1.0 (perfect positive correlation). A value of zero
indicates a lack of any correlation. As we see, the return from the savings account
is perfectly negatively correlated to the bond's return. Whether such correlation is
desirable or undesirable will be explained shortly.

The coefficient of covariance and the correlation coefficient compare returns on two assets.

Random Diversification

Random diversification sounds like disorganized investing, and in a sense, it is. However, it is probably better understood as combining assets for no purpose other than reducing risk. So, you can say that it is random only in the sense that it is not pegged to a specific investment target.

How Diversification Works We can illustrate random diversification by returning to our bond and savings account example. Suppose that after you examine the risk and return characteristics of each, you find it almost impossible to make a choice. You really cannot favor one over the other. Since you aren't restricted to investing in only one, you could consider investing a portion of your total funds in each. In this situation it might make sense to allocate half of your investment dollars to each.

You now have a new asset—the portfolio—with its own return and risk characteristics. Exhibit 4.4 shows how these characteristics are calculated. As you see, the portfolio offers an expected return of 9.4% and a standard deviation of 2.8%; its coefficient of variation is 0.298. Is this portfolio better than either of the individual assets? The answer depends upon the investor's perspective. If we compare it to the bond, we can say that it offers a lower return but it also has substantially less risk. The investor still must choose between higher return or less risk, but this portfolio might be an attractive alternative to either the bond or the savings account alone. While we can't generalize about the investor's preference for the portfolio, we can say that it represents a third alternative. To that end, diversification was effective.

EXHIBIT 4.4

Evaluating a portfolio invested evenly in a savings account and a bond

I. Calculate Possible Portfolio Returns (R_i):

Interest Rates Rise: $R_1 = (.5 \times 10) + (.5 \times 0) = 5 + 0 = 5$

Interest Rates Stay
Same: $\qquad R_2 = (.5 \times 8) + (.5 \times 10) = 4 + 5 = 9$

Interest Rates Fall: $R_3 = (.5 \times 6) + (.5 \times 20) = 3 + 10 = 13$

II. Calculate Expected Portfolio Return ($\overline{R}$):

$\overline{R} = (.2 \times 5) + (.5 \times 9) + (.3 \times 13) = 1.0 + 4.5 + 3.9 = 9.4$

III. Calculate Risk Statistics (σ^2, σ, and C):

$(R_i - \overline{R})$	$(R_i - \overline{R})^2$	$(R_i - \overline{R})^2 \times Pr$
-4.4	19.36	$19.36 \times .2 = 3.872$
-0.4	0.16	$0.16 \times .5 = 0.080$
3.6	12.96	$12.96 \times .3 = \underline{3.888}$
		$\sigma^2 = 7.840$
		$\sigma = \sqrt{\sigma^2} = 2.800$
		$C = 2.8/9.4 = 0.298$

Correlated Returns and Effective Diversification The above portfolio is an effective alternative because of the negative correlation between the bond's return and the return on the savings account. If interest rates rise, the savings account return also rises but the bond return falls, and the reverse happens when interest rates fall. Negative correlation enhances the risk-reducing power of a portfolio. In fact, if returns are perfectly negatively correlated—meaning they *always* move in opposite directions—you can arrange a portfolio to eliminate risk altogether. On the other hand, if returns are positively correlated, risk reduction is more difficult.

> The reduction of risk in a portfolio depends upon the correlation of returns among the individual assets held.

To see this, suppose the bond's return moved in the same direction as the return on the savings account. Adding the two returns together would compound the variations in return, rather than offset them. At the extreme, if assets are perfectly positively correlated, a portfolio will not reduce risk at all. Exhibit 4.5 illustrates the risk implications of holding correlated assets.

Over long periods of time, most investment returns are either positively correlated or uncorrelated. Strong negative correlations are rare, unless you get into hedging situations. Exhibit 4.6 illustrates correlations among the key financial assets. As this exhibit shows, there are some negative correlations, but they are rather weak. Strong positive correlations exist between the S&P 500 and small company stocks and between corporate and Treasury bonds. Treasury bills and the CPI are moderately correlated, while all other correlations are very weak. Various portfolios of the five assets—such as one composed of the S&P 500 (or small company stocks), corporate (or Treasury) bonds, and Treasury bills—would have offered effective reduction of risk while maintaining a reasonable return.

> A portfolio composed of the S&P 500, corporate bonds, and Treasury bills offers effective risk reduction.

The Number of Securities and Diversification How many securities must an investor hold to be adequately diversified? Suppose we are considering a broad

If Assets Are:	Value of Correlation Coefficient Is:	Combining Assets Will:
Perfectly positively correlated	+1.0	not reduce risk at all
Postively correlated	between zero and +1.0	reduce risk slightly; the lower the value, the more the reduction
Uncorrelated	0.0	reduce risk considerably
Negatively correlated	between zero and −1.0	virtually eliminate risk
Perfectly negatively correlated	−1.0	completely eliminate risk

EXHIBIT 4.5
Correlation of asset returns and reduction of risk

EXHIBIT 4.6

Correlations among key financial assets: Historical correlation coefficient values

	S&P 500	Small Companies	Corporate Bonds	Treasury Bonds	Treasury Bills	CPI
S&P 500	—	+0.82	+0.19	+0.11	−0.07	−0.02
Small Companies	—	—	+0.08	−0.01	−0.08	+0.06
Corporate bonds	—	—	—	+0.93	+0.19	−0.17
Treasury bonds	—	—	—	—	+0.22	−0.17
Treasury bills	—	—	—	—	—	+0.41
CPI	—	—	—	—	—	—

SOURCE: Roger G. Ibbotson and Rex A. Sinquefield, *Stocks, Bonds, Bills, and Inflation*, 1982 edition [Charlottesville, VA: Institute for Chartered Financial Analysts]. Updated in *Stocks, Bonds, Bills, and Inflation*, 1989 Yearbook [Chicago: Ibbotson Associates].

universe of similar securities, such as the common stocks in the S&P 500. Suppose further we select individual stocks from the 500 in some random fashion, such as by throwing darts at a page that has each of their names on it. Each stock a dart hits is then added to our portfolio. Exhibit 4.7 shows what happens to the portfolio risk as we increase the number of securities.

As you see, adding only a few securities reduces risk considerably. By the time you hold 15 to 20, you have practically eliminated all the risk that can be eliminated. This risk is called **random, or diversifiable, risk.** You can get rid of it through a portfolio. You cannot eliminate all risk, however. The remaining portion is the amount of risk you would have even if you held the entire 500 stocks in the index. It cannot be eliminated and is therefore called **market,** or **nondiversifiable, risk.**

> A portfolio of stocks can eliminate random risk, but it cannot eliminate market risk.

The reason market risk cannot be eliminated is explained in part by the fact that most individual stocks' returns are positively correlated, and any sample of sufficient size will include fewer negatively correlated or uncorrelated returns. Thus, combining stocks reduces, but does not eliminate, total risk. Since some risk remains, the only thing you can do is manage it. This idea of managing a portfolio implies an investment goal, which leads us to the topic of purposive diversification.

Purposive Diversification

> Purposive diversification attempts to achieve an investment goal.

Purposive diversification means arranging assets in a portfolio to achieve a given investment goal. In very general terms, this goal might be simply to attain a risk-return situation that we consider optimal; that is, the best possible. In other words, given our preference for greater return and our aversion to more risk, we

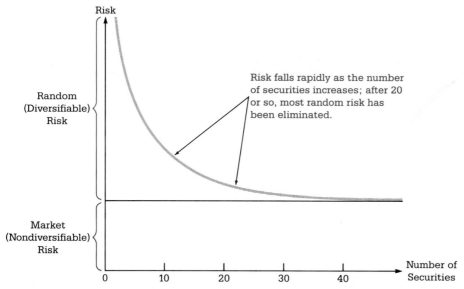

EXHIBIT 4.7
Risk and the number of
securities in a portfolio

examine many possible portfolios and find one that best accommodates our return-risk preference. Keep in mind that we continue to ignore any portfolio that is dominated by another. We will examine only those with a trade-off of greater return or less risk. Consider again the bond-savings-account example. Assume you are an investor who really dislikes risk. As far as you are concerned, the most appropriate investment goal is minimizing risk. Naturally, when you had to choose between the bond and the savings account, you picked the latter. However, even this alternative has risk, as we have seen. Now that you can combine the two assets, you wonder if it would be possible to achieve a lower risk level. The answer is yes. And, surprisingly, at the same time you actually increase your expected return.

To illustrate, assume you decide to allocate 80% of your investment funds to the savings account and 20% to the bond. Exhibit 4.8 shows the possible portfolio returns, the expected portfolio return, and risk statistics. This portfolio is clearly a vast improvement over the savings account. Your return will never be less than 8.0% and it varies only from 8.0% to 8.8%, an extremely narrow range. The expected return of 8.44% is higher than the savings account's 7.8%. Clearly, this portfolio dominates the savings account alternative.

You might wonder if there is some other allocation percentage that could reduce risk even more, although we are as low as most people might worry about going. The answer is yes; in fact, as calculated earlier, the returns are perfectly negatively correlated; so we can find a combination that reduces risk to zero. In other words, the return would be the same regardless of what happens to market interest rates. The arithmetic for finding this minimum point can be difficult, and we will not pursue it in this introductory text.

EXHIBIT 4.8

Evaluating a portfolio invested 80% in a savings account and 20% in a bond

I. Calculate Possible Portfolio Returns (R_i):

Interest Rates Rise, $\quad\quad\quad\quad\quad R_1 = (.8 \times 10) + (.2 \times \quad 0)$
$$= 8.0 + \quad 0 = 8.0$$

Interest Rates Stay The Same, $R_2 = (.8 \times \quad 8) + (.2 \times 10)$
$$= 6.4 + 2.0 = 8.4$$

Interest Rates Fall, $\quad\quad\quad\quad\quad R_3 = (.8 \times \quad 6) + (.2 \times 20)$
$$= 4.8 + 4.0 = 8.8$$

II. Calculate Expected Portfolio Return ($\overline{R}$):

$$\overline{R} = (.2 \times 8.0) + (.5 \times 8.4) + (.3 \times 8.8) = 1.60 + 4.20 + 2.64 = 8.44$$

III. Calculate Risk Statistics (σ^2, σ, and c):

$(R_i - \overline{R})$	$(R_i - \overline{R})^2$	$(R_i - \overline{R})^2 \times Pr$
−0.44	.1936	$.1936 \times .2 = .0387$
−0.04	.0016	$.0016 \times .5 = .0008$
+0.36	.1296	$.1296 \times .3 = \underline{.0389}$

$$\sigma^2 = .0784$$
$$\sigma = \sqrt{\sigma^2} = .2800$$
$$C = .28/8.44 = .0332$$

Using the Beta Concept

Beta values are used to manage market risk.

Portfolios can be arranged to meet return-and-risk targets. Doing so involves the use of another risk statistic, called the *beta weight,* or, simply, *beta.* To understand how beta works, we must first understand what it means.

Calculating Beta   **Beta** is a statistic that measures changes in an asset's return in relation to changes in the return of a broad portfolio of assets. While any broad portfolio can be considered, one that is used often is the S&P 500 stock index. Suppose you gather historical data for the annual rate of return on IBM common stock and the S&P 500 for the past ten years. You could then plot these points, as shown in Exhibit 4.9. Next, fit a line, such as the one shown in Exhibit 4.9, through the scattering of points. (You could use a freehand method to fit the line, but regression programs on a hand calculator or a computer will give a much more accurate fit. Also, you might want to read the appendix at the end of this chapter.) This line is called the asset's characteristic line, and its slope is the asset's beta value. The steeper the line's slope, the greater is beta's value, and the more shallow the slope, the less its value.

A beta value shows the risk of an individual as-set in relation to the risk of the overall market.

Interpreting Beta Values   Exhibit 4.9 should illustrate the idea that a beta value shows how changes in the return of a particular asset will be influenced by changes in returns for the overall market. For example, IBM's beta of 1.30 indicates that if the market's return increases or decreases by 10%, IBM's return

Beta measures changes in the return of a specific stock relative to changes in return of the overall market. It is an index of return sensitivity, with the overall market's index number equalling 1.0. Statistical methods are used to calculate beta. The first step is to gather return data for the stock in question and the market (the S&P 500). In this illustration, ten periods of hypothetical returns for IBM and the S&P 500 are on the left, and a graphic representation of finding beta is on the right.

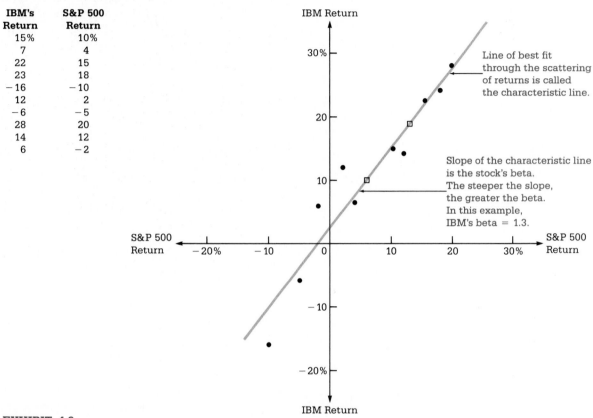

IBM's Return	S&P 500 Return
15%	10%
7	4
22	15
23	18
−16	−10
12	2
−6	−5
28	20
14	12
6	−2

Line of best fit through the scattering of returns is called the characteristic line.

Slope of the characteristic line is the stock's beta. The steeper the slope, the greater the beta. In this example, IBM's beta = 1.3.

EXHIBIT 4.9
Determining a stock's beta value

will increase or decrease by 13% (1.3 × 10). It has 30% more variation in return than the market. A beta of, say, +0.6, on the other hand, shows a stock with only 60% of the return variation of the market. Beta, then, shows risk: the higher the positive value of beta, the greater the risk, and the lower the positive value, the less the risk. Studies indicate that most assets have positive-valued betas. Negative betas indicate assets with returns that move in opposition to the direction of the market return. Such assets are rare. A negative beta has implications similar to those of negative correlation, discussed earlier, and has the same effect in reducing portfolio risk. A summary of the investment implications of beta values appears in Exhibit 4.10, and a sample of actual betas appears in Exhibit 4.11.

EXHIBIT 4.10
Investment implications
of beta values

Beta Value	Investment Implication
Negative	This stock's return moves in the opposite direction of the market; you can reduce risk substantially by holding it along with a market portfolio. However, very few stocks have negative betas.
Between zero and +1.0	This stock is less risky than the market; a portfolio of low-beta stocks would be a conservative portfolio.
+1.0	The market's beta is +1.0; any individual stock with this value is as risky as the market.
Greater than +1.0	A stock with a beta greater than +1.0 is riskier than the market; a portfolio of these stocks would show considerable variation in return over time.

Beta-Designed Portfolios   Because beta indicates nondiversifiable risk, it is useful for designing portfolios that meet individual risk dispositions. For example, if you want a conservative, low-risk portfolio, limit your investments to those with low beta values, keeping in mind that you must hold about 15 or 20 different assets to virtually eliminate the diversifiable risk. If you want an aggressive portfolio, reverse your posture and buy 15 to 20 high-beta assets. This portfolio-design approach is certainly quick and very easy, but it does present problems.

Problems with Beta   Unfortunately, the use of betas in constructing portfolios is somewhat limited, for several reasons. To begin with, unless you intend to calculate your own betas, you must use published sources, such as the *Value Line*

EXHIBIT 4.11
A sample of beta values

Company	Major Business	Beta Value
Allegheny Power	Public utility	0.70
Allied Supermarkets	Supermarket operation	0.75
Atlantic Richfield	Oil refinery	1.00
Borden, Inc.	Food products	0.95
Bristol Myers	Home products	1.00
Consolidated Edison	Public utility	0.70
Deltona Corporation	Land development	1.50
Federal Express	Overnight mail delivery	1.25
General Telephone & Electronics	Communications (established company)	0.95
MCI	Communications (new company)	1.45
Merrill Lynch	Stockbrokerage	1.75
Paine Webber	Stockbrokerage	1.80

SOURCE: *Value Line Investment Survey: Summary and Index,* August 7, 1987. © Value Line Investment Survey; used by permission of Value Line, Inc.

Investment Survey. While these are readily available for a large number of common stocks, they are generally unavailable for other kinds of assets, such as bonds, preferred stocks, or tangibles.

Secondly, research has shown that beta values are sensitive to the particular index selected to represent (serve as a proxy for) the market. For example, you might derive a beta of 1.3 for IBM using the S&P 500, whereas another index, say the Wilshire 5000 Equity Index, might give a beta of 0.9. Which do you take? There is no clear answer.

A third problem with betas is they may not remain stationary long enough to be useful. Remember that historical data are used to calculate betas. But suppose a company's situation changes; perhaps it increases its business activities in very risky ventures. Its current or future beta would be higher than its past beta, and you would understate the company's risk with the historical beta estimate. There isn't much you can do about this problem, but it might be a mistake to exaggerate it. Many decisions must be guided by historical data and the relationships they provide. There is no reason to believe the problem with historical data is more acute in investment analysis than anywhere else, or that errors are more likely to occur with a beta approach than with another. Nothing short of perfect knowledge of the future will eliminate guesswork in decision making.

> Betas give poor estimates of risk if they are not stationary.

SOURCES OF RISK

Now that we understand risk as variations in return over time, our attention can turn to sources of such variations. One broad source consists of changes in the economic environment. Another has to do with characteristics of the security issuer. An investment's risk might also be affected by its marketability and by changes in the tax law.

Changes in the Economic Environment

We live in an extremely complex economy. Not only do many domestic factors influence an investment's return, but we now must consider international factors as well. The business cycle expands and contracts, interest rates go up and down, some industries grow rapidly while others go into decline, the dollar strengthens and weakens, and other changes take place, all of them influencing the investments we make. Change is the key element in risk. If everything would work out as expected when an investment was made, risk would be minimal. The discussion below will emphasize the important role change plays.

Economic Performance Risk   **Economic performance risk** refers to return variability caused by changes in real output of the economy. Asset returns are clearly influenced by the overall performance of the national economy. A sluggish economy over a long period of time inevitably leads to poor investment returns.

Asset returns are influenced by the performance of the overall economy.

The stagnant 1970s is a good example: investors earned better returns in savings accounts than they did in many equity investments. If the economy is growing at a meager 1% or 2% annually, the average real return on all assets can hardly be much higher. Economic cycles also create investment risk by creating uncertainty. Even a robust economy, such as most of the 1960s or most of the 1980s, has periods of slow growth. The fear that a recession (or worse, a depression) might occur often depresses stock prices; when the economic outlook improves, prices rally.

Inflation risk arises when an asset's return does not match the inflation rate.

Inflation Risk   **Inflation risk** has to do with a loss of purchasing power because an investment's return fails to keep pace with the rate of inflation. During periods of high inflation, this loss can be considerable. You might recall from Chapter 3 that the historical rate of inflation has been about equal to the rate of return on U.S. Treasury bills, which means the bills' real rate of return has been about zero. In recent years, though, the real rate of return has been high, relative to the long-run historical average. One possible explanation is that investors require a higher risk premium to compensate them for the risk of making greater errors in forecasting inflation rates, which have become both higher and more unstable.

A common theme in the 1970s and early 1980s was to hedge inflation by investing in tangible assets: real estate, jewelry, art works, and particularly gold and silver. Tangible assets did indeed show relatively high rates of return during this period, and some investment advisors believe you should always have a portion of your total portfolio in tangibles to serve as the inflation hedge. No doubt, people who come from countries where high inflation is a perennial problem agree with this philosophy.

A real rate of return adjusts a nominal return for inflation.

Also, since inflation-adjusted rates of return are so important, you should see how they are calculated. The equation below solves for the real rate of return (r') on an investment, given its nominal rate of return (r) and the inflation rate (i).

$$r' = [(1.0 + r)/(1.0 + i)] - 1.0$$

As an example, suppose $r = 10\%$ and $i = 5\%$, then

$$r' = [(1.10)/(1.05)] - 1.0$$
$$= 1.0476 - 1.0$$
$$= 0.0476, \text{ or } 4.76\%$$

Notice that your answer is slightly less than if you merely subtracted the inflation rate from the nominal rate (5%), which is frequently done. The difference is trivial if we are talking about compounding an investment's return over a few years, but it can be substantial if the return is compounded over many years, as you might do in the area of retirement planning.

Inflation risk and interest-rate risk arise from an inflation-biased economy.

Interest-Rate Risk   **Interest-rate risk** has to do with a loss or gain you might experience on a fixed-income security because interest rates in general rise or fall after you purchase it. Since interest rates and inflation rates often move together,

Risk and Time: Are They Related?

A well-founded principle in investment theory is diversification. Adding securities to a portfolio reduces risk and does not necessarily reduce return. Most investors accept this rule, even though they may not adhere to it as much as they should. But what about the length of time an asset is held? Does it have any relationship to risk? Can you, for example, reduce risk by adding more years to your holding period, just as you reduce portfolio risk by adding more securities to a portfolio? Is there time diversification as well as security diversification?

The question is intriguing and some researchers have been looking into it lately. Just as good returns from some securities offset poor returns of others, leaving the overall portfolio more stable, it seems returns in good years offset those of bad years, leaving an asset's average return for a long holding period more stable. In a cursory fashion it appears that lengthening the holding period does indeed reduce return variability, as measured by customarily used risk statistics. (See the accompanying table.) The standard deviation of common stocks, for ex-

ample, declines from 21.2% when one-year holding periods are used to 6.6% for five-year holding periods. Looking at the coefficient of variation, you would have to conclude that stocks offer a better return-risk situation than Treasury bills for investors who intend to hold each for at least five years.

Regardless of any future developments in this area, it seems the research already demonstrates what many investment advisors have urged for a long time. First, identify your investment objectives, which helps formulate how long assets

will be held. If these are long periods, you need not be concerned with short-term fluctuations in value, and you have greater flexibility in choosing assets that are sometimes considered "inherently risky." Second, having the patience to hold assets for the long run is often the easiest way to success in investing. Naturally, along with time diversification, you need security diversification as well. Otherwise, you might buy one or two stocks and hold them for a long time—while the companies go into bankruptcy.

Holding Period Average Return (R), Standard Deviation (σ), and Coefficient of Variation (C) for Various Holding Period Lengths*

	Common Stocks	Treasury Bills
1-Year holding periods:		
R	12.0%	3.5%
σ	21.2	3.4
C	1.8	1.0
3-Year holding periods:		
R	10.5	3.5
σ	11.5	3.3
C	1.1	0.9
5-Year holding periods:		
R	10.0	3.5
σ	6.6	3.3
C	0.7	0.9

*Non-overlapping periods, 1926 through 1985.

interest-rate risk and inflation risk are considered separate parts of the overall problem of an inflation-biased economy.

It is important to see that interest-rate risk is associated with volatile interest rates—not simply high interest rates. Investors can adjust to high rates, as evidenced by the fact that interest rates vary considerably among different industrialized and economically stable countries of the world. In Switzerland, the rate might be 2%, while in neighboring Italy, it might be 20%. Yet, the Swiss and Italian investors seem to adjust to the different interest and inflation rates in designing their investment portfolios. (Keep in mind, also, that the real interest rates in each country are probably about the same.) The problem arises when rates become unstable: this instability creates the changes in market prices of debt instruments. We will examine interest-rate risk in more detail in the next chapter.

International and Political Risks   No sooner had inflation fears begun to subside in the mid-1980s, and investors had become disenchanted with tangibles, when a new diversification theme became popular: internationalize your portfolio. Almost overnight, mutual funds began increasing their offerings of international funds to give investors opportunities to play the theme. The same investor who five years earlier was buying gold at the gold store in a shopping center was now trying to invest in Korea, or Japan, or Australia.

What caused such interest? Surely a main cause was the expected decline in the value of the dollar relative to other currencies. It was felt that investments denominated in foreign currencies would benefit due to the weakening of the dollar and, conversely, strengthening of those currencies. Regardless of the eventual outcome for the fickle investor who likes to play themes, the experience does underscore the importance of considering the international situation in designing a portfolio. It appears that a portfolio with international diversification is more stable than one without, and often there is no reduction in return. This topic is covered in greater detail in Chapter 20.

Internationalizing a port-folio can reduce its risk.

However, there are different ways to achieve an international portfolio. Surely one of the easiest is to invest in multinational corporations, such as IBM or Exxon. Many large companies that we typically view as American are probably more accurately seen as global, since more than 50% of their sales or earnings are outside the United States. If you own a reasonable number of shares in these companies, your portfolio is already internationalized.

Political risks are part of the international investment scene and should not be ignored. The apartheid problem in South Africa, for example, has created a very unstable investment environment in that country, as investors in its huge gem- and gold-mining operations will attest. Even very stable European or Asian countries frequently scare American investors who hear of increasing socialism or some other "ism" that doesn't look favorably upon private property. True, we seem to be enjoying a period of relative economic harmony, but that can change almost overnight. Surely, as an investor you should think twice before you invest a substantial portion of your portfolio in, say, the Mexico Fund or the Korean Fund.

Characteristics of the Security Issuer

Investing means buying individual assets, whose soundness depends upon the financial strength of the organizations who issued them. As these organizations gain or lose strength, so do their securities. We can look at the characteristics of security issuers in terms of business risk and financial risk.

Business Risk   **Business risk** arises because of the nature of the business of the security issuer. We generally think of this risk in relation to common stock, although you can extend it to partnership interests and perhaps other kinds of investments. If you invest in a company that is in a risky industry—making personal computers in the early 1980s, for example—you can expect to hold a risky stock. The highest form of business risk usually comes with a company that produces only one product, or product line. The company may have played an active role in developing the product's technology and is now trying to market it. The single product makes the company particularly vulnerable to factors such as a slackening of demand, the introduction of a cheaper or better competitive product, or poor inventory management. Diversification is essential if you intend to invest in such companies and wish to avoid excessive risk. If you think genetic engineering is the coming thing, for example, try to find at least five or six companies that are in the industry and divide the amount you wish to invest in genetic engineering among them, rather than putting all of it in one company.

> Business risk depends on the company's activities and the diversification of its product or service lines.

Financial Risk   A security issuer can also increase the amount of risk its investors experience by financing itself with large amounts of borrowing. This **financial risk** is brought about by the company's level of debt obligations. Creditors rank before stockholders in both interest payments and distributions in liquidation. The larger the creditors' position, the less stockholders can expect. Moreover, debt requires the regular payment of interest, which can weaken the company's cash flow and make it difficult to operate the business. Even a company with a well-diversified product line can expose its owners to a high level of risk through excessive borrowing. And, if the single-product company borrows heavily, you have about as risky an investment as you might find.

> If a company uses large amounts of debt to finance its operations, it will have high financial risk.

There is a reason business firms use debt in their financing efforts, and you as a shareholder should be aware of it. All things considered, the use of debt—sometimes called leverage—often increases a company's earnings per share of common stock. If the company can earn more on its investments than it must pay in interest to finance those investments, then it will enhance earnings per share by investing. But the enhanced earnings per share depend upon a certain level of sales and operating income. If either of these falls to lower levels, the impact on earnings per share is disastrous; naturally, if either goes above the targets, the impact is very beneficial. In either case, the volatility of earnings per share is increased, and that is the cause of the added risks.

Other Sources of Risk

With so many different kinds of investments available, you can also find many sources of risk. Two other sources that are fairly common are marketability risk and the risk from a changing tax law.

Marketability Risk   Some investments prove to be difficult to sell after they are purchased. This difficulty commonly occurs with many tangible investments, but it can also be the case for some stocks, bonds, and particularly, limited partnership interests. **Marketability risk** arises when there is no effective secondary market for an investment. In an effective market, the investment can not only be sold, but it can also be sold at a competitively determined price and without paying excessive selling costs. There may always be a buyer for the Salvador Dalí print you just bought, but perhaps only at a price the buyer sets and at a commission of 20% of the sale.

Some stocks and bonds are so thinly traded that you should concern yourself with their marketability risk. Even if you see the stock listed in *The Wall Street Journal* each day, do not assume you will be able to sell it without difficulty. Moreover, you may pay a sizeable difference in the bid-ask spread when you trade, which further reduces your potential investment profit. This, too, should be looked upon as a cost of poor marketability.

Risks From a Changing Tax Law   A tax law that is in a constant state of flux also poses investment risk. It seems that each year the president and Congress give us a tax ''reform'' package that changes the after-tax returns on many investments. Almost immediately, the market prices of these investments change in response to an improved or worsened return picture. A dramatic example is the situation with tax-free securities, such as municipal bonds. Their attraction is based directly on their tax advantage, which in turn reflects the investor's marginal tax rate. If that rate is lowered, for example, municipal bonds lose some of their advantage over taxable issues. This leads to lower market prices on the instruments until their market yields are again competitive with taxable issues. An investor can do little to diversify against the risks of a changing tax law without knowing in advance how the law will be changed. Will capital gains be favored or disfavored this year? Will depreciation be allowed at a rapid or slow rate? Will public utilities be favored by allowing investors to defer taxes on the dividends they pay (if they take dividends in the form of new shares), or will that provision be allowed to expire? No one knows the answers to such questions. Perhaps the only diversification strategy is to hold an array of investment alternatives so that any unfavorable impacts on one type of investment may be offset by favorable impacts on another. To be sure, it's a guessing game—a game that investors are finding less fun to play as tax laws change with increasing frequency.

Marketability risk arises when there is no effective secondary market for an investment.

Changes in the tax law can create risk by favoring some investments while hurting others.

SUMMARY

The risk associated with holding an individual asset can be measured by using three statistics—the variance, the standard deviation, and the coefficient of variation—in evaluating the asset's historical returns. The greater the dispersion of returns, the higher the statistics' values, and the greater the asset's risk. Examining historical returns of key financial assets shows very low risk for Treasury bills and very high risk for common stocks, with long-term bonds' risks in the middle.

When individual assets are held simultaneously, a portfolio is created that may have a risk characteristic different from that of the assets of which it is composed. This difference results from diversification of assets and the return correlations among them. Poorly or negatively correlated asset returns reduce portfolio risk, while highly correlated returns leave risk unchanged. If securities are picked randomly and added to a portfolio, portfolio risk declines as more securities are added. The risk eliminated is called diversifiable risk; however, some risk cannot be eliminated regardless of the number of securities added. This risk is called nondiversifiable risk. Although it cannot be eliminated, it can be managed. A risk statistic used in this effort is a security's beta weight, which measures the responsiveness of a security's return in relation to changes in return for the overall securities market. High beta values indicate high risk, while low beta values show low risk. While betas are helpful, their usefulness is limited if they are difficult to calculate or do not remain stable over time.

Primary sources of risk are related to changes in the economic environment and to characteristics of the security issuer. Along with risks of an uncertain business cycle, changes in the economic environment create inflation risk, interest-rate risk, and international and political risks. Risks related to the security issuer include business risk and financial risk. Other sources of risk include marketability problems and a changing tax law.

KEY TERMS

Select the alternative that best identifies the key term.

1. expected return ($\bar{R}$)
2. variance (σ^2)
3. standard deviation (σ)
4. coefficient of variation (C)
5. coefficient of covariance (COV)
6. correlation coefficient (r)
7. random risk
8. market risk
9. beta
10. economic performance risk
11. inflation risk
12. interest-rate risk
13. business risk
14. financial risk
15. marketability risk

a. measures return sensitivity relative to the market's return
b. risk arising from a company's activities
c. the sum of possible outcomes times the probabilities of outcomes occurring
d. has to do with the loss of purchasing power
e. sum of: (actual return minus expected return)^2 × probability
f. risk from holding a security whose value is determined by market interest rates
g. risk eliminated by diversification
h. risk due to no effective secondary market
i. square root of the variance
j. nondiversifiable risk
k. standard deviation divided by expected return
l. risk arising from company borrowing
m. compares an asset's deviations of actual returns from expected return to similar deviations of another asset
n. risk arising from changes in real output
o. coefficient of covariance and standard deviations are used to calculate it

REVIEW QUESTIONS

1. What is risk? Should it be understood only as a chance of a loss? Explain.
2. What is an expected return and how is it calculated?
3. Explain what is meant by dispersion of asset returns. Indicate the statistics that measure dispersion.
4. What is meant by correlation of asset returns? Indicate the statistics used to measure correlation.
5. Discuss the historical risk statistics on key financial assets. Do the data contain any surprises? Explain.
6. How would you interpret the following values for the correlation coefficient relating returns from two assets: +0.8, −0.3, 0.0, −1.0, and +1.0?

7. How does correlation among asset returns influence the risk of a portfolio? Is it better to hold assets that are positively or negatively correlated? Explain. When can risk be eliminated completely? When can it not be reduced at all?

8. How many stocks (selected randomly from the S&P 500) must you hold to achieve reasonable diversification? Will this portfolio eliminate all risk, or will some remain? Explain.

9. Discuss the historical correlations among key financial assets. Do the values suggest that a portfolio of these assets could be effective in reducing risk? Explain.

10. Answer the following questions about the beta measurement:
    a. What is it?
    b. How is it determined?
    c. How can it be used in designing a portfolio?
    d. What are some problems in its determination?

11. NCF Corporation has a beta of 1.8. Your return from the stock last year was 10%. You expect the market to go down 20% this year. What will be your return with NCF this year? What would it be if you expected the market return to increase 20%?

12. Explain economic performance risk and inflation risk. Are these simply different perspectives on the same thing? Explain.

13. Determine an investment's real rate of return if its nominal rate is 20% and inflation is 5%.

14. Explain interest-rate risk. Is this risk related in some way to inflation risk? Explain.

15. Explain international and political risks. How can you avoid such risks?

16. Explain business risk and financial risk. How can you minimize or avoid these risks?

17. Explain marketability risk and risk from a changing tax law. Can either of these risks be minimized or avoided?

---

1. Matt McGuire is thinking of making a stock investment. As he sees it, his return can be zero, 20%, or 40%. If there is an equal probability of each return occurring, calculate: (a) the expected return, (b) the variance, (c) the standard deviation, and (d) the coefficient of variation.

   After you have your answers, compare this investment to another Matt is considering. Its statistics are: $\bar{R} = 12\%$; $\sigma^2 = 81\%$; $\sigma = 9\%$; $C = 0.75$. Compare the two investments. Does one dominate the other, or must Matt trade off risk for return? Discuss.

2. The returns from Wing Aircraft Supplies are related to strength in the overall economy, as shown below:

	Economy		
	Weak	So-So	Strong
Wing's Returns	−10%	+12%	+30%

An economic forecaster believes the economy may be headed towards a recession. When asked to be more specific, she indicated the odds of a weak economy are 3 out of 10, while the odds for a strong economy are only 1 in 10. Of course, the odds for a so-so economy are then 6 in 10. Given the above information, calculate the expected return, variance, standard deviation, and coefficient of variation for Wing's returns.

PROBLEMS AND PROJECTS

3. Suppose you were thinking of investing in Wing Aircraft, the company from problem 2. However, you would combine this investment with a bond investment that is likely to do better in a weak economy than in a strong one. This investment's returns, given the three states of the economy above, are 12%, 9%, and 6%, respectively.
    a. Determine the expected return, variance, standard deviation and coefficient of variation for this investment.
    b. Calculate the coefficient of covariance and correlation coefficient between this investment and the investment in Wing Aircraft.

4. Shown below is a table of correlation coefficients among four different investments. Assuming the returns from the investments are as follows—$A = 20\%$, $B = 10\%$, $C = 15\%$, and $D = 30\%$—which two investments would you hold together? Explain your answer.

	A	B	C	D
A	1.0	0.6	0.5	0.9
B	—	1.0	0.8	−0.5
C	—	—	1.0	0.9
D	—	—	—	1.0

5. You are planning an investment portfolio for your eventual retirement in 40 years. You feel the portfolio will show an average annual return of 12%. Unfortunately, you also think inflation will average 5% a year.
    a. Calculate your expected real rate of return.
    b. Assuming you invest $10,000 in the portfolio, determine its future *real* value.
    c. Determine the future *real* value using the approximate real rate of return of 7%. Compare this answer to part (b).

6. (*Student Project*)   Locate the *Value Line Investment Survey* at your school library and review five companies familiar to you. Find the beta for each. Are their values what you might have expected from your general knowledge of the companies? Explain.

7. (*Student Project*)   Contact a financial officer of a small company in your hometown whose stock trades in the OTC market and is reported in *The Wall Street Journal*. Ask the officer if he or she would be interested in having the stock's beta determined. If so, gather daily price data for, say, 31 days. Based on daily price changes, determine holding period returns for 30 days. At the same time, record daily closing values for the S&P 500 and calculate 30 holding period returns for it. (Ignore dividends in both cases.) Do not annualize the data, and be careful with decimal points. For example, if a stock price goes from 30 to 30⅛, record the return as +0.004167 (+0.125/30.0). When you finish, discuss your results with the officer.

CASE ANALYSES

**4.1
Janine Ricardo
Considers
Investment
Correlations**

Janine Ricardo is considering investing in the construction industry. She believes the industry will do well over time, but, of course, realizes its short-run performance may not be spectacular. Janine has narrowed her investment selections to three possible companies: (1) Home Builders, Inc. (HBI), a company that constructs single-family detached homes; (2) Home Repairs, Inc. (HRI), a company specializing in home remodeling and repair projects; and (3) National Tool Company (NTC), a firm that manufactures tools used in the construction industry.

Janine thinks a robust economy bodes well for both HMI and NTC, to varying degrees, but poorly for HRI. While Janine's investment strategy is to hold a portfolio over time, rather than to frequently trade securities, she is concerned about excessive variations in portfolio value. Before investing, she plans to analyze the portfolio implications of the three companies. Accordingly, she also has developed probability estimates for changes in the economy for the upcoming year. Additionally, she has estimated returns from the three companies, given changes in the economy. Her data appear in the following table.

	Condition of Economy		
	Weak	Average	Strong
Probability	0.25	0.50	0.25
Likely returns (%):			
HBI	−20	+18	+44
HRI	+12	+ 8	+ 4
NTC	−32	+16	+56

Questions

a. Explain why Janine probably should not invest in NTC.
b. Calculate the expected return, variance, standard deviation, and coefficient of variation for HBI and HRI. Then, discuss which is the riskier.
c. Calculate the coefficient of covariance and the correlation coefficent for the two assets' returns. Then, discuss whether combining the two in a portfolio will be effective.
d. Suppose that Janine decides to invest 90% of her funds in HRI and 10% in HBI. Calculate the expected return for this portfolio.
e. Janine feels she has a reasonable tolerance towards risk and she describes herself as a moderate risk averter. Suppose that in the upcoming year, Janine could invest in a savings account guaranteed to pay a sure return of 8% for the year. Considering your work in question d above, what advice might you offer Janine? Explain.

Lenny Young has been watching the stock of Dayton Dynamics (DDY), a small high-tech company that provides specialized engineering services to firms in the defense industry. The firm's shares are traded in the OTC market, but Lenny has been unable to obtain data about the company, other than last year's annual report to shareholders. He is sure the company represents a high-risk situation and he would feel more comfortable investing in its shares if he could assess the magnitude of that risk.

After searching a number of library sources, Lenny has given up hope of finding any information bearing upon DDY's riskiness. Consequently, he will

**4.2
Lenny Young
Needs Beta**

undertake his own study. Going back over the past ten weeks he has recorded the weekly returns for both DDY and the S&P 500. The data appear below.

Week	DDY	Market
1	8%	5%
2	16	8
3	−20	−10
4	− 5	4
5	40	25
6	25	20
7	12	8
8	− 5	− 4
9	30	10
10	39	24

a. Calculate DDY's beta. (Use any method. If you have studied the appendix to this chapter, use the techniques discussed there. Otherwise, use a graphic approach and fit in the characteristic line with a visual approximation.)

b. Comment on DDY's beta. How risky is the stock in relation to the market? Suppose the market declines 12% in the upcoming year; what is DDY likely to do?

c. Lenny is considering investing most of his funds in DDY if the return/risk situation of its stock seems attractive. Considering Lenny's approach, do you believe beta is an appropriate statistic for measuring risk? Explain.

HELPFUL READING

Barry, Christopher B., and Stephen J. Brown. "Limited Information as a Source of Risk." *Journal of Portfolio Management,* Winter 1986.

Curran, John J. "Why Investors Make the Wrong Choices." *Fortune 1987 Investor's Guide,* pp. 63–68.

Palmeri, Christopher. "Earnings Guesstimates." *Forbes,* April 17, 1989, pp. 216–20.

Reichenstein, William. "When Stock Is Less Risky Than Treasury Bills." *Financial Analysts Journal,* November/December 1986.

Rosen, Jan M. "Finding the Right Levels of Risk." *The New York Times,* November 12, 1988, p.18.

Rosenberg, Barr. "Prediction of Common Stock Betas." *Journal of Portfolio Management,* Winter 1985.

APPENDIX: ANALYSIS OF HISTORICAL RETURNS

In this chapter we have analyzed asset returns, assuming such returns were expectational in nature; that is, an investor assumes certain scenarios are important—such as changing interest rates—and estimates the probability of potential changes. The thrust of the analysis is to select assets that provide investors with acceptable risk and return combinations. Considerable investment analysis follows this mode.

However, investors also analyze historical returns in an effort to gain a better understanding of the investment environment or specific assets. While the tools of analysis are the same, they are used slightly differently. We will consider the example of estimating IBM's beta, as discussed in the chapter. However, we also show additional statistical calculations. IBM's returns and returns on the S&P 500 are taken from Exhibit 4.9.

Exhibit 4.12 shows calculations of each asset's expected return $\bar{R}$ (now more appropriately called an average, or mean, return), variance, standard deviation, and coefficient of covariance. As you see, the calculations are somewhat easier because returns are not weighted by probability numbers. This allows us simply

EXHIBIT 4.12

Statistical calculations for IBM

Period (1)	IBM R_i (2)	$(R_i - \bar{R})$ (3)	$(R_i - \bar{R})^2$ (4)	S&P 500 R_i (5)	$(R_i - \bar{R})$ (6)	$(R_i - \bar{R})^2$ (7)	(3) × (6) (8)
1	15.0	4.5	20.25	10.0	3.6	12.96	16.20
2	7.0	− 3.5	12.25	4.0	− 2.4	5.76	8.40
3	22.0	11.5	132.25	15.0	8.6	73.96	98.90
4	23.0	12.5	156.25	18.0	11.6	134.56	145.00
5	−16.0	−26.5	702.25	−10.0	−16.4	268.96	434.60
6	12.0	1.5	2.25	2.0	− 4.4	19.36	− 6.60
7	− 6.0	−16.5	272.25	− 5.0	−11.4	129.96	188.10
8	28.0	17.5	306.25	20.0	13.6	184.96	238.00
9	14.0	3.5	12.25	12.0	5.6	31.36	19.60
10	6.0	− 4.5	20.25	− 2.0	− 8.4	70.56	37.80
Sums =	105.0		1636.50	64.0		932.40	1180.00
$\bar{R} =$	105.0/10		—	64.0/10		—	—
$\bar{R} =$	10.5		—	6.4		—	—
$\sigma^2 =$	—		1636.50/10	—		932.40/10	—
$\sigma^2 =$	—		163.65	—		93.24	—
$\sigma =$	—		12.79	—		9.66	—
$Cov =$	—		—	—		—	1180.00/10
$Cov =$	—		—	—		—	118.00

to add and divide by the number of observations (periods). With the data we can calculate the correlation coefficient:

$$r = \frac{Cov: \text{IBM, S\&P500}}{\sigma_{\text{IBM}} \times \sigma_{\text{S\&P500}}} = \frac{118.00}{12.79 \times 9.66} = \frac{118.00}{123.55} = 0.96$$

This value indicates the two returns have a high degree of positive correlation. Keep in mind these are hypothetical returns. Actual returns will generally show far less correlation, either positive or negative.

IBM's beta is calculated as a final step. It is found quite easily by simply dividing the coefficient of covariance by the variance of the S&P 500; that is,

$$\text{beta (IBM)} = \frac{Cov: \text{IBM,S\&P 500}}{\sigma: \text{S\&P 500}}$$

$$= \frac{118.00}{93.24}$$

$$= 1.27$$

This is the same value (rounded to 1.3) as indicated in Exhibit 4.9, using the slope of the regression line.

PART TWO

Investing in Bonds and Other Debt Instruments

Debt instruments are important portfolio components for most investors. They are held primarily to meet liquidity needs and to accumulate funds for future expenditures, such as making a large purchase or living in retirement. On balance, they are safer than common stocks and many other assets, although recent volatile interest rates have increased their risks substantially. This change makes it important to understand the nature of debt instruments before you invest in them.

Chapter 5 uses the concepts developed in Chapter 3 to explain how returns on debt instruments are determined. It also analyzes interest-rate risk, explaining how this risk is measured and discussing its importance in selecting specific debt securities. Also covered is default risk, which is measured with ratings prepared by ratings agencies.

Chapter 6 focuses on liquidity. It explains liquidity management and identifies specific debt instruments that provide suitable liquidity. It also discusses the integration of borrowing into a liquidity management program, analyzing sources of credit often used in connection with investing.

Chapter 7 explains bondholder rights with respect to interest payments, claims on assets in liquidation, and other preferences. It identifies various forms of long-term debt, distinguishing among Treasury, federal agency, corporate, and local government debt instruments, and indicating advantages and disadvantages of each. It also explains collateralized trust receipts, which have become so popular in recent years.

CHAPTER FIVE

Risk and Return With Debt Instruments

RETURN WITH DEBT INSTRUMENTS

Cash Flows

Calculating Yields

What Investors Expect in an Interest Rate

RISKS WITH DEBT INSTRUMENTS

Bond Prices and Changing Interest Rates

Determining Interest-Rate Risk

The Reinvestment Problem

Default Risk

HISTORICAL INTEREST-RATE VOLATILITY

Short- and Long-Term Rates

Forecasting Interest Rates

BOXES

Why Have Real Rates of Interest Been So High?

Is There a Message in the Yield Curve?

After you finish this chapter, you will be able to:

- understand the cash flows with both discount and interest-bearing securities and how to calculate current yield and yield to maturity for each.

- see what investors expect to receive from an interest rate.

- identify the interest-rate risk with a debt instrument and see how it is measured with an interest elasticity coefficient or Macaulay's duration coefficient.

- understand the reinvestment problem with its reinvestment risk and rollover risk.

- recognize default risk and become familiar with quality ratings published by Moody's and Standard and Poor's.

- see that interest rates have a history of volatility and that forecasting future rates is virtually impossible.

- identify the pattern of short- versus long-term rates and understand the concept of a yield curve.

A debt instrument represents an obligation by its issuer to pay interest (if interest is promised) on a timely basis and to repay the loan at its maturity. This is a legally binding obligation, giving you the right to seek remedies in court if the issuer reneges. Despite legal protection, though, debt instruments can be risky. To begin with, a promise to pay interest and principal is one thing, and actually paying it is another. Issuers do default, leaving their creditors with partially or totally worthless claims. Then, even if the creditor meets all the obligations, you may still hold a very risky investment if it has a long maturity and if interest rates in general are very volatile.

In the previous two chapters, we saw the historical returns and risks from key debt instruments: U.S. Treasury bills, U.S. Treasury bonds, and corporate bonds. In this chapter we want to examine in greater detail how the returns from debt instruments are calculated and why debt instruments are risky. We also consider the historical volatility of interest rates and raise the issue of whether interest rates can be forecasted.

RETURN WITH DEBT INSTRUMENTS

Debt instruments offer returns in two ways: First, many pay periodic interest. A bond, for example, usually pays interest twice a year. You may have a savings account that pays interest daily and adds each day's interest to your account. Second, some debt instruments are redeemed at prices greater than their purchase prices. These latter debt instruments are called **discount securities,** while the former are often called **interest-bearing securities.** Of course, your cash flows from each are a bit different, as is the method of calculating their yields.

Cash Flows

A cash flow refers to cash you pay out or cash you receive from an investment. The time-line diagrams presented in Chapter 3 showed cash flows in a format that helped us determine present and future values. This approach is continued, but our emphasis now is on measuring investment rate of return, or yield.

Discount Securities   Since a discount security pays no periodic interest, your entire return consists of the discount. Recalling that an investment's dollar holding period return is

$$\$HPR = R + (P_1 - P_0)$$

and since $R = 0$, the return is simply $(P_1 - P_0)$. Exhibit 5.1 shows time-line diagrams for a 13-week Treasury bill and a 10-year zero coupon bond. Treasury bills are often issued with 13-week maturities. The minimum face value on a bill is $10,000.

Treasury bills and zero coupon bonds are popular discount securities.

Discount securities do not pay periodic interest. Your total
return comes from the discount—the amount you get back
at redemption minus the amount invested.

EXHIBIT 5.1
Cash flows from
discount securities

Panel *A:* Short-Term Discount Security (e.g., 13-week U.S. Treasury bill)

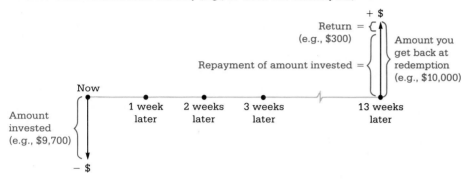

Panel *B:* Long-Term Discount Security (e.g., 10-year zero coupon bond)

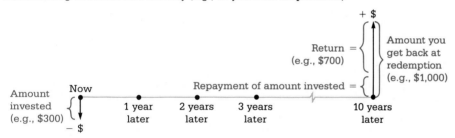

Zero coupon bonds—zeros, for short—are issued by both governments
and corporations. They have become very popular with investors who are
accumulating funds for retirement. Since they pay no periodic interest, you don't
have to worry about how to reinvest such interest to accumulate a retirement nest
egg. In striking contrast to bills, their maturities are much longer. Many zeros
have maturities of 10 years or longer, and some go as long as 40 years. The zero
shown in Exhibit 5.1 has a 10-year maturity. If you bought it for $300 and the
issuer redeemed it for $1,000 (the most common redemption value, or face value),
your return would be $700.

*Zero coupon bonds are
popular instruments is-
sued by both businesses
and government units.*

Interest-Bearing Securities   Most long-term bonds are not zeros; in contrast,
they pay interest on a regular basis. The amount of interest paid each year is
determined by their coupon rate and face value. The coupon rate is expressed as
a percent, which is then applied to the face value to determine interest dollars.
The bond illustrated in Exhibit 5.2, for example, has a 10% coupon rate and a
$1,000 face value. Interest each year will be $100 (0.10 × $1,000). Since most
bonds pay interest semiannually, you would get an interest payment of $50 every

EXHIBIT 5.2
Interest-bearing bond,
purchased and
redeemed at face value

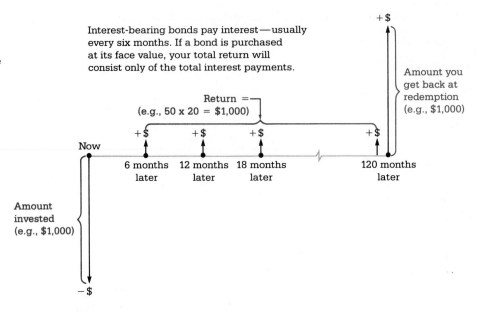

Interest-bearing bonds pay interest—usually
every six months. If a bond is purchased
at its face value, your total return will
consist only of the total interest payments.

Return =
(e.g., 50 x 20 = $1,000)

+$

Amount you
get back at
redemption
(e.g., $1,000)

Now

6 months   12 months   18 months   120 months
later   later   later   later

Amount
invested
(e.g., $1,000)

−$

six months. Exhibit 5.2 assumes you buy the bond at its face value, which means
your return consists of the 20 interest payments, or $1,000 in total.

    When bonds are issued, they are often priced at face value. However, bonds
also can be purchased in the secondary market, where their prices are usually
quite different from face value: either lower or higher, depending upon credit ease
or tightness after issuance. Exhibit 5.3 illustrates a 10-year bond bought at $750.

**A bond's price in the
secondary market might
be quite different from
its face value.**

EXHIBIT 5.3
Interest-bearing bond,
purchased at a
discount and redeemed
at face value

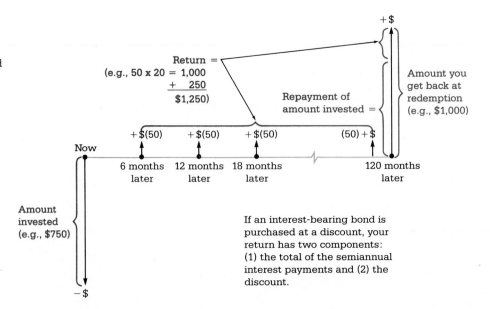

Return =
(e.g., 50 x 20 = 1,000
    +   250
    $1,250)

+$

Repayment of
amount invested =

Amount you
get back at
redemption
(e.g., $1,000)

+$(50)   +$(50)   +$(50)   (50)+$

Now

6 months   12 months   18 months   120 months
later   later   later   later

Amount
invested
(e.g., $750)

If an interest-bearing bond is
purchased at a discount, your
return has two components:
(1) the total of the semiannual
interest payments and (2) the
discount.

−$

Assuming a redemption price of $1,000 means your total return consists of both the 20 interest payments of $50 each and the discount of $250. Total return, then, is $1,250.

Calculating Yields

A statement about an investment's yield considers its dollar return in relation to the amount invested and the length of time the investment is held. However, for ease of calculation, quite often the latter item is ignored, and we refer to the yield as a **current yield.** In many instances, it is a somewhat imprecise measurement, and a more accurate yield is yield to maturity. Each of these yields, along with the Treasury bill yield, should be understood.

> A current-yield calculation does not consider the length of time an investment is held.

Current Yield   The current yield (CY) for discount securities is a meaningless concept since they offer no current return. Thus, current yield applies only to interest-bearing securities. The current yield for an interest-bearing bond bought at face value is illustrated in Panel *A* of Exhibit 5.4. As you see, maturity is ignored. The bond illustrated has a current yield of 10%. The current yield for an interest-bearing bond bought at less than face value is shown in Panel *B* of Exhibit 5.4. In this example, the CY is greater than 10%—it's 13.333%—since the bond's purchase price was $750, not $1,000.

> **EXHIBIT 5.4**
> Calculating the current yield for interest-bearing bonds

Panel *A*: A Bond Bought at Face Value

$$CY = \frac{I}{P_0}$$

I = annual interest
P_0 = market value (also amount invested)

↑ current yield

↑ ratio of annual interest to market value

Illustration assuming: I = $ 100
P_0 = $1,000

$$CY = \frac{\$100}{\$1,000} = 0.10000 \quad \text{or} \quad 10.000\%$$

Panel *B*: A Bond Bought at Less Than Face Value

Same formula as above

Illustration assuming: I = $100
P_0 = $750

$$CY = \frac{\$100}{\$750} = 0.13333 \quad \text{or} \quad 13.333\%$$

Treasury Bill Yield   Yields on discount securities are often calculated using the so-called Treasury-bill yield (TBY) formula. Exhibit 5.5 illustrates this approach with the Treasury bill indicated in Exhibit 5.1. As you see, the yield is 12.37%. This is an annualized figure that assumes an investor could earn the 13-week yield of 3.093% four times a year. A TBY calculation is not limited to Treasury bills but can be used for any discount security.

Yield to Maturity   In precise terms, the **yield to maturity (YTM)** is a specific rate that causes the present value of the debt instrument's discounted cash inflows to equal its cash outflow (the purchase price). You must remember the present value concept explained in Chapter 3 for this definition to make sense. Basically, finding a YTM means finding present values of the periodic interest and the redemption price, and adding the two together to equal the instrument's purchase price. This procedure is illustrated in Exhibit 5.6, using the 10% bond purchased at face value as an example. The present value of the coupon interest payments is $623.11 and the present value of the future redemption value is $376.89. Adding the two together equals the bond's current price of $1,000.

A YTM equates the market price (present value) of a debt instrument with its discounted future cash inflows.

Exhibit 5.7 shows how to calculate the YTM for discount securities. What do the YTMs of 12.957% and 12.795% mean? With the Treasury bill, it means $10,000 received 13 weeks after the investment date has a present value of $9,700 when discounted at the 12.957% annualized rate (3.0928% for the actual period). And with the zero, $1,000 received 10 years after investment has a present value of $300 when discounted at 12.795%.

EXHIBIT 5.5

Calculating the Treasury bill yield (TBY)

$$\text{TBY} = \left[\frac{P_1 - P_0}{P_0} \right] \times \left[\frac{52}{n} \right]$$

P_1 = redemption price
P_0 = amount invested
n = maturity (in weeks)

↑   ↑   ↑

Treasury   percent   annualization
bill yield   return   factor
          for the
          period
          held

Illustration assuming: P_1 = $10,000
                    P_0 = $ 9,700
                    n = 13

$$\text{TBY} = \frac{\$10,000 - \$9,700}{\$9,700} \times \frac{52}{13}$$

$$\text{TBY} = \frac{\$300}{\$9,700} \times 4$$

$$\text{TBY} = 0.03093 \times 4 = 0.1237 \quad \text{or} \quad 12.37\%$$

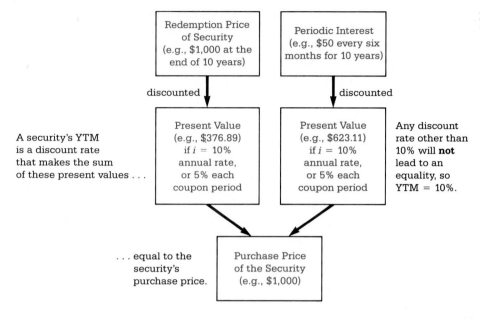

EXHIBIT 5.6
YTM illustrated

A security's YTM is a discount rate that makes the sum of these present values . . .

. . . equal to the security's purchase price.

EXHIBIT 5.7
Calculating yield to maturity for discount securities

$$YTM = \left(\frac{P_1}{P_0}\right)^{52/n} - 1.0$$

P_1 = redemption price
P_0 = amount invested
n = maturity (in weeks)*

Panel A: Treasury bill illustration, assuming: $P_1 = \$10,000$
$P_0 = \$9,700$
$n = 13$

$$YTM = \left(\frac{\$10,000}{\$9,700}\right)^{52/13} - 1.0$$

$$YTM = (1.030928)^4 - 1.0 = 1.12957 - 1.0 = .12957 \quad \text{or} \quad 12.957\%$$

Panel B: Zero coupon bond illustration, assuming: $P_1 = \$1,000$
$P_0 = \$300$
$n = 520$ (10 years)

$$YTM = \left(\frac{\$1,000}{\$300}\right)^{52/520} - 1.0$$

$$YTM = (3.3333)^{.10} - 1.0 = 1.12795 - 1.0 = .12795 \quad \text{or} \quad 12.795\%$$

*Maturity (n) can be expressed in days, rather than weeks. The numerator in the exponent of the equation is then 365, instead of 52.

You should notice the Treasury bill's YTM is a bit higher than the TBY calculated above. The difference is explained by different assumptions with each: YTM assumes each period's dollar return is reinvested in the security, while the TBY assumes such returns are withdrawn each period. In effect, with the YTM, you earn interest on interest, whereas with the TBY you do not.

Exhibit 5.8 illustrates YTM calculations for interest-bearing bonds. Panel *A* shows that YTM is the same as current yield if the bond is bought at face value. If the bond's price is more or less than face value, YTM must be calculated. Panel *B* shows the steps you take with a financial calculator. Notice that 20 (not 10) periods are involved because coupon interest is paid semiannually. Notice also that the answer is a semiannual rate of return. YTM is usually expressed as an annual equivalent, so multiply the answer by 2. As you see, the annual return for the example bond is 14.883%.

Accurate YTM measurements must consider semiannual, rather than annual, interest periods.

Without a financial calculator a solution is lengthy and less accurate. Present value tables can be used with a series of trial discount rates until the sum of the discounted interest payments and discounted redemption value equal the bond's price. This is very time consuming. A short-cut approach—also illustrated in Panel *B* of Exhibit 5.8—is sometimes used, even though its approximation of YTM can be very inaccurate. As you see, 14.286% is quite a bit less than 14.883%.

What Does the YTM Imply?   As mentioned above, YTM makes the sum of discounted cash inflows equal purchase price. But in the case of an interest-bearing bond, this also implies that its periodic interest payments are reinvested at the YTM. Is this a reasonable assumption? It may or may not be, depending on your assessment of future investment opportunities. If interest rates are expected to fall, you may not reinvest at rates as high as the YTM; and if interest rates rise, you are likely to earn higher rates. YTM is simply a measurement of profitability, and it should not be relied upon to determine future cash flows arising from reinvested interest.

A YTM calculation assumes that periodic interest payments can be reinvested at the YTM.

For example, suppose you bought the 10-year bond we have been discussing with a YTM of 10%. Assume further that you think you also can invest the $50 interest each 6-month period at 10% (5% per interest period). As shown in Exhibit 5.9, your accumulated funds at the end of 10 years is $2,653, of which $653 is interest on interest. Suppose, though, you reinvested at some other annual rate—say, 14% (7% per interest period); now, the interest on interest is $1,050. The point is, your accumulated funds depend upon both reinvestment rates and the accumulation period, and neither has anything to do with a calculated YTM. Actually, the accumulation period (maturity) has a greater impact upon the interest-on-interest factor than does the reinvestment rate. This point is underscored emphatically in Exhibit 5.10, which shows the future value of a 20-year, 10% bond. As you see, at the end of 20 years, interest on interest is $4,040, over six times as much as it is at the end of 10 years! You probably see now why zeros are popular: they avoid the reinvestment of interest problem.

Zeros are popular because they avoid the reinvestment problem.

EXHIBIT 5.8
Calculating yield to maturity (YTM) for interest-bearing bonds

---

Panel *A*: A Bond Bought at Face Value

Same amount as current yield; see Panel *A* of Exhibit 5.4

Panel *B*: A Bond Bought at Less or More than Face Value

I.   Solution using a financial calculator (the HP 12-C) and assuming a bond with a 10% coupon rate, 10-year maturity, and selling at $750; that is,

$$P_1 = \text{redemption value} = FV = \$1,000$$
$$P_0 = \text{current market price} = PV = \$750$$
$$I = \text{coupon interest} = PMT = \$50$$
$$n = \text{number of periods} = 20$$

Enter	Depress Keys	Operation
—	[f] [CLX]	Clears registers.
1000	[FV]	Enters redemption value.
750	[CHS] [PV]	Enters market price as an outlay (a negative number).
50	[PMT]	Enters semiannual coupon interest.
20	[n]	Enters number of interest periods.
—	[i]	Read *YTM* of 7.4414%. This can be annualized by multiplying by 2: 2 × 7.4414 = 14.883%.

II.   Short-Cut Approach

$$YTM = \frac{\text{annual interest} + \text{average capital gain (loss)}}{\text{average investment}}$$

$$YTM = \frac{I + \dfrac{P_1 - P_0}{n}}{\dfrac{P_1 + P_0}{2}}$$

Illustration assuming same values as above:

$$YTM = \frac{\$100 + \dfrac{\$1,000 - \$750}{10}}{\dfrac{\$1,000 + \$750}{2}}$$

$$YTM = \frac{\$100 + \dfrac{\$250}{10}}{\dfrac{\$1,750}{2}}$$

$$YTM = \frac{\$100 + \$25}{\$875} = \frac{\$125}{\$875} = .14286 \quad \text{or} \quad 14.286\%$$

EXHIBIT 5.9
Future value of a 10-year, 10% bond, assuming interest payments are reinvested at 10% or 14% annual rates

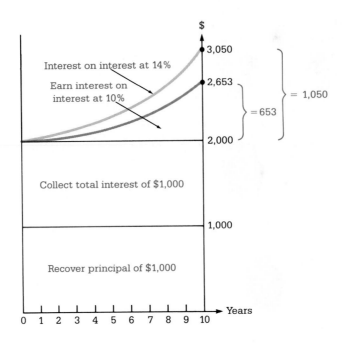

EXHIBIT 5.10
Future value of a 20-year, 10% bond, assuming interest payments are reinvested at 10% annual rate

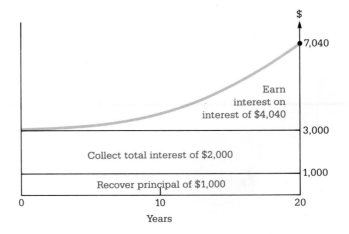

What Investors Expect in an Interest Rate

Under what conditions would you be willing to loan money to borrowers and how much interest must they pay to make the investment attractive? To answer these questions, you would have to consider your preferences for current versus future consumption, the expected inflation rate during the term of the loan, your need for liquidity, and the probability the lender will make timely interest and principal payments.

Preference for Current Consumption Given a choice between consuming goods and services today versus consuming them in the future, most of us will choose current consumption. Why not? Why should we defer consumption enjoyment unless we are compensated for doing so? Most people will not, which explains why lenders demand a reward for giving up current consumption. This reward is interest. With it, you can consume *more* in the future than you can today, making abstinence worthwhile.

Real Versus Nominal Return A nominal return means the actual dollars (or percent) an investor receives; a real return adjusts the nominal return to allow for price changes taking place during the investment period. If you made a $100, one-year loan at 10% interest, you would get back $110 a year later. If prices rose 5% during the year, however, it would cost $105 to buy the same amount of goods and services you gave up a year earlier. Your real return is obviously not $10; it is $5. Your real rate of return using current (not last year's) prices is about 4.76%. You should recall this calculation from the previous chapter where the real rate of return (r') was compared to a nominal rate (r) and the inflation rate (i):

$$r' = \frac{1.0 + r}{1.0 + i} - 1.0$$

Compensation for Giving Up Liquidity Investing means giving up holding cash, the most liquid of all assets. Since the future is uncertain, we can never be absolutely sure the cash we invest will not be needed during the investment period. Even if we can convert the investment back to cash, there usually are transaction costs and personal inconveniences involved, and we may even take a loss in selling the instrument. All other things the same, most investors prefer liquidity and demand a premium if they must forego it. The poorer the liquidity, the greater the premium.

Compensation for Assuming Default Risk If there is any question about a borrower's ability to meet his or her financial obligations, lenders will also demand a premium for this added risk, and the greater the doubt, the greater the premium. As we explained in the previous chapter, ability to handle debt is determined by both the nature of the borrower's business and the total amount of debt outstanding. If you buy the bonds of a wildcatting oil company loaded with debt, you should expect a very high premium for assuming default risk.

Putting it Together An expected interest rate must take all the above factors into consideration, as Exhibit 5.11 shows. You begin with an estimate of your required real rate of return. The next step is to estimate the period's inflation (deflation) rate to arrive at a nominal rate. This rate must be high enough to induce you to be a lender. After this is done, you add premiums for illiquidity and potential default to arrive at the total returns you need from specific debt instruments. If actual returns available in the marketplace are less than these, you

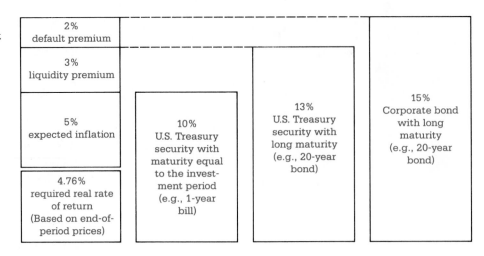

EXHIBIT 5.11
Components of interest rates (assumed rates)

will not invest; on the other hand, if some or all of the market rates exceed your required rates, you will invest.

Do investors actually go through such detailed procedures before investing? There is good evidence suggesting many do, although they don't necessarily think in terms of specific risk premiums or adjust for inflation in the same mechanical way. Keep in mind, though, we are talking about *expected* rates of return at the beginning of a period, not *realized* rates after the period is over. You may expect a real rate of 4.76%, for example, but if inflation is greater than 5%, your realized rate will be less. Such a situation seemed to exist during the inflationary period 1966–1982. Investors apparently consistently underestimated inflation, leading to very low and even negative real rates of return on debt instruments in some of those years. Moreover, some analysts argue that these estimating errors highlighted the greater risk in illiquid, long-term instruments. As a result, investors began demanding greater liquidity risk premiums in the early 1980s. This explanation may not be the only one, but it is clear that real rates of return increased substantially about then, and they have remained relatively high.

RISKS WITH DEBT INSTRUMENTS

Both liquidity and default risks must be measured in specific debt instruments. Ideally, we wish to have a quantitative estimate or qualitative ranking for each risk component. With these, it is then possible to determine if a debt instrument's expected return is large enough to warrant our investment.

Bond Prices and Changing Interest Rates

A number of different forces influence securities markets. They include actions of the federal government (the Treasury) and the Federal Reserve system (the Fed), investors' rational and emotional reactions, the need for funds by business firms, and international influences. All these are important in debt markets since their combined impacts determine the level of interest rates and the volume of credit during a period of time. Moreover, the network of cause-and-effect relationships among interest rates and financial variables is indeed complex and not fully understood by anyone. By practicing a policy of tight money, for example, the Fed may both lower and raise interest rates simultaneously. Tightness usually has its initial impact upon short-term debt instruments, increasing their rates. These higher rates, in turn, are thought to spill over into long-term markets, increasing rates there as well. But, if the Fed's policy is seen as lowering the long-term inflation rate, this could lead to a greater demand for long-term debt instruments, thereby decreasing their rates. Disentangling those separate influences may be impossible.

Regardless of what causes interest rates to change, the heart of the problem from an investor's perspective is what happens to the prices of previously purchased debt instruments while changes take place. Look at it this way: Suppose you bought a 10-year bond such as one we have been discussing, the 10% bond with a 10% YTM. You thought the bond was a good investment and planned to hold it until your retirement in 10 years when it matures. Now, imagine the day after you bought it, some extraordinary event takes place causing all interest rates to rise one full percentage point, which is a 10% increase in rates. Newly issued bonds that are identical to yours now pay investors $110 a year in interest while yours still pays only $100. Who would buy your bond for the price you paid—$1,000? No one. To sell it, you would have to lower the price so that its YTM would also be 11%. This loss in value was the liquidity risk you faced when you bought the bond.

Rising interest rates cause the prices of previously issued bonds to fall.

You might argue that if you don't sell the bond, you really won't have a loss. Of course, this is *not* so. If you don't sell, your loss is in the form of an opportunity cost. Had you waited one day, you could have bought, for the same price, a bond that provided $10 more interest each year for the next 10 years. This is no less a loss than your direct cash loss from selling. Unfortunately, your only decision is when to take the loss: you can take it quickly by selling, or slowly over 10 years by holding. True, interest rates might go back down to 10% in the future, which means the price of the bond goes back up to $1,000. But you would have a similar price increase with the 11% bond.

If you own a bond when interest rates rise, you suffer a loss; your only choice is to take it now, by selling, or take it later (and gradually) by holding.

Changes in debt instruments' prices resulting from changes in interest rates is called interest-rate risk, a topic introduced in the previous chapter. In reality, this risk is part of liquidity risk. But, in addition to potential loss of capital, liquidity risk also includes marketability risk: factors that might make selling an instrument difficult, such as a poor resale market, or high transactions costs. For securities that do not have these impediments, liquidity risk and interest-rate risk are the same thing. In the material below, we will use the narrower expression—interest-rate risk—to clearly identify the topic of concern to us.

The Importance of Maturity We showed earlier, in the discussion of reinvesting periodic interest payments, the sensitivity of a future value to the

Why Have Real Rates of Interest Been So High?

A curious situation—one that favors lenders but at the expense of borrowers—has existed recently: real rates of interest have been very high. For example, from 1981 through 1989, the inflation-adjusted rate of return on U.S. Treasury bills averaged about 4%. While that might not seem high, it's way above the long-term average of around 0.3%. Why have real rates been so high? Are they likely to stay high?

A knee-jerk response to the first question might be that lenders and borrowers have consistently overestimated inflation in shaping lending arrangements. That being the case, the after-the-fact (or, in technical terms, *ex post*) results of inflation and returns are high real rates. If this explanation is true, then the problem isn't terribly interesting, since forecasting errors of this sort happen all the time. But have real rates been high in an expected sense (or *ex ante*)? And if they have, how are they explained and what implications do they have for investors?

The three accompanying graphs indicate the trend of ex ante rates over the past 37 years. The ex ante rates in this case are estimated by analytical techniques that consider past inflation rates, past rates of economic growth, and several other variables. The methods do not give infallible results, but they are widely used in forming expectations. As the graphs show, recent ex ante rates are also high. Why? A number of interpretations have been offered.

For example, the 1982–83 period was one of changing tax policy, which supposedly increased the profitability of real investment.

Perhaps the overall reason is that volatile inflation rates have increased the risk of fixed-income investments. That being the case, investors demand—and receive—higher real rates as an inducement to invest. One thing is for sure: in recent years investing in long-term bonds has been as risky as investing in common stocks—and their total returns have been approximately the same.

SOURCE: Graphs with data through 1985 are from Steven G. Cechetti, ''High Real Interest Rates: Can They Be Explained?'' *Economic Review*, Federal Reserve Bank of Kansas City, September/October 1986. This article provides in-depth coverage of the topic through 1985. Estimates for 1986–88 have been made by the authors.

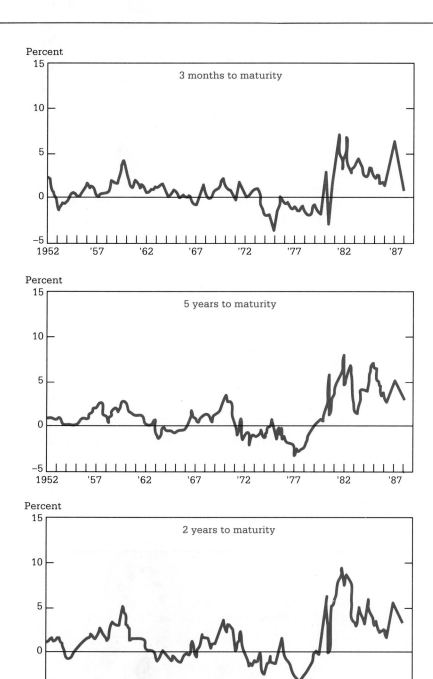

Ex ante real interest
rates on Treasury
securities

interest-on-interest accumulation factor. You should recall that extending maturity increases appreciably the importance of interest-on-interest. You should see, too, that if the reinvestment rate changes, its greatest impact will be upon securities with long maturities. The longer the maturity, everything else the same, the riskier the security. Keep in mind, though, the interest-on-interest concept is simply a way of analyzing the situation. Even securities that do not pay periodic interest—zeros, for example—also have maturity risk. In fact, they are the riskiest of all debt securities, as we will see below.

Longer maturities lead to greater bond risks.

The Importance of Coupon Rate   Why are zeros riskier than interest-bearing bonds? Because you must wait until maturity to recover any of your investment. This is not the case with interest-bearing bonds. If interest rates rise while you hold them, you will at least gradually recover your investment through the periodic interest payments, which are available to invest at the existing higher rates; but with a zero, you recover nothing until the end. This means your opportunity costs are highest, and the longer the maturity, the greater they are.

Lower coupon rates lead to greater bond risks.

Coupon rate and maturity, then, work together to produce interest-rate risk. Low coupon rates and long maturities mean considerable risk, while high coupons and short maturities mean less. For example, if you buy a zero coupon bond with a 40-year maturity, you have about the riskiest debt instrument available, not considering default risk.

Determining Interest-Rate Risk

Interest-rate risk can be determined by measuring the sensitivity of changes in a debt instrument's price in relation to changes in its YTM. There are two measurement concepts, the interest elasticity coefficient and Macaulay's duration coefficient.

Calculating the Interest Elasticity Coefficient   The **interest elasticity coefficient, E,** is defined as

$$E = \frac{\text{(Percentage Change in Bond Price)}}{\text{(Percentage Change in YTM)}}$$

Since price and YTM always move in opposite directions, the sign of E is always negative. That being the case, the negative sign is usually ignored in discussion. Exhibit 5.12 shows elasticity calculations for each security discussed so far in this chapter (numbers 1, 2, 3, and 4). Two other securities (5 and 6) have been added to provide additional examples.

Imagine that one day after you make a selection, the security's YTM increases by 10%. (This is a rather extreme jump for one day, and not likely to happen. In the past, though, 10% increases have not been uncommon for periods as short as two or three weeks.) Column 2 shows the first YTM while column 3 shows the second, which is 10% higher than the first. The YTMs shown in column

EXHIBIT 5.12

Calculating interest elasticity coefficients assuming a 10% increase in YTM

Security (1)	YTMs (%)		Prices		Elasticity Coefficient* (6)
	First (2)	Second (3)	First (4)	Second (5)	
1. 13-week T-bill	12.957	14.253	$9,700	$9,672	−0.030
2. 10-year zero	12.795	14.075	300	268	−1.183
3. 10-year, 10% bond selling at face value	10.000	11.000	1,000	940	−0.650
4. 10-year, 10% bond selling at $750	14.883	16.371	750	692	−0.845
5. 20-year zero	12.795	14.075	90	72	−2.333
6. 10-year, 30% bond selling at $2,246	10.000	11.000	2,246	2,135	−0.532

*NOTE: To avoid bias in selecting a base to determine percentage changes, the averages of the two YTMs and two prices are used. Thus, the formula is:

$$E = \frac{\dfrac{\text{Change in Price}}{(P_1 + P_2)/2}}{\dfrac{\text{Change in YTM}}{(\text{YTM}_1 + -\text{YTM}_2)/2}}$$

Applying the formula to security 2 gives the results below:

$$E = \frac{\dfrac{300 - 268}{(300 + 268)/2}}{\dfrac{12.795 - 14.075}{(12.795 + 14.075)/2}} = \frac{\dfrac{32}{284}}{\dfrac{-1.280}{13.435}}$$

$$E = \frac{32}{284} \times \frac{13.435}{-1.280} = \frac{429.92}{-363.52} = -1.183$$

2 are those calculated earlier for securities 1 through 4; security 5's YTM is assumed to be the same as security 2's, and security 6's YTM is the same as security 3's. The arithmetic in exhibit 5.12 is straightforward. Notice that averages for prices and YTMs are used to determine the bases for calculating percentage changes. This is necessary to avoid the bias favoring percentage increases over percentage decreases when the base is the first value. (See Chapter 3 for additional discussion of this topic.)

Interpreting Elasticity Coefficients   The absolute value of E (that is, ignore the negative sign) tells us how sensitive a debt instrument's price is to changes in interest rates. In doing this, it ranks debt instruments according to interest-rate risk. The elasticity numbers in column 6 of Exhibit 5.12 clearly rank the securities shown there. Security 5, the 20-year zero, is the riskiest; it is twice as risky as security 2, the 10-year zero, and over three times riskier than security 3, the 10% bond selling at face value.

> High absolute values for the interest elasticity coefficient mean greater bond price risk.

Notice also that by comparing security 2 to security 5, we have an example of the point made earlier that longer maturity means greater risk. Comparing security 3 to security 6 confirms that a lower coupon rate also adds to risk. Finally, comparing security 3 to security 4 indicates yet another factor contributing to risk—the absolute level of interest rates. To see this, assume security 4 is really security 3, but at a different point in time and with a higher YTM. Because of the higher YTM and lower price, the security is now riskier than it was previously. We can generalize from this example and say that as interest rates rise, any debt instrument you own will increase in risk. While this relationship is true, it does not have as much practical value as do maturity and coupon rate in developing a bond portfolio, unless you know in advance that interest rates will rise, or fall (in which case, risk would decrease). Few people have such knowledge.

Macaulay's Duration Concept   Like elasticity, **Macaulay's duration concept** (named after F. R. Macaulay) is an attempt to measure risk in a debt instrument. It is defined as the weighted average time required to recover principal and all interest payments. On a first reading, this statement seems confusing because we assume it takes the entire term to maturity to recover principal and all interest. The 10%, 10-year bond, for example, will pay $1,000 in total interest ($100 a year) and is redeemed for $1,000. Don't you have to hold the bond 10 years to recover this $2,000? Actually, no. If you can reinvest the periodic interest payments you receive at *any* positive rate of interest, it will take less time, how much less depending upon the reinvestment rate. The answer to the apparent riddle is the interest-on-interest concept explained earlier.

> A duration coefficient considers the weighted average time before bond principal and interest are recovered.

To see this, let's assume an extreme example: suppose you could reinvest the periodic interest payments at a 50% annual rate. The first year's interest of $100 would grow to $3,844 nine years later! You could forget the other nine years of interest and principal and have $1,844 left over. So, the three important factors determining how quickly interest and principal are recovered are maturity, coupon rate, and the assumed reinvestment rate.

Calculating the Duration Coefficient   Unlike the interest elasticity coefficient, the duration coefficient, D, is not calculated quickly, although the calculations are simple. Exhibit 5.13 shows the procedure for the 10%, 10-year bond selling at face value. The assumed reinvestment rate is the bond's YTM of 10%. The value of the duration coefficient, D, is 6.7644, which is the weighted average number of years it takes to recover the $2,000 of interest and principal. Also unlike interest elasticity, which is a "pure" number, duration is dimensioned in particular units—years.

EXHIBIT 5.13

Calculating a duration coefficient, D

(1) Year	(2) Cash Flow*	(3) PV Factor (YTM = 10%)	(4) PV of Cash Flow	(5) PV/Price	(6) (1) × (5)
1	100	0.909	90.90	0.0909	0.0909
2	100	0.826	82.60	0.0826	0.1652
3	100	0.751	75.10	0.0751	0.2253
4	100	0.683	68.30	0.0683	0.2732
5	100	0.621	62.10	0.0621	0.3105
6	100	0.565	56.50	0.0565	0.3390
7	100	0.513	51.30	0.0513	0.3591
8	100	0.467	46.70	0.0467	0.3736
9	100	0.424	42.40	0.0424	0.3816
10	1,100	0.386	424.60	0.4246	4.2460
Totals	2,000	—	1,000.00	1.0000	6.7644
			Duration Coefficient, D =		6.7644

*Annual interest is assumed for case of presentation.

Interpreting and Using D Values   What does a D value imply in terms of risk? As you might guess, the higher the value, the greater the risk, since it implies a longer recovery period. Exhibit 5.14 shows D values for the six securities shown in Exhibit 5.12, along with their previously calculated E values. The two risk measurements give the same rankings to securities 1, 2, 5, and 6 but differ on securities 3 and 4. The difference is explained by the much higher YTM with security 4. But if you assume a similar YTM for security 3, its duration would be the same as security 4's. Since it is impossible for two identical securities to sell at different prices in an efficient market, the price difference shown in Exhibit 5.12 is not realistic. Applied in a realistic setting, the two approaches will give identical rankings.[1]

High values for the duration coefficient also mean greater bond price risk.

A duration coefficient allows us to estimate how much a bond's price will change, given a change in its YTM. The steps to make the estimate are as follows:

1. Calculate an adjusted D value. This is done by dividing the known D value by (1.0 + new YTM), expressing YTM as a decimal. For the 10% bond selling at face value, we have

$$\text{adjusted } D = 6.7644/(1.0 + 0.11) = 6.7644/(1.11) = 6.0941$$

[1]Bond portfolio managers use duration more extensively than interest elasticity. However, for most applications there is little difference between the two. For an excellent discussion, see G. J. Santoni, "Interest Rate Risk and the Stock Prices of Financial Institutions," *Review*, August/September 1984, pp. 12–20. The Federal Reserve Bank of St. Louis.

2. Multiply the adjusted D by the absolute change in YTM, expressing the change in decimal form. Such change for the 10% bond is 0.01. Then, the

$$\text{percentage change in price} = 6.0941 \times 0.01 = 0.060941$$

3. Multiply the percent change in price by the initial price to determine the absolute change in price:

$$\text{absolute change in price} = 0.060941 \times \$1,000 = \$60.94$$

Duration coefficients, then, estimate risk and also provide estimates of potential losses (or gains) if interest rates happen to rise (or fall) after they are purchased. If you wish to have a low-risk bond portfolio, you should select bonds with low D (or E) values; if you want risk, expecting rates to fall, then select bonds with high values. Finally, you should note in Exhibit 5.14 the zero coupon bonds have D values equal to their terms to maturity: 10 and 20 years. This is the case with all zeros.

The Reinvestment Problem

Our discussion of interest-rate risk thus far has focused on the relationship of a bond's price to changes in its YTM. There is another aspect of changing interest rates that also concerns investors. It has to do with the problem of reinvesting periodic interest payments that will be received over the bond's remaining life. Suppose interest rates rise immediately after you buy the 10% bond that we have been discussing. The undesirable effect is the bond's price will fall. However, there also is a desirable effect insofar as you now will be able to reinvest all remaining coupon interest at higher rates. Of course, the situation works in reverse if interest rates decline; then, the desirable effect of a price increase accompanies the undesirable effect of lower reinvestment rates.

EXHIBIT 5.14

Risk rankings with D and E values

Security	D Value	Rank*	E Value (Ignoring minus sign)	Rank*
1. 13-week T-bill	0.2500	1	0.030	1
2. 10-year, zero coupon bond	10.0000	5	1.183	5
3. 10-year, 10% bond selling at face value	6.7644	4	0.650	3
4. 10-year, 10% bond selling at $750	6.2266	3	0.845	4
5. 20-year, zero coupon bond	20.0000	6	2.333	6
6. 10-year, 30% bond selling to yield 10%	5.6408	2	0.532	2

*1 = lowest risk.

Reinvestment Risk   Since future reinvestment rates are unknown, the uncertainty surrounding the accumulation of funds over a given period of time is referred to as **reinvestment risk.** Interestingly, zero coupon bonds, which have the highest price risk, also have the lowest reinvestment risk. In fact, since they have no interest to reinvest, there is no risk. That is why zeros make ideal instruments for investment goals designed to accumulate specific sums of money. In contrast, bonds with high coupon rates present greater risks, since there are greater interest amounts to reinvest. Also interesting is the fact that within this context even short-term debt instruments are risky, because each time they mature you must reinvest their redemption amounts into new issues of the same type of security, or into other kinds of securities. When maturing instruments are replaced with new instruments of the same type of security — Treasury bills, for example — the risk of reinvesting at lower rates is called **rollover risk.**

> Reinvestment risk is associated with reinvesting coupon interest at unknown future rates.

Managing Reinvestment Risk   As noted above, managing reinvestment risk can be quite simple if the investor selects only zeros. However, there may be instances when yields are better with coupon issues. So, the bond manager needs to consider each in designing a portfolio. Actually, managing reinvestment risk is simply one aspect of managing the total bond portfolio. Professional bond managers are concerned with both earnings and adequate liquidity. For example, suppose you manage a bond portfolio for the benefit of a company's retirement program. Over time, you must have sufficient cash to meet retirement obligations; but, concurrently, you want to invest funds to earn high rates of return. Balancing the two requires considerable skill and an understanding of methods and tools that are not discussed in this introductory text.

> Rollover risk arises when short-term securities mature and their redemption amounts are reinvested.

Default Risk

Default risk is generally understood as the likelihood of not receiving a debt instrument's promised cash flows. The higher this probability, the greater is default risk. Unlike interest-rate risk, which affects all debt instruments, default risk applies when the issuer's financial strength is in question. Actually, the only securities without default risk are those issued by the U.S. Treasury, which has access to the currency printing press if that is ever needed.

Estimating default risk is a difficult task, particularly as it applies to evaluating the chances of receiving a timely and full redemption, which may take place many years in the future. Despite the difficulties, estimates must be made. Fortunately, though, we need not develop our own figures; professional rating agencies do the job for us. Our tasks are first to understand what their ratings mean and then to have a realistic understanding of how yields vary among debt instruments with different quality ratings.

The Rating Agencies   The two best-known rating agencies are Moody's and Standard and Poor's. Each has its own formula for determining quality ratings.

These formulas consider a variety of factors that measure a borrower's capacity to meet its debt obligations, the most important being its liquidity, debt-carrying capacity, and earnings (these are explained in Chapter 8). Each agency evaluates proposed new debt issues and gives them a rating. These ratings are letter grades, which range from Aaa to C for Moody's and from AAA to D for Standard and Poor's. Exhibit 5.15 shows these ratings. Within each letter grade, the agencies further refine the grade: Standard and Poor's uses + or − to show that an issue is in the higher or lower end of a grade, while Moody's uses numbers. For example, an A+ or A1 rating means an issue is at the top of the A class; an A− or A3 puts it at the bottom. Incidentally, a bond with one of the first four ratings is referred to in the investment community as *investment grade,* whereas one with a lower rating is called *speculative.* These descriptions arise from requirements imposed upon many trust fund managers to limit their client purchases to securities with ratings in the first four categories. This rule serves as a simple screening device to minimize portfolio risk.

In addition to rating new issues, the agencies also evaluate outstanding debt issues and report them in their advisory services, which can be found in most major libraries. Not infrequently, an issue's rating changes because its financial strength has weakened or improved. When such a change is downward, indicating poorer quality, the market price of the issue declines substantially, if the rating change was unexpected.

Moody's and Standard and Poor's rate debt issues of both state and local governments and corporations. In addition to rating bond issues, the agencies rate commercial paper and other short-term debt instruments.

Yield and Rating It is probably obvious that a debt issue's yield depends on its rating—the lower the rating, the higher the yield—all other things held constant. Exhibit 5.16 shows how yields varied by rating class (including Treasuries, assumed to have no default risk) at three different points in time. The data show that yields and ratings are indeed inversely related, but they also show that yield differences (in these examples, called quality spreads) are not constant over time. For example, spreads on the corporate issues Aaa−Aa and Aa−A were lowest in 1988, while the spread between Treasuries and Aaa-rated issues was lowest in 1984. This spread increased dramatically in 1986 and was still rather large in late January, 1989.

The data indicate that you will be compensated for investing in poorer quality issues, but you can expect this compensation to vary (unpredictably) over time. Whether it is high enough to adequately reward you for carrying such risk is a decision you must make. Some people view the yield differences as more than adequate reward, while others confine their bond investments to Treasury issues.

HISTORICAL INTEREST-RATE VOLATILITY

To say that interest rates vary over time grossly understates the situation. In truth, they have been extremely volatile, creating an investment environment as

EXHIBIT 5.15

Moody's

Aaa Bonds which are rated Aaa are judged to be of the best quality. They carry the smallest degree of investment risk and are generally referred to as "gilt edge." Interest payments are protected by a large or by an exceptionally stable margin and principal is secure. While the various protective elements are likely to change, such changes as can be visualized are most unlikely to impair the fundamentally strong position of such issues.

Aa Bonds which are rated Aa are judged to be of high quality by all standards. Together with the Aaa group they comprise what are generally known as high grade bonds. They are rated lower than the best bonds because margins of protection may not be as large as in Aaa securities or fluctuation of protective elements may be of greater amplitude or there may be other elements present which make the long term risks appear somewhat larger than in Aaa securities.

A Bonds which are rated A possess many favorable investment attributes and are to be considered as upper medium grade obligations. Factors giving security to principal and interest are considered adequate but elements may be present which suggest a susceptibility to impairment sometime in the future.

Baa Bonds which are rated Baa are considered as medium grade obligations, *i.e.*, they are neither highly protected nor poorly secured. Interest payments and principal security appear adequate for the present but certain protective elements may be lacking or may be characteristically unreliable over any great length of time. Such bonds lack outstanding investment characteristics and in fact have speculative characteristics as well.

Ba Bonds which are rated Ba are judged to have speculative elements; their future cannot be considered as well assured. Often the protection of interest and principal payments may be very moderate and thereby not well safeguarded during both good and bad times over the future. Uncertainty of position characterizes bonds in this class.

B Bonds which are rated B generally lack characteristics of the desirable investment. Assurance of interest and principal payments or of maintenance of other terms of the contract over any long period of time may be small.

Caa Bonds which are rated Caa are of poor standing. Such issues may be in default or there may be present elements of danger with respect to principal or interest.

Ca Bonds which are rated Ca represent obligations which are speculative in a high degree. Such issues are often in default or have other marked shortcomings.

C Bonds which are rated C are the lowest rated class of bonds and issues so rated can be regarded as having extremely poor prospects of ever attaining any real investment standing.

Standard and Poor's

AAA Debt rated AAA has the highest rating assigned by Standard & Poor's. Capacity to pay interest and repay principal is extremely strong.

AA Debt rated AA has a very strong capacity to pay interest and repay principal and differs from the higher rated issues only in small degree.

A Debt rated A has a strong capacity to pay interest and repay principal although it is somewhat more susceptible to the adverse effects of changes in circumstances and economic conditions than debt in higher rated categories.

BBB Debt rated BBB is regarded as having an adequate capacity to pay interest and repay principal. Whereas it normally exhibits adequate protection parameters, adverse economic conditions or changing circumstances are more likely to lead to a weakened capacity to pay interest and repay principal for debt in this category than in higher rated categories.

BB, B, CCC, CC Debt rated BB, B, CCC and CC is regarded, on balance, as predominently speculative with respect to capacity to pay interest and repay principal in accordance with the terms of the obilgation. BB indicates the lowest degree of speculation and CC the highest degree of speculation. While such debt will likely have some quality and protective characteristics, these are outweighed by large uncertainties or major risk exposures to adverse conditions.

C The rating C is reserved for income bonds on which no interest is being paid.

D Debt rated D is in default, and payment of interst and/or repayment of principal is in arrears.

Plus (+) or Minus (−): The ratings from "AA" to "B" may be modified by the addition of a plus or minus sign to show relative standing within the major rating categories.

EXHIBIT 5.16

Yields on long-term bonds and quality spreads

Grade	1984 Yields	Spreads	1986 Yields	Spreads	1989* Yields	Spreads
U.S. Treasury	12.48%		7.85%		8.80%	
Aaa	12.71	0.23%	9.02	1.17%	9.56	0.76%
Aa	13.31	0.60	9.47	0.45	9.75	0.19
A	13.74	0.43	9.95	0.48	10.04	0.29
Baa	14.19	0.45	10.39	0.44	10.61	0.57

*For the week ended January 27, 1989.

SOURCE: *Federal Reserve Bulletin,* various issues.

risky as that of many common stocks. If this volatility continues—and many credit analysts think it will—you should give your bond investments the same concern you give common stock investment.

Short- and Long-Term Rates

Exhibit 5.17 compares current yields on short-term debt instruments—30-day T-bills—and long-term debt instruments—20-year T-bonds. Some observations seem important. First, it is clear that both yields have increased considerably in recent years. As we saw earlier, this is to be expected since inflation has also increased. Second, while bills show greater yield variability, this does not mean they are riskier. Risk is measured by holding period returns, which in turn are

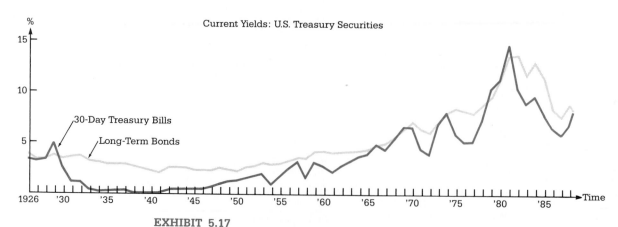

EXHIBIT 5.17

Current yields: U.S. Treasury securities (Source: *Stocks, Bonds, Bills, and Inflation: 1989 yearbook* [Chicago: Ibbotson Associates, 1989]. Data for 1989 are from Federal Reserve releases.)

heavily influenced by price changes; as we have seen, a 10% yield change for long-term bonds will have a far greater price impact than will a similar change for bills. Third, in most years the bond yield is greater than the bill yield. This might not surprise you because bonds are riskier. What might surprise you are the few years when bill yields exceeded bond yields. Bill yields were higher in four years (three since 1969) and equal to bond yields in two years. Were these periods of investor irrationality? Probably not, as we now explain.

Short-term rates are more volatile than long-term rates; however, this doesn't mean short-term securities are riskier.

The Yield Curve The concept of a yield curve can help in the explanation. A **yield curve** shows yield to maturity (YTM) in relation to maturity for debt instruments that are alike in all other respects. Such curves are usually drawn for Treasury securities, since they differ only in maturity, and the yield-curve pattern we most often find is the one represented by the February 1988 curve in Exhibit 5.18. As you see, long-term yields exceeded short-term yields, and the curve

Yield curves are usually drawn for Treasury securities.

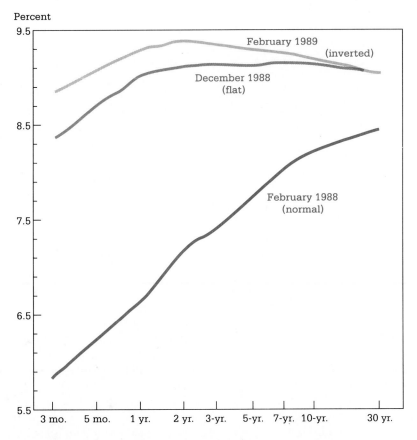

EXHIBIT 5.18
Yield curves for Treasury securities. (SOURCE: Monthly averages from the Federal Reserve Statistical Release H.15.)

Note: Three-month, six-month, and one-year U.S. Treasury instruments are quoted from the secondary market on a yield basis, all other instruments are constant-maturity series.

Is There a Message in the Yield Curve?

Investors look for omens in practically any situation, and one that has gotten a lot of press lately is the yield curve. As curves go, the yield curve is one of the easiest to find. All you need is any issue of *The Wall Street Journal* and the skill to find the curves, which are located in the financial pages (part C).

Now that you have it, what does it tell you? Well, all you will see is how interest rates on Treasury issues stacked up against their maturities on the particular day reported. But some analysts see much more. For example, if the curve is flat or slopes downward, this supposedly indicates that smart in-

vestors expect rates will fall in the future. If the curve slopes upward very sharply, the message is that rates will be rising.

Do the signs work? Some analysts think so, but the evidence is hardly conclusive. Perhaps the better way to use yield curves is in forecasting the overall economy. As the accompanying graph indicates, the onset of recessions since 1953 have been preceded by flat and inverted curves. (A zero yield spread is a flat curve, while negative spreads indicate inverted curves.) Unfortunately, investors can't make money with this information, unless someone concocts a way to take short positions on the economy.

Wait a minute, though: if it's true that flat and negative yield curves forecast a recession, can't we put such information to use? How about this approach: when the economy is at the depths of a recession, forecast that yield curves will eventually become upward-sloping. The graph shows that ought to work. If you're under 25, however, you might want to wait until you live through your first recession as an adult. You will be amazed at how difficult it is to be optimistic when gloom and doom abound. Remember, you are looking at only seven recessions, which hardly make a large data base. The eighth one might be totally different.

slopes upward. This upward-sloping yield curve is considered "normal" in that it illustrates the growing liquidity risk investors face with longer maturities and shows they demand higher rates for undertaking such risk.

Flat and Inverted Yield Curves   When yields on short-term securities are about the same as those on long-term securities, the yield curve becomes flat—the situation in December, 1988, for maturities from one to thirty years. If short-term yields exceed long-term yields, the yield curve is said to be inverted, as in February, 1989, for maturities from two to thirty years. Flat and inverted curves have appeared increasingly in recent years. Their presence is associated with

YIELD SPREAD CYCLES[a]

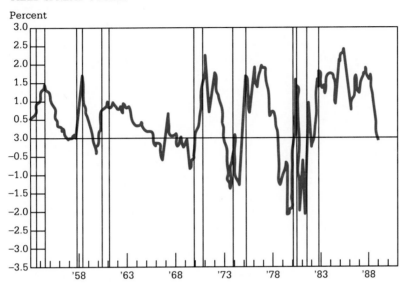

[a]Spread is the difference between the Treasury 10-year and one-year constant-maturity yield. Shaded areas represent periods of recession. Last date plotted is February 1989.
SOURCE: Monthly averages from the Federal Reserve Statistical Release H.15.

Bond portfolio managers use duration more extensively than interest elasticity. However, for most applications there is little difference between the two. For an excellent discussion, see G. J. Santoni, "Interest Rate Risk and the Stock Prices of Financial Institutions," *Review,* August/September 1984, pp. 12–20. The Federal Reserve Bank of St. Louis.

high rates in general. As you see, rates increased substantially from February 1988 to December 1988. An explanation for such curves is that both investors and debt issuers believe yields will likely fall in the future. Assuming this to be true, you can see why short-term yields will be higher.

For example, if you thought yields would decline, which of the six securities shown in Exhibit 5.12 would you wish to hold? Your answer should be the 20-year zero. It offers the greatest price-appreciation potential. If many investors feel as you do, market pressures should force prices of long-term instruments up in relation to prices of short-term instruments; and, since yields move inversely to prices, long-term yields will fall relative to short-term yields. (Keep in mind,

An inverted yield curve implies that investors expect interest rates to fall in the future.

though, that both yields are at historically high levels.) Not only will market pressures develop on the demand side of debt markets, they will also emerge on the supply side. Business firms that can choose between issuing long-term or short-term debt will choose the latter even though its current yield (cost to them) is higher. They will pay these high yields only for a short period of time, whereas if they issued long-term debt they would be saddled with high rates for many years in the future. Thus, the supply of long-term debt decreases relative to the supply of short-term debt, which adds pressure to increase its relative price.

Some investment advisors urge you to keep a close watch on yield curves if you plan to trade bonds actively. Of course, their advice is to buy heavily when yield curves are inverted and sell when they are normal. Simple enough, but, unfortunately, yield curves can stay inverted for a fairly long time. Indeed, the inverted curves can become more pronounced as time goes on. These points suggest that trading bonds to make superior returns on a risk-adjusted basis may be more difficult than it first appears. At best, this advice is probably no better than the information provided by many other market-timing signals. We'll cover these signals in greater detail in Chapter 10, which deals with technical analysis.

Forecasting Interest Rates

An appropriate final topic for this chapter is a consideration of whether interest rates can be forecasted with reasonable accuracy. The importance of the topic is obvious: if you can forecast, you can profit handsomely from any future changes in interest rates. During much of the 1960s, when interest rates were stable, forecasting was more or less taken for granted. "Experts" usually gave us their pronouncements about where they thought rates were headed, and most investors followed the line. In truth, rates changed so little that few people bothered to go back to see if the forecasts were as accurate as everyone thought them to be. In an age of volatile rates, however, fortunes are made or lost by swift and sharp changes in interest rates. As we entered this age, it became increasingly clear that no forecaster—at least no one who made his or her forecasts public information—could predict rates with any greater accuracy than the average person could achieve with very naive methods. In other words, the "experts" often could not beat a simple forecasting method such as, "next month's interest rate will equal this month's interest rate."

No one, including the so-called "experts," has consistently forecasted interest rates with much accuracy.

Ironically, despite such poor forecasting performances, there is no shortage of professional forecasters; indeed, their number has grown, probably because investors now feel a far greater need for their services. Most large banks have professional forecasters, as do the large stockbrokerage firms, along with independent forecasting firms such as Evans Economics or the Wharton Econometric Forecasting Associates. In the early 1980s, one of the most influential persons in the country was Henry Kaufman, a forecaster with Salomon Brothers. The public awaited his periodic forecasts with such anxiety that when they came, they often sent bond prices reeling or soaring. Unfortunately, Kaufman missed the big drop in interest rates that started in 1980.

If you plan to invest in long-term debt instruments, probably the best advice is to do so as part of an overall investment strategy that does not call for forecasting interest rates. Moreover, avoid the temptation to allocate a larger portion of your portfolio to long-term instruments, at the expense of short-term instruments, when interest rates have fallen and are relatively low. You should always maintain adequate liquidity—the topic of our next chapter—and not sacrifice it for higher yields.

SUMMARY

Return from a debt instrument consists of periodic interest and/or price appreciation. Discount securities offer only price appreciation while interest-bearing securities pay interest and may have price appreciation. The current yield of a debt instrument is its interest divided by its market value; a yield to maturity (YTM) is a rate that causes the present value of its cash flows to equal its market value. A YTM assumes periodic interest earned is subsequently invested at the calculated YTM. An interest rate includes elements to allow for giving up current consumption and liquidity, and to cover expected inflation and possible defaults.

Bonds may have high liquidity and default risks, which are positively related to a bond's maturity, coupon interest rate, and the level of interest rates. Liquidity risk is measured by an interest elasticity coefficient or Macaulay's duration coefficient. Reinvestment risk and rollover risk are associated with reinvesting interest and redemption amounts. Default risk is measured by quality grades provided by rating agencies such as Moody's and Standard and Poor's. Bonds with higher default risk offer higher yields.

Interest rates have been very volatile in recent years. Short-term interest rates are usually lower than long-term rates, and a yield curve shows the relationship of rates to maturity. Yield curves typically slope upward—indicating that rates increase with maturity—but on occasion are inverted, meaning rates fall as maturity increases, or are flat, meaning yields are about the same on short-term and long-term securities. Forecasting interest rates is a difficult task that has not been done accurately over the past twenty years.

KEY TERMS

Select the alternative that best identifies the key term.

1. discount securities
2. interest-bearing securities
3. zero coupon bonds
4. current yield
5. yield to maturity (YTM)
6. interest elasticity coefficient, E
7. Macaulay's duration concept
8. reinvestment risk
9. rollover risk
10. default risk
11. yield curve

a. a yield measurement that ignores time
b. deals with the weighted average time it takes to recover principal and interest
c. securities that pay no periodic interest
d. often understood as the likelihood of not receiving a debt instrument's cash flows
e. discount securities with long maturities
f. percentage change in bond price divided by percentage change in YTM
g. a discount rate that equates the sum of discounted interest plus redemption value to a security's purchase price
h. securities that pay periodic interest
i. shows the relationship of YTM to term of maturity
j. associated with reinvesting funds in the same type of security
k. eliminated with zero coupon bonds

REVIEW QUESTIONS

1. Distinguish between a discount security and an interest-bearing security. Then, construct time-line diagrams for each, making up your own dollar amounts and maturities.
2. Define current yield and Treasury bill yield.
3. Explain the concept of yield to maturity (YTM). What is implied in a YTM calculation? Include interest-on-interest in your response.
4. What factors do investors consider in evaluating an interest rate? Explain, using different types of fixed-income securities in your answer.
5. Suppose you recently purchased a bond and interest rates in general rose sharply immediately thereafter. Should this be a concern to you? Explain.
6. How is a bond's price risk related to its coupon rate and term to maturity?
7. Explain how the interest elasticity coefficient is calculated and what information it provides. How would you interpret an E value of -0.40?
8. Explain Macaulay's duration concept and interpret the following D values: $D = 0.20$; 1.00; 5.00; and 20.00. Suppose each of these is a discount security; does this information help to understand another aspect of each? Explain.
9. What is reinvestment risk? What type of security eliminates such risk? Explain. Also, identify rollover risk.

10. What is default risk? Explain whether it can be measured.
11. You plan to limit your bond investments to those with a Moody's rating of no less than Aaa. Your friend will select only Baa-rated bonds. Explain who will earn the higher yield and if you expect the yield differential to remain the same over time.
12. What is a yield curve? How would you construct one? Explain.
13. Using appropriate graphics, illustrate normal, flat, and inverted yield curves.
14. Why is the normal curve called "normal"? Explain how yield curves might be used to forecast future interest rates.
15. Is there evidence indicating certain individuals forecast interest rates accurately? Discuss.

PROBLEMS AND PROJECTS

1. C. C. Lee is thinking of investing in one of the following two securities: an 8% bond currently selling for $700 with 20 years to maturity, when it will be redeemed for $1,000; or a zero coupon bond maturing in 20 years for $1,000 and currently selling for $200. How would you advise C. C.? Be sure to use YTMs in your discussion.
2. Calculate the current yield (or the Treasury bill yield) and yields to maturity (YTMs) for the following:
   a. a 90-day Treasury bill selling for $9,800.
   b. a 12% corporate bond that matures in 8 years, selling at face value.
   c. a 10% Treasury bond that matures in 12 years, selling at $900.
3. What is meant by "interest on interest"? Explain the concept, using a 20-year, 12% bond, selling initially at face value. Then, assume a reinvestment rate of 16%.
4. Calculate interest elasticity coefficients for each bond below, assuming each is currently selling at face value when interest rates rise by 25%. Also, discuss which is the riskier bond.
   a. a 20-year, 8% bond.
   b. a 10-year, 8% bond.
5. Calculate duration coefficients for each of the following bonds and then rank them according to risk (each has a YTM of 10%):
   a. a 3-year, 10% bond, selling at par.
   b. a 3-year, 20% bond, selling at $1,249.
   c. a 3-year zero, selling at $751.
6. You are evaluating a bond with a D value of 6.25, which was calculated assuming a YTM of 9%. You expect the YTM to increase to 10%. How much will the bond's price change (and in what direction) if the current price is $1,000?
7. (Student Project) Obtain a current issue of The Wall Street Journal and find the yield curve graphs in the financial pages. Interpret the patterns shown.
8. (Student Project) Write or call a large city bank, such as Chase Manhattan, and ask if they provide interest rate forecasts to their business clients or the general public. If they do, try to get back issues, and then determine the accuracy of their forecasts.

CASE ANALYSES

5.1
The Bradys Face
Reinvestment
Problems

Ian and Karen Brady are a married couple in their mid-thirties with two children. Their combined incomes of $82,000 provide for a comfortable living, but they face substantial costs when their children begin college in ten years. They have about $20,000 to invest now, and are considering investing in fixed-income securities. Ian feels they should limit their portfolio to 10-year, zero coupon issues with yields to maturity of about 10%. Karen disagrees. She thinks the portfolio should include coupon bonds with YTMs of approximately 13%. Her bonds have a BBB rating, while Ian's are AAA-rated. Karen believes Ian is too conservative. She argues that if interest rates fall, as each expects will happen, her strategy will be better because she will have locked in the higher rates. She also thinks her strategy is better if, by some chance, interest rates rise; in that event, the larger losses will be with Ian's zeros.

    The Bradys have some liquidity apart from the $20,000 earmarked for the kids, but it is not considerable. They would like your advice on the matter. Prior to meeting with them, you have gathered yield data for selected Treasury issues:

90-day bills	11.0%
5-year notes	10.0
10-year bonds	9.0
20-year bonds	8.0

Questions

a. What will the bond portfolio be worth ten years from now if Ian's approach is followed? Is it possible to know what it will be worth if Karen's approach is followed? Explain.
b. Do you feel Karen has a correct risk perspective on their investment problem? Has she actually "locked in" higher rates? Discuss.
c. Does it seem likely that interest rates will fall in the future? Discuss your conclusion. How important to the Brady's investment objective are interest rate movements? Explain.
d. How would you advise the Bradys? If you prefer Ian's or Karen's approach, explain why.

5.2
Felix Minoso's
Bond Strategy

Felix Minoso has read recently that bonds have become almost as risky as common stocks. He doesn't understand completely why that should be the case, but it doesn't disappoint him because Felix likes to actively trade securities. He is particularly attracted to U.S. Treasury issues since there is no default risk. Considering some of the bankrupts he has encountered in common stock investing, that feature is a welcome relief.

Felix's broker has explained that bond prices go up when investors feel interest rates will fall, and vice versa. The broker sent Felix a newspaper article that highlighted economists' interest-rate forecasts for the upcoming year. Most felt interest rates would decline from present levels. The broker argued that, given Felix's objective, he should invest his funds in 30-year T-bonds, currently yielding 9%. She specifically recommends zero coupon bonds. Felix was cool to this approach. For one thing, he didn't like the idea of receiving no interest; and for another, current yields were much higher on 1-year T-bills (12%) and 5-year notes (10%). Felix decided to follow his own instincts by investing $30,000 in each of the three securities, rather than investing all $90,000 in the zeros. He purchased all the securities at their face values, and he intends to sell them after he realizes a sufficient gain in each.

Questions

a. Suppose interest rates fell very shortly after Felix invested, and new yields are 5% on the bills, 6% on the notes, and 7% on the bonds. Determine Felix's portfolio gain. Then, determine the portfolio gain if Felix had listened to his broker. Assume that no securities were sold in either case.
b. Calculate elasticity coefficients for the three securities. How could these values have helped Felix in developing his investment strategy? Would they have been applicable if interest rates had risen instead of falling? Explain.
c. Were Felix's reasons for rejecting his broker's advice sensible, given his investment objective? Explain.
d. What roles, if any, should reinvestment risk and rollover risk play in Felix's approach? Discuss.

HELPFUL READING

Benari, Yoav. "A Bond Market Timing Model." *The Journal of Portfolio Management,* Fall 1988, pp. 45–48.

Benesch, Gary A., and Steven E. Celec. "A Simplified Approach for Calculating Bond Duration." *The Financial Review,* November 1984, pp. 394–96.

CFA Readings in Income Securities Analysis. Charlottesville, VA: Institute for Chartered Financial Analysts, 1985.

Dietz, P. H., R. Fogler, and D. J. Hardy. "The Challenge of Analyzing Bond Portfolio Returns." *Journal of Portfolio Management,* Spring 1980.

Donnelly, Barbara. "Pros Offer Methods for Sizing Up Bonds," *The Wall Street Journal,* May 11, 1989, p. C1.

Maloney, Kevin J., and Jess B. Yawitz. "Interest Rate Risk, Immunization, and Duration." *The Journal of Portfolio Management,* Winter 1986.

Siconolfi, Michael. "Focus on Risk of Junk Bond Funds Is Shifting to Liquidity from Credit." *The Wall Street Journal,* July 20, 1989, p. C1.

Stevens, E. J. "Is There a Message in the Yield Curve?" *Economic Commentary,* Federal Reserve Bank of Cleveland, March 15, 1989.

Taylor, Richard W. "Bond Duration with Geometric Mean Return," *Financial Analysts Journal,* January-February 1989, pp. 78–80.

CHAPTER SIX

Investing in Debt Instruments to Meet Liquidity Needs

LIQUIDITY MANAGEMENT

Why Hold Liquid Assets?

Financial Institutions

ALTERNATIVE TYPES OF LIQUID ASSETS

Accounts at Financial Institutions

U.S. Treasury Securities

Non-Treasury-Issued Securities

Money Market Mutual Funds

BORROWING AND LIQUIDITY MANAGEMENT

Avoiding Future Borrowing

Frequently Used Sources of Investment Credit

BOXES

Where to Put Your Short-Term Funds

Pitfalls in Liquidity Management

After you finish this chapter, you will be able to:

- understand what is meant by liquidity and why investors hold liquid assets.

- identify the various financial institutions that offer checking and savings deposits.

- understand and evaluate the different types of checking and savings deposits offered by financial institutions.

- understand and evaluate Treasury securities as alternative liquid assets.

- understand and evaluate non-Treasury-issued securities as alternative liquid assets.

- structure a liquidity management strategy that considers the possibility of borrowing.

L iquid assets are the first investments many people make. Indeed, they are often called savings, rather than investments. Regardless of what they are called, they are a necessary and important part of anyone's portfolio. Investing in liquid assets is simple because every financial depository institution in the country offers them. A trip to your neighborhood bank or savings and loan can usually satisfy your entire liquidity need. However, if you are trying to increase your yield or wish to be a bit more aggressive in managing your liquid assets, you might have to shop outside the neighborhood. Thanks to deregulation of the financial institutions industry, these shopping trips are now possible and often worthwhile.

LIQUIDITY MANAGEMENT

Liquidity management (also called *cash management*) is best understood as a strategy for determining how much liquidity you will hold, in what forms, and in which financial institutions. There are many different strategies, ranging from the ultraconservative, where you hold virtually nothing other than a checking account, to the aggressive, where you hold assets that are more difficult to convert to cash and, possibly, even use tax shelters such as IRAs to enhance your return.

Why Hold Liquid Assets?

An asset is said to be liquid when it can be converted to cash easily and with very little or no loss in value. Coins and currency are obviously the most liquid of all assets. They are legal tender, which means they cannot be refused if you offer them to pay a debt. Unfortunately, currency and coins offer no positive return and actually pose the problems of easy theft or misplacement. Moving away from coins and currency, assets become less liquid. Your personal check may be accepted in most places in your hometown but it may be turned down somewhere else; thus, it has less liquidity. Your savings account is even less liquid because you must go through the inconvenience of making a withdrawal each time you need money. Much further down on the liquidity list is a certificate of deposit; with it, you may actually pay a penalty for withdrawing funds before maturity.

Generally, as liquidity increases, asset return decreases.

    Generally, as liquidity increases, asset return decreases, as Exhibit 6.1 illustrates. The deposits indicated will be explained shortly. We would prefer to have both return and liquidity, but most often it does not work that way. We must choose: either more liquidity or greater return. How much liquidity often depends upon our reasons for wanting liquidity in the first place. These reasons are to undertake transactions, to have emergency reserves, and to have a store of value.

The size and irregularity of cash flows determine how much liquidity is needed for transactions.

Undertake Transactions   We must hold some liquid assets for undertaking transactions. Our cash inflows and outflows are often irregular and somewhat unpredictable. You might get paid twice a month. Out of those payments you

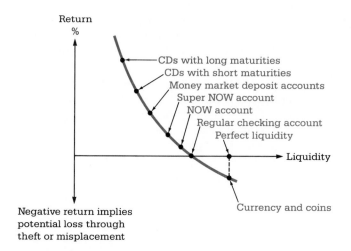

Return
%

CDs with long maturities
CDs with short maturities
Money market deposit accounts
Super NOW account
NOW account
Regular checking account
Perfect liquidity

Liquidity

Currency and coins

Negative return implies
potential loss through
theft or misplacement

EXHIBIT 6.1
Liquidity-return curve
for cash and federally
insured deposits

must make recurrent living expenditures. Your paycheck might go directly into your checking account, where checks are then issued to pay bills and to get needed currency for small items. Your balance will be relatively high twice a month and gradually diminish in the two weeks after you are paid. So, you will have an average balance for the month—a necessary investment in a liquid asset. As you might guess, this average balance depends upon various factors.

First, the larger your income and monthly expenses, the larger the average balance. If your income is $3,000 a month, you will have a larger average balance than if it is $1,000 a month. Second, the more infrequently you are paid, the larger the average balance. Someone paid weekly will have less in the checking account, on average, than someone paid monthly. Third, the more uncertain and irregular your cash flows, the larger the average required balance to protect against a possible shortage of funds. These factors are summarized in Exhibit 6.2.

Emergency Reserves An **emergency reserve** means liquid assets held to protect against unforeseen expenses or unexpected loss of income. Financial planners often recommend that you keep between three and six months of living

Your emergency reserve
should cover living ex-
penses for three to six
months.

EXHIBIT 6.2
Reasons for holding
liquid assets

Reason	Important Factors Determining Amounts Held
A. Undertake transactions	1. Amount of monthly expenses 2. Frequency of pay periods 3. Degree of uncertainty of future income and expenses
B. Hold emergency reserves	1. Amount of monthly expenses 2. Disability income protection 3. Disposition towards taking risks
C. Keep a store of value	1. Good investment vehicle 2. Temporary parking place

expenses in emergency reserves. So, if your budget shows monthly expenditures of $2,000, you need about $6,000 to $12,000, according to their advice. If you have adequate disability income insurance, you can take the lower figure; if you don't, you should plan to hold the higher amount.

For many people this reserve represents a sizeable investment in relation to their incomes. Many question whether it's really needed, and we probably will not know the answer unless we experience a financial emergency. The danger in lacking sufficient reserves is that you may have to deal with an emergency by selling other assets that you would prefer to hold. These assets could be your home, your car, even an engagement or wedding ring. In addition to having poor liquidity, these assets often hold irreplaceable sentimental value. You be the judge of the size of your emergency fund, but give it sufficient thought before you decide.

Since the emergency fund is not used for transactions, you can extend your portfolio to hold assets other than a checking account. Taking some risk to achieve higher yields is not out of the question so long as the risk is minimal. Stocks and most bonds would be poor choices, but certificates of deposit would be acceptable in most cases.

Store of Value   Liquid assets may be held simply because you feel they are the best **store of value;** in other words, your wealth will increase the most—or erode the least—with them. In this sense, liquid assets are selected because they are the best investments to hold. But when would that be the case? Perhaps in periods when interest rates in general are expected to rise rapidly. If you selected assets with long maturities and interest rates did rise, you would suffer capital losses, as we discussed in the previous chapter. When liquid assets are selected for this reason, we describe the investor as looking for a temporary parking place for his or her money. *Temporary* is the key word, since the investor would actually prefer investing in less liquid assets, and will do so when the investment horizon improves. As in the case of the emergency fund, a wider array of assets can be selected for store-of-value purposes. In many cases, investors can look for the highest-yielding liquid assets because losses or some inconveniences can be tolerated. Indeed, during periods of high rates, some investors limit their entire investment activities to selecting and managing liquid assets. They often move all their deposits to another bank or a money market mutual fund (which will be explained later in the chapter) to capture a half-percent greater yield for a period of time as short as a week. While such cases are extreme, high short-term rates make investors more aware of the importance of sound liquidity management. As we saw in Chapter 3, a small extra yield over a long period of time leads to substantial increases in wealth.

> Liquid assets are often held as a ''temporary parking place'' for funds.

Moreover, many investors considered using the individual retirement account (IRA) tax shelter to further enhance yield even though their investment objective was not necessarily to build a retirement estate. However, recent changes in the tax law have diminished the appeal of this strategy and, as Exhibit 6.3 indicates, there are points to consider before implementing it.

EXHIBIT 6.3
Points to consider in
using an IRA to shelter
short-term investments

1. Although IRAs are used typically for retirement investing, they need not be limited to this purpose. You can withdraw funds—all or some—from an IRA at any time.
2. If you make a withdrawal before age 59½, you pay a 10% penalty on amounts withdrawn.
3. If you deducted contributions to the IRA, you must include withdrawals with other taxable income and pay taxes on them, since these IRAs only *defer*—not *avoid*—taxes.
4. Funds in an IRA accumulate at your pre-tax rate of return; for example, 10%. Non-IRA accumulations are at your after-tax rate of return; for example, 7.2% if you have a 28% marginal tax rate.
5. For each dollar invested in a non-IRA, you can invest (1.0 + marginal tax rate) more in a deductible IRA. With a 28% marginal tax rate, you could invest $2,560 in an IRA versus $2,000 (maximum allowable IRA deduction) in a non-IRA.
6. If money is needed for a very short-term emergency, you could withdraw funds from one IRA and use them for a while, making sure to open a new IRA within 60 days. This is called an IRA rollover, and the law allows a 60-day period to complete it. But keep in mind that you must open the new IRA or the withdrawal is taxable (for deductible IRA contributions) and the 10% penalty applies. Also, you are allowed only one rollover a year.

Financial Institutions

As mentioned above, many alternative financial institutions offer liquid assets. Often, we deal with these institutions without giving much thought to whether or not they are the most appropriate to meet our needs, or if our deposits have adequate protection. Depositors in Ohio, for example, learned painfully that so-called state insurance on deposits provided virtually no protection in the wake of a large, failing institution. Had the state government not intervened in the crisis caused by the failure of a large savings and loan (Home State Savings), depositor losses would have been substantial. Before investing, then, determine if federal insurance protection—FDIC, SAIF, and NCUA—is provided. Exhibit 6.4 summarizes this insurance. Before examining various liquid deposits, it is appropriate to review the characteristics of the different financial institutions offering them.

Many financial institutions offer similar deposits; the most important issue is whether they are federally insured.

Commercial Banks Most commercial banks are all-purpose financial institutions, which means they offer a wide array of financial products and services. You probably have a checking or savings account with one, and you may also have a loan, either directly or through Visa or MasterCard. Commercial banks also offer trust services that are used to achieve a number of objectives. Despite competition within the financial institutions industry, most people still wish to

EXHIBIT 6.4
Federally insured financial institutions

	Insuring Federal Agency		
	Federal Deposit Insurance Corporation (FDIC)	Savings Association Insurance Fund (SAIF)	National Credit Union Administration (NCUA)
Institution insured	Commercial banks and mutual savings banks	Savings and loan associations	Federally chartered credit unions
Approximate number at 1/1/1989	14,500	2,900	15,200
Approximate insured deposits at 1/1/1989	$2.5 trillion	$970 billion	$105 billion
Amount of insurance per depositor*	$100,000	$100,000	$100,000

*It is important to note that insurance is for each depositor and not for each account. If the amount held by one depositor exceeds $100,000, another account should be opened with another financial institution.

maintain some form of business with a commercial bank. Many bank deposits are insured with FDIC, but make sure of this before you invest.

Savings and Loans (S&Ls) and Savings Banks   S&Ls and savings banks are savings institutions that historically limited their lending to mortgage loans. Many still do, although others have become much more aggressive in their lending policies (Home State, mentioned previously, was extremely aggressive, doing repurchase agreements with ESM Securities, a government bond dealer that eventually went bankrupt). Many S&Ls have experienced financial problems in recent years, making it all the more important to determine if your deposit is SAIF-insured.

Credit Unions   Investors often overlook their credit unions as a place to hold their liquid deposits. This is unfortunate, since many offer very competitive interest rates—both when you invest and when you borrow—along with NCUA protection. The credit union also may be the most convenient place to do business. Be careful if NCUA protection is not provided; events in the financial institutions industry have taught us that no institution is free of default risk. Think twice before you invest more than a modest amount in any institution that is not federally insured.

Credit unions can offer competitive rates to their members.

Consumer Banks   A consumer bank is any financial institution that limits its lending or depositing activities to individuals and excludes businesses. Large S&Ls and commercial banks are attempting to expand their business over state lines by setting up consumer banks. To investors, this expansion provides new opportunities to earn higher rates. Again, though, it is necessary to determine the

Where To Put Your Short-Term Funds

Some years ago, if you asked investors how their short-term funds were doing, you might be lucky to arouse a loud yawn. Unless you had at least $10,000 to invest, your choices of where to put your money were few and not very meaningful if you were looking for higher yields. Banks and S&Ls gave away toasters, not higher interest rates.

Not so today. Money market mutual funds in the 1970s, followed by deregulation in the 1980s, have created an investment atmosphere rivaling the stock market in competitive activity. If you see a group of enthusiastic investors poring over the financial pages, don't assume they're looking for the IBM of the future; a more likely guess is they're checking Banxquote (a service of Masterfund, Inc.) to see which federally insured financial institution in the U.S. is offering the highest savings rate this week. Or they might be checking yields and portfolio maturities of their favorite money market mutual funds.

The yields on money market investments now appear routinely in many newspapers and even on the business news on television. Investors often look at yields on money market instruments they will never invest in directly—such as Treasury bills or commercial paper—simply because their fund invests in them and they hope to anticipate its yield in the future. A high level of interest rates, of course, adds excitement to the quest. But it's the differential in rates that investors seek, and these can be high even when overall rates are low.

So, getting current yield information is important. The accompanying table shows what you would have found if you were in the market around the middle of May, 1989. It's clear that yield differentials existed, and shifting short-term funds could have been worthwhile.

Item	Minimum Investment	Days to Maturity	Yield (%)
U.S. Treasury bills	$ 10,000	90	7.81
High-grade commercial paper	25,000	90	9.63
Negotiable ("jumbo") CDs	100,000	90	9.34
Deposits at federally insured institutions:			
Money market accounts:			
Highest in U.S.	(a)	instant	10.47
National average	(a)	instant	7.12
3-month CDs:			
Highest in U.S.	(a)	90	10.47
National average	(a)	90	8.64
1-year CDs:			
Highest in U.S.	(a)	365	10.67
National average	(a)	365	9.28
Money market mutual fund (Merrill Lynch Ready Assets)	(b)	—	9.52

(a) Minimum deposits range from $500 to $2,500.

(b) Yield is based on performance over the past 30 days.

SOURCE: Deposit information from Banxquote online Deposits, for Thursday, May 11, 1989, as reported in the May 12, 1989, issue of *The Wall Street Journal*, p. C17. Banxquote is a registered trademark of Masterfund, Inc., New York. Other rates reported in the same issue of the *Journal*, p. C12.

safety of deposits. Anything other than federal insurance should call for a very close examination of potential default.

Stockbrokerage Firms Your stockbroker can also provide liquid instruments. Many offer money market mutual funds (explained later in this chapter) and they can purchase other instruments, such as Treasury bills or commercial paper.

Stockbrokerage firms offer liquid assets as part of their money management accounts.

Probably one advantage of using your broker is that cash balances in your securities account can be transferred immediately to liquid assets. Not only is this convenient, your funds are invested for longer periods of time because you avoid mail delays. Merrill Lynch was the originator of so-called "sweep accounts" with its cash management account (CMA), a type of all-purpose checking, saving, borrowing, and investing account. Despite a high initial investment of $20,000, this account is exceptionally popular with investors. Other brokerage firms and other financial institutions have entered the market with similar accounts, but doing so is difficult because Merrill Lynch successfully patented the account and defended against infringements by Dean Witter and Paine Webber.

ALTERNATIVE TYPES OF LIQUID ASSETS

The array of liquid assets offered today is indeed very wide. Many investors are not familiar with them, and the best advice someone might offer at the outset is to shop around. Federal regulation of financial institutions has virtually ended with respect to maximum interest rates and minimum deposit amounts, so any remaining restrictions are set by the institution.

Accounts at Financial Institutions

Many investors limit their liquid investments to deposits at financial institutions. They may do so because deposit rates are often competitive with rates on other liquid assets but require smaller minimum investments, or because they are convenient and federally insured, or because inertia keeps them from searching for alternatives. Exhibit 6.5 shows an array of liquid assets, which includes the most popular ones at financial institutions.

Checking and NOW Accounts Most of us understand a checking account, but a **NOW account** is often less familiar. NOW stands for *negotiated order of withdrawal,* a term used to describe checks issued by institutions other than commercial banks. That distinction is meaningless today and it is better to understand a NOW account simply as a checking account that pays interest. You may have heard of a super-NOW account. This is merely a NOW account that pays more interest than a regular NOW and probably has a higher minimum balance requirement.

Checking and NOW accounts are needed for transaction purposes.

Each, though, is a checking account in every respect. Their advantage is obvious: your balances held for transactions purposes earn interest. This is not a

	Average March Balances (billions)	
	1988	**1989**
Currency	$200.7	$215.6
Checking accounts at commercial banks	288.4	284.3
NOW accounts at all financial institutions	267.5	279.1
Money market deposit accounts	525.5	480.3
Savings deposits:		
Passbook accounts	419.2	418.5
Nonnegotiable (small) CDs	955.8	1,064.6

EXHIBIT 6.5
Currency and popular deposits at financial institutions

SOURCE: *Federal Reserve Statistical Release H.6,* May 4, 1989.

trivial advantage, but it must be weighed against a possible disadvantage if the minimum balance requirement forces you to keep more in the account than you would otherwise. If this is the case, and if you could earn a higher rate on the excess amount somewhere else, then you should consider holding a regular checking account with a lower minimum requirement and investing the difference elsewhere. For example, suppose you normally keep an average balance of $400 in your regular checking account. You are considering opening a super-NOW account that pays 6% interest and has a $2,500 minimum average balance requirement. Assuming your balance would average the $2,500 minimum means the account would earn $150 interest a year. However, if you could invest the extra $2,100 at, say, 10%, you would be $60 a year better off maintaining a regular checking account and investing the difference.

A checking account with a side investment account might offer a higher return than a NOW account.

Savings Accounts A number of different kinds of savings accounts are available, as Exhibit 6.5 shows. The simplest is the **passbook account,** so named because a passbook is often used to record activity in the account. This savings account allows an unlimited number of withdrawals each period, but usually pays the lowest rate of interest. The passbook account is rapidly being replaced by statement accounts. Instead of a passbook, you receive monthly statements, as with a checking account.

    Money market deposit accounts (MMDAs) are savings accounts that pay money market rates, which means the rates change over time in step with interest-rate changes in the money markets. To investors with limited funds, this feature is very attractive. It allows them to participate in the money market, which usually excludes them because of high minimum investment amounts. (Another alternative is the money market mutual fund.) MMDAs have minimum balance requirements, usually around $2,500, and offer limited access to funds, with perhaps only three withdrawals or other transfers a month.

    Another attractive savings vehicle is the **certificate of deposit (CD)**. These are available in practically any amount and with a wide array of maturities, ranging from one week to over ten years. A CD is quite different from an MMDA. An interest rate is locked in for the CD's maturity; that is, it has a fixed rate of return. Obviously, if you feel interest rates will decline in the future, you would prefer the CD to an MMDA; but, if you think they will increase, you would pick the MMDA. Because the yield curve tends to have a normal shape more often than it is inverted, CDs usually offer higher rates than MMDAs. You would expect this to be the usual case, since CDs tie up your funds for a given maturity. They should offer a higher return to compensate you for accepting the risk involved in possible interest-rate fluctuations. But suppose you want to cash in the CD before its maturity? Be prepared to pay a penalty for early redemption. The amount of the penalty will be at the discretion of the issuing financial institution. Make sure you ask about such penalties before investing in CDs.

Money market accounts and CDs are primarily savings instruments, but CDs have early-withdrawal penalties.

Know How Your Savings Account Earns Interest   Surprising as it may seem, there is no established pattern of paying interest that all financial institutions follow. Some compound interest quarterly or annually, while others compound it daily or even continuously. Some require that your funds be invested for an entire month or quarter before interest is paid at all; others credit your account daily. Are these differences trivial? Very often they are not.

For example, Exhibit 6.6 shows the accumulation of $1,000 invested for various periods of time assuming an 8% stated annual rate and compounding at different intervals. At the end of sixteen years, daily compounding adds $170.19 ($3,596.13 − $3,425.94) more to your account—and remember, you invested only $1,000 at the start.

Also, the method the institution uses to determine what balances qualify to earn interest has a considerable effect on the amount of interest earned. Exhibit 6.7 shows four widely used methods applied to assumed quarterly activity.

Day of Deposit to Day of Withdrawal.   This method means interest is earned on each day's balance. Notice, though, this is not the same as daily compounding, where each day's interest is added to your account to earn future interest (compound interest). The calculations in Exhibit 6.7 actually assume simple

EXHIBIT 6.6
Funds accumulated at 8% interest ($1,000 invested)

Frequency of Compounding	Years Deposit Is Held				
	1	2	4	8	16
Annually	$1,080.00	$1,166.40	$1,360.49	$1,850.93	$3,425.94
Semiannually	1,081.60	1,169.86	1,368.57	1,872.98	3,508.06
Quarterly	1,082.43	1,171.66	1,372.79	1,884.54	3,551.49
Weekly	1,083.22	1,173.37	1,376.79	1,895.55	3,593.11
Daily	1,083.28	1,173.49	1,377.08	1,896.35	3,596.13
Continuously	1,083.30	1,173.51	1,377.13	1,896.48	3,596.62

EXHIBIT 6.7
Determining savings
balances that qualify for
interest

Activity in the Account		
Day	Deposit (Withdrawal)	Balance
1	$1,000	$1,000
30	1,000	2,000
60	(900)	1,100
90	Closing	1,100

Interest Calculations

1. Day of deposit to day of withdrawal:
   a. $1,000 × 30/360 × .06 = $ 5.00
   b. $2,000 × 30/360 × .06 = $10.00
   c. $1,100 × 30/360 × .06 = $ 5.50
                Total $20.50

2. Minimum balance:
       $1,000 × 90/360 × .06 = $15.00

3. FIFO:
   a. $ 100 × 90/360 × .06 = $ 1.50
   b. $1,000 × 60/360 × .06 = $10.00
                Total $11.50

4. LIFO:
   a. $1,000 × 90/360 × .06 = $15.00
   b. $ 100 × 60/360 × .06 = $ 1.00
                Total $16.00

interest calculations where interest earned (I) equals principal (P) times rate (r) times time (T); that is,

$$I = P \times r \times T$$

Minimum Balance. This method pays interest only on the minimum balance in the account for the period. As you see in Exhibit 6.7, this method can lead to very little interest if you make withdrawals during the period. Moreover, deposits made during the period usually must be received before a given date—such as before the tenth day of the first month of the quarter—to earn any interest for the quarter. This method obviously does not benefit depositors.

FIFO. FIFO means first-in, first-out. It assumes any withdrawals you make during the period reduce your earliest balances—another assumption in the bank's favor. So, the $900 withdrawal made two months after the quarter began is assumed to reduce the opening balance of $1,000.

Be wary of the minimum balance and FIFO methods.

LIFO. LIFO means last-in, first-out. In contrast to FIFO, it assumes withdrawals reduce your later, rather than earlier, balances. Here, the $900 withdrawal is assumed to reduce the $1,000 deposit made on the 30th day.

LIFO is more to your advantage than FIFO but is still less generous than the day of deposit to day of withdrawal method. If you feel that some activity will occur in your savings account fairly often, you should probably try to select an institution offering the day of deposit to day of withdrawal method over those offering the minimum balance, FIFO, or LIFO methods.

U.S. Treasury Securities

Because they are free of default risk, Treasury securities are often favored by investors seeking safety of principal. Actually, there is little difference between Treasury securities and currency itself; the former is interest-bearing debt of the Treasury while the latter is non-interest-bearing debt. The non-interest-bearing type is preferred only when perfect liquidity is more important than earnings. The instruments shown in Exhibit 6.8 and discussed below are popular Treasury securities held for liquidity.

Treasury Bills   **Treasury bills** are debt obligations of the U.S. Treasury sold on a discount basis with maturities ranging from three months to a year. At the beginning of 1989, there was about $414 billion of Treasury bills outstanding. Bills are issued in minimum denominations of $10,000, and they are actively traded in the secondary market. Treasury bills can be purchased through commercial banks or stockbrokerage firms. However, buying them directly from the Treasury is just as easy and avoids commissions. All that is needed is a tender form, available from 37 Treasury Direct Servicing Offices. This is a simple form that you complete and submit to the Federal Reserve Bank in your area. You also must

EXHIBIT 6.8
Popular short-term investments other than deposits at financial institutions

	End-of-Year Amounts (billions)		
	1988	1987	1986
Treasury Debt:			
Bills	$414.0	$389.5	$426.7
Savings bonds	107.6	99.2	90.6
Non-Treasury Issuers:			
Commercial paper	455.0	357.1	330.0
Negotiable (jumbo) CDs[a]	537.8	487.4	438.9
Money market mutual funds[a,b]	239.6	221.1	208.0

[a]Average daily balance.
[b]Excludes funds that are offered only to businesses or other institutional owners.
SOURCE: *Federal Reserve Bulletin,* May, 1989.

establish a Treasury Direct Account that will be connected with your checking or savings account. All payments from the Treasury are wired directly to the account. However, active T-bill investors usually roll over maturing bills into new issues.

Bills are now sold only in "book entry" form, which means buyers must have accounts with the Treasury. New issues of bills with less than one year maturity are sold at auction every Monday morning (those with a year maturity are auctioned only once a month). Both stock market and credit analysts frequently watch the outcomes in these auctions in an effort to gauge future interest rates. Whether these observations are of much help is another matter, but we do know the T-bill rate is volatile and very sensitive to changes in the supply and demand for credit.

Bonds and Notes with Short Remaining Maturities   Treasury bonds and notes will be explained in greater detail in the next chapter, but for now let us recognize that they can also serve as liquid instruments. There is also a very active secondary market for bonds and notes, again making it possible to buy them with varying maturities. Buying a T-bond with 3 months remaining to its maturity is little different from buying a 3-month T-bill. In fact, investors will prefer the bond if its yield to maturity is better. As you guess, the active secondary market keeps the yields to maturity about equal on all Treasury debt of equal maturity. You can purchase Treasury bonds and notes in the same ways you purchase Treasury bills, including direct purchase from the Treasury.

U.S. Series EE Bonds   **U.S. Series EE bonds,** usually called savings bonds, are nonnegotiable instruments of the Treasury sold on a discount basis and issued primarily for the benefit of small investors. They are replacing the old Series E bond, considered in the past as an investment "dog" because its yield was low in relation to yields elsewhere. But the Series EE bond has changed the "dog" image and many investment advisors now view savings bonds as good short-term vehicles. About $108 billion was invested in EE bonds at the start of 1989.

Exhibit 6.9 summarizes the most important characteristics of savings bonds. Notice that their yields are indexed to other Treasury securities; specifically, they yield 85% of the actual average interest earned on an index of Treasury securities for the five-year period prior to their redemption. The yield is changed every six months, and the 7.81% yield that began May 1, 1989, was quite good in relation to other short-term rates available then. Other features that appeal to some investors are federal income tax deferral on the interest until you redeem the bond, and no state or local income taxes. Moreover, federal income taxes may be avoided altogether if interest on the bond is used to pay for a child's college or vocational education. Currently, single individuals earning $40,000 or less and married couples jointly earning $60,000 or less earn a full exclusion of all Series EE bond interest. For incomes from $40,000 to $50,000 (single return) and $60,000 to $90,000 (joint return), partial exclusion is available; and for incomes

You can avoid commissions by buying Treasury bills through a Federal Reserve Bank.

Because they offer both a minimum return and indexed returns, Series EE bonds are attractive liquid assets.

EXHIBIT 6.9

Important facts about U.S. Series EE savings bonds

PURCHASE PRICE	☐ $25 to $5,000, maximum investment is $30,000 per individual
YOUR RETURN	☐ No less than 4.27% if held one year
	☐ No less than 6.0% if held five years or longer
	☐ Actual return after five years indexed to returns on U.S. Treasury securities (six-month annualized yield beginning May 1, 1989 = 7.81%; this rate changes every six months)
WHERE TO BUY	☐ Through payroll deduction plans
	☐ At most banks and other financial institutions
	☐ Through the mail from Bureau of Public Debt, Washington, DC 20226
REDEMPTION	☐ Must wait six months, unless there is an emergency
	☐ Redeem at any bank, but be careful not to redeem immediately before an interest date (there are two a year), since you can lose several months' interest even if you redeem only several days too early
OTHER ADVANTAGES	☐ No buying or selling charges, fees, or commissions
	☐ Federal income taxes can be deferred until redemption, or possibly avoided altogether if bond interest is used for a child's education
	☐ No state or local income taxes

over $50,000 and $90,000, no exclusion is allowed. Clearly, this possible avoidance of taxes on Series EE bonds makes them very attractive and highly competitive with all other debt instruments—those with long maturities as well as those with short maturities. So, savings bonds may not have the same conveniences as savings accounts, but their other advantages should be considered carefully in constructing the investment portfolio. To obtain current rates on the bonds, call the Series EE Bond Information Center at 1–800–872–6637.

U.S. Series HH Bonds   **U.S. Series HH bonds** are also issued by the Treasury. You cannot buy them, however; you can acquire them only by exchanging Series EE bonds (or series E bonds, an older version of Series EE). The HH series differs from the EE series in that interest is paid semiannually at a fixed 6% rate and the bonds mature in ten years (but can be extended to 30 years). An appealing feature of HH bonds is that deferred interest on EE bonds can be continued by the exchange. However. semiannual interest is taxable.

Non-Treasury-Issued Securities

Although the Treasury is considered the safest insurer of securities, there are other issuers. Corporations such as GM and IBM often sell commercial paper as a means of borrowing on a short-term basis, and commercial banks sell negotiable certificates of deposit.

Commercial Paper **Commercial paper** is a short-term, unsecured debt obligation of a corporation. About 1,000 corporations issue commercial paper in denominations usually starting at $25,000 and with maturities ranging from 1 to 6 months. Because of SEC restrictions, commercial paper's maturity is limited to 270 days or less. The high minimum investment puts commercial paper out of reach to many investors, although some banks and S&Ls may have a program that allows you to participate with smaller amounts in pooled weekly purchases. Commercial paper is also sold on a discount basis, and its issuers must have strong credit histories, but even so, they are not as safe as the Treasury. Thus, commercial paper rates are higher than T-bill rates. Investing on your own, you may not be able to have a reasonably diversified portfolio of commercial paper, but many money market mutual funds are buyers. Investing in them opens the market to you and allows you to earn the higher rates without taking considerable extra risk. There was approximately $455 billion of commercial paper outstanding at January 1, 1989.

Commercial paper and negotiable CDs have very high minimum investments, putting them out of reach for small investors.

Negotiable CDs **Negotiable CDs** are bank debt instruments sold to investors who negotiate both yield and maturity. They are also negotiable instruments; if you own one, you can sell it directly to someone else. This feature makes them different from the CDs previously discussed, and there are other important differences. The minimum denomination of a negotiable CD is $100,000, and maturities usually range from one month to one year. Their yields are also higher than T-bill rates and tend to be on a par with commercial paper rates. The high minimum investment obviously means that most of us will own negotiable CDs the same way we will own commercial paper; that is, through a pooling arrangement such as the money market mutual fund. Negotiable CDs had an average daily balance of about $538 billion at the beginning of 1989.

Money Market Mutual Funds

A **money market mutual fund (MMMF)** is a pooling arrangement; specifically, it is a fund that invests in short-term debt instruments, primarily of the type discussed above. The MMMF has been, and still is, the most popular of all mutual funds. After MMDAs were introduced in late 1982, the popularity of MMMFs fell sharply, but it has gradually returned as investors continuously seek higher yields or look for greater conveniences. There was an average daily investment of about $240 billion in MMMFs as of January 1, 1989.

By investing in MMMFs, you enjoy the higher yields of money market instruments that otherwise might be unavailable.

Characteristics of MMMFs   MMMFs are easy to establish. You usually do it directly with the fund rather than through a broker. You can find convenient listings of most funds, including addresses and phone numbers, in various issues of *Forbes* and *Money* magazines, who also evaluate fund performance. All funds have a minimum initial investment, which can range from $500 to over $10,000. Subsequent deposits can be much smaller, and you typically access your funds by writing a check, which usually also has a minimum amount requirement. The funds requiring larger initial investments often allow unlimited check-writing privileges that in effect make the account a NOW account.

MMMFs are exceptionally convenient, particularly if you also invest in other funds offered by the same family or group—for example, the Fidelity Family of funds or the Vanguard Group. The convenience arises because you can transfer cash balances among the individual funds within the family, usually at no cost (although the number of transfers might be limited). This is a distinct advantage for investors who move their balances from stocks to bonds to money markets, and so forth. Another advantage is that most transactions, including fund switching, can take place over the phone.

Varieties of MMMFs   There are different kinds of MMMFs, ranging from those that invest only in short-term Treasury securities to those investing in so-called "junk paper." This paper usually consists of commercial paper with a low quality rating or negotiable CDs issued by lesser-known banks. Some MMMFs invest in municipal bonds with short maturities. These provide tax-free income to investors, but their yields are usually two to three percentage points below MMMFs that invest in taxable securities. Nevertheless, if you have a high marginal tax rate they may provide a better after-tax return.

Not all MMMFs are the same; check their portfolio maturities and the types of instruments they hold.

The Safety Record of MMMFs   The MMMF industry points out that no MMMF has ever held a security that defaulted. Several faced an illiquidity crisis some years ago because they had overextended the maturity of their portfolio, but they were rescued by other MMMFs. True, the record has been excellent. But does this mean it will continue to be so in the future? If the trend continues to "junk," then investors must be very cautious. The situation is not unlike having a loaded gun in the house: the fact that it has never accidentally fired in no way lessens its potential danger. Since many people have invested so much of their total savings in MMMFs, it is vitally important to be aware of their risks. If you wish to be aggressive, you should at least consider diversifying among the aggressive funds, rather than investing in only one. The additional yield you can expect for being aggressive varies over time, but often is in the range of 0.5% to 0.75%. Actually, the single most important factor influencing the yields on MMMFs is the size of the management fee. Some funds have fees as low as 0.25% of assets, while others are as high as 1.5%. All things considered, you should search for a low-cost fund since it probably will offer a relatively high yield.

BORROWING AND LIQUIDITY MANAGEMENT

Generally, we think of investment borrowing as being undertaken to acquire long-term investments where, it is usually assumed, you will earn a higher rate than the rate of interest on the borrowed funds. However, if investors hold both short- and long-term investments, it is purely arbitrary to say they borrow to invest long, since they could just as easily sell the short-term investments and avoid borrowing altogether. We could, in fact, raise the issue that they really borrow to invest in short-term assets. The situation is illustrated in Exhibit 6.10.

Since interest rates on short-term loans are usually higher than interest rates on short-term investments, the more interesting question is why investors are willing to pay this differential. Why not forget the emergency reserve and use the funds to reduce any short-term debt we might be carrying, whether it was used to buy securities, to finance a new car, or for any other purpose? If an emergency does arise in the future, we can always borrow then, as we need the funds. However, many investors do not follow that approach, preferring instead to maintain rather permanent amounts of short-term debt.

Avoiding Future Borrowing

Borrowing *today* to keep short-term investments means you might avoid borrowing in the *future,* a course of action that would be dictated if an emergency

A. Traditional view often sees short-term borrowing
    financing long-term investments.

B. But many investors hold both short- and long-term
    investments; thus, short-term borrowing finances both.

C. This arrangement is often more desirable than
    converting short-term investments to long-term
    and holding little or no funds for an emergency.

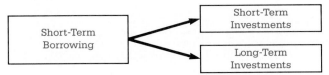

D. With no short-term investments, a future emergency
    would dictate selling long-term investments at possible
    losses or borrowing under unfavorable conditions.

EXHIBIT 6.10
Borrowing and investing

did arise and if you had sold your short-term investments. Waiting until an emergency arises is the riskier approach in two ways: First, you face a possibility that funds might not be available. Suppose you have a good income now and are viewed as a good credit risk. Borrowing is easy. But if the emergency in some way impairs your credit standing—you lose your job, for example—obtaining credit may become more difficult or more expensive. Second, even if your credit standing is unchanged, you face the risk of unknown future interest rates: they might be lower, but they could be higher. In either event, your risk is greater because you face a greater array of possible outcomes. The interest differential, then, is the price investors must pay if they wish to both invest in long-term assets and simultaneously reduce risk. Managed effectively, though, it may not be an exorbitant cost to pay.

Borrowing today avoids unknown loan rates and possible lack of credit availability in the future.

Frequently Used Sources of Investment Credit

Investors who use borrowed funds usually favor sources that are relatively cheap or convenient. The loan sources below are used frequently.

The Margin Account   The mechanics of a margin account were explained in Chapter 2. It was noted there that a margin account is easy to establish and that you typically pay the prime rate of interest plus one or two percentage points on amounts actually borrowed. Also, you need not borrow with a margin account; instead, you can put up the full value of securities purchased and retain borrowing power for later, if it is needed. Our attention below is on the leverage aspect of margin investing.

   Exhibit 6.11 illustrates a situation where an investor is considering borrowing $10,000 to invest in long-term securities. We assume she does not wish to sell her short-term securities to do so, although that would be a possibility. It

EXHIBIT 6.11
Leverage illustrated

	No Leverage	Leverage Profit	Leverage Loss
Amount invested in short-term assets	$10,000	$10,000	$10,000
Amount invested in long-term assets	-0-	10,000	10,000
Total invested in assets	$10,000	$20,000	$20,000
Less amount borrowed	-0-	10,000	10,000
Net invested capital	$10,000	$10,000	$10,000
Short-term return (8%)	$ 800	$ 800	$ 800
Long-term return ($+30\%$, -30%)	-0-	3,000	$-3,000$
Interest on $10,000 borrowed (12%)	-0-	$-1,200$	$-1,200$
Total return	$ 800	$ 2,600	$-3,400
Rate of return on invested capital	$+8\%$	$+26\%$	-34%

is also assumed the short-term assets will yield a certain 8% while the long-term investment could show a +30% return or a −30% return. If she doesn't use margin, her rate of return is simply 8%. If she margins, she can leverage the return on her invested capital to +26% if the +30% return is achieved on the long-term investment. However, if the −30% return occurs, leverage works the other way: now her portfolio return falls to a −34%. This analysis ignores taxes, which would dampen the differences somewhat, but it serves to show that leverage is a two-edged sword, cutting both for and against us.

A margin account is an easy source of credit, but it creates leverage.

Using Securities as Loan Collateral   The above example illustrates what takes place in a margin account with the broker acting as an intermediary. However, you can arrange your own loans by taking your securities to a bank and pledging them as collateral. You probably will pay the same interest, so why not use the broker and avoid the trouble? Indeed, most people do just that. But if you prefer holding your certificates rather than leaving them with the broker, using your securities as collateral might appeal to you.

Borrowing on Whole Life Insurance Policies   A whole life insurance policy may be the cheapest source of funds anywhere, particularly if you bought the policy some time ago. The policy will have loan values printed within it, making it possible to determine how much you might borrow. It also will specify a guaranteed borrowing rate that could be considerably below current market rates. If that's true, it makes virtually no sense to borrow anywhere else, assuming you have made up your mind to borrow. Don't be dissuaded by an insurance representative's arguments that you are robbing your beneficiaries. If that's true, any loan that must be repaid after your death is robbing your beneficiaries. The simple truth is that if you can borrow at a low rate, say 6%, it makes sense to do so.

A life insurance policy may be a low-cost source of credit, but don't invest in life insurance just because of its liquidity characteristics.

However, be careful with some new insurance policies that are being marketed as though they offer short-term liquidity. They also allow policyholders to borrow, and at rates that seem attractive. However, a policy loan then means that earnings on the policy fall from high market rates (the ones touted when the policies are promoted) to much smaller guaranteed rates.

In general, it is not advisable to buy life insurance specifically for its ability to provide liquidity. It simply does not accomplish that goal effectively. If you already have a policy with loan features, then carefully examine the policy in comparing it to other loan sources, if you are seeking a loan.

Borrowing from Retirement Plans   Borrowing from a retirement plan sounds almost as terrible as robbing beneficiaries. It isn't, unless you wish to assume the borrower takes the money and loses it in reckless abandon. Assuming contrarily that you are intelligent and not prone to childish behavior, why then borrow somewhere else at higher rates or, far worse, never establish a tax-deferred plan in the first place because the money might be needed in the future?

Pitfalls in Liquidity Management

Few investors question the wisdom of holding a portion of their portfolios in liquid assets, the kind that convert to cash readily and with no loss in value. Let interest rates rise, though, and it's amazing how quickly liquidity can be shunted aside in an effort to "capture" or "lock in" higher rates. While we are supposed to know better, the creative promotional hype of some financial institutions makes it hard to settle for low rates when much higher ones seem to be there for the taking. But are they? Below are some pitfalls you might want to consider before investing.

Noninsured Institutions Investing in these places to gain a slight additional yield is perhaps the gravest error you will ever make in short-term investing. S&L failures are now as common as corporate bankruptcies. Putting funds in a noninsured institution is courting danger, because the willingness, or even the capacity, of the federal government to bail out such institutions in the future is questionable. Handling the mess with insured S&Ls will strain even the government's resources.

Noninsured Deposits Some insured institutions recently have begun offering investments that might fool you into thinking they are insured savings deposits. They definitely are not. One form, called "subordinated capital notes," are more like junk bonds: long-term debt obligations with high yields but poor investor protections. Actually, they can be worse than junk bonds because there is no secondary market for them. This means you hold the notes until their maturities, which can be as long as twelve years.

Teaser Ads How would you like a 3-year CD paying 20%? If you see this type of ad, be sure to read the fine print. You can bet the 20% will apply for only a very short period of time, such as a month or even less. For the remaining time, the rate will be much lower, perhaps 8%. Another teaser is advertising high rates in large print and minimum deposit amounts—often in the $25,000 range—in minuscule print.

Mutual Funds with No Fees Some mutual funds have started advertising that they will waive management fees. This could be a good deal: research indicates that variability of returns among money market mutual funds depends considerably upon management fees; that is, better performing funds have low fees, and vice versa. With the new funds, however, the waiving may be a gimmick because the fund can start charging fees in the future. If money market funds appeal to you, consider investing only in those that have established a reputation for low fees. The Vanguard Prime Portfolio and the Kemper Money Market Fund are two such funds.

Net Cost Loans on Life Insurance Policies A big pitch with some insurance companies lately is that their policies offer everything, including easy access to your money through very low-cost policy loans. The so-called "net cost" procedure means that you pay, say, three percentage points over the policy's guaranteed earning rate. So, if the guaranteed rate is 5%, the borrowing rate is 8%. On the surface, that seems reasonable. Keep in mind, though, that you might have invested funds in another vehicle, such as a money market fund, and earned a substantially higher rate than 5%. Say you could have earned 10%; the true cost of the loan, then, is 13%. Clearly, there are other factors to consider in evaluating an insurance policy, but if you intend to use it for back-up liquidity, make sure you understand its effective rate of return. The high (nonguaranteed) rate—say, 12% for the above example—touted by the company applies only if you *don't* borrow. What good is it, then, if you use the policy for liquidity purposes?

Tax-deferred investing is one of the best techniques for accumulating wealth (see Chapter 20 for a discussion). If you are investing in an employer-provided 401(k) plan or a tax-deferred annuity, or if you have your own Keogh plan, you will have borrowing privileges. There are restrictions that you should understand before borrowing, but these are not particularly burdensome. By all means, ask your employer or your tax advisor for details before you undertake major debt obligations elsewhere.

Consumer Credit   While we don't usually associate consumer credit with investing, since both go on simultaneously with many investors, it would be a mistake to ignore it. Several observations seem particularly important.

First, consumer credit tends to be very expensive credit, and interest cannot be deducted for income tax purposes. Visa and MasterCard arrangements were charging over 20% interest in periods when the interest earned on short-term investments was around 8%. In this situation you would be better off trying to reduce the debt by selling short-term assets, or to look for alternative sources of debt.

Second, using credit simply as a shopping convenience and paying your monthly bill on a timely basis to avoid interest makes sense. In fact, it's like an interest-free loan for the amount of your average monthly charges. Surely, take the loan and invest it. With some cards, however, interest is charged from the day a purchase is made, which eliminates this advantage.

Use consumer credit only as a shopping convenience, not as a source of short-term funds.

SUMMARY

Liquid assets are held to undertake transactions, or to serve as emergency reserves or a store of value. Financial institutions offer many liquid assets to investors. Such institutions include commercial banks, savings and loans (S&Ls) and savings banks, credit unions, consumer banks, and stockbrokerage firms.

Accounts at financial institutions include checking and NOW accounts, and savings accounts, which may be passbook accounts, money market deposit accounts, and certificates of deposit. Financial institutions determine interest on savings accounts in many different ways. Liquid assets also include U.S. Treasury securities (bills and bonds, or notes with short maturities); U.S. Series EE and HH bonds; and non-Treasury-issued securities such as commercial paper, negotiable CDs, and money market mutual funds.

Liquidity management must consider the possibility of borrowing to meet liquidity needs. The advantage of holding both short-term assets and debt is that it avoids the possibility of borrowing in the future. Frequently used sources of credit are margin accounts, bank loans (using securities as collateral), whole life insurance policies, retirement plans, and consumer credit such as Visa and MasterCard.

KEY TERMS

Select the alternative that best identifies the key term.

1. liquidity management
2. emergency reserve
3. store of value
4. NOW account
5. passbook account
6. money market deposit accounts (MMDAs)
7. certificate of deposit (CD)
8. Treasury bills
9. U.S. Series EE bonds
10. U.S. Series HH bonds
11. commercial paper
12. negotiable CDs
13. money market mutual fund (MMMF)

a. negotiable short-term Treasury debt
b. negotiable short-term corporate debt
c. negotiable short-term bank debt
d. advisors recommend an amount equal to 3 to 6 times monthly expenses
e. non-negotiable Treasury debt issued to benefit small investors
f. how much liquidity, in what forms, and in what institutions
g. convenient, but offers lowest interest
h. acquired through an EE rollover
i. a checking account that pays interest
j. a savings account offering money market interest rates
k. a non-negotiable savings deposit with a given maturity
l. a pooling arrangement to invest in short-term instruments
m. reason for holding an asset

REVIEW QUESTIONS

1. Discuss what is meant by liquidity management. Include in your discussion the meaning of liquidity and the relationship between liquidity and asset return.
2. Explain three reasons why investors want to hold liquid assets. If your monthly expenditures are $3,000, about how much should you hold in an emergency fund? When would short-term investments be used as a temporary "parking place"?
3. Describe the five kinds of financial institutions discussed in this chapter. Explain whether it is worth your time to shop around if you are looking for one.
4. Identify the key characteristics of the following deposits: (a) checking, NOW, and super-NOW accounts, (b) passbook account, (c) money market deposit account (MMDA), and (d) certificate of deposit (CD).
5. Does it matter how often interest is compounded on a savings account? Explain.
6. Indicate four different methods savings institutions use to determine interest on a savings account. Indicate which is the best method for investors.
7. Identify the key characteristics of U.S Treasury bills, including a discussion of how you might purchase them.
8. Identify the key characteristics of U.S. Series EE bonds. What feature enhances their appeal to investors concerned about inflation and rising interest rates?
9. Explain commercial paper and negotiable CDs. Are these popular securities with small investors? Explain.

10. Discuss money market mutual funds, describing their characteristics, varieties, and safety record. Do you feel they are as safe as money market deposit accounts? Indicate your personal preference for one over the other, explaining the reason(s) for your choice.

11. If you examine balance sheets of many investors, you find that some have both long- and short-term investments and some form(s) of short-term debt, such as a margin account or installment loans. Is it correct then to argue that borrowed funds are used to acquire long-term investments? Discuss.

12. Can a margin account be used as a source of loan funds? Is this similar to borrowing from a bank, pledging securities as collateral? Explain.

13. Are life insurance policies a source of loan funds? Explain, discussing the implication of "robbing from your beneficiaries."

14. What form of borrowing "robs from your retirement?" Explain, indicating whether you feel this source of funds should be used.

15. Should consumer credit sources, such as Visa or MasterCard, ever be used? Explain.

PROBLEMS AND PROJECTS

1. Which is the better savings account: one offering a 12.25% rate compounded annually, or another offering a 12.0% rate compounded quarterly? Indicate the total accumulation with each account after 5 years, 10 years, and 40 years.

2. Tito Francola has a savings account that determines interest quarterly. It offers an 8% rate computed on an annual basis and determines interest quarterly. Qualifying balances for interest are based upon the minimum balance method. Activity in Tito's account last quarter was as follows:

Opening balance at day 1	$1,000
Deposit, 60 days after day 1	500
Withdrawal, 75 days after day 1	600
Balance at end of the quarter	900

Calculate Tito's interest and compare it to the amount he would have earned with other methods of determining interest: (a) day of deposit to day of withdrawal, (b) FIFO, and (c) LIFO.

3. Tom Lustie's investment portfolio now consists of $5,000 of short-term investments that yield about 10% a year. He is considering opening a margin account and using it to borrow $5,000 to invest in common stocks that he expects will appreciate 20% in value next year. He estimates his margin interest at 12% and does admit the stocks have an equal chance of declining 20% in value. Determine Tom's possible rates of return on his invested capital if he goes ahead with his plan. Compare your answers to his rate of return if he does not. What would you advise Tom to do? What would you do personally?

4. (Student Project) Obtain a current issue of The Wall Street Journal and find rates on the securities and deposit accounts discussed in this chapter. Compare them to the rates indicated in the boxed feature called "Where to Put Your Short-Term Funds." Discuss your comparisons.

5. (Student Project) Contact a Federal Reserve Bank in your area and ask for a tender

form for 13-week bills. You also can contact the U.S. Treasury Bureau of the Public Debt at 1–202–287–4113 for information.

6.   *(Student Project)*   Call the Series EE Bond Information Center at the number given in the text and obtain current rate information. Also, present an argument favoring investment in such bonds.

CASE ANALYSES

6.1 The Hamiltons Consider a Short-Term Portfolio

Melanie and Frank Hamilton are a professional couple with two young children. Their combined income is $72,000 a year, consisting mostly of salaries and dividends from their stock investments. The Hamiltons are avid investors and enjoy a stock and bond portfolio (about equally weighted) worth approximately $81,000; however, they have no short-term investments other than a checking account that has an average balance of around $800. Frank thinks short-term investments are not suitable for their goals, which consist primarily of an educational fund for their children and a retirement fund. Moreover, Frank argues that stocks can always be sold if a cash emergency arises.

Melanie disagrees. Her casual reading of investment literature suggests that most investment advisors recommend that some short-term investments be held all the time. Accordingly, she has prepared the following list of vehicles, along with current rates, to consider as possible additions to their portfolio. The Hamiltons have a very low risk tolerance with respect to achieving their major goals. Also, the Hamiltons do not have particularly good disability insurance, although they do have excellent life insurance coverage.

1.   U.S. Treasury bills (7.5%)
2.   U.S. Series EE bonds (6.5%)
3.   MMDA (8.0%)
4.   MMMF—low risk (8.5%)
5.   3-year CDs (9.5%)
6.   10-year CDs (10.5%)
7.   Commercial paper (8.75%)
8.   Negotiable CDs (9.0%)
9.   Money Market Life Insurance Policy (current rate of 11.0% but guaranteed rate of 4.5%; policy loans—up to a maximum of $10,000—are available at 7.5%, but policy then earns the guaranteed rate)

Questions

a.   Do you agree with Frank that short-term investments are not suitable for their investment goals? Explain.

b.   What portion, if any, of the Hamiltons' portfolio would you recommend be invested in short-term securities? Would you sell stocks, bonds, or both to rearrange the portfolio?

c. Select short-term securities for the Hamiltons, indicating a total investment and a breakdown of amounts to be invested in the vehicles you feel are appropriate.

Lucinda Mendoza is a young woman starting a legal career with a well-known law firm. Her professional activities have prevented her from giving much attention to investing, and her financial situation is a bit confused. Lucinda currently has $4,000 of U.S. Series EE bonds and $10,000 of common stocks. She also has borrowed $3,000 (the limit) on her life insurance policy (fixed 8% rate), $2,000 on her margin account (variable rate, currently 11%), and $2,000 on MasterCard (1.5% per month rate).

Lucinda has consulted with a college friend, Shirley Wosnanski, asking her advice. Shirley thinks Lucinda is foolish to pay so much interest each year and she suggests selling the Series EE bonds, and paying off as much debt as possible. While Shirley believes the bonds will yield 8% if Lucinda holds them ten more years, she also believes interest rates on Lucinda's debts will exceed this amount.

a. Do you agree with Shirley? If so, explain which debts you would reduce.
b. Regardless of your response to question *a*, suppose Lucinda increased the loan balance in her margin account to $4,000. However, she now is considering selling $4,000 of stocks to eliminate the broker's loan. Assuming the stocks might either increase by 20% or decrease by 20%, illustrate Lucinda's stock returns if she sells versus her returns if she does not.

6.2 Lucinda Mendoza Considers a Short-Term Investment Strategy

Questions

HELPFUL READING

Bittner, Jill. "Beware of 'Savings Accounts' Bearing Junk-Bond Yields." *The Wall Street Journal,* December 13, 1988, p. C1.

"Endless Dealing: U.S. Treasury Debt Is Increasingly Traded Globally and Nonstop." *The Wall Street Journal,* September 10, 1986, p. 1.

Langley, Monica. "Bank Ads Trumpet Interest Rates, but Keep the Real Yield Hidden." *The Wall Street Journal,* January 10, 1986, p. 17.

Liscio, John. "How To Buy a Treasury Bill." *Barron's,* January 16, 1989, p. 32.

"Managing Debt." *Money,* April 1987, pp. 90–170. (This is a series of six articles dealing with personal debt management.)

Schifrin, Matthew. "Beware of Bankers Bearing Shares." *Forbes,* December 26, 1988, pp. 41–43.

Slater, Karen. "Money Fund Levies Are a Vital Variable." *The Wall Street Journal,* March 31, 1989, p. C1.

Winkler, Matthew. "A CD Guaranteed to Beat Inflation Has Some Firms Aiming To Ape It." *The Wall Street Journal,* March 13, 1989, p. C1.

Yakov, Amihud, and Haim Mendelson. "Liquidity and Stock Returns." *Financial Analysts Journal,* March-April 1986.

CHAPTER SEVEN

Investing in Debt Instruments for the Long Term

CORPORATE BONDS

Bondholders' Rights

Special Bond Features

The Mechanics of Buying Corporate Bonds

U.S. TREASURY AND AGENCY ISSUES

Treasury Debt

Collateralized Treasury Receipts

Federal Agency Bonds

MUNICIPAL BONDS

The Income Tax Advantage

Kinds of Municipal Bonds

Default Risk in Municipal Bonds

BOXES

Pity the Poor Bondholder, Or a Lesson in Applied Financial Theory

If You See a Liability—Securitize It!

After you finish this chapter, you will be able to:

- understand the nature of a corporate bond, recognizing what rights you possess as a bondholder and how these rights are protected.

- see the various features of corporate bonds and read corporate bond quotations in the financial pages.

- understand the characteristics of Treasury bonds and notes and read their quotations in the financial pages.

- distinguish a collateralized trust receipt from an actual Treasury issue and determine whether a trust receipt is an appropriate investment for you.

- identify the key characteristics of federal agency debt and recognize how it differs from Treasury debt.

- calculate the income tax advantage of municipal bonds and evaluate them for investment suitability.

W hy invest in bonds? In some respects they are the worst of all possible worlds: they lack the potential for substantial capital appreciation that many common stocks offer; yet, as we saw in Chapters 4 and 5, they still involve considerably more risk than short-term debt instruments. So why not construct a portfolio of stocks and short-term investments and forget bonds altogether? In fact, many investors moved in that direction in the 1970s and early 1980s, as fluctuating interest rates put bond prices on a roller coaster and persistently increasing inflation drove their prices to all-time lows.

But, as the 1980s moved on, bonds made a remarkable recovery. Declining inflation and interest rates sent bond prices soaring. Undoubtedly, some investors turned to bonds in an effort to improve their portfolio return, which suffered when short-term yields fell. Perhaps they saw bonds as substitutes for short-term debt. You recall from Chapter 5, though, they are not substitutes. Your investment goal with bonds should be long-term in nature—not short-term—because bonds lack liquidity. But why not invest exclusively in higher-return common stocks if you are going for the long term? The answer, put simply, is that bonds are less risky. There is far less risk of losing most of your investment through default, and there is, overall, less price risk. Perhaps the most important advantage of a bond is that you know what your cash flows will be if you hold the bond until maturity. With common stock, you are never guaranteed future cash flows. Which would you rather have if you are investing to achieve a future goal that is extremely important to you? If you consider the alternatives, you will understand why bonds play a key role in investing.

This chapter explains important characteristics of both corporate and government bonds. The government bonds examined are those issued by the U.S. Treasury, the federal agencies, and state and local governments.

CORPORATE BONDS

A **corporate bond** is essentially a debt obligation (an IOU) of the corporation that issued it. When a business borrows large sums of money, corporate bonds are created in the process. The amount borrowed is far too large for any one creditor to handle, so the business cannot simply go to a bank or some other financial institution to take care of its needs. A bond, then, is a small fractional part of a large business loan the issuer has with many creditors, rather than just one. In this sense, a bond is very similar to a single share of common stock, except it probably has a much higher market price. Its more important differences, though, are legal in nature.

A corporate bond is a debt obligation—an IOU of the issuer.

Bondholders' Rights

If you own a bond, such as the one illustrated in Exhibit 7.1, you are a creditor. As such, you enjoy a far better legal position than does an owner of common stock. You also rank ahead of any preferred stockholders. The coupon rate of

EXHIBIT 7.1

NCR's corporate bond. (Courtesy of National Cash Register Company.)

interest—7.7% in Exhibit 7.1—is a legal obligation of the issuer and it must be paid. If it isn't, you can take legal action to force payment. Common or preferred stock dividends, on the other hand, are paid at the discretion of the company.

Additionally, the company is legally bound to redeem your bond at its face value, which is also called the bond principal and is almost always $1,000 for a corporate bond. And, if the issuer faces financial difficulties and is forced to sell assets in bankruptcy proceedings, any amount owed you for either interest or principal must be paid first before any payments are made to common and preferred stockholders. The right to receive interest and timely redemption of principal and the right to share first in asset distributions are basic bondholder rights. These are discussed in greater detail below.

The Bond Indenture   The **bond indenture** is a legal agreement between the issuer and the bondholders. It provides details about the basic bondholder rights, such as the coupon rate, when interest will be paid, how redemption will take place, and others. It also usually places restrictions on the issuer's future activities. These restrictions serve to strengthen the bondholders' position, and they include items such as: (1) a limitation on issuing future debt, (2) a limitation on paying dividends on common or preferred stock, and (3) a provision that prevents the company from selling fixed assets, merging with another company, or undertaking any activity that would materially change the nature of the business. These restrictions are extremely important in preserving the issuer's solvency.

> An indenture includes restrictions designed to strengthen the bond-holders' position.

Despite them, many issuers do fail and are forced into liquidation. If the company fails to pay interest or principal on a debt issue, it is in default. Most bond indentures will also require that a default on any other issue leads to default on the one under this specific indenture. Liquidation in bankruptcy seldom provides bondholders with a 100% recovery of their investments. Settlements are more likely to range from thirty to forty cents on the dollar, and often are less. Default risk was discussed in Chapter 5, but you should be mindful of it as we move through this chapter. If you buy low-rated bonds, you will carry more risk than with high-rated bonds. It is important to review a bond's rating in Moody's or Standard and Poor's before investing.

> Liquidation in bank-ruptcy seldom provides 100% recovery of a bond investment.

The Trustee   The issuer would find it impossible to have a separate contract with each bondholder. Instead, the indenture covers all bondholders. But who enforces the indenture on behalf of the bondholders? That is the function of the **trustee,** which is typically a large commercial bank. The trustee's primary function is to seek legal action if the issuer fails to meet the indenture's terms.

Mortgage Bonds   Corporations often pledge collateral to strengthen a bond issue. When this is done, the bond is called a **mortgage bond**. An announcement of a mortgage bond issue is shown in Exhibit 7.2. The corporation might choose this type of issue in an effort to get a lower interest rate, or simply out of necessity because it cannot borrow on the strength of its general credit standing. Collateral

New Issue / February 12, 1986

$150,000,000

Commonwealth Edison Company

First Mortgage 10½% Bonds, Series 56, due February 15, 2016

Price 99.50% and accrued interest from February 15, 1986

Morgan Stanley & Co. Incorporated	**Salomon Brothers Inc**
The First Boston Corporation	**Goldman, Sachs & Co.**
Merrill Lynch Capital Markets	**Prudential-Bache** Securities
Shearson Lehman Brothers Inc.	**Dean Witter Reynolds Inc.**

Bear, Stearns & Co. Inc.	**Alex. Brown & Sons** Incorporated	**Dillon, Read & Co. Inc.**
Donaldson, Lufkin & Jenrette Securities Corporation		**Drexel Burnham Lambert** Incorporated
E. F. Hutton & Company Inc.	**Kidder, Peabody & Co.** Incorporated	**Lazard Frères & Co.**
PaineWebber Incorporated		**L. F. Rothschild, Unterberg, Towbin, Inc.**
Smith Barney, Harris Upham & Co. Incorporated		**Wertheim & Co., Inc.**
William Blair & Company	**A. G. Edwards & Sons, Inc.**	**McDonald & Company** Securities, Inc.
Robert W. Baird & Co. Incorporated	**Blunt Ellis & Loewi** Incorporated	**Dain Bosworth** Incorporated
Piper, Jaffray & Hopwood Incorporated		**Prescott, Ball & Turben, Inc.**
Rodman & Renshaw, Inc.		**Stifel, Nicolaus & Company** Incorporated

EXHIBIT 7.2

Announcement of a mortgage bond issue appearing in *The Wall Street Journal.*
(Courtesy Commonwealth Edison Company.)

can consist of real estate, such as land, buildings, and factories, and personal property, including machinery, equipment, and anything else not permanently attached to buildings. While corporations of all kinds issue mortgage bonds, the public utility industry is unquestionably the largest issuer. This is partially explained by the fact that public utility property usually will hold its value for many years in the future, which may not be true of many other businesses.

A mortgage bond has collateral supporting it, while a debenture does not.

A bond that is not supported by collateral is called an unsecured bond, or a **debenture**. You will find a large number of both mortgage bonds and debentures outstanding. On the surface, a mortgage bond seems the safer of the two; after all, with specific collateral to support the loan, if the issuer goes into liquidation, any proceeds from the sale of the collateral must be used first to pay off the mortgage bonds. In general, they are safer, but not always. If the collateral is poor and the corporation has financial weaknesses, the bond's strength is diminished accordingly. You would be better off with debentures of a financially strong company rather than mortgage bonds issued by Fly-by-Night Airlines using its dilapidated hangars and World War II vintage aircraft as collateral.

Equipment Trust Certificates   A particular type of mortgage bond is called an **equipment trust certificate**. Such certificates are issued by companies that are financing transportation equipment, such as railroad cars, jet airplanes, and containers used on oceangoing and inland water vessels. In the past, this collateral was referred to as ''rolling stock,'' since the only equipment was railroad boxcars. Often, such items make excellent collateral: they are durable, can be taken over easily if the borrower defaults, and, because their construction is so standardized, they have a good resale market. Exhibit 7.3 shows an announcement of an equipment trust certificate issue.

Subordinated Debentures   As mentioned above, most indentures will restrict the corporation's future borrowing activities in an effort to protect the bondholders' position. Naturally, the more debt a corporation issues, the riskier it is. Without such a provision, bondholders would be in serious trouble whenever the issuer decided it needed more capital.

A subordinated debenture gives its claim on assets to another class of debtholders.

To overcome the restriction against future borrowing, the indenture might allow the corporation to sell additional bonds if the position of the new bondholders is subordinated to (made inferior to) the position of the existing bondholders. The additional bonds issued under such a condition are called **subordinated debentures**. (It should be noted that a bond issue also can be subordinated to other debt claims, such as commercial paper.) The investor's position is materially weakened with this type of bond. Exhibit 7.4 shows how subordination works. The corporation has two bond issues outstanding: the debentures and the subordinated debentures. Each has total principal of $4 million, and there are $2 million of general creditor claims. If the company's assets are sold for $6 million, the debentures would be paid in full because they are entitled to their own share plus the subordinated debentures' share. In contrast,

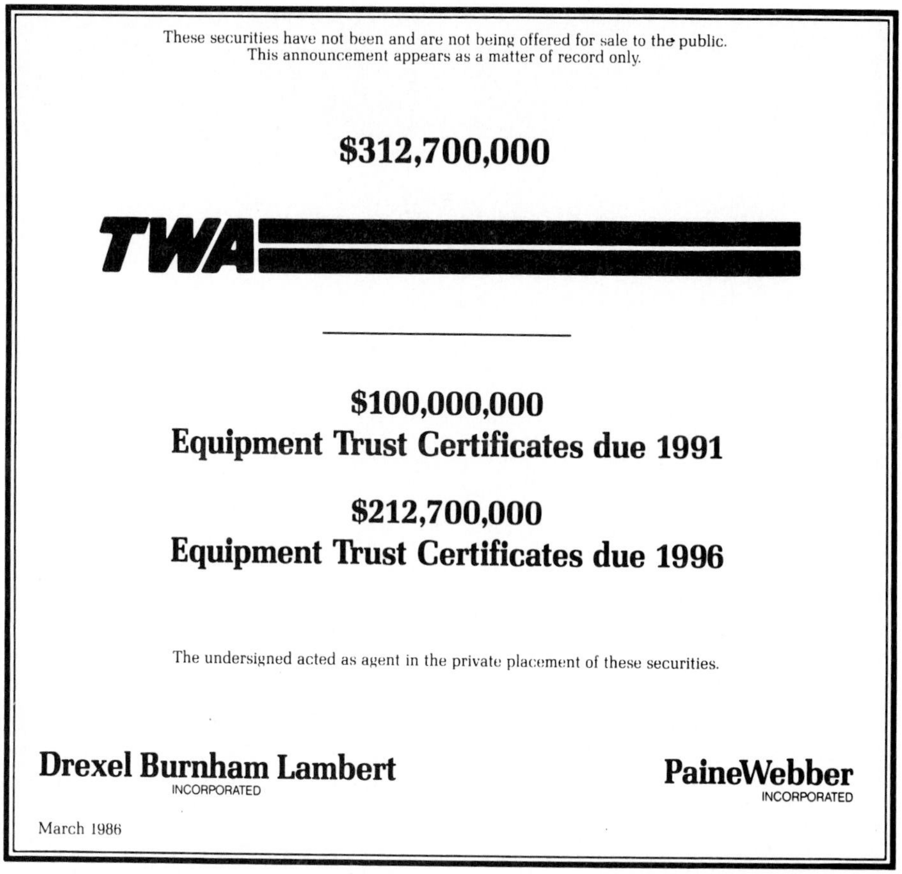

These securities have not been and are not being offered for sale to the public.
This announcement appears as a matter of record only.

$312,700,000

TWA

$100,000,000
Equipment Trust Certificates due 1991

$212,700,000
Equipment Trust Certificates due 1996

The undersigned acted as agent in the private placement of these securities.

Drexel Burnham Lambert
INCORPORATED

PaineWebber
INCORPORATED

March 1986

EXHIBIT 7.3
Announcement of an
equipment trust
certificate issue
appearing in *The Wall
Street Journal*.
(Courtesy TWA.)

the subordinated debenture holders receive only $800,000, a loss of $3.2 million, or $0.80 on each $1.00.

Because of the greater potential default risk, yields on subordinated debentures are higher than those on mortgage bonds and debentures, all other things held constant. Indeed, the lower-quality issues (referred to as ''junk'') often have yields rivaling those on common stocks. Some analysts feel that such bonds are actually more closely related to equity than to debt. Their market prices, for example, are strongly influenced by events affecting the issuers as well as by changes in market rates of interest. This is reasonable, since any factor that strengthens or weakens an issuer will clearly help or hurt the prospect of receiving the subordinated debentures' promised interest payments and redemptions.

Subordinated debentures' prices are greatly influenced by events that strengthen or weaken the issuers.

Payment of Interest   All corporate bonds issued today are **registered bonds,** which means the bonds are registered in the name of their owners. If you wish, you can receive a bond certificate such as the one shown in Exhibit 7.1. Interest

EXHIBIT 7.4
How subordination
works

	Debt Outstanding			
	Debentures	Subordinated Debentures	General Creditors	Total Debt
Amount	$4,000,000	$4,000,000	$2,000,000	$10,000,000
Percent of total	40%	40%	20%	100%
Percents applied to amount received from sale of assets	$2,400,000	$2,400,000	$1,200,000	$ 6,000,000
Subordination allocation	+ 1,600,000	− 1,600,000		
Final distribution	$4,000,000	$ 800,000	$1,200,000	$ 6,000,000

is mailed to you, usually every six months. In the past, many corporate bonds were **bearer bonds**. These bonds were owned directly, rather than in certificate form, and ownership was transferred by simply exchanging the bonds with someone else. To receive interest, you clipped an appropriate coupon attached to the bond and presented it to the bank acting as trustee. Corporate bearer bonds are no longer issued since the Internal Revenue Service's ruling that interest is subject to withholding; however, many are still in existence and will remain outstanding until their eventual redemption.

We noted before that bond interest payments are a legal liability of the issuer. However, there is one exception: an **income bond** pays interest only if the issuer has sufficient earnings to make such payments. Income bonds are seldom issued by corporations except when reorganizations are brought about by financial difficulties. A type of income bond called a revenue bond is issued frequently by municipalities. Revenue bonds are discussed later in this chapter.

Another unique bond, with respect to interest payments, is a payment-in-kind bond, called a **PIK bond**. Interest from this bond may not be paid in cash; rather, the issuer has the option of paying cash or paying in additional bonds. For example, suppose a PIK issue has a 15% annual coupon rate and semiannual interest is due. The company can choose to pay the $75 in cash, or it can choose to issue 0.075 of an additional bond. Typically, the PIK interest period is for a limited number of years (usually five to ten), after which cash interest is then paid. These bonds have been issued in buyout situations, such as the RJR Nabisco leveraged buyout in 1989. While the present number of issues is rather small, both PIK bonds and PIK preferred stock have grown in popularity and more are likely to be issued in the future. However, they present certain risks to investors that are not clearly understood at this time. For one thing, an issuer can be expected to exercise the payment option to its own advantage, not to the investor's. So, if

Interest on a PIK bond can be paid in cash or in additional bonds.

interest rates rise, interest will be paid in additional bonds; and if rates fall, interest will be paid in cash. While yields are exceptionally high, caution is necessary until a performance history develops.

Redemption Provisions   All bonds issued in the United States have finite maturities; that is, issuers are obligated to redeem them. (Interestingly, since the Napoleonic Wars, Great Britain has issued bonds, called consols, that never mature.) However, since maturity is often so far in the future, bond investors are rightfully concerned about the issuer's ability to make good on the redemption promise. To safeguard their interest, some bond issues require a **sinking fund,** which means the corporation must set aside funds (usually with the trustee) for the exclusive use of redeeming the bonds. This is done by calling (this term will be explained shortly) a portion of the bonds each year, or by buying them in the secondary market. Also, some bond issues are divided into a series of redemption dates, in which case retirement is called **serial redemption.**

A sinking fund strengthens an issue by providing for its redemption.

It is important to know that an issuer's liability to pay interest ceases once a bond is called for redemption. If you fail to offer a called bond, you cannot collect any interest after the call date, although the issuer is obligated to pay the principal. If you delay for a long period of time, the loss of interest could be substantial. Clearly, bond investors must watch serial redemptions very closely, both for corporate and municipal bonds.

Special Bond Features

The supply of and the demand for bonds are in a constant state of flux. Very often, to attract investors, bond issuers must add certain features, called sweeteners, to make the bonds more saleable. At other times, an issuer's market exists, and sellers then take away the sweeteners or add features that are of greater benefit to them. Let us see what some of these sweeteners and features are.

Convertibility   A **convertible bond** is one that can be converted into shares of the common stock of the issuing corporation. Another type of convertible bond that is used very infrequently is one that converts into the common stock of another company. For example, General Cinema Corporation has a bond issue that converts into the common stock of RJR Nabisco. A holder of this bond presents it to General Cinema, which makes the exchange from shares of RJR Nabisco that it owns. An announcement of a conventional convertible issue appears in Exhibit 7.5. (You might notice this issue is also a subordinated debenture; most convertibles are.) The convertible feature is sometimes viewed as the ultimate sweetener because you enjoy the safety and high yield of a bond while simultaneously having a stake in the company's future growth. But you pay for this sweetener, as we shall see in more detail in Chapter 12. For now, though, notice the Porex bond offers a mere 7% coupon rate, while the Commonwealth Edison mortgage bond shown in Exhibit 7.2 offers a 10.5% rate. The convertible feature on the Porex is not cheap.

A convertible bond converts into shares of the issuer's common stock.

This announcement is neither an offer to sell nor a solicitation of an offer to buy these securities.
The offer is made only by the Prospectus.

$50,000,000

Porex Technologies Corp.

7% Convertible Senior Subordinated Debentures due February 15, 1998
(Interest payable February 15 and August 15)

Price 100%
plus accrued interest from February 15, 1986

Copies of the Prospectus are obtainable in any State from the undersigned
and such other dealers as may lawfully offer these securities in such State.

Drexel Burnham Lambert
INCORPORATED

February 12, 1986

A floating rate bond
does not have a fixed
coupon rate.

Floating Rate Bonds   A **floating rate bond** is one that has its periodic interest payments indexed to some broad market interest-rate index. As the rate on this index goes up or down, so do the interest payments on the floating rate bond. As you can see, a bond such as this will protect you against interest-rate risk. Most of these bonds have been issued by commercial banks and other kinds of financial institutions, although some industrial concerns have also issued them. On balance, they have not been exceptionally popular with investors, probably because their yields are not exceptionally generous. Normally, yields are set at one to two percentage points above the 90-day Treasury bill rate, which is a rather modest premium for undertaking the potential default risk. The slowing-down of inflation has reduced further the public's interest in the protection offered by floaters, but if prices and interest rates heat up again, they may regain popularity.

Put Bonds   A **put bond** is one that allows the holder to sell ("put") the bond back to the issuer at a set price. In other words, you have a guaranteed redemption price that you can exercise any time. Puts of this sort are most popular in municipal bond issues, although nongovernmental issuers have also used them. The put option again eliminates interest-rate risk. If rates rise, forcing down bond prices, you can avoid a loss by exercising your put right; in effect, you "bail out." Unfortunately, a sweetener this good also comes with a price, which is a substantially reduced yield. Investors, then, must determine if they are any better off owning an instrument such as this versus simply owning short-term instruments. Most corporate issuers are not fond of put bonds because they disrupt financing operations. Corporate treasurers must consider the possibility of being forced to redeem a bond issue through puts, most likely at a time when they would be forced to borrow at increasingly higher interest rates.

A new kind of put was introduced into bond indentures in 1989 as a result of an upheaval in the corporate bond market brought about by the takeover movement. The new put, called a **super poison put,** forces a company to redeem a bond issue in the event of a buyout, takeover, or other massive recapitalization. Bondholder fears motivating the new put were well founded. A number of takeovers around that time led to substantial declines in the market values of existing bonds because the takeovers relied so heavily on additional debt. Unfortunately, there were no provisions in existing indentures prohibiting shareholders from selling their shares to other buyers, who purchased them almost entirely with borrowed funds. The situation was so bad that a new form of risk was introduced into the investment literature—**event risk**. This risk refers to the potential weakening of current bondholder claims by virtue of a takeover or other recapitalization. The super poison put is designed to protect bondholders from event risk.

A super poison put is designed to deal with event risk, which arises from buyouts or other capital restructurings.

The Right to Call   Most corporate bond issues give the issuer the **right to call** the bonds for an early redemption. Whereas the put feature benefited bondhold- ers, the call feature benefits the issuer. Why do issuers want the call option? Very simple: it gives them greater flexibility in future financing. For example, a corporation may have issued 20-year bonds at 16% interest in 1986. Suppose the total issue was for $20 million. This means the corporation must pay $3.2 million each year in bond interest. Now it's 1990, and 16-year bonds of the same quality are yielding only 12%. The company would clearly benefit—to the tune of $800,000 each year—if it would issue new bonds and use the proceeds to retire the old bond issue. This is called refunding, and it's an ongoing function in most large corporations.

Calls benefit bond issu- ers, not investors.

If a call benefits the issuer, it obviously works against the investor. You may have purchased the 16% bond and then were looking for $160 interest each year for the next 20 years. Now you find the bond being taken away from you. Because this is undesirable, bonds with call features typically have a **call premium** for some time after the issuance. For example, the above bond might be callable at $1,100 for 5 years after issuance, the $100 being a premium you receive for an early redemption. If you buy a bond that is selling at a price above its call value, you must consider the risk that a call will take place. If you assume the market price quickly adjusts to the call price, you will take a capital loss that could exceed the call premium. It is dangerous to pay more than the call price, even though some issuers seldom exercise their calls.

Pity the Poor Bondholder, Or a Lesson in Applied Financial Theory

Most people have little sympathy for bondholders, who are usually professional money managers who should know what they're doing. That's true, but keep in mind the pros aren't buying bonds for their own portfolios; on the contrary, they manage other people's money, much of it in retirement and other benefit plans. So, if they take a hit, it is our lifestyles—not theirs—that stand to suffer. And, there have been plenty of hits lately.

The big ones have risen from the corporate takeover binge. When the massive RJR Nabisco leveraged buyout was announced, the company's existing bonds (about $5.4 billion) declined almost 20%. Other companies, such as Kroger and Quantum Chemical, accomplished the same end by thwarting takeover attempts; their defense was to pay a massive cash dividend. Either situation leads to considerably greater debt loads and, naturally, greater risk to existing debt holders. The situation was so bad after the RJR debacle that new corporate bond offerings virtually disappeared, and companies needing funds were forced to issue much shorter-term securities. How long the market will stay in a shell-shocked state is anybody's guess.

Hard-up issuers are being forced to consider new restrictive covenants in their bond indentures. A recent addition is the super poison put, which gives bondholders the right to recover their initial investments if the company is taken over, merged, or recapitalized. Companies such as Grumman Corporation and Becton-Dickinson have taken this route. Investors are coping with the situation in several ways. One is to identify potential takeovers in advance, and then avoid their bonds. Another is to hedge the bond investment by also buying an issuer's common stock. Theoretically, a hit on the bonds should be offset by a profit on the stock.

Interestingly, finance academicians have long theorized the notion that common stockholders have an incentive to create very high risk levels in an effort to achieve high profit levels. If things work out, they take most of the gain; and if they don't, they leave bondholders holding the bag. It looks as though some financial entrepreneurs are putting the theory to good practice.

The Mechanics of Buying Corporate Bonds

Most corporate bonds can be purchased as easily as you buy common stocks. There is an active secondary market for bonds, although many issues are thinly traded, meaning they have very little trading volume. Such issues tend to be more sensitive to changes in demand and supply and usually are more price-volatile. Bonds are traded on the New York Bond Exchange (part of the New York Stock Exchange), the American Bond Exchange (part of the Amex), and the over-the-counter market. By far the largest volume of bond trading is done in the OTC market, since all governmental issues and many corporate issues are traded there.

Bonds can be purchased with margin.

Bonds can be owned in a margin account and used as collateral for a broker's loan, just as you might use stocks for that purpose. In fact, the margin requirement for some bonds may be less than it is for stocks. You should ask your broker for details and, of course, also determine his or her commissions. Before investing in corporate bonds, you should understand their price quotations.

Reading Corporate Bond Quotations   Bond prices, along with other informa-tion, are reported in the financial pages of many newspapers, local and national. *The Wall Street Journal,* of course, reports information daily on bonds traded on the New York and American exchanges. Exhibit 7.6 shows two typical listings. (The NCR bond is the same one illustrated in Exhibit 7.1.)

Corporate bond prices are reported in the financial pages of many newspapers. Typical listings and explana-tions are shown below.

Bond			Cur Yld	Vol	High	Low	Close	Net Chg
NWA	7½	10	cv.	24	104	103¾	104	− ½
NCash	7.7s	94	8.3	7	92¼	92¼	92¼	+ 1⅝
(1)	(2)	(3)	(4)	(5)	(6)	(7)	(8)	(9)

1. Name of the issuer: *NCash* is an abbreviation for National Cash Register Company. This company has changed its name and is now known as NCR.
2. Coupon rate of interest: *7.7s* tells us the bond pays $77 a year interest, which is 0.077 × $1,000 (the face value of the bond).
3. The year the bond matures: NCR's bond matures in 1994.
4. *Cur Yld* means the bond's current yield: NCR's current yield of 8.3% is determined by dividing the annual interest of $77 by the bond's closing price of $922.50. The symbol *cv.* in the Cur Yld column tells us the bond is a convertible, and current yields are not calculated for convertibles. The NWA bond is a convert-ible.
5. *Vol* means the number of bonds traded: seven NCR bonds traded on the day being reported.
6. *High* is the highest price the bond traded at during the day: NCR's highest price is 92¼. However, this reported price is one-tenth the actual price; so, to get the actual price, you must multiply the reported price by ten:

$$\text{actual price} = 10 \times \text{reported price}$$
$$= 10 \times 92¼$$
$$= 10 \times 92.25$$
$$= 922.50$$

7. *Low* is the lowest price during the day: NCR's lowest price is the same as the highest price, $922.50.
8. *Close* is the last price of the day: NCR's is again $922.50.
9. *Net Chg* means the difference between the closing price of the day being reported and the closing price of the previous day: NCR's price increased (+) by 1⅝, which means the price was up $16.25 (10 × 1⅝ = 10 × 1.625 = 16.25) for the day. The NWA bond was down $5.00 (10 × 0.5) for the day.

EXHIBIT 7.6
Reading corporate bond quotations

Exhibit 7.6 requires little elaboration, but you might note the current yield calculation is the same one explained in Chapter 5. We indicated there that current yield is often not the most appropriate yield measurement and that yield to maturity, YTM, should also be considered in evaluating a potential bond purchase. Using a financial calculator to find YTM, we can determine NCR's is 9.08%. There were eight years (assumed) remaining to maturity when the calculation was made (in early 1986). As you see, this is somewhat higher than the current yield of 8.3%.

Corporate Bond Commissions and Spreads   Most major brokerage houses charge corporate bond commissions on a sliding scale on which the commission per bond declines as more bonds are purchased. The scale below is typical:

Number of Bonds Purchased	Commission
First 5 bonds, or $5,000 of par value	$10 per bond, or per $1,000 of par value
Next 20 bonds, or $20,000 of par value	$7.50 per bond, or per $1,000 of par value
Amounts above 25 bonds, or $25,000 of par value	$5 per bond, or per $1,000 of par value

If you purchased 27 bonds, the commission would be $210 [(5 × $10) + (20 × $7.50) + (2 × $5) = $50 + $150 + $10 = $210]. Assuming you paid $1,000 for each bond would make the commission percentage equal to 0.7% ($210/$27,000), which is relatively inexpensive. However, you should determine if there is a minimum commission per transaction. Discount brokers often charge a minimum that is usually no less than $25. A purchase of only one bond, then, would involve a 2.5% ($25/$1,000) commission rate in this case.

Bond commissions are reasonable, but be careful of spreads.

While commissions are reasonable, you also pay a spread for bonds purchased in the over-the-counter market, where about 90% of all bond trading occurs. The spread is the difference between the bid and asked prices, and since many bonds are thinly traded, spreads can be relatively large. In some cases they can be as much as $50 a bond, although $10 to $20 spreads are more common. Even these smaller amounts, though, add substantially to transactions costs and make frequent bond trading an expensive activity.

U.S. TREASURY AND AGENCY ISSUES

The federal government, through the Treasury and its various agencies, issues a considerable amount of debt, as Exhibit 7.7 shows. There is a strong demand for government debt because it is considered the safest to hold. Treasury bills were explained in the previous chapter; our attention now is on Treasury notes and bonds. Notes and bonds are similar in that each has a coupon rate of interest and pays interest semiannually. They differ in that notes have maturities of two to ten

	End-of-Year Balances (Billions)		
	1986	1987	1988
Treasury debt:			
Bills	$ 426.7	$ 389.5	$ 414.0
Notes	927.5	1,037.9	1,083.6
Bonds	249.8	282.5	308.9
Total	$1,604.0	$1,709.9	$1,806.5
Federally sponsored agency debt:			
Federal Home Loan Banks	$ 88.9	$115.7	$135.8
Federal Home Loan Mortgage Corporation	13.6	17.6	18.4
Federal National Mortgage Association	93.6	97.1	106.0
Farm Credit Banks	62.5	55.3	53.8
Student Loan Marketing Association	12.7	16.5	20.1
Total	$271.2	$302.2	$334.1

EXHIBIT 7.7
U.S. Treasury and federal agency debt outstanding

SOURCE: *Federal Reserve Bulletin*, May, 1989.

years, while bonds have maturities greater than ten years. Of course, these are maturities at the time of issuance. Since many bonds and notes were issued in the past and are in the process of maturing, you can buy them in the secondary market to achieve practically any maturity you wish. We will discuss important aspects of government debt in the sections below.

Treasury Debt

As we indicated in the previous chapter, Treasury debt is considered the safest of all debt and, in fact, is as safe as currency since it is also backed by the full faith and credit of the U.S. government. While some cynics might regard such faith as ill-founded, it has served us well in the past. In addition, if the Treasury ever defaults on its debt, few other investments will be worth holding. Gold or other tangibles, perhaps, but even they aren't sure bets if the federal government is bankrupt.

One advantage of investing in Treasury securities is that interest is exempt from state and local income taxes. If you live in an area with high local taxes, this advantage will not be trivial. For example, suppose the local tax has a marginal rate of 10% and you have a 33% marginal federal rate. Assume further that you could earn 10% on a Treasury bond and 12% on a corporate. The pre-tax difference is two percentage points but, as Exhibit 7.8 shows, the after-tax difference is only 0.78% (7.48% − 6.70%). The added risk with the corporate may not be worth a spread as small as this; thus, you should consider both your federal and local income tax situations in deciding between treasuries and corporates.

Interest on Treasury debt is free of state and local taxes.

Reading Quotations on Treasuries With over $900 billion of Treasury notes and bonds outstanding, investors have a wide array of coupon rates and

EXHIBIT 7.8
Comparing after-tax
returns of Treasury and
corporate bonds

	Treasury Bond	Corporate Bond
Assumed amount invested	$ 1,000	$ 1,000
Pretax interest earned (10%, 12%)	100.00	120.00
State and local income tax (10% rate)	-0-	− 8.31*
Federal income tax (33% rate)	− 33.00	− 36.86*
After-tax return	$ 67.00	$ 74.83
After-tax rate of return	6.70%	7.48%

*State and local taxes can be deducted in determining the federal tax liability and federal taxes can be deducted in determining the state and local tax liability. If L = the local tax liability and F = the federal tax liability, we then have the following equations:

$$L = .10 (120 − F) \quad \text{and} \quad F = .33 (120 − L)$$

Solving,

$$L = .10 [120 − .33(120 − L)]$$
$$L = .10 [120.00 − 39.60 + .33L]$$
$$L = 12.00 − 3.96 + .033L$$
$$.967L = 8.04$$
$$L = 8.314$$
$$F = .33(120.000 − 8.314) = .33(116.686) = 36.856$$

maturities to consider. Information on price and yield to maturity is reported in the financial pages of many newspapers in the format shown in Exhibit 7.9. The reported information is similar to that of corporate bonds, except fractional parts are in thirty-seconds rather than in eighths. The decimal point in front of the fractional part is a bit confusing to the first-time reader: you automatically assume the quote is in decimals, which it is not. You should also notice that yield to maturity is reported, rather than current yield as in the case of corporate bonds. As mentioned before, yield to maturity is the more useful yield figure. Having it readily available makes the process of evaluating specific bonds much simpler.

Buying Treasury Bonds   Treasury bonds can be purchased through your broker or directly from a Federal Reserve Bank. The latter approach saves commissions but does take some effort. Purchases can be handled through the mail, and if you wish to buy any Treasury security in this fashion, you can begin with a call to the Federal Reserve Bank closest to you, or you can write the Bureau of the Public Debt, Department F, Washington, DC 20239–0001, for more information.

Collateralized Treasury Receipts

In the early 1980s a new Treasury security appeared on the scene—the **collateralized Treasury receipt** (called **CAT,** for short). Actually, this wasn't a new Treasury security at all; in reality, it was simply a trust receipt that gave its holder an ownership right to a fractional interest in a pool of "stripped" Treasury securities. This definition requires further elaboration.

Cats and TIGRs are collateralized Treasury receipts.

EXHIBIT 7.9

A sample listing of Treasury notes and bonds at early February, 1986

Rate	Mat.	Date		Bid	Asked	Bid Chg.	Yld.
13¾s	1992	May	n	111.22	111.26	+.08	9.17
8s	1994	July	n	95.10	95.14	+.16	9.12
10¾s	2003	May		112.03	112.09	+.15	9.17
(1)	(2)		(3)	(4)	(5)	(6)	(7)

1. *Rate* refers to coupon rate. The third bond has a coupon rate of 10¾% (10.75%).
2. *Mat.* and *date* refer to the year and month of the bond's maturity. The third bond doesn't mature until May, 2003.
3. The symbol *n* indicates the instrument is a note rather than a bond. The first two instruments are notes; the third is a bond. It is common practice to refer to both bonds and notes as bonds.
4. *Bid* is the highest price bond dealers were offering to buy the bond. Fractional prices are quoted in 32nds of $10; thus, the third bond's fractional price of .03 means $\frac{3}{32}$ of $10, or $0.9375. To find the price per $1,000 of par value, multiply the whole number by 10 and add the fractional part. Thus, 10 × 111.22 = $1,120; $1,120 + $0.9375 = $1,120.9375.
5. *Ask* is the lowest price dealers were accepting. The third bond's ask price was 112.09, or $1,122.8125.
6. *Bid Chg.* shows the difference in the bid price between the day of the quotation and the previous day. So, the third bond was up $\frac{15}{32}$ (.46875) of $10, or $4.6875 per $1,000 par value.
7. *Yld.* means yield to maturity. The third bond has a yield to maturity of 9.17%.

How Are Collateralized Trust Receipts Created? To create the instrument, a large brokerage house such as Merrill Lynch purchases a huge portfolio of Treasury securities with widely varying maturities. Combining both redemptions and interest payments, the brokerage house creates pools with varying maturities. Exhibit 7.10 shows an excerpt from a Merrill Lynch announcement for its collateralized receipts, which it calls TIGRs (Treasury investment growth receipts). These securities were issued around November of 1983, and notice that you could have bought some to mature as early as February 15, 1984, or as late as August 15, 2013. In total, there were 50 different pools of serial TIGRs with 50 different maturities: a pool matured each February 15 and August 15, beginning in 1984 and ending in 2008. But keep in mind that you actually buy a trust receipt to the underlying Treasury securities and their related interest payments; you don't buy the Treasury securities themselves.

How Safe Are CATs and TIGRs? Since these instruments are not actually Treasury securities, are they as safe as Treasury securities? The consensus seems to be they are "about as safe," but not "just as safe." Since the Treasury securities and the related interest payments are held in a trust, CATs are removed from any risk associated with the originator (Merrill Lynch, for example). The originator can go into bankruptcy and the trust is unaffected. Nevertheless, there

CATs and TIGRs are considered very safe, but they are not backed by the Treasury.

EXHIBIT 7.10
Excerpt from an announcement of TIGRs appearing in *The Wall Street Journal.*
(Courtesy Merrill Lynch.)

Maturity Date	Aggregate Face Amount (in millions)	INITIAL PRICES Price as % of Face Amount(1)	Yield to Maturity(2)	Minimum Denominations Face Amount	Rounded Price(1)
		Serial TIGR's			
February 15, 1984	$ 30.0	98.056%	9.60%	$3,000	$2,942
August 15, 1984	30.0	93.025	10.50	3,000	2,791
February 15, 1985	30.0	88.081	10.80	3,000	2,642
August 15, 1985	30.0	83.434	10.90	3,000	2,503
February 15, 1986	30.0	78.463	11.30	3,000	2,354
August 15, 1986	30.0	74.172	11.35	3,000	2,225
February 15, 1987	30.0	69.870	11.50	3,000	2,096
February 15, 2007	30.0	7.801	11.30	12,000	936
August 15, 2007	30.0	7.384	11.30	12,000	886
February 15, 2008	30.0	7.151	11.20	12,000	858
August 15, 2008	30.0	6.772	11.20	12,000	813
	1,500.0				
		Callable TIGR's			
August 15, 2013	800.0	4.729	10.90	40,000	1,892
	$2,300.0				

(1) Plus accrued amortization, if any, of original issue discount from December 1, 1983 to date of delivery.
(2) Compounded on a semiannual basis.

is a trustee who is responsible for administering the trust. This trustee is not the U.S. Treasury: he, she, or they are mere mortals capable of errors and fraud. True, this is a minor and probably insignificant factor to consider. But if it would bother you to know your money is not actually in the hands of the Treasury, then the above information is relevant.

Why Are CATs and TIGRs So Popular?   The collateralized trust receipt has been called the most imaginative security ever created. Investors—large and small—bought them so rapidly that originators found it difficult to form pools quickly enough to meet demand. Unquestionably, many investors bought them without ever understanding exactly what they were buying. Some thought they were investing in a security that had no risk—default or interest-rate risk—whatsoever. Brokerage firms promoted them extensively, calling attention to their yield and safety but minimizing potential risks. Some investors actually believed they were buying a money market fund that invested in government securities.

CATs and TIGRs are popular because of their zero coupon form.

The main reason for such popularity can be found in two words—zero coupon. The collateralized trust receipt is a zero coupon instrument. As we saw in Chapter 5, a big advantage of a zero is that you avoid the problem of reinvesting the periodic interest you receive on conventional bonds. This makes them ideal instruments for locking in future cash flows. Imagine that you are investing for your retirement and then consider how useful the TIGRs shown in Exhibit 7.10 would be in your planning. You can buy them to mature in any year you choose, but you should remember from Chapter 5 that zeros have much greater interest rate risk than do conventional bonds, for a given maturity. As an exercise, you might refer back to Chapter 5 and evaluate the TIGR in Exhibit 7.10 that matures on August 15, 2008, and is priced at $67.72 per $1,000 of redemption value. Your analysis should show that it is hardly a money market instrument!

Two final comments on CATs and TIGRs: First, the IRS gives them an unfavorable tax treatment. You must accrue interest each year and report it as taxable income even though you don't actually receive it. While this tax treatment appears as a major disadvantage, it is not if you own the CATs in an IRA where your tax is deferred. Surely, many investors hold them in this form. If you don't, it makes more sense to own the Treasury securities outright. You would pay the same amount of tax on the earned interest, but since you actually receive the interest, your after-tax rate of return over the security's life would be greater. Second, if you are considering buying a new issue, determine the originator's spread, commissions, and other costs. These often are quite high in relation to the amount of funds invested, and they are deductible immediately from the initial investment. If you hold the bonds for only a short period of time, you might be surprised to find that your return is substantially less than what might have been expected, based upon returns of the underlying Treasury bonds.

Federal Agency Bonds

A **federal agency bond** is a bond issued by an agency of the federal government. To carry out its objectives, the federal government has many separate agencies, some of which become involved directly and indirectly in various financing arrangements. Such financing creates agency bonds. An announcement of an agency bond is shown in Exhibit 7.11. Agency bonds are also backed by the full faith and credit of the Treasury (with the exception of most passthrough securities, which will be explained shortly). Since the yield on agency debt is slightly higher than the yield on Treasury debt, you might improve your portfolio return by making a substitution, either partially or completely. However, you should consider the items below before investing in agency debt.

Characteristics of Agency Debt With some exceptions, agency debt is very similar to Treasury debt. The minimum denomination varies from $1,000 to $50,000, depending upon the particular security. Maturities at issuance also vary from 9 months to 40 years. Agency debt quotations are identical to Treasury quotations, and you can find them daily in *The Wall Street Journal*.

Lately, investors have shown considerable interest in agency issues that are quite different from Treasury bonds and notes. These securities are mortgage-backed passthrough participation units issued by the Government National Mortgage Association (Ginnie Mae), the Federal National Mortgage Association (Fannie Mae), and the Federal Home Loan Mortgage Corporation (Freddie Mac).

Passthrough securities such as Ginnie Maes have become very popular.

EXHIBIT 7.11
Announcement of a federal agency bond issue appearing in *The Wall Street Journal*.

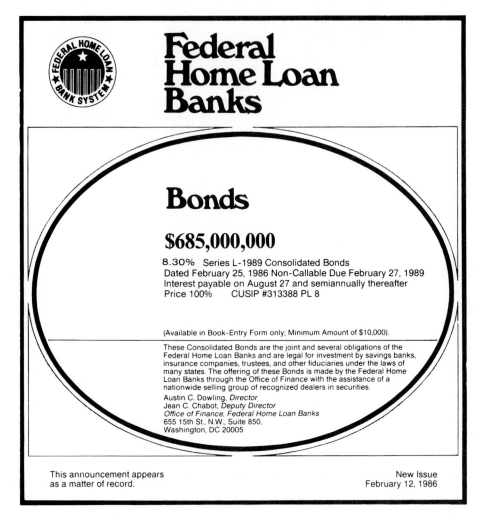

Participation units are created when an agency buys mortgages from S&Ls, commercial banks, or other lenders, and packages them in a large pool; then, individual units are sold that "pass through" mortgagee payments of interest and principal to investors. If you buy one of these units, you are acting indirectly as a mortgage lender. You will receive monthly payments of both interest and principal, and eventually your entire investment is recovered as all the mortgages in the pool are repaid.

It is important to recognize that even though the individual mortgages in the pool may have maturities of 25 and 30 years, the pool's life is very unlikely to be that long, because most mortgages are repaid well before their maturities. A 12-year average is often used in evaluating passthroughs, but shorter maturities are possible and very likely if interest rates fall substantially, since borrowers will

If You See a Liability—Securitize It!

Creating new securities seems to be a game of considerable interest to investment bankers, professional money managers, and other financial participants whose compensation rests heavily on the V word (volume). Simply to list the financial innovations since the mid-1960s would fill a magazine (or textbook) page.

One of the more popular creations is the mortgage-backed passthrough bond. By creating a pool of mortgages, an originator can issue bonds that, in effect, give investors the same risks and cash flows derived from the mortgages. Targeted originally as investment vehicles for S&Ls, the bonds also are popular with individual investors. Approximately $95 billion of such bonds were outstanding at the beginning of 1989.

Not to be outdone by Ginnie Mae or Freddie Mac, large brokerage firms have started packaging their own debt instruments. In a typical deal, an underwriter will buy $50 million or so of consumer loans from a lender, such as a commercial bank. The loans are then repackaged and sold to individual investors. Maturities are often four years or less, and yields are 0.5% to 1.0% above prevailing Treasury bill rates. What kind of consumer loans are being used as collateral? Practically any kind, but the major sources are auto loans and credit cards. Recent deals, though, have been written on mobile home loans, boat loans, airplane loans, and auto leases.

Why all the interest in securitizing? In a word, profit. How do you like this scenario? A commercial bank makes credit card loans with a 21% annual rate of interest. It then packages the loans and sells them to investors to yield 9.5%, pocketing the difference, less the underwriters' commissions. Clearly, a "passthrough" security this isn't.

refinance their existing mortgages. Thus, you will be disappointed if you buy a high-yielding passthrough, expecting to enjoy this return for 25 years or longer, and then find most of the mortgages are repaid within 3 or 4 years.

Ginnie Mae passthroughs are backed by the full faith and credit of the U.S. Treasury, but other passthroughs are not. There are no particular tax advantages to passthrough issues. Any amounts you receive that are designated as principal payments represent a return of your capital and are therefore nontaxable. But this is true of any investment. Interest payments are fully taxable at the federal, state, and local levels, which means passthroughs are taxed like corporate debt. (Most other agency debt is free of state and local tax.)

Investment Appeal of Agency Issues Other than the higher yield of agency issues versus Treasury issues, little justification exists for the unusual public interest in agency debt, specifically the passthrough units. Moreover, this yield advantage may diminish if you live in an area with high local taxes on income. Also, be cautious of ads, such as the one shown in Exhibit 7.12, that create an impression of virtually no risk with agency debt. You might note the ad tells you that prices and yields fluctuate, but the message comes after "Ready liquidity"

Falling interest rates shorten the average life of a mortgage pool and reduce a passthrough's average maturity.

EXHIBIT 7.12
Advertisement for a
Ginnie Mae mutual
fund appearing in *The
Wall Street Journal*.
(Courtesy Dreyfus Corp.)

and is situated to look more like an advantage than a disadvantage. This fund would have considerable interest-rate risk; you could be in for a real shock if you had to sell your shares on short notice and if interest rates had increased since you purchased the shares.

Passthroughs can have high price volatility.

MUNICIPAL BONDS

Technically, a municipality is an incorporated political subdivision within one of the 50 states. However, the term municipal bond refers to a debt instrument of practically any political unit—city, village, school district, water district, pollution control district, county, or state—other than one of the federal government. The right to tax and borrow is a state right, one often exercised by the states and their political subdivisions in myriad ways.

The Income Tax Advantage

The popularity of municipal bonds arises primarily from the fact that the interest they pay escapes federal income taxation, although capital gains and losses resulting from trading such bonds are considered in determining taxable income. Being tax-free is no small advantage, as Exhibit 7.13 shows. An investor in a 33% bracket must earn a pre-tax return about 1.5 times the amount of the municipal's return to do as well in a taxable bond. Even at the lower 15% and 28% rates, the tax advantage is important.

Municipal bond interest is free of federal income tax.

The formula below is used to determine the pretax yield equivalent of a municipal bond assuming a yield of $Y\%$ and a marginal tax rate of MTR:

$$\text{Pretax yield equivalent (\%)} = \frac{Y\%}{(1.0 - MTR)}$$

If $Y = 8\%$ and $MTR = 0.33$, then

$$\text{Pretax yield equivalent (\%)} = \frac{8\%}{(1.0 - 0.33)} = \frac{8\%}{0.67} = 11.94\%$$

Sample calculated values (%)·

			Bond Yield (Y)%				
MTR	**5%**	**6%**	**7%**	**8%**	**9%**	**10%**	**11%**
0.15	5.88	7.06	8.24	9.41	10.59	11.77	12.94
0.28	6.94	8.33	9.72	11.11	12.50	13.89	15.28
0.33	7.46	8.96	10.45	11.94	13.43	14.93	16.42

EXHIBIT 7.13
The income tax advantage of municipal bonds

However, this advantage can turn to a disadvantage whenever Congress decides to lower marginal tax rates. (Naturally, it becomes an even bigger advantage when rates are increased.) By referring to the formula in Exhibit 7.13, you can see that the pre-tax yield equivalent would fall as the marginal tax rate falls. Other bonds would thus become more attractive relative to municipals, and to remain competitively priced with other bonds, municipal bond prices would also fall. On balance, the threat of a changing federal tax rate structure increases the overall price volatility of municipals.

While all municipal bond interest is free of federal income tax, it may be subject to state or local income taxes if you own bonds issued by political subdivisions outside your home state or city. In response to investor demand to lower taxes, some mutual funds are offering double and triple tax-free bonds to investors residing in certain states (New York, Ohio, and Michigan, for example). Investing in these funds is one way to pay no tax whatsoever on interest earned.

Kinds of Municipal Bonds

Almost all municipal bonds are issued in $5,000 denominations. They are purchased in registered form and have a variety of features. Some of the more important ones are discussed below.

General Obligation Versus Revenue Bonds   A **general obligation bond** is one backed by the full taxing authority of the issuer. A **revenue bond** is one that is issued to finance a specific revenue-generating project, such as a highway or a hospital. It is backed only by the revenues the project generates. An advertisement showing various revenue bonds issued in Illinois is shown in Exhibit 7.14. All things considered, a general obligation bond is a far stronger bond than a revenue bond. Nevertheless, new municipal bond issues are predominantly the latter, by a margin of almost three to one. Practically all general obligation bonds are retired serially, while revenue bonds have a set term to maturity.

General obligation bonds are safer than revenue bonds.

Zero Coupon   A number of recent municipal bond offerings have been in zero coupon form. The popularity of CATs and TIGRs has not gone unnoticed by promoters of new security issues, and a zero coupon municipal bond overcomes the disadvantage of paying taxes on accrued interest on a taxable zero. So, you need not limit your purchases of zeros to those you will hold in an IRA.

Zero coupon municipals are finding a variety of uses, some obviously not dreamed of when they were first introduced. Car dealers, for example, are advertising: ''Buy a new $15,000 car today and we'll give you a government bond for $10,000.'' What you get are two zero coupon municipals that can be redeemed for $5,000 each in thirty or forty years. We will leave the determination of the present value of those bonds up to you, but it should be obvious that you are not buying the car for $5,000!

The Put Feature   Within the past several years, we have also seen the introduction of the adjustable-rate option bond. These are municipal bonds that

EXHIBIT 7.14
Advertisement of
various revenue bonds
issued in Illinois,
appearing in *The Wall
Street Journal.*

$15,990,000

Village of Oak Park, Illinois

Multi-family Housing Revenue Bonds
(The Oak Park Partnership)

Prudential-Bache
Securities

$7,200,000

Illinois Development Finance Authority

Floating/Fixed Rate Industrial Project
Revenue Bonds
(Webster-Wayne Shopping Center Ltd. Project)

Prudential-Bache
Securities

8,500,000

of Tinley Park, Illinois

Housing Mortgage Revenue Bonds
(lk IIIA and IIIB Project)

ential-Bache
Securities

$6,510,000

Village of Palatine, Illinois

Multi-family Housing Revenue Bonds
(Clover Ridge Apartments Project)

Prudential-Bache
Securities

give holders an option each year to sell back the bond at its face value to the issuer. The adjustable rate feature means the interest rate is also adjusted each year in step with changing market rates of interest. Such a bond provides excellent protection against interest-rate risk, but, as you expect, offers considerably lower yields than conventional municipals with long maturities. Actually, these bonds are more appropriately considered for short-term liquidity investing, as we discussed in the previous chapter.

Default Risk in Municipal Bonds

Municipals, like corporate bonds, carry default risk. That fact was brought home dramatically when the Washington Public Power Supply System defaulted on $2.25 billion of bonds that had been issued to finance the construction of two new

"Woops" provided a lesson in municipal bond default risk.

plants. The failure gave WPPSS its nickname of Woops, and caught investors—large and small—completely by surprise. Some cases were tragic, as families lost much of the life savings they had invested for eventual retirement. Two important lessons should be learned from this tragedy.

First, municipal bonds are evaluated by Moody's and Standard and Poor's (see Chapter 5) in the same manner as are corporate bonds. If you invest without consulting these ratings, you are ignoring an important step in the evaluation process. Don't assume the words "government" and "safety" mean the same thing. They obviously don't.

Second, regardless of a bond's rating, never limit your investments to a few individual issues. A portfolio is absolutely essential to eliminate random risk. Considering how many local governmental units are now issuing revenue bonds—and even general obligation bonds—of dubious quality, you should expect defaults to occur. If you can't diversify adequately on your own, you should consider buying an insured municipal bond. There are two municipal bond insurers: the American Municipal Bond Assurance Company (AMBAC) and the Municipal Bond Insurance Association (MBIA). Each of these companies is rated triple-A by Moody's and Standard and Poor's, which means the bonds they insure also carry that rating. In the municipal bond investment community, this insurance is called "sleep insurance." The fact that about one-fourth of all new long-term issues in 1985 carried such insurance probably tells us that investors place a premium on sleeping. Of course, a good night's sleep costs something—a lower yield than what you could get with a poorer-rated issue.

You can buy insured municipal bonds.

SUMMARY

Corporate bonds offer certain bondholder rights, which are detailed in the bond indenture. A trustee is appointed to make sure the issuing corporation meets the terms of the indenture. A mortgage bond is backed by specific real property, while a debenture is not supported by any collateral. An equipment trust certificate is a mortgage bond, backed by transportation equipment. Subordinated debentures have positions inferior to straight debentures. All U.S. corporation bonds are registered (rather than held in bearer form) and have finite maturities; some have special redemption provisions that include sinking funds and serial redemption. Special bond features include convertibility into common stock, floating rates, and put options; a feature favoring the issuer is a right to call the bond before its maturity. Bonds are purchased on organized exchanges or in the over-the-counter market, and their prices are reported daily in the financial pages of many newspapers. Commissions on bonds can be relatively high, particularly if bid-asked spreads are involved.

Treasury bonds are considered free of default risk. They can be purchased through a broker or directly from a Federal Reserve Bank. Collateralized Treasury Receipts (CATs) are not Treasury issues but, rather, are trust certificates to a pool of Treasury securities, including their future interest payments. CATs are often issued in zero-coupon form and have become very popular recently. Their safety appears high but is still untested. Agency bonds are issued by agencies of the federal government. Passthrough certificates— a type of agency issue—have also been popular lately because of their apparent high yields; these yields may not be realized, though, as mortgages are prepaid.

Municipal bonds are issued by state and local governments. Their primary investment appeal is the lack of federal taxation on their interest. Municipal bonds can be general obligation bonds or revenue bonds. Most are interest-bearing, although zero coupon issues are becoming popular. Some offer put features to minimize interest-rate risk. Investors should be aware of default risks in municipal bonds and use quality ratings in making selections.

KEY TERMS

Select the alternative that best identifies the key term.

1. corporate bond
2. bond indenture
3. trustee
4. mortgage bond
5. debenture
6. equipment trust certificate
7. subordinated debentures
8. registered bonds
9. bearer bonds
10. income bond
11. PIK bond
12. sinking fund
13. serial redemption
14. convertible bond
15. floating rate bond
16. put bond
17. super poison put
18. event risk
19. right to call
20. call premium
21. collateralized Treasury receipt (CAT)
22. federal agency bond
23. general obligation bond
24. revenue bond

a. money set aside to retire a bond issue
b. you own these bonds directly, rather than in certificate form
c. "rolling stock" serves as collateral
d. bond issued by a corporation
e. bond backed by the full taxing power of the municipality
f. a bond interest rate that fluctuates
g. its trust consists of "stripped" Treasury securities
h. contract between a corporation and its bondholders
i. a bond not supported by collateral
j. a bond issued by a federal government agency
k. a bond supported by collateral
l. retirement of a bond at a price above par
m. they rank below debentures
n. you can get common stock with it
o. gives the issuer the right to redeem the bond before its maturity
p. supported by the revenues the municipal project provides
q. a portion of the bond issue is retired before maturity
r. your name appears on this bond
s. the institution that enforces the indenture
t. allows the holder to sell the issue back to the issuer
u. a leveraged buyout can create it
v. designed to protect bondholders from event risk
w. interest is paid only if the issuer earns profits
x. issuer can pay interest in cash or in additional bonds

REVIEW QUESTIONS

1. What is a corporate bond? What basic rights do bondholders have and how are these rights protected?
2. How does a mortgage bond differ from a debenture? Explain which kind of bond is an equipment trust certificate.

3. What is a subordinated debenture? Discuss the risks associated with this type of bond.

4. Identify and explain the following bond characteristics: *(a)* registered bond versus bearer bond; *(b)* sinking fund and serial redemption; *(c)* convertible bond; *(d)* floating rate versus put bond; *(e)* the right to call and the call premium.

5. Explain an income bond, indicating the circumstances usually associated with its issuance.

6. Explain a PIK bond and discuss possible risks associated with it.

7. Explain event risk and discuss how a super poison put deals with it.

8. You are thinking of buying seven bonds issued by Duke Power. They have a face value of $1,000 and a market price of $800. How much commission can you expect to pay on the purchase?

9. Briefly explain Treasury debt, indicating your opinion of its safety and adequacy of return (include taxes in your response).

10. Explain a collateralized Treasury receipt, indicating its investment advantages and disadvantages.

11. What are agency issues? Are these ''good'' substitutes for Treasury issues? Discuss.

12. What are mortgage-backed passthrough participation units, such as Ginnie Maes? Explain why falling interest rates might be a concern if you own such units. Finally, do you regard a mutual fund investing in Ginnie Maes to be about as safe as a money market fund? Explain.

13. How does a general obligation municipal bond differ from a municipal revenue bond? Which one is safer? Which is more popular?

14. Is there any advantage in owning a zero coupon municipal or an adjustable-rate option municipal? Explain each.

15. Since municipalities are governments, is it really necessary to exercise precautions in selecting municipal bonds? Explain, indicating what precautions, if any, you might take. Include in your answer a discussion of ''sleep insurance.''

PROBLEMS AND PROJECTS

1. You purchased three subordinated debentures and two debentures ($1,000 face value for each) of Dekline Corporation several years ago. Recently, the company has gone into bankruptcy and all its assets have been sold for $3 million. You have learned the company issued $2 million of subordinated debentures, $2 million of debentures, and has $4 million of general creditor claims. Assuming you paid face value for your bonds, how much will you lose in the bankruptcy?

2. You are reading a bond quotation in the morning newspaper:

    Ace   9s   11   9.7   25   93⅛   92⅛   92¼   +1¼

    a. Briefly explain what each item above means, putting prices in dollars and cents.
    b. Using a financial calculator, determine the bond's YTM and compare it to its current yield. Assume it is 1991.

3. Interpret the following Treasury quotation (put prices in dollars and cents):

    10s   2010   Feb   102.8   102.24   +.4   9.92

4. You can invest in a municipal bond yielding 8% or a corporate bond yielding 10%. Show which one is the better of the two, assuming marginal tax rates of: 15%, 28%, and 33%.

5. Assume the yield on AAA-rated corporate bonds is 8.5% while Treasuries with similar maturities are yielding 7.9%. If you have a 33% federal income tax rate and a 12% combined state and local income tax rate, which bond offers the higher after-tax yield?

6. *(Student Project)*   Obtain a recent issue of *The Wall Street Journal* and in the third section find the column indicating yields on corporates, Treasuries, and municipals. Discuss the yield situation.

7. *(Student Project)*   Public utilities usually have very complex capital structures. If one is located in your area, contact the public relations department and request the most recent financial report. Then, determine the different bond issues the company has outstanding. Look for key differences among the issues.

CASE ANALYSES

**7.1
Terry Lee's
Bond Adventure**

Terry Lee, a recent college graduate, is considering investing $10,000 in speculative bonds. He has narrowed his selection to one of the following: *(a)* a PIK bond with a 16% coupon rate, or *(b)* a subordinated debenture with a 14% coupon rate. (Assume each bond pays interest annually at year end.) The PIK option lasts for five years, after which interest must be paid in cash. Terry has a high risk tolerance and is seeking maximum return from his investments. Unfortunately, evaluating the two bonds is proving to be a problem.

To begin with, each bond has a 25-year maturity and is callable after 2 years—the subordinated debenture at a 15% premium over par and the PIK at par. Secondly, Terry believes interest rates will be stable (or rise slightly) over the next 2 years, but then decline sharply. He forecasts current yields on the bonds as follows:

End of Year	PIK Bond	Subordinated Debenture
1	18%	15%
2	19	16
3	16	14
4	15	13
5	13	11

Questions

a. Assuming the PIK bond's interest is paid in additional bonds in years 1, 2, 3, and in cash in years 4 and 5, determine the accumulated value of the investment at the end of 5 years. Assume cash interest is reinvested to earn 10%.

b. Determine the accumulated value of the subordinated debenture investment, assuming interest is reinvested to earn 12% in years 2 and 3, and 10% in years 4 and 5.

c. Considering your responses to questions *a* and *b,* which bond is the more attractive?
d. Which is the more attractive if each is called after 3 years?
e. Do you recommend either of these bonds, considering Terry's investment objective?

7.2 Florence Mims Seeks a Bond Portfolio

Florence Mims has been divorced recently. The divorce settlement has provided her with a $90,000 portfolio, invested heavily in growth stocks. Florence is in her late 30s. She has a good income as an independent accountant, but lacks a retirement plan. She intends to establish one and believes that bonds should occupy a key position in it. However, she is unfamiliar with bond investment and has turned to you for advice. Her future marginal tax rate for federal income tax is 33%, and she lives in a state with no state or local income taxes. Prior to your meeting with Florence, you have jotted down a number of bonds and their present yields to maturity (see the following list). Some, or possibly all, of these bonds may not be appropriate for her situation. However, your assignment is to develop a $60,000 bond portfolio for Florence. Of course, this assumes she will leave $30,000 invested in growth stocks. Also, you can assume that Florence will manage her portfolio in the future, and that she doesn't mind the related work.

Bond Sample *(all have long maturities; assume 20 years)*

(a) Florida Power and Light mortgage bond   9%
(b) Coca Cola subordinated debentures   10.5%
(c) Frionics, Inc. (growth company) subordinated debenture   14.0%
(d) RJR Holdings Capital Corporation PIK subordinated debenture   14.0%
(e) Treasury bond   8%
(f) Federal agency bond   8.5%
(g) GMAC debentures   9.5%
(h) State of New York general obligation bonds   7.5%
(i) Collateralized Treasury receipts   7.8%
(j) Ginnie Mae passthrough certificates   9.0%
(k) State of California revenue bonds (zero coupon)   8.1%

Questions

a. Indicate those bonds you feel are most appropriate for Florence.
b. Design a bond portfolio, indicating specific bonds selected and amounts invested in each.

HELPFUL READING

Beckett, Sean. "The Prepayment Risk of Mortgage-Backed Securities." *Economic Review,* Federal Reserve Bank of Kansas City, February 1989, pp. 43–57.

Bittner, Jill. "New Mortgage Security Has High Yields But Also an Unpredictable Income Stream." *The Wall Street Journal,* July 19, 1988, p. C1.

Hector, Gary. "The Bondholders' Cold New World." *Fortune,* February 27, 1989, pp. 83–86.

Peers, Alexandra. "Municipal Bond Industry Is Phasing Out a Popular—But Often Abused—Security." *The Wall Street Journal,* August 22, 1988.

Sandler, Linda. "TWA to Sell $300 Million Notes Secured in Part by Light Bulbs." *The Wall Street Journal,* June 2, 1989, p. C1.

Schifrin, Matthew. "Zombie Bonds." *Forbes,* April 3, 1989, p. 70.

Winkler, Matthew. "Mortgage Market Goes from Feverish to Sick." *The Wall Street Journal,* April 25, 1989, p. C1.

Winkler, Matthew, and James A. White. "Shock Still Clouds Blue-Chip Corporate Bond Market." *The Wall Street Journal,* March 22, 1989, p. C1.

PART THREE

Investing in Equities

E quity instruments provide ownership interests in the corporations that issue them. There are two quite different types of equities— common stock and preferred stock. While the latter is equity in a legal sense, in the marketplace it is more closely identified with debt because of its fixed dividend payments. Common stock is by far the more important of the two, and it is used extensively by investors to help them achieve long-term goals.

Chapter 8 explains return and risk characteristics of common stock investing. It identifies different opportunities in common stocks and categorizes risk into diversifiable and nondiversifiable sources, explaining how investors can deal with each. It also discusses how required rates of return can be derived for common stocks, and how earnings and dividend approaches are used to select securities.

Chapter 9 explains the tools of fundamental analysis of common stock. It identifies key components of a company's balance sheet and income statement and shows how ratio analysis is useful in measuring financial strength and earnings performance. It also indicates how changes in the overall economy or a particular industry affect specific firms.

Chapter 10 discusses and evaluates technical analysis, viewing selected technical indicators in depth. It introduces the topic of efficient security markets. Also, the efficient market hypothesis is explained, and empirical tests of the hypothesis are reviewed.

Chapter 11 explains preferred stock investing. It indicates the advantages and disadvantages of straight preferred in relation to bond investment. It also discusses the investment characteristics of adjustable-rate preferred stock, and explains interest-rate risk and default risk in relation to preferreds.

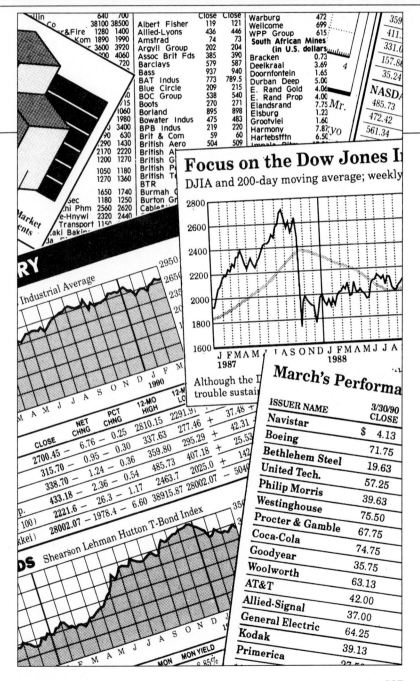

	640	700
Co	38100	38500
r&Fire	1280	1400
Kom	1890	1990
	3600	3920
		4060
		720

	Close	Close
Albert Fisher	119	121
Allied-Lyons	436	446
Amstrad	74	73
Argyll Group	202	204
Assoc Brit Fds	385	390
Barclays	579	587
Bass	937	940
BAT Indus	773	789.5
Blue Circle	209	215
BOC Group	538	540
Boots	270	271
Borland	895	898
Bowater Indus	475	483
BPB Indus	219	220
Brit & Com	59	60
British Aero	504	509
British A		
British G		
British P		
British Te		
BTR		
Burmah		
Burton Gr		
Cable		

Warburg	472
Wellcome	699
WPP Group	615
South African Mines	
(in U.S. dollars)	
Bracken	0.73
Deelkraal	3.69
Doornfontein	1.65
Durban Deep	5.00
E. Rand Gold	4.06
E. Rand Prop	4.00
Elandsrand	7.75
Elsburg	1.23
Grootvlei	1.60
Harmony	7.87
Hartebstftn	6.50

359
411.
331.0
157.86
35.24

NASDA
485.73
472.42
561.34

Focus on the Dow Jones I

DJIA and 200-day moving average; weekly

J F M A M J J A S O N D J F M A M J J A
1987 — 1988

Although the D
trouble sustai

March's Performa

ISSUER NAME	3/30/90 CLOSE
Navistar	$ 4.13
Boeing	71.75
Bethlehem Steel	19.63
United Tech.	57.25
Philip Morris	39.63
Westinghouse	75.50
Procter & Gamble	67.75
Coca-Cola	74.75
Goodyear	35.75
Woolworth	63.13
AT&T	42.00
Allied-Signal	37.00
General Electric	64.25
Kodak	39.13
Primerica	

Industrial Average

CLOSE	NET CHNG	PCT CHNG	12-MO HIGH	12-M LO
2700.45 −	6.76 −	0.25	2810.15	2291.9
315.70 −	0.95 −	0.30	337.63	277.46 + 37.48 +
338.70 −	1.24 −	0.36	359.80	295.29 + 42.31 −
433.18 −	2.36 −	0.54	485.73	407.18 + 25.53
2221.6 −	26.3 −	1.17	2463.7	2025.0 + 142
28002.07 −	1978.4 −	6.60	38915.87	28002.07 − 5040

Shearson Lehman Hutton T-Bond Index

CHAPTER EIGHT

Return and Risk in Common Stocks

COMMON STOCK CHARACTERISTICS

Stockholders' Rights

Opportunities in Common Stocks

Reading Stock Quotations

RISKS IN COMMON STOCKS

Liquidity and Inflation Risks

Firm-Specific and Industry Risks

Market Risk

ESTIMATING A STOCK'S REQUIRED RETURN

The CAPM and the SML

Using the SML

DETERMINING EXPECTED RETURNS

The Earnings Approach

The Dividend Approach

Valuation with Multiple Growth Rates

Other Valuation Methods

BOXES

Some Information About Dividends

Where to Look for Value

After you finish this chapter, you will be able to:

- identify the basic rights of common stockholders, and understand what it means to have a residual interest.

- recognize different return opportunities in common stocks that are provided through cash dividends or price appreciation.

- recognize the risks of common stock investing, including firm-specific, industry, and market risks.

- determine a required rate of return to evaluate stock opportunities by constructing and using a securities market line (SML).

- understand and apply the earnings approach and the dividend approach to stock evaluation and selection.

- apply the dividend model with multiple growth rates.

- identify other valuation methods, based on asset approaches, break-up value, and rules of thumb.

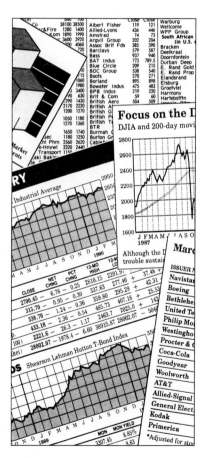

To many people, investment and common stock mean the same thing. All funds not needed for liquidity are invested in common stocks. For these investors, "playing the market" is an obsession not terribly different· from "playing the horses," and they know less about the stocks they trade than racing enthusiasts know about horses they bet on. The lure is the super return. Most of us have read that $1,000 invested in IBM 30 years ago, or McDonald's 20 years ago, would have made us rich, and we saw in Chapter 3 that simply investing $1,000 in the smallest companies on the New York Stock Exchange 63 years ago would have made us millionaires today. With profits this high and so easily earned, who can resist?

To be sure, common stocks do offer the potential for returns higher than those usually available on money market instruments and long-term bonds. Earning these returns, though, is not easy and demands that you take risks. Risk means variability of return: the chances of taking substantial losses with common stocks are high even if you do your homework and invest intelligently. And if you plan to be an investor who "plays the market," rather than "invests in the market," your losses can be extraordinary. The intent of this chapter and the next two is to help you be an intelligent common stock investor.

COMMON STOCK CHARACTERISTICS

A share of **common stock** represents an ownership interest in the issuing corporation. When you invest in common stocks, you acquire certain ownership rights, and you are looking for various return opportunities. Before investing, you should understand these rights and opportunities.

Stockholders' Rights

Suppose you are thinking of investing in Mead Corporation—a paper and forest products company with other diversified interests—by buying 100 shares of its common stock at $40 a share. Along with receiving a stock certificate (such as the one shown in Exhibit 8.1) evidencing your ownership, you will become one of about 30,000 other investors who own some 63 million shares of Mead common stock. Your 100 shares will give you a 0.00000160 (100/63,000,000) interest in the company. Although your holding is minuscule, you are an owner. True, you have far less power than someone who owns a million shares, but you have identical privileges. Each of you has the right to vote for members of the board of directors or in other matters affecting the company, the right to maintain a proportionate interest in the company, and the right to share in its distributions of assets or earnings.

Shares of a company's common stock represent an ownership interest, which can be large but is usually very small.

The Right to Vote   In general, your **voting right** means one vote for each share of stock. A corporation is not a democracy allowing one vote for each shareholder. The person who holds a million shares to your hundred has 10,000 times more say

Voting rights usually allow one vote for each share of stock; cumulative voting is an exception.

EXHIBIT 8.1
A share of Mead common stock (Courtesy of the Mead Corporation.)

in the business than you do. However, some corporations have a system of voting—called cumulative voting—that gives more power to shareholders with a minority interest. Suppose nine members are to be elected to nine seats on a corporation's board of directors. With traditional voting, if you own 100 shares, you can cast 100 votes for each seat; but with cumulative voting, you could cast 900 votes for only one director, giving up your right to vote for the other eight seats. With this method, minority interests might be able to pool their votes to elect at least one or several directors.

The Pre-Emptive Right   As small as it is, you still have a right to maintain your proportionate interest in Mead. This is called a **pre-emptive right**. Without such a right, your ownership interest could be diluted by simply selling more shares to others and not to you. If Mead wanted to sell 10 million more shares to raise capital, you would have a right to buy 16 ($0.00000160 \times 10,000,000$) more shares. Most investors do not put a great deal of emphasis on the pre-emptive right and

You keep a proportionate ownership interest with the pre-emptive right.

many corporate charters (the document that creates the corporation) are amended to allow investors to give up the right so that management has greater financing flexibility.

The Right to Share in Earnings or Asset Distributions   The **right to share** in earnings or other distributions is the right that appeals most to investors. With common stock you have the right to participate (in proportion to the number of shares you own) in any distribution of earnings or assets. This right is limited, however. For example, most states prohibit any distribution that would impair the firm's capital and subject its creditors to greater risk. In addition, if the corporation has any preferred stock outstanding, all current or past unpaid dividends must be paid on it before any cash distributions can be made to common stockholders. As a common stockholder, therefore, you stand last in the distribution line, behind both bondholders and preferred stockholders. You are said to have a **residual claim**; that is, you get what is left. While this sounds dismal, getting what is left is why you buy common stock in the first place. While bondholders and preferred stockholders have prior claims, the amounts they are entitled to are generally fixed each year, which means that regardless of how well (or poorly) the company does, the amount they get is the same. In contrast, the amounts available to common stockholders vary in direct proportion to the company's profits. Exhibit 8.2 illustrates this situation.

Shareholders rank last in earnings and asset claims.

EXHIBIT 8.2

Illustration of common stock's residual interest

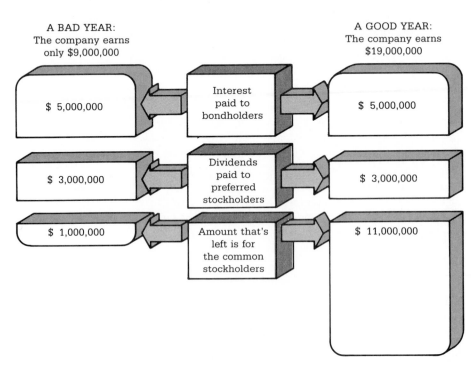

A BAD YEAR:
The company earns
only $9,000,000

A GOOD YEAR:
The company earns
$19,000,000

$ 5,000,000 — Interest paid to bondholders — $ 5,000,000

$ 3,000,000 — Dividends paid to preferred stockholders — $ 3,000,000

$ 1,000,000 — Amount that's left is for the common stockholders — $ 11,000,000

The company has bonds outstanding requiring $5 million a year in interest, and preferred stock requiring $3 million a year in dividends. This represents $8 million of fixed obligations that must be paid before any earnings are available to common stockholders. Thus, in a bad year, when profits are only $9 million, common stockholders' claims on earnings would be $1 million; but in a good year, when profits jump to $19 million, they are entitled to $11 million. It should be noted the corporation may not pay all the common stockholders' claims in dividends. Indeed, it is more common to retain a large portion of earnings for reinvestment in the business. The proportion of earnings (E) paid in dividends (D) is called the **payout ratio**; that is,

$$\text{payout ratio} = D/E$$

We will use this ratio later and in the next chapter, but you can see now that companies with high ratios usually represent poor growth opportunities. It is difficult for the company to grow when it pays out a large proportion of its earnings in dividends.

Stock Dividends and Stock Splits   When we speak of a distribution to common stockholders, we do not include stock dividends or stock splits. A **stock dividend** is a distribution of additional shares of the company's own common stock. For example, Mead might declare a 10% stock dividend, which means every stockholder would receive shares totalling 10% of the amount owned. Your 100 shares would thus entitle you to 10 more. Of course, you seem wealthier, since your ownership has gone up 10%; unfortunately, the price per share will go down 10%, leaving your wealth unchanged. Neither you nor any other shareholder can be made wealthier simply by increasing the number of shares outstanding.

> Stock dividends and splits increase the number of shares outstanding.

A **stock split** works exactly like a stock dividend except more new shares are usually issued. For example, the most popular stock split is two-for-one, which means you receive one additional share for each share held. Stock splits also have no impact on your wealth. Why then do so many companies have stock dividends and stock splits? There is probably no simple or single answer to this question. It is often believed that a stock's price should be kept within a popular range, say, $30 to $60, to make the shares more marketable. A very high price, for example, might exclude some investors who lack sufficient capital. So, if price increases beyond this range, a stock dividend or split will return it. Along this line, you will sometimes see a reverse split, such as one for ten. Now, the stock's price has decreased too much, suggesting a deteriorated company. Most academic researchers doubt the argument of an optimal price range, since it supports the notion of increasing shareholder wealth by increasing or decreasing the number of shares outstanding.

> It is questionable whether stock dividends and splits influence market value.

Another argument advanced in favor of stock dividends is that they let shareholders know that earnings are good, but the company wishes to retain cash for internal investment rather than paying a dividend. It is extremely doubtful, however, that shareholders require a stock dividend to provide them with information.

Opportunities in Common Stocks

Unlike conventional bonds and money market instruments that have a rather narrow investment purpose, common stocks offer an array of investment opportunities. A discussion of the more important of these opportunities is provided in the sections below.

Growth Stocks   All of us like to get in on the ground floor of a company that we think has a bright future. We are looking for growth in such an opportunity. A **growth stock** can be described as one investors feel will show greater growth in earnings than the expected growth in the overall economy. Of course, there are all sorts of growth companies: IBM is one, Lotus Development is another. IBM has a proven track record of growth, and its position in the computer industry gives rather good assurance that it will enjoy future growth. Lotus, on the other hand, is a newcomer. It has had remarkable success with its software, but it is in an extremely competitive industry where fortunes are made—and then lost—almost overnight. Obviously, the more rapid the expected growth, the riskier the company. Moreover, the mere presence of growth should not be seen as a guarantee of a good investment. The market price of the stock might be so high that even if the expected growth materializes, you still have a bad investment.

A growth stock is expected to show price appreciation.

Income Stocks   An **income stock** is one that offers a fairly high dividend yield. Public utility stocks stand out as examples. Yields with these stocks are often on a par with yields available on corporate bonds. This appeals to investors who look for good current yield along with some potential for price appreciation. However, don't assume your dividend yield has the same protection as a bond yield. Dividends can be—and frequently are—cut if the company faces a disruptive situation. After the nuclear reactor leak at Three Mile Island, General Public Utilities (GPU) suspended its dividend, and the price of its stock fell from $17 to under $5. (However, the stock has rebounded since then and currently sells above $17.)

An income stock has a high dividend yield.

Growth and Income Stocks   A **growth and income stock** offers a reasonable dividend yield—perhaps one equalling the rate you might earn on a passbook savings account—along with good potential for long-term price appreciation, although at a slower rate than that of a growth stock. A public utility in a growing metropolitan area, such as Florida Telephone, is an example.

Blue Chips   The term **blue chip** is often used to describe a stock that is thought to be of high quality. Again, IBM or Xerox easily come to mind. However, the term itself is ambiguous, since high quality can be achieved in a variety of ways. A growth stock can have high quality, but so can an income stock, or a stock with any particular characteristic. Perhaps we should think of a blue chip stock as one with a very high probability of achieving whatever it promises—growth, income, or something else.

Blue chip denotes quality.

Some Information About Dividends

Receiving a dividend check is surely one of the joys of investing in stocks. The following information will increase your familiarity with dividends.

Dividend Dates

Date of Record   The company's board of directors sets the date of record. If your name appears in the firm's stock ledger on this date, you are entitled to receive the dividend. As an example, assume this date is October 10.

Ex-Dividend Date   The stock exchanges set the ex-dividend date, usually four business days before the date of record, or October 6 in our example. Beginning with the ex-dividend date, a stock sells without ("ex") the dividend. For example, if ABC, Inc., closes at $50 a share on October 5 and a $2 dividend has been declared, on October 6 its stock will open at $48 a share. If you buy it on that date or later, you do not get the dividend.

Payment Date   The date the company will mail dividend checks is called the payment date, and it is also set by the board of directors. The date selected might be October 31.

Dividend Reinvestment Plans

Many companies allow shareholders to reinvest their dividends by using them to purchase additional shares of stock. The main advantage of a reinvestment plan is eliminating a stockbrokerage commission; a secondary advantage might be that it is a form of forced savings.

Liquidating Dividends

Liquidating dividends are not true dividends but, rather, are distributions of capital. In effect, the company is reducing its size, or going out of business altogether, and is in the process of selling assets and distributing cash to shareholders. These distributions may or may not be taxable, depending upon your investment in the stock. If you receive them, you will probably need help in filing a tax return.

Stock Repurchases

Although stock repurchases aren't true dividends either, they probably have the same effect: you receive cash by selling a portion of your shares back to the company. So, you have cash but fewer shares, which, on the surface, looks like a wash; however, the market price of the stock typically increases with fewer shares outstanding. You might have the cash plus no loss in *the value* of your investment.

Stock Dividend

A dividend paid with shares of the company's stock is called a stock dividend. On the surface, it seems a good deal, since it increases your share holdings. However, the market price of the stock adjusts downward to reflect the proportionate increase in shares, so *the value* of your investment remains the same.

Cyclical Stocks   **Cyclical stocks** are more responsive to changes in the business cycle than are other stocks. Companies in the capital goods industries, such as Cincinnati Milacron, experience far greater volatility in earnings than companies in the food or beverage businesses, such as Heinz or PepsiCo. Other volatile industries are those associated with housing, mining, or transportation. The Big Three automakers are fairly cyclical stocks because their dominant product is a consumer durable, the purchase of which is easily postponed in an economic slowdown.

Defensive Stocks   The return of a **defensive stock** is expected to vary in opposition to the cycles of the overall economy. Defensive stocks' returns are not as volatile as the overall market return. Put more concretely, these are stocks with low betas, as discussed in Chapter 4. (The beta concept will also be used later in this chapter.) Holding a defensive stock is a good idea, but defensive stocks are not always easily found. Companies dealing in consumer perishables or consumer services often have betas less than 1.0—meaning they are less risky than the overall market—but it is virtually impossible to find stocks with negative betas. For example, not 1 stock out of 1,700 in the Value Line survey has a negative beta, and fewer than 2% have betas of 0.5 or less.

It was often felt that investors should attempt to play an economic cycle by investing in cyclical stocks when an economic expansion was anticipated, and then sell these stocks and invest in defensive issues as the cycle moved towards contraction. Surely, there are still many who advocate this approach, but growing evidence indicates that few people can forecast the cycle with any recurring accuracy, much less design an investment program to benefit from it.

Speculative Stocks   A **speculative stock** can involve practically any type of situation. The term is about as ambiguous as blue chip and is used just as frequently. Probably, most investors understand *speculative* to mean an opportunity for a very fast profit, such as you might earn in a takeover or merger, or the unexpected development of a new product. Of course, we also might think of a speculative stock as simply a high-risk stock, one with a high beta or a high absolute measure of risk such as the standard deviation. Thinking of risk in these more concrete terms is the better way to do it, as we shall see later in this chapter.

Reading Stock Quotations

Many stocks are quoted daily in the financial pages of local and national newspapers. Prior to investing, you may follow a stock in the paper, and after you make a selection, your curiosity will probably lead you to keep watching it. Exhibit 8.3 shows a typical listing for Mead Corporation and explains how to interpret the data. As you see, quite a bit of information is provided on one small line. Pay particular attention to items 5 and 6 since they will be applied later in the chapter.

Mead's stock is traded on the New York Stock Exchange. A listing on the Amex is exactly the same. However, less information is provided for over-the-counter stocks. If the stock is on the OTC National Market Issues list, you are provided with all the information given on a NYSE or Amex issue, except current yield and the P/E ratio. If the listing is on NASDAQ's Bid and Asked Quotations, limited data, such as that shown for Cascade Corporation, are provided.

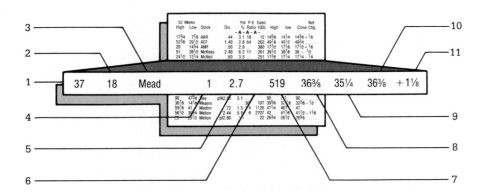

52 Weeks High	Low	Stock	Div.	Yld %	P-E Ratio	Sales 100s	High	low	Net Close Chg.
		· A - A - A ·							
17¾	7⅞	AAR	.44	3.1	18	12	14⅝	14¼	14⅜ + ⅛
52⅜	29½	ACF	1.40	2.8	64	262	49⅞	49½	49¾ ....
20	14¾	AMF	.50	2.9	..	380	17½	17⅜	17½ + ⅛
51	39½	McKess	2.40	6.2	11	201	39½	38⅞	39 - ½
24½	13¼	McNeil	.60	3.5	..	251	17⅜	17¼	17¼ - ¼

37	18	Mead		1	2.7		519	36⅜	35¼	36⅜ +1⅛

90	47⅝	Mea	ptA2.50	3.1	..	30	90	32⅜	90	32⅜ - ½
36⅞	14⅛	Measrx				107	39⅝	3⅛	47	
59⅞	41	Medtrn	.72	1.5	24	1126	47¼	46⅝	47	
56½	36¾	Mellon	2.44	5.9	6	2707	42	41⅛	41½ - 1⅛
	15½	Mellon	pf2.80		..	22	26¾	26½	26⅝	....

1. The highest price per share paid in the past year; prices are quoted in dollars and eighths of dollars, so a price of 10⅛ = $10.125 a share. Mead's highest price was $37.

2. The lowest price per share paid in the last year. Mead's lowest price was $18.

3. The company's name, which may be abbreviated. Mead's is not.

4. The indicated regular dividend in the current year based upon what the company has paid in the last quarter or six months. Some companies also pay extra dividends in good earnings years, but these are not shown. Mead's regular dividend was estimated at $1 a share.

5. The current yield, which is found by dividing the current year regular dividend by the closing price of the stock. Mead's current yield is 2.7 percent.

6. The price-earnings ratio, which is the company's earnings over its last fiscal year divided into the closing price of the stock. There is no entry if earnings are negative, as in Mead's case.

7. The number of shares sold on that day, in hundreds. For example, 519 means 51,900 shares of Mead stock.

8. The highest price paid for the stock that day. Mead's was 36⅜ ($36.375)

9. The lowest price paid for the stock that day. Mead's was 35¼ ($35.25)

10. The last price paid that day. Mead's was 36⅜.

11. The difference between the closing price that day and the closing price of the previous day. For example, Mead's closing price on Monday was 1⅛ ($1.125) higher than its closing price on Friday.

EXHIBIT 8.3

Typical listing of a common stock in the financial pages of many newspapers

Name and Indicated Regular Dividend	Sales (100s)	Bid	Asked	Net Change
Cascade Cp .60	63	35½	37⅛	+½

Cascade's regular indicated dividend is $0.60 a share. On the reported day, 6,300 shares traded. The bid price of 35½ means you would have received $35.50 if you wanted to sell a share, and the 37⅛ asked price means you would have paid $37.125 to buy a share. The spread between the bid and the asked price is part of the broker's commission (or profit) for making a market in the stock. As you can judge, it is a significant amount and it can reduce your profits substantially if you are an active trader of OTC stocks. The net change of +½ indicates an increase of $0.50 a share from the bid price on the reported day versus the bid price of the previous trading day.

RISKS IN COMMON STOCKS

A groundwork for understanding risk in common stocks was built in Chapter 4. We will continue to build on that foundation in this chapter.

Liquidity and Inflation Risks

Common stocks have high liquidity risks.

Practically all common stocks have high degrees of both liquidity and inflation risk. The lack of liquidity is probably clear to you, if you remember that liquidity means not only being able to sell an asset quickly and at low cost, but also being able to sell it with no loss in market value. Common stocks offer no guarantee of price and, so, lack liquidity.

Less clear, though, might be why common stocks are high inflation risks. In fact, you may have heard just the opposite: that you should invest in common stocks to hedge inflation. The logic behind this advice is that business firms can raise prices of their products and services to match the inflation rate, thereby maintaining profit margins on sales and preserving real returns for investors. Unfortunately, the logic hasn't always held. While common stocks did perform well in what was then considered ''the inflationary 1950s,'' they did poorly during much of the 1970s and early 1980s, when the inflation rate far exceeded that of the 1950s. The underlying reasons for such a poor performance are not completely clear. We do know that a high and volatile inflation rate increases business risk within firms and dampens their willingness to expand or to make needed investments in new technology or product development. Eventually, profitability suffers. Simultaneously, the inflation forces investors to require higher rates of return from common stocks, both to match the higher rates available on alternative investments, particularly tangibles and money market instruments, and to compensate them for what is now perceived as a riskier investment medium. On balance, it is better to hold other assets for inflation hedges and to hold common stocks for other reasons.

Common stocks have not always been good inflation hedges.

Firm-Specific and Industry Risks

When you invest in a common stock, you invest in a specific company with products or services competing in specific industries. If you buy Exxon, you are in the international oil business—for better or worse. While we will cover firm and industry analysis in detail in the next chapter, an overview of the risk factors is appropriately included here.

Strong market position is often a key to a company's success.

Declining Market Position   Probably the greatest risk of all arises from a deteriorating market position. An individual firm—such as Chrysler, before its resurgence—can lose its market position when it fails to compete in its industry. An entire industry—the railroads, for example—may decline, or become less able to compete with foreign producers, as the U.S. auto industry has suffered from competition with the Japanese. Whatever the cause, the long-run impacts are usually both a riskier stock and a less profitable one. While we are frequently told to avoid stocks in declining market situations, following that advice is not usually easy to do. Has Chrysler made a sound recovery and is it no longer in financial danger? Is GM now the high-cost producer? Will the Big Three learn how to control quality and costs, and once again resume world leadership in manufacturing automobiles? Perhaps. Perhaps not.

To some extent, any company faces a threat of an eroding market. Even public utilities have seen consumers cut demand through energy conservation and alternative heating sources, such as solar energy, firewood, and kerosene. Few companies and industries are free of competition or insulated from economic misfortune. The best advice is probably not to attempt to decide which firms or which industries will do spectacularly well or poorly, but, rather, to diversify among firms and across industry lines.

Inability to Control Costs   Even companies with bright futures can experience difficulties if they can't control costs. The list of bankrupts each year usually includes as many from this category as ones with declining market positions. Young growth firms are especially vulnerable. Often, their ability to sell products and services far exceeds their skill at business management. One month you will read of how well things are going, and the next month the company files bankruptcy. Osborne Computer, a leader in the development of personal computers and an eventual bankrupt, is a classic example, but there are many others.

Heavy dependence on natural resources may make some costs difficult to control.

Companies with a heavy dependence upon natural resources—public utilities, for example—or with a product line connected to the natural resources industries—manufacturers of oil drilling equipment, for example—are particularly vulnerable to cost changes beyond their control. Although utility rates soared when the world price of oil shot up, it would be a mistake to think that most public utilities simply passed on all the cost increase to consumers. Some of the increases were absorbed by the utilities and the shareholders who owned them. Similarly, when the price of oil fell, manufacturers of oil drilling equipment found their market had largely disappeared as drilling for new oil slowed considerably. Using *Value Line* or another advisory service, check the earnings reports and the historical movements of the market price of Schlumberger, a leading manufacturer in this industry, and the message will become clear.

Other factors that present cost control problems are an extensive use of unionized labor and special environmental problems. An alleged reason for the auto industry's problems are the high wages and benefits paid to its unionized workers. (In early 1986, hourly wages and benefits were estimated at $25 in the United States versus $13 in Japan. Each of these countries, though, was in fear of a newcomer—South Korea—with a figure of $2.16.) Costs to control environmental pollution are legendary in some cases. Nuclear power is most likely a dead industry because of the enormous costs of meeting pollution-control requirements. For example, nuclear reactor facilities have been abandoned by Cincinnati Gas and Electric and Long Island Lighting Company. If you dislike

Where To Look for Value

With 20,000 or so stocks in the U.S., trying to find undervalued ones can be difficult and time-consuming, even with easy access to data. The problem is where to look. Savvy analysts have identified certain "winner" characteristics over the years and recent academic research, while certainly not conclusive, does offer support for some of them. Here's a very limited list you might want to consider. After reading about them, your investment approach will be to buy shares (at the end of a year) in small companies that are not followed by professional analysts or investors, and have dull product or service lines, a large inside ownership, and low debt levels and P/E ratios.

Small Company Stocks   Over fairly long periods of time, small company stocks do substantially better than large company stocks. They do so even after taking risk into consideration. Be careful, though. It seems small company stocks register their biggest gains in the month of January. In fact, if you take the January effect out of the picture, small stocks just about match the performance of big stocks. The reasons for this anomaly aren't perfectly clear, but researchers believe it has to do with investors' year-end portfolio adjustments for income-tax

purposes. If you are interested in small companies, buy their shares in late December or early January.

Neglected Stocks   A neglected stock is one that is not actively followed by many professional analysts or professional investors. The logic here is that a large following draws attention to a stock, which in turn drives up its price. Neglected stocks can be those of both large and small companies, but you likely will find more of the latter.

Large Inside Ownership   An insider is someone with a significant interest in a company; for example, someone who owns a large number of shares, is on the board of directors, or is a company officer. When the inside-ownership stake is large, stock returns often are higher. The rationale for this factor is old-fashioned self-interest. People who run the company seem to do a better job of it when they have much to gain—or lose.

Low P/E Ratios   A P/E ratio is simply a company's earnings per share divided into the market price of its stock. Analysts often believe that companies with low P/E ratios do not have good earnings growth opportunities. They might be "dull" companies selling very basic prod-

ucts or services, as opposed to the "exciting" ones selling esoteric items: Johns Manville and gypsum board versus Genentech and genetically engineered gene splices. Low P/E stocks tend to do better simply because their prices have not been driven excessively high. They represent a solid return based upon actual performance, rather than a hypothetical return based upon assumed earnings growth rates that may never be achieved. Be careful, though: some of the very low P/E stocks might represent companies destined for bankruptcy, particularly if the earnings figure is for a past, rather than a current or future, year.

Low Debt Levels   A small amount of debt obviously reduces the risk in a stock, but there is some evidence that it might also indicate better performance. Again, reasons are unclear here. Perhaps a management that spends too much time on financing, instead of producing and marketing, winds up with less profit for shareholders. But the superior performance might simply reflect the fact that fewer low-debt companies go bankrupt over time. When you take a total loss in a stock, your portfolio had better contain some exceptional winners, or your overall results will be poor.

investment risks, you should look closely at firms or industries for particular situations that could lead to uncontrollable cost increases, and avoid these businesses when selecting your stocks.

Excessive Use of Debt   Measuring the impact of a company's borrowing upon earnings and risk is much easier than determining similar measurements for many of the factors discussed above. All you need is the firm's current balance sheet. A heavy reliance upon debt means a greater number of fixed claims in front of your residual claim. All things being equal, it also means a riskier stock. It is simple to avoid this risk by limiting your investments to companies with little debt or preferred stock outstanding.

Market Risk

Market risk can be understood as the risk of a stock's price increasing or decreasing because of changes in the overall stock market. Over time, the prices of most stocks tend to move in the same direction, up or down. When we speak of the market going up or down, of course, we must remember the market is merely an aggregation of individual stocks. Usually, we are referring to a broad index of the market, such as the Dow Jones 30-Stock Industrial Average or the Standard and Poor 500 Stock Index. It is these 30 or 500 stocks, then, that "average" an increase or decrease.

What Causes Market Risk?   Fundamentally, the strengths, weaknesses, and uncertainties of the economy are the causes of volatile stock prices. The poor performance of stocks in the 1970s is most likely explained by an equally bad performance of the economy. Per capita real growth in income, for example, lagged far behind similar figures in the 1960s and 1950s. Conversely, the strong performance of stocks during most of the 1980s reflects resurgent strength in the economy. We mentioned the poor performance of stocks during inflationary periods; we should now recognize the real problem is one of poor economic performance, a situation most likely exacerbated by high inflation.

While changes in the economy lead to changes in stock prices, it is wrong to think there is some simplistic connection between the two. You may hear the evening newscaster make a comment such as, "The government's latest figures on unemployment led to lower prices on Wall Street today." Did the news lead to lower prices? Perhaps, if it was quite unexpected news. By and large, though, most news of this sort is not news to investors. Unemployment figures are anticipated far in advance of news releases, which more often merely confirm what most analysts expected. So, if you are trying to use economic data to forecast future stock prices, consider this: The Bureau of Economic Analysis does exactly the opposite; they consider stock prices one of their better *leading* indicators of future economic performance.

Market performance is embedded in the performance of the overall economy.

Managing Market Risk   It should be clear that market risk cannot be eliminated and must be faced if you plan to invest in common stocks. However,

Market risk can be managed using the beta concept.

it affects stocks differently. Cyclical stocks, as we noted, will tend to be influenced more than defensive stocks. The key to managing market risk is to first measure it and then determine how much additional return you require for undertaking it. Our discussion in Chapter 4 of measuring market risk led us to the beta concept. You should recall that beta is a quantitative estimate of the variability of returns of an individual stock in relation to the variability of returns of the overall stock market. While theoretically beta values can be positive or negative, as noted above, the overwhelming majority are positive, and we will limit our discussion to them. Keep in mind, then, what a beta value means:

From zero to 1.0:   a stock with less return variability than the market; the lower the number, the less the variability and the less risky the stock.

Equal to 1.0:   a stock with return variability and price risk equal to the market's.

Greater than 1.0:   a stock with greater return variability than the market; the higher the number, the greater the variability and the more risky the stock.

We will now use betas to estimate required returns for individual stocks.

ESTIMATING A STOCK'S REQUIRED RETURN

How much return should you get from a stock—15% a year, 20%, or what? Intuitively, you know that your return should be better than what you can receive investing risk free, such as in Treasury bills. Otherwise, why take the risk of a common stock? But determining how much better it should be is a difficult task. We shall attempt to answer the question by using the **capital asset pricing model (CAPM)** and one of its constructs, the **securities market line (SML)**.

The CAPM and the SML

The CAPM is a theory about asset returns.

The CAPM is essentially a theory that attempts to explain how asset returns are determined. An important underpinning to the theory is that returns depend upon the degree of risk investors are willing to undertake—the higher the risk, the greater the return. But returns do not depend upon total risk; rather, they depend only upon market risk. Why is that so? Because, as we discussed in Chapter 4, a diversified portfolio can eliminate firm-specific and industry risks without reducing expected return. The theory argues that the competitive behavior of thousands of investors eventually drives asset returns to a point where investors are compensated only for actual risks assumed. Since industry and firm-specific risks can be eliminated, investors will not be compensated for undertaking them. Thus, market risk is the only risk we need consider in evaluating a stock, and we can limit our assessment of an asset's risk to its market risk indicator—the beta weight.

For example, before you decide to invest in any individual stock, you first might consider limiting your investing to two assets: Treasury bills and a mutual fund that is an exact duplicate of the S&P 500 stock index. (Such funds actually exist. They are called index funds, and the largest is offered by the Vanguard Group of mutual funds.) If you put all your funds into T-bills, you would have no risk and a certain return; let us assume it is 6.0% for the upcoming investment period. If you put all your funds into the S&P 500 (call it the "market"), you would have a risk estimated by a beta value of 1.0 and an uncertain return for the period. You could put half your funds in each, thereby giving your portfolio a beta of 0.5 and a return mid-way between 6.0% and the market return. Let us first estimate the required market return and then look at the required return and risk characteristics of many portfolios composed of simply T-bills and/or the market. We'll also allow you to borrow funds to achieve higher returns and greater risks.

What Is a Reasonable Estimate of the Required Market Return? Our primary means of determining a reasonable estimate of the required market return is to look in the past. Rather than finding an absolute number, though, we should try to determine the amount of excess return over the return on T-bills. This figure is far more useful because both the T-bill rate and the market rate are very volatile from one year to the next. The study by Ibbotson Associates, cited in Chapter 3, indicated that over the period 1926–1988, the premium of stock returns over the T-bill return—called the market risk premium—was about 6.5%, based on the geometric average return of each. Suppose we wish to continue earning this average over an extended number of years in the future. We need to plan a somewhat higher premium on a year-by-year basis in order to achieve this average. As Ibbotson Associates point out (1986 *Yearbook,* p. 89), we actually should target the arithmetic average each year. Of course, some years' returns will be over this average and some years' returns will be under, but setting the arithmetic average as a goal should lead us to earn the geometric average as a long-run return.

> The market risk premium helps in determining a required return for the market.

So, to determine a required return for an upcoming year, estimate the T-bill rate and add the risk premium based on arithmetic averages—8.5% (see Chapter 3). In the current example, the target required return is 14.5% (6.0% + 8.5%). It is important to remember this is a total return. As such, it will consist of dividends and price appreciation. For example, if dividend yield is estimated at 4.0%, price appreciation is expected to be 10.5%.

Required Returns When Betas Are 1.0 or Less Exhibit 8.4 will help us understand the securities market line, or SML. For the time being, focus your attention on the segment of the line beginning at 6.0% on the y-axis and going out to the point where beta equals 1.0 on the x-axis. In effect, the SML is simply a line that connects the two points: 6.0% and zero beta (point 1), and 14.5% and beta = 1.0 (point 2). There is more than geometry involved, though. Any point on the line—such as point *A*—represents a portfolio of T-bills and the market. The characteristics of three portfolios are shown in Exhibit 8.5.

> The SML indicates a required return for portfolios with different beta values.

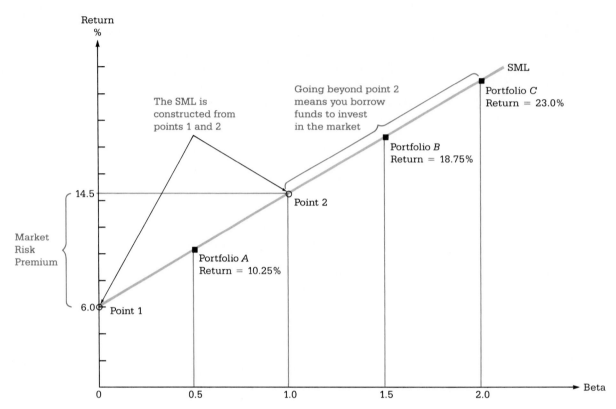

EXHIBIT 8.4
Constructing and using the SML

Portfolio *A,* for example, is invested half in bills and half in the market. Its beta of 0.5 is the weighted average: (1.0 × 0.5 + 0.0 × 0.5). Its return of 10.25% is the weighted average: (6.0 × 0.5 + 14.5 × 0.5). Another way to determine a portfolio's return (R_i) is to express it in terms of the risk-free rate (R_F), the portfolio beta (β_i), and the market risk premium (MRP), which is simply the difference between the market return (R_M) and R_F; that is, MRP = $R_M - R_F$. The following relationship holds:

$$R_i = R_F + \beta_i \text{ (MRP)} \tag{8.1}$$

As we see in the case of portfolio *A*:

$$10.25 = 6.0 + 0.5 \text{ (8.5)}$$

Required Returns When Betas Are Greater Than 1.0   The above relationships seem simple enough to understand, but you might wonder how an investor could ever construct a portfolio with a beta greater than 1.0 with only T-bills and the

	Portfolios		
T-bill return (or cost) = 6.0% Market return = 14.5%			
	A	B	C
Percent invested in T-bills	+ 50	− 50*	− 100*
Percent invested in the market	+ 50	+ 150	+ 200
Required return:			
(+0.5 × 6) + (0.5 × 14.5) =	10.25%	—	—
(−0.5 × 6) + (1.5 × 14.5) =	—	18.75%	—
(−1.0 × 6) + (2.0 × 14.5) =	—	—	23.0%
Portfolio betas	0.5	1.5	2.0

EXHIBIT 8.5
Characteristics of three portfolios composed of Treasury bills and the market

*Minus sign indicates borrowing.

market. If you are limited to investing only your own funds, you can't. But suppose you borrow and actually invest an amount greater than your own funds. To keep things simple for the time being, let's assume you can borrow at the T-bill rate. This assumption allows us to extend the SML beyond point 2 in Exhibit 8.4.

Borrowing has two impacts: it increases our portfolio beta beyond 1.0 and it increases our expected portfolio return. Exhibit 8.6 shows the effects of borrowing different amounts. For example, portfolio B assumes you have $1,000 to invest. But you want to increase your return and are willing to take risks to do so. Thus, you borrow $500 and invest $1,500 in the market. As you see, your net return is an expected $187.50, or 18.75% on your invested funds. Again, you could calculate this return using the weighted average return indicated above.

A portfolio with a beta greater than 1.0 involves leverage.

$$18.75 = -0.5\ (6.0) + 1.5(14.5) = -3.0 + 21.75$$

Now, the T-bill return is actually a cost—hence, the negative sign—and the weight (0.5) shows the proportion of borrowed funds to your own funds invested. In this case, you borrow $0.50 for each $1.00 of your own funds.

	Portfolios	
	B	C
Amount of your funds to invest	$1,000.00	$1,000.00
Amount of funds you borrow	500.00	1,000.00
Total invested in the market	$1,500.00	$2,000.00
Total return (market return = 14.5%)	$ 217.50	$ 290.00
Less interest paid (6%) on borrowed funds	30.00	60.00
Net return	$ 187.50	$ 230.00
Rate of return on your invested funds	18.75%	23.0%

EXHIBIT 8.6
Determining the rate of return on portfolios using borrowed funds

The portfolio beta is determined by dividing your funds into total funds invested, so 1.5 = $1,500/$1,000. You should be able to see now how the returns and betas for portfolios B and C in Exhibit 8.4 were determined. More important, you should see that the SML is a line that connects points representing all possible risk and return combinations from holding a risk-free asset (as a borrower or lender) and the market.

Shifts in the SML   Keep in mind that an SML is constructed at a given point in time. The line isn't set in stone, and we should expect that it will shift over time. Indeed, as the risk-free rate increases or decreases, the SML will shift upwards or downwards. For example, if the T-bill rate increased to 8.0%, the SML would shift upwards, as shown in Exhibit 8.7. This means all rates of return would increase by 2 percentage points. The market return would be 16.5% and a 0.5-beta portfolio's return would be 12.25%. The SML could also change its slope, but this implies a changing risk premium. While a change is possible, we prefer to think of the risk premium as being fairly constant over an extended period of time. If the

Changes in the risk-free rate shift the SML.

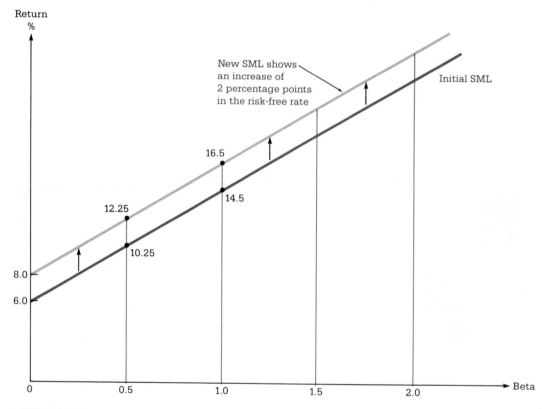

EXHIBIT 8.7
A shift in the SML

scope of our investment is long term, this assumption is reasonably realistic and does not diminish the analysis.

Before moving on, we should discuss the topic of borrowing at the risk-free rate. Is this a realistic assumption? Most likely, it is not. While you may have access to some funds at very low rates, such as a life insurance policy, you eventually reach a borrowing point where interest costs exceed the risk-free rate. While we won't pursue the implications of this point in greater detail, let us simply note that a rate higher than the T-bill rate would reduce the slope of the SML for all beta values greater than 1.0. Such a slope is illustrated in Exhibit 8.8, and the practical application is that portfolios with betas greater than 1.0 earn proportionately less return in relation to their risk than those with betas of 1.0 or less.

Using the SML

The SML provides us with a clear estimate of the *minimum* return we can require from investing in any specific stock. For example, if you were thinking of

The SML indicates the minimum return a stock must offer.

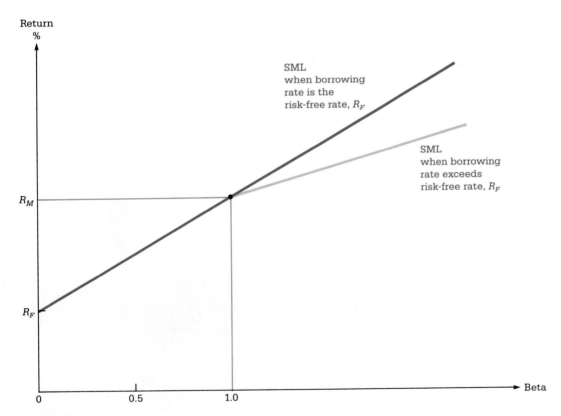

EXHIBIT 8.8
SML under two assumptions of the borrowing rate

investing in a stock that has a beta of 0.5, you should require a return of at least 10.25%. Why should you settle for less when you can very easily achieve this much through the simple portfolio of 50% in the market and 50% in T-bills?

Choosing stocks, then, is a straightforward process of comparing their required returns with their expected returns. The process is illustrated for the three stocks shown in Exhibit 8.9. Stock E is definitely chosen, since its expected return greatly exceeds its required return. Stock F is definitely rejected because its expected return is much less than its required return, and stock G is a borderline case, since its expected return barely exceeds its required return (you might flip a coin to decide this one). A graphic illustration of the selection process is shown in Exhibit 8.10. You can generalize from this graph that any stock represented by a point below the SML is rejected, any above is accepted, and any almost on the line leaves us indifferent between accepting or rejecting.

DETERMINING EXPECTED RETURNS

The next step in the stock-selection process is estimating expected returns. There are two widely used approaches: the earnings approach and the dividend approach. Actually, the two approaches are very similar and are better understood as two perspectives on the same process.

The Earnings Approach

An **earnings approach** consists of estimating future earnings and dividends per share of a selected stock and from them deriving a holding period return. As an alternative procedure—one that is computationally easier—we can use the stock's required rate of return to calculate the present value of the future cash flows we expect to receive. If this present value exceeds the current market price of the stock, we know its expected rate of return exceeds the required rate, and the stock should be purchased. An example will help illustrate the process.

Suppose we are thinking of investing in the stock of DAX, Inc., a company that has a long history of earnings and dividends. Its stock has a beta of about

Stocks	Beta	Required Rate of Return	Expected Rate of Return	Decision
E	0.5	10.25%	14.00%	Definitely accept; expected rate well exceeds required rate
F	1.5	18.75	15.00	Definitely reject; expected rate is far below required rate
G	2.0	23.00	23.25	A borderline case; flip a coin to make your choice

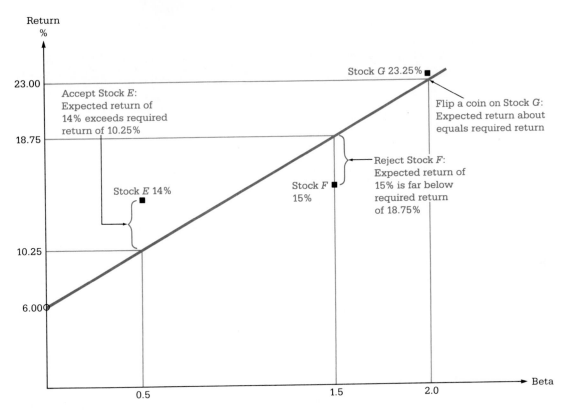

EXHIBIT 8.10
Graphic illustration of selecting stocks using the SML

0.71. Assume further the risk-free rate is again 6.0% annually. DAX, Inc., then, has a required rate of return of about 12%: 12.0 = 6.0 + 0.71(8.5). For simplicity, we will assume a three-year holding period and a current price of $20 a share for the stock. Exhibit 8.11 summarizes the analysis, and the important steps in the process are discussed below.

Estimate Future EPS   The earnings approach begins by estimating the stock's future earnings per share (EPS). With DAX, Inc., EPS in the past year was $2. Assuming EPS will grow at a 10% annual rate will give future EPS amounts of $2.20, $2.42, and $2.66. There are many difficulties involved in estimating the growth rate, but it is the key to the analysis and you should devote most of your time to this task. Candidly, this is what securities analysts are paid handsomely to do (or, more specifically, to do well). You might get a first guess at future growth by looking at a company's historical rate of growth. If you believe this growth rate will continue, then you can use it to project future earnings.

EXHIBIT 8.11

Analysis of DAX, Inc., using the earning approach

	Year 1	Year 2	Year 3
Current market price of DAX = $20 a share			
Current EPS = $2			
1. Future EPS (10% growth rate)	$2.20	$2.42	$ 2.66
2. Future DPS (50% payout ratio)	1.10	1.21	1.33
3. P/E ratio at end of year 3	—	—	10
4. Market price at end of year 3	—	—	$26.60
5. Annual cash flows (lines 2 + 4)	$1.10	$1.21	$27.93
6. Present value of $1 factors ($i = 12\%$)	0.893	0.797	0.712
7. Present value of future cash flows (line 5 × line 6)	$0.98	$0.96	$19.89

Present value of the stock = $0.98 + $0.96 + $19.89 = $21.83

Decision: buy the stock, because its present value of $21.83 exceeds its current market price of $20.00.

Actual rate of return (using HP 12C calculator) = 15.5%. This exceeds the required rate of return of 12% and further confirms the buy decision.

Estimate the Payout Ratio   The payout ratio tells us how much of the future earnings will be distributed to stockholders. There must be a logical connection between the EPS growth rate and the payout ratio in the sense that a high payout ratio dampens EPS growth, and vice versa. Growing companies must retain and invest earnings, rather than pay them out as dividends. So, if you are using a company's historical growth rate in EPS, you should also use its historical payout ratio. It would be a mistake, for example, to assume a high EPS growth rate along with a high payout ratio. On the other hand, a slower growth rate may be associated with a higher payout ratio.

Estimate DPS   The payout ratio applied to EPS gives dividends per share, DPS. Dividends paid represent actual cash inflows to investors. EPS amounts, in contrast, benefit shareholders only indirectly.

Estimate a Future P/E Ratio   If you follow an earnings approach, you generally believe stocks will sell at some multiple of their current or future EPS. This multiple is called the **P/E** (price/earnings) **ratio**. For example, the stock's past year's EPS is $2 and the market price is $20; thus, the P/E ratio is 10 ($20/$2). If you feel that ratio will stay the same, the stock's price at the end of three years will be $26.60, or 10 times its EPS of $2.66 in year 3.

Find and Discount the Annual Cash Flows   The annual cash flows consist of the dividends received plus the future price of the stock; that is, its price at the end of year 3 in our example. After the cash flows are determined, they must be discounted at the stock's required rate of return: 12% in the example. Discounting involves finding present value of $1 coefficients from Appendix A.3 and multiplying them by the cash flows. Adding the discounted cash flows gives us their present value of $21.83, as indicated in Exhibit 8.11.

Make a Decision   Since the present value of the cash flows exceeds the current market price of DAX, Inc., the stock should be purchased. This decision is further confirmed by calculating the internal rate of return on the investment. It is 15.5%, which exceeds the required rate of 12%. Thus, we can do better in DAX, Inc., than we can in a portfolio invested 29% in T-bills and 71% in the market. Assuming we are reasonably diversified to begin with, DAX, Inc., should be bought.

The Dividend Approach

An alternative method for evaluating a stock purchase is a **dividend approach**. While this approach can be applied in a variety of ways, the most frequently used is to express the expected total return (*TR*) of a stock as the sum of its current return and its future return. The current return (*CR*) is simply what you expect the stock to yield in the first year that you own it; that is, its upcoming annual dividend (D_1) divided by its current price (P_0). Its future return (*FR*) is usually expressed as the expected percentage growth (*g*) of dividends in the future. We then have:

> The dividend approach considers current return and future return.

$$TR = CR + FR = \frac{D_1}{P_0} + g \tag{8.2}$$

   Return to DAX, Inc., as an example of this approach. If we felt its EPS growth rate would stay at 10% and its payout ratio would remain 50%, then its dividend growth rate would also be a constant 10%. With these assumptions, we can find its *TR*:

$$TR = \frac{\$1.10}{\$20.00} + 0.10 = .055 + 0.100$$
$$= 0.155, \text{ or } 15.5\%$$

You should see that its upcoming annual dividend is $1.10, and the current price is $20. Notice also this return is exactly the same as the one determined using the earnings approach. This result is no coincidence because the assumption we made regarding a constant rate of dividend growth assures this outcome. Each method, in effect, determines a present value as a function of future dividends and the discount rate. If we discounted the cash flows in Exhibit 8.11 at 15.5%, the present value would be the stock's current price, $20. Equation 8.2 can be rearranged also to solve for current price; that is,

$$P_0 = \frac{D_1}{(TR - g)} \tag{8.3}$$

And,

$$\$20 = \frac{\$1.10}{(0.155 - 0.10)} = \frac{\$1.10}{(0.055)}$$

A dividend approach often assumes dividends will grow at a constant rate.

Equation 8.2 assumes a constant dividend growth rate forever, which may or may not be realistic. Obviously, if you have reason to believe the growth rate would change, then more extensive methods would be needed to determine a stock's present value. One such approach is presented in the following section.

Valuation with Multiple Growth Rates

The earnings or dividend models can be modified to accommodate various earnings or dividend growth rates over time. Actually, computer spreadsheet programs make it relatively easy to change any of the valuation variables and then determine the change's impact upon the value of the stock. To illustrate the impact of different growth rates, let us rework the DAX, Inc., case.

An Example   Instead of assuming that DAX's dividends will grow at a 10% rate forever, suppose that after three years the growth rate falls to 5%, which is then expected to continue forever. What impact does this have on share value? To solve the problem, we break it down into two parts: First, determine the present value of dividends received *during* the higher growth period; second, determine the present value of the expected market value of the stock *at the end of the* higher growth period.

The earnings and dividend approaches are adapted easily to an assumption of multiple growth rates.

Calculations for the first part follow. The discount rate is 12%, which is the assumed required rate of return as in previous examples with DAX.

Year	Dividend	Present Value of $1 Factor	Present Value
1	$1.10	0.893	$0.98
2	1.21	0.797	0.96
3	1.33	0.712	0.95
Present value of dividends			$2.89

These are the same calculations (with the exception of year 3) as those in Exhibit 8.11.

To determine the market value of the stock at the end of the higher growth period, we apply equation 8.3 with some modifications. First, the value will be at the end of a future year, not at the present time; and second, instead of using total return (*TR*), we use required return (*RR*). This gives us the following

$$P_t = \frac{D_{t+1}}{(RR - g)} \qquad (8.4)$$

which is applied in the present example.

$$P_3 = \frac{D_4}{(RR - g)}$$

$$P = \frac{\$1.33 \times 1.05}{(0.12 - 0.05)} = \frac{\$1.40}{0.07} = \$20.00$$

So, DAX, Inc., stock will be worth $20 a share at the end of year 3. (Notice that the dividend in year 4 is determined by increasing year 3's dividend by 5%.) However, we are interested in the present value of that future value. Thus, we discount, using the appropriate present value of $1 factor; that is,

Present Value of P_3 = $20.00 × 0.712 = $14.24

The last step is to add $14.24 and $2.89 to arrive at the present value of the stock—$17.13. According to this approach, investors should be willing to pay up to $17.13 for a share of DAX common stock.

Discussion Notice that DAX is worth less, given the new assumption of lower dividend growth after year 3. All things held constant, this is what you might expect, since a lower growth rate implies lower future dividends. You should note also that we did not make any new assumption about DAX's payout ratio after the higher-growth period is over. A more realistic assumption would be that the payout ratio increases as earnings growth decreases. In that event, the dividend in year 4 would be greater than $1.40. Assume the payout ratio increases to 60%. Since earnings in year 4 is $2.80 (5% increase over year 3), the dividend would be $1.68 (0.60 × $2.80). This implies a share value of $24 at the end of year 3 ($1.68/0.07) instead of $20. The present value of $24 is $17.09. Adding this to $2.89 gives a total present value of $20.98, which is greater than $17.13, although it is still slightly less than the $21.83 associated with the constant 10% growth.

This method is particularly useful in evaluating growth stocks, which typically have very high dividend and/or earnings growth rates. Surely, these rates cannot continue forever, and the analyst must consider that at some future date, or dates, the growth rates will fall. Failure to make this consideration can lead to very inflated stock values. While our example considers only one change in the growth rate, it is fairly straightforward to consider more changes using the same method.

Other Valuation Methods

The earnings and dividend models are used extensively to evaluate stocks. However, other approaches are also employed. Some of the more popular alternatives are explained here.

Asset Approaches Rather than focusing on earnings and dividends, some methods focus on asset values. One of the oldest approaches is the **Ben Graham NCAV** (net current asset value) **rule**. This rule argues that any stock with a

Ben Graham's NCAV rule looks at current assets minus total liabilities.

market value less than the company's net current assets per share is a good buy. Graham's net current assets are simply current assets minus total liabilities. An asset is current if it is cash or will convert to cash within a year, while liabilities are a company's debt obligation. (These are explained and used in greater detail in the next chapter.) Clearly, this is a simple rule to follow, but in recent years there have been relatively few companies selling below net current assets.

Break-Up Value   Some analysts attempt to determine **break-up value,** which arises with companies that supposedly are worth more broken up than left intact. Such companies may have divisions that do not mesh well with their overall operations, or business interests that cannot be managed well because of inexperience or lack of expertise. Other reasons may increase a company's break-up value, such as a more favorable tax situation to other companies. Such undervalued companies become targets for either friendly or unfriendly takeovers. The raider hopes to acquire the stock at a price below break-up value per share and then turn a profit from breaking the company apart. Small investors, of course, can hardly become corporate raiders; however, by buying takeover candidates they can realize substantial price appreciation when a raider begins to act. Typically, the raider drives up the market price of the stock in trying to gain control. The situation becomes very profitable for small investors if a bidding war between two (or more) raiders begins. The theory is good, and there have been a number of good applications. Unfortunately, determining break-up value is difficult, and there is no guarantee a raider will show interest in a potential target.

Rules of Thumb   There are numerous rules of thumb for determining value, and we will briefly discuss only two. One rule holds that a company's P/E (price/earnings) ratio should equal its expected growth in earnings. So, if you expect IBM's earnings will grow at a 12% rate in the future, its stock price should be 12 times its current earnings per share (EPS). If EPS is $8, then IBM's price should be $96 a share. As a rough rule, this might work reasonably well, but its use is questionable if you are capable of undertaking more rigorous work, such as the earnings or dividend approaches.

Another rule argues that stocks in general are good buys whenever dividend yields are high relative to Treasury bill yields. For example, when stock yields are, say, 75% of bill yields, they should be purchased. Conversely, if their yields fall to, say, 50% of bill yields, they should be sold. This rule of thumb can be modified and applied to specific companies, taking into consideration their growth character-istics. Is it worth the effort, though? Again, applying an earnings or dividend approach is relatively simple and usually provides far better insights on the valuation process. For example, as we have already seen, if Treasury bill yields change, so will required rates of return, which in turn influence the present values of stocks. It makes more sense to work with these relationships directly, rather than indirectly through rules of thumb.

Some companies may have greater value if some of their operations are sold.

Rules of thumb should be unnecessary for trained investors.

SUMMARY

Common stock provides investors with a right to vote, a right to maintain their proportionate interest in the corporation, and a right to share in earnings or asset distributions. Investors have various opportunities in common stocks: growth (price appreciation), current income, a combination of growth and income, blue chips (considered high quality stocks), cyclical price behavior, defensive (countercyclical) price behavior, and speculative situations. Price and other information on common stocks are reported daily in the financial pages of many newspapers.

Common stocks have liquidity and inflation risks, firm-specific and industry risks, and market risk. Market risk is often measured by a stock's beta weight, which allows investors to manage market risk by framing required rates of return.

A required rate of return can be derived from a securities market line (SML), which is constructed by using a risk-free rate of return and an estimate of the market's rate of return. Once established, points on the SML indicate required asset returns given their beta weights. The SML can be used to evaluate specific investments by comparing their required rates of return with their expected rates of return. Assets with expected rates greater than required rates should be purchased or held; assets with expected rates less than required should not be bought or should be sold.

Expected rates of return can be estimated using an earnings approach or a dividend approach. The former requires estimates of future earnings per share, the payout ratio, and future price/earnings ratios. The latter uses a current return percentage and an estimate of dividend growth infinitely into the future. While the two approaches can be different, in many applications they are virtually identical and lead to similar expected rates of return. The methods can be used also under an assumption of multiple growth rates. Other approaches can be used to determine stock value; these include asset approaches, break-up value, and rules of thumb.

KEY TERMS

Select the alternative that best identifies the key term.

1. common stock
2. voting right
3. pre-emptive right
4. right to share
5. residual claim
6. payout ratio
7. stock dividend
8. stock split
9. growth stock
10. income stock
11. growth and income stock
12. blue chip
13. cyclical stocks
14. defensive stock
15. speculative stock
16. capital asset pricing model (CAPM)
17. securities market line (SML)
18. earnings approach
19. P/E ratio
20. dividend approach
21. Ben Graham NCAV rule
22. break-up value

a. dividends divided by earnings
b. prices of these stocks are heavily influenced by economic cycles
c. market price divided by EPS
d. two-for-one is the most common
e. a high-quality stock
f. represents an ownership interest
g. a line connecting points showing returns and betas
h. a stock with a high dividend yield
i. you get one of these for each share you own
j. similar to a stock split
k. this entitles you to "what's left"
l. expresses expected return in terms of current and future returns
m. you buy these if you expect an economic slowdown
n. finds the present value of future cash flows, discounting at the required rate of return
o. you buy these when you expect a quick profit
p. earnings and dividend growth should exceed growth of the overall economy
q. your interest must be considered in any cash distribution
r. growth may be less than the overall economy's but current yield is good
s. allows you to maintain your proportionate interest in the corporation
t. a theory explaining investment returns
u. a takeover might be needed to realize profit from this valuation method
v. based upon current assets minus total liabilities

1. As an owner of common stock, you have three basic rights. Identify and explain each, indicating which of the three you feel is most important to most investors.
2. How does a stock dividend differ from a cash dividend? How are stock dividends and stock splits similar, and why do companies have them? Does either increase your wealth? Explain.
3. Explain the investment opportunities offered by the following kinds of stocks: *(a)* growth stock, *(b)* income stock, *(c)* growth and income stock, *(d)* blue chip, *(e)* cyclical stock, *(f)* defensive stock, and *(g)* speculative stock.
4. What are liquidity and inflation risks? Explain whether or not stocks have been good hedges against inflation.
5. What are firm-specific and industry risks? Explain specific sources of such risks.
6. Define market risk and explain its causes. Also explain how market risk can be managed.
7. How can you construct a securities market line (SML); that is, what information is necessary to construct it?
8. If the risk-free rate changes, what changes might occur to: *(a)* the slope of the SML, *(b)* the position of the SML, and *(c)* the value of the market risk premium? Explain your responses.
9. An SML provides required rates of return: Explain what this statement means.
10. Suppose investors cannot borrow at the risk-free rate. Explain the implication of this limitation upon the SML.
11. What is an expected return? Indicate how it differs from a required return.
12. Indicate six steps in utilizing an earnings approach to stock valuation.
13. Provide the basic formula for the dividend approach. How does it differ from an earnings approach? Does each lead to a similar decision regarding a stock, if a constant dividend growth rate is assumed?
14. What implications does a situation of multiple growth rates have upon stock valuation? Is such a situation a realistic approach for growth stocks? Explain.
15. Identify and briefly explain other methods of stock valuation.

1. You are looking at a quotation of AT&T in the morning newspaper. You see:

    25⅜ 19⅞ AT&T 1.20 5.6 16 40387 21⅝ 21⅛ 21½ −⅜

    Explain what each entry means.
2. Construct a securities market line (SML) assuming the risk-free rate (T-bill rate) is 6% and the market risk premium is 8.5%. Then, calculate the return for a stock with a 0.75 beta value and explain the implication of this return in terms of deciding to invest in the stock.
3. Referring to question 2, construct a new SML under the assumption the risk-free rate increases to 10%. What implication does such an increase have in terms of investing in specific stocks?
4. Again referring to question 2, suppose investors can lend at the T-bill rate of 6% but borrow at an 8% rate. Construct a new SML to reflect this situation. Does it influence the selection of the 0.75 beta stock? Would it influence the selection of a stock with a 1.5 beta? Explain.

5. You are thinking of investing in one or possibly all three stocks listed below. Assuming a risk-free rate of 8.8% and a market risk premium of 8.5%, explain which—if any—of the stocks should be purchased.

	Ace Co.	King Inc.	Queen Inc.
Beta values	0.400	0.612	1.800
Expected rates of return (%)	11.5	16.6	19.0

6. In addition to the information provided in problem 5, you have other data for King, Inc. You know the current market price of the stock is $15 a share and last year's EPS was $1.50. The company's payout ratio was—and will be in the future—60%, and EPS is expected to grow at a 10% rate each year. Determine the present value of a share of King, Inc., stock, assuming a three-year holding period. Does your answer confirm your decision about the stock in problem 5? Explain.

7. Using information provided in problems 5 and 6, use the dividend approach to show that King, Inc.'s, expected rate of return is, in fact, 16.6%.

8. (Student Project) P/E ratios are published in each issue of The Wall Street Journal and Barron's. From the library, reference an issue of either one and draw a sample of 20 companies: 10 with very low P/E ratios and 10 with very high ratios. Do not select companies with negative earnings, or any company whose price performance over the year is known to you. Now, with a current issue of either paper, obtain current prices and evaluate performances of the two groups. Write a brief essay describing your experiment.

CASE ANALYSES

8.1
The Zumwalts' Interest in Common Stocks

Larry and Barb Zumwalt are a young couple in relatively strong financial shape. Each has a professional career and earns around $40,000 annually. In addition, they have accumulated about $20,000 that can be earmarked for speculative investing. They intend to develop a common stock portfolio, making their own security selections rather than utilizing pooling arrangements. The Zumwalts have done a reasonable amount of reading on the topic of common stock investing, although they hardly consider themselves experts. They admit they have no idea of what kinds of stocks to buy, or what amounts of return they should expect from their investments.

To illustrate their problems, Barb feels they should invest heavily in public utility stocks because their dividend yields are quite good at around 9%. She does not favor growth stocks because of their low yields, but also because they seem difficult to find. Barb likes the three public utilities operating in their region of the state, and she would invest at least $5,000 in each of them. Larry disagrees with Barb. He favors growth stocks and feels yearly returns of 30% are very likely if the right stocks can be found. Larry hopes to find the right stocks by subscribing to an investment advisory service that claims a very successful past history. Larry sees little risk in this strategy, but he admits that Barb's utility stocks are probably less risky.

Questions

a. The Zumwalts indicate a willingness to undertake speculative investing. However, do they have concrete investment plans? Discuss.

b. Explain whether the Zumwalts comprehend risk and return possibilities from common stock investing. Suppose they ask you to advise them in this regard. Indicate specific risks and discuss how these risks might be managed. Then explain how sensible estimates of required return can be generated, given an understanding of risk.

c. Do either public utility stocks or growth stocks seem appropriate for the Zumwalts? Discuss.

d. How would you advise Larry and Barb as to specific selections of stocks? Explain.

**8.2
Analytical
Evaluation of
the Darden Tool
Company**

The Darden Tool Company had an initial public offering of its common stock last year. The company produces specialized tools and components used in manufacturing cellular telephones. The spectacular growth of this industry has created exciting opportunities for Darden, and the price of its stock reflects this potential. Its current price is $40 a share, which is 25 times its earnings per share in the previous year. EPS has grown at a 20% annual rate for the past four years and analysts anticipate this rate will continue for at least four more years. They also believe the current P/E ratio will continue for four more years. Darden's management does not favor a large dividend, preferring instead to reinvest earnings; the current payout ratio is 40%. At present, the risk-free rate is 6.0%, the market risk premium is 8.0%, and the company's beta is 1.5.

Questions

a. Determine the present value of the stock, using the earnings approach. Does the stock represent a good purchase? Explain.

b. Calculate the stock's total return, using the dividend approach. Does this approach indicate a good buy? Explain.

c. Determine the stock's present value assuming the following: (i) after four years, earnings and dividend growth falls to a 12% annual rate, which will continue indefinitely; and (ii) the payout ratio increases to 60%, beginning in the 5th year. Do these new assumptions change your recommendations in parts a and b? Explain.

**HELPFUL
READING**

Clements, Jonathan. "Value is Where You Find It." *Forbes*, March 20, 1989, pp. 62–64.

Donnelly, Barbara. "Dividend Indicator Yields Crop of Critics." *The Wall Street Journal*, May 17, 1989, p. C1.

Kuntz, Mary. "Compared to What? Growth Stocks Are Relatively Cheap." *Forbes*, February 23, 1987, p. 154.

Long, J. B. "The Market Valuation of Cash Dividends: A Case to Consider." *Journal of Financial Economics,* June-September 1978.

Lynch, Peter, with John Rothchild. *One Up on Wall Street: How to Use What You Already Know to Make Money in the Market.* New York: Simon and Schuster, 1989.

Ozanian, Michael. "Dividend Play." *Forbes,* December 15, 1986, pp. 202–4.

———. "Bird in Hand Theory." *Forbes,* February 23, 1987, pp. 104–8.

Palmeri, Christopher. "Earnings Guesstimates: Uncertain or Unstable Earnings Forecasts Mean Opportunity for Investors." *Forbes,* April 17, 1989, pp. 216–20.

Serwer, Andrew Evan. "To Find Tomorrow's Hot Stocks, Go Where the Big Boys Aren't." *Fortune,* February 27, 1989, pp. 29–30.

Sharpe, W. F. "Capital Asset Prices: A Theory of Market Equilibrium Under Conditions of Risk." *Journal of Finance,* September 1964.

CHAPTER NINE

Fundamental Analysis of Common Stocks

FINANCIAL STATEMENTS

The Balance Sheet

The Income Statement

EVALUATING FINANCIAL PERFORMANCE

Measuring Balance Sheet Strength

Measuring Earnings Strength

Was NCR an Undervalued Security?

Using Ratio Analysis

EVALUATING THE ECONOMY AND THE INDUSTRY

Brief History of U.S. Cycles

Forecasting Economic Cycles

Industry Analysis

BOXES

Should PSRs Replace P/E Ratios?

If You Think Economic Forecasting Is Chaotic, You Could Be Right

After you finish this chapter, you will be able to:

- understand a business balance sheet, including what it does and does not show.

- understand an income statement in terms of what it shows and what its limitations are.

- evaluate balance sheet strength by understanding liquidity and solvency ratios.

- evaluate earnings strength by understanding earnings ratios.

- see how earnings and dividend growth relate to the market price of a common stock.

- grasp how economic performance moves in cycles and realize the importance of forecasting future economic activity.

- understand the nature of industry analysis.

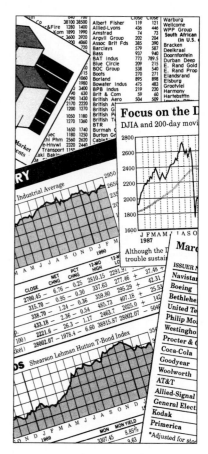

I f the key to successful investing is finding undervalued securities, the important question is, How is it done? Two broad approaches—the earnings approach and the dividends approach—were explained in the previous chapter. They are a part of securities analysis called fundamental analysis, and someone working in this area is referred to as a fundamentalist. Fundamentalists believe it is possible to determine the intrinsic value of common stock. This value may reflect factors such as a company's earning power, its asset structure, the quality of its management or product lines, or its potential for being acquired in a merger or other takeover. Fundamentalists are often seen as professional securities analysts, many having been trained in securities evaluation techniques and some holding the designation Chartered Financial Analyst (CFA). The CFA has undergone rigorous testing and has met other professional requirements to earn the title. This chapter will not make you a CFA, but it will help you understand the nature of fundamental analysis.

FINANCIAL STATEMENTS

All financial analysis requires data, and a good starting point for obtaining data is a company's annual financial report, particularly the financial statements. As an investor you should be familiar with the two most important of these—the balance sheet (also called a statement of financial condition) and the income statement.

The Balance Sheet

A balance sheet shows assets, liabilities, and net worth.

A **business balance sheet** shows the assets and liabilities of a business and the difference between the two, which is referred to broadly as net worth. Assets are things of value to a business: its cash, accounts receivable, inventories, machinery and equipment, land and buildings, and many others, including intangible items such as patents and copyrights. Liabilities are amounts a business owes its creditors over both the long and short term. Net worth, as the difference between assets and liabilities, indicates what the business is worth, in an accounting sense. If the business is a corporation, net worth is usually referred to as shareholders' equity.

Exhibit 9.1 shows the balance sheet for NCR Corporation for the three years ended December 31, 1988, 1987, and 1986. NCR is a large multinational corporation with total assets of $4.72 billion and about 60,000 employees. It develops, manufactures, markets, installs, and services business information processing systems, operating on a worldwide basis with approximately 50% of its sales earned outside the United States. An analyst would probably describe NCR as a high-quality (blue chip) growth company.

Assets, Liabilities, and Shareholders' Equity Most of the assets, liabilities, and shareholders' equity accounts are probably clear to you and do not require

EXHIBIT 9.1

NCR Corporation's balance sheet. (Source: *NCR Annual Shareholders' Report,* 1988. Courtesy of NCR.)

	December 31		
Consolidated Statement of Financial Position	1988	1987	1986
	(in thousands)		
Assets			
Current assets			
Cash and cash equivalents	$ 534,573	$ 488,592	$ 433,115
Short-term investments	288,723	223,479	236,471
Accounts receivable, net	1,174,395	1,172,873	1,055,793
Inventories	743,885	762,835	671,804
Other current assets	264,957	227,609	182,801
Total Current Assets	3,006,533	2,875,388	2,579,984
Long-term receivables, net	288,836	283,570	278,280
Rental equipment and service parts, net	207,280	222,444	226,057
Property, plant and equipment, net	907,466	835,740	734,225
Goodwill, net of amortization	115,538	120,353	126,174
Other assets	191,664	203,341	138,231
Total Assets	$ 4,717,317	$ 4,540,836	$4,082,951
Liabilities and Shareholder's Equity			
Current liabilities			
Short-term borrowings	$ 266,078	$ 399,713	$ 53,713
Accounts payable	251,479	247,006	173,292
Taxes payable	288,401	258,842	190,415
Payroll payable	189,534	213,245	157,152
Customers' deposits and deferred service revenue	395,618	368,380	319,653
Other current liabilities	384,930	371,497	327,437
Total Current Liabilities	1,776,040	1,858,683	1,221,662
Long-term debt	222,254	109,844	129,417
International employees' pension and indemnity liabilities	135,138	131,159	104,218
Deferred income taxes	137,533	104,129	98,166
Minority interests	206,177	175,502	133,156
Shareholders' Equity			
Common stock	544,125	544,125	544,125
Retained earnings	3,136,958	2,782,643	2,443,192
Accumulated translation adjustments	36,755	17,444	(78,763)
Less treasury stock at cost	(1,477,663)	(1,182,693)	(512,222)
Total Shareholders' Equity	2,240,175	2,161,519	2,396,332
Total Liabilities and Shareholders' Equity	$ 4,717,317	$ 4,540,836	$4,082,951

The Summary of Significant Accounting Policies and Notes to Consolidated Financial Statements are an integral part of the statement.

elaboration. Others, though, are not so clear. The asset, "Goodwill, net of amortization," is better understood as simply "goodwill." It means NCR acquired some companies and paid more for them than their net asset value, also called book value. Amortization is a form of depreciation, and in this case, it means the goodwill value is being reduced each year to show that it is being used and eventually will cease to exist.

The liability, "Customers' deposits and deferred service revenue," indicates NCR has collected payments from customers for services it will provide in the future. Rather than showing the collection of these payments as revenues, it is more appropriate to show them as liabilities until NCR actually performs the services. "Minority interests" is an account that comes into existence when one company takes over another but does not acquire all of the common shares outstanding. These remaining shares are called the minority interest. The account is actually a hybrid—not a liability, since the acquirer is under no obligation to purchase the remaining shares, and not part of shareholders' equity. In evaluating a company, most analysts treat the minority interest as a liability.

> A minority interest is a hybrid account.

The shareholders' equity account, "Accumulated translation adjustments," has to do with applying a dollar value to NCR's operations abroad. Since these operations are denominated in foreign currencies—not dollars—a translation to dollars must be made for reporting purposes. As the dollar strengthens or weakens relative to other currencies, leading to translation gains or losses, this account will increase or decrease. Often, these gains or losses are substantial and have a significant impact on the company's profits and financial position.

The shareholders' equity account, "Treasury stock," indicates the purchase value of shares of the company's own stock that management has bought and not retired. These shares are said to be held in the treasury; thus, the name treasury stock. Companies buy back their shares for a variety of reasons. Small amounts are usually purchased for eventual distribution through employee stock option plans. However, a major purchase usually means management feels the shares are undervalued and represent good buying opportunities. Notice that NCR has accumulated a substantial amount of treasury stock through 1988. It did so as part of a share repurchase strategy, since NCR's management felt the shares were undervalued.

What the Balance Sheet Shows   The main function of the balance sheet is to show what a company is worth at some point in time, using accounting concepts to measure worth. The worth of a business corporation is shown by the value of shareholders' equity. NCR was worth $2,240,175,000 at December 31, 1988. If we divide this figure by the number of shares of common stock outstanding on that date, we then have shareholders' equity per share, more commonly referred to as **book value per share;** that is,

> Book value shows what the company is worth in an accounting sense.

$$\text{book value/share} = \frac{\$2,240,175,000}{79,437,775} = \$28.20$$

Was each share of NCR stock really worth $28.20? Since the market price of each share at that time was about $53, we could conclude that something was wrong: either investors were paying too much, or book value is not a good measurement of true value. While both alternatives could be true, keep in mind that book value is purely an accounting concept. As such, it depends upon certain accounting conventions and regulations for determining value. One of the most important of these is the use of historical cost as a basis for measuring asset values; in effect, companies show the values of most of their assets at the price paid for them less any depreciation the companies have taken to allow for loss of productivity or obsolescence. But is cost the same as value? Not in most cases, and in some there are huge differences. When you begin fundamental analysis, book value can be a starting point, but you must go beyond it in almost every situation for a more comprehensive view of value.

> Cost is not the same as value, and in many cases the two are quite different.

What the Balance Sheet Doesn't Show   Apart from the problem of reporting values that are more appropriately described as historical costs, a balance sheet may not even list all of a company's assets or its potential liabilities. For example, unless a company actually purchases an asset or expends funds to develop and produce it, the asset will not be shown on the balance sheet. Furthermore, any increases in value attributable to inflation or increased demand is also ignored. This means Coke's and PepsiCo's formulas, trademarks, copyrights, and many other intangible assets are not even shown. Walt Disney's library of films, reportedly worth hundreds of millions of dollars, is shown at a tiny fraction of that figure and there are many other examples. These hidden assets are in some cases worth far more than assets revealed on the balance sheet. In recent years, fundamentalists have devoted considerable research time looking for **hidden asset plays**. A *play* is Wall Street jargon for finding a way to profit from an undervalued or overvalued situation. If the market price of a company's stock is far below its book value, which includes values of the hidden assets, then the company may be a good candidate for a takeover. Buying the stock now and waiting for the takeover is the play.

> Many valuable assets may not appear on balance sheets.

Certain potential losses might also not appear on a company's balance sheet. Although CPAs must indicate potential losses and contingent liabilities when reasonable evidence suggests they will occur, it is not cut and dried as to what makes up reasonable evidence, or how much the future amounts will be. It is extremely important to read all parts of a company's financial report, including the footnotes, since expected future adversities may be reported there and no place else.

The Income Statement

The **income statement** is a listing of revenue and expense accounts that show the results of a company's operations over some time period. Since the generation of income is the primary function of most businesses, the income statement is regarded as the most important statement the company prepares. Exhibit 9.2

> The income statement is a company's most important statement.

EXHIBIT 9.2
NCR Corporation's income statement. (Source: *NCR Annual Shareholders' Report,*
1988. Courtesy of NCR.)

	Year Ended December 31		
Consolidated Statement of Financial Position	1988	1987	1986
	(in thousands, except per share amounts)		
Revenue			
Sales and rentals	$3,892,631	$3,688,777	$3,156,463
Services	2,097,278	1,951,890	1,725,178
Total Revenue	5,989,909	5,640,667	4,881,641
Costs and Expenses			
Cost of sales and rentals	1,900,851	1,811,366	1,503,614
Cost of services	1,301,402	1,233,809	1,081,457
Marketing, general and administrative	1,621,098	1,518,795	1,387,449
Research and development	416,429	356,594	320,718
Interest expense	45,907	29,515	35,563
Other (income) expenses, net	(82,944)	(75,162)	(69,841)
Total Costs and Expenses	5,202,743	4,874,917	4,258,960
Income before Income Taxes	787,166	765,750	622,681
Provision for income taxes	347,900	346,420	286,157
Net Income	$439,266	$419,330	$336,524
Per Common Share			
Net income	$5.33	$4.51	$3.42
Cash dividends declared	1.24	1.00	.92
Weighted Average Number of Common Shares Outstanding	82,423	93,067	98,306

The Summary of Significant Accounting Policies and Notes to Consolidated Financial Statements are an integral part of this statement.

shows NCR's income statements for the years ended December 31, 1988, 1987, and 1986. The term "consolidated" indicates NCR has income from its subsidiary corporations that has been incorporated into these statements.

What the Income Statement Shows The objective of the income statement is to show the amount of net income (or net loss) the company earned for the period indicated. As you see, NCR's net income in 1988 was $439,266,000, up from $419,330,000 in 1987. Investors are less interested in total earnings than they are in earnings per share of common stock (EPS). Exhibit 9.2 shows the weighted average number of common shares outstanding each year and also shows each EPS, which in 1988 was $5.33, up from $4.51 in 1987. Exhibit 9.2 also reports the dividend per share NCR paid each year. It was $1.24 in 1988 versus $1.00 in 1987.

Investors are interested in earnings per share (EPS).

Limitations of the Income Statement   Like the balance sheet, the income statement should not be relied upon as the absolute truth of a company's earnings performance. Keep in mind that net income is an accounting concept, shaped and formed by accounting rules, regulations, and conventions. Some of these make a great deal of sense for determining value, while others are more controversial.

For example, we mentioned previously the accountant's insistence that historical cost be used to state asset values. These same historical costs, then, form the basis for depreciation, which is taken as an expense on the income statement. No one questions that depreciation is an economic reality that must be recognized in measuring earnings. But should the annual allocation be based upon what an asset actually cost when it was purchased, or what it could be sold for today, or how much it would cost today to replace it? Depending on your view, you could have three substantially different depreciation figures. Even if we agree on what basis to depreciate, we may then disagree on our estimates of the asset's life, which also gives us different depreciation amounts. Many financial analysts have become so skeptical of depreciation figures that they have chosen to ignore them altogether by calculating cash flows. A **cash flow** is simply net income plus depreciation (or amortization); that is,

Depreciation expense might be based on an asset's historical cost, its replacement cost, or its market value.

Many financial analysts prefer cash flow because it is uninfluenced by depreciation amounts.

$$\text{cash flow} = \text{net income} + \text{depreciation}$$

It has become an important concept, so you should be familiar with it. Like earnings, it is often shown on a per share basis.

Unfortunately, NCR does not list its depreciation on the income statement. It is found elsewhere in the report, however, and the amounts, along with cash flow figures, are as follows:

	1988	1987	1986
Depreciation	$297,053,000	$294,243,000	$277,294,000
Net income	$439,266,000	$419,330,000	$336,524,000
Total cash flow	$736,319,000	$713,573,000	$613,818,000
Cash flow per share	$8.93	$7.67	$6.24

As you can tell, the depreciation amounts are quite large in relation to net income.

Do cash flow figures help in determining a company's value? Some analysts believe strongly they do, while others are less convinced. Cash flow figures are generally more useful in comparing one company to another than in looking at a single company's historical data, because companies may differ considerably in using depreciation methods. In effect, cash flows remove these differences.

Along with depreciation, there are other areas where accounting principles are often applied differently. Important differences arise in valuing inventories, with some companies choosing to value them at their more recent purchase prices while others value them at older prices. It often takes an expert to unravel the differences in income produced by these different valuation methods. Fortunately, during periods of stable prices the differences are not very large.

Accounting differences arise in valuing inventories.

Accounting-determined net income is not perfect, and in some situations you should go beyond it to judge a company's capacity to generate earnings. But ignoring net income altogether would be a mistake. In the overwhelming majority of cases, it provides a reasonable estimate of a company's earnings strength.

EVALUATING FINANCIAL PERFORMANCE

The balance sheet and income statement by themselves provide a good overview of a company's financial strengths and weaknesses. If you have reviewed Exhibits 9.1 and 9.2 closely, you most likely have formed an impression of NCR. You can sharpen that impression by examining the data more extensively and critically through ratio analysis, which is a technique of looking at one account value in relation to another. It often provides insights that are missed when looking at accounts independently.

Historical ratio analysis uses trends and averages.

Ratio analysis is often performed by looking at the historical data of one company over a period of time. With this method, called *historical analysis,* trends and averages are used to evaluate a given year's performance. Another approach, called *cross-sectional analysis,* compares one company's ratios to those of others or to industry averages. A thorough financial review includes both approaches, although we will limit our discussion to historical analysis. Various financial reports provided data on NCR for the 13-year period ending December 31, 1988.

Measuring Balance Sheet Strength

Is NCR a financially strong company, a candidate for bankruptcy, or somewhere in the middle of these extremes? Is it sufficiently liquid to pay its bills on an ongoing basis, or is it burdened by excessive short-term debt? Ratio analysis can shed light on these questions.

Liquidity   One balance sheet strength is adequate liquidity. A company is liquid when it has sufficient current assets to pay its current liabilities. The term *current* usually means the asset can be converted to cash within the firm's normal operating cycle, usually presumed to be one year; a current liability is one that must be paid within one year. Total liquidity is measured by net working capital (NWC), defined as current assets minus current liabilities. Exhibit 9.1 shows NCR's net working capital in 1988 was $1.231 billion ($3,006,533,000 − $1,776,040,000) at year end. Given current assets, current liabilities, and net working capital (NWC), two liquidity ratios can then be calculated.

Low ratios of NWC to sales or current assets to current liabilities indicate a potential liquidity problem.

NWC/Sales.   NWC typically must increase as sales increase. NCR could not be expected to run its business with no more NWC than the corner grocer. If NWC lags considerably behind sales growth, the company could face a future liquidity problem. NCR's **NWC/sales ratio** was .205 ($1.231 billion/$5.990 billion) in 1988. Exhibit 9.3 indicates this ratio is below the 13-year average value of .297.

The Current Ratio. The **current ratio** is defined as current assets divided by current liabilities; that is,

$$\text{current ratio} = \frac{\text{current assets}}{\text{current liabilities}}$$

NCR's 1988 current ratio is

$$\frac{\$3,006,533}{\$1,776,040} = 1.69$$

A current ratio of 1.69 means NCR had $1.69 in current assets for each $1.00 of current liabilities. Exhibit 9.3 indicates this is also below the 13-year average of 2.01.

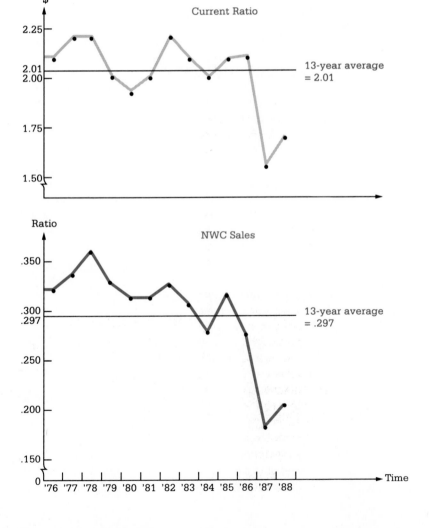

EXHIBIT 9.3

NCR's liquidity ratios

Liquidity is an elusive quality to measure. The previous two ratios suggest a deteriorating position, although they do not show a liquidity crisis. To gain further insights at this point, an analyst would consider using industry comparisons to determine how NCR's liquidity position compares to other firms in the computer industry. An unfavorable comparison would be considered in determining the intrinsic value of the company's stock.

Solvency takes a longer view than liquidity.

Solvency   Solvency is different from liquidity: liquidity is a short-term concept while solvency takes a longer view. Each, though, has to do with evaluating a company's debt position. Solvency is particularly important to a company's bondholders. They are concerned that interest and principal payments can be met over the bond issue's life and that the company is not forced into bankruptcy. In the latter case, the bondholders' claims are more likely to be paid if there is a small amount of debt in relation to assets. Two ratios are often used to measure the firm's debt structure: the total debt ratio and the debt/equity ratio.

The Total Debt Ratio.   The **total debt ratio** shows total liabilities divided by total assets; that is,

$$\text{total debt ratio} = \frac{\text{total liabilities}}{\text{total assets}}$$

The following equation shows NCR's 1988 total debt ratio:

$$\frac{\$1,776,040 + \$222,254 + \$135,138 + \$137,533 + \$206,177}{\$4,717,317} = \frac{\$2,477,142}{\$4,717,317} = .525$$

At the end of 1988, NCR's total liabilities were about 53% of its total assets; thus, asset values could shrink 47% before creditors would face a potential loss in selling assets to cover their claims. Of course, this assumes assets could be sold at book values, which may not be true. Exhibit 9.4 shows NCR's debt ratio has shrunk since 1976 but was above its 13-year average in 1988.

The Debt/Equity Ratio.   Since the total debt ratio includes current liabilities in the calculation, it duplicates some information available with the current ratio. To measure the long-term financial structure, analysts use the **The debt/equity ratio describes the long-term financial structure.** **debt/equity ratio**. Its calculation is shown below:

$$\text{debt/equity ratio} = \frac{\text{long-term debt}}{\text{total shareholders' equity}}$$

NCR's 1988 figure is determined as follows:

$$\frac{\$222,254 + \$135,138 + \$137,533 + \$206,177}{\$2,240,175} = \frac{\$701,102}{\$2,240,175} = .313$$

Exhibit 9.4 indicates this ratio is above its 13-year average of .248, and has risen rather sharply since 1985. This recent trend shows clearly how NCR has increased its use of long-term debt relative to owners' equity. While the company's solvency

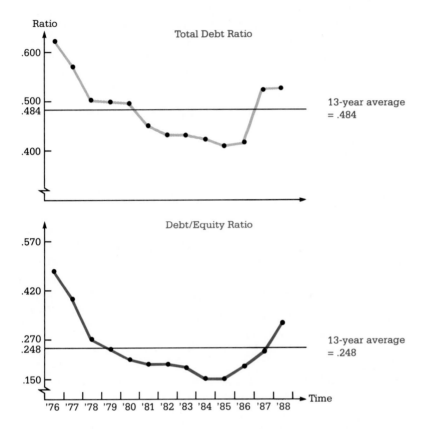

EXHIBIT 9.4
NCR's solvency ratios

position has deteriorated somewhat, one might argue it was too strong in the past. NCR's share repurchases have contributed to the recent rise. Very often earnings per share can be increased by using borrowed money. If so, the shareholders' position is not enhanced by low levels of debt; in effect, they are better off if borrowed funds are used to invest in earning assets.

Measuring Earnings Strength

While balance sheet strength is important, earnings strength is even more so. In fact, balance sheet strength usually arises from earnings strength. Despite how strong a company might be to start with, it cannot sustain constant losses without eventually facing bankruptcy. You can measure earnings strength by examining key ratios, and earnings and dividend growth rates.

Earnings Ratios   Earnings ratios indicate profitability in relation to certain charges that must be covered each year—such as interest—and to funds invested in the business. Three often-watched ratios are the times-interest-earned figure and the returns on investment and equity.

Times-Interest-Earned Ratio.   A company's earnings must be used first to pay bond interest. Only after it is paid can the company pay dividends to shareholders or retain any funds for reinvestment. The **times-interest-earned ratio** indicates the adequacy of earnings to pay interest, and it is calculated as follows:

$$\text{times-interest-earned ratio} = \frac{\text{net income before interest and taxes}}{\text{interest}}$$

NCR's 1988 times-interest-earned ratio is

$$\frac{\$787{,}166 + \$45{,}907}{\$45{,}907} = \frac{\$833{,}073}{\$45{,}907} = 18.15$$

In 1988, NCR had $18.15 of earnings, before interest and taxes, for each $1.00 of interest, which is excellent coverage. Exhibit 9.5 shows that coverage is substantially above the 13-year average of 12.15. NCR should have virtually no trouble meeting its existing interest obligations.

Return on Investment.   **Return on investment (ROI)** indicates the company's ability to generate profits from its assets. The ratio is shown below:

$$\text{ROI} = \frac{\text{net income}}{\text{average asset investment}}$$

Average asset investment is often calculated as the average of the end- and beginning-of-year asset values. NCR's 1988 ROI is

$$\frac{\$439{,}266}{(\$4{,}717{,}317 + \$4{,}540{,}836)/2} = \frac{\$439{,}266}{\$4{,}629{,}077} = .095, \text{ or } 9.5\%$$

NCR earned about 9.5% in 1988 on its asset investments. Is this a good return? Relative to the 13-year average of 7.7%, it would seem so. However, ROI is an after-tax return, and you might compare it to similar returns, such as those on long-term municipal bonds. Using this yardstick, we would conclude it was not exceptional, since municipal bonds yielded about 7% for most of 1988 and offered less risk. Moreover, Exhibit 9.5 shows that ROI has never been above 10.0% and has been somewhat volatile over the 13-year period. The most likely explanation for this poor performance is that NCR was reinvesting much of its profits to make assets and earnings grow. Many of these investments were in product research and development—areas that do not immediately show high returns. If these investments ultimately prove profitable, NCR's ROI's in the future could be much higher.

Return on Equity.   ROI does not consider how the company's assets were financed; as such, it measures the return to total investment, not the return to the stockholders' investment. A direct measurement of this latter item is the **return on equity (ROE)**. It is calculated in the following way:

EXHIBIT 9.5
NCR's earnings ratios

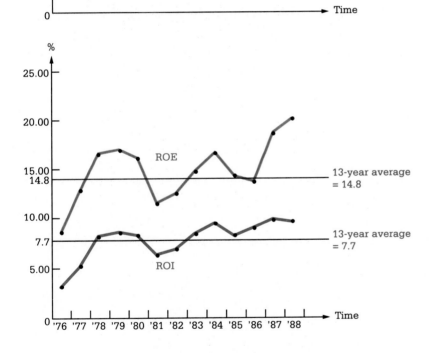

$$ROE = \frac{net\ income}{average\ shareholders'\ equity}$$

where average shareholders' equity is end-of-year value plus beginning-of-year value divided by two. NCR's ROE in 1988 is

$$\frac{\$439,266}{(\$2,240,175 + \$2,161,519)/2} = \frac{\$439,266}{\$2,200,847} = .200, \text{ or } 20.0\%$$

Exhibit 9.5 shows the 13-year history of this ratio and indicates that 1988's value is remarkably better than the average of 14.8%. NCR's ROE figures are more impressive than its ROIs, illustrating the beneficial effect of using borrowed funds to enhance the return to owners.

Earnings and Dividend Growth   NCR's improved earnings ratios most likely explain why the price of its common stock has increased so dramatically since 1976, as Exhibit 9.6 shows. Exhibit 9.6 also indicates NCR's net income per share of common stock (EPS) grew from $0.52 in 1976 to $5.33 in 1988. This increase represents an annual rate of growth of 19.6%, which is slightly above the annual rate of growth of the stock's price (18.3%). Increasing at a slightly lower annual rate (16.0%) were NCR's dividends per share.

Comparing prices of the common stock to EPS amounts in Exhibit 9.6 gives us NCR's historical price/earnings (P/E) ratios. Over the ten-year period, this ratio varied between a high of 14.0 (1987) and a low of 5.2 (1981). Clearly, the P/E ratio has been volatile. This volatility somewhat diminishes its usefulness for determining future stock values, but some analysts feel its major limitation rests in the easy manipulation of earnings, a topic discussed earlier in this chapter. Despite its limitations, it is widely used and will continue its popularity until more appropriate analytical tools are developed.

Is NCR a blue chip growth company? The ratios we have examined seem to support that title. Notice carefully, though, the implications of investing in growth companies such as NCR. Clearly, a large portion of your investment return hangs on the company being able to sustain a high rate of growth, and any disruption of that ability will lead to substantial declines in the price of its common stock. Fortunately for NCR's investors, the company has sustained high rates of earnings and dividend growth over a long period of time.

Was NCR an Undervalued Security?

At a market price of $53⅜ at the end of 1988, was NCR undervalued? Using the dividend approach developed in the previous chapter, some preliminary comments can be made. First, calculate the expected total return (*ETR*). The total return (*TR*) formula is:

$$TR = \text{current return} + \text{future return} = \frac{D}{P} + g$$

where D = the dividend expected in the upcoming year (1989),

P = the current price of the stock ($53.375), and

g = the expected growth of dividends in the future (16.0%, using the 13-year historical rate).

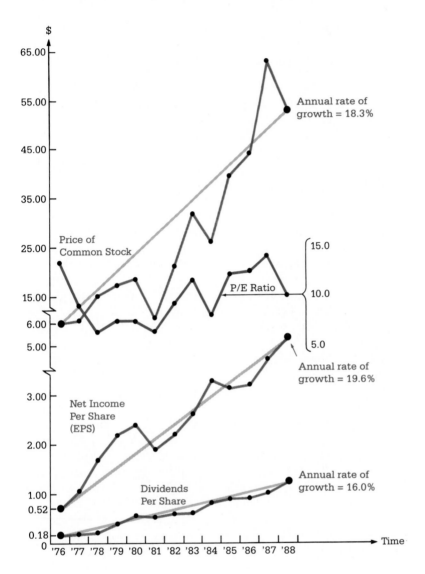

EXHIBIT 9.6
NCR's growth rates

D can be estimated by multiplying the 1988 dividend of $1.24 per share by 1.16, which assumes the 1989 dividend will increase by 16.0%. Then D = $1.4384, or simply $1.44. Now,

$$ETR = (\$1.44/\$53.375) + .160 = .027 + .160 = .187, \text{ or } 18.7\%$$

The next step is to calculate the required return (RR). To do this, we need NCR's beta value (β_i), the market risk premium (MRP), and an estimate of the risk free rate (R_F) available at the beginning of 1989. These are fitted into the equation:

$$RR = R_F + \beta_i(MRP)$$

Should PSRs Replace P/E Ratios?

According to one investment advisor, Kenneth Fisher, PSRs should replace P/E ratios. Why? Because earnings are influenced too heavily by management discretion (or indiscretion). Different accounting methods among companies or changes in methods within a company over time can cause huge distortions in corporate earnings, making true profitability in an economic sense virtually impossible to determine. Fisher's point has merit. Even financial analysts often err badly in forecasting earnings, due as much to accounting problems as to the difficulty of the task.

So what is a PSR and why is it better? PSR stands for price-to-sales ratio. You calculate it by multiplying the market price of a company's stock by all its shares outstanding, and dividing this product by its sales. For example, suppose XYZ stock is selling at $8 a share, there are 2 million shares outstanding, and its sales are $20 million. Its PSR is 0.80 ($8 × 2,000,000 = $16,000,000; $16,000,000/ $20,000,000 = 0.80). Fisher believes sales are less easily influenced by accounting assumptions and conventions, making the ratio more indicative of a company's underlying financial strength. He advises using the ratio contrarily; that is, companies with low PSRs are the most desirable. Fisher recommends avoiding stocks with PSRs over 1.5, and definitely selling a stock when the PSR is between 3 and 6.

Fisher writes a column regularly in *Forbes,* so it is easy to read about PSR applications and to track the performance of his recommendations. Recently, though, Evan Sturza has suggested several modifications to the basic PSR to make it more effective (*Forbes,* March 6, 1989, pp. 162–63). First, Sturza believes a company's debt should also be included in the calculation. He proposes doing this by adding debt to the market value of the stock. So, if XYZ had $8 million in debt, its total capitalization is $24 million and its PSR increases to 1.2 ($24,000,000/ $20,000,000). Sturza's second point is that a company's industry should be considered, since PSRs vary so much among industries. To accommodate this factor, he suggests that a PSR be divided by the average PSR of the industry. If XYZ's industry average PSR is 2.0, then its relative PSR is 0.6 (1.2/2.0). Finally, investors should select stocks on the basis of relative PSRs.

Should you use PSRs—the basic or the improved version—to select securities? Probably not, if you intend to limit your analysis to this single factor. Investment value is a complex concept that is seldom captured in one perspective on a company. Use all the tools, P/E ratios *and* PSRs, and all other ratios that pinpoint strengths and weaknesses.

NCR's beta at the end of 1988 was estimated at about 1.2. U.S. Treasury securities with a one-year maturity were yielding about 9%. Assuming an *MRP* of 8.5% (the 63-year arithmetic average) gives the following value for *RR*:

$$RR = .09 + 1.2(.085) = .09 + .1020 = .1920, \text{ or } 19.2\%$$

An undervalued security has an expected return greater than its required return.

Since an undervalued security is one that has an expected return greater than its required return, we conclude NCR was overvalued, rather than undervalued. The difference, though, of 0.5% (19.2% − 18.7%) is not large. In fact, we might conclude that NCR was fairly valued. Was it a good investment buy, then? Not particularly, although growth-oriented investors may have favored it. Exhibit 9.7 shows what one investment advisory service thought of NCR in October, 1988. As you see, this service regarded the stock quite highly, giving it an A rating.

Using Ratio Analysis

Ratio analysis has been in use for a number of years, and its application in investments was pioneered by Ben Graham, who was mentioned in the previous chapter. Until the advent of the personal computer and easily accessible data bases, only professional investment advisors made widespread use of the techniques. Today, however, for a rather modest investment, amateurs also can perform ratio analysis on a wide array of companies. Selecting companies is often done by screening, using so-called **filters**.

Screening with Filters   The first step is to access a data base, such as the Compustat Tapes. Then, you must decide which ratios are important. After your selection, the data base is screened to select companies that meet criteria imposed by your ratio selections.

For example, suppose you are a cautious investor and do not wish to invest in any company with a debt ratio greater than 0.50. By entering this requirement as a command, you might find that, say, 3,000 firms of the total on the data set meet this requirement. Next, you also want to invest in companies with good earnings records. So, of the 3,000 initial firms, you impose a second requirement that annual growth in EPS over the past ten years must equal or exceed 20%. This might screen out 2,500 firms, narrowing the list to 500. Since this is still too large, and since you also like some dividend income, your last command might be that only firms with dividend yields of 4% or better are desired. This last ratio might leave only 12 remaining firms, from which you make your selections. Of course, success with the method depends on the usefulness of the filters selected and the bold assumption that selected firms will continue their desired characteristics in the future. There are obvious problems and risks that should be considered.

Screening refers to selecting securities using predetermined criteria (filters).

The Usefulness of Ratios   Clearly, ratios help us understand the financial characteristics of a firm. Do you believe that you understand NCR better as a result of the simple ratio analysis in this chapter? And do you now have a basic understanding of which ratios might be important in a screening operation? Few people argue that ratios are not helpful in such efforts. Unfortunately, some people believe that a single ratio, or some simplistic use of ratios, can distinguish "good" stocks from "bad" ones. At best, ratios are rough indicators of financial strength. In some respects, they are quite similar to various tests a medical doctor might use to measure your bodily strength or health. If your temperature exceeds 98.6 degrees, or if your blood pressure is above 120/80, or if your cholesterol count exceeds 200, you have a greater risk of encountering a physical problem. Do these

A financial analyst using ratios is similar to a medical doctor examining certain health indicators.

NCR Corp.

1570T

NYSE Symbol NCR Options on CBOE(Mar-Jun-Sep-Dec) In S&P 500

Price	Range	P-E Ratio	Dividend	Yield	S&P Ranking	Beta
Nov. 8'88	1988	11	1.24	2.2%	A	1.13
55¼	69⅛-52⅝					

Summary

This company manufactures business information processing systems, including a range of computer systems, automated teller machines, point-of-sale terminals, and data communications products. Over the past two years NCR has aggressively introduced new products across all product lines, both for its proprietary families and for those based on industry standards. Earnings are expected to continue to reflect the wider availability of those products in 1989, as well as a share buyback program.

Current Outlook

Earnings for 1989 are expected to increase to $6.05 a share from the $5.50 estimated for 1988.

Dividends could be raised from the current $0.31 quarterly in early April, 1989.

Revenues in 1989 are expected to show only single digit growth. Domestic sales will continue to reflect economic uncertainties and international revenues are not expected to benefit from a lower dollar. However, demand for banking automation systems and the Tower UNIX-based multiuser systems should continue to be strong and several new products should improve orders. Operating margins should be fairly stable with cost containment efforts, although spending on research and development is likely to remain high. Share earnings will continue to benefit from stock repurchases.

Revenues (Million $)

Quarter:	1989	1988	1987	1986
Mar.	....	1,281	1,122	961
Jun.	....	1,497	1,360	1,169
Sep.	....	1,407	1,340	1,177
Dec.	....	....	1,819	1,575
		5,641	4,882

Revenues for the nine months ended September 30, 1988, rose 9.6%, year to year, aided by the weaker U.S. dollar. Profitability improved, and pretax earnings were up 11%. After taxes at 44.3%, versus 45.0%, net income rose 12%. Share earnings were up $3.49 (on 12% fewer shares), versus $2.74.

Common Share Earnings ($)

Quarter:	1989	1988	1987	1986
Mar.	E0.95	0.88	0.65	0.51
Jun.	E1.50	1.36	1.05	0.80
Sep.	E1.40	1.26	1.05	0.75
Dec.	E2.20	E2.00	1.76	1.39
	E6.05	E5.50	4.51	3.42

Important Developments

Oct. '88— NCR said that orders in the third quarter posted a broad-based decline geographically and across all product lines, with the exception of the TOWER family of supermicrocomputers and self-service financial terminals. NCR added that little or no revenue growth was expected in the fourth quarter compared with a year earlier.

Next earnings report expected in mid-January.

Per Share Data ($)

Yr. End Dec. 31	1987	1986	1985	1984	1983	1982	1981	¹1980	¹1979	1978
Book Value	24.30	24.15	22.51	19.63	18.16	16.92	16.17	14.72	12.98	12.35
Earnings²	4.51	3.42	3.15	3.30	2.64	2.19	1.93	2.38	2.20	1.81
Dividends	1.00	0.92	0.88	0.80	0.65	0.60	0.55	0.50	0.40	0.25
Payout Ratio	20%	26%	27%	23%	24%	28%	28%	21%	18%	14%
Prices³—High	87¼	57	42½	33	34¼	24¾	18⅞	20½	20½	16⅞
Low	44⅞	38⅝	24⅞	20⅝	20½	9¾	9⅛	12⅛	14⅛	9¼
P/E Ratio—	19-10	17-11	13-8	10-6	13-8	11-4	10-5	9-6	9-6	9-5

Data as orig. reptd. Adj. for stk. div(s). of 300% May 1984. 1. Reflects merger or acquisition. 2. Bef. results of discont. opers. of +1.16 in 1978. E-Estimated.

Standard NYSE Stock Reports
Vol. 55/No. 222/Sec. 18

November 16, 1988
Copyright © 1988 Standard & Poor's Corp. All Rights Reserved

Standard & Poor's Corp.
25 Broadway, NY, NY 10004

NCR Corporation

1570T

Income Data (Million $)

Year Ended Dec. 31	Revs.	Oper. Inc.	% Oper. Inc. of Revs.	Cap. Exp.	Depr.	Int. Exp.	Net Bef. Taxes	Eff. Tax Rate	Net Inc.	% Net Inc. of Revs.
1987	5,641	1,024	18.1	389	294	26.5	782	43.9%	³419	7.4
1986	4,882	875	17.9	361	277	35.6	634	44.7%	337	6.9
1985	4,317	791	18.3	309	251	40.3	³575	43.1%	315	7.3
1984	4,074	772	19.0	315	249	42.7	³572	38.3%	315	8.4
1983	3,731	723	19.4	317	246	45.9	³531	44.3%	288	7.7
1982	3,526	634	18.0	322	239	51.6	³435	44.9%	³234	6.6
1981	3,433	586	17.1	362	244	72.5	³363	41.3%	208	6.1
⁵1980	3,322	683	20.6	371	227	55.9	³469	43.0%	255	7.7
²1979	3,003	626	20.8	322	210	39.7	³449	47.0%	235	7.8
²1978	2,611	561	21.5	220	186	47.8	³365	43.6%	194	7.4

Balance Sheet Data (Million $)

Dec. 31	Cash	Assets	Curr. Liab.	Ratio	Total Assets	Ret. On Assets	Long Term Debt	Common Equity	Total Cap.	% LT Debt of Cap.	Ret. On Equity
1987	712	2,768	1,609	1.7	4,187	10.8%	110	2,162	2,447	4.5	19.5%
1986	670	2,512	1,252	2.0	4,015	8.6%	129	2,396	2,659	4.9	14.6%
1985	794	2,569	1,207	2.0	3,940	8.4%	232	2,318	2,650	8.7	14.5%
1984	495	2,280	1,147	2.0	3,589	9.9%	225	2,076	2,377	9.5	17.1%
1983	517	2,194	1,048	2.1	3,560	8.3%	325	2,045	2,445	13.3	14.5%
1982	412	2,111	966	2.2	3,373	6.9%	341	1,937	2,340	14.6	12.3%
1981	182	2,172	1,099	2.0	3,387	6.2%	300	1,853	2,221	13.5	11.7%
1980	119	2,237	1,200	1.9	3,366	8.0%	322	1,704	2,091	15.4	15.9%
1979	148	1,947	965	2.0	2,918	8.5%	345	1,476	1,877	18.4	16.9%
1978	248	1,781	815	2.2	2,596	7.9%	348	1,298	1,700	20.5	16.7%

Data as orig. reptd. 1. Bef. results of disc. oper. in 1978. 2. Excludes discontinued operations. 3. Incl. equity in earns of noncons. subs. 4. Reflects accounting change. 5. Reflects merger or acquisition.

Business Summary

NCR manufactures business information processing systems. Revenues in recent years were:

	1987	1986
Industry-specific workstations	21%	23%
Multiuser systems	15%	13%
Workstations	8%	7%
Large computer systems	6%	6%
Communications processors & other	6%	5%
Business forms/supplies	8%	9%
Components	2%	2%
Services	35%	35%

Foreign operations contributed 55% of revenues in 1987 and 52% of operating profits.

Industry-specific workstations, such as point-of-sale and automatic teller terminals, are primarily sold into the retail and financial markets. General-purpose workstations include personal computers, office automation workstations and terminals. Multiuser systems are small and mid-sized computers for departmental use and interactive and batch processing. Large systems are designed for on-line transaction processing and batch processing. Other related products and ser-vices include communications processors, semi-conductors and components, and software.

Dividend Data

Dividends have been paid since 1934. A dividend reinvestment plan is available. A "poison pill" stock purchase right was adopted in 1986.

Amt. of Divd. $	Date Decl.	Ex-divd. Date	Stock of Record	Payment Date
0.31	Jan. 20	Mar. 7	Mar. 11	Apr. 22'88
0.31	Apr. 20	Jul. 1	Jul. 8	Aug. 5'88
0.31	Oct. 19	Oct. 7	Oct. 13	Nov. 11'88
		Jan. 9	Jan. 13	Feb. 10'89

Next dividend meeting: late Jan. '89.

Finances

NCR repurchased some 2.8 million of its common shares in the first half of 1988 and 10.7 million shares in all of 1987.

Capitalization

Long Term Debt: $105,768,000.

Minority Interest: $175,502,000.

Common Stock: 81,430,813 shs. ($5 par).
Institutions hold about 64%.
Shareholders of record: 37,848.

Office—1700 South Patterson Blvd., Dayton, Ohio 45479. Tel—(513) 445-5000. Chrm—C. E. Exley, Jr. Pres—C. P. Williamson. VP-Secy—C. P. Russ III. Treas—N. A. Cocke. Investor Contact—Jim Valenio. Dirs—C. A. Anderson, W. S. Anderson, W. G. Bowen, N. F. Brady, C. E. Exley, Jr., C. H. Hardesty, Jr., H. Holiday, Jr., J. J. Horan, C. S. Morawetz, H. A. Poling, E. J. Schlegel, R. E. White, G. P. Williamson. Transfer Agent & Registrar—Bank of Boston. Incorporated in Md. in 1926. Empl—62,000.

Information has been obtained from sources believed to be reliable, but its accuracy and completeness are not guaranteed. Melanie McCrossen

---

EXHIBIT 9.7

Standard & Poor's report on NCR—October 30, 1988

measurements mean you are "unhealthy"? Or, do they tell a doctor specifically what's wrong with you, if you complained of not feeling well? Not necessarily. Similarly, financial ratios can only indicate greater potential risks; they seldom can tell us what is fundamentally wrong or right with a company.

EVALUATING THE ECONOMY AND THE INDUSTRY

Determining how well an individual company might do in the future often requires a prior assessment of the likely performances of the overall economy and the company's industry. This top-to-bottom approach is illustrated in Exhibit 9.8 and is discussed throughout the following sections.

Brief History of U.S. Cycles

The history of the U.S. economy is one of uneven growth. Changes in economic activity over time—referred to as the business cycle—have been persistent, sometimes taking place at moderate and reasonably predictable rates, other times changing so wildly that all you can do is guess about the future. The business cycle influences the economic fortunes of the industries and firms that are part of it. Few of them escape the misfortunes of a recession, and many of them prosper during the upswings. Exhibit 9.9 demonstrates one aspect of this correlation.

The exhibit shows that since 1952 the economy generally has been in a period of expansion; however, there have been seven recessions with varying

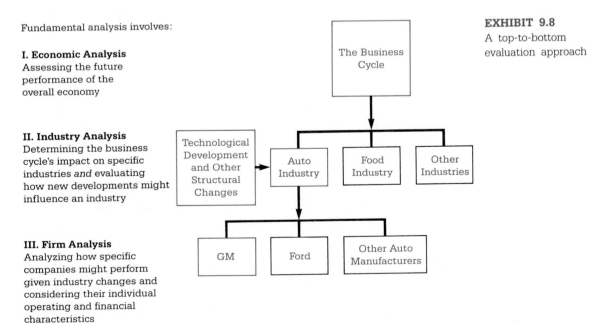

Fundamental analysis involves:

I. Economic Analysis
Assessing the future performance of the overall economy

II. Industry Analysis
Determining the business cycle's impact on specific industries *and* evaluating how new developments might influence an industry

III. Firm Analysis
Analyzing how specific companies might perform given industry changes and considering their individual operating and financial characteristics

The Business Cycle

Technological Development and Other Structural Changes → Auto Industry

Food Industry

Other Industries

GM

Ford

Other Auto Manufacturers

EXHIBIT 9.8
A top-to-bottom evaluation approach

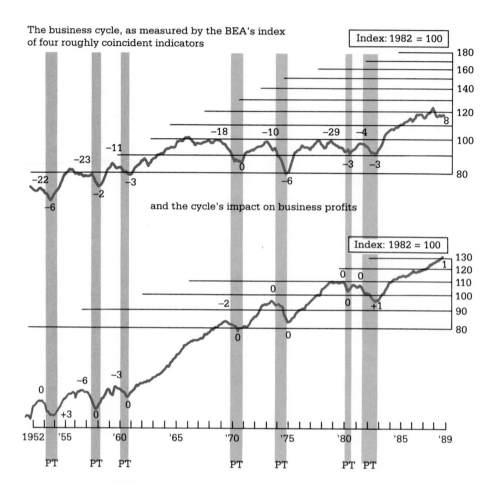

The business cycle, as measured by the BEA's index
of four roughly coincident indicators

and the cycle's impact on business profits

degrees of intensity. As you see, business profits are very sensitive to the
economic cycle, declining measurably as the economy falters. Very few firms
escape the downward drag of the cycle, although some feel it far worse than
others. Particularly sensitive to the cycle are industries that produce capital goods
(machinery, equipment, and so forth) or consumer durables (autos, housing, and
major appliances). Less sensitive are industries that provide services or produce
perishable consumer goods. NCR was not immune from the business cycle.
Exhibit 9.6 shows its EPS fell in 1981 to $1.91 from $2.38 a year earlier. The 1980
recession most likely contributed to this decline.

Forecasting Economic Cycles

While the cycle may cause serious economic harm, it actually represents good
purchase or sale opportunities to investors. Good, that is, if investors could
forecast coming cyclical changes with a fair degree of accuracy. Investors,

economists, and practically everyone else have been trying to do so almost from the time a business cycle was first observed. Although forecasting techniques have improved considerably over the years, not even professional forecasters have a high degree of accuracy. Forecast errors are still quite large, particularly those pertaining to cyclical turning points, which are unquestionably the most difficult parts of the cycle to forecast. Despite these problems, if you are doing fundamental analysis, you must consider the economy's impact upon the firm you are reviewing. To keep abreast of the economy, get in the habit of reading financial publications to gain a general awareness of where the economy is and, perhaps, where many of the "experts" feel it may go. Two methods will help in this effort: following the government's publication of its leading economic indicators, and determining the nature of the consensus among experts.

Even professionals cannot forecast cyclical turning points with much accuracy.

The Leading Indicator Series   Each month the Bureau of Economic Analysis (BEA) publishes its comprehensive list of economic indicators in a publication called *Business Conditions Digest,* available in many public and school libraries. Of particular importance is a list of eleven indicators called the leading indicators. The **leading indicator series (LIS)** includes eleven variables that have tended to change direction prior to changes in the business cycle; thus, they lead the cycle. The eleven were chosen from among hundreds that were tested to perform this function. Exhibit 9.10 shows how the LIS has tracked the business cycle. As you see, it generally turns down before the peak of an economic cycle is reached and turns up before the trough of a recession occurs. Notice, however, that the number of months elapsing between the cue given by the LIS and the eventual

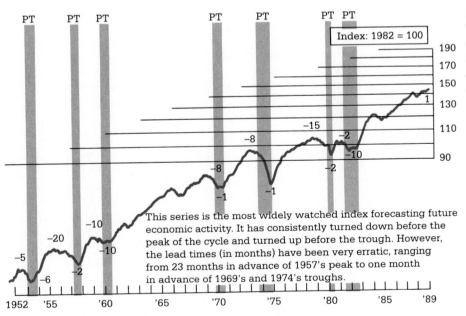

EXHIBIT 9.10

The BEA's index of eleven leading indicators. (Source: *Business Conditions Digest,* February, 1989.)

If You Think Economic Forecasting Is Chaotic, You Could Be Right

The plain truth of the matter is that economists don't forecast very well. Most professional forecasters missed the 1982 recession, and a large number thought the market crash in October of 1987 would send the economy into a tailspin. It actually showed a robust 6+ percent annualized gain in the fourth quarter of that year. Why do such large errors exist? Is the science of forecasting deteriorating? Let's review the two basic forecasting methods and then return to the question.

Extrapolative Techniques

These methods essentially forecast the future by extending the behavior of a historical time series. A trend line is one of the simplest techniques; others, such as ARIMA or Box-Jenkins models, can be very complex. All share the same basic premise that the future will in some fashion be similar to the past.

Econometric Methods

Econometrics is a blending of economic theory, mathematics, and statistics. It rests on the creation of a model, which supposedly represents the structure of the overall economy. A key feature of the model is the so-called structural coefficient that links performance of one indus-

try to that of others. Thus, industry changes can indicate and provide measurements of changes in the aggregate economy. Econometric methods also can be relatively simple; more often, though, they are very complex, reflecting complicated and extensive models.

With all this math and theory going for them, why, then, such bad forecasts? To begin with, forecasting is a snap if the economy is in a trend. Either method will do quite nicely. The trick is forecasting turning points; that is, when an expansion stops and recession begins, or vice versa. As you can appreciate, a simple trend line will never indicate a turning point, and the more complex extrapolative techniques aren't much better. They all have built into them a set periodicity (up and down patterns) that often do not repeat. Years ago, economists frequently talked about 8-year cycles; you hardly hear the term nowadays.

While an econometric model has a greater capacity to forecast turning points, unfortunately, most fail at the task. The reason is the structure of the economy seems to change constantly; it is described as dynamic, rather than static. A model built on the old structure isn't much better than a simple

trend. A case in point is consumer demand. Few forecasters foresaw the strength in this sector during most of the 1980s, and no one expected our national saving rate to hit the lowest levels since the Great Depression. So, when the stock market crashed in October, 1987, the professional forecasters thought a recession was in the wings. But the economy went through the market crash as though it never existed.

Perhaps there is hope for the future, though. A new approach to economic analysis is emerging, one that has its roots in a new field of mathematics called "chaos theory." This new math emerged to help explain chaotic events, such as earthquakes, or lightning strikes. Some economic events surely seem chaotic: the October 1987 crash, or reaction to the oil embargo in 1973, or the German hyperinflation of the 1920s. Economic reactions to chaotic events may be predictable with the new theory. If so, we should be able to increase our understanding of how economic systems work. Will we then forecast more accurately? Probably not, unless we also learn how to predict the next chaotic event. Slim hope here, unless we get a crystal ball that actually works.

peak or trough varies considerably. This wide variation in lead times has serious implications for using the LIS to profit from forecasting, but we think you will understand this point better in an investment setting. We will therefore defer discussion to the next chapter, where technical market indicators are explained and evaluated.

Changes in the LIS are usually headline news, particularly when they change direction, foreshadowing a downturn or upturn. If you are even a casual viewer of the evening news or reader of the newspaper, you will catch the announcements. Naturally, so will everyone else. This publicity means that even if the forecasts are correct, you probably will find it difficult to take any investment action that other investors are not also taking. Therefore trying to ''market time'' purchases or sales in anticipation of changes in the business cycle will not increase your investment return; in fact, the increased commissions will probably lower it.

Changes in the LIS make headline news.

Consensus of Experts   In one respect, following the LIS is a form of using expert opinion, because the list itself has been prepared by experts. However, it does not offer interpretation, nor does it provide estimates of future activity. These functions are undertaken by many professional forecasters who are more than willing to share their results and opinions with us. Most full-service brokerage houses and many commercial banks have economic forecasters on their staffs. If you are a client, you can get their advice immediately through your representative. If you are not a client, you must wait until it is made available to the public.

The key to using forecasts is getting a consensus, because individual forecasters have been so terribly incorrect at various times. Even the well-known Henry Kaufman from Salomon Brothers—considered the most accurate interest-rate forecaster—has had huge errors. In 1982 he forecasted sharp increases in interest rates, even though they were already at historically high levels. His forecast sent the stock market reeling, but eventually proved incorrect as interest rates then entered a period of dramatic declines. Several institutions have attempted to formalize the consensus approach by obtaining forecasts from an array of well-known forecasters. For example, *The Wall Street Journal* undertakes a consensus forecast each December and June and publishes the results in one of its issues. The National Association of Business Economists obtains a consensus among its members bimonthly and publishes the results in its newsletter *NABE News*. This consensus is growing in stature, and many newspapers and TV stations are now reporting the results.

Rather than relying upon one forecaster, you can use the consensus of many.

Perhaps the best-known consensus forecast is *The Blue Chip Indicators,* published by Robert Egger in Sedona, Arizona. Egger polls some 40 economists on a variety of cyclical issues. Distinct advantages of his series are that it is available monthly, and that it not only provides the average forecast but also the variations about the average. Thus, you can see if there is reasonable agreement or disagreement among the forecasters. A wide variation alerts us to wide differences of opinion and probably indicates greater risk in accepting the average. Unfortunately, Egger's series is rather expensive for small investors, at

The best-known consensus forecast is The Blue Chip Indicators.

about $330 a year. It has a very large circulation—over 1,000 clients, most of whom are businesses—indicating that many find the consensus approach appealing.

Industry Analysis

An industry links the individual firm to the overall economy. The financial analyst often develops industry outlooks and forecasts that shape his or her projections for the firm. Industry analysis usually consists of three activities: correlating industry performance to performance of the overall economy, finding new developments within the industry, and correlating industry performance to performance of the firm.

The Industry and the Business Cycle We mentioned earlier that few industries are immune from variations in the business cycle. Particularly sensitive industries are those with activities in some way dependent upon interest rates. Housing is a classic example, since interest payments typically constitute the single largest expense of home ownership. The sale of new homes is very dependent upon changes in interest rates on mortgage loans, as Exhibit 9.11 shows. Changes in the housing industry induce repercussions in many other industries, such as home appliances or financial lending. High real rates of interest also influence activities of business firms, who often curtail their capital spending programs; so, industries producing capital goods are also heavily influenced by the cycle.

Some industries are very sensitive to economic changes; others are not.

In contrast to cyclical industries, other areas of the economy tend to go through the cycle without experiencing its forces to any large extent. The food

EXHIBIT 9.11
Housing construction and interest rates. (Sources: *Statistical Abstract of the United States,* 1988, and *Survey of Current Business,* March 1989.)

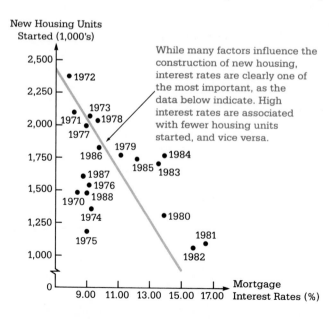

and beverage industries, for example, do not show wide variations in sales. Nor do many service industries, such as health and life insurance. Some industries may even be countercyclical; that is, their sales increase during economic slowdowns. Home gardening and other do-it-yourself industries supposedly perform this way.

Whether the analyst uses very sophisticated statistical tools or simple, back-of-the-envelope calculations, he or she must express quantitatively an estimate of the expected change in industry performance given a change in the overall economy. For example, if the economy is expected to grow at a 3% real rate in 19XX, what will be the percentage change in this industry's sales that *result from* this growth? An answer to this question completes the first part of industry analysis. Of course, the analysis can grow more complex as you try to link industry sales to specific components of the economy, such as interest rates, or changes in the money supply.

Financial analysts must determine industry changes, given changes in the overall economy.

New Developments in the Industry   Apart from cycle-induced changes, new developments may be taking place within the industry that would lead analysts to increase or decrease their estimates of industry performance. New developments, such as the introduction of the personal computer in the early 1980s, may influence analysts to increase their sales estimates. Other developments may lead them to revise profit estimates; an example is the auto industry's conversion to greater use of robotics and other capital-intensive production techniques. New developments also include favorable or unfavorable legislation, including the impact of federal income tax legislation. Changes in the tax law in 1986 have been particularly hard on industries requiring heavy capital investment, since one of the changes repealed the investment tax credit. Also, any material changes in union contracts, or increase in unionization of the work force, could lead to significant cost changes.

Clearly, uncovering all new trends in an industry may be a very difficult task. And, measuring their impacts upon industry performance may be far less accurate than measuring the impacts of the business cycle. Despite the problems, though, you cannot ignore emerging trends. While they often lead to higher rates of return, they also increase risk, particularly in the formative stages.

Uncovering new trends in an industry may be difficult.

Linking the Industry to the Firm   Just as all industries do not march in perfect step with the economy, all firms will not keep exact pace with the industry. There are various explanations for the differences. For one thing, firms have different cost structures, some relying heavily upon fixed costs, with others having higher variable costs. Public utilities, for example, have very different cost configurations, depending upon whether their generating equipment uses hydroelectric or nuclear power, with their high fixed costs, or coal or oil, with their high variable costs. A decline in industry demand will have much more devastating results on profit for firms with high fixed costs than it will for those with high variable costs.

Another factor to consider is each firm's product mix. Some might offer top-of-the-line items that do well when the economy is operating robustly, while

Changes in an industry can lead to important changes in a firm's earnings.

others might offer more basic product lines that sell better when the economy is in modest growth. Then, too, you need to consider geographic differences. A firm servicing one geographic region of the country might show booming sales while firms located in other regions do poorly. The housing market, for example, was booming in Boston in the mid-1980s, driving the median price of a home to the highest in the nation, while in Houston, the housing industry declined as a result of a slump in the oil industry brought about by the sharp drop in oil prices. Five years earlier, the situation was just the reverse. And, at the end of the 1980s, the California market replaced the Northeast as the booming market.

Linking industry changes to performance of specific firms is an important step in industry analysis.

Determining how the individual firm will respond to industry changes completes industry analysis; you could also make the point that it is the beginning of firm analysis. Whatever the perspective, it is important to focus your attention upon how changes in the industry lead to changes in a firm's earnings. Exhibit 9.12 shows how GM's earnings per share have been influenced by changes in activity in the auto industry. Of course, GM is a major part of the industry; the high correlation between its EPS and industry sales is not surprising. Nevertheless, similarly high correlations are found in many other industry-firm relationships.

Most of the large stockbrokerage firms and the independent advisory services, such as Standard and Poor's, Moody's, and Value Line, employ security analysts who specialize in specific industries. Along with becoming very knowledgeable about an industry, they also increase their understanding of the industry's individual firms. This background enables them to make specific recommendations for purchases or sales. As an individual investor, you might find it difficult to do your own research on a level comparable to theirs, and it is to your advantage to use these sources.

SUMMARY

The key financial statements of a business are the balance sheet and the income statement. The balance sheet shows assets, liabilities, and shareholders' equity. Items not shown on the balance sheet can be important also. These include hidden assets and contingent liabilities. An income statement shows the company's earnings and dividends. The major limitation in using income statements is a lack of uniformity in presenting such items as depreciation and inventory costs. Investors often prefer a cash flow concept that attempts to measure the company's ability to generate cash.

Ratio analysis is a technique for evaluating a company's economic performance. Balance sheet strength is measured by liquidity and solvency ratios. Earnings strength is measured by the ability to cover interest charges, the return on investment, the return on equity, and earnings and dividends growth.

Evaluating a security requires an assessment of future economic activity overall and in specific industry sectors. A leading indicator series and the

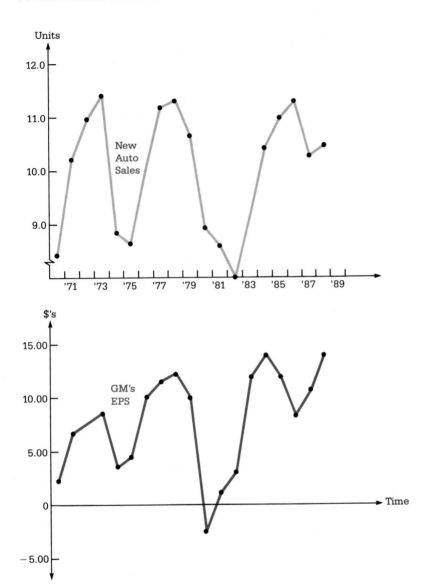

EXHIBIT 9.12
New automobile sales
and GM's earnings per
share.

consensus of experts are used to forecast economic cycles. Industry analysis begins by relating changes in the industry to changes in the overall economy. It then looks for new developments in the industry that might accelerate or reduce its historical growth patterns. The final step in industry analysis is to link the industry with specific firms in it. The analyst attempts to determine how specific firms will respond to anticipated industry changes.

KEY TERMS

Select the alternative that best identifies the key term.

1. business balance sheet
2. book value per share
3. hidden asset plays
4. income statement
5. cash flow
6. NWC/sales ratio
7. current ratio
8. total debt ratio
9. debt/equity ratio
10. times-interest-earned ratio
11. return on investment (ROI)
12. return on equity (ROE)
13. filters
14. leading indicator series (LIS)

a. current assets divided by current liabilities
b. a listing of revenues and expenses showing the results of operations
c. a direct measurement of profitability for the stockholders
d. perspective on the firm's long-term capital structure
e. one estimate of the worth of the business
f. 11 variables that change direction prior to changes in the business cycle
g. attempts to profit from finding companies with valuable assets *not* shown on their balance sheets
h. net income plus depreciation
i. indicator of a company's ability to earn profits from its assets
j. (current assets minus current liabilities)/sales
k. a measurement of earnings capacity to service long-term debt
l. shows assets, liabilities, and net worth of a business
m. total debt divided by total assets
n. ratios selected for screening purposes

REVIEW
QUESTIONS

1. Briefly explain items typically listed on a balance sheet.
2. Explain the following items that, although not common, might be found on a business balance sheet: *(a)* goodwill, net of amortization; *(b)* customers' deposits and deferred service revenue; *(c)* minority interests; *(d)* accumulated translation adjustments; and *(e)* treasury stock.
3. Define book value per share and then explain if you believe it is a good estimate of the true value of a common stock.
4. Explain why a balance sheet might not show all items of value to a company. Also, what is a hidden asset, and a hidden asset play?
5. What is the objective of the income statement? Briefly explain items typically found on the statement.
6. Discuss several limitations of an income statement.
7. What is cash flow, and how does cash flow per share differ from EPS?
8. Offer a brief debate on the topic, ''Is EPS an ideal indicator of a firm's earning performance?'' Take the side favoring the issue.

9. Define net working capital. Then, indicate two ratios that measure a company's liquidity position.
10. In what way does solvency differ from liquidity? Then, indicate two ratios that measure a company's solvency position.
11. Indicate three ratios that measure a company's earnings strength. Which of the three is the best measurement from the perspective of a *shareholder's* investment?
12. The growth rates of which variables usually influence the growth rate of a company's common stock price?
13. What is meant by screening with filters and how are ratios used in the process? Suppose you are a very growth-oriented investor but wish to avoid excessively risky companies. Select three screening ratios that you would apply to a data base. Explain your selections.
14. Briefly describe the performance of the overall economy since 1952 and its implication for business profitability. Also, explain the LIS and its relationship to the overall economy.
15. What is meant by the consensus of experts? Explain the advantages of such an approach.
16. Explain three aspects of industry analysis. Which aspect do you feel is the most difficult to do? Explain.

PROBLEMS AND PROJECTS

1. Given the following data (in millions of dollars), what evaluation do you have for the Endicott Company's liquidity and solvency positions? Explain.

	1991	1990	1991 Industry Average
Current assets	$478	$532	$236
Fixed assets	489	346	513
Total assets	$967	$878	$749
Current liabilities	$341	$327	$104
Long-term debt	225	174	251
Shareholders' equity	401	377	394
Total liabilities and shareholders' equity	$967	$878	$749
Sales	$879	$843	$815
Interest expense	23	14	25
Net income	38	36	43
Dividends	14	10	17
Depreciation	20	16	15

2. Given the data in Problem 1, evaluate the Endicott Company's earnings strength, comparing it to the industry average.
3. In addition to the data in Problem 1, you also know the Endicott Company had 10 million shares of common stock outstanding during each year; the industry average number of shares outstanding was 11 million during each year. Determine EPS and cash flow per share; then, evaluate the company relative to the industry average. Do

you believe the market price of Endicott's stock is higher or lower than the average stock price of its industry competitors? Explain your reasoning.

4. Financial data for Blunt Enterprises appear in the following table, arranged in alphabetical order.

Account	19X2	19X1
common stock (100,000 shares)	$ 200,000	$ 200,000
cost of products sold	9,270,000	8,850,000
current assets	456,000	421,000
current liabilities	282,000	205,000
dividends	181,000	161,000
interest expense	22,000	24,000
long-term debt	180,000	200,000
other expenses	1,042,000	993,000
plant and equipment, net	810,000	683,000
retained earnings	604,000	499,000
sales	14,080,000	13,290,000
selling expenses	3,260,000	2,980,000
income taxes	200,000	190,000

a. Rearrange the data to produce the balance sheet and the income statement for each year.

b. Discuss the company's liquidity position and solvency position using appropriate ratios for each.

c. Using appropriate ratios, discuss the company's earnings strengths, comparing the two years.

d. Calculate the percentage increases in earnings per share and dividends per share and, assuming the dividend per share percentage growth continues in the future, explain if Blunt is over or undervalued if its market price is $60 a share. (Assume: Blunt's beta = 1.7, R_F = 8%, and MRP = 8.5%.)

e. Calculate Blunt's 19X2 book value per share and discuss it in relation to the market price of $60.

5. *(Student Project)* Obtain a financial report for a company of interest to you. Reports are often kept at university libraries, or you can call a local company and request one. Then, using the ratios developed in this chapter, evaluate the company. If possible, find its beta value (try Value Line's *Investment Survey*) and make a comparison between the company's expected return and its required return. Check the return on Treasury securities for your R_F rate.

6. *(Student Project)* Make sure you read in this chapter the boxed item, "Should PSRs Replace P/E Ratios?" Then, utilizing 1988 data available for NCR, calculate its basic PSR and the adjusted PSR that considers debt. Work with total debt, as reported on the balance sheet.

7. *(Student Project)* Obtain the most recent issue of *Business Conditions Digest* from your school library. Reviewing the LIS, determine where the economy is headed six months in the future. Prepare a brief report on your findings.

CASE ANALYSES

9.1
Rob Dexter Looks for the Right Stock

Rob Dexter is a conservative investor who is concerned greatly with preservation of capital. However, he does seek growth as an investment objective. Two companies have come to his attention lately, and he is considering investing in one of them. Both are in the same industry. Consider the following ratios and recommend one of the companies to Rob, explaining the reasoning for your selection.

	Fleet, Inc.	Dirge, Inc.
Current ratio	1.8	1.9
NWC/sales	0.5	0.6
Debt ratio	0.6	0.3
Debt/equity ratio	1.5	0.4
ROI	8%	10%
ROE	20%	14%
Times interest earned	4.5	7.2
10-year growth rates:		
Earnings per share	15%	12%
Dividends per share	17%	11%
Price of common stock	14%	9%
Current share price of stock	$50	$99
Last year dividend per share	$ 2	$ 6
Beta	1.5	0.8

Risk-free rate = 8%
Market risk premium = 8.5%

9.2
Allison Demming Undertakes an Industry Analysis

Allison Demming is considering investing in Precision Tools, a leading firm in the machine tool industry. Her research leads Allison to believe that Precision is a sound company with reasonably good earnings possibilities. However, she is concerned about the machine tool industry, which tends to be somewhat volatile. Allison has gathered quarterly data for Precision, the machine tool industry, and the overall economy. She hopes the data might reveal certain linkages that can help her plan an investment strategy. The data appear in the accompanying table. The industry sales index, the economic activity index, and Precision Tool's per-share stock price are values at the beginning of each quarter.

Year Quarter	Precision Tool's EPS	Industry Sales Index	Economic Activity Index	Precision Tool's Stock Price
1988: I	$1.62	125	108	$83.50
II	1.98	133	114	78.25
III	2.09	136	118	60.00
IV	2.17	142	125	67.38
1989: I	1.27	140	127	46.88
II	1.66	135	124	39.13
III	0.81	121	120	40.13
IV	0.65	113	116	32.50
1990: I	−0.10	103	111	34.75
II	1.05	106	113	45.38
III	1.54	112	118	62.50
IV	2.12	126	122	77.25
1991: I	2.33	142	133	91.63
II	1.55	152	145	73.75
III	1.23	158	148	83.50
IV	3.06	165	155	92.13
1992: I	—	—	—	88.75

Questions:

a. Calculate Precision Tool's EPS for each of the above years and determine a P/E ratio based upon the stock price: (1) at the beginning of the year, (2) at the end of the year, and (3) average for the year.

b. Plot the above time series on a piece of graph paper. Explain any correlations you observe.

c. Do the time series indicate a trading strategy Allison might use? Explain.

d. What advice might you offer Allison with respect to her intended investment?

HELPFUL READING

Amal, Kumar Naj. "Clouds Gather Over the Biotech Industry." *The Wall Street Journal,* January 30, 1989, p. B1.

Arnott, Robert D., and William A. Copeland. "The Business Cycle and Security Selection." *Financial Analysts Journal,* March-April 1985.

Bernstein, Peter L., and Theodore N. Silbert. "Are Economic Forecasters Worth Listening To?" *Harvard Business Review,* September-October 1984.

Clements, Jonathon. "Compound Interest Machines." *Forbes,* August 21, 1989, pp. 43–44.

Donnelly, Barbara. "Stock-Picking Tools May Need Repair." *The Wall Street Journal,* July 19, 1989, p. C1.

Dorfman, John R. "Two Money Managers Duke It Out in Debate on Stock-Value Theories." *The Wall Street Journal,* July 17, 1989, p. C1.

Guerard, John B., Jr. "Combining Time-Series Model Forecasts and Analysts' Forecasts for Superior Forecasts of Annual Earnings." *Financial Analysts Journal*, January-February 1989, pp. 69–70.

Jasen, Georgette, and Tom Herman. "How Managers Predict Direction of Rates." *The Wall Street Journal*, February 7, 1989, p. C1.

Lunzer, Francesca. "Cash Flow Confusion." *Forbes*, April 7, 1986, pp. 72–75.

Ozanian, Michael. "Grapes of Math: An Old Fashioned Analyst Bets on Return on Equity." *Forbes*, October 6, 1986, pp. 195–96.

Piccini, Raymond. "Stock Market Behavior Around Business Cycle Peaks." *Financial Analysts Journal*, July-August 1980.

Pouschine, Tatiana. "Count the Cash and Go Home Early." *Forbes*, May 29, 1989, pp. 124–128.

Sturza, Evan. "New, Improved Version." *Forbes*, March 6, 1989, pp. 162–63.

CHAPTER TEN

Technical Analysis, Market Timing, and Efficient Markets

USING PRESSURE INDICATORS

Who is Buying or Selling?

Interpreting Market Activity

Investor Psychology

Evaluating Pressure Indicators

USING CHARTS AND GRAPHS

Constructing Graphs

Interpreting Graphs

Evaluating the Use of Graphs

EFFICIENT MARKETS

What Are Efficient Markets?

Implications of the EMH

BOXES

Watch the Super Bowl and Be a
Super Forecaster

Do Insiders Really Beat the Market?
And, Can Outsiders Following
Insiders Do As Well?

Screening for Big Winners

After you finish this chapter, you
will be able to:

- understand pressure indicators
  that show who is buying and selling securities, that measure market activity, or that reveal investor
  psychology.

- evaluate pressure indicators, judging their reliability, accuracy, and
  timeliness.

- understand the graphic approach
  to technical analysis.

- evaluate the graphic approach to
  technical analysis by understanding the nature of randomness.

- determine what is meant by efficient markets and review evidence in support of the efficient
  market hypothesis.

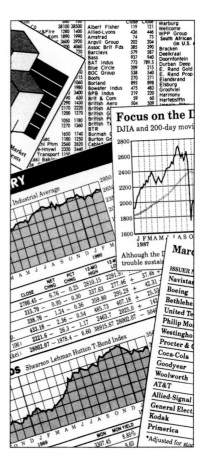

As we have just seen, fundamental analysis attempts to discover underlying strengths and weaknesses in the overall economy and its component industries and firms. It involves considerable work with no assurance of investment success, even if the work is done well. Indeed, a market technician (someone who uses technical analysis) might argue that you are wasting your time with fundamental analysis. After all, you most likely are using published information available to anyone. If you are successful at finding an undervalued security, isn't it likely that many others will find it too? Thousands of investors are using the same data as you and employing the same analytical techniques. If they all come to the conclusion that a security is undervalued, won't they quickly rush to buy it, thereby pushing up its price so that eventually it is no longer undervalued?

The above arguments have been made by technicians and others for quite some time. To them, finding undervalued securities must be done with other methods. This chapter explains and discusses some of these methods. We also evaluate both technical and fundamental analysis within the framework of a body of investment literature that is called *the efficient market hypothesis*.

USING PRESSURE INDICATORS

To begin, let us define **technical analysis** very broadly as any security selection method that does *not* look at investment fundamentals. Supposedly, one of the large stockbrokerage firms employs a technician who refuses any information about a particular company, or industry, or the economy overall. He works in a shuttered room, alone with his graphs and other forecasting devices, to protect against "alien fundamental information" that might influence his chart readings. If you watch the immensely popular *Wall Street Week* on PBS, you will hear the host, Louis Rukeyser, refer to the gnomes, or "cave-dwelling" technicians who prepare the technical market indicators used on the show. This abhorrence of fundamentals is typical of many market technicians, although some feel more strongly about recommendations that are supported by positive conclusions from fundamental analyses.

Many market technicians abhor fundamentals.

In using pressure indicators, technicians are usually attempting to forecast the future direction for the overall market, even though some of their indicators can be applied to forecast future prices of specific securities. There are three popular sets of indicators: those that show what kinds of investors are buying or selling stocks, those that measure market activity, and those that reveal investor psychology.

Who Is Buying or Selling?

If you have reason to believe some buyers are smarter than others, then you might wish to time your purchases and sales in conjunction with those of the smart investors—if they can be identified. Also, if you notice the smart buyers are not buying, but choosing instead to increase their liquidity positions, then you might wish to do the same. This approach involves two steps: first, you must decide who are smart investors; second, you must find information that reveals what they are doing.

The Odd-Lot Ratio The **odd-lot ratio** shows the ratio of odd-lot purchases to odd-lot sales: that is,

$$\text{odd-lot ratio} = \frac{\text{odd-lot sales}}{\text{odd-lot purchases}}$$

Remember that an odd lot is an order for less than 100 shares. What can such a ratio reveal? If you take the view that odd-lot traders are probably unsophisticated investors with little capital to invest, while round-lot traders are just the opposite, then an increase in the ratio indicates greater selling activity among unsophisticated buyers. And, if you are willing to assume the unsophisticated buyer is generally *wrong* about the market, then you should be buying, or at least not selling. Conversely, a decrease in the ratio would be interpreted as a selling signal.

> Some technicians feel odd-lot traders are unsophisticated investors.

Of course, if you bought or sold every time the indicator changed direction, you might be buying and selling constantly. Most technicians feel that minor changes in an indicator are not meaningful and should not be acted upon immediately. Rather, they believe a time series of the indicator—such as the one shown in Exhibit 10.1—should be constructed, and trading cues taken from significant changes in the series. But how do you measure a significant change? While many technicians feel it is a subjective skill, they do use some objective criteria, such as looking for trend reversals. To help in this effort, moving averages are often determined.

To calculate a moving average, you first must decide upon a meaningful length of time for establishing trading rules. Assuming, for example, that we work

EXHIBIT 10.1

The odd-lot ratio

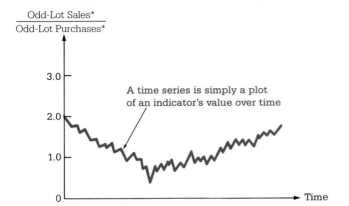

Odd-Lot Sales*
─────────────
Odd-Lot Purchases*

A time series is simply a plot of an indicator's value over time

3.0

2.0

1.0

0

Time

*Measured in shares or dollars.

with weekly odd-lot data available in *Barron's,* we might decide that five weeks is a reasonable time period. The moving average is then calculated by adding a new value each week and subtracting the value that is then five weeks old. To illustrate, a five-period moving average is calculated in Exhibit 10.2. With a moving average line, we are then in a position to derive trading rules based upon the series performance in relation to the moving average. Rule 1, for example, might be to buy stocks whenever the time series has been below its moving average but has just crossed over it, moving upwards. Rule 2 could be to sell stocks when the series has been above the moving average but has just crossed over, moving downwards. These trading rules are illustrated in Exhibit 10.3.

A moving average is a type of trend line; it is also used to establish trading rules.

Five periods are usually not enough for establishing moving-average trading rules, because frequent trend reversals will occur, which in turn lead to frequent buying and selling. Working with daily observations, most technicians will use 30- to 270-day moving averages to reveal what they call minor and major trends. We will not comment on the usefulness of this approach at this point, but we should note that the moving-average technique can be applied to any time series, not just that of the odd-lot ratio.

Odd-Lot Short Sales   Since short selling is generally left to investment professionals, **odd-lot short sales** are supposed to show the very worst of odd-lotters' decisions: when they sell short. A persistent increase in their short selling is interpreted as practically a sure sign the market is headed upwards—the opposite direction from what the odd-lotters think—while decreases signal a bear market. Again, to measure this pressure indicator, you could construct a time series, such as the one shown in Exhibit 10.4.

Institutions' Cash Positions   Rather than doing the opposite of what odd-lotters are doing, which is actually an indirect approach, why not try to identify

EXHIBIT 10.2

Calculating a five-period moving average for the odd-lot ratio

Period	Value	Moving Average Calculation
1	2.0	—
2	1.8	—
3	1.9	—
4	1.7	—
5	1.2	(2.0 + 1.8 + 1.9 + 1.7 + 1.2)/5 = 8.6/5 = 1.72
6	1.0	(1.8 + 1.9 + 1.7 + 1.2 + 1.0)/5 = 7.6/5 = 1.52
7	0.6	(1.9 + 1.7 + 1.2 + 1.0 + 0.6)/5 = 6.4/5 = 1.28
8	0.8	(1.7 + 1.2 + 1.0 + 0.6 + 0.8)/5 = 5.3/5 = 1.06
9	1.2	(1.2 + 1.0 + 0.6 + 0.8 + 1.2)/5 = 4.8/5 = 0.96
10	1.6	(1.0 + 0.6 + 0.8 + 1.2 + 1.6)/5 = 5.2/5 = 1.04
11	1.8	(0.6 + 0.8 + 1.2 + 1.6 + 1.8)/5 = 6.0/5 = 1.20
12	1.2	(0.8 + 1.2 + 1.6 + 1.8 + 1.2)/5 = 6.6/5 = 1.32
13	0.6	(1.2 + 1.6 + 1.8 + 1.2 + 0.6)/5 = 6.4/5 = 1.28
14	1.4	(1.6 + 1.8 + 1.2 + 0.6 + 1.4)/5 = 6.6/5 = 1.32

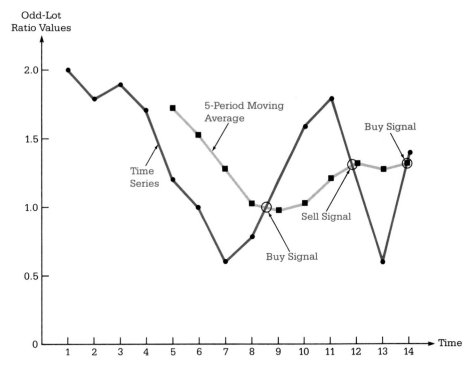

Odd-Lot Ratio Values

5-Period Moving Average

Time Series

Buy Signal

Sell Signal

Buy Signal

EXHIBIT 10.3

The odd-lot ratio. Time series and five-period moving average

intelligent investors and follow their leads directly? Of course, we must be able to identify smart investors and also find objective indicators of their trading activities. Who are smart investors? One answer might be professional money managers, individuals who manage the portfolios of pension funds, mutual funds, and other investment pools.

Mutual funds, for example, report their cash positions each month; that is, they indicate the proportion of their investment portfolio held in cash and marketable securities. By watching this information over time, you could determine if the managers were making significant changes in their cash positions. Increasing them would be interpreted as a sign managers were becoming more pessimistic about the market, while decreases in cash positions would indicate optimism.

Insider Activity Portfolio managers may be smart, but surely the smartest investor of all should be a company insider, someone who knows firsthand what the company plans to do in the future. Corporate directors, officers, and stockholders with significant ownership interests in the corporation must report any purchases or sales of their company's stock to the SEC, which makes this information publicly available. With it, you can trade exactly as the insiders do: if they are buying, so can you, and you can sell when they sell. Unfortunately, the

Professional money managers are supposedly smart investors.

EXHIBIT 10.4
Odd-lot short sales

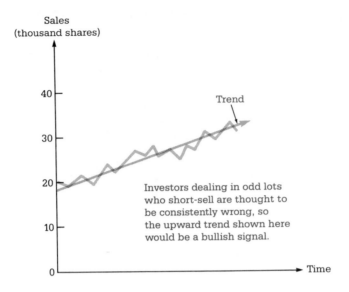

Sales
(thousand shares)

40

30

20

Trend

Investors dealing in odd lots
who short-sell are thought to
be consistently wrong, so
the upward trend shown here
would be a bullish signal.

10

0   Time

**Insider trading must be
reported to the SEC.**

information may be several months old by the time it is released, which diminishes its timeliness. Another shortcoming occurs if insiders are both buying and selling. Then, investors must establish some way to discern which influence is the stronger.

Interpreting Market Activity

Along with attempting to identify buyer and seller groups, many technicians feel it is important to gauge buying and selling pressures for the overall market. To do this, they often look at the Dow theory, trading volume, the advance/decline index, and the new highs/new lows index.

The Dow Theory   The **Dow theory** is probably the oldest formal technical approach to the market. In broad terms, the theory holds that a market's strength is measured by the relative performance of two averages: the industrials and the railroads (now broadened and called the transportation average). A strong market—bullish or bearish—is one in which both averages are moving in the same direction. A weak or indecisive market exists when they are moving in **The Dow Theory looks at the industrials and transportation averages.** opposite directions. People who still hold to the Dow theory are looking for movements in the two averages that will confirm a broad market trend. For example, if the industrials were in an uptrend while the transportation average was waffling up and down with no clear pattern, a sudden, persistent upward movement in the latter average would confirm that a major bull market was underway.

Volume and Price-Related Volume   Substantial price increases and decreases are often accompanied by heavy trading activity. To a technician, the volume of shares traded over a particular period might be as important as the change in a market index, (such as the Dow Jones 30 Industrials). Suppose that over the past four weeks the index increased five percent each week, but the number of shares traded each week consistently declined. The technician sees this as a sign of weakness and would be less enthusiastic about future price increases than would be the case had volume increased each week.

Some technicians link volume to price by noting the specific number of shares traded when the price of a stock increased, when it decreased, and when it was unchanged. Exhibit 10.5 shows how this data might be used to construct an index. Joseph Granville, probably the best-known technician, first popularized this method by constructing the **on-balance volume index,** such as the one

An on-balance volume index links volume to price changes.

Period	Price of Stock	Shares Traded	Volume +	Volume −	On-Balance Volume
1	$ 10	10,000	—	—	—
2	9	12,000	—	12,000	− 12,000
3	8⅛	30,000	—	42,000	− 42,000
4	9⅛	16,000	16,000	—	− 26,000
5	9	20,000	—	20,000	− 46,000
6	9¼	60,000	60,000	—	+ 14,000
7	10	40,000	40,000	—	+ 54,000
8	10	25,000	—	—	+ 54,000

EXHIBIT 10.5

Volume indicators

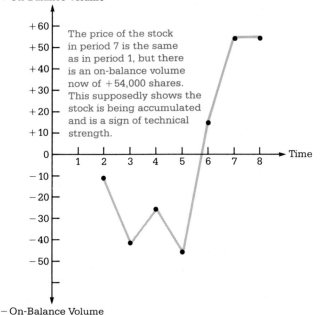

+ On-Balance Volume

The price of the stock in period 7 is the same as in period 1, but there is an on-balance volume now of + 54,000 shares. This supposedly shows the stock is being accumulated and is a sign of technical strength.

− On-Balance Volume

shown in Exhibit 10.5. He also developed specific trading rules based on the index. Generally, a consistent upward trend in the index is bullish, while a downward trend is bearish.

The Advance/Decline Index   The **advance/decline index** simply plots the number of issues advancing in price divided by the number declining in price each day (or other period). As long as the series remains in an uptrend, many technicians would remain bullish about the market, while a downtrend calls for bearishness. Exhibit 10.6 illustrates the advance/decline index. Issues advancing and declining are reported daily in *The Wall Street Journal,* which provides a source of data to construct the index.

The New Highs/New Lows Index   The **new highs/new lows index** is constructed from periodic data that show the number of new issues that traded at their highest 52-week price divided by the number of issues that traded at their lowest 52-week price. Exhibit 10.7 illustrates this index, which is often used as a companion to the advance/decline index and is interpreted in the same manner.

Investor Psychology

Some technicians believe that investor psychology is the dominant force in the market. If investors are cautious and conservative, the market will not do well. Conversely, investor optimism will eventually lead to higher prices and a robust market. Of course, the trick is to measure optimism and pessimism. Three indexes are used often: Barron's Confidence Index, the slope of the yield curve, and activity in low-priced stocks.

Investor optimism and pessimism can influence market prices.

Barron's Confidence Index   **Barron's Confidence Index** is calculated by dividing the yields of the best-grade bonds by the yields of intermediate-grade bonds; that is,

EXHIBIT 10.6
The advance/decline index

Number of Issues Advancing in Price / Number of Issues Declining in Price

EXHIBIT 10.7
New highs/new lows
index*

Number of Issues at 52-Week Highest Price
Number of Issues at 52-Week Lowest Price

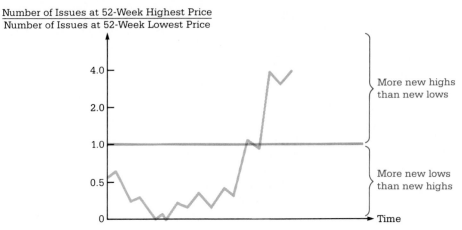

*To show the magnitude of new highs and new lows, this series is
sometimes shown as new highs minus new lows. The graph must
then allow for negative values.

$$\text{Barron's Confidence Index} = \frac{\text{Yield: Best-Grade Bonds}}{\text{Yield: Intermediate-Grade Bonds}}$$

You would expect the index to always have a value less than 1.0, but the amount
less indicates the degree of bond market enthusiasm. A downward trend in the
index, such as that shown in Exhibit 10.8, might show that investors are
demanding greater yields to compensate them for the higher risk associated with
poorer quality bonds. This demand for higher yields, in turn, shows growing
investor pessimism and, perhaps, a future decline in the stock market as this

EXHIBIT 10.8
Barron's Confidence
Index

Yield: Best-Grade Bonds
Yield: Intermediate-Grade Bonds

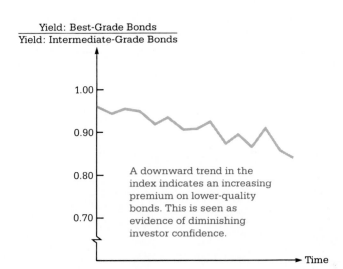

A downward trend in the
index indicates an increasing
premium on lower-quality
bonds. This is seen as
evidence of diminishing
investor confidence.

pessimism spills out of the bond market. On the other hand, an upward trend in the index indicates optimism and potential future market strength.

Slope of the Yield Curve   The yield curve was explained in Chapter 5. You should remember that it shows the relationship between debt instrument yields to maturity and maturity. A normal yield curve is considered one that has positive slope; that is, the longer an instrument's maturity, the greater its yield to maturity. Occasionally, though, yield curves become inverted, as shown in Exhibit 10.9. On the surface, an inverted yield curve seems an anomaly: why should investors receive lower yields on debt instruments with longer maturities, which are clearly riskier than those with short maturities? The answer lies in the fact that investors expect interest rates to fall, and as they do, investors will earn greater price appreciation with longer maturities.

> An upward trend in Barron's Confidence Index indicates investor optimism.

The market technician feels bond investors are smart investors, and their belief that interest rates will fall is a cue to begin buying stocks. Some technicians also believe a steeply sloped positive yield curve can provide evidence that interest rates will rise in the future. Although not as strong a signal, such a curve is seen as a selling cue.

> Some technicians believe bond investors are smart investors.

Activity in Low-Priced Stocks   The activity in low-priced stocks supposedly heats up as a bull market comes to an end. Why is this so? Again, because it

EXHIBIT 10.9
Yield curves and future interest rates

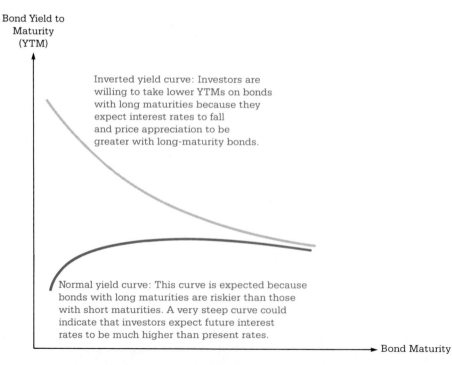

Bond Yield to Maturity (YTM)

Inverted yield curve: Investors are willing to take lower YTMs on bonds with long maturities because they expect interest rates to fall and price appreciation to be greater with long-maturity bonds.

Normal yield curve: This curve is expected because bonds with long maturities are riskier than those with short maturities. A very steep curve could indicate that investors expect future interest rates to be much higher than present rates.

Bond Maturity

indicates increased activity of small investors, who are attracted to low-priced stocks. It also shows that all investors are disregarding fundamentals in favor of securities that simply have low prices, because investors see better percentage gains in low-priced issues as opposed to high-priced issues. *Barron's* constructs an index of low-priced stocks and reports it each week in its statistics section.

Small investors may favor low-priced stocks.

Evaluating Pressure Indicators

You might be interested in using indicators as a forecasting method, but before you do, consider some questions about their effectiveness. Basically, pressure indicators are similar in use to the leading economic indicators discussed in the previous chapter. To be effective a leading indicator must: (1) give a correct signal, (2) give the signal with sufficient lead time for appropriate action, and (3) have consistent lead times. Exhibit 10.10 illustrates how a perfect market indicator would work. Notice that it gave four correct signals — two increases and

EXHIBIT 10.10

Illustration of a perfect market indicator

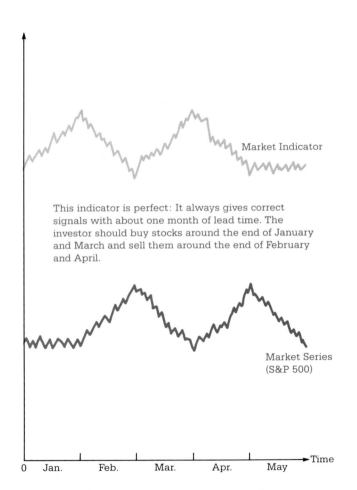

Market Indicator

This indicator is perfect: It always gives correct signals with about one month of lead time. The investor should buy stocks around the end of January and March and sell them around the end of February and April.

Market Series (S&P 500)

Time

0   Jan.   Feb.   Mar.   Apr.   May

two decreases—with a consistent one-month lead time, which would have been enough time for an investor to take action. This perfect market indicator is a pure fiction, existing only in theory. Actual indicators show a much more confused picture.

Correct Signals   Many indicators do not consistently give correct signals; that is, they might signal a market increase, but the market subsequently goes down. Exhibit 10.11 illustrates how most market indicators actually work. As you see, the pattern of relationships between the two time series is very hazy. True, a quick or casual glance gives the impression of a close correlation between them, but a more detailed examination might show the indicator is virtually useless as a forecasting tool. If you look closely, you can see that a false signal was given from mid- to late February. The indicator was showing a market increase that never came, or at least did not come until the middle of March. The indicator fell sharply in late February and early March, leaving us to wonder whether the increase or the decrease was appropriate.

Many indicators give false signals.

EXHIBIT 10.11

Illustration of most market indicators

This is how most indicators move in relation to the market. Is it clear the indicator leads the market—or does the market lead the indicator? Mathematical techniques would probably show no significant leads or lags between the two time series.

Market Indicator

Did the January trend in the indicator foreshadow the sharp market increase in late January and early February? And if it did, was the trend clear enough by late January to give investors sufficient lead time to act?

Market Series (S&P 500)

0   Jan.   Feb.   Mar.   Apr.   May   Time

Sufficient Lead Time Even if an indicator provides a correct signal, by the time it is interpreted, the market may have already moved. Is it clear the upward January trend in the indicator was recognizable in sufficient time to get in the market? Notice that the indicator's trend wasn't actually established clearly until the last week or so in January. By then, the market was also moving up sharply. If you hesitated a day or so, you most likely missed most of the gains.

Many indicators fail to give sufficient or consistent lead times.

Consistent Lead Times Exhibit 10.11 shows very inconsistent lead times between the indicator and the market. Indeed, the pattern is so confusing that you could just as easily argue that the market leads the indicator, rather than the indicator leading the market. For example, the market clearly turned up in mid-March before the indicator, and seems to have done so in mid-April as well. The false signal in mid-February mentioned earlier could also be interpreted as the market signaling a downturn in the indicator. If we analyzed the two series with mathematical techniques, we probably would find they tend to move together rather than one leading the other. If this is true, the market indicator is best described as a coincident, rather than a leading, indicator. Unfortunately, coincident indicators have little value in forecasting.

An Appraisal Can pressure indicators help you make better investment decisions? Consider this: If you plan to use them, you obviously also intend to time your purchases and sales of securities to what you believe are market cycles. However, the investment literature contains strong evidence that timing often does no better than a simple buy-and-hold approach, and that when commissions are considered, it usually does worse.

To the uninitiated investor, the technician's pressure indicators and price graphs (these are covered in the next section) often appear to be highly mathematical and complex constructs that must be good because they are impossible to understand. Most are not that mathematical, nor are they very complex. If we can't understand them, it probably reflects a lack of substance on their part rather than our ignorance. The underlying rationale for many of the indicators simply does not exist. For example, there is no clear evidence showing odd-lot traders are any worse—or better—than their round-lot counterparts. Moreover, the record of mutual fund managers is hardly one of superior performance; in fact, mutual funds so often perform more poorly than an unmanaged market index that you might be better off doing the opposite of what the managers do.

The underlying rationale for many indicators does not exist.

Even when an indicator's underlying logic seems more substantial, there are still problems to consider. For example, it is true that all inverted yield curves have been followed by falling interest rates and rising stock prices. But the lead times between when the curve became inverted and when interest rates and stock prices moved have been highly unpredictable. Using the yield curve to forecast would have been no more effective than using some simple, naive approach, such as always buying stocks whenever their prices have fallen 30% and selling them after they increase 50%.

Watch the Super Bowl and Be a Super Forecaster

Want to get your portfolio started right each year? Forget technical analysis, fundamental analysis, expert advice, and anything else that takes a lot of work and might have some connection to the stock market. Instead, enjoy a football game. Specifically, watch the Super Bowl each January and if one of the old NFL teams wins, buy; if one of the expansion AFL teams wins, don't buy (for even better results, go short). Sounds crazy, right? Well, the accompanying table shows how you would have done with this strategy since the Super Bowl began. You would have missed the market direction in only 2 of 23 years, which is remarkable. (And, the misses were so close that a few points change at year's end could have given a perfect record.) Indeed, the chances of doing this well by luck are about 2 in 1,000. With performance this good, why use anything else?

Let's be serious. Stock market performance and the Super Bowl are definitely independent events. The fact that they appear not to be is unusual. But, if you looked at an endless number of independent events, you should find one eventually that forecasts the market as well or better than the Super Bowl. If you understand the point here, you should also understand why some supposedly more sophisticated forecasters show remarkable forecasting results. Keep this in mind: with thousands of professionals forecasting, the odds are excellent that we can find one or two who do it almost perfectly. Are they lucky, or are they good? You make the decision.

Super Bowl Forecast Results

Year	Winner	League	Change in the Market
1967	Green Bay Packers	NFL	+20.09%
1968	Green Bay Packers	NFL	+ 7.66
1969	New York Jets	AFL	−11.42
1970	Kansas City Chiefs	AFL	+ 0.16*
1971	Baltimore Colts	NFL	+10.79
1972	Dallas Cowboys	NFL	+15.63
1973	Miami Dolphins	AFL	−17.37
1974	Miami Dolphins	AFL	−29.72
1975	Pittsburgh Steelers	NFL	+31.55
1976	Pittsburgh Steelers	NFL	+19.15
1977	Oakland Raiders	AFL	−11.50
1978	Dallas Cowboys	NFL	+ 1.06
1979	Pittsburgh Steelers	NFL	+12.31
1980	Pittsburgh Steelers	NFL	+25.77
1981	Oakland Raiders	AFL	− 9.72
1982	San Francisco 49ers	NFL	+14.76
1983	Washington Redskins	NFL	+17.27
1984	Los Angeles Raiders	AFL	+ 1.39*
1985	San Francisco 49ers	NFL	+26.34
1986	Chicago Bears	NFL	+14.63
1987	New York Giants	NFL	+ 2.03
1988	Washington Redskins	NFL	+12.41
1989	San Francisco 49ers	NFL	+27.50
1990	San Francisco 49ers	NFL	?

*Shows incorrect forecasts.

USING CHARTS AND GRAPHS

Not all technicians employ pressure indicators as their primary forecasting devices. Many prefer using price charts and graphs. Even if you are not a technician, you might find that a price graph helps you to understand a security's historical price movements. Apart from its use as a forecasting tool, a price graph provides some indication of a security's price volatility and, thus, its risk. The discussion below, though, focuses on the forecasting aspect of price graphs.

Constructing Graphs

The most popular price graph is a **time graph,** which simply plots the periodic (daily, weekly, quarterly, or whatever) price of a security over time. The top graph in Exhibit 10.12 shows a typical time graph. The analyst appears to be recording the price of the stock every other or every third day. As we see, price has shown an up-down pattern, gradually increasing from $15 to $26 a share, and then declining to $21. Constructing a time graph is obviously simple and can be done by anyone.

However, many of the price changes over the five months are inconsequential: up a half or a quarter, down a half or a quarter, and so forth. Some analysts feel it is unnecessary to record all prices, and a more effective use of time would be to record only important changes. Defining important is arbitrary; in the case of a stock selling at $15, you might decide any price change of $1 or more is important and will be recorded. You ignore, then, any change less than this amount. The lower graph in Exhibit 10.12 illustrates the construction of a graph using this approach. It is called a **point-and-figure (P and F) graph**.

A point-and-figure graph records only significant price changes.

Assuming you start the graph when the price is $15, no entries are made until the middle of January, when the price reaches $16. You then enter an X to show an increase of $1. As you see, price continues increasing until $20 is reached towards the end of January. So, keep entering Xs up to $20 on the P and F graph. Then in late January, price begins to fall and continues falling until mid-February, eventually reaching $16.50. These decreases are recorded with three Os. Using the same methods, you record and condense the entire five months of price activity on the P and F chart. As you see, P and F charts require less time to maintain, which enhances their appeal to technicians who are watching many individual stocks. However, excellent computer software packages can now automatically record and analyze data available from various data banks, so saving time is no longer a problem, and P and F graphs should eventually become obsolete.

A P and F chart is easy to maintain, but with computer systems available, this advantage is no longer as important.

Interpreting Graphs

Whether a time or a P and F graph is used, the price movements must be interpreted. There are probably as many interpretation methods as there are technicians using them, so attempting to explain even a small portion of them

EXHIBIT 10.12
Price Graphs

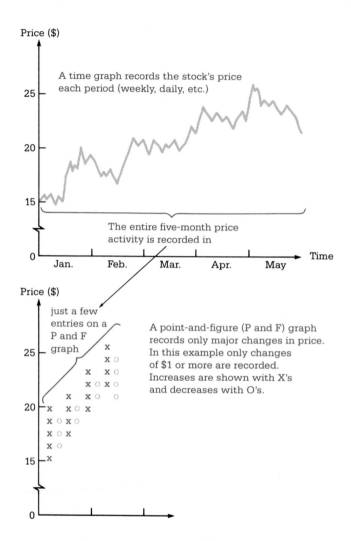

Price ($)

A time graph records the stock's price each period (weekly, daily, etc.)

The entire five-month price activity is recorded in

Time

Jan.   Feb.   Mar.   Apr.   May

Price ($)

just a few entries on a P and F graph

A point-and-figure (P and F) graph records only major changes in price. In this example only changes of $1 or more are recorded. Increases are shown with X's and decreases with O's.

would take the rest of this text. We will discuss two methods that are widely used: support and resistance lines, and the head and shoulders pattern. Interpretation methods are usually the same for time and P and F graphs.

Support and resistance lines are trend lines.

Support and Resistance Lines **Support and resistance lines** are actually trend lines drawn through a series of high and low prices. The top graph in Exhibit 10.13 provides an illustration. As you see, this stock's price has been trending upwards, reaching a string of highs and lows along the way. By drawing lines through the highs and lows, you create the support and resistance lines. Why use these names? Notice that as price reached its highs, selling pressures increased (technicians might describe this as "investors taking their profits") and

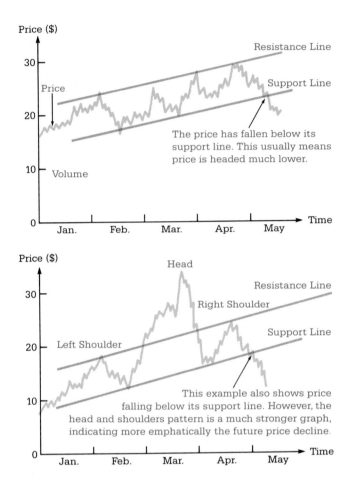

EXHIBIT 10.13
Interpreting price
graphs

price fell; that is, there was resistance to greater price increases. Each time the support line was reached, buying pressures mounted, giving support to the price.

A logical question to ask is, "So what?" What do support and resistance lines have to tell us about future price? Many technicians believe that as long as price remains within its support and resistance lines, it is safe to hold the stock, but there are no compelling reasons to either buy or sell it. However, if the resistance line is penetrated from below, a buying situation exists; if the support line is penetrated from above, a selling situation exists. Exhibit 10.13 illustrates the latter, and the interpretation is that price is headed much lower. Most technicians also watch volume. If a breakthrough is accompanied by heavy volume (as shown in Exhibit 10.13), the signal is considered even stronger.

Trading actions are prompted when a support or resistance line is penetrated.

A Head and Shoulders Pattern   A **head and shoulders pattern** is simply a price pattern that looks like a head and two shoulders, such as the one shown in the lower part of Exhibit 10.13. Many stock prices exhibit such patterns, although it sometimes takes a vivid imagination to see them. Technicians revel when they see a head and shoulders pattern, because it is thought to be one of the strongest technical price indicators. The interpretation is about the same as it is for support and resistance lines. In the example, price has again gone through the support line, indicating continued price weakness. Had it not penetrated the support line, but, instead, increased above the resistance line—formed by passing a line through the tips of the two shoulders—the technician would probably feel price would continue to increase, eventually going above the head. Since a head and shoulders is considered a stronger pattern than simple resistance and support lines, the technician most likely would have greater confidence in his or her forecast.

Moving Averages   A moving average was introduced and explained earlier in this chapter. While moving averages can be used to evaluate any time series, they play a very important role in the technical analysis of price graphs. The graph shown in Exhibit 10.3 can represent a price time series, instead of an odd-lot ratio (simply imagine the vertical axis shows prices). In this case, the buy and sell signals would be the same. The effectiveness of using moving averages depends very much upon the price movements of the market. A rather flat market with a repeating up-down pattern will generate numerous signals, leading to frequent buying and selling, large commissions, and large investor losses. The method is used more successfully when longer trends take place.

Price Momentum   Many technical analysts evaluate a stock's **price momentum,** which refers to the relative speed of its price increases or decreases. Momentum can be measured in numerous ways. One method involves calculating percentage changes each period (usually weekly or quarterly). For example, suppose over the past three weeks, a stock price goes from $10 to $11 to $12⅛ to $13⅜. Calculating percentage changes indicates price is rising at about a constant 10% rate, which is its momentum. Increasing momentum—considered desirable—would be reflected in a series such as: $10 to $11 to $13¼ to $17⅛, which shows first a 10% increase, then a 20% increase, and finally a 30% increase. Rather than calculating percentage increases, some analysts weight each period's return, giving more weight to more recent periods. These are called *relative strength* indicators. Suppose price over three weeks goes from $10.00 to $10.50 to $11.00 to $12.00, and the analyst weights the most recent week at 0.6 and the two previous weeks at 0.2 each. Then, weighted weekly performance is shown below:

$$
\begin{array}{llll}
\text{week 1:} & + \ \$0.50 \times 0.2 = & + & \$0.1 \\
\text{week 2:} & + \ \ \ 0.50 \times 0.2 = & + & 0.1 \\
\text{week 3:} & + \ \ \ 1.00 \times 0.6 = & + & 0.6 \\
& \text{total} = & & +\$0.8
\end{array}
$$

Price increased $2 over the three weeks, and the relative strength of the third week is 0.667 ($0.6/$0.8).

Trading rules are then established based upon recent periods' relative strengths. A buy signal in the above example might be a relative strength of 0.6 or better. As with a moving average technique, the analyst hopes to find a stock on the verge of a sustained upward trend in price.

Relative strength ratios can also compare the price movement of one stock to its industry average, or the relative strength of an industry to the overall market. The calculations for these comparisons are similar to those illustrated for comparing performances during different periods. The purpose of the comparisons is the same.

Evaluating the Use of Graphs

There is a mystique about price graphs that appeals to many investors. How can you not be impressed by the patterns often seen in the graphs? Surely, all you need to do is find the interpretation key to unlock the mystery the graphs hold. Support and resistance lines are one of the keys, but there might be others that are even more effective. Believe it or not (and most technicians don't), most of the patterns you are likely to see are easily explained by random processes.

What is Randomness?   You can understand randomness better by creating your own price chart. Take a coin and flip it 250 times, recording each time the head or tail that results. (This experiment goes much faster if you can find a few friends to help you.) Now, on a piece of graph paper, assume you are watching a stock that is currently selling at $25. Assume each flip of the coin represents one day. Each time you get a head, assume price increases by $1; if you get a tail, assume it decreases by $1. For example, if the first flip was a head, you assume price increased to $26 on the first day; if the second flip is a tail, price falls back to $25 on the second day. After 250 flips, you will have about a year's price graph (allowing days off for weekends and holidays).

What do you think this graph might look like? You probably agree that flipping a coin is a random process, and the graph should then show randomness. Would randomness appear as a series of up $1 and down $1 on a rotating basis, such as the top graph in Exhibit 10.14? That would be almost mathematically impossible. Instead, you are likely to have series of ups and downs called *runs,* and your graph more likely will look like the one at the bottom of Exhibit 10.14. Such a time series is often called a **random walk**. You might get three or four heads in a row, followed by a couple of tails, and then two or three more heads, and so forth. In short, you surely would expect a series of runs, and some might be quite long. When you are finished, you might be amazed at how closely your graph resembles many actual price graphs. Indeed, you may turn up a head and shoulders pattern or two, and you probably will have little trouble finding some support and resistance lines. And, consider that coin flipping is only one of many randomizing techniques that could be used to create the price graph. A more complicated one might provide an even better facsimile.

A random walk shows a process with no predictable patterns.

The Implications of Randomness   If a price graph can be explained by random processes, is it likely there are any predictive patterns in the time series that can

EXHIBIT 10.14
Hypothetical price
graphs

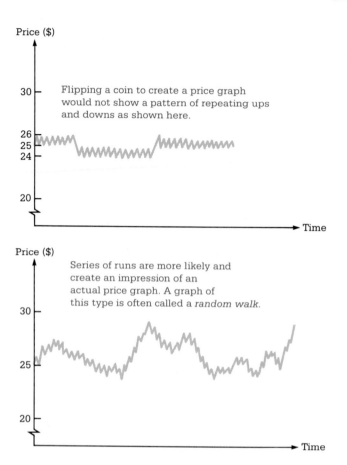

be used to forecast future prices? The simple answer is no. As you begin your coin-flipping experiment, what is your best guess for the stock's price one year later? The right answer is $25, since you logically expect about an equal number of heads and tails after 250 flips. It would be very unlikely, however, that you would get exactly 125 heads and 125 tails. Rather than picking one specific future price, you would prefer to think in terms of a likely price range. For example, the odds are fairly good the future price will be somewhere between $20 and $30.

**Technicians often be-
lieve they see patterns
in random processes.**

Unfortunately, our conclusion about the effectiveness of price graphs to improve investment performance is they are no better than pressure indicators. You can do as well with most simple random methods—something to consider before you pay several hundred dollars or more a year for a chart service.

EFFICIENT MARKETS

We have discussed the two broad approaches to security evaluation and selection: the fundamental approach and the technical approach. Proponents for each contend their methods allow them to identify undervalued and overvalued securities, and, over time, to earn returns in excess of what might be earned by simply buying a random portfolio of securities, or by buying a broad market index such as the S&P 500. Earning this extra return is referred to as **beating the market**. In the sections to follow, we'll look at the empirical evidence that relates to these beating-the-market claims. First, though, we must understand that comparing performances is legitimately undertaken only when risk is held constant; that is, if an analyst consistently recommends securities far riskier than the market, you should expect a return in excess of the market return. The important question is whether the extra return was adequate compensation for the added risk. As we saw in Chapter 8, with respect to common stocks, this means earning a return above that which you would expect given the stock's beta value.

Claims of beating the market must consider risks undertaken.

What Are Efficient Markets?

There are several definitions of market efficiency, but the one most appropriate for investment purposes defines an **efficient market** as one in which a security's price reflects all existing information that bears on its expected return in the future. This information includes both technical data, such as historical prices and volume, and fundamental data, such as past or projected earnings and balance sheet strength. Assuming investors make decisions based upon such information, and further assuming a sufficient number of investors in the market so that no single investor can influence market price with his or her trading, then a market price is described as being in equilibrium. This means it is a relatively stable price with no pressure to push it either up or down. This stability may be short-lived, however, since new information can arise that might change investor expectations, leading to greater buying or selling pressures that push price to a new higher or lower equilibrium.

Prices in an efficient market reflect all information available to buyers and sellers.

In such a market, an investor can earn excess profits only by knowing in advance the new information causing an equilibrium shift. Market analysts who believe investors cannot consistently have such information express their view in what is called the **efficient market hypothesis (EMH)**. Put simply, those who hold to the EMH argue that no one can consistently beat the market, and they have conducted many tests to determine if the EMH can be supported by factual evidence.

EMH proponents argue that no one can consistently beat the market.

The Weak Form of the EMH   The EMH was first tested by evaluating the effectiveness of technical analysis, primarily charting techniques. As we saw, chartists believe that historical price patterns offer clues to future price movements. With the aid of the computer, testing charting techniques is relatively easy, since most trading strategies can be expressed in a mathematical format. For example, support and resistance lines can be found, and trades based on their penetrations can be determined and evaluated. Many such tests have been conducted, and the overwhelming evidence indicates charting techniques

Tests of the EMH indicate technicians cannot beat the market.

Do Insiders Really Beat the Market? And, Can Outsiders Following Insiders Do As Well?

You would think if there is one group of investors who might have an edge, it would be corporate insiders: officers, directors, and people who own a lot of the company's stock. If they don't know what's going on in their own companies and, more important, what's likely to happen in the future, then there is little hope for the rest of us. While the proposition that corporate insiders do indeed earn superior investment returns seems obvious and might be taken as an act of faith, market analysts have said, "No, it needs to be tested, as do all other theories suggesting some investors beat the market."

There has been no shortage of tests, since information is readily available by virtue of the SEC requirement that insiders report transactions in their com-panies' stocks by the tenth day of the month following the transactions. The information is then

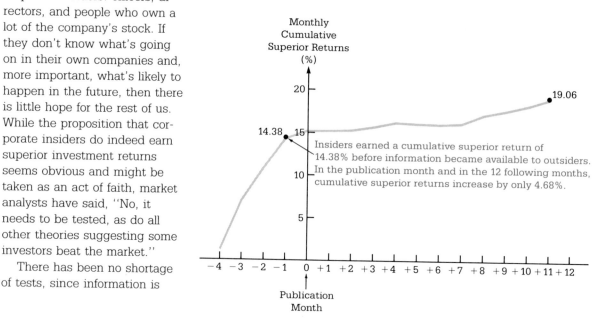

Monthly Cumulative Superior Returns (%)

Insiders earned a cumulative superior return of 14.38% before information became available to outsiders. In the publication month and in the 12 following months, cumulative superior returns increase by only 4.68%.

Publication Month

do *not* beat the market. You will do just as well with a simple buy-and-hold strategy, selecting securities randomly.

The failure of technical approaches to beat the market is described as weak support for the EMH, or the **weak form of the EMH**. The adjective *weak* suggests that merely showing the failure of technical analysis does not provide a strong argument in favor of efficient markets. Most sophisticated fundamentalists felt that technical analysis was closer to voodoo forecasting than genuine security analysis, anyway. So, it came as no surprise to learn that what they long suspected was indeed true. However, they felt much stronger evidence was needed to sustain the EMH.

The Semistrong Form of the EMH   Such evidence was not long in coming, and much of it was directed against fundamental techniques. Several studies showed

published in the SEC *Official Summary*. It is also available through private newsletters that often devise methods of interpreting trading activity to rate stocks as to the extent of inside buying or selling.

So, what does the research tell us? On balance, it confirms what we thought: insiders apparently do earn abnormally high returns, meaning they beat the market on a risk-adjusted basis. While not overwhelming, the evidence is strong enough to suggest that if insiders can do it, outsiders can follow their trading cues and do it, too. This proposition is far more interesting because, if true, it offers us all an opportunity to improve our investment performance.

Before you rush out to look at the *Official Summary* or buy one

of the newsletters, be cautious. The evidence is far less convincing that we can mimic insiders to earn returns as high as theirs. A study by Gary A. Benesh and Robert A. Pari indicates the problem.* They tested investment performance of both insiders and outsiders, using the Consensus of Insiders (COI) newsletters published by Perry Wysong as the source of information outsiders used to determine insider trading. Each month the COI provides its subscribers a list of the 20 highest-rated stocks, based on insider trading over the previous four months. How well would you have done following the monthly lists? The accompanying figure shows the answer.

Adjusting for market performance and risk, outsiders

earned a monthly cumulative superior return of about 4.7% over a 13-month period from the time the insider trading took place. Not bad, except that none of the monthly superior returns was significant in a statistical sense. In other words, the 4.7% cumulative figure could be due to luck or any other random event. Luck is not the explanation for superior insider returns, though. They clearly beat the market (with statistical significance). Unfortunately for us, they did it in the four months before trades were published in the COI.

*Benesh, Gary A. and R. A. Pari, "Performance of Stocks Recommended on the Basis of Insider Trading." *The Financial Review 22,* February, 1987, pp. 145–58.

that buying securities because their shares were to be split (a favorite technique in years past and still occasionally heard of today) was a complete waste of time. So too were strategies based upon changes in certain macroeconomic variables, such as interest rates, GNP, or the money supply. Other studies showed that earnings announcements by managements had virtually no effect upon their firms' stock prices. First-time investors are often very much surprised when the stock market, or an individual stock, fails to react to good (or bad) news about the economy, or about the company. For example: IBM announces record earnings, and the stock falls in price. Investors must learn (some the hard way) that current prices already reflect the expected news. Indeed, it is only "news" if the information is different from what had been anticipated.

The **semistrong form of the EMH** argues that any public information—not only historical prices—cannot be used to earn above-expected

Evidence is inconclusive as to whether fundamental analysts can beat the market.

returns. This means that fundamental analysis using, for example, a company's financial report as a data source is as much a waste of time as drawing a chart of its price history. While the early studies supported the semistrong form, recent studies offer mixed evidence. Buying stocks with low P/E ratios has been found to produce above-expected returns. Also, there appears to be an advantage in buying small company stocks. We saw in Chapter 3 that small companies did show much greater returns than the S&P 500, although they also showed greater risk. In effect, the current research seems to indicate the added return was worth the added risk. You would have been better off buying them than leveraging the S&P 500 to achieve an equivalent degree of risk (beta).

The Strong Form of the EMH   The **strong form of the EMH** argues that investors cannot consistently earn above-expected profits using *any* information—public or private. This form does not mean that someone with privileged information cannot make an occasional windfall; obviously, many corporate insiders have possessed such information and have used it to their advantage. What the strong form does say is that even insiders cannot consistently earn superior returns by virtue of their information monopoly. Since federal law requires directors, officers, and important shareholders (those owning 10% or more of a company's total stock) to report transactions in their companies' stocks to the SEC, there is ample information to test the strong form. The results of such tests are mixed, although the evidence leans mostly in the direction that insiders do earn superior returns on a risk-adjusted basis. The strong form of the

Insiders apparently beat the market, but outsiders following insider trading cues do not.

EMH must therefore be rejected. Can other investors—outsiders—also earn superior returns by following the trading patterns of insiders? This issue has also been tested, and while evidence again is mixed, it leans most heavily in the direction that outsiders cannot earn superior returns.

Another test of the strong form determined whether professional money managers could beat the market. On the surface, it is logical to expect that they could. They have extensive research facilities and most likely are the first to receive information about a company. So, what is their performance record? Surprisingly, a large majority actually show below-expected returns for their clientele when commissions and administrative expenses are considered. In fact,

A majority of professional money managers do not beat the market.

their performance has been so poor over the years that many institutional investors have given up on them and turned their money over to funds that simply buy the market. These are called index funds. They make no pretense to earn superior returns, and their success is measured strictly by how well they correlate with a market index such as the S&P 500. A high correlation guarantees the fund will earn at least as much as the index and have the same degree of risk. Obviously, an index fund doesn't beat the market, but it doesn't lose to it, either. Over $100 billion is invested in such funds and the total grows larger each year.

Implications of the EMH

Is the evidence supporting the EMH strong enough to encourage you to abandon your effort to find undervalued securities or superior-performing mutual funds

Screening for Big Winners

A stock that doubles or triples in value in one year is surely a big winner, and finding one is a big task. Some might say it's an improbable task, where luck plays a greater role than skill. A recent study, though, by Marc Reinganum ("The Anatomy of a Stock Market Winner," *Financial Analysts Journal,* March-April 1988, pp. 16–28) might provide investors with clues to help give them an edge.

Reinganum studied 222 stocks that turned in super one-year performances during the period 1970–1983. He then studied characteristics of these winners and reached some interesting conclusions. For example, he found that both fundamental and technical indicators pinpointed potential winners. The most important of these were:

1. Price to book ratio less than 1.0 (fundamental)
2. Acceleration in quarterly earnings (fundamental)
3. Price momentum (technical)
4. Less than 20 million shares outstanding (technical)

Using these four characteristics, Reinganum then selected stocks from a broad universe of stocks that did not contain the original 222. His results were amazing: holding the selections for one year produced a return of 16.67% in *excess* of the market return; over two years, the excess return was 37.14%.

Actually, he worked with a broader set of variables—nine instead of four—and achieved even better results. However, some of the variables in the broader set are not readily available. The study is interesting, not only in that it refutes the efficient market hypothesis, but also in that the successful predictors differ somewhat from those usually associated with beating the market. For example, small firms did not have an edge over large ones. (Reinganum himself found an advantage with small firms in earlier studies.) "Smart money" variables, such as insiders' activities, were ineffective. Also, following a contrarian approach (buying stocks with depressed prices)

didn't work since most of the big gainers were trading at prices within 15% of their previous two-year highest price. Says Reinganum, "This suggests that there may be more than one way to skin the performance cat."

Hide-taking aside, there are some issues you should consider before you use the four variables to find winners. First, the study found 10,543 buy signals over the 13-year period. If you acted on each one, you made 811 purchases annually. Clearly, this amount of buying far exceeds that of most investors. Perhaps, selecting randomly from this large list might produce a smaller portfolio with equally good results, but we're not sure. Second, the study's results are not extended beyond two years, so we also don't know how selections perform in a longer-run period. Of course, with one- and two-year results this good, who cares? Finally, commissions should be considered, although they seem a trivial matter in this setting.

and, instead, put your money in an index fund? There may not be a simple yes-or-no answer to this question. The following points are worth considering:

1. The evidence appears sufficiently strong to discourage the use of graphing and other technical approaches. In fact, strategies based on them typically involve such frequent trading that you probably will do much worse than the market and enrich only your broker.

2. The evidence also seems strong enough to discourage your use of fundamental analysis if it is based exclusively on public information and uses techniques used by everyone else. This advice is particularly appropriate if you are analyzing large companies thousands of other analysts are watching. Being realistic, what can we hope to find, for example, in IBM's financial report that other analysts will not find? You also should give little attention to research reports prepared by professional analysts if their analysis goes no further than reworking the company's financial report, or repeating information management has made available to the public. Surprisingly, many such reports are limited to these activities with, perhaps, a broad overview of the effectiveness of the company's management or its position in the industry. Very few investors show superior returns with these reports.

3. Your best hope is to concentrate on small companies, trying to find information other investors do not have. Your odds might be better if you limit your investigations to companies in your home area (where you might have an advantage in getting information) or to those in an industry in which you have a particular expertise. If several such firms interest you, then prepare a fundamental analysis, using the tools highlighted in the previous chapter and risk analyses explained in Chapter 4. And, by all means, make sure you have adequate diversification. If you can find only one or two companies that appeal to you, consider investing only a limited portion of your available funds in them. Is this approach risky? Indeed it is; in a sense, you are becoming as entrepreneurial as the people who founded the company and possibly still hold a large portion of its common stock. But, this may be what it takes to beat the market.

SUMMARY

Technical analysis attempts to discover profitable investments using methods that do not rely upon measuring the intrinsic strengths of a company, industry, or overall economy. It uses pressure indicators that show who is buying or selling, levels of market activity, and investor psychology. Specific indicators include the odd-lot ratio, odd-lot short sales, institutions' cash positions, insider activity, the Dow theory, volume and price-related volume, the advance/decline index, the new highs/new lows index, Barron's Confidence Index, slope of the yield curve, and activity in low-priced stocks. There is little evidence to show that using pressure indicators leads to better investment decisions. Indicators often give false signals, signal too late to be effective, or have inconsistent lead times.

Market technicians also use charts and graphs. These can be time graphs or point-and-figure graphs. Interpreting graphs is not a precise science and often involves subjective evaluation. There is little evidence to show that using graphs or charts helps improve investment decisions. Many so-called chart patterns are actually random patterns.

An efficient market is one in which a security's price reflects all existing information that bears on its expected future return. An efficient market hypothesis implies that investors cannot consistently outperform the overall market on a risk-adjusted basis. The hypothesis has been tested in various settings, and has been supported in some and rejected in others. Implications of the tests for investors include a general rejection of technical analysis for security selection; a rejection of fundamental analysis, if it is performed on companies with a large following; and some support for fundamental analysis when it is applied to small companies with few followers.

KEY TERMS

Select the alternative that best identifies the key term.

1. technical analysis
2. odd-lot ratio
3. odd-lot short sales
4. Dow theory
5. on-balance volume index
6. advance/decline index
7. new highs/new lows index
8. Barron's Confidence Index
9. time graph
10. point-and-figure (P and F) graph
11. support and resistance lines
12. head and shoulders pattern
13. price momentum
14. random walk
15. beating the market
16. efficient market
17. efficient market hypothesis (EMH)
18. weak form of the EMH
19. semistrong form of the EMH
20. strong form of the EMH

a. no information can be used to beat the market consistently
b. not meaningful unless risk is considered
c. ratio of the number of securities setting 52-week high prices to the number setting 52-week lows
d. examines the industrial and transportation indexes
e. shows meaningless patterns called "runs"
f. public information cannot be used to beat the market
g. security selection approach that ignores fundamentals
h. ratio of the number of securities increasing in price to the number decreasing
i. plots only important price movements
j. no one can consistently beat the market
k. indicates what unsophisticated investors are doing
l. considered one of the strongest technical indicators
m. a security's price reflects all existing information
n. links volume to price changes
o. shows price movements over time
p. a technician can't beat the market
q. indicates the very worst investment decisions
r. examines yields on high- and low-grade bonds
s. trend lines drawn through high and low prices
t. relative speed of price increases or decreases

REVIEW QUESTIONS

1. Explain the following: *(a)* the odd-lot ratio, *(b)* odd-lot short sales, *(c)* institutions' cash positions, and *(d)* insider activity. Discuss how these indicators are supposed to help you make better investment decisions.
2. Explain how a moving average line is constructed and discuss its purpose in time series analysis.

3. Explain the following: *(a)* the Dow Theory, *(b)* on-balance volume index, *(c)* advance/decline index, and *(d)* new highs/new lows index. What investment implications do these indicators have? Explain.
4. Explain the following: *(a)* Barron's Confidence Index, *(b)* slope of the yield curve, and *(c)* activity in low-priced stocks. Indicate the rationale behind these indicators.
5. Discuss three important attributes of a successful leading indicator. Is it likely that you will find technical indicators with all three? Explain.
6. Explain a time graph and a point-and-figure graph, comparing the two with respect to construction and interpretation.
7. Explain support and resistance lines.
8. Explain a head and shoulders pattern.
9. Discuss how moving averages are used in interpreting a price graph.
10. What is meant by momentum? How is it measured?
11. Explain the nature of randomness. Construct a line showing a random walk.
12. Discuss what is meant by an efficient market and what it means to beat the market.
13. Explain the efficient market hypothesis and evidence supporting it. Classify the evidence in the weak form, semistrong form, and strong form.
14. Given the research supporting (or failing to support) the EMH, discuss some investment implications arising from such evidence.

PROBLEMS AND PROJECTS

1. You have recorded the following prices for a stock over the past 25 days:

1	$17	6	$23	11	$24	16	$24	21	$23
2	18	7	26	12	22	17	22	22	25
3	20	8	24	13	20	18	25	23	27
4	20	9	21	14	21	19	26	24	26
5	22	10	23	15	23	20	22	25	23

a. Construct a time graph for the stock. Also, construct a 5-day moving average line and indicate buy and sell points.
b. Given the cues from your answer to question *(a)*, determine your profit or loss assuming you bought 100 shares on day 1 and followed the trading cues thereafter. Assume commissions were 1% of the trade amount. Compare your performance with this trading strategy versus buying 100 shares on day 1 and holding them through day 25.
2. For the past 5 days, you have recorded the price of a particular stock and volume of shares traded. Below are the data:

Day	Price	Volume
1	$54	28,000
2	52	34,000
3	51	22,000
4	52	51,000
5	53	97,000

a. Determine on-balance volume for days 2 through 5.
b. Do you think the stock should be bought or sold? Explain.

3. Monsanto's price was $45 a share one year ago. End-of-quarter prices since then are: (Q1) $46, (Q2) $48, (Q3) $52, and (Q4) $60.
    a. Determine price momentum by calculating quarterly percentage changes. Is momentum increasing? Explain.
    b. Suppose you weight quarterly changes as follows: 40% for the most recent quarter, and 20% for the three other quarters. If you require a relative strength of 0.65 as a condition for purchase, is Monsanto a buy? Illustrate your answer.

4. Be sure to read the boxed item in this chapter, "Watch the Super Bowl and Be a Super Forecaster." Using the market return data, evaluate the following trading strategy: buy stocks the year before an election year and hold them until the election year is over. Election years were 1988, 1984, 1980, 1976, 1972, and 1968. Compare the returns from this strategy versus the one of being guided by the Super Bowl winner. For simplicity, assume you buy when an NFL team wins and hold for the year. If an AFL team wins, assume you invest in a savings account that pays 7%. Also use the geometric progression and geometric mean as an evaluation method. (See Chapter 3 if you need a review.) Finally, compare performances of the election-year strategy and the Super Bowl strategy to a simple buy-and-hold approach.

5. (Student Project)   Simulate the price movement of a stock with a deck of cards. Here are the rules: current stock price = $30; each card represents one trading week; price changes as follows:

    > any diamond—up 2 points
    > any heart except the king—up 1 point
    > king of hearts—up 20 points
    > any club—down 2 points
    > any spade except the queen—down 1 point
    > queen of spades—down 13 points

    Shuffle, go through the entire deck and then answer the following.
    a. Prepare a time graph and indicate any interesting patterns.
    b. What must be the closing price of the stock one year from now? Explain.

6. (Student Project)   Select a random sample of 10 stocks from Value Line's *Investment Survey*. For a 4-year period prior to the most current year, determine for each the ratio of market value per share to book value per share, the number of shares of stock outstanding, the percentage increase (decrease) in earnings per share, and price momentum. Rank each stock for each performance indicator and then determine an aggregate rank. Finally, see if the aggregate rank correlates well with price appreciation or depreciation in the most current year.

CASE ANALYSES

10.1 Agnes Wade: Junior Technician

Agnes Wade is employed by ABC, Inc., a firm involved in hauling dangerous and hazardous materials. While Agnes does not have any privileged information about the company, she does know business is brisk and expected to remain so in the foreseeable future. Agnes has saved some money and is considering investing it in ABC's common stock. She does not understand financial statement data, but she has read material about technical analysis and thinks she can utilize some of the simpler methods to determine if the stock is a good buy. Accordingly, she has collected price and volume data for the company for the past 20 days.

Day	Price	Volume	Day	Price	Volume
1	9.50	3,000	11	12.00	8,000
2	9.75	2,000	12	11.88	6,000
3	10.13	6,000	13	11.25	9,000
4	10.13	4,000	14	11.38	4,000
5	10.00	7,000	15	11.00	10,000
6	10.25	5,000	16	11.25	5,000
7	10.75	9,000	17	10.50	16,000
8	11.63	12,000	18	10.38	9,000
9	11.50	7,000	19	10.25	14,000
10	11.75	15,000	20	11.50	7,000

With the data Agnes will construct the following graphs: *(a)* a time graph of price, *(b)* a 5-day moving average of price (show on graph to *a*), *(c)* an on-balance volume graph, and *(d)* a point-and-figure graph, assuming an important price movement is $0.50.

Questions

a. Construct the graphs indicated above.
b. Agnes thinks ABC is a good stock to buy. Explain whether you agree with her.

10.2
Troy Darnell
Looks at the
Indicators

Troy Darnell believes he can invest successfully if he can discover a way to determine how the overall market is likely to perform. He recalls from his college investments course that technical analysis deals with the topic of market forecasting, and he is considering using some of its methods. He has accumulated a substantial amount of monthly data, which he will analyze. The data appear in the accompanying table. Bond yields are based upon high-grade and intermediate-grade corporate issues, and upon Treasury issues with maturities of over 20 years (long) and 3 months (short).

| Year/ Month | Market Indexes | | | Bond Yields | | | |
| | Indus-trials | Trans-portation | New Highs/ New Lows | High Grade | Int. Grade | Maturities | |
						Long	Short
1/1	100	100	8.5	9.0%	12.0%	8.0%	6.0%
2	104	102	9.2	9.5	12.1	8.2	6.4
3	106	101	7.2	9.7	12.6	8.3	6.7
4	108	103	6.3	10.3	13.7	8.8	6.5
5	107	103	6.7	10.1	13.8	8.8	7.1
6	104	101	2.1	9.8	13.9	8.9	7.7
7	102	102	1.5	10.3	14.6	9.4	8.3
8	96	98	1.7	10.6	14.8	9.7	9.1
9	92	99	0.4	10.8	14.7	9.9	10.2
10	93	96	0.5	10.5	14.2	9.5	10.4
11	91	96	0.6	10.2	14.0	9.2	10.5
12	95	95	1.3	10.1	13.5	9.0	10.2
2/1	98	100	4.2	9.8	12.7	8.9	9.1
2	104	102	3.8	9.6	12.1	8.8	8.6
3	109	106	2.7	9.1	12.0	8.4	8.8
4	116	109	3.1	8.7	11.3	8.1	8.6
5	123	107	2.8	8.4	10.4	7.8	7.6
6	120	112	4.8	8.1	9.6	7.3	6.8
7	126	114	3.9	8.0	9.5	7.4	6.2
8	124	116	5.3	8.2	9.5	7.5	5.9
9	127	122	6.9	8.3	9.4	7.6	5.3
10	127	124	8.2	8.5	9.6	7.5	5.1
11	131	125	8.5	8.6	9.6	8.1	5.1
12	124	120	2.6	8.9	10.8	8.3	5.2

Questions

a. What technical indicators are the above series intended to reflect? Discuss each briefly and *how* each is supposed to work.

b. Suppose Troy is attempting to forecast the index for the industrials. How well does each of the indicators perform this task? Discuss.

c. Is it clear that each indicator leads the industrials, or do the industrials lead the indicator? Explain.

d. Utilizing whatever method(s) you believe are suitable, forecast the industrials for each of the first three months of year 3. How strongly do you feel about your forecasts? Discuss.

HELPFUL READING

Anders, George. "Here's How Stock-Market Experts Decide Which Rumors to Act On." *The Wall Street Journal*, February 4, 1986, p. 27.

————. "Stock Market's Technical Analysts Get New Respect after Price Drop." *The Wall Street Journal*, July 11, 1986, p. 19.

Clements, Jonathon. "The Almost-Perfect-Market Thesis." *Forbes,* February 6, 1989, pp. 150–51.

Garcia, Beatrice E. "Market Signs: Call them Unreliable." *The Wall Street Journal,* April 21, 1986, p. 33.

Gottschalk, Earl C., Jr. "Using Utility Stocks as Market Indicator." *The Wall Street Journal,* June 5, 1989, p. C1.

Merrill Lynch, Pierce, Fenner & Smith, Inc. *The Merrill Lynch Guide to Technical Analysis.* New York: latest edition.

Norris, Floyd. "Odd-Lot Short Sales: An Old Indicator's New Lease on Life." *Barron's,* August 25, 1986, p. 21.

Pinches, G. "The Random Walk Hypothesis and Technical Analysis." *Financial Analysts Journal,* March-April 1970.

Queenan, Joe. "Prophet Without Honor." *Forbes,* April 17, 1989, pp. 129–33.

Reinganum, Marc R. "The Anatomy of a Stock Market Winner." *Financial Analysts Journal,* March-April 1988, pp. 16–28.

Sivy, Michael. "How a Technician Spots a Trend." *Money,* April 1986, pp. 131–38.

Slater, Karen. "Opinions on 'Moving Averages' Wander Across the Spectrum." *The Wall Street Journal,* May 18, 1989, p. C1.

CHAPTER ELEVEN

Investing in Preferred Stocks

PREFERRED STOCK CHARACTERISTICS

Basic Stockholder Rights

Other Features of Preferred Stock

PREFERRED STOCK RETURNS

Straight Preferreds

Adjustable Rate Preferred Stock

RISKS IN PREFERRED STOCKS

Interest Rate Risk

Default Risk

BOXES

Hungry for Some Dividend Sweets? How About a Preferred Dividend Roll?

Buying Preferred Stock at Dutch Auction

After you finish this chapter, you will be able to:

- recognize the important characteristics of preferred stocks, understanding how they differ from bonds and common stocks.

- identify the terms included in the preferred stock agreement.

- calculate the return from a perpetuity and the yield to call.

- compare preferred stock returns to bond returns and understand the nature of adjustable rate preferred stock.

- identify and measure interest rate risk and use ratings guides to assess default risk in preferred stocks.

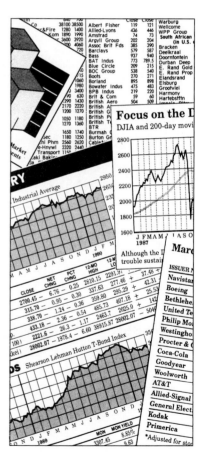

P referred stock is often called a hybrid security, because it has characteristics of both common stock and bonds. It is similar to a bond in that it usually pays a fixed dividend each year, but from a legal perspective it is considered equity. Your rights as a preferred stockholder are stronger than those of the common stockholders, but considerably weaker than bondholder rights. In the event of a forced liquidation, the lowest-ranking subordinated debenture's claim must be satisfied in full before any distribution is allowed to even the highest-ranking preferred stock. This feature alone would seem to be enough to discourage most investors, but when you consider that yields on preferred stock are often less than yields on bonds, it is a wonder that anyone buys them. However, they do have some appealing features that we will study in this chapter.

PREFERRED STOCK CHARACTERISTICS

Many corporations issue preferred stock by default: they would prefer to issue bonds, but their financial position may be too weak to support a bond issue, or there may be restrictions from an existing bond indenture that prohibits it. Why is preferred the second choice? Very simple: bond interest can be deducted in determining taxable income and dividends cannot. Consider, then, a corporation facing a marginal tax rate of 34%. If it issues preferred stock, it must earn about $1.52 for each $1 of dividends it pays ($1.00/.66), but it must earn only $1 to pay $1 of interest. With a penalty this severe, corporate financial officers clearly prefer to issue bonds. Indeed, as Exhibit 11.1 shows, considerably more long-term funds are raised by issuing bonds than by issuing common and preferred stock combined.

The tax law favors the issuance of bonds over preferred stock.

As you see, for the years indicated, corporations raised only 3.4% of their long-term funds with preferred stock. Moreover, since 1982 a large portion of the total preferreds has been types with floating dividends that change with

Adjustable rate preferred stock now dominates the preferred stock market.

EXHIBIT 11.1
New security issues of corporations (in billions of dollars)

	1986	1987	1988	Total	Percent
Stocks					
Common	$50.3	$43.2	$35.9	$129.4	16.2%
Preferred	10.5	10.1	6.5	27.1	3.4
Total	$60.8	$53.3	$42.4	$156.5	19.6%
Bonds*	274.5	233.6	132.5	640.6	80.4
Total stocks and bonds	$335.3	$286.9	$174.9	$797.1	100.0%

*Excludes private placements.
SOURCE: *Federal Reserve Bulletin,* May 1989.

changing market rates of interest. These new versions have accounted for over 50% of all preferred issues in recent years. So, the preferred stock market is a small one, dominated by one type of issue. If you plan to buy preferreds, keep in mind that volume may be very light in the stock you are considering. In a thin market such as this, paying or receiving competitively determined prices could become a problem.

Basic Stockholder Rights

Preferred stockholders have certain basic rights, including conditional voting rights, the right to receive dividends, and the right to share in asset distributions in liquidation. These rights are explained below.

Voting Rights   Unless specified to the contrary in the articles of incorporation, preferred stock is nonvoting stock; however, the trend toward greater shareholder representation in corporate matters has led some issuers to extend voting rights to the preferred. This right may take the form of absolute voting rights, with the preferred shareholders voting along with the common shareholders whenever a vote is taken; or, it may be conditional upon certain events taking place. These events include not paying a dividend (called **passing the dividend**), or proposing a new long-term debt issue or a new preferred offering, or a potential merger.

Preferred stock often has conditional voting rights.

A Right to Dividend Distributions   Preferred holders have a right to receive their indicated dividends. However, this right is legally contingent upon the board of directors actually declaring them. In contrast to bond interest, which becomes a legal liability of the corporation the moment it is due, preferred dividends require a specific declaration by the board.

Until the late 1970s and early 1980s, most preferred stock was issued with a $100 par value. Since then, however, there has been a trend towards issuing preferreds with smaller par values, probably to increase their marketability. Dividends may be expressed in dollars or as a percent of par. In the latter case, par must be known to determine the dollar amount. Once issued, the yield on a preferred will be determined by the dollar dividend and its market price, as we will discuss later in this chapter.

Cumulative Versus Noncumulative Dividends   If dividends are **cumulative,** all passed dividends must be paid before any dividend can be paid to common stockholders. If dividends are noncumulative, any passed dividend is lost forever. Allowing the corporation to pass a dividend and never be concerned about repaying would create an almost intolerable situation for the preferred holders. Therefore, practically all preferred is cumulative. Exhibit 11.2 shows a share of preferred stock issued by the Mead Corporation. It looks very similar to a share of common stock, and you should notice that it is cumulative and voting. It is also

Practically all preferred is cumulative.

EXHIBIT 11.2
A share of Mead Corporation preferred stock. (Courtesy of the Mead Corporation.)

convertible into shares of the common stock, and it pays an annual dividend of $2.80 a share.

Participating Versus Nonparticipating   Most preferred stock receives a fixed dividend each quarter. If the preferred is nonparticipating, it receives no more than its stated amount, but if it is **participating,** it receives an additional dividend after an initial dividend is paid to the common stockholders. The participating feature was needed in the 1930s to help sell preferred during very depressed market periods. However, you are no longer likely to encounter a participating preferred except, possibly, in closely held corporations where stock issues can be shaped to meet unique circumstances. No participating preferred is traded on the New York Stock Exchange, the last having been retired in the early 1960s.

Payment-in-Kind (PIK) Preferred   We described in Chapter 7 payment-in-kind bonds. With these instruments borrowers have the option of paying interest either in cash or in additional bonds. Similar preferred stock, called **PIK preferred,** has been issued, usually as part of a financing package for a leveraged buyout. The issuer can choose to pay quarterly dividends either in cash or in additional preferred shares.

Of course, your return with a PIK security depends upon whether the dividend is in cash or additional securities. For example, suppose you buy 100 shares of a PIK preferred with a 4% quarterly dividend rate (16% annually) on a par value of $100 a share. Suppose during the year, the issuer paid all dividends in additional shares, giving you 117 shares at year end ($1.04 \times 1.04 \times 1.04 \times 1.04 \times 100$). Assume the year-end market price of the stock is $90 a share, and that you paid $100 at the beginning of the year to acquire the stock. The holding period return then is:

The return on PIK preferred depends upon whether dividends are paid in cash or additional shares.

$$HPR = [(117 \times \$90) - (100 \times \$100)]/(100 \times \$100)$$

$$= (\$10,530 - \$10,000)/\$10,000 = \$530/\$10,000 = 0.053$$

If the dividends were paid in cash and the ending price was $90, then the *HPR* is 6%, as shown below.

$$HPR = [\$1,600 + 100(\$90 - \$100)]/(100 \times \$100)$$

$$= (\$1,600 - \$1,000)/\$10,000 = \$600/\$10,000 = 0.060$$

The slight difference arises from additional shares associated with the PIK preferred in relation to the number of shares that could have been purchased by reinvesting quarterly cash dividends—17 versus 16—*assuming* additional shares would have been purchased at $100 a share. Naturally, that is merely an assumption. For example, if the price fell to $90 before the first quarterly dividend and remained there until year end, then more shares—17.78 ($1,600/$90) versus 17.00—could have been acquired by reinvesting cash dividends.

Because of their newness, the risks of PIK preferred are unclear because of a lack of performance history. They carry attractive dividend yields, but because they are callable, this advantage could be eliminated quickly if interest rates fall. Moreover, as noted earlier, preferred stockholders have a far weaker position in bankruptcy than bondholders—an important consideration with leveraged buyouts involving substantial fixed-income financing.

A Right to Assets in Liquidation   Preferred stockholders stand between bondholders and common stockholders when assets are distributed in liquidation. Because bonds are debt instruments, they must be paid first, including all principal and accrued interest. If corporate assets are adequate to meet these claims, then any remaining funds are distributed to the preferred shareholders before any distributions are made on the common. Since in the overwhelming majority of failures, assets are insufficient to meet creditor claims, it is unlikely that preferred stockholders receive anything in a forced liquidation. Thus, the

Preferred shareholders often receive nothing in a forced liquidation.

advantage of ranking ahead of the common should not be viewed as a valuable one.

In recent years some preferred stock is being referenced as *preference stock*. Such stock is a weaker form of preferred in that it ranks behind regular preferred issues with respect to both dividend and asset distributions. However, it still ranks before the common.

Other Features of Preferred Stock

A public issue of preferred stock is accompanied by a prospectus, which details shareholder rights and specifies corporate obligations. The prospectus can be viewed as an agreement between shareholders and the issuer. Some of the more important features of the agreement are explained below.

Dividend Payments   The agreement details when dividends will be paid. It also specifies the amounts or how the amount is to be calculated, if the dividend is participating or adjustable. The agreement also explains the cumulative feature and indicates when passed dividends must be paid. Since dividends are the primary reason investors buy preferreds, provisions dealing with dividends should be understood thoroughly before investing.

Retirement, Call, or Convertible   Until recently, most preferred stock was issued in perpetuity, which means it is never retired. Current trends, though, are towards preferred with a call feature, or a convertible feature coupled with a call. The call feature gives the corporation an option to retire the issue if it so chooses. Of course, it typically does choose to do so when interest rates have fallen below the preferred's rate. If you bought preferred with a high yield and expected that yield to continue, you might be disappointed if the corporation calls the stock. The company may establish a sinking fund to retire a portion of the issue each year, either by exercising the call or through purchases in the open market. However, sinking funds are not mandatory and must be provided in the agreement.

> The trend is towards preferred with a call.

Much preferred stock is convertible into shares of common stock. The preferred stock agreement must specify conversion terms, the most important being the number of common shares into which each share of preferred converts. Frequently, this conversion ratio decreases over time. Also, to force eventual conversion, the issuer must attach a call feature. Otherwise, investors might hold the preferred to receive a larger dividend than they could earn on the common, knowing the price of their preferred will increase if the common increases, since it can always be converted into the common. The investment opportunities and risks of convertible securities are discussed in the next chapter.

> Many preferred issues are convertible.

Restrictive Covenants   Preferred stock agreements are similar to bond indentures in placing restrictions on certain company activities. These restrictions often ban the company from issuing more bonds or preferred stock; they might

Hungry for Some Dividend Sweets? How About a Preferred Dividend Roll?

f sitting around and waiting three months for a corporation's regular dividend is not your idea of action, you might consider rolling in and out of different stocks to capture dividends on a more frequent basis. In other words, buy a stock about to pay a dividend, then dump it after it does and reinvest in another that is ready to pay. With luck, you might receive a dividend every other week. Sounds dumb, because the first thing an investor learns about dividends is that when the stock paying them goes ex-dividend, its price falls an amount equal to the dividend.

How do you get ahead on that arrangement, considering you must pay a commission to the broker on each ''roll of the dividend?''

You don't, which might make it hard to understand why some investors are playing the game, and why some choose preferred stocks. If you look closely, you'll notice most of the players are corporations. They face a different tax situation than we do, and taking dividends might be to their advantage even if the declines in stock prices make the deal a wash. Preferreds are often chosen because they are thought to have greater price

stability than common stocks, although that assumption can be questioned.

Even corporations find preferred dividend rolls much riskier than conventional money market instruments. Some attempt to lower this risk by hedging with options or futures contracts, but too much hedging reduces any gains to amounts you might earn on a conventional portfolio. So, if you are a corporate treasurer, you might want to brush up on what's new in cash management; if you are an individual investor, relax and put in the three months.

require that a minimum level of working capital be maintained; they might restrict dividends on the common stock; or they might call for voting rights, as we saw earlier. These covenants attempt to keep the issuer in strong financial condition, thereby safeguarding the preferred shareholders' interests.

It is important to recognize, however, that legal recourses available to preferred stockholders in the event the issuer fails to meet terms of the agreement are quite different from those available to bondholders. Preferred holders' rights derive ultimately from the articles of incorporation creating the company, not from a legal contract such as the bond indenture. Moreover, taking action against the issuer could force it into bankruptcy—a situation where preferred holders seldom gain any advantage.

Legal recourses available to preferred holders are relatively weak.

PREFERRED STOCK RETURNS

Many preferred stocks are reported in the financial pages of most newspapers. The quotes, illustrated in Exhibit 11.3, are interpreted as you interpret common stock quotes, explained in Chapter 8. Preferred stock quotes, though, have more diversity, and additional information is needed to understand them. The list in

	High	Low	Stock	Div.	Yld. %	P-E Ratio	Sales 100s	High	Low	Close	Net Chg.
1.	50¾	46¼	USX pf	4.81e	10.1	—	44	48¼	48¼	48¼	+⅛
2.	30⅝	26⅝	Am Brands pf	2.75	10.2	—	5	27¼	27	27	−⅛
3.	17⅜	11⅞	Talley Ind pf	1.00	5.4	—	5	18⅝	18⅝	18⅝	+⅛
4.	45⅛	34	LIL pf U	—	—	—	6	44	44	44	—

Comments on above stocks:
Stock 1: The e symbol after the dividend indicates a varying dividend payment; this issue is probably adjustable rate.
Stock 2: The high yield of 10.2% suggests a straight preferred.
Stock 3: The low yield is a good indication of a convertible issue.
Stock 4: The lack of a yield figure indicates dividends are not being paid.

EXHIBIT 11.3
Preferred stock listings in the financial pages

Exhibit 11.3 was selected to show some of this diversity. The comments below the list show some "clues" that help identify the type of preferred listed. For example, USX's changing dividend suggests an adjustable rate preferred (which it is). The relatively high yield on American Brands indicates a straight preferred, while the low yield on Talley Industries suggests a convertible (which it is). The absence of a yield on the Long Island Lighting Preferred Series U tells us the current dividend has been passed and there may be dividends in arrears—unpaid dividends that have accumulated under the cumulative feature. Further research would show this is the case and that $20.19 per share was in arrears as of April 15, 1989, about a month before the date of the listings.

> Preferred dividend arrearage arises with the cumulative feature.

Your return from an investment in preferred stock depends broadly upon whether you have straight preferred or preferred with sweeteners. If it is straight preferred, your periodic holding period returns (HPRs) will correlate closely with returns on bonds. If you have a sweetener, such as a convertible or an ARPS, your HPRs will be influenced by other factors. Straight preferred's returns and returns on ARPS are discussed in the following sections, while convertible returns are covered in the next chapter.

Straight Preferreds

The return from a straight preferred is measured with the same time-value-of-money techniques explained in Chapter 3. The calculations depend upon whether the preferred is issued in perpetuity or if it has a call that is likely to be exercised.

A Perpetuity If the preferred is a perpetuity, its cash flows would appear as indicated by the example in Exhibit 11.4. Assuming the investor pays $10 for a

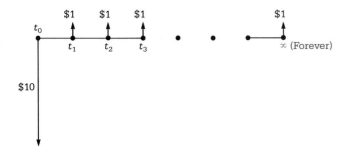

EXHIBIT 11.4

Cash flows from a perpetuity

share of preferred that promises to pay a $1 a year dividend forever, the current yield (CY) is found with the formula below:

$$CY = \frac{D}{P}$$

where D = the annual dividend, and

P = the current price of the preferred.

This is the same formula you use to determine the current yield on a savings account. In effect, a perpetuity is identical to a savings account (assuming interest, but not principal, is withdrawn each period). When you put your money in a savings account, you expect to receive the indicated interest rate for as long as the funds are deposited; forever, if you never withdraw principal.

Yield to Call   If a call seems likely, a more appropriate yield calculation is **yield to call (YTC)**. This yield involves finding the discount rate that equates the present value of the future dividends and the call price to the current market price. Exhibit 11.5 provides two examples. Preferred A is selling at a price below the call. In this case, the investor believes interest rates will fall, thereby increasing the preferred's price up to the call value. Preferred B is selling at a price in excess of its call value. If the investor actually expected the issue not to be called until the end of three years (the preferred agreement might indicate this is the case), then the yield to call calculation would be a realistic one to use in deciding whether or not to buy the stock. However, paying a price in excess of call value can be very risky if the issue is immediately callable. The YTC figure shown for preferred B could be a fiction if the call takes place sooner.

A yield to call calculation is needed if a call is likely.

Comparison to Bond Yields   Exhibit 11.6 shows that yields on straight preferreds are closely correlated to bond yields. You expect this correlation, since both are fixed income securities. What you might not expect is that preferred stocks offer lower yields than bonds. Considering their lower ranking in asset distributions, most people guess that preferred yields should be higher—not lower—than bond yields. The tax law again explains the riddle. Under the present code, corporations are allowed to exclude 70% of most dividend income

Although riskier, preferred stocks often yield less than bonds.

The tax law explains the riddle.

Preferred *A*: selling at less than its
call price of $9 and expected to be
called at the end of three years

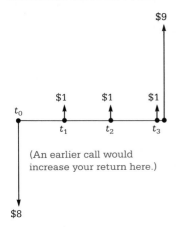

(An earlier call would
increase your return here.)

Preferred *B*: selling at more than its
call price of $9 and not expected to be
called until the end of three years

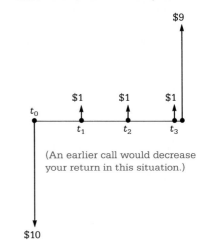

(An earlier call would decrease
your return in this situation.)

$$\$8 = \left\{ \frac{\$1}{(1 + YTC)^1} + \frac{\$1}{(1 + YTC)^2} + \frac{\$10}{(1 + YTC)^3} \right\}$$

Solve for *YTC*
YTC = .1606, or 16.06%

$$\$10 = \left\{ \frac{\$1}{(1 + YTC)^1} + \frac{\$1}{(1 + YTC)^2} + \frac{\$10}{(1 + YTC)^3} \right\}$$

Solve for *YTC*
YTC = .0689, or 6.89%

EXHIBIT 11.5
Yield to call (YTC) calculations

they receive, while they cannot exclude any interest income. The impact of this
law on after-tax income and rate of return is considerable, as the example below
shows:

	Preferred Stock	Bond
Assume the price of each is	$10.000	$10.000
Annual dividend or interest	1.000	1.000
70% exclusion	0.800	—
Taxable income	0.300	1.000
Tax, assuming 34% rate	0.102	0.340
After-tax income	0.898	0.660
After-tax rate of return	0.0898	0.066
	8.98%	6.60%

Given a choice between the preferred and the bond, you would choose the
preferred if return was your major investment criterion. Indeed, you might even
accept a somewhat lower before- tax return on the preferred, since the after-tax
advantage is so large.

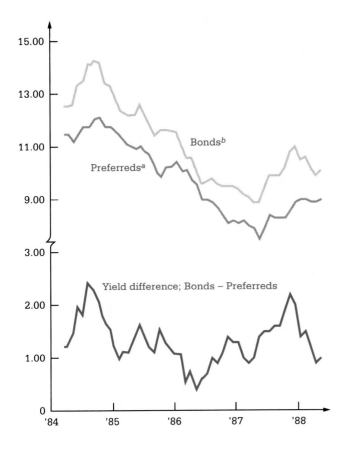

EXHIBIT 11.6
Preferred stock and bond yields. (Source: Standard and Poor's *Statistical Service,* April 1989 and January 1989. Standard and Poor's Corporation, 25 Broadway, New York, NY, 10014.)

[a]Standard and Poor's Preferred Stock Index: Consists of ten high quality straight preferreds.
[b]Standard and Poor's Composite Bond Index of *A*-rated issues.

Many corporate investors are so inclined, which explains why preferred yields are less than bond yields. You must consider carefully whether you, as an individual investor, wish to compete with corporate investors in the preferred markets. If you are interested in straight preferreds, you should be advised not to invest, because you receive no preferential tax treatment on dividend income. However, if you have your own corporation or are associated with your family's corporation, or if you manage corporate funds, preferred stock may be a very desirable investment.

Adjustable Rate Preferred Stock

An entirely new form of preferred stock was introduced in May of 1982—the **adjustable rate preferred stock (ARPS)**. Corporate interest in preferred stock

Buying Preferred Stock at Dutch Auction

You've heard of a Dutch treat, but what is a Dutch auction? Buying preferred stock at Dutch auction is an ingenious way for corporations to more or less borrow from other corporations at very low rates of interest that are negotiated (reset) every seven weeks. That surely doesn't sound like the preferred stock familiar to most of us—the kind that pays a fixed rate and is never retired. But it has been the hottest preferred in the market in recent years, and many analysts think it will continue to be so, unless the government steps in and changes the tax law. As it stands, corporations can exclude 80% of dividend income in determining their taxable incomes. That sets up all kinds of possibilities.

Dutch auction rate preferred stock (DARPS) evolved from adjustable rate preferred stocks (ARPS) that hit the market in a big way in May of 1982. Both are designed to overcome a major disadvantage of most pre-ferred stocks—the sensitivity of their market prices to changes in interest rates. So, a corporate cash manager who wants the tax advantage of dividends no longer needs to give up the price stability of a money market instrument, such as commercial paper. At least that was the thinking when ARPS were created; but, despite their rate adjustments (which take place on a quarterly basis, indexed to rates on Treasury securities), they have shown far greater price volatility than many cash managers are willing to bear.

In contrast to ARPS, DARPS guarantee a fixed price—the par value—to investors, if they hold their shares seven weeks. At that time, they can either sell them to other investors at par, or they can compete in an auction that determines the yield for the next seven-week period. All investors submit the lowest yield they will accept and the actual yield for *all* shares is then set by the *highest* bid that clears the market. Clearing takes place when the number of shares demanded by investors equals the total shares outstanding. So, if you own shares and submit a bid above the clearing yield, you must sell to others who submitted lower bids; if your bid was below the clearing yield, you will be pleasantly surprised to receive the higher figure.

It's a clever idea, and it has worked. DARPS now dominate the adjustable-rate market, and their yields have fallen considerably. Indeed, triple-A-rated issues often have yields of 20% below yields on commercial paper with comparable maturities. These are pre-tax yields; on an after-tax basis, many investors are still better off with the DARPS. Are the issuing corporations any better off? If their tax rates are low, the answer probably is yes. Surely, a lot of investors and issuers must be better off, or the DARPS innovation would have flopped at the outset.

was always strong; however, many corporate cash managers were reluctant to buy straight preferred because of its interest-rate risk. The apparent solution to this problem was to create a preferred stock with an adjustable dividend rate.

An ARPS has its rate indexed to rates on Treasury securities.

How the Adjustable Rate Works   An ARPS rate is indexed to yields on U.S. Treasury securities. Specifically, its dividend is reset each quarter in step with the *highest* of the following three rates: the 90-day T-bill rate, the 10-year T-note rate, or the 20-year T-bond rate. The reset rate is specified in terms of basis points above or below the appropriate Treasury rate. For example, USX has an issue that offers 35 basis points above the Treasury rate. When the ARPS market began, resets were very generous; however, they have declined over time, and it is more common now to have resets at 100, 200, or even 300 basis points below the Treasury rate. Other factors, such as issuer quality, also determine resets, and every issue has a collar—a minimum rate and a maximum rate. USX's collar, for example, is 7.5% and 15.75%.

A new version of ARPS is an ingenious creation in that it allows the dividend rate to be set by an auctioning process every seven weeks. (Stocks must be held 45 days for the corporation to earn the 80% exclusion.) It is called **Dutch auction rate preferred stock (DARPS)** and it has become exceptionally popular with corporate money managers.

> Dutch auction preferred is a new form of ARPS; its dividend is determined every seven weeks in an auction process.

ARPS Performance   Surprisingly, dividend resets on traditional ARPS did not stabilize prices as much as ARPS promoters anticipated, which explains the popularity of the Dutch auction variety. Commercial banks were first to issue ARPS, and they dominated the market at the beginning. However, the banking industry experienced shocks in 1983 and 1984—fear of Latin American debt repudiation and the collapse of Continental Illinois—that caused their ARPS prices to be very unstable. The commercial bank segment of the market, then, created considerable price volatility that could not be offset by rate adjustments. Since 1984, the market has stabilized somewhat, although a fair amount of price risk still remains.

If risks have exceeded expectations, so have ARPS returns. Several studies have shown they have done very well on a risk-adjusted basis. Given such performance, individual investors might be as much interested in ARPS as are corporations. Since the market is still relatively new and, perhaps, still in flux, you should consult your broker or do your own research before investing. You might compare the ARPS yields to yields on floating rate bonds or yields available on three- to five-year CDs. By all means, do not assume you can always sell an ARPS at your cost or a higher price. You face a serious risk of capital loss if you are forced to sell.

DARPS Performance   DARPS have followed a performance history somewhat similar to ARPS. Because of investor unfamiliarity, early issues were priced above other comparable money market instruments such as 60-day commercial paper. However, as investor experience increased, yields fell below such instruments. Shearson Lehman Hutton prepares indexes of DARPS yields, which can be found in the weekly issues of *Barron's*. To illustrate yield differences, the general index showed a yield of 7.85% for the week ended May 29, 1989. For the same period, the yield on 60-day commercial paper was 9.40%. As you see, if you are a noncorporate investor, commercial paper is the far better alternative.

RISKS IN PREFERRED STOCKS

If you invest in straight preferred stocks, you will have a risk situation almost identical to that involved in bond investing. You must be concerned with both interest rate risk and default risk.

Interest Rate Risk

Because preferred stocks are fixed income securities, their market prices are affected by changes in the overall level of interest rates. It is important to measure the degree of interest rate risk. You should remember from Chapter 5 that two measurement tools are used: the interest elasticity coefficient (E) and Macaulay's duration coefficient (D). We will limit the current discussion to the interest elasticity approach.

The interest elasticity coefficient can be used to measure interest rate risk with preferreds.

Risk with a Perpetuity   To calculate the interest elasticity coefficient for a perpetuity, we can use the formula:

$$E = \frac{\text{percentage change in preferred's price}}{\text{percentage change in preferred's CY}}$$

The elasticity formula requires two price-CY points. Returning to the example of a preferred that pays a $1 annual dividend and is currently selling for $10, by selecting a second point we can find an E value. Let's assume interest rates rise by 10%, which causes this preferred's CY also to increase by 10%, going from 10% to 11%. For CY to increase, price must decrease. To find the new price, we simply rearrange the CY formula and solve for it:

$$CY = \frac{D}{P} \quad \text{or} \quad P = \frac{D}{CY}$$

Since the new $CY = 0.11$, the new $P = \$9.09$ ($1.00/0.11). The change in P is $-\$0.91$, which is a 9.1% ($0.91/$10.00) decrease in price. Therefore, $E = -.91$:

$$E = \frac{-9.1}{+10.0} = -0.91$$

Suppose we go the other way and assume CY declines to 9%—a 10% decrease. Now, price increases to $11.11 ($1.00/0.09), which is an 11.11% increase ($1.11/$10.00); and:

$$E = \frac{+11.11}{-10.00} = -1.11$$

As you see, you get a different value, depending upon whether CY increases or decreases. Actually, what causes the difference is the way we normally measure percentage changes. As pointed out in Chapter 5, to avoid the problem,

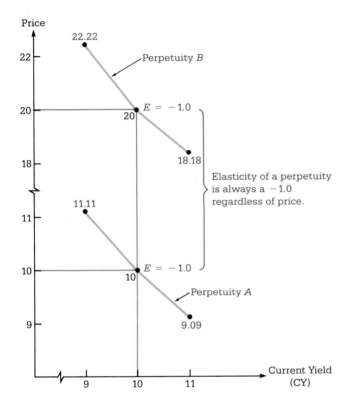

Price

EXHIBIT 11.7
Elasticity of a
perpetuity

22.22

Perpetuity B

$E = -1.0$

18.18

Elasticity of a perpetuity
is always a -1.0
regardless of price.

11.11

$E = -1.0$

Perpetuity A

9.09

Current Yield
(CY)

simply average the two. By doing so, we obtain the approximate value of -1.0 [(0.91 + 1.11)/2].

The interest elasticity of any perpetuity is -1.0.

The elasticity value of -1.0 is very important because it applies to any perpetuity, regardless of its price. For example, suppose we had a preferred that paid a $2 dividend and was presently selling for $20 a share. Going through the above calculations again would show that its elasticity is also -1.0. Exhibit 11.7 shows graphically the relationship between CY and price for both securities.

If you buy a perpetuity, then, you can expect its percentage changes in price to be about the same as percentage changes in long-term bond yields. This implies considerable price risk—something to be considered carefully in making your investment selections.

Risk With a Callable Issue   The interest rate risk of a callable issue depends upon the length of time until the call takes place—the longer this period, the greater the risk. To find the elasticity coefficient, you must assume two *YTC*s and find two corresponding prices. Since this procedure is identical to the one shown in Chapter 5 that deals with bond price elasticity, we will not repeat it here, but simply refer you to that section.

Default Risk

Investors in preferred stock must be concerned with the issuer's ability to meet future dividend payments and to retire the issue if it is not a perpetuity. You should expect that serious financial difficulties in the firm will in all likelihood lead to passed dividends. This does not mean most issuers pass the preferred dividend at the drop of a hat, but, in a financial crisis, they really have no choice. As a result, you can find some issues with dividends in arrears, an expression that means unpaid dividends have accumulated with the cumulative feature. Before investing, then, you should consult a rating agency to determine the quality of the issue you are considering.

Moody's and Standard and Poor's rate preferred issues.

The Rating Agencies   Both Moody's and Standard and Poor's rate preferred issues. Their rating systems are similar to those used in rating bonds, although there are some differences. Exhibit 11.8 illustrates Standard and Poor's rating guide. The individual ratings reflect Standard and Poor's estimate of both the issuer's asset protection (ability to avoid bankruptcy) and its ability to pay dividends in the future. The value of such a rating guide should not be underestimated. The individual investor is seldom in a position, or skillful enough, to do his or her own ratings of preferred issues. Moreover, these services also provide information on individual preferred issues that you usually need if you are a potential buyer. They indicate any dividend arrearages, information certain investors find vital to their investment strategy.

Investing in Preferreds with Dividend Arrearages   This investment approach seems excessively foolhardy and, indeed, it may be. However, investors who are willing to take considerable risks to earn considerable returns often find it worth their while. Earlier in this chapter we noted that Long Island Lighting—a public utility in the New York area—had a preferred issue with an arrearage of $20.19 a share. Additional research shows the annual rate on this issue is $4.25 a share. For sake of example, suppose you bought a share at the price of about $44 (mid-May, 1989) and the company's fortunes changed, allowing it to resume dividends. You would pick up the entire arrearage immediately, along with the quarterly dividend of $1.0625 ($4.25/4)—not a bad return! Keep in mind, though, LIL was mired in difficulty as a result of its Shoreham nuclear facility and had about $344 million in total arrearages on all its preferred issues. Supposedly, the company expected to pay all arrearages by the first quarter of 1989. Obviously, since arrearages still existed at mid-May, it failed to do so.

The strategy for investing in preferred issues with dividends in arrears is to find one selling at a very low price relative to what its value should be if the arrearage were paid and regular dividend payments resumed. There are two guides to finding such an issue: First, look for a company in a turnaround situation with respect to its earnings. Earnings improvement is the key to resuming preferred dividends, particularly if the company has a history of paying dividends on the common stock and hopes to resume these payments. Second, you might consider companies that are likely to be taken over by others. Part of

"AAA" This is the highest rating that may be assigned by Standard & Poor's to a preferred stock issue and indicates an extremely strong capacity to pay the preferred stock obligations.

"AA" A preferred stock issue rated "AA" also qualifies as a high-quality fixed income security. The capacity to pay preferred stock obligations is very strong, although not as overwhelming as for issues rated "AAA."

"A" An issue rated "A" is backed by a sound capacity to pay the preferred stock obligations, although it is somewhat more susceptible to the adverse effects of changes in circumstances and economic conditions.

"BBB" An issue rated "BBB" is regarded as backed by an adequate capacity to pay the preferred stock obligations. Whereas it normally exhibits adequate protection parameters, adverse economic conditions or changing circumstances are more likely to lead to a weakened capacity to make payments for a preferred stock in this category than for issues in the "A" category.

"BB," "B," "CCC" Preferred stock rated "BB," "B," and "CCC" are regarded, on balance, as predominately speculative with respect to the issuer's capacity to pay preferred stock obligations. "BB" indicates the lowest degree of speculation and "CCC" the highest degree of speculation. While such issues will likely have some quality and protective characteristics, these are outweighed by large uncertainties or major risk exposures to adverse conditions.

"CC" The rating "CC" is reserved for a preferred stock issue in arrears on dividends or sinking fund payments but that is currently paying.

"C" A preferred stock rated "C" is a nonpaying issue.

"D" A preferred stock rated "D" is a nonpaying issue with the issuer in default on debt instruments.

NR indicates that no rating has been requested, that there is insufficient information on which to base a rating, or that S&P does not rate a particular type of obligation as a matter of policy.

EXHIBIT 11.8
Standard and Poor's preferred stock ratings. (Source: Standard and Poor's *Stock Guide,* May 1989. Standard and Poor's Corporation, 25 Broadway, New York, NY, 10014.)

the takeover agreement might stipulate that preferred stock be retired at its face value and any arrearages be paid.

Keep in mind that neither of these tasks is done easily and the strategy itself is extremely risky. You stand a very good chance of buying an issue that never pays a dividend and eventually becomes worthless as the company enters bankruptcy. Professionals who play this investment theme are usually well diversified among low-quality preferreds. If you can't achieve this same degree of diversification, you would be wise to seek your risky investments somewhere else.

Investing in preferreds with large arrearages is very risky.

SUMMARY

Dividends on preferred stock cannot be deducted in determining taxable income, while bond interest can, which makes preferred stock an undesirable instrument for raising capital. As a result, very little is issued, and in recent years most new preferred issues have had adjustable—rather than fixed—dividend rates. Preferred stockholders usually do not vote, but they do have dividend rights that are usually cumulative and nonparticipating. They also have a right to assets in liquidation, which rank ahead of common stockholder rights, but are inferior to those of bondholders. A preferred stock agreement indicates dividend payments and other characteristics of the issue. It also details restrictive covenant features.

The return from a straight preferred is determined using a perpetuity formula if the issue is not callable; in the event it is callable, a yield-to-call calculation is more appropriate. Yields on preferreds are often below bond yields, which seems unusual because preferreds have a weaker position. The explanation is that corporate investors favor preferreds over bonds because of a dividend exclusion allowed in determining corporate taxable income. Adjustable rate preferred stock (ARPS) was introduced to minimize interest-rate risk that accompanies fixed-rate preferreds. Rates adjust each quarter in step with changes in rates on Treasury securities. Actual ARPS performance, though, has been considerably more volatile than expected. Dutch auction rate preferred stock (DARPS) followed ARPS. It is viewed as an improvement insofar as its dividend is determined by an auction process that takes place every seven weeks.

Risks in preferred stocks include interest-rate risk and default risk. The latter risk is estimated by rating agencies: Standard and Poor's and Moody's. Some investors pursue a risky investment approach that calls for purchasing preferred issues with substantial dividend arrearages. They hope issuers will recover financially and resume dividend payments on both common and preferred stock. In this event, all arrearages must be paid.

KEY TERMS

Select the alternative that best identifies the key term.

1. passing the dividend
2. cumulative
3. participating
4. PIK preferred
5. yield to call (YTC)
6. adjustable rate preferred stock (ARPS)
7. Dutch auction rate preferred stock (DARPS)

a. possibly earns an extra dividend
b. unpaid dividends are in arrears
c. indexed to yields on Treasury securities
d. a dividend not declared
e. may not be realized if the preferred's price is very high
f. dividend is determined every seven weeks
g. dividend may be paid in additional shares

REVIEW QUESTIONS

1. Explain why preferred stock is called a hybrid security and why most corporations prefer not to issue preferreds, choosing bonds instead. Also, indicate the relative importance of the three financing media: common stocks, preferred stocks, and bonds.

2. Briefly explain the basic rights of preferred stockholders, comparing their rights to those of common stockholders and bondholders.
3. Compare the following: cumulative versus noncumulative; participating versus nonparticipating.
4. Explain PIK preferred.
5. Explain three different ways a preferred stock may be terminated; that is, not have a perpetual life.
6. Indicate similarities between preferred stock and bonds with respect to requirements imposed upon the corporation. Explain whether preferred holders have equal legal recourses if issuers fail to meet the requirements.
7. You are interested in investing in preferreds and have been following some in the financial pages. You are confused, though: one seems to have a much lower yield than the others and another shows no yield at all. Explain these oddities.
8. A perpetuity formula is used often to evaluate a preferred stock. What is the assumption when such a formula is used? Explain when it might be inappropriate, and indicate a more appropriate valuation formula in these instances.
9. Why are yields on preferred stocks often less than bond yields, even though they typically represent greater investment risk? Also, indicate if the yields on bonds and preferred stocks move together or in opposite directions.
10. Explain why each was created and how its periodic dividend is determined: (a) ARPS, (b) DARPS.
11. What is the elasticity value for any perpetuity? Explain how to interpret this value and use it in making investment decisions.
12. How can you determine potential default risk with preferred stocks? Explain potential rewards and risks from investing in issues that have dividend arrearages.

PROBLEMS AND PROJECTS

1. Blant Corporation has a cumulative preferred issue outstanding with an indicated annual dividend of $2 a share. There are 50,000 shares issued, and there are 150,000 shares of common stock outstanding.
   a. Assuming Blant declares a total dividend of $200,000, indicate the per share distribution to the preferred and the common. Indicate amounts for each if dividends of $80,000 or $400,000 were declared.
   b. Assume Blant was forced to pass dividends for two full years. Things have improved and it wishes to resume paying dividends. In the first quarter that dividends resume, how much must be paid the preferred before any distribution is made to the common?
2. Jane Frawley is considering buying 100 shares of a new PIK preferred to be issued by Newjon Corporation. The issue has a 12% annual dividend rate with quarterly dividend payments. Par value is $50 a share, the price Jane would pay if she invests. Calculate Jane's return if dividends are paid in additional shares and the price of a share is $45 at year end.
3. Determine the current yield (CY) for a perpetuity that pays $4 a year in dividends and has a price of $50 a share. Suppose the issue has a call at $48 a share that can be exercised by the company at any time. However, you feel it will not be called for two years. Estimate your yield to call (YTC) in this case. Suppose your assumption is wrong and the issue is called one year later. What is your actual return?
4. Randalay, Inc., has excess temporary funds. It is considering investing them in Dutch auction rate preferred stocks, expected to yield 8% over the upcoming year. Indicate

if this represents a better investment than commercial paper with an expected yield of 10% for the same period. Randalay will have a 39% marginal tax rate.

5. Northern Power and Light has experienced serious difficulties with respect to a nuclear energy facility under construction. Two years ago, the company suspended all quarterly dividends on its preferred stock, which has a par value of $100 and a stated yield of 12%. The market price of the stock fell sharply after the suspension and it currently trades at around $60 a share. You have heard that a favorable court ruling might allow the company to complete the facility and raise rates sufficiently high to recover its cost plus a reasonable return to investors. If such a ruling takes place, the company would resume paying dividends and would be in sound financial shape to continue paying them in the future. Preferred stock issues similar to Northern's currently offer around a 10% current yield.

   a. If a favorable ruling takes place, determine the dollar and percentage return on your investment, assuming all arrearages are paid *and* the market price of the stock adjusts to reflect the new situation.

   b. Explain the risk in such an investment.

6. (*Student Project*)   Try to survey several financial executives in your home town. Ask if they have invested in preferred stocks, for either short- or long-term purposes. If their responses are "no," ask if they disregard the tax savings, or if they consider preferreds too risky. If neither of these options apply, determine the nature of their resistance to preferreds.

7. (*Student Project*)   Consult a current issue of *Barron's* and find the Shearson index of DARPS at the end of the "Market Laboratory" section. Compare the rate on the composite index to the rate on 60-day commercial paper (in the same section). Then, determine if the rate difference seems "reasonable" in light of the income tax situation on dividend income to corporations.

CASE ANALYSES

**11.1
Arnold Savain
Considers
Straight
Preferreds**

Arnold Savain is considering investing to establish a retirement nest egg. He knows very little about stocks or bonds but feels that following a conservative investment program should reduce his portfolio risk to reasonable levels. His Uncle Mort has told him that preferred stocks are better and safer investments than common stocks. As Mort says, "That's why they're called preferred." Mort shows Arnold stock listings in the newspaper and indicates that many preferred issues have 10% and 11% yields, while yields on most common stocks are under 5%. Mort has picked three preferreds that he particularly likes and he recommends that Arnold invest all his funds in them. Details for these stocks follow.

	Consolidated Retailers	Pacific Utilities	Southern Telephone
1. Par value	$100	$25	$75
2. Dividend yield	12%	10%	8%
3. Maturity	10 years	20 years	perpetuity
4. Callable	immediately	3 years	no
5. Call price	par	$30	—
6. Current market price	$105	$24	$48
7. Advisory service rank	AA	BBB	B

While Arnold appreciates Uncle Mort's advice, he thinks a second opinion is needed. For one thing, Mort's strategy seems too simple, and for another, he notices that yields on U.S. Treasury bonds are quoted in the newspaper at 10%. As Arnold sees it, a yield this high is as good as Pacific Utilities' and better than Southern Telephone's. So, if he decides to invest in preferreds, Consolidated Retailers seems the only logical selection.

Questions

a. Calculate current yields for each security.
b. Calculate yields to maturity for Consolidated Retailers and Pacific Utilities. Is it likely each issuer will allow the preferreds to remain outstanding until maturity? Explain.
c. Calculate yields to call for Consolidated Retailers and Pacific Utilities, assuming the former is called in one year and the latter is called in three years.
d. What is the interest elasticity for the Southern Telephone preferred? Explain your answer.
e. Do you agree with Uncle Mort's advice? Discuss, indicating specific points of agreement or disagreement.
f. Assuming that Arnold wishes to invest some of his funds in one of the three securities, which do you recommend? Explain reasons for your choice.

11.2 The Hughes Venture Into Risky Preferreds

Wayne and Mary Beth Hughes are a young, recently married couple. They have no dependents and enjoy a combined income in excess of $100,000 annually. Their financial advisor has suggested that they consider certain preferred stocks as additions to their portfolio. Specifically, she recommends a PIK preferred issued by Star International—a recent leveraged buyout—and Midwest Public Power, a public utility that has suspended dividend payments on all its preferred stocks.

The Star stock has a 16% annual rate, while Midwest's rate is 8%. Each "pays" dividends quarterly, and Midwest has an arrearage of $12 a share going into the current year. Star's current market price is $80 a share (par = $100), while Midwest trades at $28 a share (par = $50). The advisor believes the upcoming year will feature rising interest rates and that Star will pay its dividends in additional shares. She anticipates a year-end price of $75 a share. She also feels Midwest will not resume dividend payments in the upcoming year, and the year-end price will fall to $24 a share. However, she sees a turnaround in the second year. She expects Star's price to rebound to $100 and Midwest to resume dividend payments at the end of the fourth quarter. Star will most likely pay dividends in cash in the second year. Finally, she expects Midwest to be priced to yield 12% going into the third year. (It is a perpetuity.)

The advisor feels the Hugheses should put $5,000 into each stock. She also recommends that another $5,000 be invested in conventional preferred, yielding 10%.

Questions

a.   Given the advisor's assumptions, calculate year 1 and year 2 HPRs for each preferred stock. Which offers the higher return over the two-year period?

b.   The Hugheses indicated to the advisor that they have a moderate risk tolerance. Are her recommendations in line with this indication? Explain.

c.   Explain whether you agree or disagree with her recommendation of conventional preferreds.

d.   All things considered, explain whether you believe she made sound recommendations for the Hugheses.

HELPFUL READING

Alderson, Michael J., Keith C. Brown, and Scott L. Lummer. "Dutch Auction Preferred Stock." *Financial Management,* Summer 1987.

Garcia, Beatrice E. "Trading to Nab Dividends Captures Investors' Fancy." *The Wall Street Journal,* May 19, 1986, p. 17.

Joehnk, M. D., O. D. Bowlin, and J. W. Petty. "Preferred Dividend Rolls: A Viable Strategy for Corporate Money Managers." *Financial Management,* Summer 1980.

McDaniel, W. R. "Sinking Fund Preferred Stock." *Financial Management,* Spring 1984.

Rose, Robert L. "A Little-Known Type of Convertible Bond Can Be a Profitable Investment for Some." *The Wall Street Journal,* June 9, 1988, p. 21.

Winger, Bernard J., Carl R. Chen, John D. Martin, J. William Petty, and Steven C. Hayden. "Adjustable Rate Preferred Stock." *Financial Management,* Spring 1986.

Winkler, Matthew. "More Issuers Prefer Issues of Preferred." *The Wall Street Journal,* August 17, 1989, p. C1.

PART FOUR

Leverage-Inherent Investments

Leverage-inherent investments provide opportunities to shape investment portfolios in ways otherwise unattainable. They can be used to increase potential return *or* to reduce risk. In this latter capacity, they often perform an insurance function—guaranteeing certain outcomes, but at a cost. Leverage-inherent investments are also called derivative instruments, because their value derives from that of the underlying securities to which they have claims.

Chapter 12 explains the nature of an option security. It indicates how the market value of an option depends upon its specific characteristics and also upon certain market factors. Warrants, rights, and convertibles are explained and discussed in detail, with emphasis placed upon their investment advantages and disadvantages.

Chapter 13 extends option analysis to put and call options. It identifies their unique characteristics and how they are used in speculative and hedging situations. Covered option writing is also explained and evaluated in terms of its risk and potential for increasing return.

Chapter 14 discusses uses of commodity and financial futures in investment portfolios. It indicates their hedging and speculating opportunities, and describes how they can be used in place of other investments such as common stocks or bonds.

CHAPTER TWELVE

Warrants, Rights, and Convertibles

OPTION VALUE

Option Features

Options and Leverage

Determinants of Market Value

Predicting Market Values

WARRANTS AND RIGHTS

Characteristics of Warrants

Characteristics of Rights

CONVERTIBLES

Characteristics of Convertibles

Investment Opportunities in
Convertibles

A Sample of Convertibles

BOXES

Why Get Excited? It's Only an
Academic Formula

Convertible Securities: Look Closely
Before Investing

After you finish this chapter, you
will be able to:

- understand the nature of an option security and identify its key
  characteristics.

- determine an option security's formula value and option premium.

- recognize and understand the factors that influence the market
  value of an option.

- understand the characteristics of
  warrants and reasons for investing
  in them.

- understand the characteristics of
  rights and recognize why it is important to take action within
  rights' maturities.

- understand the characteristics of
  convertibles, comparing and contrasting them to warrants.

- use a method that helps to evaluate a convertible issue and judge
  its investment suitability.

W arrants, rights, and convertibles (covered in this chapter) and put and call options (covered in the next chapter) share a common characteristic: they give you the right to buy or sell an underlying security. You may have heard of options being used in other areas, such as someone holding an option to purchase a parcel of land, or a professional sporting team having an option to acquire the contract of a certain player. While options have many uses, they are most prevalent in financial markets, where their trading has become highly standardized and extremely efficient. The beginning investor often sees option securities as nothing more than wagering tickets, but that perception is not completely accurate. Surprisingly, options can be used both to increase and decrease investment risk, as we shall see.

OPTION VALUE

An option's value depends upon the value of an underlying security.

An **option security** derives its value exclusively from the value of the underlying security to which it has a claim. Exhibit 12.1 illustrates the relationship with a hypothetical IBM option. This option is referred to as a call since it gives its holder the right to buy (''call'') the underlying security from someone else. In contrast to calls, there are also put options, which allow holders to sell (''put'') shares of the underlying security to others. For ease of presentation, the discussion in this section is limited to call options; also, we are discussing option value in general, and not specific options. However, the general principles apply to all types of option securities.

Because of the value relationship between an option and its underlying security, options are called derivative instruments. Moreover, changes in their value correlate almost perfectly with changes in value of the underlying security. Suppose the option in Exhibit 12.1 allowed its holder to buy one share of IBM stock at $150 a share anytime within the next six months. The value of this option would depend upon the market price of IBM.

An option must have a minimum value.

Exhibit 12.2 shows the **minimum** (or **formula**) **value** of the option, given different prices of the stock. The minimum value is the lowest possible market

EXHIBIT 12.1

Illustration of an option security

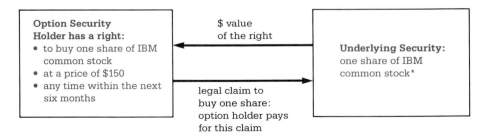

*Standard option contracts (explained in Chapter 13) deal with 100 shares of the underlying stock. However, it is usually easier for beginners to understand option principles by considering one share for one option.

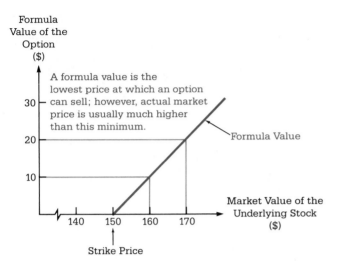

Formula
Value of the
Option
($)

A formula value is the
lowest price at which an option
can sell; however, actual market
price is usually much higher
than this minimum.

Formula Value

Market Value of the
Underlying Stock
($)

Strike Price

EXHIBIT 12.2

Illustration of an
option's formula value

value of an option; the formula for determining this value will be discussed shortly. In this example, if the stock's price is $160, the minimum value of the option should be $10. Why can't it be less? Suppose it were $5: you could make an easy, risk-free profit by buying the option and using it to buy one share of IBM at $150. Your total investment would be only $155, and you could immediately sell the share for $160 to net $5 on the deal. Of course, everyone is free to do this, and buying pressures should arise to push the price of the option up to its formula value of $10. Indeed, some investors might think so highly of the option they would bid its price beyond the formula value. For example, if IBM's price is $149, its formula value is zero. But, would you be willing to pay something for an option that allows you to buy a share at the fixed price of $150 anytime you want within the next six months? Clearly, the formula value is simply a starting point to estimate an option's market value. Before examining market value, though, we need to understand very well the important features of an option.

An option price less than its minimum value presents a risk-free profit opportunity.

Option Features

The important features of an option are its nature as a right, its strike price, and its maturity. These are explained below.

A Right, Not an Obligation   An option provides a *right* to buy or sell the underlying security. There is no obligation to do so. You are not forced to buy IBM at $150 a share. If its market price is less than this at the end of the option's life, you will discard the option as you would a losing lottery ticket. Any amount you paid for it is a total loss.

The Strike Price   The **strike price** (also called exercise price) is the price you must pay to acquire the underlying security. It is fixed for the life of the option,

A strike price is fixed for the life of an option.

so you know in advance how much it will cost to acquire the security. Without an option, you must endure the risk of a changing price. Suppose it is important that you pay no more than $150 for IBM: without the option there is no guarantee, and you run the risk of being unable to make the purchase. As you see, this aspect of an option reduces risk.

The strike price in relation to the market price of the underlying security determines an option's formula value. Specifically, for a call option:

$$\text{formula value} = (\text{market price of stock} - \text{strike price})$$

Maturity   Maturity refers to an option's life, which is the length of time available to exercise it. If a call option is about to expire, and if its strike price is below the underlying security's market price—a situation called **"in the money"**—you would choose to exercise the option even if you did not want the underlying security. You can always sell it at the market price and earn the profit the option provides. However, if the option is **"out of the money"**—strike price is greater than the underlying security's market price—you discard the option and let it expire worthless. The expression **"at the money"** means the strike price is equal to the market price. If this occurs at maturity, the option is still worthless.

The relationship between strike price and market price of the stock determines whether an option is "in the money," "out of the money," or "at the money."

Options and Leverage

In addition to being called derivative investments, options are called leverage-inherent investments. An option investment by itself can allow you to control many more shares of the underlying security than you could by investing the same amount directly in the security. This leverage is illustrated with the example in Exhibit 12.3.

Options offer a high degree of leverage.

Suppose you have $16,000 to invest and you are thinking of buying 100 shares of IBM currently selling at $160 a share. As an alternative, you also are considering buying 1,600 of the six-month, $150-strike-price options at $10 each. Assuming you hold the options until their maturity and then either exercise or discard them, you will lose the entire $16,000 if IBM's last price is $150 or less; if it is $160, you break even; and, at $170, you make $16,000 profit. With the stock itself, your profit or loss is much less—only $1,000. In effect, the options give the price action of 1,600 shares, rather than only 100, over the six-month period. This is an exceptionally high degree of leverage that often appeals to risk-seeking investors.

EXHIBIT 12.3
Profit (losses) from investing in IBM stock versus investing in IBM options

	Closing Price of IBM Stock		
	150	160	170
1. $16,000 invested in 100 shares of common stock	$ (1,000)	$-0-	$ 1,000
2. $16,000 invested in 1,600 options with a $150 strike price	$(16,000)	$-0-	$16,000

Determinants of Market Value

The contractual features of an option—the number of shares it controls, its maturity, and its strike price—play a role in determining its market value. Also important are the price of the underlying stock and its market volatility, and the overall level of interest rates.

Number of Shares Controlled   An option does not necessarily have a one-to-one relationship to the underlying security; that is, it may take more or less than one option to buy (or sell) the security. For example, First Executive Corporation has warrants outstanding that require 2.280 warrants to buy one share of its common stock. Of course, the greater the number of options required per share, the lower the market value of each option.

> The greater the number of shares controlled, the greater an option's market value.

Strike Price and Underlying Security's Market Price   For any given strike price, the market value of an option will increase as the market value of the underlying stock increases. This is so because the option is deeper in the money and worth more in terms of its formula value. For example, suppose IBM's stock price increases to $200. The formula value of the option now is $50 ($200 − $150), and the market value of the option must be at least this amount. However, as an option increases in market value it offers less leverage; if IBM's stock price increased to $1,000, there would be virtually no leverage since the option's formula value would be $850. Investing in the option would require almost as much money as investing in the stock. The loss of leverage means investors are less willing to pay a market price for the option that is much *above* formula value. This point will be illustrated more fully later in this chapter.

> The greater an option's formula value, the greater its market value.

Maturity   All things the same, the longer the maturity of an option, the greater its market value. For an option to have value at its maturity, it must be in the money; and, the longer the period of time before maturity, the greater the probability this price movement will take place. Suppose IBM is selling at $140 and you are considering the option with the $150 strike price. You might not pay much for one that matures in a week, realizing there is very little remaining time for IBM to gain $10 or more. On the other hand, you might pay quite a bit for a six-month option, because IBM has a good chance of increasing by $10 over such a long period.

> The longer an option's maturity, the greater its market value.

Price Volatility of the Underlying Security   If you were considering the six-month option just mentioned, you would also be concerned about the price volatility of IBM's stock. The greater the volatility of the stock, the greater the probability your option will be in the money. So, options on volatile stocks are worth more than similar options on stable ones. Beginning investors sometimes find this relationship confusing because they associate greater volatility with greater risk and less—not more—value. An option, though, presents a different situation. Keep in mind that you are not taking any downside price risk beyond the amount you pay for the option. If you paid, say, $15 for the above option and

> The greater the volatility of the underlying stock, the greater an option's market value.

IBM fell to $100 a share, your loss is still only $15. Someone who bought the stock would lose $40. Options allow investors to play volatile stocks with limited and known risks. Investors are willing to pay for this advantage, and the riskier the stock, the more they are willing to pay.

Level of Interest Rates   It is not intuitively clear why interest rates should have any bearing on the market prices of options, but they do. The connection arises from the leverage-inherent nature of options. The simplest way to see this connection is to view options as an alternative to other leverage techniques, such as buying securities with a margin account. Suppose you are considering the two alternatives: margin or options. If the interest rate on the margin account is high, you should prefer options, and you also should be willing to pay more for them than if margin interest was low. Thus, high interest rates are associated with high option prices, and vice versa.

Higher levels of interest rates lead to greater option values.

Exhibit 12.4 can help you remember the five important factors influencing option value. The exhibit assumes an increase in each factor, so you should realize that a decrease would have the opposite effect of the one shown.

Predicting Market Values

Considerable research has been done in the area of determining market values for options. Given the factors discussed above, it is possible to construct a model that indicates what the market price of an option should be. The most widely used such model is one developed by Fischer Black and Myron Scholes called the **Black-Scholes Model (BSM)**. Exhibit 12.5 shows theoretically predicted market values for the $150 IBM option, along with the formula values. Note that the market value of the option is $15 when the market price of the stock is $160.

The Black-Scholes Model is used to predict option values.

Also, notice the option has value even when the stock's market price is far below the strike price of $150. As long as there is even a small possibility that IBM's price could increase sufficiently within six months to put the option in the money, investors would be willing to pay some amount for the option. Also, you can see that the spread between an option's market value and its formula value decreases as the stock's price increases. This demonstrates the point mentioned

EXHIBIT 12.4

Factors influencing an option's market value

	Change in Factor	Change in Option Value
1. Number of options to acquire one share of the underlying stock	+	−
2. Market price of the underlying stock	+	+
3. Option's maturity	+	+
4. Price volatility of the underlying stock	+	+
5. The overall level of interest rates	+	+

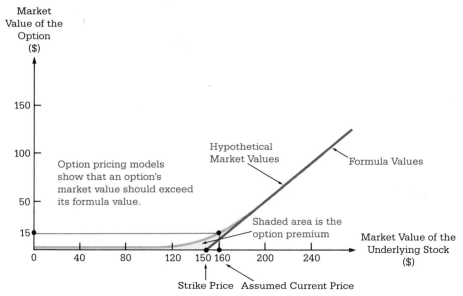

EXHIBIT 12.5
Market value of an
option and option
premium

earlier that as leverage decreases, investors are less willing to pay a premium to hold the option instead of the stock. This spread is called the *option premium,* and the relationship below shows how it is determined:

option premium = (market value of option − formula value of option)

So, the option premium is $5 ($15 − $10) when the price of the stock is $160. (The graph does not show negative formula values; while these are theoretically possible, they have no practical application. Also, the market price of an option is sometimes called the *premium*. It is unfortunate the same term is used to describe different items, but our usage will be strictly as shown above.) Finally, all options should have a positive premium, as shown in Exhibit 12.5.

> Option premium refers
> to the excess of an op-
> tion's market value over
> its formula value.

Do market prices of options actually behave in the manner predicted by the BSM? On balance, they appear to, making the BSM one of the most useful theoretical constructs to come from the field of finance. Its worth is dramatically shown by the fact that practically every option specialist uses it to look for overvalued or undervalued options. You can buy BSM software for your computer, and there are programmed hand calculators utilizing the model. The important point to recognize is that option trading is a highly specialized and sophisticated area—not one where you trade on the basis of guesswork and hunches.

WARRANTS AND RIGHTS

Warrants and rights are issued by corporations as part of their financing plans. They are typical option securities insofar as they entitle their owners to acquire other securities at a fixed price for a given period of time. However, there are

> Warrants are issued by
> corporations.

Why Get Excited? It's Only an Academic Formula

What jogging has become for the seeker of fast physical and mental well-being, a formula known as Black-Scholes and its descendants became for people seeking to turn investing into a science. The formula underlies such practices as portfolio "insurance," index arbitrage, and other forms of program trading. This innocent bit of academic arcanum ended up costing people a lot of money and scaring the whole world on October 19, 1987.

The formula first appeared in an article by Fischer Black and Myron Scholes in the May-June issue of the *Journal of Political Economy*. At the time, they were professors at the University of Chicago's Graduate School of Business, but they had been working on their theory for years, since meeting at MIT in the late 1960s.

Black-Scholes probably would have remained academic had it not appeared around the very time when active, liquid options markets were starting in Chicago, . . .creating securities for Black-Scholes to value. . . . Like a rock precipitating an avalanche, Black-Scholes encouraged index arbitrage. . .and a

host of arcane, computer-based strategies that allowed brokerage houses such as Goldman, Sachs & Co. and Salomon Brothers to generate high short-term yields for corporate treasurers via complicated arbitrages.

[However, the original] article's warnings are explicit. For their formula to work, Black and Scholes said, markets must be open and orderly. There must be no problem executing trades or selling securities short. The volatility of the option's underlying common stock must remain constant. Unfortunately, during market panics, none of these conditions hold: Markets are disorderly, it's difficult to execute trades, the uptick rule inhibits short selling, and volatility increases.

Had the practitioners of the new arts returned to Black and Scholes' original article and noted its confessed limitations, they might have proceeded more carefully. In their haste to make money, the practitioners ignored the warnings. Greed conquered common sense.

The two men have a fine sense of the absurd, and laughingly admit they got murdered when they tried to use their

new formula in the market. In 1973 they plunged into what their formula said was the most undervalued warrant around—the warrant to buy a share of Gene Klein's National General Corporation for $40, expiring in 1978. Whoops! Scholes, now a professor at Stanford, notes wryly that the market knew something Black-Scholes didn't: that Carl Linder's American Financial was soon going to buy National General on terms that slaughtered the warrant holders.

What now? Pretty much business as before. Portfolio "insurance" has obviously been discredited, and perhaps half of it is no longer in force. But index funds are still using arbitrage. Corporate treasurers still use complex arbitraging strategies to lock in short-term yields. Big brokerage houses are still doing program trading.

People are reluctant to give up on formulas that promise easy riches even when those formulas prove seriously flawed.

SOURCE: Excerpted from Allan Stone and Richard L. Stern, "How $V_0 = V_S\,N\,(d_1) - E/e^{rt}\,N\,(d_2)$ led to Black Monday," *Forbes*, January 25, 1988, pp. 55–59.

similarities and dissimilarities between them, which are explained in the sections that follow.

Characteristics of Warrants

Warrants typically come into existence as "sweeteners" as part of a corporate financing plan. They often are attached with bonds or common stock. An example of the latter is illustrated in Exhibit 12.6, which shows an announcement of an offering made by Clevite Industries. The offer is a unit, consisting of one share of common stock and one warrant that allows its owner to buy one-third of a share of common stock at a price of $12.875 per share.

Trading Warrants   Within a specified time after purchasing a unit, you may strip the warrants and do with them as you please; that is, you can choose to hold or sell them. They have their own investment lives, and often are traded on the organized exchanges or in the over-the-counter market. If you look at stock quotations in the financial pages of a newspaper, you will find them listed in the same place you find stocks, and you identify them with the symbol *wt* after the issuer's name. Generally, commissions on warrants follow the same schedules brokers use for common stocks.

> The trading of warrants is similar to that of common stocks.

At the time of issuance, warrants usually have maturities between three and ten years, but there are exceptions, and you can even find a few perpetual warrants. Strike prices are typically fixed over the warrants' lives, although increasing strike prices are not uncommon. This feature often forces investors to use their warrants to acquire the common stock, if the warrant is in the money. Practically every warrant calls common stock; however, in a few instances warrants might call a corporation's preferred stock or one of its bonds.

A Sample of Warrants   Exhibit 12.7 provides a small sample of warrants. The information was provided by *Value Line Options and Convertibles*, the weekly survey published May 1, 1989. Value Line is an excellent reference source for all option securities. The six issues shown were selected to show diversity in characteristics, rather than to support some argument. However, you should notice that the plus or minus sign in column 5 indicates if an issue is in the money (+) or out of the money (−) and the dollar amount shows by how much. Notice further that issues 4 and 5—First Executive Corporation and Eli Lilly—are deepest in the money and have the lowest option premiums on an adjusted basis (which is necessary because the issues differ considerably in strike price).

> A sample of warrants reflects key option characteristics.

As you see, the issues also vary considerably in both maturity and volatility. First Executive Corporation's low values for each helps explain its low option premium, while Pan Am's high values support its high premium. Examining the six, which one would you prefer to buy? Buying Eli Lilly's is very similar to buying the stock outright. It is a sizeable investment because of the high price of the warrant. In contrast, you pay only $0.94 for a Pan Am warrant, but you are asking for quite a price increase in the common stock (from $4.38 to $8.00) before the

EXHIBIT 12.6

Announcement of a stock issue with detachable warrants, appearing in *The Wall Street Journal* (Courtesy of Clevite Industries, Inc.)

New Issue

2,000,000 Units

Clevite Industries Inc.

Each Unit Consists of One Share of Common Stock and a Warrant to Purchase One-Third Share of Common Stock

Each Warrant entitles the holder to purchase one-third share of Common Stock at a price of $12.875 per share, subject to adjustment. The Common Stock and the Warrants will not be separately transferable prior to July 27, 1986, or such earlier date as may be determined by the Representatives of the Underwriters, as more fully described in the Prospectus.

Price $11.50 Per Unit

Copies of the Prospectus describing these securities and the business of the Company may be obtained from any of the undersigned in States in which such underwriters may legally offer these securities. This announcement is neither an offer to sell nor a solicitation of an offer to buy these securities. The offer is made only by the Prospectus.

Prudential-Bache Securities	**Donaldson, Lufkin & Jenrette** Securities Corporation

Bear, Stearns & Co. Inc.	Alex. Brown & Sons Incorporated	Hambrecht & Quist Incorporated
PaineWebber Incorporated L. F. Rothschild, Unterberg, Towbin, Inc.		Smith Barney, Harris Upham & Co. Incorporated
Allen & Company Incorporated		A.G. Edwards & Sons, Inc.
Oppenheimer & Co., Inc.		Thomson McKinnon Securities Inc.
Arnhold and S. Bleichroeder, Inc.	Robert W. Baird & Co. Incorporated	Sanford C. Bernstein & Co., Inc.
Blunt Ellis & Loewi Incorporated Cowen & Co.	Dain Bosworth Incorporated	First Albany Corporation
First of Michigan Corporation		J.J.B. Hilliard, W.L. Lyons, Inc.
Interstate Securities Corporation	McDonald & Company Securities. Inc.	Neuberger & Berman
The Ohio Company		Piper, Jaffray & Hopwood Incorporated
The Chicago Corporation	R.G. Dickinson & Co.	Gabelli & Company, Inc.
The Illinois Company Incorporated Jesup & Lamont Securities Co., Inc.		Laidlaw Adams & Peck Inc.
The Milwaukee Company	Parker/Hunter Incorporated	Raffensperger, Hughes & Co. Incorporated
Rodman & Renshaw, Inc.	Roney & Co.	R. Rowland & Co. Incorporated

June 30, 1986

EXHIBIT 12.7

A sample of warrants

(1) Issuer	(2) Ratio: Stock to Warrant[a]	(3) Strike Price	(4) Market Price of the Common Stock	(5) Formula Value[b]	(b) Market Price of the Warrant	(7) Premium[c]	(8) Adjusted Premium[d]	(9) Months to Maturity	(10) Price Volatility
1. Bank of New York	1.00	$62.00	$45.25	$−16.75	$8.63	$25.38	.409	102.0	80%
2. Genesco	1.00	8.00	6.13	−1.87	1.25	3.12	.390	46.0	155
3. Hotel Investors	1.00	16.95	8.50	−8.45	0.75	9.20	.543	90.5	70
4. First Executive Corporation	0.656	13.34	14.63	+0.85	3.25	2.40	.179	18.0	130
5. Eli Lilly	2.00	37.99	53.50	+31.02	38.00	6.98	.184	23.0	80
6. Pan Am	1.00	8.00	4.38	−3.62	0.94	4.56	.570	47.6	140

[a]The conversion ratio: for example, 2.00 means one warrant buys 2.00 shares of stock.

[b]Formula value = column (2) × [column (4) − column (3)].

[c]Premium = column (6) − column (5).

[d]Adjusted premium takes into consideration differences in strike prices; it is column (7) divided by column (3).

[e]This volatility measurement is calculated by Value Line. It is the standard deviation of the security's price relative to the standard deviation of the average common stock covered by Value Line.

SOURCE: *Value Line Options and Convertibles*, May 1, 1989, published by Arnold Bernhard and Company, Inc. 711 Third Avenue, New York, NY, 10017 © Value Line, Inc. Reprinted by permission.

warrant will be in the money. Can Pan Am do it? It's a risky proposition but one a risk-seeking investor might be inclined to take. Obviously, your preference for any option security should begin with your preference for the underlying stock. To this extent, you cannot divorce option analysis from stock analysis. However, once you have pinpointed a company that appeals to you, then it is necessary to decide whether to invest directly in the stock or indirectly through an option security. Now, option analysis, such as that provided by the Black-Scholes Model, can be used to determine if the warrant is overvalued or undervalued.

Characteristics of Rights

Rights are also issued by corporations, but they have much shorter maturities than warrants.

Rights are also created in connection with corporate financing plans. They are issued to investors who own a company's common stock, allowing them an opportunity to acquire additional shares of stock at a price below the current market price. So, rights are always in the money, at least when they are issued. In contrast to warrants, though, rights have very short lives—usually only several weeks.

Trading Rights   After rights have been issued, they trade in securities markets as any other option security. If you are a shareholder of a company issuing rights, you must decide whether you will use them to acquire additional shares or sell them before they expire. It is extremely important that you act within the right's maturity, because if you fail to do so, the right will expire and you will suffer a loss if the right is in the money, which it usually is. Many shareholders in the past have ignored their rights for whatever reason and have suffered unnecessary losses. An advantage in exercising rights is that you save commissions in acquiring additional shares of stock. However, there is really no advantage in using your rights to buy at the lower strike price. While this may seem an advantage, it isn't, because you give up the opportunity to sell your rights. Due to their very short lives, rights have limited uses as option instruments.

Failure to sell or exercise a right leads to an unnecessary loss.

Exercising rights can save brokerage commissions.

Formula Value of a Right   Since you may come in contact with rights as a shareholder, it is useful to understand how the formula value of a right is determined. This value depends essentially on two factors: the number of rights (N) it takes to acquire one new share of the common stock, and the subscription (strike) price (SP) of the rights offering. Suppose you have learned that Ralston Purina is planning a rights offering to raise $500 million. You know there are 40 million shares of common stock outstanding, so 40 million rights will be issued; each share always receives one right. You determine the company will set a subscription price at $25 a share, and the current market price (MP) of the stock is $35 a share.

Before calculating the formula value for each right, you must first determine how many rights will be required to buy one new share. You can do this by first dividing the amount of funds to be raised by the subscription price to determine the number of new shares to be issued. The answer is 20 million ($500,000,000/$25); then, since 40 million rights will be issued, it will take two rights (plus $25) to buy one new share. The formula value (V) for each right is:

$$V = \frac{(MP - SP)}{(N + 1)} = \frac{(\$35 - \$25)}{(2 + 1)} = \frac{\$10}{3} = \$3.33$$

Assuming you own 100 shares, you would receive 100 rights with a total value of $333.33. While this seems like a good deal, actually the company is not providing a gift. After the rights are issued, the market price of the stock will fall by the value of each right. In our example, the price will fall to $31.67 ($35 minus $3.33). Suppose you decide to sell your rights. You will then have $333.33 plus stock worth $3,166.67; obviously, you are no better or worse off after the rights offering.

Exercising the rights won't increase your net worth, either. The following calculations demonstrate this point by comparing the two alternatives.

	Exercise Rights	Sell Rights
Number of rights granted	100	100
Number of new shares purchased	50	-0-
Cash used to buy new shares @ $25 each	$1,250	-0-
Market value of stock owned:		
150 shares @ $31.67	$4,750	—
100 shares @ $31.67	—	$3,167
Cash from selling rights	—	333
Cash retained by not buying new shares	—	1,250
New worth after taking action	$4,750	$4,750

This comparison shows there is no particular advantage in either selling or exercising rights. If you care to increase your investment on a commission-free basis, then you should exercise; if that is not important, then sell the rights. What is important is taking action within the rights' maturity. Failure to do so in the above example leads to an unnecessary loss of $333.33.

CONVERTIBLES

A **convertible security** is usually one that can be exchanged for shares of common stock of the issuer; however, there are a few convertibles that exchange into preferred stock or bonds. Convertibles are an important financing medium for many corporations and they are used extensively. There are both convertible preferred stocks and convertible bonds. Listings of each can be found in the financial pages where other preferred stocks and other bonds are listed. The symbol *cv* appears after the name of the issuer if it is a convertible bond; however, convertible preferreds have no identifying symbol.

Convertibles, also issued by corporations, have very long maturities.

Characteristics of Convertibles

Convertibles are complex financial instruments. In contrast to a bond with detachable warrants that allow investors to strip the option value from the debt security, a convertible's option value is permanently fixed to it and embedded in its market price. Investors, then, must evaluate both debt and option characteristics of convertibles in forming portfolios.

Debt Characteristics   Exhibit 12.8 shows an announcement of a convertible bond issued by Dreyer's Grand Ice Cream. If you were thinking of buying this bond, you would want to know its coupon rate (6.5%), its maturity (May 25, 2011), and any other debt characteristic—such as quality rating, call provisions, sinking fund availability, and more—that might help you evaluate the instrument as a

EXHIBIT 12.8

Announcement of a convertible bond issue appearing in *The Wall Street Journal* (Courtesy Dreyer's Grand Ice Cream)

This advertisement is neither an offer to sell nor a solicitation of an offer to buy these securities. The offering is made only by the Prospectus. These securities are redeemable prior to maturity as set forth in the Prospectus.

<u>NEW ISSUE</u>

$50,000,000

6½% CONVERTIBLE SUBORDINATED DEBENTURES DUE 2011

The Debentures are convertible into Common Stock of the Company at any time on or before May 25, 2011, unless previously redeemed, at a conversion price of $32 per share, subject to adjustment under certain conditions.

Price 100%

(Interest payable June 1 and December 1 in each year)

Copies of the Prospectus may be obtained in any State only from the undersigned as may lawfully offer these securities in such State.

HAMBRECHT & QUIST
INCORPORATED

June 2, 1986

debt security. Since these have been covered in Chapter 7, we will not repeat them here.

A first point of interest, though, to the convertible investor is how much interest return he or she is giving up by buying a convertible rather than a straight bond. At the time the Dreyer's issue came to market, 25-year Treasury bonds were yielding about 7.5%. Clearly, without the convertible feature, the Dreyer's bond would yield much more than 6.5%; it might yield, say, 9.5%. Thus, you give up about $30 a year on each bond to hold the convertible option. However, you hold a debt instrument with whatever protections it provides in the event of default. This issue might have greater appeal than Dreyer's common stock with its far greater bankruptcy risk.

Option Characteristics The most important option characteristic is the instrument's **conversion ratio**. This ratio tells us the number of common shares into which the instrument converts. The announcement in Exhibit 12.8 does not give the conversion ratio but it does show a conversion price of $32. Knowing that, we can determine the conversion ratio by also knowing that most bonds have a face value of $1,000. The calculation is shown below:

$$\text{conversion ratio} = \frac{\$1,000}{\text{conversion price}} = \frac{\$1,000}{\$32} = 31.25$$

The Dreyer's convertible converts into 31.25 shares of Dreyer's common stock. While practically all bonds have both conversion ratios and conversion prices, many convertible preferred stocks have only conversion ratios. For example, Anheuser-Busch has a convertible preferred that converts into 1.935 shares of the common. The lack of a conversion price is not a material item because it does not have any influence upon conversion value.

Along with the conversion ratio, other important information would be how long the conversion right lasts (the full 25 years in Dreyer's case) and whether or not the conversion ratio is fixed over the life of the issue. Frequently, this ratio decreases over time, serving as an incentive to investors to convert into the common earlier rather than later. Any call provisions on the bond are also important, because a call could shorten the option period, thereby lowering the option value.

Investment Opportunities in Convertibles

Convertibles are sometimes called "the best of both worlds." This lavish praise arises from the fact that, as a bond, a convertible offers a relatively safe investment, while at the same time providing participation in the issuer's growth through the convertible feature. True, a convertible does possess these features, but you pay for them through its higher market price. As with every investment, there is the inevitable trade-off of risk and return.

Convertible Values Illustrated   Given its particular debt and option characteristics, the value of a convertible at any time depends primarily upon the market
price of the underlying common stock and the general level of interest rates. The
influence of these factors for the Dreyer's bond is illustrated in Exhibit 12.9.

Value as Straight Debt.   If you bought the bond, you might argue the worst
that could happen (short of bankruptcy) would be a sharp drop in the price of the
common stock. Even if that happened, you would still hold a bond paying 6.5%
interest each year, or $32.50 every six months. Assuming it will be redeemed at
$1,000 at the end of 25 years, and also assuming an opportunity investment rate
(what you could earn by investing in a similar bond without a conversion option)
of 9.5%, allows us to determine the bond's value as straight debt. We do this by
simply calculating its present value, using the methods explained in Chapter 5.
This value is $715.23. The Dreyer's bond, then, should have a market price at least
this high, as long as interest rates don't change. In Exhibit 12.9, the value as
straight debt is shown as a horizontal line that implies this value is not influenced
by the price of the common stock. At low prices of the common stock, this value
dominates other values, which is indicated by the color portion of the line. At high
prices of the common stock, the value as straight debt is unimportant, because
conversion value becomes dominant.

Conversion Value.   A convertible's **conversion value** is its value as a
common stock. To determine this value, you multiply the price of the common
stock by the conversion ratio. If the common stock price is zero, conversion value
is also zero; as the price increases, conversion value increases in proportion to the
conversion ratio, as illustrated in Exhibit 12.9. Notice that when the price of the
common stock is $26 a share—the actual market price of Dreyer's common when

> **Even if the price of the common falls, a convertible has value as straight debt.**

> **Conversion value increases as the price of the common increases.**

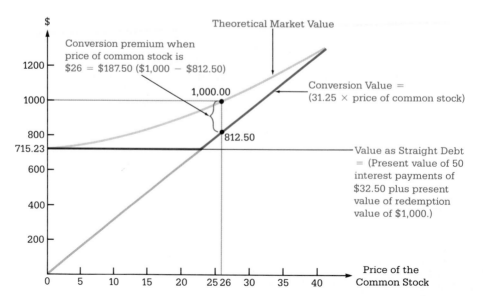

EXHIBIT 12.9
Dreyer's Grand Ice
Cream convertible bond

Conversion premium when
price of common stock is
$26 = $187.50 ($1,000 − $812.50)

Theoretical Market Value

1,000.00

Conversion Value =
(31.25 × price of common stock)

812.50

Value as Straight Debt
= (Present value of 50
interest payments of
$32.50 plus present
value of redemption
value of $1,000.)

Price of the
Common Stock

Convertible Securities: Look Closely Before Investing

On the surface, a convertible security—bond or preferred—seems a good idea: high current return plus a play on the underlying stock. But, caution should be exercised by the prudent investor. Here are a few warnings:

☐ If you are interested in bonds, keep in mind that buying only a few bonds can be expensive in terms of commissions and dealers' spreads. If preferreds are your choice, many are inactively traded, or traded in the over-the-counter market where reports of prices and volume may be sparse or inaccurate. Bid and ask spreads can be a problem here, too.

☐ Convertibles are complex securities. Investment professionals use elaborate option pricing methods to determine intrinsic values. If you aren't doing the same, you could be at a disadvantage in finding undervalued or overvalued securities.

☐ Buying a convertible as an alternative to buying the underlying stock generally means you pay a premium over the market value of the stock. While you hope to recoup the premium over time through larger current returns, the strategy might be defeated if the convertible is called shortly after issuance.

☐ While a convertible offers greater protection against price decreases in the common, that hardly constitutes a reason for buying it. If you think the common is likely to decrease in price, you should avoid it *and* the convertible.

☐ There is scant evidence that portfolios of convertibles are appreciably less risky than portfolios of stocks and fixed-income securities, or even of stocks alone. Data in the accompanying table show returns from three closed-end funds that invest primarily in convertibles. These are compared to the S&P 500 and, as you see, these three funds offer no particular return or risk advantage for the period covered.

Returns of Three Convertible Funds Versus the S&P 500 and Corporate Bonds					
	Funds				
Year	American Capital	Bancroft	Castle	3-Fund Average	S&P 500
1988	15.3%	4.9%	10.1%	10.1%	16.8%
1987	− 0.8	1.8	− 6.7	− 1.9	5.2
1986	14.8	12.6	− 2.2	8.4	18.5
1985	27.4	27.4	27.8	27.5	32.2
1984	1.7	6.6	2.9	3.7	6.3
1983	25.2	19.0	24.4	22.9	22.5
1982	36.5	13.0	42.8	30.8	21.4
1981	7.6	− 3.9	18.5	7.4	− 4.9
1980	37.2	36.2	22.8	32.1	32.4
1979	24.3	30.9	17.8	24.3	18.4
1978	15.2	6.7	2.3	8.1	6.6
Average	—	—	—	15.8	15.9
Standard Deviation	—	—	—	11.9	11.6

the convertible was issued—conversion value is $812.50 (31.25 × $26). As you see in Exhibit 12.9, when conversion value reaches $715.23, at a price of $22.89 for the common ($715.23/31.25), it dominates the value as straight debt. The color portion of the line indicates that conversion value dominates. The entire color line, then, represents minimum values for the convertible. It should never sell below these prices in efficient markets.

Theoretical Market Value.   Using an option pricing model, such as the **The Black-Scholes Model can predict the market value of a convertible.** Black-Scholes Model, you could generate theoretical market values similar to those shown in Exhibit 12.9. As we have seen before in this chapter in discussing option premium, the conversion premium—the difference between market value and conversion value—becomes smaller as the price of the underlying stock increases. At high prices of the stock, owning the convertible is very much like owning the stock outright: interest yield will be low and price risk will be about the same as with the stock. At low prices of the stock, the conversion premium has little value, and owning the convertible is similar to owning a straight bond: interest yield is high and price risk is connected more closely with changes in interest rates (not demonstrated in the diagram) than with changes in the price of the stock (except, of course, for very large increases in price).

Investors must weigh each of these situations in selecting convertibles. Many prefer to buy convertibles that are in price situations similar to the Dreyer's bond; they want a bond with a conversion price about 20% to 30% above the current market price of the stock. They hope the price will increase sufficiently over time to produce capital gains; meanwhile, they enjoy an interest yield that is usually much better than what could be earned in dividends with the common stock. Investors such as these often use a payback method to evaluate a convertible.

Using a Payback Method to Evaluate a Convertible   Suppose you felt Dreyer's was a good investment opportunity and you planned to invest in it. However, you wondered: should the investment be in the common stock or in the convertible? If you chose to buy 31.25 shares of stock, your investment would have been the conversion value of $812.50; you would have saved the conversion premium of $187.50. But Dreyer's common stock did not pay a cash dividend at the time the convertible was issued. Looking at the situation this way, one might argue that the bond's interest each year will eventually recoup the premium. From that point on, you are better off with the bond because of the greater current return each year. How many years will it take to recover the convertible's **Payback period refers to the number of years required for a convertible's extra current return to recover the conversion premium.** premium? The answer to this question is called the **payback period,** or break-even time. The formula below calculates the payback period (N):

$$N = \frac{\text{conversion premium}}{(CR \text{ convertible} - CR \text{ common stock})}$$

where: conversion premium = market value of the convertible
minus conversion value,

$$CR \text{ convertible} = \text{the current return in dollars of the convertible, and}$$

$$CR \text{ common} = \text{the current return in dollars on the number of common shares into which the convertible converts.}$$

The payback period for Dreyer's is:

$$N = \frac{\$187.50}{(\$65 - \$0)} = 2.89 \text{ years}$$

Is 2.89 years good, bad, or indifferent? Although convertible investors surely look at many other factors in making a decision, any payback period of less than four years is considered a fairly quick payback. So, an argument could be made to buy the convertible rather than the stock. Given its better position in the event of financial trouble, this advice seems even more appropriate. Dreyer's might represent an excellent growth company, and at the end of 2.89 years, you may have wished that you invested the entire $1,000 in the common stock to buy 38.46 shares ($1,000/$26). On the other hand, if the price of the common stock falls, you will take less loss with the convertible, and by then you will have recovered the entire conversion premium. As you see, a convertible represents an interesting investment alternative, but is not quite the *best* of both worlds.

A short payback period favors owning the convertible rather than the common stock.

The Problem of an Early Call   We noted earlier that if a convertible is called, investors may not earn the return they had anticipated. Most convertibles have calls and many companies exercise the call as soon as it is to their advantage to do so. Indeed, convertibles often are issued at times when managements believe their firms' common stocks are undervalued, or long-term interest rates are too high, or both. Their intent is to call as soon as economic conditions turn more favorable.

An early call can upset expected return with a convertible.

To understand the implications of an early call, let us assume that Dreyer's common stock increases to $35 a share shortly after issuance of the convertible, and that the convertible is callable—say, at $1,050—at any time. The market value of the convertible when the price of the common is $35 should be about $1,175 (you can see this in Exhibit 12.9). However, the conversion value is $1,093.75 (31.25 × $35); and if the bond is called, investors clearly would choose to convert to the common, rather than honor the call, since this provides $43.75 ($1,093.75 − $1,050.00) more. Either alternative, though, is substantially below the theoretical market value of $1,175. If that value did in fact exist, and if investors purchased bonds at that price, they would lose $81.25 ($1,175.00 − $1,093.75) as a result of the call. It is highly unlikely a price of $1,175 would exist unless investors felt very strongly that the bond issue would not be called. Given the trend towards early calls, this possibility is remote.

Thus, the bond's price probably would be close to $1,093.75. Now, suppose you bought the bond at its initial offering in preference to the common stock, and a call takes place, say, one year after issuance. How does your choice compare to the alternative of investing directly in the stock? The gain on the bond is $93.75 ($1,093.75 − $1,000.00). Adding this to one year's interest of $65 gives a total gain of $158.75. But, had you invested $1,000 and bought 38.46 shares of the common, your gain would have been $346 [($35 × 38.46) − $1,000]—over twice as much. While our example is hypothetical, the message is clear: investors should examine call provisions very closely before investing. Payback periods have little meaning if an issue is likely to be called sooner.

Convertibles as Defensive Issues   In the above example, the common stock increased in value. Suppose, though, it declines. For example, assume Dreyer's price falls to $20 a share at the end of one year. The bond's price declines to about $900 (again, inspect Exhibit 12.9), leading to a loss of $100 a bond. This is partially offset by the $65 of interest, resulting in a net loss of $35 for the year. But, buying 38.46 shares of the common would have led to a far greater loss of $231 [$1,000 − (38.46 × $20)]. Convertibles, then, are the better choice if price declines seem likely. In this sense, they are viewed as defensive issues.

Return Volatility with Convertibles   Since upside potential is poorer with convertibles vis-a-vis the common stock, while downside protection is better, convertibles should exhibit historical return patterns that are less volatile than those of common stocks. In short, they are less risky. Given this situation, over time their returns also should be less. Assuming investors hold portfolios of convertibles, they should determine whether that strategy is better than an alternative of simply holding a portfolio consisting of equities and debt instruments that might achieve a similar risk exposure. There is little evidence indicating a portfolio of convertibles is the better choice.

A Sample of Convertibles

Before leaving convertibles, it is instructive to examine a small sample to see their diversity. Exhibit 12.10 shows two convertible preferreds and two convertible bonds. Part *A* provides basic information about the convertible and the underlying stock, while Part *B* prepares a payback analysis for each issue. As you see, B. F. Goodrich has the quickest payback, while IBM has the longest. Also, current yields are fairly attractive (except B. F. Goodrich's) considering that long-term Treasury bonds were yielding about 8.3% at the time.

   B. F. Goodrich has a relatively small conversion premium and a relatively quick payback period. However, the issue was callable at $52.40 within about seven months. So, it is unlikely the conversion premium will go much higher in the immediate future. As previously discussed, the existence of a call—and most convertibles are callable—imposes a constraint upon conversion premium whenever a call seems likely. Would B. F. Goodrich call the issue at the first possible call date? That is difficult to say. The current yield on the convertible of 6.76% was not terribly high at that time. If the issue was to be refinanced, it is

Margin notes:

Early calls make ownership of a convertible a poorer choice than outright ownership of the stock.

A convertible offers greater downside protection than does the common stock.

Convertibles should be less volatile than underlying stocks.

EXHIBIT 12.10
A sample of convertible issues

	Preferred Stocks		Bonds	
	American International	B.F. Goodrich	Hills Dept. Stores	IBM
Part A: Basic Information:				
1. Conversion price	$ —	$ —	$ 14.00	$153.66
2. Conversion ratio	2.985	.909	71.43	6.508
3. Annual dividend or interest	$ 2.00	$ 3.50	$ 87.50	$ 78.75
4. Maturity	—	—	2002	2004
5. Market price of the convertible	$22.88	$51.75	$947.50	$991.25
6. Price of the common stock	$ 5.75	$52.63	$ 7.75	$113.50
7. Annual dividend per share on the common stock	$ 0	$ 2.00	$ 0	$ 4.42
8. Total dividends = line 7 × line 2	$ 0	$ 1.82	$ 0	$ 28.76
Part B: Payback Analysis:				
9. Conversion value = line 2 × line 6	$17.16	$47.84	$553.58	$738.66
10. Conversion premium = line 5 − line 9	$ 5.72	3.91	393.92	252.59
11. Extra current return with the convertible = line 3 − line 8	2.00	1.68	87.50	49.99
12. Payback years = line 10 ÷ line 11	2.86	2.33	4.50	5.05
13. Current yield on the convertible (percent) = line 3 ÷ line 5	8.74	6.76	9.23	7.95

SOURCE: *Value Line Options and Convertibles*, May 1, 1989, published by Arnold Bernhard and Company, Inc.
© Value Line, Inc. Reprinted by permission.

likely the new issue would offer a yield at least that high. However, if refinancing could take place at, say, 5.5%, a call would seem likely.

SUMMARY

An option security provides a right to buy or sell an underlying security, and derives its value from the value of that underlying security. An option must have a strike price and most have fixed maturities. Options provide leverage, an appealing feature to some investors. The value of an option is determined by the number of shares it controls, its strike price in relation to the underlying security's market price, its maturity, the price volatility of the underlying security, and the level of interest rates. Option market values are often predicted with the Black-Scholes Model.

A warrant is created as part of a corporate financing package. Warrants are traded on organized exchanges and in the over-the-counter market. Rights are created as part of a stock offering. They have very short lives, and their market values tend to follow their formula values.

A convertible security has both debt and option characteristics. As such, they offer unique investment opportunities. Their market values are determined in light of their values as common stock or straight debt. The Black-Scholes Model can be used to predict their market values. Convertibles are often evaluated by using a payback method that compares owning them to owning the underlying stock directly.

KEY TERMS

Select the alternative that best identifies the key term.

1. option security
2. minimum (formula) value
3. strike price
4. "in the money" call
5. "out of the money" call
6. "at the money"
7. Black-Scholes Model (BSM)
8. warrants
9. rights
10. convertible security
11. conversion ratio
12. conversion value
13. payback period

a. option security with a very short life
b. the number of common shares per convertible
c. the lowest possible market value of an option
d. gives the right to buy or sell another security at a fixed price over a given period of time
e. option value cannot be separated from the security
f. strike price greater than market price
g. strike price below market price
h. predicts an option's market value
i. length of the time required for extra current return to equal conversion premium
j. can be detached and sold separately
k. price at which the underlying security can be bought
l. conversion ratio × market price of the stock
m. strike price equals market price

REVIEW QUESTIONS

1. Explain why an option is called a derivative instrument.
2. What is meant by the formula value of an option? What assurance do we have that option prices must always equal or exceed their formula values?
3. Identify three key features of an option security.
4. Explain why options are considered leverage-inherent securities.
5. Identify five factors that determine an option's market value. Working with each individually, indicate what effect—if any—a *decrease* in the value of the factor would have upon the market value of the option.

6. Why should the general level of interest rates have any bearing on an option's market value? Explain, creating your own example.

7. Explain the nature of warrants and some aspects of trading them. Do the warrants illustrated in Exhibit 12.7 show characteristics of option securities? Explain.

8. What is a right? How are rights created? Do they represent "long-term" investment vehicles? Explain.

9. What is a convertible security? Explain some of its characteristics, such as: conversion ratio, conversion price, conversion value, conversion premium, value as straight debt, and theoretical market value.

10. Indicate several advantages of investing in a convertible security as opposed to investing directly in the underlying stock.

11. How is a payback method used to evaluate a convertible?

12. Most convertibles have calls that allow their issuers to retire them before maturity. Explain how a call influences your evaluation of a convertible.

13. Do convertibles offer protection against downside risk? Explain.

14. Over time, convertibles should have *greater* price volatility than their underlying stocks. Explain your agreement or disagreement with this statement.

PROBLEMS AND PROJECTS

1. You are thinking of investing $10,000 by purchasing 100 shares of XYZ, Inc., at $100 a share. As an alternative, you are considering buying 1,000 options that would allow you to acquire XYZ at $90 a share anytime within the next six months. Each option costs $10. Assuming the price of XYZ's shares is $90, $100, or $110 six months from now, indicate your profit or loss with each alternative. Then explain why an option is described as "leverage-inherent."

2. Using your best judgment, complete the following table.

Price of the Common Stock	Formula Value	Expected Market Value	Option Premium
$40	$_____	$20.50	$_____
35	_____	_____	_____
30	_____	11.00	_____
25	5.00	_____	_____
20	-0-	4.00	_____
15	-0-	_____	_____
10	-0-	0.13	_____
5	-0-	_____	_____
0	-0-	-0-	_____

3. Suppose you own 100 shares of ABC Company, which has just announced a rights offering. You will be able to purchase one share of common stock at $20 a share plus four rights. The current market price of the stock is $25 a share.
   a. What will each right be worth after the rights are issued and begin trading?
   b. Is it to your advantage to: sell the rights, use the rights to buy more shares, or discard the rights? Explain your answer, using a numeric example.

4. You are thinking of buying a convertible bond issued by Lancer Industries. The bond matures in 10 years, has a coupon rate of 6% (interest paid semiannually), and is

currently selling at its face value of $1,000. You notice that similar bonds without a convertible feature currently have a yield to maturity of 9%. The Lancer bond has a conversion price of $40 a share. Lancer's common stock is currently selling at $30 a share and pays an annual dividend of $0.20 a share. You believe the dividend will increase substantially in the distant future but do not anticipate any increases over the next 5 years. The stock has considerable price risk, as indicated by its beta value of 1.6.

   a. Determine the bond's current conversion value, conversion premium, value as straight debt, and payback period.

   b. Discuss whether you would prefer investing in the convertible bond or the common stock.

5. Pete Martinez is thinking of investing in the convertible bond of United Conglomerates, Inc., currently selling at par. The conversion price is $100, the coupon rate is 8%, and the bond is callable in one year at $1,100. United's common stock currently sells at $80 a share, but it is fairly risky, having a beta of 1.2. Pete anticipates the common will rise in value to $100 a share by year end, but he agrees there is an equal chance it could fall to $60 a share. His broker has given him Black-Scholes theoretical values for the bond in both cases: $1,120 and $900. United pays no dividends on its common stock.

   a. Outline the profit/loss situation for the upcoming year with both the bond and an equal investment in the common stock, assuming United calls the bond if the common increases in value as anticipated.

   b. Suppose the bond is callable at $1,200 instead of $1,100 and after three years instead of one. Assume further that the price of the common stock after three years is projected to be $110 a share. With these new conditions, how would you advise Pete with respect to buying the bond or the stock? Explain, using time value of money and a 10% discount rate (Pete's assumed opportunity investment rate).

6. (*Student Project*)   Review current issues of *The Wall Street Journal* until an ad for a convertible appears. Contact a brokerage firm that is part of the underwriting syndicate and request a prospectus. Read the provisions concerning conversion feature and call provisions. Then, find information on the common stock—its price and expected dividend—and evaluate the convertible.

CASE ANALYSES

12.1
Ken Loggia
Feels His
Options Warrant
Consideration

Ken Loggia invested $10,000 in one-year certificates of deposit that are about to mature. Ken can roll over the CDs at an 8% rate, but he is hesitant to do so since he believes the stock of DNX Pharmaceuticals is primed for a major price increase. The company has recently developed a new over-the-counter pain reliever that has considerable profit potential. Ken is willing to take some risk in playing his feeling about DNX, but he doesn't want to lose the entire amount.

   DNX common stock is currently selling at $50 a share. Several years ago the company issued warrants that allow a holder to buy one share of the common at $40 a share. The current market price of the warrants is $14 each and they mature in four years. Also, put and call options on DNX are available. A call option with a 6-month maturity and $55 strike price is available for $2.00 a share, or $200 per 100-share contract.

Ken is somewhat familiar with common stocks but he has little understanding of options and warrants. His first thought was to invest the entire $10,000 by buying 200 shares of the common stock. The stock should pay a quarterly dividend of $0.50 a share, and Ken hopes its price will increase to $58 a share by mid-year. Ken realizes his price appreciation estimates could be at least 20% off the mark—higher or lower—depending upon first-year sales of the new product. The warrants and options alternatives were suggested to Ken by a friend who, unfortunately, also knew very little about their mechanics. Ken believes he can make a better decision if he could determine potential profit or loss from each alternative, given his most likely price estimates *and* the possible 20% variations.

Questions

a. Developing profit/loss estimates first requires estimating the market values of the options and warrants at the end of six months. The following table presents alternative values, given the three possible stock prices. You must select the most realistic price in each case.

		Price of the Common Stock		
		$46.40	$58.00	$69.60
Possible values of the call options (per share):	(1)	−8.60	3.00	-0-
	(2)	-0-	8.00	19.60
	(3)	−3.60	-0-	14.60
Possible values of the warrants (per warrant):	(1)	6.40	17.00	32.00
	(2)	−3.60	21.00	40.00
	(3)	11.00	25.00	50.00

b. With your value selections from question *a,* develop profit/loss estimates, assuming $10,000 is invested in the common stock, or in warrants, or in call options.
c. Which alternative do you recommend for Ken? Explain.
d. Suppose you could allocate the $10,000 among the three alternatives. Develop a portfolio of the three for Ken, explaining your rationale.

**12.2
Mona Giles
Looks at a
Convertible**

Mona Giles has decided to invest in Parkhurst Industries, a company that Mona feels will do well in the years ahead. She was ready to purchase 100 shares of the common stock at $20 a share when her broker told her that she might consider buying two 25-year convertible subordinated debentures the company was about to issue at par. The convertible issue has a conversion price of $25 a share and an 8% coupon rate. The bonds have a call price of $1,100 but they cannot be called for three years.

At present, the company pays a dividend of $1 a share on the common stock. Dividends are not likely to increase in the near future since the company needs cash to complete an expansion project. Parkhurst issued the convertibles as an alternative to issuing straight subordinated debentures that would have carried a 12% coupon rate.

Mona is finding it difficult to choose between the two alternatives. She feels interest rates will remain stable in the years ahead but the price of Parkhurst's common stock will be volatile, ranging from a possible low of $10 a share to a possible high of $40 a share. Her best estimate is that price will increase 10% a year. Mona needs help in determining profit/loss estimates for the convertibles, and she needs advice in making a selection. She describes herself as a definite risk averter.

Questions

a. Given Mona's high and low estimates for the price of the common stock, determine profit or loss amounts from investing $2,000 in each investment alternative—the common stock or the convertibles. Assume a 3-year holding period and consider dividends and interest. To determine the price of the convertibles, consider the alternatives listed in the following table. Select the most realistic alternative given each possible price of the common stock. (Do not consider time value of money in your work and assume Mona would hold either securities at the end of three years.)

		Prices of the Common Stock	
	$ 10.00	$ 26.62	$ 40.00
Possible prices of a convertible: (1)	400.00	1,000.00	1,620.00
(2)	690.00	1,300.00	1,000.00
(3)	1,000.00	1,100.00	2,000.00

b. Calculate the payback period for the convertible.
c. Which security do you recommend for Mona? Give reasons for your choice.

HELPFUL
READING

Black, F. "Fact and Fantasy in the Use of Options." *Financial Analysts Journal*, July-August 1975.

———, and M. Scholes, "The Pricing of Options and Corporate Liabilities." *The Journal of Political Economy*, May-June 1973.

———. "How We Came Up With The Option Formula." *The Journal of Portfolio Management*, Winter 1989, pp. 4–8.

Choie, Kenneth S., and Frederick Novomestky. "Replication of Long-Term with Short-Term Options." *The Journal of Portfolio Management*, Winter 1989, pp. 17–19.

Cox, J., S. Ross, and M. Rubenstein. "Option Pricing: A Simplified Approach." *Journal of Financial Economics*, September 1979.

Donnelly, Barbara. "Convertible Bond Game Becomes Riskier." *The Wall Street Journal,* March 7, 1987, p. C1.

Patakala, A. L. "There is a Free Lunch." *Financial Analysts Journal,* September-October 1988, pp. 82–87.

"Smoother Ride in Convertibles." *Barron's,* March 6, 1989, pp. 26–27.

Winkler, Matthew. "Big Spring Rally Has Corporate Treasurers Driving Convertibles." *The Wall Street Journal,* May 25, 1989, p. C1.

CHAPTER THIRTEEN

Put and Call Options

PUT AND CALL
CHARACTERISTICS

Trading Puts and Calls

Reading Put and Call Quotations

Buyers and Sellers

Contract Settlement

Brokerage Commissions

PUT AND CALL TRADING
STRATEGIES

Naked Positions

Hedge Positions

Spreads

Arbitrage Opportunities

OTHER PUT AND CALL USES

Covered Option Writing

An Option-Bills Portfolio

Hedging Market Risk

BOXES

Synthetic Fibers, Synthetic Fuels,
and Now, Synthetic Stocks

Arbitrageurs, Program Trading, and
Ivan Boesky

After you finish this chapter, you
will be able to:

- understand the characteristics of
  standardized put and call contracts and why investors use
  them.

- understand what is involved in
  contract settlement and recognize
  the importance of commissions in
  option trading.

- identify profit opportunities and
  risks in various trading strategies
  involving naked positions, hedges,
  spreads, and arbitrage.

- understand profit opportunities
  and risks in covered option writing.

- recognize advantages and disadvantages of using market index
  options in an option-bills portfolio
  or as a hedge against market risk.

W arrants, rights, and convertibles are issued by corporations as part of their
financing plans. In contrast, put and call options can be created by anyone.
As an individual, you can create a put or call by simply calling your broker and
giving the instruction to sell a contract. One can usually be sold within minutes,
and you will be wealthier by the amount the buyer agrees to pay. Just as IBM can
raise funds by selling option securities, so can you; and, just as IBM incurs risks
and gives up certain rights in the process, so will you.

In addition to selling options, you also can buy them. Indeed, buying is
probably more often undertaken by beginning investors. In this chapter we will
examine the investment uses of puts and calls from both buyers' and sellers'
perspectives.

PUT AND CALL CHARACTERISTICS

A **call option** is the type of option examined in detail in the previous chapter. The
term *call* means a right to buy the underlying security at the strike price anytime
during the option's life. A **put option** is new to us: it gives the right to sell the
underlying security at the strike price anytime during the option's life. Like a call,
a put can be used to increase investment return and risk, or to reduce each.

A call is a right to buy; a put is a right to sell.

Trading Puts and Calls

Puts and calls are traded on organized exchanges in a fashion similar to stock and
bond trading. There are five major exchanges: the Chicago Board Options
Exchange and the American Exchange are the two largest, with the smaller ones
being the Pacific Exchange, the Philadelphia Exchange, and the New York
Exchange. As Exhibit 13.1 shows, contracts are available for individual stocks
(such as IBM), stock indexes (such as the S&P 500), debt instruments (Treasury
notes and bonds), foreign currencies (such as the British pound), and a large array

EXHIBIT 13.1
Put and call options
available

Underlying Assets	Example	Number of Different Contracts
Individual common stocks	IBM	over 300
Stock indexes	the S&P 500	15
Treasury bonds and notes	the 8⅛% due 2/2019	4
Foreign currencies	the British pound	11
Futures contracts	gold	48

*Approximate numbers; new contracts are introduced frequently.

of futures contracts on various commodities and financial instruments (such as soybeans, gold, and Eurodollars). Option contracts have proliferated so rapidly in the 1980s that even experienced investors find it difficult to be familiar with all of them. Fortunately, all options work on the same general principles discussed in the previous chapter and in this one. It is more important to understand these principles than to memorize details about specific contracts.

Options are available on a wide array of intangible and tangible assets.

Reading Put and Call Quotations

Puts and calls are reported in a separate section of the financial pages of many newspapers. Typical quotations are shown in Exhibit 13.2. The underlying securities are IBM common stock and Sears common stock. IBM options are very popular and actively traded. As you see, options are available with maturities in three separate months. Sears options are less popular and more representative of the majority of options on individual stocks. Their maturities are on a three-month basis.

Each contract involves 100 shares. You must multiply the prices shown, which are on a per-share basis, by 100 to determine the contract's value. For example, the IBM February 160 call is worth $75 ($¾ × 100): a buyer pays this amount and a seller receives it. The prices shown in Exhibit 13.2 once again demonstrate that option prices are influenced by how deeply they are in the money (or, far out of it) and by maturity. We find the IBM February 150 call is worth more than the February 160 call (5¼ versus ¾); and the March 160 call is worth more than the February 160 call (2⁷⁄₁₆ versus ¾).

A standardized contract involves 100 shares.

Notice that put values move in the opposite direction of call values in the sense that as the underlying stock's price increases (decreases), a put's value

IBM	Strike Price	Calls			Puts		
		Feb.	Mar.	Apr.	Feb.	Mar.	Apr.
155	150	5¼	7⅜	8⅞	1³⁄₁₆	2⁹⁄₁₆	3⅝
155	155	2³⁄₁₆	4½	6¼	3⅜	4¾	5⅝
155	160	¾	2⁷⁄₁₆	3⅞	6⅞	8	8½
Sears		**Mar.**	**Jun.**	**Sep.**	**Mar.**	**Jun.**	**Sep.**
40⅛	35	5¼	5½	6⅜	³⁄₁₆	½	⅞
40⅛	40	1⁵⁄₁₆	2⅜	3⅛	1¼	2¹⁄₁₆	2⅞
40⅛	45	³⁄₁₆	¾	1³⁄₁₆	r	6¼	r

The symbol *r* means the option did not trade that day.

Closing prices of the underlying stocks

Closing prices of the option contract. Quoted price is per share of the underlying stock. Since the standard contract requires delivery of 100 shares, multiply by 100 to determine a contract's total value.

EXHIBIT 13.2
Typical newspaper listings of option quotations

decreases (increases). A right to sell IBM at 160 is worth more than the right to sell it at 150, and each increases in value as the price of IBM falls.

Since many examples in this chapter involve formula values, let us recall that the formula value for a call (illustrated in the previous chapter) is: market price of the stock minus strike price of the option. The formula value of a put is exactly the opposite; that is: formula value equals strike price of the put minus market price of the stock. So, the formula value on each of the IBM 150 calls is $5 a share ($155 − $150), while the formula value on each of the IBM 160 puts is also $5 a share ($160 − $155).

Buyers and Sellers

Put and call options help shape a portfolio's risk exposure and potential return. Options can make it more flexible by allowing investors to take many positions in different securities at relatively low cost. They also serve as a form of insurance by converting unknown and potentially huge losses into known, manageable costs.

Who Buys Options, and Why?   Option buyers tend to fall into two groups. The first group seeks higher investment returns through the leverage quality of options. We reviewed leverage in the previous chapter and can note here that it works the same way with puts and calls. The standard option contract on individual stocks involves 100 shares of the underlying security, which means you control quite a few shares with a relatively small investment. The second group of option buyers is looking for the insurance protection of options.

Some option buyers are looking for insurance protection.

The insurance aspect comes into play when an investor wishes to lock in a known price for a security. For example, suppose you bought 100 shares of IBM at $100 a share. It is now $155, and you have a $5,500 profit that you are happy with, but you feel IBM might increase further in price. Not willing to risk the loss of most of your profit, you buy the 155 April put for $562.50 ($5⅝ × 100). This move gives you about ten weeks of protection (assuming this is the first week in February); if IBM is above $155 at maturity, you discard the option as you would an expired insurance policy on your car, but if it is below $155, you can exercise the option and sell your shares at that price. Paying about $56 a week to insure the value of your stock might seem very stiff insurance, but the alternative of losing a substantial sum of money might be far less appealing.

Puts are used to protect a portfolio value.

While locking in selling prices with puts is the most common form of option insurance, you also can lock in a buying price by buying a call. This insurance could be important if you sold a stock short and have a profit that you wish to protect. In this situation the call performs the same function as does a put for a long position.

Who Sells Options, and Why?   Option sellers also tend to fall into two groups. The first group is made up of speculators who sell options for the income provided. They believe the options will expire out of the money, freeing them of the obligation to sell or buy shares at strike prices. Keep in mind it is the seller's responsibility to make good on the option, which can be very expensive. For example, suppose you sold an IBM April 150 call for $887.50 ($8⅞ × 100; see Exhibit 13.2). April's maturity now arrives and IBM is selling at $170. You have an obligation to deliver 100 shares at a price of $150, and assuming you must buy them in the market, you will lose $2,000 [($170 − $150) × 100] meeting the obligation. Your net loss would be $1,112.50 ($2,000.00 − $887.50).

The second group of option sellers consists of investors seeking additional income from shares they own. These sellers are called **covered option writers,** and their plan is to sell the options as an alternative either to selling their shares immediately or to holding them uncovered; that is, without offsetting options. Covered option writing is very popular and it will be covered in greater detail later in this chapter.

Some option sellers are covered option writers.

Contract Settlement

As an option approaches and eventually reaches its maturity, some action must be taken. There are three ways to settle a contract: reverse a position, take or make delivery of the underlying security, or receive (pay) cash.

Reverse a Position   **Reversing a position** means you take action opposite to your initial action, before the contract expires. For example, suppose you bought an option that is now considerably in the money and has a high market value. You really don't want the underlying security and are content with the profit in the option. So, you sell the option, reversing your original long position. It is likely that over 90% of all option contracts are settled in this fashion. The option, having performed its function, is eliminated from the portfolio and, perhaps, replaced with another having a longer maturity or a different strike price.

The majority of option contracts are settled by reversing positions.

Take or Make Delivery   If an option is in the money, you might wish to **take (make) delivery**. For example, you might exercise an IBM put and choose to sell your shares at the strike price; or, you might exercise a call and take delivery to the shares at the strike price. Option trading has become highly organized and very efficient. Your contract is actually with a central clearing organization called the Options Clearing Corporation (OCC), formed by the option exchanges to facilitate trading. An important function of the OCC is to simplify settlement. Without going into details, let us simply note two important implications for option traders: First, you are assured of performance on your contract; if you have a call, for example, you need not worry about another party being able to deliver 100 shares of the underlying stock when you want them. Second, as an option writer, you face the risk the OCC might call your number, so to speak, to honor your obligation before an option's maturity. To honor option holder demands, a random process of allocating performance responsibilities to writers is used. As a writer, you could be forced to sell or buy shares far ahead of the time you anticipated you would have to act, if your anticipation date was the option's maturity. Option writers must be aware of this provision in the option contract.

The OCC facilitates option trading.

Beginning option investors sometimes worry that if they fail to take action with an in-the-money option before maturity, they will lose whatever it might be worth, just as you take losses when you fail to act with stock rights. This is not true with options. If you take no action prior to maturity, your broker automatically buys or sells shares to complete the option contract. So, if you bought a call option with a strike price of $50 and then forgot about it, when the option expires, your broker will notify you that you bought 100 shares of the stock at $50. The confirmation slip will also show that you paid a commission to buy the shares. This commission could be far more than the commission to reverse a position, and if you didn't want the shares it would be foolish to let the option expire. If you trade options, you must be an alert investor.

Cash Settlement   In a **cash settlement** no underlying security is delivered; rather, you receive (or pay) cash equal to the difference between the strike price and the market price of the underlying instrument at maturity. For example, suppose you bought a call on the S&P 500 index with a strike price of 200. At maturity, the index stands at 250, giving you a 50-point profit. Since this contract requires payment at 100 times the index value, you receive a cash settlement of $5,000 ($50 × 100). Someone selling the call under the same circumstances would pay $5,000.

Cash settlement is more efficient than share delivery and is characteristic of a mature options market. It is absolutely necessary for instruments that could not possibly be delivered, such as the S&P 500 index. Actually, there is no reason why it cannot be used for individual stocks, even though delivery is possible.

Brokerage Commissions

Trading options can be very expensive if you deal in small quantities or low-priced options. Exhibit 13.3 indicates a small sample of option commissions and shows how they depend on the number of contracts involved and the market price of the option. The important point to see is not the absolute dollar amount, but, rather, the commission as a percent of funds invested. Buying one contract at a price of $0.25 a share leads to a commission of only $5.89, which seems reasonable. However, it is actually about 24% of invested funds. Keep in mind, too, that option trading may involve two transactions if the option is in the money; for example, you may reverse a position and pay another option commission, or you may take delivery and pay a stock commission. And, if you don't want the stock and eventually sell it, a third commission comes into play. Small wonder most stockbrokers are enthusiastic about option trading.

PUT AND CALL TRADING STRATEGIES

Investors use puts and calls in an almost endless variety of techniques. There are three basic approaches: naked positions, hedges, and spreads. Each is explained in the sections that follow.

EXHIBIT 13.3
Illustrative put and call
commissions of a full-
service stockbroker

	Number of Option Contracts Traded			
Option Cost/Share	**1**	**5**	**10**	**15**
$ ¼	$ 5.89(a)	$14.45	$ 27.82	$ 41.20
½	8.56	27.82	54.57	81.32
1	26.75	58.15(b)	101.12	132.31
5	26.75	88.76	150.55	209.65(c)

Commission as a percent of contract value:

(a): $\dfrac{\$5.89}{(\$0.25 \times 100 \times 1)} = \dfrac{\$5.89}{\$25.00} = 0.236\ (23.6\%)$

(b): $\dfrac{\$58.15}{(\$1.00 \times 100 \times 5)} = \dfrac{\$58.15}{\$500.00} = 0.116\ (11.6\%)$

(c): $\dfrac{\$209.65}{(\$5.00 \times 100 \times 15)} = \dfrac{\$209.65}{\$7,500.00} = 0.028\ (2.8\%)$

Naked Positions

While it sounds exciting, a **naked position** is nothing more than owning or writing a put or call without having an offsetting position in another security. Naked positions are generally the riskiest of all positions, particularly to put and call sellers, although buyers face risks as well.

Naked positions usually involve the greatest amount of risk.

Calls: Buyer's and Seller's Perspectives   Exhibit 13.4 illustrates a profit-loss graph with a call from the perspective of both the buyer and the seller. The amounts shown are based on the formula value of an option, which implies we are looking at the situation at the option's maturity. It is assumed the call is traded at a price of $600 and has a strike price of $50.

From the buyer's perspective, the most he can lose is $600; he will lose this much if the price of the underlying stock at maturity is $50 or less. As the price of the stock increases above $50, he begins to earn a contribution to profit. At a price of $56, he breaks even, the profit on the option being just enough to offset its cost. At prices greater than $56, positive trading profit appears. At $70, for example, he makes a profit of $1,400.

The seller's perspective is directly opposite to that of the buyer. She earns her maximum profit whenever the stock's market price is less than the strike price. As the market price increases, her profit diminishes: she also breaks even at $56 and begins taking losses for prices beyond that figure. At $70, her loss is $1,400. As you examine the graph, you should see that the seller has a great deal to lose if the stock's price increases dramatically. Many writers deal with this problem by setting maximum loss limits and immediately reversing a position whenever the maximum is reached.

Buyers' and sellers' profit positions are directly opposite.

EXHIBIT 13.4
Profit-loss graph: Naked
position in a call

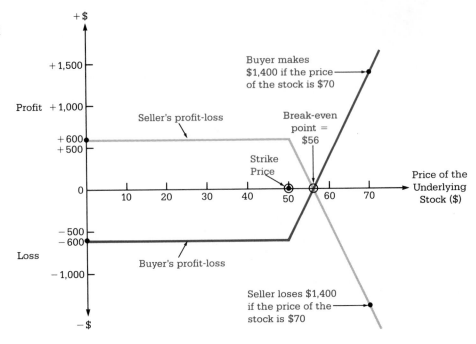

Puts: Buyer's-Seller's Perspectives   A put option has identical implications to
the call option. Now, however, the buyer's profit increases as the price of the
stock falls, while the seller's profit decreases. Exhibit 13.5 illustrates the profit-loss
graph for a put. Again, the most the buyer can lose is $600, while the seller's
losses can be much greater.

Hedge Positions

A **hedge** is usually viewed as taking two positions simultaneously in two different
assets in order to reduce risk. We discussed earlier in this chapter how options

*Insurance is a form of
hedge.*

serve as insurance. Insurance is a hedge in the sense that it will reduce your
portfolio's return by the cost of the insurance, but it simultaneously reduces risk.
If you own a house or a car, you can look at the asset itself and the insurance
policy covering it as a combination of assets; not insuring would be cheaper, but
riskier. So it is with stock ownership, and Exhibit 13.6 illustrates changes in your
net worth that would result from straight ownership (the solid line) or the
combination of stock plus the put option (the dashed line). The put illustrated is
the same one shown in Exhibit 13.5. As you see, with the put, your net worth will
never go lower than the cost of the put ($4,400), while straight ownership of the
stock could lead to a zero net worth.

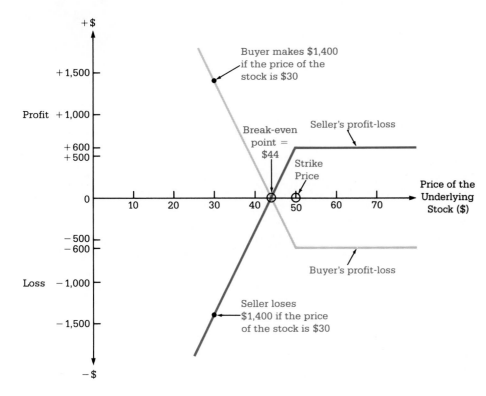

EXHIBIT 13.5
Profit-loss graph: Naked
position in a put

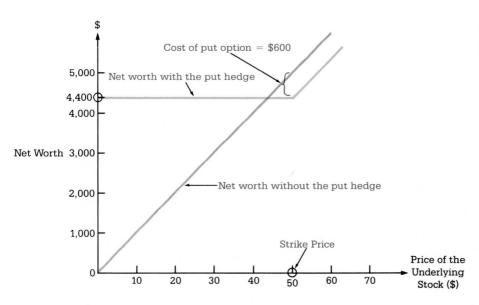

EXHIBIT 13.6
Illustration of a put
hedge to ensure a
minimum net worth

Synthetic Fabrics, Synthetic Fuels, and Now, Synthetic Stocks

If your tastes run towards the "real thing," you aren't going to like a synthetic stock, but here it is. How do you get the imitation? First, find the stock you are thinking of buying and see if options are traded on it. If they are, *buy* a call and *sell* a put. Presto—instant stock!

Put and call options give their buyers rights to buy or sell stocks at set prices over set periods of time. If you own a call, you have a right to buy the stock, while a put gives you the right to sell it. To create the synthetic, you buy the call, which gives you any price appreciation the stock makes above the call price. Obviously, that's also what you get when you own the stock. When you sell the put, you must make good to its buyer any price depreciation below the put price. You lose on this end, which is also what happens when the

stock falls in price. As you see, there's no difference between holding the stock and the synthetic creation, as far as price changes are concerned. That being the case, why not own the stock outright and save time and effort—*and* commissions? Because there are times when owning the synthetic is cheaper than owning the stock.

The accompanying table illustrates a synthetic stock based on the prices of Digital Equipment in early June, 1989. Digital closed on June 7 at $93.875 a share. To create the synthetic, you should look for options with strike prices about the same as the price of the stock, and you need an appropriate account with a broker and sufficient equity to support the shorted put. Assuming you deposited $9,387.50 worth of Treasury bonds, which yielded about 8.3% at the time, you would

have earned interest of the amounts shown in the table. On the same day, put and call options closed at the prices shown. Three commissions will apply: one to open each position and another to close one of the two. (One of the options must close in the money, and the assumption is you would buy it back before its maturity. The other option expires out of the money.)

Everything now considered, the July synthetic provides a $62 advantage over owning the stock outright ($552 annualized; you would repeat the deal every 41 days). The October synthetic has a $4 advantage ($11 annualized).

While this example appears moderately attractive for the July options, other factors must be considered. If the stock pays a dividend, the synthetic may be less desirable. For that rea-

Spreads

Spreads are similar to hedges, but usually involve more risk.

Spreads are similar to hedges insofar as several positions are taken in different securities, but they differ in that their intent is to earn profit rather than to simply reduce risk. Spreads are generally less risky than naked positions, and consequently, have less profit potential. Put and call traders devise many spread situations involving different maturities or different strike prices. (Our discussion does not distinguish between spreads, straddles, and other names used to identify different situations.) What they hope to create is a very low-risk profit opportunity. Let us consider a number of examples.

son, non- or low-paying stocks like Digital are often selected. Also, you might have to deliver shares on the put if your number is called by the option clearing house, which adds another commission cost. To lower this probability, you should close positions before the options mature. But doing so also increases the annual cost by increasing the number of deals you need to transact in a year. To reduce this cost, it is helpful to have maturities as long as possible, which also saves annual commission costs.

Is creating a synthetic worth it? Perhaps, if you have a lot of time to watch for option prices that enhance the deal—high put price and low call price—and if you can reduce commissions through a discounter or by trading in larger volumes. Otherwise, you are probably better off directly in the stock.

Finally, some investors like to tip the numbers in their favor by selling a put at a strike price above the strike price of the call—say, a $100 price for the put in the Digital example. The reasoning here is the stock's price is expected to increase and the put will be out of the money at the option's maturity. For example, the Digital July put

at $100 had a price of $638. Selling it increases income by $300. Naturally, this sweetens the deal, but is the stock price likely to increase 6⅛ points in 41 days? You are expecting a lot if you think so. At any rate, the difference in strike prices creates an instrument that is not a "pure" synthetic—for better or worse.

Cost of Creating a Synthetic Digital Equipment Stock

	July Maturities		October Maturities	
	Price	Amount	Price	Amount
Buy a call (strike price = ($95)	2⅞	(288)	6⅝	(663)
Sell a put (strike price = $95)	3⅜	338	4¾	475
Estimated commissions		(75)		(90)
Estimated interest earned		87		282
Net advantage		$ 62		$ 4
Net advantage annualized		$552		$11

A Maturity Spread   Suppose you see a call with a three-month maturity selling for $200. You also see another call with a six-month maturity selling for $400. Assume each has a strike price of $40 a share, and the current market price of the stock is also $40 a share. So, you think: "Why not short-sell the longer maturity and use the money to buy two of the shorter maturities? If the price of the stock jumps, I should earn about twice as much on my long position as I will lose on my short position. Even a little additional gain is worth it, since I have virtually no investment in the deal." This is an example of a **maturity spread,** which involves offsetting positions in options with the same strike price but with different

A maturity spread involves offsetting positions in options with different maturities.

maturities. It sounds good, and on rare occasions you might actually find a price structure, such as in this example, that makes maturity spreading attractive. There is risk in this spread, though. Suppose the stock's price fell and the two shorter maturity calls expire worthless. You still hold—now, naked—the short position in the longer maturity. You probably would reverse this position, but that involves a cost and means you lose on the hedge. Then, too, don't forget commissions that must be paid on each transaction.

A Neutral Spread   Suppose you are neither bullish nor bearish about a particular stock. In fact, you think its price will be flat over the near term. Given such a feeling, you might consider selling a **neutral spread**. This means you sell both a put and a call on the same stock at the same strike price and with the same maturity. Exhibit 13.7 illustrates a profit-loss graph for such a spread involving a put and a call with strike prices of $50 for each.

A neutral spread reflects a flat view of the market.

If the stock's price at maturity is exactly $50, each option expires worthless and you are free to pocket the amount received from selling the two—assumed to be $500 each, or $1,000 in total. Now, if the stock's price is higher or lower than $50, one of the options will be in the money and the other will be worthless. You will earn some profit on this spread for all stock prices between $40 and $60, which are the two break-even prices. If price exceeds $60 or goes below $40, you will suffer losses, as shown in Exhibit 13.7. At a price of $70, for example, the call will be worth $2,000, which offsets the $1,000 you received from selling both options, leaving you with a $1,000 loss.

A Volatile Spread   If you reverse the assumption of a neutral spread and assume instead that a stock's price will move dramatically either up or down,

EXHIBIT 13.7
Profit-loss graph for a neutral spread

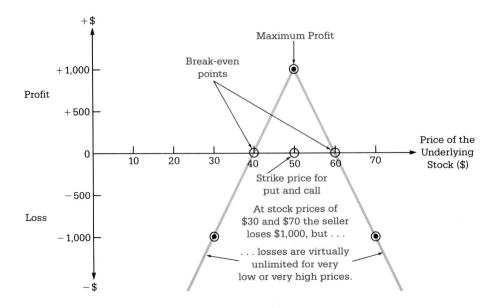

then you *buy* both the put and the call rather than selling them. The profit-loss graph for this spread would be the exact opposite of the one shown in Exhibit 13.7. You show losses where the neutral spreader shows profits, and vice versa. A **volatile spread** might be appropriate for a stock that has been the subject of takeover rumors and has run up in price. If one of the rumors proves correct, its price might jump still higher; if all the rumors are false, prices might fall sharply.

A volatile spread assumes the market will make an important move—either up or down.

Bull and Bear Spreads   A **bull or bear spread** assumes you have definite feelings about the future price of a stock, but your feelings are not strong enough to take naked positions. For example, you might feel reasonably sure a stock will make a move but that it has a better chance of increasing in price than decreasing. In this situation, a spreader might buy two calls and one put. This is a bull spread, and it is illustrated with the profit-loss graph shown in Exhibit 13.8. As you might guess, a bear spread might consist of buying two puts and one call. You can reinforce your understanding of a profit-loss graph by constructing one for this bear spread.

A bull spreader might buy two calls and one put; a bear spreader buys two puts and one call.

Arbitrage Opportunities

An **arbitrage** is usually understood as taking offsetting positions in an investment situation in an attempt to exploit unusual price disparities without

An arbitrage is an attempt to exploit price disparities to earn a profit with little or no risk.

EXHIBIT 13.8
A bull spread: Buy two calls and one put

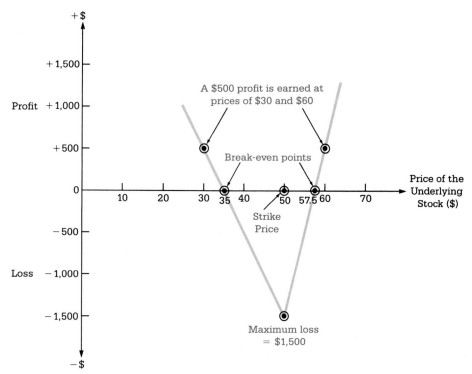

Arbitrageurs, Program Trading, and Ivan Boesky

What do arbitrageurs, program trading, and Ivan Boesky have in common? They all deal with risk and each is misunderstood. Webster's defines an arbitrager (*arbitrageur* is French and sounds classier) as someone who buys in one market for immediate resale in another at a higher price. By doing this, arbitrageurs keep markets efficient. For example, if the price of GM's stock is $70 a share in California and $68 in New York, they will sell in California and buy in New York. As a result, GM's price will very quickly move to one value in both markets. As you see, arbitrageurs take no risks—their profits are assured before they trade.

Program trading became popular with the development of options and futures contracts on market indexes. These contracts allow investors to place bets on the future price direction of an entire index of stocks, such as the S&P 500. Theoretically, the market value of these contracts should correlate very closely to the market values of the stocks in the index. As a practical matter, though, they sometimes don't. Enter the arbitrageurs who buy in one market (say, options or futures) and sell in another (say, the underlying stocks; of course, you could reverse the process just as easily). If price disparities are huge, the arbitrageurs profit considerably without taking much risk. However, disparities are generally quite small, and so are the arbitrage profits. Are markets made more efficient by these activities? You would think so, but program trading has been criticized by those who allege that it enhances price volatility and abuses the little investor who lacks the megabucks to be a program trader. The SEC is reviewing the matter and some rules governing program trading might be in the offing.

What does Ivan Boesky have to do with risk? You might recall that Boesky was described in the press some years ago as an arbitrageur. His activities led him into trouble with the SEC and he eventually agreed to pay a $100 million fine for using inside information that reportedly earned him over $300 million. Of course, having information before anyone else is the ideal way to reduce risk and make big profits at the same time, which gives a whole new meaning to the word arbitrage. Maybe Webster's needs to expand the definition. Or, it might be better to call Boesky something other than an arbitrageur.

taking risk. At the beginning of Chapter 12, we noted that options must sell at prices equal to or greater than their formula values, or potential arbitrage profits arise. Another example of an arbitrage profit might involve a maturity spread, as discussed previously in this chapter. Suppose the price of an April call option is $400 while a July call is $350. Clearly, this is a price disparity that can be exploited: sell the April option and buy the July. If the stock price increases, each option should increase approximately the same amount; if price decreases and both options expire worthless, you still net $50 (before commissions) with no risk.

Such opportunities are virtually nonexistent with individual securities, but index options and the securities represented by an index occasionally show such possibilities. Let us note also that the expression *arbitrage* has now been extended to include price disparities that may not offer risk-free opportunities, but do offer favorable opportunities in relation to hypothetically correct prices. Normally, these "correct" values are those derived from option pricing models, such as Black-Scholes. To illustrate with the previous example, assume the correct prices are $400 for the April call and $420 for the July. Suppose the July's actual price is $410; thus, it is undervalued and should be bought. The trader in this case arbitrages the deal by selling the April. Doing so is less risky than holding the July naked, but also has far less profit potential. Indeed, the trader anticipates profiting only to the extent that other investors eventually recognize the July underpricing and bid its price up to the "correct" value, whereupon the positions are reversed and arbitrage profits taken.

Today's dynamic trading looks for arbitrage situations in futures contracts as well as options. We will therefore return to this topic in the next chapter.

OTHER PUT AND CALL USES

As mentioned earlier, puts and calls provide many investment opportunities to investors. Covered option writing became popular as the standard option contract was developed and the organized options exchanges were created in the early 1970s. Moreover, the creation of various index options challenged investors to devise new investment strategies—and they responded. The index options became the most actively traded of all options, and program trading—a strategy that hedges between options on an index and the underlying stocks in the index—became so popular that its influence was thought to be a major force causing periodic sharp increases or decreases in the stock market.

Covered Option Writing

Covered option writing means that you sell call options against securities you own. (Short sellers can also sell puts against stocks they have shorted; however, this activity is far less popular.) The idea is to improve your investment performance by receiving income from the sale of the option. However, there are risks the covered option writer should know. These risks are best understood by looking at an example.

> Covered option writing involves selling options against securities you own.

An Example If an investor plans to hold a security in the long term but does not feel its price will increase very much in the near future, then writing a call option against it can be advantageous. This is illustrated in Exhibit 13.9. Assume you own 100 shares of IBM, currently selling at $155 a share. You regard IBM as a permanent part of your portfolio, but you do not believe its price will increase much over the next ten weeks. Since you can sell a $155 call option for $625, you see no reason not to and so earn this extra income. You face two problems, however: first, if you guess wrong about IBM's price, you must buy back the option; second, you must pay at least one commission and possibly two.

EXHIBIT 13.9

An example of covered option writing

Assumptions:
1. Investor owns 100 shares of IBM with a current price of $155.
2. A call option that expires in 10 weeks can be sold for $625; the option's strike price is $155.
3. If the option is in the money, the position is reversed.

	Closing Price of IBM ($)				
	145	**150**	**155**	**160**	**165**
Income from selling option	$ 625	$625	$625	$625	$ 625
Less commissions:					
Selling the option	27	27	27	27	27
Reversing the position	—	—	—	30	30
Less cost of option repurchased	—	—	—	600*	1200*
Net option income (loss)	$ 598	$598	$598	($ 32)	($ 632)
Gain (loss) in stock's price	(1000)	(500)	-0-	500	1000
Net gain (loss) from covered option writing	($ 402)	$ 98	$598	$468	$ 368
Net gain (loss) from holding IBM uncovered	(1000)	(500)	-0-	500	1000

*Assumes the investor pays a 20% premium above formula value to repurchase the option and reverse the position.

Exhibit 13.9 compares the alternatives of writing versus not writing the option. Since you probably would reverse your option position before maturity, we must assume you will pay more than formula value for the option. For simplicity, we assume a 20% premium above formula value is paid. The comparisons are straightforward: as you see, writing the option is to your advantage if the price of the stock is around $160 or less. At higher prices, though, you would do better owning the stock uncovered.

However, our example can be modified to assume the position is held long enough so that the option premium declines from 20%. Suppose only a 10% premium exists when the option is repurchased. Profit then increases by $50 at the $160 price and by $100 at the $165 price. In fact, covered option writers anticipate earning profit from the decay in option premium over time.

Generalizations on Covered Option Writing From the previous example, you should see that covered option writing improves investment return only under certain conditions. It does not guarantee greater returns or less risk all the time.

Covered option writing does not guarantee greater returns or less risk.

Moreover, trying to time option sales because you think you can forecast the short-run price of a stock is often a mistake. Few people can forecast this accurately.

Moreover, it could be a mistake to buy a stock if your sole intent is to write options against it. Exhibit 13.9 shows that if IBM's price falls below $150, your losses will be substantial. Meanwhile, the most you can gain is $598. If you are a risk-averse investor, you should understand that writing a covered option is a riskier strategy than owning stock uncovered.

All things considered, the best stocks to write options against are usually those that have little expected price variation and that pay high dividends. You might wish to hold these stocks for the long run and you don't expect their prices to be very volatile. Unfortunately, options on such stocks have market values less than those on volatile stocks, which lowers the net option income.

An Option-Bills Portfolio

A market index option can be used conveniently to create an **option-bills portfolio**. Such a portfolio consists of investing most of your funds in Treasury bills and a small portion in a call option on a market index. For example, suppose you have $30,000 earmarked for stock investment. However, you know stocks are risky and you could lose a substantial portion of your funds if you invested directly in them. On the other hand, you are aware of the growth potential of stocks over time and you wish to participate in that growth, if it takes place. In other words, you want to have your cake and eat it too. A possible solution: put most of the funds in Treasury bills and use a portion periodically to buy call options on the market. If the market jumps during some period, your long position in the calls will ensure that you participate in the jump. On the other hand, if the market is flat or declines, you discard the options and appreciate the wisdom of investing only a fraction of your funds in them.

In investments, you can almost never have your cake and eat it too, and an option-bills portfolio is no exception to this rule. Index options are relatively expensive, as Exhibit 13.10 shows. The index in this case is the S&P 100, which includes 100 active stocks from the S&P 500. This is by far the most popular of all

> An option-bills portfolio holds Treasury bills and call options on a market index.

Strike Price	Calls			Puts		
	June	July	August	June	July	August
300	5⅝	10	11¾	1⅞	4¾	6¼
305	2½	6⅛	6⅜	4	6¾	8½
310	15/16	4⅛	4⅜	7⅞	9⅝	10½

Closing value of the index on day of the quotes = 302.57
Market value of an option = 100 × quoted price

EXHIBIT 13.10
A sample of price quotations on the S&P 100 index (June 9, 1989)

the index options. You can see that buying about ten weeks of coverage (the August maturity) cost $637.50 ($6⅜ × 100) for the 305 call. An investor with about $30,000 to invest could have considered placing about $29,360 in T-bills and $640 in the option.

Over time, an option-bills portfolio will have less return than holding stocks outright.

Over an extended period of time, total outlays on the options will be considerable, and the net return from the option-bills portfolio is likely to be less than that from a portfolio consisting of stocks only. The strategy seems more appropriate, then, in a short-run setting where safety of principal is important but the investor feels that a market jump is imminent.

A recent innovation in an option-bills portfolio has been developed by Chase Manhattan Corporation. This company offers a series of plans that involve investing in certificates of deposit with option rights to price appreciation on the S&P 500. Essentially, investors choose to receive less interest than current market CD rates in exchange for a stake in any appreciation. For example, one plan provides a 4% yield on a three-month CD, plus the right to receive 25% of any price appreciation at the end of the three months. When the plan was offered, a conventional three-month CD paid about 5.75%. In effect, the investor gives up 1.75% yield to buy an option. Other plans offer different maturities, guaranteed rates, and sharing proportions, the last item increasing as you choose longer maturities and lower guaranteed rates. The Chase plan is clearly an advantage to small investors, since it requires a minimum investment of only $1,000 and eliminates the work and sophisticated knowledge required with self-directed plans. However, its yield may be less because Chase must build into the pricing arrangement its administrative costs and profit.

Hedging Market Risk

Index options also make it possible to **hedge market risk**. To see an application of this type of hedge, suppose you believe you can select stocks that will outperform the overall market. However, even if you are successful, you may still show investment losses if the overall market moves against you during an investment period. In a major market cycle, most stock prices tend to move in the same direction. So, a decline in the market will probably drag your stocks along with it. But if you really are capable of picking superior stocks, their price declines should be less than the overall market's, just as you would expect them to increase more rapidly than the market in an upswing.

Hedging market risk typically involves buying puts on a market index.

Since you cannot control the market, your strategy is to hedge it by buying an index put. If the market does poorly, the put should increase in value to partially offset some of the losses you might take on your stocks. If the market does well, you discard the put and enjoy the superior returns on your stocks. In either case, the return you realize should be as good as—or better than—the return if you simply invested in the stocks alone. This put hedge is illustrated in Exhibit 13.11. The example assumes you can always do twice as well as the market. If it declines by 10% your stocks will fall only 5%; and if it increases 10%, your stocks will jump 20%. The three assumed changes in the market show how

	$20,000 Invested in:	
	Stocks Alone	Stocks Hedged
Market Declines 10%		
Change in portfolio (−5%)	$−1,000	$−1,000
Change in put's value (+10%)	—	+2,000
Cost of the put	—	− 750
Profit or loss	$−1,000	$+ 250
Market Declines 2%		
Change in portfolio (−1%)	$− 200	$− 200
Change in put's value	—	+ 400
Cost of the put	—	− 750
Profit or loss	$− 200	$− 550
Market Increases 10%		
Change in portfolio (+20%)	$+4,000	$+4,000
Change in put's value	—	—
Cost of the put	—	− 750
Profit or loss	$+4,000	$+3,250

EXHIBIT 13.11
Example of a market risk hedge

this hedge affects portfolio returns. It is true that you will have positive profits *before* considering the cost of the option. However, when this cost is considered, minor changes in the market will lead to insufficient changes in your stocks to cover the option cost. In such a situation, you would have been better off simply holding the stocks unhedged.

SUMMARY

A put or call option provides its holder with a right to sell or buy an underlying asset at a given price over a given period of time. Anyone—including individual investors—can both buy and sell such options. Option buyers try either to increase a portfolio's return or to lower its risk. Option sellers are seeking speculative profits or additional income through covered option writing. Buyers and sellers must settle option contracts by reversing their positions, taking or making delivery of underlying shares, or transferring cash. They must be aware of commissions in determining option strategies.

These strategies include naked positions, hedge positions, spreads, and arbitrage positions. Naked positions offer the most profit potential but also are the riskiest; hedges are designed primarily to reduce risk; spreads have a variety of risk and return opportunities; and arbitrage positions exploit temporary price disparities.

Covered option writing is a popular practice that involves selling call options on stocks an investor owns. The intent is to earn option income that exceeds possible price appreciation of the underlying security while the option is held. An option-bills portfolio holds market index call options along with Treasury bills as an alternative to holding stocks. Index options are used to hedge market risk. In this activity, an investor buys securities he or she thinks will outperform the market and hedges against an adverse movement of the market by purchasing a market index put. The put reduces risk but also reduces potential profit.

KEY TERMS

Select the alternative that best identifies the key term.

1. call option
2. put option
3. covered option writers
4. reversing a position
5. take (make) delivery
6. cash settlement
7. naked position
8. hedge
9. spreads
10. maturity spread
11. neutral spread
12. volatile spread
13. bull or bear spread
14. arbitrage
15. option-bills portfolio
16. hedge market risk

a. assumes a stock's price will either increase or decrease
b. owning an option outright
c. allows you to buy an underlying security
d. you want to participate in market advances but not suffer losses in market declines
e. settle by using transfers of the underlying security
f. assumes prices will be flat
g. allows you to sell an underlying security
h. based on the assumption you can outperform the market
i. similar to hedges, except they attempt to earn a profit
j. sells calls while owning the stock
k. a weak belief a stock's price will increase or a weak belief it will decrease
l. buying back an option
m. necessary when it is impossible to deliver an underlying security
n. taking offsetting positions simultaneously
o. earns a profit by exploiting temporary price disparities
p. offsetting positions in options with the same strike price but with different maturities

REVIEW QUESTIONS

1. How does a put differ from a call? What types of underlying securities do puts and calls cover, and how are they traded?
2. Discuss two different groups of put and call buyers and sellers.
3. Explain how put options can be used as portfolio insurance.
4. Explain three different methods of settling an option contract. Discuss if you must take action or run the risk of suffering losses when an in-the-money contract expires.

5. What is a naked position? Who has the greater risk—buyer or seller—in such a position? Discuss your answer.
6. What is a hedge position and what is its primary intention?
7. What is a spread and what is its primary intention? Briefly explain the following spreads: (a) maturity, (b) neutral, (c) volatile, (d) bull, and (e) bear.
8. What is an arbitrage position? Give several examples of arbitrage opportunities with options.
9. How is covered option writing accomplished, and what is its primary purpose?
10. Explain generalizations that seem appropriate to covered option writing. Explain whether risk-averse investors should engage in this activity.
11. Discuss how an option-bills portfolio works and when it may be an appropriate investment strategy.
12. How can you use an index option to hedge market risk? When should you consider using such a hedge, and is it true that this hedge can assure a profit regardless of changes in the stock market? Explain.

PROBLEMS AND PROJECTS

1. Interpret the put and call quotations below, indicating which set is associated with each type of option.

NCR	Strike Price	Dec.	Mar.	Jun.
52⅛	45	7¾	9⅛	10¼
	50	2⅞	4⅜	6¼
	55	⅞	1¾	2½
52⅛	45	¼	⅞	1⅜
	50	1⅛	2⅛	3¼
	55	3¼	5⅛	6⅞

2. Referring to problem 1 above, determine your brokerage commission if you bought a December 45 put (one contract); then, explain whether you think this commission is reasonable or expensive.
3. Referring to problem 1 above, construct a profit-loss graph for the June 50 call from both the buyer's and seller's perspective (naked positions). What is the profit or loss for each for stock prices of $40, $45, $50, $55, and $60? What is the break-even price?
4. Referring to problem 1 above, construct a profit-loss graph for the June 50 put. Respond to the same questions asked in problem 3.
5. Referring to problem 1 above, construct profit-loss graphs for the following strategies: (a) a neutral spread—June maturity, 50 strike, (b) a volatile spread—June maturity, 50 strike, (c) a bull spread—June maturity, 55 strike, and (d) a bear spread—June maturity, 55 strike. Find breakeven points.
6. Do you see any arbitrage profits in the data of problem 1? Discuss. Change one of the prices to create an arbitrage opportunity.
7. Referring to problem 1 above, suppose you own 100 shares of the stock in question and plan to keep it in your portfolio. However, you are concerned the price of the stock might fall. Explain how you can "insure" against potential losses, using an appropriate option (use a 55 strike price and June maturity). Show your response graphically.

8. Referring to problem 1 above, suppose you own 100 shares of the stock in question and plan to keep it in your portfolio. However, you are considering writing a call option against it. Assuming you write the June 50 and pay a $30 commission for each option transaction, evaluate the decision to write the option. Assume stock prices of $40, $45, $50, $55, and $60 and a 20% premium above formula value if the option is repurchased.

9. (*Student Project*)   Evaluate your skill in making profits from daily forecasts of the stock market. Each day, forecast the market and then buy 10 appropriate options on the S&P 100. Assume you reverse your position at the end of the day. Do this daily for 10 days, recording your gain or loss each day. Also, charge commissions of $150 on each transaction. Report your trading performance at the end of the period.

CASE ANALYSES

13.1
The Hendersons Hedge Their Retirement Fund

The Hendersons, Robert and Angela, are nearing retirement. Bob will leave his employer in a year and they will move to St. Petersburg, Florida. Bob has about $400,000 in a retirement plan where he works, and the funds currently are invested in a broad portfolio of common stocks. The plan is a so-called money purchase plan (also called a defined contribution plan); it allows Bob the flexibility of deciding how his funds should be invested, such as in a stock fund, bond fund, or money market fund.

The stock market crash of October 19, 1987, has scared the Hendersons enormously. They shudder to think how their retirement nest egg could be depleted by a prolonged bear market. On the other hand, another robust year could add substantially to their retirement funds. Angela thinks the prudent course of action is simply to transfer all amounts to the money market fund. While Bob basically shares this view, he wonders whether other courses of action might be available. For example, he has read how some investors use options as insurance protection. The Hendersons are in a quandary and have asked your advice. The S&P 100 is now at 302.5.

Questions

a. Explain how an option-bills portfolio might work in the Hendersons' case. You can assume that Bob would transfer his retirement funds into a money market fund and that he would trade options on his own.

b. Refer to the option quotations in Exhibit 13.10 and assume they would be representative of the situation facing the Hendersons for the upcoming year. Assume the August contract has 10 weeks before maturity. Determine the number of contracts needed and the cost of engaging in an option-bills portfolio, assuming the 305 strike was selected. Then, determine the net cost assuming the money market fund earns 8% for the year.

c. Suppose the Hendersons decided to leave their funds invested in the stock fund, but to hedge the situation they will buy puts on the S&P 100. Assuming the August 305s are selected, how much will this insurance cost the Hendersons for the year? Assume the stock fund pays a 3% dividend and correlates closely with the S&P 100 with respect to price changes.

d. Considering each approach, make a recommendation to the Hendersons. Do you believe either plan is appropriate, or would they be better off putting the $400,000 in the money market fund? To answer this question, you should assume different possible outcomes for the market over a ten-week period, such as: down 4%, down 2%, unchanged, up 2%, up 4%, and up 6%.

13.2 Rachel Elliot Considers a Market Risk Hedge

Rachel Elliot seems to have a unique skill at finding undervalued stocks. Her picks always seem to beat the market on a risk-adjusted basis but she always seems to find them when the market heads south. Unfortunately, investment patience is not one of Rachel's better traits, so she usually sells before the market recovers and takes losses in the process. Rachel has done well in bull markets but she is looking for a way to improve her performance in bear markets.

An examination of her past trades reveals that she usually does 5 percentage points better than the overall market. So, if the market goes up 10%, Rachel's portfolio is likely to go up 15%; and if the market goes down 10%, her portfolio will go down only 5%; and she would show a 5% return if the market is unchanged. Rachel has $61,000 to invest. She is considering using a market risk hedge because she is concerned that the market may perform rather poorly in the months ahead. Rachel describes her tolerance for risk as fairly low.

Questions

a. Using the option prices shown in Exhibit 13.10 (August maturities and 305 strike price), evaluate a market risk hedge. Assume the following possibilities for the market: down 10%, unchanged, and up 10%. Also, assume the closing value of the index on the day of the quotes is 302.50.

b. Do you recommend a market risk hedge for Rachel? Explain your response.

HELPFUL READING

Angrist, Stanley W. ''Why Option Buyers Face Stacked Deck.'' *The Wall Street Journal,* August 31, 1989, p. C1.

Block, Stanley B., and Timothy J. Gallagher. ''How Much Do Bank Trust Departments Use Derivatives?'' *The Journal of Portfolio Management,* Fall 1988, pp. 12–15.

Donnelly, Barbara. ''Bank CD Offers Ways to Hedge in Stock Market.'' *The Wall Street Journal,* March 31, 1987, p. 33.

Feinstein, Steven P. ''Forecasting Stock-Market Volatility Using Options on Index Futures.'' *Economic Review,* Federal Reserve Bank of Atlanta, May/June 1989, pp. 12–30.

Greenleaf, Robert W. ''Synthetic Instruments.'' *Financial Analysts Journal,* March-April 1989, pp. 71–73.

Ritchken, Peter. *Options: Theory, Strategy, and Applications.* Glenview, IL: Scott, Foresman and Company, 1987.

Torres, Craig. ''Small Investors Help Option Volume Soar.'' *The Wall Street Journal,* June 26, 1989, p. C1.

CHAPTER FOURTEEN

Commodity and Financial Futures

CHARACTERISTICS OF FUTURES

The Futures Contract

Trading Futures

Organized Exchanges and the Clearinghouse

COMMODITY FUTURES

Speculative Trading

Hedging

Investing in Commodity Futures

FINANCIAL FUTURES

Currency Futures

Interest Rate Futures

Index Futures

BOXES

The Changing Structure of the Chicago Board of Trade

Are Spreads a Low-Risk Way to Play the Market?

After you finish this chapter, you will be able to:

- understand the characteristics of futures contracts and how to read commodity futures quotations.
- identify important aspects of trading futures contracts, including the use of margin and selecting a broker.
- see the uses of commodity futures and distinguish among trading strategies that are speculative, hedging, or investment-oriented.
- appreciate that speculative trading involves substantial risks and is seldom conducted profitably by either amateurs or professionals.
- evaluate the uses of financial futures in speculative, hedging, or investment applications.
- understand quotations of financial futures, with particular emphasis on Treasury bond and bills futures quotations.

L ike options, commodity and financial futures can make investment portfolios more flexible by broadening the array of assets from which to choose and by providing new opportunities for managing risk. Although futures have a long history in the United States, going back to the early part of the nineteenth century, many investors ignored them until very recently. Looking for ways to hedge inflation and to deal with volatile interest rates, investors turned their attention to the futures markets in the 1970s. What they found was a remarkably efficient and sophisticated trading system, very similar to the more familiar stock and bond markets. With the inflation rate subsiding considerably by the mid-1980s, some of the appeal of futures was gone, and so were many of the trend-following investors. A few were wealthier, but the majority probably paid their dues to learn that futures trading is not for the novice investor unwilling to learn its fundamentals or appreciate its risks. This chapter attempts to explain each.

CHARACTERISTICS OF FUTURES

Investing in futures is, in a sense, investing in the future. Suppose your business is milling wheat, corn, and other grains into flour. You need a constant supply of these grains to continue operating and, since you are a prudent person, you are concerned about their future availability and future price. Without a **futures market**—a market where futures contracts are traded—all you could do is worry about the future. You must buy the grains in the **cash market** (a market where the actual commodity is traded; a grain elevator, for example) when the need arises and pay the prevailing prices. However, a futures market allows you to negotiate for the future delivery of the needed grains.

A futures market allows you to negotiate for future deliveries of commodities.

Now, suppose you entered into an agreement in January for deliveries in April, but when April arrives you find there is an ample supply of grains available for purchase at lower prices than those negotiated. Can you simply discard your agreement, as you would an option that expires valueless? The answer is an emphatic no, and that is the major difference between owning an option and entering into a futures contract: An option is a right, not an obligation; a futures contract is an obligation to perform. You buy an option, but you do not buy a futures contract. If you buy an option, your potential losses are known and limited; if you take a naked position in a futures contract, your potential losses are virtually unknown and unlimited. Understanding a futures contract is essential before you consider trading futures.

The Futures Contract

A **commodity futures contract** involves the future delivery of a commodity or financial instrument. It has specific terms and conditions that must be met.

Contract Specifications   A futures contract must specify clearly the rights and obligations given each party to the contract. The following provisions are important:

☐ The commodity must be defined precisely in terms of quality, purity, weight, or any other characteristic that might influence market value.
☐ The time and place of delivery must be certain.
☐ The quantity of the commodity or amount of the financial instrument must be indicated.
☐ The price at which delivery will take place must be established.

The flour miller in our previous example would be concerned with each of the above provisions, because he or she would probably intend to actually take delivery to the grains per the conditions of the contract. However, that would be a very rare occurrence, since the overwhelming majority of contracts never involve delivery.

As in the case of options, most futures contracts are closed by reversing a position. This procedure is used even more often with futures trading, where it is estimated at least 97% of all positions are reversed. Even the miller who needs the grains often will find it more convenient to buy them in the cash markets rather than by a futures contract delivery. The contract served its function during the uncertain period, and when it is over, it can be eliminated through reversal.

> Most futures contracts are closed through position reversal.

Reading a Futures Quotation   Exhibit 14.1 shows a typical commodity quotation. Commodity quotes can be found in the financial pages of many newspapers, although they are not reported as extensively as stocks, bonds, and options. *The Wall Street Journal* and *New York Times* have comprehensive daily listings, and *Barron's* has one each week.

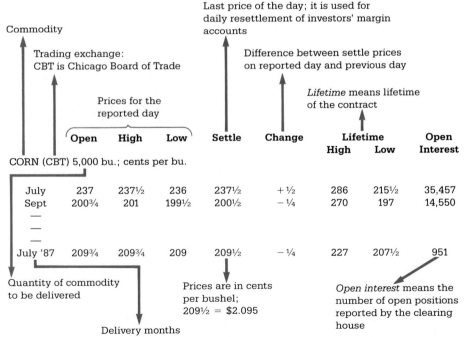

EXHIBIT 14.1
Explanation of a typical commodity futures quotation

The commodity illustrated is corn, and while Exhibit 14.1 is self-explanatory, it is important to realize that the total value of a contract is not reported. To determine total value, simply multiply the contract quantity—in this case, 5,000 bushels—by the settle price. For example, the July contract closed at $2.375 a bushel; multiplying this by 5,000 gives a total market value of $11,875. This figure is sometimes called your **money at risk**. If you traded one July contract, you should look at your investment—your money at risk—as $11,875, regardless of how much, or little, of your own funds were used to trade the contract. As you see, one contract involves a substantial sum of money.

A long position accepts delivery: it is called a "buy."

Buyer—A Long Position   As we mentioned earlier, you do not actually buy a contract, although the terms *buy* and *buyer* are often used. A buyer takes a long position, which means he or she will *accept* delivery of the commodity according to the contract provisions. Since buyers accept delivery at the established contract price, they are of the opinion that the actual price in the cash market at the time of delivery will be higher. If true, they could exercise their right to buy at the lower contract price and immediately sell the commodity at the higher market price to earn a profit. Viewed more simply, buyers expect the commodity's price to increase in the future. If it does, the value of the futures contract—like the value of a call option—will increase right along with it, as Exhibit 14.2 indicates. The buyer probably has no intention of holding the contract to maturity and may reverse his or her position at a profit (or loss) five minutes after it is opened.

A short position makes delivery: it is called a "sell."

Seller—A Short Position   A "seller" (again, a misnomer) agrees to make delivery of the commodity. Clearly, the seller expects the price of the commodity to fall in the future, in which case the commodity could be purchased at the lower cash market price for a quick profit. Very few sellers will hold contracts on the settlement day; they, like buyers, will reverse their positions. As with put and call options, one investor's profit is another's loss, as Exhibit 14.2 shows. Keep in mind, though, with a futures contract the buyer's potential losses are virtually unlimited, whereas, for the buyer of an option, the maximum loss is the cost of the option.

One helpful way to view a futures contract is to visualize it as a wager between two investors about a future price of the commodity. One bets it will increase while the other bets it will decrease. The loser then pays the winner the contract quantity times the difference between the contract price and the actual market price at the end of the trading period, which is every day (as we will see shortly).

Trading Futures

Trading futures is relatively easy to do. All you need are sufficient funds and a commodity account with a broker. Trading is very similar to stock trading, with the same orders—market, limit, and stop-loss—and margin being used.

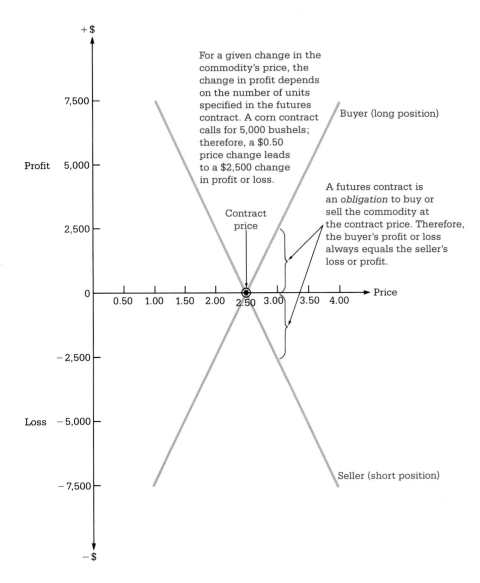

For a given change in the commodity's price, the change in profit depends on the number of units specified in the futures contract. A corn contract calls for 5,000 bushels; therefore, a $0.50 price change leads to a $2,500 change in profit or loss.

Buyer (long position)

A futures contract is an *obligation* to buy or sell the commodity at the contract price. Therefore, the buyer's profit or loss always equals the seller's loss or profit.

Contract price

Seller (short position)

EXHIBIT 14.2
Profit-loss graph for a corn futures contract

Opening an Account Because futures are inherently very risky, most brokers require that you meet certain net worth or income requirements before you can open a commodity trading account. Assuming you meet these requirements, most brokers then require an initial deposit (margin) that must be maintained as long as the account is open. This deposit varies among brokers, but is usually $5,000 or more. Keep in mind this is an idle, nonproductive investment. Many brokers will allow the deposit of Treasury bills, but they may then insist on a larger deposit, say, $10,000.

In addition to the initial deposit, each contract you trade has its own margin requirements. For example, a corn contract has an initial margin requirement of $1,000, which is quite low in relation to the contract's total value. Small margin requirements are characteristic of all futures contracts, as Exhibit 14.3 indicates. Along with the initial margin requirement, brokers impose their own maintenance margin requirements. In the case of corn, this requirement might be set at $750. If you took a position in corn with the minimum margin of $1,000, and price moved against you by only five cents ($250/5,000) a bushel, you would get a margin call. Since margins are often slim in futures trading, margin calls are frequent. If you can't make the call, your broker will immediately close the position with you taking the loss. [Exhibit 14.3]

It should be noted also, as a point of information, that margin in futures trading is not actually margin in the sense that it represents your equity in the purchase of an asset; as we have seen, you do not buy or sell an asset. Margin in futures trading is more in the nature of a performance bond: if you do not live up to the terms of the futures contract, your broker is free to use the funds in settlement of any deficiency. The term *margin,* though, is used extensively in futures trading and most investors view it no differently than they view margin to trade stocks or other securities.

Selecting a Broker   Full-service stockbrokers also provide commodity brokerage services. You probably will deal with the same representative who handles your other securities. Commissions with full-service brokers vary, but are in the neighborhood of $80 a ''round turn.'' This means you pay one commission to open and close a position. Some brokerage firms specialize in commodity trading, and these firms often discount commissions, with charges of $40 a round turn being fairly common. To attract you as a customer, many of the discounters will offer very low commissions for a limited period of time or for a limited number of orders.

EXHIBIT 14.3

Illustrative futures contracts and initial margin requirements

Commodity or Financial Instrument	Initial Margin
Cocoa	$1,000
Corn	1,000
Cotton	1,000
Gold	3,500
Live cattle	1,500
Lumber	1,200
Japanese yen	1,800
Pork bellies	1,500
Soybeans	1,500
S&P 500 stock index	7,500
Treasury bills	2,500

Futures margins are slim, and margin calls are common.

Of course, each broker claims to be the best or the most economical, or to offer some other advantage. The full-service (expensive) brokers usually provide research reports on various commodities, which are supposed to improve your trading profits. Whether they do or not can be argued, but any broker worth dealing with should explain very carefully the risks of futures trading. For every one successful trader who made a fortune starting with a shoestring, there are probably nine failures. Often, a failure is a sad story of someone who trades a few contracts successfully and thinks he or she cannot lose. But losses come quickly and heavily in this market segment and absolutely no one is perfect, or even very good.

Investor Protection   Commodity trading is regulated to some degree, although your protections are not as strong as with stocks and bonds. The Commodity Exchange Authority (CEA), a division of the Department of Agriculture, is responsible for enforcing federal regulations that pertain to commodity transactions and commodity exchanges. These regulations, though, have more to do with establishing uniform trading standards than with protecting investors.

> Investor protections are not strong in commodity trading.

In 1974, Congress created the Commodity Futures Trading Commission (CFTC), which was intended to be a regulatory commission, enforcing federal laws in the futures and options markets. It has come under fire in recent years for failing to prevent abusive practices to some investors. In 1989, the FBI made public the details of a sting operation in the commodities exchanges, which indicated some floor traders were arranging trades in a fashion that benefited them at the expense of their clients. Such illegal practices were supposed to be monitored by the CFTC. An in-depth review of the commission was ordered by the House Agriculture Committee, with the key issue being why the CFTC failed to curb trading abuses.

Organized Exchanges and the Clearinghouse

An organized futures exchange is similar to an organized stock or bond exchange. It is owned and operated (on a nonprofit basis) by its members, who hold seats on the exchange. Its primary function is to provide an arena for the orderly and efficient trading of futures contracts. The largest in the United States is the Chicago Board of Trade, but there are quite a few important other exchanges, as Exhibit 14.4 indicates.

Each exchange has a clearing system that involves a **clearinghouse**. The clearinghouse facilitates trading by eliminating the need for buyers and sellers to deal directly with each other. Instead, each deals with the clearinghouse. So, if you buy or sell a futures contract, your obligation is to the clearinghouse and you can expect contract performance from it, not from a person on the other side of the contract. The clearinghouse, in turn, must take steps to make sure each trader can meet his or her obligations. It does so through the margin requirements and through daily resettlement of accounts. This resettlement is also called **marking to market,** and it means that at the end of the trading day, each one of your

> "Marking to market" means your commodity account is updated daily for profits or losses.

EXHIBIT 14.4
Important commodity
exchanges in the U.S.
and Canada

Chicago Mercantile Exchange (CME)
Chicago Board of Trade (CBT)
International Monetary Market of the CME
Commodity Exchange, Inc.
Mid-America Commodity Exchange
Minneapolis Grain Exchange
New Orleans Commodity Exchange
Kansas City Board of Trade
New York Cotton Exchange
New York Futures Exchange (a division of the NYSE)
New York Mercantile Exchange
Winnipeg Commodity Exchange

futures positions is updated using the commodity's settlement price given for the day. For example, suppose you bought a corn contract at $2.50 in the morning and the settlement price at the end of trading was $2.55; your account would show the day's profit of $250 ($0.05 × 5,000).

You are free to withdraw this gain in cash, if you wish. However, if price moved against you, it would be necessary to deposit additional margin equal to the loss. In effect, with futures trading there is no such thing as a ''paper loss,'' or a ''paper profit,'' although many traders do not make daily withdrawals or daily deposits. (They have excess margin as a buffer.)

COMMODITY FUTURES

Commodity futures have been in existence longer than any other futures contract. Exhibit 14.5 provides a list of the major commodities for which futures contracts are available; as you see, the list is quite extensive. Investors deal in commodity

EXHIBIT 14.5
Commodity futures
contracts available

Commodity Group	Specific Commodities
Grains and oilseeds	Corn, oats, soybeans, soybean meal, soybean oil, wheat, barley, flaxseed, rapeseed, and rye
Livestock and meat	Feeder cattle, live cattle, hogs, and pork bellies (bacon)
Food and fiber	Cocoa, coffee, cotton, orange juice, world sugar, and domestic sugar
Metals and petroleum	Copper, gold, platinum, palladium, silver, crude oil, heating oil, gas oil, and NY gasoline—leaded regular and unleaded regular
Wood	Lumber

futures for reasons similar to those for using options—to either speculate or to hedge against risks inherent in production or merchandising activities that require commodities. Additionally, in recent years commodity futures have been used to protect portfolios against inflation and to reduce overall portfolio risk.

Speculative Trading

Commodity futures have considerable speculative appeal. As with options, traders can take naked positions or spreads (see Chapter 13). The extremely low margin requirements allow many people to participate in the market with relatively high risk exposure. Where else, for an initial ante of $10,000 or so, can you control $50,000 to $100,000 worth of investments? And, where else, if you guess right, can you make as much as $1,000 to $2,000 a day on your $10,000 ante—and withdraw it at the end of the day? Finally, where else can you compete on a reasonably fair footing with most other "players," who probably don't know any better than you what will be the future price of corn, or pork bellies (bacon)? The speculative appeal of commodity futures is great but there are facts you should consider before you attempt to trade.

Most Individual Speculators Lose   Studies of the trading performances of individual speculators are not encouraging. In fact, the overwhelming majority—as high as 90%—lose in futures trading and many lose very heavily. Most engage in frequent trading, opening and closing positions daily and even several times during the day. As you suspect, commissions eventually consume most of the profit of those fortunate enough to show any before commissions. Despite such frequent trading, very often speculators stay with one position that they are convinced will make a big profit. More often than not, price moves against them, and their losses become enormous and eventually wipe out their margin balances.

The beginning speculator should be advised also that trading based on reaction to a natural calamity is exceptionally risky. You may hear that Florida has just been hit by a cold wave, freezing the entire orange crop. Now is a good time to buy orange juice futures, since price must increase. The problem is that everyone is hearing the same news and reacting the same way. By the time you enter the market, price may have already peaked. Later, when the news indicates the cold wave really wasn't as bad as first feared, you are still holding a long position when price plummets. Before you trade on the basis of rumor or news, or for any other reason, you should take the time to first trade on paper only. Be very honest with yourself as you record trades executed, and measure your performance. Put everything in writing *before* you trade, and don't forget commissions. Do this for a while, perhaps a year or longer, and if you are not discouraged at the end of this time, then you can consider "trading for keeps."

Many Professional Traders Also Lose   Individual investors can take heart that professional traders' performances are not much better than theirs. Many

Exceptionally slim margins appeal to speculators.

Commodity speculation based on reaction to a natural calamity is very risky.

commodity pooling arrangements, such as limited partnerships, were begun in the late 1970s when interest in commodity trading heightened. Their trading performances are a matter of public record and were, for a while, reported regularly in *Barron's*. What does the record show? It is not one of overwhelming success; indeed, professionals do not perform much better than rank amateurs. There are some with exceptionally high returns, but there are many more with very low and negative returns. Many of the professional traders base their trading systems on technical analysis, which was described in Chapter 10. Trading signals based on moving averages, for example, are very popular. However, these mechanical systems apparently work no better here than they do in trading common stocks.

The record of professional commodity traders is not a successful one.

Hedging

Earlier in this chapter, we saw an example of a miller who might wish to use futures contracts to remove uncertainties from the business. Many businesses and individuals face similar risks. For example, a farmer with corn growing in the field has no choice but to have a long position in corn. Many jewelers have natural long positions in gold or silver, while a building contractor who has sold a house that is yet to be built has a natural short position in lumber. That these people wish to hedge is not surprising; indeed, you wonder why hedging doesn't always take place. Why wouldn't farmers hedge their crops at planting time? And if the futures price is not high enough to make a profit on the crop, why even bother to plant? Commodity hedging sounds simple, but there are risks to consider.

On the surface, it seems reasonable that most farmers should hedge.

Mechanics of a Hedge Suppose it is April and a farmer has just planted enough seed to harvest 10,000 bushels of corn in September. Not willing to take risks, he sees that a September corn futures is selling at $2 a bushel and he immediately sells two contracts (10,000 bushels). As the growing season moves along, suppose corn shortages appear likely because of a poor growing season and the price of corn rises to $3 a bushel by September. This is bad luck for the farmer, who now wishes he had not hedged in April. The crop is harvested and sold for $30,000, but he must then close his short position in the futures market at a loss of $10,000. His net gain from the crop is $20,000.

But suppose the price of corn fell to $1 a bushel by September. Now the crop is sold for only $10,000, but the futures contract provides an additional profit of $10,000. Again, the net gain is $20,000. As you see, the hedge locks in the price of the commodity on the futures contract; in this case, $2 a bushel. This example also illustrates a **perfect hedge,** which means any gain or loss in the cash market is offset *exactly* by loss or gain in the futures market. (Gain or loss is measured by the difference in price between when the futures position is opened and when it is closed. Gain or loss in the cash market assumes the commodity could be sold in the cash market at the time the futures position is taken. In the case of the farmer with unharvested corn, this is obviously an assumption.)

Hedging Problems   People who must use hedges often argue that hedges work better in textbooks than they do in the real world. Clearly, they think perfect hedges are seldom found. The farmer, for example, hopes to harvest 10,000 bushels, but he may not. His fields may yield more or less, which means he may have under- or over-hedged, either of which exposes him to risk. For example, suppose the yield is 5,000 bushels and corn's September price is $3 a bushel. The crop is sold for $15,000, but the loss of $10,000 on the two futures contracts reduces the net gain to only $5,000.

Perfect hedges are diffi-
cult to execute in the
real world.

   Another problem confronting short-term hedgers is a divergence of prices in the futures and cash markets. One assumes that the price of a commodity in the futures market should be almost identical to its price in the cash market. However, that may not be true because they are actually two different markets. The price of corn on a September futures contract need not be the same as the cash price of corn in April. For example, suppose the cash price for corn in April was $1.90 a bushel. Instead of a farmer growing corn, let us now assume a grain elevator operator holding 10,000 bushels in inventory. To hedge her position, she also shorted corn at $2 for September delivery. Much to her surprise, a week later she receives a big order to ship 10,000 bushels immediately to a customer. Her price—the cash market price—is $1.85 a bushel; but when she reverses her position in the futures contracts, she finds the September price has actually risen to $2.05 a bushel. Price decreased in the cash market and increased in the futures market.

   In this case, basis moved against the hedger. **Basis** is defined as the difference between the cash price and the futures price. Adverse changes in basis are common in commodity hedging, with risk being greater as the two prices are more separated in time. As a contract reaches its maturity, basis converges to zero, as Exhibit 14.6 shows. Why zero? Any positive or negative basis would set up a virtual risk-free trading opportunity: buy at the low price and immediately resell at the high one. For example, suppose that one day before the September corn contract expires, the futures price is $2 while the cash price is $1.95. You immediately sell a futures contract and at the same time call a grain elevator and buy 5,000 bushels in the cash market. You then deliver these bushels to fulfill the futures contract and pocket $250 ($0.05 × 5,000) in profit. Efficiency in the futures markets makes such opportunities almost impossible.

Adverse movements in
basis are common in
commodity hedging.

Arbitrage guarantees
that basis converges to
zero.

Investing in Commodity Futures

Investing in commodity futures represents a third general use of these instruments. Investing differs from trading or hedging in several respects. First, it implies a perpetual long position, since your intent is really to invest directly in commodities but the futures contract is used as a more efficient substitute. Second, far less leverage is used even though it is available.

Advantages   Investing a portion of your portfolio in tangible assets is considered advantageous during inflationary periods. Prices of many tangibles keep

EXHIBIT 14.6
Basis illustrated

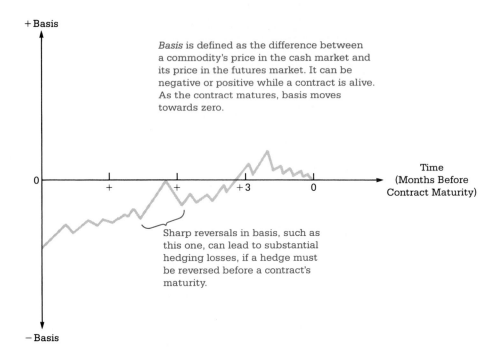

Basis is defined as the difference between a commodity's price in the cash market and its price in the futures market. It can be negative or positive while a contract is alive. As the contract matures, basis moves towards zero.

Sharp reversals in basis, such as this one, can lead to substantial hedging losses, if a hedge must be reversed before a contract's maturity.

pace with inflation. Since a long position in a futures contract allows you to own tangibles indirectly at relatively low cost, a perpetual long position may be a more attractive alternative than owning tangibles directly. Even gold and silver, which are the easiest tangibles to own, present the ownership problems of safe storage, insurance, and eventual resale.

Futures contracts allow for possible greater diversification among commodities. If you try to hedge inflation with a single commodity such as gold, you could be frustrated if gold's price is upset by other events. Excess production in the U.S.S.R. or South Africa, for example, might depress price. Moreover, diversifying among an array of actual tangibles may be impossible or undesirable. Where would you store 5,000 bushels of corn or 15,000 pounds of orange juice?

A third advantage of investing in futures is revealed by several studies that have shown their returns to be poorly correlated to returns from common stocks. Poor correlation is an advantage if you are considering holding the assets in portfolio, because it leads to lower portfolio risk. Portfolios of stocks and futures have been shown to be less risky and about as profitable (over time) as holding each separately. Thus, you can argue that an efficient portfolio should include both.

Hedging inflation with commodity futures can lead to large losses if disinflation occurs.

Disadvantages   There are problems with using commodity futures. To begin with, unless you are quite wealthy or wish to use considerable leverage, adequate diversification among an array of contracts may be difficult. Few investors could afford to have unleveraged positions in, say, ten different contracts. You would need well over $100,000, depending on the contracts chosen. The pooling arrangements mentioned earlier are helpful here but you must be sure their investment objective is inflation hedging. If it is speculating, they are unsuitable to meet your goal. Secondly, there are some costs to consider. While commissions are not high, they may be frequent if you select contracts with short maturities; and, of course, if your initial margin is not in the form of Treasury bills, you forego interest that could be earned elsewhere.

Perhaps the biggest disadvantage in hedging inflation is that most investors are not prepared to take the losses that must come if disinflation occurs, as it did beginning in the early 1980s. Most commodity prices fell sharply, leading to substantial losses for holders of long positions. You might argue that the inflation hedge worked exactly as it should have—stock and bond prices increased while commodity prices decreased—but few investors were prepared to take such losses. What they actually wanted was inflation protection *and* stock price appreciation *and* high interest rates on their bonds. What they wanted was impossible, or at least very unlikely to happen. An attempt to have all three requires buying options, not futures contracts. But, as we saw in the previous chapter, this is tantamount to buying insurance and paying the heavy premiums.

FINANCIAL FUTURES

Financial futures are identical to commodity futures in most respects, except the underlying asset is an intangible, financial asset rather than a tangible commodity. While currency futures have been in existence for some time, interest rate futures first made their appearance in late 1975, and index futures were not available until 1982. Today, financial futures are as popular and as widely used as commodity futures, and Exhibit 14.7 shows a partial listing of contracts available.

Currency Futures

A **currency futures contract** calls for delivery of a specified number of units of a given currency: pounds, francs, yen, and others. Exhibit 14.8 illustrates a

Financial Group	Specific Financial Instruments
Currencies	British pround, Canadian dollar, Japanese yen, Swiss franc, W. German mark, and U.S. dollar index
Interest-Rate Securities	Eurodollars, Treasury bonds, Treasury bills, Treasury notes, GNMA passthroughs, bank CDs, and stripped Treasuries
Indexes	Municipal bond index, S&P 500 index, NYSE composite index, KC Value Line index, major market index, and the CRB index

EXHIBIT 14.7
Financial futures contracts available

EXHIBIT 14.8

Explanation of a typical currency futures quotation (See Exhibit 14.1 for previously explained items.)

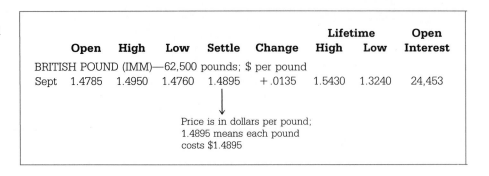

	Open	High	Low	Settle	Change	Lifetime High	Low	Open Interest
BRITISH POUND (IMM)—62,500 pounds; $ per pound								
Sept	1.4785	1.4950	1.4760	1.4895	+.0135	1.5430	1.3240	24,453

Price is in dollars per pound;
1.4895 means each pound
costs $1.4895

Currency futures allow for speculation or hedging in foreign currencies.

quotation for British pounds. At the settle price, the pound cost $1.4895 for September delivery of 62,500 pounds; so, the contract was worth $93,093.75.

Who cares to trade currency futures? Again, there are three interested parties: speculators, hedgers, and investors. The speculator hopes to profit by guessing correctly the future prices of currencies. For example, he or she might anticipate future economic problems in Great Britain that will weaken the pound. Given this conviction, shorting the pound is the correct strategy, because the speculator believes its value will fall relative to the dollar. If you thought the dollar would weaken relative to the pound, you would take a long position in the pound, expecting its price to increase. If these are naked positions, they will be extremely risky, as are naked positions in commodity futures.

Hedgers in currencies hope to manage risks that arise in connection with their business activities. If you own a business in Great Britain, your profits are earned in pounds, not dollars. Of course, you ultimately want dollars and perhaps will convert the pound earnings to dollars at a future date for transfer to the United States. Until the transfer takes place you are at the risk of a weakening pound. You may have £62,500 earnings when the pound is worth $1.50; but if it falls to $1.45 in the interim, you will lose $3,125 ($0.05 × 62,500). To hedge this risk, you short one futures contract. If the pound does fall, your position will show a profit to offset the loss in holding the pound.

Investors might consider using currency futures to internationalize their portfolios. As the dollar weakened in the mid-1980s, it became fashionable to add an international "flavor" to one's portfolio to reduce risk. There is merit in the effort; however, using foreign currencies to accomplish the task is both difficult and risky. For most investors, it would be more efficient to use mutual funds specializing in foreign investment, or to invest in companies that are international in scope, such as IBM or Exxon.

Interest Rate Futures

An **interest rate futures contract** also has the same features as a commodity contract, except the underlying asset is a debt instrument. Exhibit 14.7 indicated the availability of contracts for Treasury securities, stripped Treasury bonds (see

Chapter 7 for details on these securities), GNMA passthroughs, and bank CDs. The popularity of futures on Treasury securities is simply incredible: the volume of trading in the Treasury bonds and bills contracts alone on any given day probably has a greater market value than the market value of all commodity contracts combined. Ironically, when the first interest rate futures were introduced, there was some doubt that sufficient demand would exist for them.

Futures on Treasury securities have been unexpectedly popular.

Reading Quotations   Exhibit 14.9 shows how to interpret a typical quotation for a Treasury bond futures contract. This contract assumes delivery of $100,000 face value of Treasury bonds with an 8% coupon rate (paid semiannually) and a maturity of 20 years. Actual settlement, though, can be made with many different Treasury bonds. (The details are rather complicated and not essential to our understanding of the futures contracts.) Once again, however, the most common form of settlement is position reversal.

As you read Exhibit 14.9, notice the large open interest, comparing it to the corn future shown in Exhibit 14.1. At the settle price of $96,438, the value of the open interest is $16.11 billion ($96,438 × 167,036); by contrast, the value of corn's open interest was $421.1 million ($2.375 × 5,000 × 35,457). Also, the settle price of $96,438 is the present value you find by discounting (at an annual rate of 0.08370) the (*a*) $4,000 semiannual coupon interest for 40 periods, and (*b*) the redemption value of $100,000 at the end of the 40th period.

The Treasury bond futures contract is based upon an 8% coupon rate and a 20-year maturity.

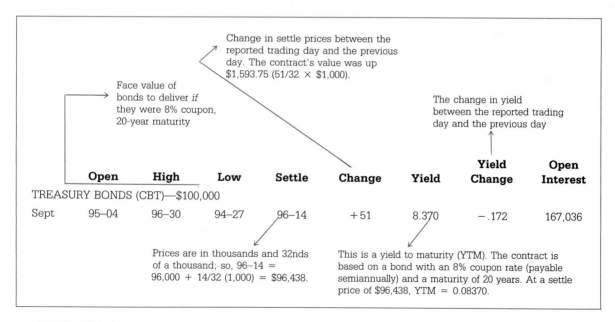

EXHIBIT 14.9
Explanation of a typical Treasury bond futures quotation (See Exhibit 14.1 for previously explained items.)

The Changing Structure of the Chicago Board of Trade

Mention the Chicago Board of Trade (CBT) and a lot of people conjure up images of a place where wheat, corn, and other commodities are traded, along with some live animals like cows and pigs. They imagine an "Old MacDonald's Farm" right in downtown Chicago. Naturally, those in the know understand the CBT has nothing to do with the physical trading of grains or meats; it specializes in trading futures contracts on such commodities, right? Well, partially so; but today the CBT is better characterized as a place where bankers, insurance companies, and many other financial institutions hedge their risk positions. Rather than trading wheat, corn, pork bellies, and the like, bankers and insurance executives deal in con-

tracts applicable to the fodder of their businesses—things such as interest rate and stock index futures, foreign currencies, and options on futures.

Formed in the late 1840s as a centralized marketplace to accommodate grain buyers and sellers, the Board now describes itself as "the world's premier agricultural and financial risk-management institution." Underscore the word financial. As the accompanying graph shows, trading in financial instruments now dominates trading on the Board. As you see, financial instruments futures exploded from about two million contracts in 1979 to almost 80 million in 1988. Options on futures, which didn't begin trading until 1983, recorded over 25 million contracts in 1988.

What does the future hold? Few people see the trends reversing, although the pickup in commodity prices in 1987 and 1988 sparked renewed interest in the traditional commodity contracts. To be sure, the proliferation of contracts can hardly continue, so a shaking-out seems imminent, with the superfluous contracts being abandoned. But those meeting real risk needs are likely to survive and, indeed, flourish. Today's financial executives are becoming much more sophisticated in the use of hedging techniques—almost as sophisticated as your average grain elevator operator.

SOURCE: Data for graph from the Chicago Board of Trade's 1989 Report.

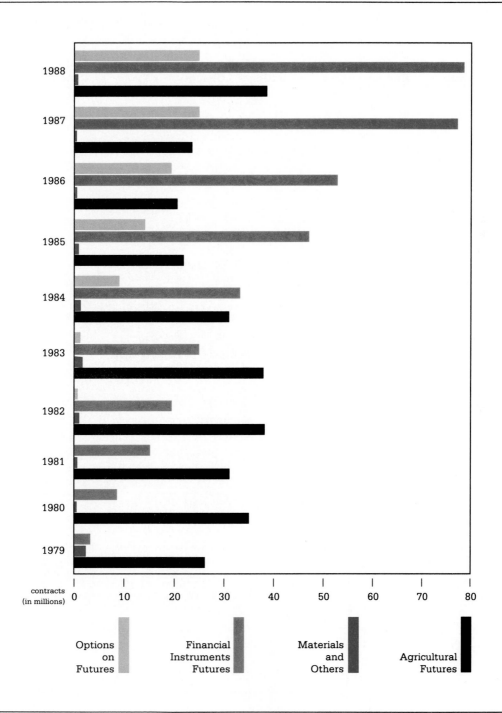

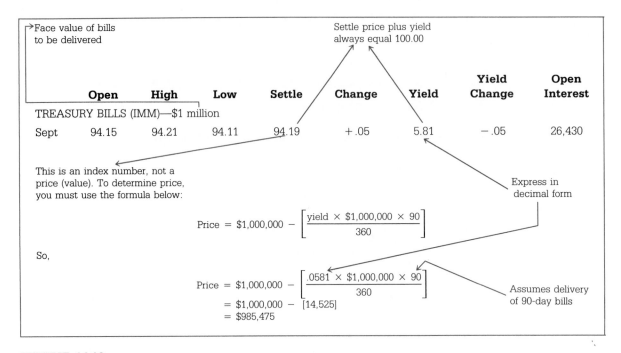

EXHIBIT 14.10

Explanation of a typical Treasury bill futures quotation (See Exhibit 14.1 for previously explained items.)

Exhibit 14.10 shows a typical quotation for a Treasury bills futures contract. Its reporting features are somewhat different from those for bonds. The most confusing aspect is the reported price, which really isn't a price. It is an index number, and to determine price, you must apply the mathematical manipulation shown in the exhibit. The contract illustrated has a price (market value) of $985,475. As you see, one contract involves a substantial amount of money. Moreover, even though the open interest in bills of 26,430 positions is much smaller than the bonds' open interest, it actually has a greater market value—$26.05 billion ($985,475 × 26,430) versus $16.11 billion. Notice also that the day's change in yield is the same number as the change in settle price, but with the opposite sign. This is always the case, since the index number representing price is simply 100.00 minus the yield; that is, 94.19 = 100.00 − 5.81. People who trade bills frequently know that a one-basis-point change in yield leads to an opposite $25 change in contract value. So, the reported yield change of −0.05 means a minus 5 basis points, which in turn means an increase in contract value of $125 ($25 × 5).

The Treasury bills futures contract assumes delivery of $1,000,000 (face value) of 90-day Treasury bills.

Trading Interest Rate Futures   In relation to contract value, margin requirements for Treasury futures are quite low, generally in the $2,000 to $3,000 range. Obviously, this low margin adds to their speculative appeal. Since we have covered speculative trading in detail already, we will not elaborate further here except to say that interest rate futures have shown as much price volatility as many commodities, and if interest rates in the future continue to vary as much as they have in the past, this volatility should continue. A danger unique to interest rate futures has to do with believing that someone can forecast future interest rates. Put bluntly, no one can—or at least no one who makes his or her forecasts public information has demonstrated an ability to do so in the past. Unfortunately, many people act as though they can forecast successfully. You might be skeptical if people tell you they know what corn's price will be next year, but you are more likely to believe a well-dressed banker with an impressive aura who announces authoritatively, "Interest rates will rise next year!" Don't rush out and short a Treasury bond contract on the basis of such news. Many investors have, and many have lost substantially.

Interest rate futures also are used extensively in hedging. Suppose, for example, you have accumulated $200,000 in 8%, 20-year Treasury bonds in your employer's retirement plan. You will retire in about a year and will receive a lump-sum distribution of the value of the bonds at that time. You are very concerned that interest rates might skyrocket during the year, driving the value of the bonds down considerably. What to do? Simple: short two Treasury bond contracts for delivery in one year. If interest rates do rise, your losses in the pension plan should be offset by profits on the futures contracts. And, if you guess wrong and interest rates fall, your losses on the futures contracts should be offset by price appreciation of your bonds. The costs of this hedge in terms of a commission and setting up an account with appropriate margin may be relatively high for only two contracts, but the alternative could be even more costly. Hedges such as this by pension plans themselves and by many other types of financial institutions are very common. Indeed, the hedging applications of interest rate futures are only recently being understood and used. One complicating factor involves matching changes in the value of the bond portfolio to changes in the futures contract. Dealing with the problem requires the use of hedge ratios.

Interest rate futures can be used to hedge a retirement plan.

Hedge Ratios   The problem confronting an interest-rate hedger arises when the instrument to be hedged does not have an exact counterpart in a futures contract. For example, suppose your retirement fund contains 8% Treasury securities with 6-year maturities, instead of those with 20-year maturities. Unfortunately, a futures contract based upon 6-year Treasuries does not exist. However, you still could consider a hedge, utilizing the existing contract, if you realize that price fluctuations of the futures contract will be greater than those of your bonds. This is because a 20-year bond is more volatile than a 6-year bond, all other things held constant. (If you do not understand why, you need to review Chapter 5.)

To illustrate, suppose both 6-year bonds and 20-year bonds are selling at par ($1,000) when interest rates rise and yields to maturity on each bond increase to 10%. The value of a 6-year bond will fall to $913, while a 20-year bond declines to $830. The ratio of the changes in value (20-year to 6-year) is 1.95 ($170/$87). Thus, to hedge your position, you must short 0.513 (1.0/1.95) of a futures contract for

Hedging complications arise when the securities to be hedged are not exact counterparts of the security in the futures contract.

Are Spreads a Low-Risk Way to Play the Market?

The introduction of stock index futures some years ago created a marriage made in the pits, critics say. When the Kansas City Commodity Exchange started trading futures contracts on the Value Line stock index, stock traders learned there was a whole new game to be played—not on the pompous stock exchanges, but amidst the yelling, screaming, and unruly behavior of the commodities futures markets. And when other futures contracts on other indexes were created, they learned there wasn't only one new game, but several.

Enter the spread, which is a sort of cross between a naked position (where you can lose your shirt overnight) and a hedge (where you might reduce risk but can't make a profit). Spreads come in many varieties, but in the stock index game a popular play is to go long in one index while shorting another. On the surface, this seems to be a hedge; you would think that both indexes will move in the same direction. So, how can you make any money on this deal? The trick is that you believe they will move in the same direction *but not by the same amount*. What you hope to do is guess correctly the change in each.

For example, suppose at the end of January, 1989, you thought the market was ready for a big increase. But you are a bit squeamish on your feeling and you aren't willing to risk big bucks that you will be right. You reason, though, that if the market jumps, smaller stocks with high betas should increase more than stable stocks with low betas. What to do? Go long on the Value Line index, which consists of about 1700 small and large stocks, and short the less volatile S&P 500 index, which contains only the big blue chips. This is an example of a bull spread.

The spread at January 30 was 35.60 index points (see the accompanying table). Suppose that six weeks later you reverse the positions. Now the spread is 29.05 and the gain is 6.55 (35.60 − 29.05) points; at 500 times the gain, your profit is $3,275. Even allowing for commissions of $120 or so, the six-week profit is great. What's greater is you would have needed only about $1,200 margin to do the spread, versus about $7,000 if you had simply shorted (or gone long on) one of the index contracts.

By the way, don't take complete credit for the successful spread: the market actually went down from January, to the middle of March. What happened was apparently a rally in small stocks. Once again, luck wins over brains in the pursuit of profit, although you can take credit for avoiding a naked long on the S&P 500.

Example of a Bear Spread (Spreader Expects Spread to Increase)

	Price (in points)	
At January 30:		
Buy the Value Line index	260.70	
Sell the S&P 500 index	296.30	
Spread	35.60	
At March 13: reverse positions		
The Value Line index	264.95	4.25 profit
The S&P 500 index	294.00	2.30 profit
Spread	29.05	
Increase in spread	6.55	6.55 profit

each $100,000 in the retirement fund. With $200,000 invested, you must short 1.026 contracts. Since you can't deal in fractional parts, you must settle for second best, which is to short one contract. The number of contracts needed to hedge perfectly an existing position is called a **hedge ratio**—0.513 in our example. Hedge ratios are usually not important in commodity futures, but they play critically important roles in certain financial futures, primarily interest rate and stock index futures.

> A hedge ratio compares value changes between portfolio securities and futures contracts.

Of course, our example is simplified for ease of presentation. In actual settings, hedge ratios may be more complicated to determine, for several reasons. First, the bonds to be hedged are likely to have coupon rates other than 8%. Secondly, hedge ratios must be calculated each time interest rates change and as maturities of the underlying instruments change. For example, one year later, your portfolio of bonds will have 5-year maturities (not 6), and a new hedge ratio will apply. (Keep in mind the 20-year maturity of the assumed Treasury bond utilized in the futures contract never changes—it is assumed always to be 20 years.)

Index Futures

An **index futures contract** is based upon values of a particular index. As in the case of index options, index futures cannot be settled by delivery. Cash settlement stands in place of delivery, but once again the most popular form of settlement is position reversal. Exhibit 14.11 shows a typical quotation on the S&P 500 index. The value of the contract is 500 times the index number. So, the settle price of 248.15 means the September contract was worth $124,075 ($248.15 × 500.) As you can tell from the large open interest, the S&P 500 futures is very popular.

> Speculating in the stock market with an index futures contract might be easier than trading stocks directly.

Speculative Positions   Anyone who wishes to speculate in the stock market might find it is easier to do so with a stock index futures than by trading stocks

Settlement is always in cash								
						Lifetime		**Open**
Open	**High**	**Low**	**Settle**	**Change**	**High**	**Low**		**Interest**
S&P 500 INDEX (CME) 500 times index								
Sept	246.90	248.20	245.45	248.15	+.80	252.70	187.00	31,409
Value of a contract = 500 × Index								
Therefore, Value = 500 × $248.15 = $124,025								

EXHIBIT 14.11
Explanation of a typical index futures quotation (See Exhibit 14.1 for previously explained items.)

directly. Suppose, for example, that you had $124,000 to invest in stocks and that you planned to buy stocks similar to those in the S&P 500. Rather than doing this, you deposit $124,000 in Treasury bills with your broker (far more than what is needed to meet a margin requirement, but we do not want to introduce leverage into the example), and then buy one S&P 500 futures that eventually expires. While it is held, though, your risk exposure is about the same either way. The only relevant factors to consider then are: (1) interest on the T-bills that you earn with T-bills and not with the stocks; (2) dividends earned on the stocks but not with T-bills; and (3) commissions each way, which would be a one-time occurrence with the stocks (assuming you buy and hold) but occur periodically with the futures as you renew each expiring contract. In many cases, the futures approach is the better alternative. Unfortunately, it involves a fairly large investment, putting it out of reach for investors with limited funds.

Market timers, though, have become avid users of stock index futures because it gives them far greater flexibility than the alternative of frequently trading in and out of stocks. They adjust their portfolios easily, and at much lower cost, by simply holding Treasury securities and taking long or short futures positions in line with their outlook on the market.

Hedge Positions   Hedge positions are also extremely popular with professional money managers. We noted earlier how a retirement fund invested in bonds can be hedged with interest-rate futures; similarly, one invested in stocks can be hedged with stock index futures. Just as hedge ratios were important before, so are they now. For example, your retirement portfolio might be invested in securities only half as risky as, say, the S&P 500. Instead of hedging on a one-to-one basis, you hedge one-half to one. For example, if the index was 250.00, the value of one contract would be $125,000. If you had $250,000 invested in the retirement fund, you would hedge it by shorting one contract. Assume the market declines 10%: your retirement fund should go down 5%, from $250,000 to $237,500. But, your short position should increase 10% in value, assuming the S&P declines to 225.00. The profit here is $12,500 (500 × 25.00 points), which offsets exactly the loss in the retirement fund.

> Stock index futures also can hedge a retirement plan.

Arbitrage Positions   We discussed in the previous chapter how options enter into arbitrage opportunities. Similar opportunities exist with index futures. This is because a futures index should have a theoretically correct value in relation to the securities that compose the index. Actual values, however, might be slightly different from the theoretical values. For example, suppose a futures contract on the S&P 500 that will expire in one month is quoted at 250.00 when the index itself has a value of 248.00. In other words, there is negative basis of 2.0 points. Suppose that all 500 stocks in the index, in their proper proportion, could be purchased and held for one month. Assume further that all transactions costs, including an allowance for interest on funds that could have been invested elsewhere, amount to 0.5% of the purchase amount. In relation to the index value of 248.00, transactions costs are 1.24 (248.00 × 0.005). Adding this figure to the index value of 248.00 gives 249.24, which is the theoretically correct value.

Since the futures contract is quoted at 250.00, an arbitrage opportunity is available: buy the stocks and short the index. You lock in a risk-free profit of 0.76 points (250.00 − 249.24), which amounts to $380 per contract (0.76 × 500). On the surface this procedure seems simple, but in reality it is quite difficult to carry out. The major impediment is actually buying the underlying stocks in an index. Modelling the S&P 500 perfectly would require a considerable amount of money, and trades would have to take place very quickly to exploit favorable price differences. An arbitrager must execute trades in both the futures market and the stock market to realize the expected gain. If, in our example, the stock purchases lagged behind the futures sale, stock prices might increase, thereby eliminating the small profit margin. Of course, they also could decrease, improving the deal, but in either event risk increases—a situation arbitragers try to avoid.

While arbitraging a stock index is possible, it is difficult.

Such arbitraging has become very popular, primarily because large brokerage firms have simplified it by creating *market baskets,* which are smaller versions of stocks in an index. For example, 20 key stocks might show price variations almost identical to those of the S&P 500. If so, this basket can be used as a substitute for the 500 stocks. A further simplification was created with the *designated order turnaround (DOT) system,* which allows arbitragers to place coordinated buy or sell orders (using computers) for a number of stocks on the floor of an exchange. This form of arbitraging is referred to as **program trading**. Clearly, it is not completely risk-free since a market basket may not correlate perfectly with its intended index; however, risks are minimal.

Market baskets and the DOT system of placing stock orders has made arbitrage possible.

SUMMARY

A futures contract is an obligation to buy or sell a specific amount of a certain commodity or financial instrument at a set price at some future point in time. The contract must provide specific details about each of these items. Futures information is provided daily in many newspapers. Long and short positions are possible with a futures contract; long means acceptance of future delivery and short means making such delivery. Trading futures is similar to trading stocks or options in that an account is opened with a broker. Most futures traders make extensive use of margin, which is more technically known as a performance bond. There is little investor protection, and trading is conducted through organized exchanges, facilitated by clearinghouses.

Commodity futures are available for a wide variety of commodities such as corn, soybeans, and pork bellies. Speculative trading is a highly risky activity premised on forecasting future commodity prices. Hedging is often undertaken to reduce risk. There are advantages and disadvantages to both speculative trading and hedging.

Financial futures are available for a wide variety of financial instruments, such as Treasury securities, foreign currencies, and stock indexes. These futures are quoted in the financial pages in a format similar to that of commodity futures and are used by speculators and hedgers in similar trading activities.

KEY TERMS

Select the alternative that best identifies the key term.

1. futures market
2. cash market
3. commodity futures contract
4. money at risk
5. clearinghouse
6. marking to market
7. perfect hedge
8. basis
9. currency futures contract
10. interest rate futures contract
11. hedge ratio
12. index futures contract
13. program trading

a. total market value of a futures contract
b. you might use one if you had a business in Japan
c. if you need a commodity, you probably buy it here
d. if you wish to hedge a position in a commodity, you probably do it here
e. updating your futures positions at the end of a day
f. calls for delivery of a debt instrument
g. eliminates the need for buyers and sellers to deal directly with each other
h. you can buy one on pork bellies
i. gains or losses in the cash market equal losses or gains in the futures market
j. settlement cannot be made by delivery
k. difference between the cash price and the futures price
l. uses market baskets and the DOT system
m. number of contracts required to hedge a position perfectly

REVIEW QUESTIONS

1. Define a futures market and then compare it to a cash market. If you used wheat in your baking business, in which market would you buy it?
2. List four important provisions of a futures contract.
3. What do the following terms in a futures quotation mean? *(a)* settle price and *(b)* open interest? How do you determine your money at risk in a futures contract?
4. Do you actually buy or sell a futures contract? Explain. And, is margin really the same type of margin you use in trading stocks? Explain.
5. What role does a clearinghouse play in futures trading? What steps are taken by the clearinghouse to make sure traders can meet their obligations? Explain.
6. What makes speculative trading of commodity futures extremely risky? Does discussion in this chapter encourage speculation? Explain.

7. You operate a grain elevator that currently holds 100,000 bushels of corn. You could sell the corn today for $2.40 a bushel, but you plan to hold it for three months, when you feel price will be higher. Discuss how you might hedge this position.

   Suppose a week after you executed a hedge, you want to reverse it, but your broker exclaims, "Your hedge wasn't perfect and basis has moved against you!" What does this mean?

8. Discuss advantages and disadvantages of investing in commodity futures contracts.

9. Broadly, how do financial futures differ from commodity futures? Also, discuss the relative importance of each.

10. Discuss one hedging example involving each of the following: *(a)* a currency futures, *(b)* an interest rate futures, and *(c)* an index futures.

11. What is a hedge ratio? Explain its use in hedging situations involving interest-rate futures.

12. The following settle prices were found for futures quotations:
    a. Treasury bonds—98–08
    b. Treasury bills—93.20
    c. S&P 500—250.22
    Determine a contract's market value for each of the above.

13. Why would market timers be interested in stock index futures?

14. Discuss arbitrage opportunities in stock index futures.

15. Explain program trading, including in your discussion an explanation of why stock baskets and the DOT order system are necessary.

---

1. In mid-June 1989, Andy Metz notices the following settle quotations for an ounce of gold (100 ounces to the contract):

June	361.90
August	365.80
June 90	385.30

   He also saw on the evening news that gold closed on the day of the quotes at $361.19 an ounce.
   a. Determine the amount of basis for each contract. Is basis converging towards zero? Explain.
   b. Suppose Andy shorted the August contract. By the end of July, gold's price jumped considerably with the August contract closing at 410. Calculate Andy's gain or loss on his naked position.
   c. Suppose Andy could borrow $36,119 at an interest rate of 8%. He is contemplating the following strategy: Buy 100 ounces of gold now, simultaneously taking a short position in one August 90 gold futures contract. Total commissions would be $100. Evaluate this strategy.

2. Margo Fibber is convinced the dollar will weaken against other currencies over the next six months. The current exchange rate is 1.5000 dollars to the pound. The most recent settle price for a British pound futures contract maturing in six months is 1.4500 dollars to the pound.
   a. Do other investors share Margo's outlook on exchange rates? Explain.
   b. What strategy should Margo follow (given her conviction), assuming she will trade

PROBLEMS AND PROJECTS

the pound contract? Also, determine her profit or loss if she reverses her position at an exchange rate of 1.5500.

c. Suppose Margo owned a boutique on Downing Street in London. She anticipates having a cash flow of 185,000 pounds available at the end of six months. Assuming Margo wants to be sure to have the dollar equivalent ($277,500) available for wiring home at that time, what strategy should she pursue? Explain and illustrate.

3. The settle price on a Treasury bond futures contract is 101–16 and its quoted yield is 7.85%.

a. What is the price in dollars?

b. Reviewing material from Chapter 5, if necessary, explain how the yield is calculated.

c. Suppose interest rates rose and the yield increased to 8.0%. Determine the change in settle price and the amount of change per basis-point change in yield.

4. The settle price on a Treasury bills futures contract is 92.22 and its quoted yield is 7.78%.

a. What is the price in dollars?

b. What is the relationship between yield and settle price?

c. Suppose interest rates fall and yield is quoted at 7.00%. By how much will the futures price (in dollars) rise?

5. Many interest rate forecasters attempt to forecast changes in the yield curve, rather than changes in interest rates as such. Suppose you thought the yield curve, which is now upward-sloping, would flatten within the next month. Specifically, suppose you thought 90-day Treasury bills would go from 6% to 9% while 20-year bonds would go from 8% to 9%. Given these assumptions, what strategy would you take with futures contracts? Provide specific details in your answer.

6. *(Student Project)* Select any futures contract and follow its price variations for a 10-day period. To make the exercise more exciting, take a position in the contract at the beginning of the period. Calculate your gain or loss at the end of the period.

7. *(Student Project)* Some commodity traders often act on certain unexpected events. For example, a frost might hit Florida, potentially damaging the citrus crop. Follow the news fairly closely for such events—look in particular for international crises—and if you find one, develop a strategy to play the event with futures contracts. Record daily price quotations and evaluate performance after, say, a 10-day period.

CASE ANALYSES

14.1
Corey Darwin
Seeks Protection
for His
Inheritance

Corey Darwin will inherit within the next year approximately $600,000 in bonds that are part of his grandmother's estate. Corey intends to sell the bonds, using the proceeds to buy a condominium and a Porsche 928. He is scared that interest rates might rise sharply during the probate period, thereby lowering the bond prices. Afraid that this occurrence could cost him the Porsche, Corey is searching for ways to cope with potential losses in the bonds' values during the waiting period.

The bonds consist mainly of Treasury securities with an average maturity of 8 years, an average coupon rate of 8%, and an average yield to maturity of 8%. A friend of Corey's has suggested that he short sell bonds now as a hedge. If bond prices fall, profit from the short sales will offset losses on the bonds he will inherit. That seemed an ideal approach until Corey learned that he must provide margin for the short sale—both initially and perhaps later if bond prices rise instead of falling. Another friend then suggested that Corey use futures contracts as a hedge. Unfortunately, Corey knows very little about this approach.

Questions

a. Does the use of futures contracts seem a viable alternative for Corey? Describe briefly the approach he will take.
b. Must Corey worry about margin and margin calls with this approach? Explain.
c. Reviewing material from Chapter 5, determine the possible loss in Corey's portfolio value if yield to maturity increased to 10%.
d. Determine the decrease in value of a Treasury bond futures contract if its yield to maturity increases from 8% to 10%.
e. Calculate the hedge ratio for Corey's situation and give him specific instructions on how to use Treasury bond futures to solve his problem.

**14.2
Sue Hagan
Considers an
Arbitrage**

Sue Hagan follows the stock market fairly closely. Recently, she notices the settle price on the S&P 500 index futures is 305 for a delivery date one month in the future. The actual index value currently is 301. Sue doesn't understand why these two values are different and she believes the difference represents an arbitrage opportunity.

Sue feels that she can construct a basket of five stocks that will have price variations closely correlated to movements of the index. Dealing in 100-share lots and with an average share price of $75, she estimates that $37,500 would be necessary to buy one basket. She believes commissions would be 0.5% on both purchases and sales of the stocks and $80 (round turn) on one futures contract. Sue also estimates the cost of funds at 0.6% a month, although she is not sure this cost is a relevant consideration.

Questions

a. Is Sue correct in her reasoning that the settle price on the futures contract should equal the index value? Would she be correct if there was one day remaining before the contract's maturity? Explain.
b. Can Sue arbitrage successfully? Explain with calculations.
c. What potential risk or problem do you envision in this arbitrage? Explain.

HELPFUL READING

Angrist, Stanley W. ''Beating the Odds in Commodity Trading.'' *The Wall Street Journal,* February 13, 1989, p. C1.

———. ''Commodity Markets Get Taste of Program Trading.'' *The Wall Street Journal,* June 26, 1989, p. C1.

———. ''Put Options Can Help Protect Portfolios.'' *The Wall Street Journal,* February 28, 1989, p. C1.

Chicago Board of Trade. *Commodity Trading Manual.* Chicago: 1985.

Lee, Susan. ''What's With the Casino Society?'' *Forbes,* September 22, 1986, pp. 150–58.

Morris, Charles S. ''Managing Interest-Rate Risk with Interest Rate Futures.'' *Economic Review,* Federal Reserve Bank of Kansas City, March 1989, pp. 3–20.

Sebastian, Pamela. ''How Program Trading Works and Why It Causes Controversy in the Stock Market.'' *The Wall Street Journal,* January 10, 1986, p. 10.

Sturza, Evan. ''A New Kind of Arbitrage.'' *Forbes,* July 19, 1989, p. 128.

Torres, Craig. '''Yield-Curve Arbitrage' Rewards the Skillful.'' *The Wall Street Journal,* July 27, 1989, p. C1.

PART FIVE

Pooling Arrangements

M ost investors lack sufficient resources to establish adequately diversified portfolios on their own. Consequently, they often turn to pooling arrangements. These investments not only diversify a portfolio, they also enable investors to use the skills of professional money managers, and to invest in areas they might otherwise avoid, such as real estate, or gas and oil drilling ventures.

Chapter 15 explains advantages, disadvantages, and investment mechanics of investment companies. It indicates differences among funds in terms of both their structure and their investment objectives. It also provides an analytical framework for evaluating fund performance.

Chapter 16 describes other pooling arrangements. It examines the mechanics, advantages, and disadvantages of unit investment trusts, real estate investment trusts, limited partnerships, and self-directed pooling arrangements such as investment clubs and money manager limited partnerships.

CHAPTER FIFTEEN

Investment Companies

TYPES OF INVESTMENT
COMPANIES

Closed-End Funds

Open-End (Mutual) Funds

FUND OBJECTIVES AND
SERVICES

Fund Objectives

Mutual Fund Services

EVALUATING FUND
PERFORMANCE

Understanding Returns

Measuring Risk

How Good Are Fund Managers?

Popular Press Fund Evaluations

BOXES

Are Discounts on Closed-End Funds
Worth Anything?

Is the Load on the Load Fund
Worth It?

After you finish this chapter, you
will be able to:

- recognize the differences between
  closed-end and open-end investment companies (funds).

- understand a fund's net asset
  value (NAV) and the investment
  implications of premiums or discounts on closed-end funds.

- identify the various expenses of
  investing in open-end mutual
  funds, including front-end and
  back-end loads.

- recognize the many different fund
  objectives.

- identify various services funds
  provide.

- understand how beta values are
  determined as part of the process
  of evaluating fund performance.

- understand how to evaluate a
  fund on a risk-adjusted return
  basis.

M any investors allocate most, or even all, of their portfolios to investment companies. In recent years, some 20 million investors in the United States have invested almost $600 billion in them. An investment company offers important advantages over the alternative of selecting and managing individual securities. However, such companies should not be viewed as the end of all your investment troubles. Monitoring and measuring the performance of an investment company is as important as watching your individual securities. All companies, for example, are not equally successful, and, perhaps more important, many may not be suitable for your specific investment goals. Since you probably will invest in fewer individual investment companies than in individual securities, you should take the time to become very familiar with any group of companies you are considering.

TYPES OF INVESTMENT COMPANIES

Investor demand for non-money market funds increases in bull markets but fades in bear markets.

An organized investment company (often called a **fund**) pools the resources of many individuals to buy securities issued by businesses, governmental units, and others. It is characterized primarily by active portfolio management and a wide range of services offered to its shareholders. Currently, the popularity of funds is exceptionally strong, as Exhibit 15.1 indicates. The public's interest in non-money market mutual funds, however, seems to rise and fall with the stock market. When the market is strong and bullish, investors turn to mutual funds as a way to participate in the boom. The long bull market that began in 1982 brought with it an explosive increase in investor demand; however, the decline in non–money market assets in 1988 (after the market crash in late 1987) shows how

EXHIBIT 15.1
Total assets of investment companies—selected years (in billions of dollars)

| | Open-End Funds | | Closed-End Funds |
Year	Non–Money Market	Money Market	
1988	$426.6	$312.4	$38.8
1987	453.8	298.6	15.8
1986	424.8	274.7	10.7
1982	76.8	180.5	7.2
1980	66.7	71.6	8.1
1976	47.5	3.6	6.6
1972	59.8	0.0	6.7
1962	22.4	0.0	2.8
1952	3.9	0.0	1.0

SOURCE: Reprinted with permission from Weisenberger Investment Companies Services, 1989 Copyright © 1989. Warren, Gorham, & Lamont, Inc., 210 South Street, Boston, MA 02111. All rights reserved.

this demand fades when prices fall. Notice also a similar decline in 1976 relative to 1972, which reflects the severe recession in 1974–75. While some observers believe we may have entered a new era of pooled-resource investing, that conclusion may be premature. What we do know is there are now many more funds from which to choose, and their diversity of investment objectives is constantly expanding. If there is an investment theme to be played, you probably can find a fund playing it.

Funds can be classified into two broad categories: closed-end funds and open-end funds. A further classification of the open-end funds divides them into load and no-load funds. Exhibit 15.2 indicates how open-end funds dominate the industry.

Closed-End Funds

A **closed-end fund** was the first type of fund created. The key distinction between it and an open-end fund involves their capital structures: a closed-end fund has a relatively fixed capital structure, while an open-end fund's capital structure is changing constantly. This means the number of shares to a closed-end fund is practically constant, while the number to an open-end fund increases or decreases in response to shareholder demand. You buy and sell shares of closed-end funds as you do the shares of any company, and you find their quotations on the same financial pages of your newspaper. Stockbrokers offer the same trading assistance, and commissions are the same as for any trade. In short, trading shares of a closed-end fund such as Adams Express is no different from trading shares of IBM.

> A closed-end fund has a fixed capital structure, and its shares trade as do the shares of any company.

Determining Net Asset Value (NAV) The prices of closed-end fund shares, then, are market-determined; you might pay $20 a share for Adams Express. However, the market price should bear some relationship to the market values of the securities Adams holds minus any liabilities it might owe. Indeed, this underlying value is usually the first piece of information an investor wants in evaluating a fund, whether open- or closed-end. It is called a fund's **net asset**

> NAV is usually the first piece of fund information an investor wants.

EXHIBIT 15.2
Numbers of
funds—selected years

Year	Open-End	Closed-End
1989*	2,150	160
1988	2,111	144
1987	1,782	93
1986	1,356	62
1985	1,071	39

*Authors' estimates.

SOURCE: Reprinted with permission from Weisenberger Investment Companies Services, 1989 Copyright © 1989. Warren, Gorham, & Lamont, Inc., 210 South Street, Boston, MA 02111. All rights reserved.

Are Discounts on Closed-End Funds Worth Anything?

Closed-end funds selling at discounts are prized by many investors, including Burton Malkiel, a former Wall Street professional, highly respected finance academician, and author of the immensely popular paperback, *A Random Walk Down Wall Street: Second College Edition* (New York: W. W. Norton and Company, 1981). With these funds, you can buy well-known stocks at less than their market prices. In this age of computer-assisted investment programs and mathematical trading models, how can something this simple give you an edge? There must be a catch.

Malkiel argues there really is none. He believes discounts generally reflect a lack of enthusiastic promotion of closed-end funds, in contrast to the hype that characterizes many open-end funds. The fact that the closed-end fund has a fixed number of shares gives the fund's manager little reason to spend money to promote it. Many investors don't even know such funds exist, much less that they can be bought cheaply.

However, if a discount is very large, be careful, because something other than a lack of promotion is probably at work. For example, the capital shares of a dual fund sell at huge discounts. (Dual funds consist of income shares that receive all the dividends from the portfolio, plus capital shares that take all the capital appreciation or losses.) The fact that the capital shares of such funds sell at discounts means nothing, because the net asset value calculation assumes the fund would be liquidated tomorrow and proceeds used to redeem the income shares. Liquidation, however, will not take place for many years, so the discount shows nothing more than the time value of money. Other large discounts might show un-favorable tax situations, such as a fund having huge unrealized profits that, when taken, will increase shareholders' taxable incomes.

While Malkiel plays down the importance of some explanations for the discounts, even he would probably advise that you get more information if one fund's discount dwarfs those of its counterparts. In mid-1989, some of the foreign funds showed rather large discounts (50% for the Brazil Fund, for example). A partial explanation was, supposedly, fear of an adverse move in currency exchange rates. (The dollar was expected to strengthen against other currencies.) What you might see in this situation is not only an opportunity to buy foreign stocks at reduced prices, but also an opportunity to play your hunch on changes in exchange rates. But, that's a different game—good luck if you play it.

value (NAV) and its determination is illustrated in Exhibit 15.3. In this simplified example, the fund owns common stock shares in three companies. Collectively, the shares are worth $59,000. After deducting the fund's liabilities of $1,000 and then dividing by the 1,000 shares the fund has issued, the NAV of $58 per share is determined. If this is a closed-end fund, you could say its intrinsic value is $58 a share. The market price may be higher than this figure—the shares are then trading at a premium—or lower, in which case the shares trade at a discount. There are investment implications of premiums and discounts that should be considered.

Shares Held and Market Value per Share	Total
100 IBM @ $150 per share	$15,000
200 Xerox @ $80 per share	16,000
400 GM @ $70 per share	28,000
Total	$59,000
Less fund liabilities	1,000
Total net asset value	$58,000
Shares outstanding to the fund = 1,000	
Net asset value per share (referred to as NAV)	$ 58.00

EXHIBIT 15.3
Illustration of net asset value (NAV) per share

Discounts and Premiums A closed-end fund selling at a discount seems a good investment opportunity. If you can buy shares in IBM, Xerox, and GM through a fund and pay less for them than if you purchased directly, why not take advantage of it? Indeed, many investors have done so because it is a good opportunity. As Exhibit 15.4 shows, discounts can vary considerably over time, and the reasons for the relatively small discounts from 1982 through 1986 are not clear.

Funds selling at discounts may be good investments.

There also are some funds selling at premiums, which raises the question: are they worth it? To have a premium, a fund must offer investors something they

You might pay a fund premium if it is difficult to make a similar investment in some other way.

Year	Discount
1988	16%
1987	18
1986	4
1985	5
1984	2
1983	4
1982	5
1981	12
1980	15
1979	22
1978	25
1977	19
1976	23
1975	23
1974	24

EXHIBIT 15.4
Year-end discounts from NAV: Eight diversified closed-end funds

SOURCE: Reprinted with permission from: Weisenberger Investment Companies Services, 1989 Copyright © 1989. Warren, Gorham, & Lamont, Inc., 210 South Street, Boston, MA 02111. All rights reserved.

cannot achieve easily on their own. For example, several closed-end funds, such as the Mexico Fund or the Japan Fund, specialize in foreign investment. You might find it inconvenient and difficult to invest directly in securities of these countries, so you will pay a premium for the advantage of investing indirectly. Other funds might command premiums because they offer leverage opportunities, or tax savings of one type or another. It would be a mistake to pay a premium without determining why it exists. The underlying reason might make sense and work well in your portfolio design. On the other hand, it might not reflect any item of importance to you. If you are not sure, ask your broker or contact the fund and request a prospectus.

Open-End (Mutual) Funds

An **open-end fund** is appropriately referred to as a mutual fund, although that term is also used often to denote closed-end funds. In contrast to the closed-end fund with its fixed number of shares, an open-end fund sells new shares to anyone wishing to buy them. Moreover, it buys back shares from anyone wishing to sell them. All trades take place at the fund's NAV (plus or minus possible commissions), which has the same calculation as that of a closed-end fund. So, with an open-end fund you usually deal directly with the fund, rather than through a broker (although brokers can be used to trade shares). This feature appeals to many investors who have become disenchanted with their brokers' advice and commissions, but it does mean you must find an open-end fund's address or telephone number to open an account. This inconvenience should be minor because many funds advertise in the popular press, and magazines such as *Forbes* and *Money* provide regular mutual fund evaluations that include such information.

You usually deal directly with an open-end fund.

Before an account can be opened, the fund must provide a prospectus that describes the fund and indicates its past performance. It is important to read this document thoroughly in order to understand the nature of the fund. Of course, its performance history is of interest, but determine also what charges the fund may impose on your account and the nature of its investment objectives. Most newspapers provide quotations on open-end funds, so you can monitor the fund's progress. Exhibit 15.5 shows how to interpret a typical quotation. You should consider first if the fund charges a purchase commission: if so, this is typically the largest single expense you will pay with the fund.

A front-end load is a commission to purchase fund shares.

Front-End Loads   As you see in the exhibit, the fund "ADTEK" is listed as N.L., which means no load. A load is a commission, and in this case it means no commission is charged to buy shares of the fund. The other three funds have offer prices greater than their NAVs; the differences are purchase commissions. ABT Funds would be referred to as a "family" of funds. Purchase commissions, or **front-end loads** are the most common form of investor charge, and about a third of all open-end funds have a front-end load. Some charge less than 5.0%, while

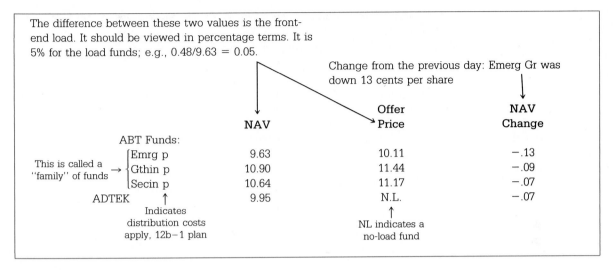

The difference between these two values is the front-end load. It should be viewed in percentage terms. It is 5% for the load funds; e.g., 0.48/9.63 = 0.05.

Change from the previous day: Emerg Gr was down 13 cents per share

	NAV	Offer Price	NAV Change
ABT Funds:			
Emrg p	9.63	10.11	−.13
Gthin p	10.90	11.44	−.09
Secin p	10.64	11.17	−.07
ADTEK	9.95	N.L.	−.07

This is called a "family" of funds →

↑ Indicates distribution costs apply, 12b−1 plan

↑ NL indicates a no-load fund

EXHIBIT 15.5
Explanation of an open-end fund quotation

some charge as high as 9.3%. This is hardly a trivial figure and you should logically wonder why anyone would pay it, given that alternative no-load funds are available. Surely, the load funds must perform better than the no-loads. This is *not* true, as studies on relative performance have shown. By all means, thoroughly review no-loads that meet your investment objectives before considering load funds. There is no reason to spend 9.3% of your investment funds each time you purchase.

There is no evidence indicating load funds outperform no-load funds.

Other Fund Charges   Rather than a front-end load, some funds have charges for redeeming shares, called **back-end loads**. These charges are usually in the 1% to 2% range. Along with loads, funds have begun imposing other kinds of charges. You should determine if the fund has a start-up cost when you open the account or if it has an annual maintenance fee. Another possibility is a deferred sales charge, which means you are charged a commission if you do not hold shares a sufficient length of time. Be particularly alert to any **12b−1 plan** that allows a fund's management to use up to 1.25% of the fund's net assets each year to pay promotion costs that can include commissions to selling agents. In effect, a 12b−1 plan passes on the usual front-end load as an operating cost of the fund. Either way, directly or indirectly, fund shareholders pay the load.

The trend in recent years is towards increasing shareholder charges. Indeed, some observers believe that true no-load funds may eventually disappear. For example, by 1989 about 600 funds had initiated 12b−1 plans, up from only 10 funds with them in 1984.

Is the Load on the Load Fund Worth It?

The answer to the above question, in a word, is *no*. So why do so many mutual fund investors put their money in load funds? Probably because they are promoted so heavily and because investors don't take enough time to read prospectuses or study fund performance histories that take risk into account.

Naturally, any list of the top-performing funds is likely to include some with loads. Since approximately 60% of all funds have front-end loads, the law of averages should put some there. For example, *Changing Times* made a comparison between load and no-load funds (February 1989, pp. 35–40), and found 14 of the top 25 equity funds for a five-year period ending November 30, 1989, were load funds. Actually, that's a little less than what you would expect (0.60 × 25 = 15) based on a probability estimate. Interestingly, of the top 10 performers, 5 are front-end load funds before the load is considered in determining return; after it is considered, only 3 make the list.

So what should an investor do? Simple: ignore load funds— at least those with very high loads—and concentrate on no- or low-load ones, since there are plenty from which to choose. But don't overlook other fund charges, such as those in connection with 12b–1 plans. Over time, these could be more expensive than front-end loads. Also, be careful to review a fund's operating costs. If these are considerably above 1.0% of net assets, the fund's management would seem to be excessively expensive. For example, the Vanguard Index Trust, a no-load fund that simply attempts to mimic the S&P 500, has a cost percentage of around 0.3%. In contrast, some equity funds have ratios in excess of 2.0%. Are their managers worth it? Have they done that much better over time than the Index Trust on a risk-adjusted basis? Look very closely before you buy.

FUND OBJECTIVES AND SERVICES

Investment company selection begins by identifying those funds with investment objectives similar to your own. Next, you consider the importance of various services they might offer.

Fund Objectives

As mentioned earlier, fund objectives are quite diverse. Generally, a fund invests in securities that help achieve its stated objectives, although some of the specialized funds cannot always do so. For example, the collapse of energy stocks several years ago prompted some managers of energy funds to invest elsewhere. One of these funds—New Era Fund—held as much as 40% of its portfolio outside the energy sector by 1986. Had you invested in New Era because you wished to have part of your portfolio in the energy sector, your effort would have been partially defeated. When you read the fund's prospectus, review its current holdings to determine if they are reasonably supportive of its objectives.

Review a fund's holdings to see if they conform to its stated investment objectives.

Of course, it is important to realize that a fund may not achieve its objectives, just as you as an individual investor may not achieve yours. Many growth funds, for example, have selected securities that haven't grown very much; on the other hand, some funds that strive for high current income might show remarkable price appreciation if interest rates fall. Also, you must allow a reasonably long period of time to judge whether or not the fund is fairly successful in achieving its stated goals. A one-, two-, or even ten-year evaluation period may be too short. The discussion below focuses on the most common fund objectives.

Growth Funds   A **growth fund** attempts to achieve long-term price appreciation in the shares it purchases. There are two main subgroups: some funds invest primarily in established growth companies while other funds seek small companies with untested growth results. The latter group is considerably riskier than the former, but, as Exhibit 15.6 shows, such funds usually provide greater price appreciation. As a group, growth funds are one of the most popular of all forms of funds. Many investors prefer using growth funds to achieve growth goals in their portfolios, while investing on their own—primarily using deposits at financial institutions—for current income. Finding good growth companies does involve considerable research effort and skills, so shifting the effort to a fund is often a sensible alternative.

Finding good growth companies is difficult, making the selection of a growth fund a sensible alternative.

Maximum Capital Appreciation Funds   **Maximum capital appreciation funds** seek quick capital gains and use a variety of investment approaches to achieve them. Many search for merger or takeover candidates; others use call options, short sales, margin accounts, and other leverage techniques. For the period shown in Exhibit 15.6, these funds enjoyed some success as a group. Be very careful of specific funds, though, since they are exceptionally risky. For example, the 44 Wall Street Fund was an outstanding performer from 1976 to early 1980 ($10,000 invested on 1/1/76 was worth about $50,000 at 12/31/80) and a complete failure from then to the end of 1985 (the $50,000 value had shrunk almost to the initial $10,000). The fund's spectacular successes and failures stem from its risky investment strategies, which have included buying stocks out of favor and those of small technology companies, using margin, and limiting the number of stocks held (sometimes holding as few as ten).

Maximum capital appreciation funds can be very risky.

Income Funds   An **income fund** invests primarily in fixed-income securities—bonds and preferred stocks—in an attempt to provide a high current return to its shareholders. Price appreciation is not its target, although it might be achieved in an environment of falling interest rates. While price depreciation is hardly one of its objectives, that too is possible if interest rates rise. In short, an income fund may have considerable interest-rate risk if the maturity of its portfolio is rather long. It might also present default risks if it invests exclusively in high-yielding, low-rated issues. These so-called junk funds became popular as interest rates fell in the early 1980s, appealing to investors who were willing to give up quality to preserve yield. How these funds will perform in a serious

Many junk funds have yet to be tested in a serious economic recession.

EXHIBIT 15.6
Mutual funds:
Objectives and
performance (excludes
money market funds)

Number of Funds	Type of Fund	Total Reinvested Cumulative Performance 3/31/74–3/31/89
	General Funds	
258	Growth	+605.08%
76	Small company growth	+772.38
156	Maximum capital appreciation	+714.32
56	Equity income	+638.72
216	Growth and income	+558.86
	Specialized Funds	
10	Health/Biotech	—[a]
16	Natural Resources	+529.63
25	Science and Technology	+469.97
13	Utility	+427.33
45	Specialty	+430.03
37	Global	+910.21
69	International	+593.21
35	Gold-oriented	+181.21
5	Option growth	—[a]
19	Option income	+464.41
1,036	All equity funds' average	+608.63
30	Convertible	+594.63
66	Balanced	+485.63
19	Income	+445.50
37	World income	—[a]
529	Fixed income	+282.75
1,717	All funds' average	+555.72
	S&P 500	+518.95

[a]Funds not in existence for 15 years.
SOURCE: Lipper Analytical Services, Inc.; as reported in *Barron's*, May 15, 1989, p. 82.

economic downturn remains to be seen, but some analysts feel there could be massive defaults that would hurt even supposedly well-diversified portfolios of the funds. If a fund advertises "maximum yields," it is a junk fund and you should give it more than a casual review before investing.

Balanced Funds A **balanced fund** is one seeking a combination of current income plus price appreciation. Its portfolio typically includes bonds, preferred stocks, and common stocks in varying proportions, reflecting its relative preferences for income or growth. These are often conservative funds with beta values less than 1.0. Some people question the need for a balanced fund, since investors can achieve their own "balancing" by combining income and growth funds. This alternative approach is worth considering, if you are willing to do the extra work in reviewing two types of funds.

Money Market Funds   A **money market fund** invests exclusively in short-term debt obligations of businesses and government units. The average maturity of most funds' portfolios is between 10 and 40 days, which means they are very liquid. They do differ in potential default risk, as we discussed in Chapter 6. Most money market funds hold a combination of corporate and government debt instruments, although some specialize. For example, you can find funds that invest exclusively in Treasury issues. Others invest only in federal tax-exempt securities. These money market municipals have lower pre-tax yields than their fully taxable counterparts, but often have an after-tax yield advantage to investors in high tax brackets.

Sector Funds   A **sector fund** invests exclusively in one industry. In 1990, for example, the Fidelity family had no fewer than 35 different sector funds investing in industries such as energy, health care, telecommunications, leisure, and precious metals. Sector funds appeal to investors who feel a particular industry might perform better than the overall economy but who lack sufficient resources to diversify within that industry. The idea is appealing, but keep in mind it rests on the presumption that you can identify the better-performing industries early enough in the investment cycle to be profitable. That may be hard to do. For example, everyone knows that as the economy moves out of recession, the housing industry typically does very well. So, why not buy the housing sector? The trouble is that, indeed, everyone does know, which means prices of stocks in the housing industry tend to increase well before the industry actually enters recovery. If you wish to speculate, you must buy the sector while the economy is in deep recession—clearly a riskier proposition than buying later in the cycle.

> A sector fund invests in one industry, such as health care.

Also, keep in mind a sector fund is riskier than a fund investing in a cross-section of industries. A high percentage of your investment funds committed to one industry can be exceptionally dangerous. And, if you diversify across sectors, you might question whether that policy is any better than simply investing in a conventional equity fund that could offer lower commissions and operating costs (in relation to assets).

> A sector fund is generally riskier than a conventional equity fund.

Specialized Funds   A **specialized fund** is one with a unique investment objective or one with a particular investment approach. Although we treated sector funds separately because of their importance, they are clearly specialized funds. There are many others; for example, some funds invest in foreign companies, allowing you to internationalize your portfolio. Others use put and call options, both as buyers and as covered option writers. Some funds invest in only one type of security, such as GNMA passthroughs. Again, it is important to recognize that a specialized fund can present a high-risk situation if a large percentage of your portfolio is invested in it. Once that is understood, these funds then can be used to enrich portfolio diversity, possibly reducing its overall risk or increasing its return.

Index Funds   An **index fund** is one that invests in securities represented in an index. The idea is to provide an investment portfolio that matches a popular index. The best-known such fund is Vanguard's Index Trust. It is a huge fund that is based on the S&P 500 index, and its performance correlates almost perfectly with it. On the surface, an index fund does not seem an appropriate fund in which to invest; surely you would expect a fund manager to do better than an unmanaged index. The popularity of this fund suggests that many investors think otherwise. We'll look at this topic later in this chapter. For now, consider an index fund a convenient and possibly very worthwhile investment vehicle. You might also note in Exhibit 15.6 that of the 905 funds reviewed, the average performance of +555.72% was somewhat higher than the S&P 500's performance of +518.95%.

Dual Funds   A **dual fund** is a unique arrangement that has the appearance of a balanced fund seeking modest growth and reasonable current return. Its uniqueness arises from the fact that two classes of stock are issued to investors when the fund is formed, each representing half of the total money raised. The first class— called *income shares*— receives all the dividend and interest from the portfolio and is redeemed at a set price at some future date. The second class— called *capital shares*— receives all the capital appreciation of the portfolio. In effect, each class has a leveraged position with respect to its return objective. For example, the income shares receive twice the dividends and interest as they would if they were to put up all the money to acquire the fund's portfolio. Likewise, the capital shares receive twice the capital appreciation.

It should be noted that dual funds are closed-end. Also, they have a maturity; that is, at a future date, the fund ceases operating by redeeming the income shares and distributing all capital appreciation to the capital shares. Moreover, as we have seen before, leverage implies risk, and dual funds are no exception to the rule. A number of such funds were formed in the late 1960s and their performance record showed greater volatility than traditional funds holding similar portfolios. All these funds have reached maturity and no longer exist, but a number of new ones have been formed. They should be as risky as their predecessors and require careful analysis before you invest. Typically, income shares sell at premiums, while capital shares sell at discounts. The analytical task is to determine the appropriateness of the premium or discount.

Mutual Fund Services

In recent years, mutual funds have begun offering a wide assortment of services to their shareholders. Fidelity, for example, operates customer service centers that look like combined commercial bank and stockbrokerage offices. The larger

Investing in the "market" is possible with index funds.

A dual fund consists of income shares and capital shares; each offers a leveraged position.

fund families seem to be growing even larger, while the smaller individual funds are finding it more difficult to compete. The trend towards the financial supermarket appears prevalent in the mutual fund industry, since investors prefer to have most of their investment needs satisfied in one institution. The services discussed below are those most investors find useful.

Telephone Transactions   While the Fidelity service center appeals to some investors, many more prefer transacting by phone. After you establish an account, all additional purchases or sales can be made in this manner. You must be sent a prospectus for each fund in which you invest, and you need to file a separate application for each, but this takes very little time. You also can have funds wired to your bank to avoid a mail lag involved with a check.

Reinvestment of Dividends and Capital Gains   You have a number of reinvestment options with a fund. You can choose to have all dividends and capital gains mailed to you, you can take dividends in cash and reinvest capital gains by buying additional shares to the fund, or you can reinvest both in additional shares. Many funds, particularly income funds, allow you to withdraw a given amount each month as an annuity. If the fund's earnings exceed the annuity, the excess is automatically reinvested in the fund; and, in the reverse situation, shares are automatically sold to make up the annuity amount.

> Many funds offer a number of reinvestment options.

Also, some funds charge loads on reinvestments. This policy is seldom highlighted in the fund's prospectus, but is in effect whenever reinvestment takes place at an offer price, rather than NAV.

Fund Switching   A fund-switching privilege allows you to sell shares in one fund and reinvest the proceeds in another if each fund is a member of the same family. This service seems to be exceptionally well received by investors, particularly since a number of switches can be made each year without incurring any separate charges. However, loads may apply to load funds and there also may be an annual limit on the number of free switches, so it is important to read the fund's literature to understand the situation. Switching particularly appeals to investors who try to do market timing. You can invest in a growth or other equity fund when you feel the market will be bullish and then switch to a money market fund when your outlook turns bearish. We mentioned earlier playing sector funds to time the business cycle, which is made easier by fund switching. The growing number of investors who use switching services indicates that many people at least think they can time the market successfully; however, as we noted in Chapter 10 and elsewhere, there is little evidence to suggest they can. While convenient, fund switching also makes it easy to show investment losses if you can't time the market properly.

> Fund switching is particularly appealing to investors who do market timing.

Adaptability to Retirement Plans   Most mutual funds are readily adaptable to individual retirement plans such as IRAs and Keoghs. Making your investment an IRA, for example, requires nothing more than completing a simple form that

Using a fund for your
IRA is as easy as setting
up a bank deposit for
that purpose.

allows the fund to serve as a trustee. The set-up cost and annual maintenance
fees are competitive with those charged by commercial banks and other financial
institutions. Apparently, mutual funds are doing very well competing for IRA
deposits; their share of the market has increased rapidly. Finally, a number of
investors use fund switching among their IRA accounts, because any gains
escape current taxation. (Unfortunately, any losses do not offset other taxable
income.)

EVALUATING FUND PERFORMANCE

After you have identified a number of funds that meet your investment objectives,
how do you decide which funds are the best? Most investors attempt to find a
partial answer to this question by examining the fund's historical performance.
You can do this yourself using data from the fund's prospectus and annual
financial report, or from a library source such as Weisenberger's *Investment
Companies,* or you might simply rely upon evaluations provided in publications

It is important to under-
stand how fund evalua-
tions are made.

such as *Forbes, Money,* or *Business Week*. Even if you take the easy approach,
though, you should understand how evaluations are made. The procedures are
explained in the following sections.

Understanding Returns

Most funds make periodic cash distributions designated as dividends from
investment income or as distributions from realized gain on investments. Exhibit
15.7 shows a ten-year performance summary for Fidelity Fund, a very large
growth fund that invests primarily in blue chip issues. This reporting format is

Most funds use a similar
format to report share-
holder distributions.

standard and used by practically all funds. Notice that lines 4 and 6 show the
dividend and capital gain distributions. In 1984, for example, shareholders
received $0.71 in dividend distributions and $4.40 in capital gain distributions.
Notice also the NAV values at the beginning (line 8) and end (line 9) of each year.

Holding Period Return for A Single Year As a shareholder, you should be
interested in determining a holding period return (HPR). Using the information in
Exhibit 15.7, we can calculate the HPR for 1984 as follows:

$$\text{HPR} = \frac{\text{Distributions} + \text{Change in NAV}}{\text{Beginning of Year NAV}}$$
$$= \frac{(\$0.71 + \$4.40) + (\$14.82 - \$19.89)}{\$19.89}$$
$$= \frac{\$5.11 - \$5.07}{\$19.89} = \frac{\$0.04}{\$19.89} = 0.002, \text{ or } 0.2\%$$

Your rate of return in 1984, then, was two-tenths of a percent. It should be noted
the above calculation assumes you withdraw the distributions and do not reinvest
them in the fund; also, it assumes they are made at the end of the year.

EXHIBIT 15.7

Past performance of Fidelity Fund

				Years Ended December 31						
	1988	1987	1986	1985	1984	1983	1982	1981	1980	1979
1. Investment income	$ .65	$ .56	$ .74	$ .81	$ .84	$ .98	$ 1.01	$ 1.07	$ .93	$ .89
2. Expenses	.10	.11	.11	.11	.10	.14	.12	.14	.13	.12
3. Investment income—net	.55	.45	.63	.70	.74	.84	.89	.93	.80	.77
4. Dividends from investment income—net	(.56)	(.48)	(.66)	(.72)	(.71)	(.84)	(.89)	(.85)	(.80)	(.75)
5. Realized and unrealized gain (loss) on investments—net	1.85	.28	2.08	3.33	(.70)	2.96	3.89	(1.65)	4.65	2.02
6. Distributions from realized gain on investments—net	—	(2.72)	(4.08)	(.05)	(4.40)	(1.97)	(3.00)	(1.39)	(.68)	(.79)
7. Net increase (decrease) in net asset value	1.84	(2.74)	(2.03)	3.26	(5.07)	.99	.89	(2.96)	3.97	1.25
Net asset value:										
8. Beginning of year	13.58	16.05	18.08	14.82	19.89	18.90	18.01	20.97	17.00	15.75
9. End of year	$15.42	$13.58	$16.05	$18.08	$14.82	$19.89	$18.90	$18.01	$20.97	$17.00
10. Ratio of expenses to average net assets	.67%	.67%	.60%	.66%	.66%	.71%	.73%	.74%	.73%	.75%
11. Ratio of net investment income to average net assets	3.69%	2.75%	3.48%	4.25%	5.06%	4.34%	5.65%	4.88%	4.43%	4.76%
12. Portfolio turnover rate	175%	211%	214%	215%	200%	210%	165%	103%	67%	68%
13. Shares outstanding at end of year (000 omitted)	57,821	64,053	48,640	42,116	41,671	33,629	31,123	27,217	27,342	28,683

SOURCE: Fidelity Fund *Prospectus*, February 28, 1989. p. 3. © Fidelity Investments. All rights reserved.

Most fund annual reports, however, show rates of return based upon a reinvestment assumption. To calculate this rate, you must know when distributions took place during the year and the NAV at the times distributions were made. Exhibit 15.8 shows how the HPR is calculated, given these assumptions. As you see, it is a lengthy process and does not give the same HPR figure. This calculation shows an HPR of 1.5%, versus the previously calculated 0.2%. Since the HPR shown in Exhibit 15.8 is used so often, you should be aware of how it is determined. Of course, if you lack intra-year distribution information, you have no choice but to use the simpler HPR.

HPRs over Time The year 1984 was selected arbitrarily to illustrate HPR calculation methods for a single year, but you would be interested in HPRs for all years. Fortunately, the Fidelity Fund *Prospectus* (February 28, 1989) shows them, along with similar figures for the S&P 500, for each year from 1979 through 1988. Exhibit 15.9 presents the information. It should be noted that the 5- and 10-year summary percentages are geometric—not arithmetic—accumulations. For example, the 82.6% accumulation for Fidelity Fund for the five years ended 1988 is determined as follows:

$$0.826 = [(1.000 + 0.015) \times (1.000 + 0.277) \times (1.000 + 0.158)$$
$$\times (1.000 + 0.033) \times (1.000 + 0.178)] - 1.000$$

EXHIBIT 15.8
Calculating an HPR assuming dividend reinvestment

Date (1984)	Activity	(1) Distri- bution	(2) NAV	(3) Shares Acquired (1)/(2)	(4) Total (2) × (3)
1/01	Initial investment	$ —	$19.89	1.0000	$19.89
1/30	Capital gain of $4.40/share	4.4000	14.84	0.2965	—
	Account total	—	14.84	1.2965	19.24
2/27	Dividend of $.135/share	0.1750	14.16	0.0124	—
	Account total	—	14.16	1.3089	18.53
5/29	Dividend of $.135/share	0.1767	13.28	0.0133	—
	Account total	—	13.28	1.3222	17.56
9/04	Dividend of $.135/share	0.1785	14.50	0.0123	—
	Account total	—	14.50	1.3345	19.35
12/17	Dividend of $.305/share	0.4070	14.43	0.0282	—
	Account total	—	14.43	1.3627	19.66
12/31	End of year	—	14.82	1.3627	20.19

$$1984 \text{ HPR} = \frac{20.19 - 19.89}{19.89} = \frac{+0.30}{19.89} = +0.015 \ (1.5\%)$$

Years Ended 12/31	Fidelity Fund's Total Return	S&P Total Return
1979	18.7%	18.5%
1980	33.9	32.5
1981	−3.3	−4.9
1982	34.4	21.5
1983	22.4	22.5
1984	1.5	6.2
1985	27.7	31.6
1986	15.8	18.6
1987	3.3	5.3
1988	17.8	16.6
Five years ended 1988	82.6	103.5
Ten years ended 1988	362.2	352.3

EXHIBIT 15.9
Historical total returns: Fidelity Fund and the S&P 500

$$0.826 = [1.015 \times 1.277 \times 1.158 \times 1.033 \times 1.178] - 1.000$$
$$0.826 = 1.826 - 1.000$$

This calculation tells us that $1 invested in the fund at the beginning of 1984 would have grown to $1.826 by the end of 1988. The geometric average also can be calculated from the above figure (see Chapter 3 for a discussion of this average). Simply take the fifth root (there are five periods) of 1.826 and subtract 1.000 from it. We have

The geometric average is a better measurement of fund performance than the arithmetic average.

$$\text{Geometric average return} = [1.826]^{1/5} - 1.000$$
$$= 1.128 - 1.000 = 0.128, \text{ or } 12.8\%$$

Before going on, let us calculate the geometric average returns for the Fidelity Fund for ten years and the S&P 500 for both five and ten years. The calculations are shown below:

$$\text{Fidelity (10 years)} = [4.622]^{1/10} - 1.000 = 1.165 - 1.000$$
$$= 0.165, \text{ or } 16.5\%$$
$$\text{S\&P 500 (5 years)} = [2.035]^{1/5} - 1.000 = 1.153 - 1.000$$
$$= 0.153, \text{ or } 15.3\%$$
$$\text{S\&P 500 (10 years)} = [4.523]^{1/10} - 1.000 = 1.163 - 1.000$$
$$= 0.163, \text{ or } 16.3\%$$

So, Fidelity Fund's performance for the 5-year period is quite a bit poorer (12.8% versus 15.3%) than the S&P 500. However, it did show a slight advantage (16.5%

versus 16.3%) for the 10-year period. The next question is: how did the fund perform on a risk-adjusted basis?

Measuring Risk

A fund's risk can be measured with the techniques explained in Chapter 4. The beta measurement seems particularly appropriate because many funds' returns show a high degree of statistical correlation to the overall market's return. This gives analysts greater confidence in using the statistic to make investment decisions. Along with the beta measurement, we derive a fund's alpha value, which shows if it outperformed the market *on a risk-adjusted basis*.

Determining Alpha and Beta   Using the data provided in Exhibit 15.9, the graph in Exhibit 15.10 is prepared. It illustrates a regression of Fidelity Fund's

EXHIBIT 15.10
Determining Fidelity Fund's beta value

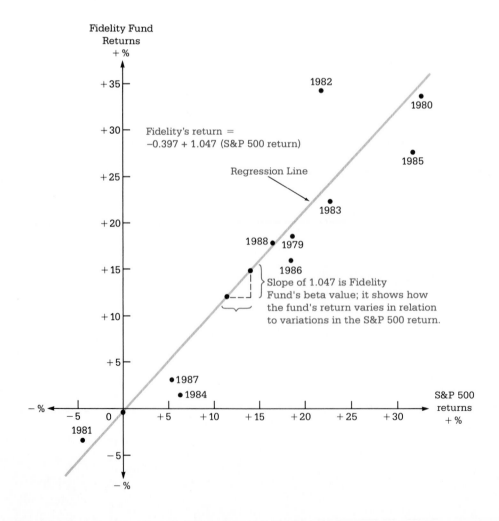

Fidelity's return =
−0.397 + 1.047 (S&P 500 return)

Slope of 1.047 is Fidelity Fund's beta value; it shows how the fund's return varies in relation to variations in the S&P 500 return.

returns on the S&P 500 returns. The return for each in a given year is one data point on the graph. The regression line is a line of best fit through the 10 data points. You could fit this line free hand, but a more accurate fit is provided by a calculator or computer.

The slope of the regression line is the fund's beta value. As the figure shows, Fidelity's beta was 1.047, which means it was slightly riskier than the overall market with its beta of 1.0. So, while Fidelity had a slightly higher return than the market over the 10-year period, we are not sure whether this higher return reflects superior fund management or simply greater fund risk. To analyze this issue further, we can determine Fidelity's **alpha value**. Exhibit 15.11 is helpful in this effort.

Over the 10-year period, the average return on short-term Treasury bills was about 9.0%. With this figure and the 16.3% rate of return on the S&P 500, the securities market line (SML) is drawn. You should remember the SML discussion from Chapter 8, but note the line in Exhibit 15.11 has a different shape because it is derived from only 10 years of data. Moreover, use of the SML in the present situation is somewhat different. In Chapter 8, the SML was constructed on the basis of *expectation;* that is, although historical data were used, the thrust of the analysis was to determine expected future returns for all portfolios consisting of different combinations of a risk-free asset and a market asset. These returns then served as minimum required returns to evaluate specific assets with given beta values. In the present application, the SML is used to evaluate what has *actually*

The SML is used to determine a fund's alpha value.

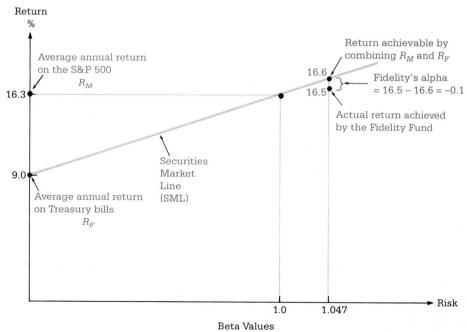

EXHIBIT 15.11
Illustration of Fidelity Fund's alpha value

happened over some period of time. It is called an *ex-post* (after-the-fact) SML, while the expectative SML is called *ex-ante* (before the fact).

While the perspectives are quite different, the mechanical use of the SML is identical. Now, we wish to know what return (R_i) could have been achieved by investing in only the two assets—the S&P 500 (R_M) and Treasury bills (R_F)—in a proportion that would have led to a portfolio beta of 1.047. The answer is determined below:

$$R_i = R_F + \beta_i(R_M - R_F)$$

$$R_i = 9.0\% + 1.047 \, (16.3\% - 9.0\%)$$

$$R_i = 9.0\% + 1.047 \, (7.3\%)$$

$$R_i = 9.0\% + 7.6\%$$

$$R_i = 16.6\%$$

Since this return is higher than the actual return of 16.5% achieved by Fidelity, we conclude its management underperformed the market on a risk-adjusted basis. You would have been slightly better off investing on your own in a market index and Treasury bills. The difference between Fidelity's actual return of 16.5% and the return on the SML of 16.6% is Fidelity's alpha value: −0.1%. If a fund's return is greater than the corresponding value on the SML, it has a positive alpha, which suggests good fund management.

Choosing a Fund   As a general rule, you should select funds that show positive alpha values and avoid those with negative alpha values. That is a simple rule to follow, but how do you choose among funds that all have positive alphas, assuming each meets your investment objective? There are a number of responses to this question. One method ranks funds on the basis of alpha and chooses those funds with the higher values. If another fund had an alpha of, say, 2.0%, it would be a better choice than Fidelity.

Choosing among funds with positive alpha values requires a decision rule.

Another widely used approach compares a fund's excess return to its beta weight. In this case, excess return is defined as actual return minus the risk-free return. The comparison is called the **Treynor Index (TI),** and it is calculated for Fidelity Fund below.

$$TI = \frac{R_i - R_F}{\beta_i} = \frac{16.5\% - 9.0\%}{1.047} = \frac{7.5\%}{1.047} = 7.16\%$$

Fidelity's 7.16% value could be compared to TI values of other funds and a selection made on the basis of the highest value.

Finally, an approach that is employed more quickly than the above two simply compares the fund's beta-adjusted return to the market return. This **risk-adjusted rate of return (RAROR)** is shown below.

$$RAROR = \frac{R_i}{\beta_i} - R_M$$

$$= \frac{16.5\%}{1.047} - 16.3\% = 15.8\% - 16.3\% = -0.5\%$$

Funds are then ranked by RAROR values and those with higher values are favored. The advantage of this approach is it eliminates the need to use the risk-free rate. From a theoretical perspective, though, it is less rigorous than either the alpha ranking or the Treynor Index.

How Good Are Fund Managers?

If you read fund advertisements in the popular press, you probably conclude that fund managers are geniuses at selecting securities. The advertisements are almost always return-oriented and almost never mention risk in any useful way. Moreover, they are fond of illustrating by how much they beat the S&P 500, but they never tell you what risks they took to do so.

Mutual fund managers usually tout their performances but say little about risks undertaken.

Since performance information is readily available, the subject of evaluating performance has been well researched by finance academicians. Results of earlier studies were fairly uniform and indicated that very few funds outperformed the S&P 500 index on a risk-adjusted basis, as we have just explained it (see Exhibit 15.12). And, those that did better in one year were not likely to repeat this accomplishment in a following year. In short, they might have been lucky, as you would expect any small set out of a large group of investors to be in any given year. Some newer studies, though, have indicated partially conflicting results. They indicate that some funds have consistently done better than the market. These funds apparently achieve their success by selecting and holding securities that perform well, rather than through clever market-timing techniques. An

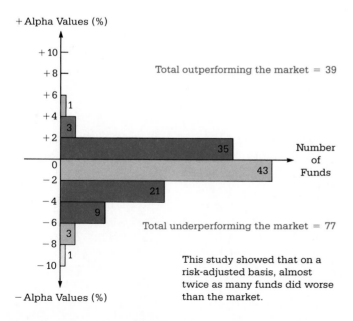

EXHIBIT 15.12
Mutual fund performance (Source: Michael C. Jensen, "The Performance of Mutual Funds in the Period 1945–64." *Journal of Finance,* May 1968, pp. 389–416.)

implication of these studies is that investors should avoid funds with high turnover ratios and rapidly changing beta weights.

Fidelity Fund is a case in point. If you refer to Exhibit 15.7 and review line 12, you see that its turnover ratio has increased dramatically since 1979. A turnover of 215% in 1985 is exceptionally high, indicating the fund turned over its entire portfolio of securities 2.15 times during the year. Moreover, you might note the turnover ratio increased sharply in 1981. Now, review Exhibit 15.9 and see if the fund did better in the high turnover years than it did in the low turnover years. Again, comparing performance to the S&P 500, it did not do better: in the early years it beat the S&P 500, while in the later years it underperformed the index.

Popular Press Fund Evaluations

Evaluating mutual funds is a regular feature of some financial magazines. *Forbes* has an annual survey of mutual funds, which includes an evaluation of performance. It attempts to rank funds on the basis of how well they do in both bull and bear markets. Its rankings are given as letter grades, such as A, B, and so forth. This is an attempt to bring risk into the picture, but it falls somewhat short of the ideal, because the connection between return and risk is not expressed quantitatively or rigorously. *Money* magazine follows a similar approach in its evaluations and receives the same criticism. If you select your funds by using either of these sources, you should at least review several years (or more) of evaluations to see if their current high-rated funds have performed well in the past.

Forbes, Money, and *Business Week* prepare reasonably thorough fund evaluations; each considers return and risk.

Business Week also has an annual fund evaluation appearing in one of the February issues. Its review appears to use the beta approach explained above to rank funds on a return-risk basis. By following its rankings, or those of *Forbes* or *Money,* you can select funds that have performed well and avoid those that have not. However, you still might wish to consider other fund characteristics, particularly loads. As noted previously, there is no evidence supporting superior performance by load funds, and it is difficult to justify investing in a fund with a heavy initial load.

SUMMARY

Investment companies are popular pooling arrangements. A closed-end fund has a fixed number of shares that are traded like other stocks. A fund share has a net asset value (NAV), but closed-end fund shares can trade at discounts or premiums to NAV. Open-end funds—which are far more popular than closed-end funds—sell additional fund shares and redeem them (each at NAV) in response to investor demand. These funds may have front-end loads and other charges.

It is important to understand a fund's investment objective: growth, income, money market, sector, specialized, or index. Funds offer many investment conveniences, such as telephone transactions, automatic reinvestment of dividends or capital gains, fund switching, and adaptability to retirement plans.

Investors should evaluate fund performance before making specific selections. Holding period returns should be used and geometric averages determined. Fund risk can often be measured with a beta weight, and the beta method also indicates superior or inferior performance by the fund in relation to the overall market. Some fund managers tout their performances in the popular press but often neglect to indicate risk. Moreover, fund evaluation in the popular press usually does not link risk and performance in an adequate fashion. So, it is important for investors to be capable of making their own evaluations.

KEY TERMS

Select the alternative that best identifies the key term.

1. fund
2. closed-end fund
3. net asset value (NAV)
4. open-end fund
5. front-end loads
6. back-end loads
7. 12b−1 plan
8. growth fund
9. maximum capital appreciation funds
10. income fund
11. balanced fund
12. money market fund
13. sector fund
14. specialized fund
15. index fund
16. dual fund
17. alpha value
18. Treynor Index (TI)
19. risk-adjusted rate of return (RAROR)

a. allows a fund to charge shareholders for promotion costs
b. invests in one industry
c. organized investment company that buys securities
d. actual return minus beta-related return on SML
e. its shares outstanding are constantly changing
f. acquires shares expected to show price appreciation over time
g. (actual return − risk-free return) divided by beta
h. its shares outstanding are relatively constant
i. might invest in gold company shares
j. invests in growth shares and income shares
k. underlying value of a mutual fund share
l. its performance matches the market
m. purchase commission
n. seek quick price appreciation
o. (actual return divided by beta) minus the market return
p. invests in liquid assets
q. selling commission
r. invests in fixed-income securities with long maturities
s. offers income shares or capital shares

REVIEW QUESTIONS	1. Discuss the current popularity of investment companies. Which form—open-end or closed-end—is more popular?
	2. Describe the characteristics of a closed-end fund. Is there any advantage in investing in closed-end funds selling at discounts or premiums? Explain.
	3. What is a fund's net asset value (NAV)? How might this differ from its offer price? Explain.
	4. Describe the characteristics of an open-end fund. Do you buy its shares in the same manner as you buy shares in a closed-end fund? Explain.
	5. Explain the following terms: (a) front-end load, (b) back-end load, (c) 12b–1 plan, and (d) fund family.
	6. Briefly explain eight fund objectives. Which might be the most important to you personally?
	7. How does a dual fund work? Discuss whether it is more or less risky than a traditional fund offering a similar portfolio.
	8. Briefly discuss four important fund services. Which might be the most important to you personally?
	9. How might an investor measure his or her *annual* return from a fund?
	10. How do most funds calculate return measurements reported to shareholders?
	11. Explain the terms *beta value* and *alpha value* as they apply in mutual fund evaluations.
	12. How does the market risk premium differ in measuring fund performance as opposed to its use in finding under- or over-valued securities?
	13. Explain the Treynor Index, indicating how it is calculated.
	14. What is a RAROR and how is it calculated?
	15. Describe the performance evidence of mutual fund managers and sources of fund evaluations in the popular press.

PROBLEMS AND PROJECTS	1. The Zoom Fund has 10,000 shares outstanding. It owns 100 shares of DuPont (selling at $80 a share) and 500 shares of Exxon (selling at $50 a share). Calculate its NAV if it also has $500 in liabilities.
	2. The Radiant Fund made two distributions last year. The first was a dividend of $1.00 a share and the second was a capital gain of $3.00 a share. NAV was $30 at the beginning of the year, $20 when the dividend was distributed, $15 when the capital gain was distributed, and $25 at year end.
	a. Calculate Radiant's HPR assuming all distributions took place at year end and were not reinvested.
	b. Calculate its HPR taking into consideration when dividends were paid and assuming they were reinvested when received. Compare and discuss this return to the one calculated in *a*.
	3. Annual returns for the Sun Fund, the Moon Fund, and the S&P 500 are shown below.

Year	Sun	Moon	S&P 500
1	8.0%	4.0%	5.0%
2	−1.0	3.0	2.0
3	27.0	11.0	15.0
4	36.0	12.0	20.0
5	−23.0	−2.0	−10.0

   a. Calculate the arithmetic average return for each. Then determine the geometric accumulation for each. If you have an appropriate calculator, show that the geometric average returns are 7.3%, 5.5%, and 5.9%, respectively. Finally, discuss which is the best-performing fund.

   b. Your highest return is with the Sun Fund; but is it high enough to offset its added risk? To answer this question, begin by determining Sun and Moon funds' beta values. Use any method, including a graphic plot of the return of each fund versus the S&P 500's returns. Then determine alpha values (assume the average risk-free return was 2.0%), Treynor Index values, and RARORs. Discuss your findings, indicating clearly the best investment: the Sun Fund, the Moon Fund, or a portfolio of the S&P 500 and the risk-free asset.

4. (*Student Project*) From a library, request a year of back issues to *Forbes, Money,* and *Business Week*. For each publication, find the issue that evaluates mutual funds. Then select a sample of 10 or so funds and compare evaluations. In reviewing the *Forbes* issue, compare fund operating costs (expressed as a percent of net assets) and note the wide variations. Does it appear that funds with high ratios have better performance histories? Discuss.

5. (*Student Project*) From one of the sources indicated in Project 4 above, find the toll-free numbers of several funds. Call them and request a prospectus, the last annual report, and the most recent quarterly report. When these publications arrive, evaluate each fund, utilizing the methods explained in this chapter. Prepare a report on your findings.

CASE ANALYSES

The Ankeneys, Nick and Karla, are a recently married couple with two small children. They have a modest combined income, but plan to save and invest $1,000 a year to meet future goals. They are seeking a balanced portfolio invested in common stocks, bonds, and money market instruments. Nick and Karla have some understanding of securities and security analysis, but hardly consider themselves proficient in the area. Nick is a carpenter and Karla works part-time as a legal assistant. Both are very busy right now and have little free time.

   Initially, they planned to do their own security selection, but lately they have been leaning towards investment companies, even though their knowledge of this investment medium is very limited. They have been contacted by a representative of a securities firm. She has indicated the firm can service all the Ankeneys' needs, including mutual funds. She also provided literature on various stock funds which indicate rather good performances over the past 20 years.

   a. Which method of investing do you feel is more appropriate for the Ankeneys? Explain your answer.

**15.1
Are Mutual
Funds
Appropriate for
the Ankeneys?**

Questions

b. Should the Ankeneys consider investing in funds on their own, or should they rely exclusively upon the securities firm representative? Cite and discuss specific factors in reaching your conclusion.

c. Assuming the Ankeneys choose to invest in funds on their own, indicate the steps they should take in the process. How should they select appropriate funds, how can they establish accounts, and what decisions should they make with respect to reinvesting dividends. Also, indicate data sources the Ankeneys can consider in evaluating and following fund performances.

15.2 Roger Maltbey Examines a Mutual Fund Report

Roger Maltbey intends to invest in a mutual fund that specializes in investing in the common stock of small companies. The fund seems to have done quite well over the past 10 years and Roger thinks it also should do well in the future. A popular personal finance magazine gives the fund a high ranking, which is encouraging, but Roger is a bit skeptical since a similar rank is given to many other funds. He requested literature from the fund and received a preliminary report indicating performances for the past two years. Unfortunately, Roger doesn't completely understand the data. He has requested your help.

He would like you to advise him on the relative attractiveness of the fund and whether it is suitable for him. He describes his primary investment objective as long-term capital accumulation and indicates that he has an average tolerance for risk. Information on the fund appears in the following table.

	Past Year	Two Years Ago
1. Investment income	$ .90	$ .97
2. Expenses	.15	.12
3. Investment income—net	.75	.85
4. Dividends from net investment income	(.80)	(.81)
5. Realized and unrealized gain (loss) on investments—net	2.84	1.13
6. Distributions from realized gains	(4.14)	(.28)
7. Net increase (decrease) in net asset value	(1.35)	.89
8. Beginning of year	15.57	14.68
9. End of year	14.22	15.57
10. Ratio of expenses to average net assets	1.57%	1.03%
11. Portfolio turnover	186%	112%

To help in responding to Roger, you did some research and found that yields on 90-day U.S. Treasury bills averaged 7% in the past year and 10% two years ago. Additionally, the overall market showed a return of 18% a year ago and 9% two years ago. You also have found the fund's beta value, which is 1.8.

a. Determine holding period returns for each of the two years.
b. Evaluate the fund's performance for each of the two years utilizing alpha values, Treynor Index values, and RARORs.
c. Would you advise Roger to invest in the fund? Explain your answer.

HELPFUL READING

Baldwin, William. "The Fund: Keep It Simple." *Forbes,* February 9, 1987, pp. 128–29.

Chen, Carl R., and S. Stockum. "Selectivity, Market Timing, and Random Beta Behavior of Mutual Funds." *Journal of Financial Research,* Spring 1986.

Clements, Jonathon. "Faulty Arithmetic." *Forbes,* May 15, 1989, p. 112.

————. "Smart Money?" *Forbes,* June 12, 1989, p. 131.

————. "Twins But Not Identical Twins." *Forbes,* May 1, 1989, pp. 402–3.

Gottschalk, Earl C., Jr. "Fees for Reinvestment Could Lurk Within Your Fund." *The Wall Street Journal,* June 14, 1989, p. C1.

Lowenstein, Louis. "Ignorance Isn't Bliss." *Barron's,* May 29, 1989, p. 11.

Schiffers, Manuel, and Priscilla Brandon. "Loads vs. No-Loads: The Winner is. . ." *Changing Times,* February 1989, pp. 35–40.

Siconofli, Michael. "Account Transfers Can Be a Real Circus." *The Wall Street Journal,* March 13, 1989, p. C1.

————. "Firms' Pay Policies for Fund Sales Can Put Broker, Investor at Odds." *The Wall Street Journal,* March 3, 1989, p. C1.

————. "Locked In: Mutual Funds' Use of Exit Fees Stirs Investors' Complaints." *The Wall Street Journal,* March 13, 1989, p. A1.

Walbert, Laura. "Buyer Beware." *Financial World,* February 7, 1989, pp. 48–49.

CHAPTER SIXTEEN

Other Pooling Arrangements

INVESTMENT TRUSTS

Unit Investment Trusts

Real Estate Investment Trusts

LIMITED PARTNERSHIPS

Business Activities

Investment Potential

SELF-DIRECTED POOLING
ARRANGEMENTS

Investment Clubs

Money Manager Limited
Partnerships

BOXES

Unit Investment Trusts—What You
See May Not Be What You Get

Investment Clubs Are for Real

After you finish this chapter, you
will be able to:

- understand the nature of a unit
  investment trust and its advantages for investing in municipal
  bonds, GNMA passthroughs, and
  other assets.

- understand the nature of a real
  estate investment trust and distinguish among different types of
  trusts.

- evaluate the potential return from
  a real estate investment trust, including a determination of share
  premium or discount.

- understand the nature of a limited
  partnership, including its unique
  income tax situation.

- recognize advantages and disadvantages of investing in limited
  partnerships.

- understand the nature and operation of self-directed pooling arrangements and recognize advantages and disadvantages of
  investment clubs and money
  manager limited partnerships.

While the organized investment company is the most common form of pooling arrangement, there are other important forms. Investment trusts are used in a variety of settings to invest in assets ranging from Treasury bills to precious gems. Some limited partnerships offer certain tax advantages not available in other pooling forms, and with an investment club you not only receive interest and dividends from your investing activities, but possibly a good time as well. This chapter discusses the advantages and disadvantages of these other pooling arrangements.

INVESTMENT TRUSTS

A **trust** is a legal document that allows one person or institution to hold title to assets and to manage them for the benefit of others. Trusts are common in estate planning, where they are often used in conjunction with wills to help in the process of transferring wealth, both during a person's lifetime and at his or her death. These so-called "private trusts" differ somewhat from "public trusts" that are used in investing. The private trust has a *grantor* who transfers assets to a *trustee* who in turn manages them for the benefit of *beneficiaries*. In an investment trust, the grantor is replaced with a trust originator who purchases assets and then transfers them to a trustee. The originator in turn sells units to the trust to investors, who stand in place of beneficiaries. The trustee's role, however, is the same in each case.

   With a unit investment trust, the ownership instruments are simply called *units,* but in a real estate investment trust, they are called *shares*. The two types of trusts differ in important ways in addition to terminology, as we shall see.

Unit Investment Trusts

A **unit investment trust (UIT)** is formed usually to invest in intangible assets, the most popular being debt instruments of one type or another. However, some trusts do invest in tangible assets. Units are often priced at $1,000 each and most trusts require a minimum purchase of two to five units. Most unit investment trusts have finite lives that are pegged to the maturities of the assets they own, while others are terminated as of a certain date (with assets being sold and proceeds distributed to unit holders). In most cases, the originator of the trust makes a market in trust units, which means you as an investor can sell your units at any time, as you can with an open-end mutual fund. Obviously, this feature enhances the investment's marketability considerably, but you should understand that units are repurchased at the current market values of trust assets. If these assets are subject to price variability, you run the risk of poor liquidity even though the units are readily marketable. The more common investment trusts are explained below.

Trust originators usually redeem trust units, but only at their market values.

Municipal Bond Trusts   At present, the **municipal (muni) bond trust** is probably the most popular of all UITs. Approximately $130 billion was invested in all UITs in early 1989 (compared to over $800 billion in mutual funds), with most of it in muni trusts. A muni trust is usually formed by a brokerage house or other originator specializing in them, such as John Nuveen and Company—one of the largest. Exhibit 16.1 illustrates the formation process. Obviously, muni trusts appeal to investors in the highest federal income tax brackets. Some of these trusts have been formed to offer both state and local tax exemption as well, but these often have lower yields than nationally invested trusts and may not offer a significant after-tax advantage. Moreover, since their portfolios are limited to very narrow geographical and taxing regions, they typically involve higher risk because of the shortage of suitable securities available for an adequately diversified portfolio.

As an investor, you face the choice between muni trusts and muni mutual funds, and you also must decide whether either one is more desirable than buying muni bonds on your own. A minimum investment in a trust or fund is typically $1,000 to $5,000, while at least $15,000 is needed to achieve adequate diversification when investing on your own. Exhibit 16.2 compares other aspects of the three investment approaches. Trusts typically have front-end loads of about 4.5% and charge annual operating fees of about 0.2%. These fees are about one-fourth those of the mutual funds. In addition, a trust has a 2.0% spread to sell. Considering these costs together suggests that the longer the holding period, the better alternative a trust will be. With an annual savings of 0.6% (0.8% − 0.2%), it takes almost 11 years (6.5/.06) for the total costs to be the same with each.

Minimum investment in a trust is usually $1,000 to $5,000.

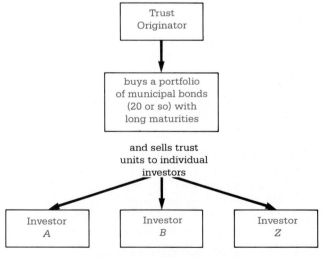

EXHIBIT 16.1
Formation of a municipal bond trust

EXHIBIT 16.2

Investing in municipal bonds: Three approaches

Item to Consider	On Your Own	Unit Trust	No-Load Mutual Fund
Selecting and Holding Bonds	Your job: make sure of adequate diversification	Originator picks and holds 15 to 40 issues	Portfolio manager holds and actively manages over 40 issues
Managing the Portfolio	Your job: avoid excessive trading	Virtually no management	Considerable: avoid funds with excessive turnovers
Payments	Semiannual payments	Monthly checks, if desired	Monthly checks or reinvestment
Commissions and Fees	Commission is usually a 2.0% spread between buying and selling	2% buy-sell spread, plus 4.5% front-end load, plus 0.2% operating costs	No load and no spread, but 0.8% operating costs
Insurance	Yes, a must for a small portfolio	Available, but will reduce yield	Unnecessary because of large portfolio
Investor Appeal	Experienced investor with no less than $10,000 to invest in munis	Casual investor willing to hold 10 years or longer	Investor with shorter horizon or one who wants other mutual fund services

The default risk with a trust is usually very low. Some originators have taken greater risks recently, however, so it is important to review a trust's prospectus to examine the quality of the portfolio it will hold. If more than, say, 20% of the issues are rated below BBB (Standard and Poor's minimum investment grade) or Baa (Moody's), there is potential for default losses, and you must decide whether you will feel comfortable with this situation. About half the trusts being formed in recent years offer default insurance. While reducing risk, insurance also reduces yield by as much as 40 basis points. A muni fund generally has sufficient diversification to eliminate the problem of default risk; however, it may offer higher interest rate risk if its portfolio includes bonds with longer maturities. A fund's portfolio is constantly changing, so gauging its interest rate risk is more difficult than it is with a trust with its fixed portfolio. (Actually, a trust's portfolio is not always fixed: it may sell bonds if the trustee judges a deterioration in their quality; however, it is legally prevented from buying additional bonds. Also, if bonds default or are called, the trust's income can change.)

No UIT can guarantee a rate of return because defaults or called issues cannot be known with certainty.

GNMA Trusts   Most large stockbrokerage houses have formed **GNMA trusts** that invest in Ginnie Mae passthrough securities. These UITs have also been very popular, because investing directly involves difficulties, primarily the $25,000 face

Unit Investment Trusts—What You See May Not Be What You Get

On paper, a unit investment trust (UIT) makes a lot of sense: A sophisticated money manager designs a relatively safe portfolio of securities (usually municipal bonds), puts them away (so to speak) for the benefit of trustholders, and then bows out of the picture. As the years roll by, trustholders enjoy the income with very low operating costs to pay, and eventually the bonds mature and trustholders' units are redeemed with the proceeds. Surely that favorite expression of sophisticated bond traders—"locking in a return"—must apply here. What could go wrong?

What can go wrong in today's market environment is that, as competition heats up for the bond investor's funds, some originators bend the rules a bit to offer high-yielding deals. So you might find a portfolio laced heavily with zero coupon bonds that mature beyond the trust's termination. Since they are very cheap, the trust has plenty of excess funds to invest in premium bonds, which enhance its quoted yield to investors, but

what the zeros will be worth at termination time is anybody's guess. This practice locks in very little.

Even worse, some originators include bonds of questionable quality, and under arrangements that appear as conflicts of interest. For example, an SEC investigation of the Washington Public Power Supply System (the infamous Woops) indicated that two originators were also lead underwriters for several bond offerings, while other originators were part of underwriting syndicates. Naturally, any defaults in the trust portfolio will diminish return below the supposed locked-in rate.

Finally, many bonds today are callable. If and when they are called, the trust portfolio is altered accordingly. Again, the locked-in rate disappears. The call feature is particularly onerous to trusts since they are prohibited from buying other bonds. Indeed, doing so would make them more of a managed, rather than unmanaged, fund.

It's unfortunate that the shabby behavior of originators

has permeated a medium that is designed for small investors. Apparently, however, the SEC plans no serious investigation of the industry other than a review of advertising regulations. What to do? The first and easiest step is to avoid UITs; fortunately, there are mutual funds available to serve the same investor needs. If you won't take the time to study a UIT's prospectus and review an originator's track record, this is the only way to go (other than investing on your own).

The second alternative is to take the time. If your broker suggests a UIT, ask for the following *before* you invest: (1) a prospectus, and (2) details of other UITs the firm has sponsored, including a history of performance. What return did the previous UITs offer, and what did they deliver? If the broker doesn't respond to the latter request, look for another investment. Keep in mind that brokerage commissions on UITs are surely high enough (4% to 5% range) to make the broker interested in selling them.

value of a single security. Most trusts pass both interest and principal payments to trust holders each month, thus providing a steady cash flow.

Mutual funds also invest in mortgage-backed securities, so the logical question is whether you are better off with a mutual fund or a UIT. As in the case of a muni trust, it's difficult to generalize, so you really must read the prospectus of any fund or trust you are considering. The funds may not have a front-end load, while the trusts usually charge about 4% or 5%. On the other hand, a fund's yearly management fees are typically higher. The funds offer better services involving reinvestment of interest or principal, withdrawals, and fund switching, which might be important if you are investing in other funds within a family.

Other UITs   UITs have been formed to invest in other kinds of assets. **Liquid investment trusts** were very popular before money market mutual funds were formed. These trusts invested in short-term securities that provided investors with higher short-term yields than those available on savings deposits.

Exhibit 16.3 shows an advertisement of an unusual trust. Its objective is to assure investors of getting back an amount at least equal to what they invested. This is accomplished by investing half the funds raised in zero coupon bonds guaranteed to double at maturity. The other half of the initial ante is invested in shares of an equity mutual fund that is expected to show good growth over the trust's life. Actually, this trust is nothing more than a balanced fund, whose weights will change over time in response to the annual appreciation of the zeros and the performance of the equity fund. If a balanced fund appeals to you, then this "Double Play Trust" might make sense, particularly if annual management fees are low.

UITs have been formed to achieve many different objectives; investing in precious gems, for example.

Another interesting use of a UIT was the "Jefferson Trust" formed by Thomson McKinnon, a stockbrokerage firm. It purchased high-quality diamonds, offering investors an efficient means of participating in the precious gems market. Launched in December of 1980 at $994 a unit, this trust has been a huge disappointment, with the value of a unit being only $115 at May 31, 1989 (the trust terminated in 1990). This failure, however, does not diminish the usefulness of the trust vehicle for making such investments. It underscores, however, the necessity of evaluating carefully the assets in which the trust will invest.

A bond index trust simply attempts to match the performance of a bond index.

Finally, a very recent trust innovation is one that invests in a bond index. These trusts are similar to stock index funds and appeal to bond investors for the same reasons stock index funds appeal to equity investors. The idea is that most bond investment managers cannot do as well as an unmanaged index. So, why pay for the so-called professionally managed portfolio when one linked to an index does better? There is growing evidence that bond management has not been an outstanding success. For example, one study showed that 69% of bond managers reviewed did not do as well over a four-year period (ended September 30, 1985) as the Shearson-Lehman Brothers' Bond Index. Another study covering an eight-year period showed that 58% underperformed the index. **Bond index trusts** have had very large minimum deposits because they were originally intended for institutional investors. However, Vanguard offers one to the general public with a $3,000 minimum investment.

EXHIBIT 16.3
Advertisement for an unusual trust appearing in *Money* magazine (Courtesy Kemper Sales Company)

Real Estate Investment Trusts

A **real estate investment trust (REIT)** invests in assets related to the real estate industry. While its legal characteristics make it a trust, investors often view and evaluate a REIT as though it were a closed-end investment company. There are similarities: each has a relatively fixed capital structure with shares traded on the organized exchanges and the over-the-counter market, and each pays most of its earnings in dividends. But there is an important difference: a mutual fund invests exclusively in securities, while REITs invest in both securities and tangible assets.

A congressional act in 1960 regulated REITs extensively. To operate as one and to enjoy the federal income tax exemption, the trust must meet five conditions:

1. 75% of its assets must be in real estate, mortgages, cash, or government securities at the end of each quarter;
2. 75% of its gross income must come from real estate or mortgages;
3. it must distribute 90% of its income to beneficiaries (shareholders);
4. it must have at least 100 beneficiaries; and
5. 50% or more of its shares cannot be controlled by any five or fewer beneficiaries.

REITs are usually classified as equity or mortgage trusts.

Types of REITs   There are differences among REITs, and with about 130 from which to choose, it is necessary to identify these differences. They are highlighted in Exhibit 16.4 and discussed in the following sections. [Exhibit 16.4]

Equity Trusts.   An **equity trust** invests in tangible, real property. Some hold interests in a wide variety of real estate assets—commercial and office buildings, shopping centers, warehouses, and more—throughout the United States, while others either specialize in a particular type of property or limit their investing to a small geographical area. The principal assets of Santa Anita Realty, for example, are the Santa Anita racetrack and a 50% interest in an adjacent enclosed shopping center.

Mortgage Trusts.   A **mortgage trust** invests in mortgages backed by real estate. If you invest in one, in effect you are participating in the commercial mortgage-lending business. Commercial lending involves large sums of money and often complex lending arrangements. Clearly, a small, inexperienced investor cannot enter this area easily without a pooling arrangement.

Finite-Life REITs.   A **finite-life REIT,** called a **FREIT,** is a relatively recent innovation. It is designed to sell all its properties at the end of ten or fifteen years and distribute any capital gains to the shareholders. The rationale for a FREIT is that it should overcome the tendency for REITs to sell at discounts from the appraised values of the properties they own. With a definite termination point, investors should be willing to pay share prices that reflect the intrinsic value of the FREIT. Investors apparently have been willing to accept the rationale, since

Margin notes:

REITs are regulated extensively and must meet certain requirements to be exempt from federal income taxes.

FREITs are designed to overcome the tendency of REITs to sell at discounts from appraised values.

EXHIBIT 16.4

Types of REITs

Type	Activity	Investment Appeal
Equity Trust	Invests in tangible property, mostly real estate	A convenient way to invest in real estate on a diversified basis
Mortgage Trust	Invests in mortgages	Higher yields of commercial loans available to investors with limited funds
Finite-Life REIT (FREIT)	Invests in real estate	Properties sold in 10 to 15 years and trust liquidated; REIT shares may not sell at large discount from equity per share
Single-Purpose REIT	Invests in properties of a single company	Very attractive return, *if* lessee company remains financially sound
CMO REIT	Buys mortgage-backed passthroughs; sells collateralized securities backed by them	Opportunity to earn a spread between short-term and long-term interest rates

FREIT shares typically sell at higher multiples of earnings than comparable equity trusts.

Single-Purpose REITs. A **single-purpose REIT** is also a new innovation. It is established to buy properties of a single company, such as chains of fast-food restaurants or tire stores. It then leases these properties back to the business. An investment in one of these can be quite risky, because the REIT is completely dependent upon the success of the leasing business.

CMO REITs. A **CMO REIT** is also a fairly recent innovation, the first being created in 1985. It actually does not invest in either properties or mortgages; rather, it performs a brokering function by buying mortgage-backed passthroughs (see Chapter 7 for a discussion) and then selling to institutional investors debt instruments backed by the mortgage passthroughs. These debt instruments are called collateralized mortgage obligations (CMOs). Investors in a CMO REIT, then, expect to earn income from a spread (called a ''residual'') between returns on the passthroughs and interest paid on the CMOs.

Unfortunately, some CMO REITs have become disasters, for several reasons. First, the CMO security essentially offers variable short-term rates while the passthroughs are relatively long-term fixed rates. Rising short-term rates, then, cause the residuals to disappear. Second, passthrough income is influenced considerably by refinancings. As these occur when interest rates decline, revenue sources are depleted. These factors sent one large CMO REIT—Residential Resources Mortgage Investments Corporation—into a Chapter 11 reorganization and depressed CMO REIT prices. Obviously, CMO REITs deserve close scrutiny. Their proferred yields, going as high as 20%, may be totally illusory.

CMO REITs offer high current returns that may never be realized; several have experienced financial difficulty.

The Return from a REIT   As noted earlier, 90% of a REIT's earnings must be distributed as dividends. The current return on many REITs is therefore fairly high, but also volatile, a factor you should not overlook if a stable return is important to you. Similar to the net asset value (NAV) of a mutual fund, the equity per share (EqPS) of a REIT can be determined by dividing assets minus liabilities by the number of shares outstanding; that is,

Equity per share is the equivalent of a mutual fund's NAV.

$$EqPS = \frac{(REIT\ assets\text{-}liabilities)}{REIT\ shares\ outstanding}$$

EqPS is an important figure to investors who wish to know if the market price of a REIT share is selling at a discount or premium to it. However, you should understand that assets are measured at their book—rather than appraised—values. If a REIT acquired properties some years ago, there is a good possibility that book value will be substantially below appraised value. So, it is important not to attach excessive importance to the EqPS figure.

Exhibit 16.5 presents a small sample of three equity trusts and three mortgage trusts to illustrate REIT performance and value characteristics. As you see, they vary considerably in realized dividend growth over the past 5- and 10-year periods (columns 5 and 6). Projecting future price appreciation based upon the 10-year historical rate, and combining it with the current dividend yield leads to some rather optimistic expected total returns, as shown in column 9. Of

EXHIBIT 16.5
Historical performance of six REITs, May 12, 1989

REIT	BETA	Premium or (Discount)		Div/Share Growth		Current DPS		Total Return
		1975	1988	5 Yr.	10 Yr.	$	Yield	(6) (8)
(1)	(2)	(3)	(4)	(5)	(6)	(7)	(8)	(9)
Equity REITs								
BRE Properties	.70	(54%)	69%	14.0%	18.8%	2.40	8.0%	26.8%
Federal Realty	.70	(43)	199	9.6	12.8	1.55	8.1	20.9
HRE	.60	(45)	(8)	−3.5	2.9	1.80	7.2	10.1
Mortgage REITs								
L & N Mortgage	.60	(50)	(10)	9.2	11.4	2.30	15.2	26.6
Mortgage & Realty	.70	(72)	(1)	7.7	9.4	2.00	11.8	20.2
MGI Properties	.75	(67)	16	3.9	9.8	1.38	10.7	20.5

SOURCE: Value Line, *Investment Survey: Real Estate Investment Trust Industry,* May 12, 1989.

course, you must be very cautious in using these projections, since the assumption that past dividend growth will continue in the future may not hold true. This was the case when Exhibit 16.5 was prepared, since many analysts were bearish on REITs.

It should be noted also that the market prices of many REIT shares had increased rapidly from the early 1980s. These percentage price increases were often in line with the realized dividend growth rates (as would be expected in view of the dividend model discussed in Chapters 8 and 9). Notice, though, the considerable swing in the difference between market price and EqPS from 1975 through 1988. In each case, the 1975 discount either turned into a premium or was reduced substantially. Federal Realty shows the most dramatic swing, going from a 43% discount to a 199% premium over the period. Apparently, what a REIT share should be worth in relation to the book value of its shares can change considerably in the minds of REIT investors. This change underscores the intrinsic risk of REITs. Their beta values are quite low, suggesting low price volatility with respect to stock price changes, but their prices should not be viewed as historically stable. Some, particularly mortgage trusts, are likely to be more sensitive to interest rate changes than to factors influencing stock prices. If you plan to invest in REITs, a diversified assortment seems appropriate, and the low betas suggest holding REITs in conjunction with stock investments to increase portfolio efficiency.

Many REIT prices now exceed their equity-per-share figures.

Historical Experience with REITs

Historical Experience with REITs   The history of REITs clearly illustrates the risks associated with excessive leverage. During the early 1970s, REITs borrowed considerable amounts of capital and invested it at rates only slightly higher than those they paid to borrow the funds. As long as defaults were few and interest rates fairly stable, their earnings were impressive. But the rapidly escalating rates that began in 1973, coupled with the serious recession of 1974–75, meant disaster for many REITs. Loans went into default and tenants were breaking lease arrangements routinely. Not a few REITs filed bankruptcy, and those that remained went through very hard times to regain some financial strength. Investors abandoned REIT shares, leading to the substantial discounts shown in column 3 of Exhibit 16.5.

REITs used extensive leverage in the past, which led many into financial difficulty.

Can disasters of this magnitude happen again? Apparently they have with CMO REITs; however, many analysts think traditional REITs are much safer. They point out that leverage is used less extensively today than in the dismal past, and some REIT managers even attempt to hedge their interest rate exposure with appropriate futures or options. In addition, REIT managements are presumably more aware of real estate peculiarities and intricacies, which apparently eluded them earlier. Whether or not these managements have improved enough to justify some of the very generous premiums that now exist remains to be seen. Additional information about REITs is available from the National Association of REITs, 1129 20th Street NW, Suite 705, Washington, DC 20036 (telephone 202–785–8717).

Less leverage and supposedly better management increase the current appeal of REITs.

LIMITED PARTNERSHIPS

A **limited partnership** is a legal arrangement that combines features of a corporation and a general partnership (see Exhibit 16.6). It is similar to a corporation in that its investors (called *limited partners*), like corporate shareholders, have limited liability for business losses. They also are inactive in managing the business, preferring instead to turn over these responsibilities to a person called the *general partner*. A limited partnership resembles a general partnership in that profits or losses are passed directly to the partners, rather than being profits or losses of the business.

Prior to the 1986 Tax Reform Act, the appeal of many limited partnerships was taxpayer ability to deduct partnership losses from other taxable income in filing the individual federal income tax. These deductions could turn mediocre or poor business ventures into rather profitable investments for individuals with high marginal tax rates. However, such deductions are no longer allowed (with some exceptions for oil and gas shelters), and with tax advantages eliminated, limited partnerships are losing much of their investment importance. For example, sales of public syndications (explained shortly) fell from around $13 billion in 1986 to $10.4 billion in 1988. Moreover, approximately half of all sales in 1988 were real estate syndications. While popularity has declined, limited partnerships are likely to continue in situations that have genuine economic potential and where the limited partnership form of conducting business is considered the most appropriate.

The 1986 Tax Reform Act deprived many limited partnerships of their investment importance.

Business Activities

The most important business activities undertaken by limited partnerships are in real estate and energy resources. Others include equipment leasing deals and livestock feeding and breeding programs.

EXHIBIT 16.6
Illustration of a limited partnership

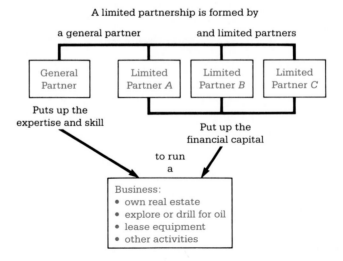

Real Estate   **Real estate limited partnerships,** the most popular form, acquire and manage properties of all types. Some emphasize current income and immediate cash flow, while others seek long-term capital appreciation. A limited partnership may be a *public syndicate.* (Exhibit 16.7 shows an announcement for an unusual one.) A public syndicate is marketed very much like a new distribution of common stock. A *private syndicate,* on the other hand, restricts the number of limited partners. A public syndicate is often a *blind pool*—totally or partially—which means the properties the partnership will acquire are not known

Public syndicates are often blind pools.

This announcement constitutes neither an offer to sell nor a solicitation of an offer to buy these securities. The offering is made only by the Prospectus, copies of which may be obtained in any State from such of the undersigned and others as may lawfully offer these securities in such State.

December 5, 1986

2,600,000 Units

Boston Celtics

Limited Partnership

Price $18.50 per Unit

Smith Barney, Harris Upham & Co.
Incorporated

Bear, Stearns & Co. Inc.	The First Boston Corporation	Alex. Brown & Sons Incorporated
Donaldson, Lufkin & Jenrette Securities Corporation	Drexel Burnham Lambert Incorporated	Goldman, Sachs & Co.
Hambrecht & Quist Incorporated	Kidder, Peabody & Co. Incorporated	Lazard Frères & Co.
Merrill Lynch Capital Markets	Montgomery Securities	PaineWebber Incorporated

Prudential-Bache   Robertson, Colman & Stephens   L. F. Rothschild, Unterberg, Towbin, Inc.
Securities

Salomon Brothers Inc   Shearson Lehman Brothers Inc.   Dean Witter Reynolds Inc.

A. G. Edwards & Sons, Inc.	Robert W. Baird & Co. Incorporated	Blunt Ellis & Loewi Incorporated

J. C. Bradford & Co.   Dain Bosworth   McDonald & Company   The Ohio Company
Incorporated   Incorporated   Securities, Inc.

Piper, Jaffray & Hopwood   Stifel, Nicolaus & Company   George K. Baum & Company
Incorporated   Incorporated

The Chicago Corporation   R. G. Dickinson & Co.   Parker/Hunter
Incorporated

EXHIBIT 16.7
Limited partnership announcement appearing in *The Wall Street Journal.* Limited partnerships are formed to engage in a variety of business activities. This one makes you a part owner of the Boston Celtics. (Courtesy Boston Celtics Limited Partnership)

at the time partnership interests are sold. These interests are typically $1,000 each and, in general, you must buy at least five units. In contrast, many private syndicates are formed to buy a specific property, such as a shopping center or office building, and this property is identified to the prospective partners. Such a limited partnership interest often requires an investment of $25,000 or more.

Energy Resources **Energy resources limited partnerships** are in the business of finding, extracting, and transporting all forms of energy resources. However, they are most popular in the oil and gas industry, where three types of programs exist. An *exploratory program* searches for new fields in areas that appear fertile, but where strikes have not yet been made. The fact that fewer than 15 out of 100 drillings find oil indicates these programs are extremely risky, but a strike can be very profitable. Investing in one of these programs is often compared to investing in an untested, very small growth company.

A *developmental program* drills wells in areas that already have producing wells. The success rate here is considerably greater, but each well's payoff is much smaller. An investment in a developmental program can be compared to investing in a tested growth company such as General Electric. The third alternative is an *income program,* which buys producing wells with known reserves. This investment is similar to buying a corporate bond. The annual production of crude is fairly uniform over time, just as is the payment of bond interest. Its value, however, is highly unpredictable because it depends on the price of oil, just as the value of a bond is unpredictable because interest reinvestment rates in the future are so volatile.

Of course, the return from any energy resource program depends heavily upon the price of energy. In the late 1970s and early 1980s, energy prices were very high and programs proliferated, many offering fairly attractive returns. But when the price of oil fell to around $10 a barrel in 1986, these same programs and many like them became disasters. Very large originators, such as Petro-Lewis, faced bankruptcy and most limited partnership interests fell considerably in value. Despite some tax concessions to the oil and gas industry, public syndications of energy limited partnerships were particularly hard hit by the 1986 tax law. Offerings fell from $1.2 billion in 1986 to around $589 million in 1988.

Other Business Areas In the past, limited partnerships have been active in other business areas such as equipment leasing and livestock feeding or breeding programs. In an *equipment leasing deal,* the partnership buys equipment—such as a computer installation—that is needed by a particular business. It then leases the equipment to that business under a standard lease agreement that provides the business an opportunity to buy the equipment at the end of the lease period. In *livestock feeding programs,* a limited partnership is formed to buy stock from farmers or ranchers and to feed the animals until they are ready for market; *breeding programs* operate somewhat differently, holding the stock as a producing asset rather than selling it after a short period of time.

As previously mentioned, much of the success of these limited partnerships in the past was attributable to the then-existing income tax structure, rather than

[margin note] Declining energy prices sent some limited partnerships into bankruptcy.

[margin note] Equipment leasing and livestock programs are also organized as limited partnerships.

to any economic advantages of the arrangement. Why shouldn't the business buy its own computer, or ranchers feed their own cattle? Very often it was desirable for certain corporate entities to shift business expenses or tax credits to individuals because they had much higher marginal tax rates. Limited partnerships were ideal vehicles for making such shifts. The 1986 tax law, however, greatly reduces the marginal rate disparities and does away with other tax incentives to form limited partnerships.

Investment Potential

The tax advantages of limited partnerships once made them particularly attractive investments, but they offer few other advantages to offset their disadvantages. The key disadvantages are high promotion and syndication costs, and poor liquidity.

Without tax advantages, limited partnerships are not particularly attractive investments.

     Public syndicates are very expensive to form and market. As much as 20% of total funds raised commonly go into areas not related to the actual buying of real estate, or drilling of wells, or whatever the business might be. Selling costs run in the 7% to 10% range, the general partner usually takes an acquisition fee of 5% or so, and other items add another 5% to 10%. An investment must offer a fairly good and continuous return to offset an initial burden of this magnitude.

     Practically all limited partnership interests have poor liquidity. Although some efforts have been made to form a secondary market for such interests, it is questionable how successful this market will be in the new tax environment. Without a secondary market, selling your interests becomes difficult. The large brokerage firms that help market the public syndicates might be able to find potential buyers. But determining the intrinsic value of an interest might be impossible, which means you have no way of knowing if the price you are offered is a fair one; and, of course, there will be a selling commission. Given these obstacles, you should consider a limited partnership interest as having the poorest marketability and liquidity of practically any intangible investment you will make.

Limited partnership interests may have the poorest marketability and liquidity of all intangible investments.

     Moreover, another worry with limited partnerships has surfaced in the form of general partners with financial difficulties. Large Southmark Corporation in Dallas, a general partner in numerous arrangements, sought Chapter 11 bankruptcy in late 1988; and, six months later, Cardinal Industries, Inc.—a Columbus, Ohio, general partner—followed suit. Legally, a limited partnership is distinct from the general partner, and its economic viability should continue. As a practical matter, however, that may not be the case. A general partner wrapped up in protecting itself may prove to be a poor property manager. Only time will tell how investors have fared in these two cases and possibly others to follow.

SELF-DIRECTED POOLING ARRANGEMENTS

Mutual funds, trusts, REITs, and limited partnerships are formed and managed by others. You have no influence on the securities or other assets they purchase or the dividends and interest they pay. Your only choices are to buy or sell them.

However, there are several pooling arrangements that allow you to take an active role in the pool operation. These are investment clubs and a money manager limited partnership.

Investment Clubs

An **investment club** is simply an informal association of individual investors who pool their resources for investment purposes. Although clubs are often viewed with disdain by investment professionals, their number is growing rapidly, and some evidence suggests their investment performance is not as bad as the experts might think. For example, Exhibit 16.8 shows that from 1976 through 1983, the clubs beat the S&P 500 every year. However, their performance has lagged somewhat behind since then. Their poorer performance in 1984 and 1985 is attributed to the large influx of new clubs drawn by the bull market. (New clubs typically show poorer results than established clubs.) Many clubs affiliate with the National Association of Investment Clubs (NAIC).

The investment performance of many investment clubs is quite good.

Why have investment clubs become popular? First, a long bull market, such as the one that began in 1982, often attracts first-time investors, both to the market and eventually to an investment club. Second, many experienced investors have also joined. These individuals have become disenchanted with the advice of their brokers or the performance of their mutual funds. To illustrate this point, consider that an association called the American Association of Individual Investors (AAII), formed as recently as 1979, now has about 110,000 members. The AAII takes a very serious and professional perspective on investments and is active in sponsoring academic research relating to individual investing. Its

EXHIBIT 16.8
Performance of investment clubs (Source: National Association of Investment Clubs, 1515 East 11 Mile Road, Royal Oak, MI 48067)

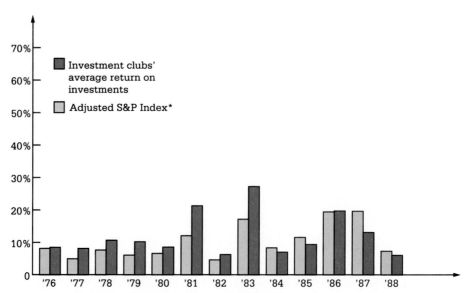

*Adjusted to include dividends as well as appreciation

Investment Clubs Are for Real

Disdained by yuppies who prefer spending to investing, good old-fashioned investment clubs are definitely back "in." Typical is the Farmerette Investment Club of Greene County, Ohio. Once featured in *U.S. News and World Report,* the club consists of 23 members from a rural community who meet every month at Curley's Restaurant, a local favorite, to buy and sell stocks. Like most clubs, their portfolio includes a lot of companies that sell products familiar to members. So, you find Bob Evans and Ralston Purina among the Farmerette's holdings.

When you think about it, buying what you know is not bad investment advice, particularly if you take the time to do adequate research and try to buy it before its price reaches the stratosphere. But, regardless of their selection methods, investment clubs have shown results many money managers would be proud to claim. For example, 53.2% of clubs affiliated with the National Association of Investment Clubs (NAIC) equalled or exceeded the S&P 500 in 1988. This probably exceeds the proportion of professional investors who did as well. Admittedly, this number was up considerably from 22.2% in 1987—but that was a tough year for most investors.

The NAIC, based in Detroit, provides assistance to any group wishing to form and affiliate with it. Of an estimated 20,000 clubs in existence, about 7,000 are members. One advantage of affiliation is the NAIC's Investment Advisory Service, which helps clubs select stocks. This service has also compiled an enviable record against market indexes. NAIC also publishes a monthly magazine, *Better Investing,* which contains useful information on stock selection, model portfolios, and analytical methods, such as fundamental and technical analysis. A separate unit, called the National Association of Investors (NAI), serves members of disbanded clubs who wish to continue their affiliation with the organization.

Extolling a conservative, get-rich-slow approach to investing, NAIC's president, Thomas O'Hara, apparently practices what he preaches. He has been a member of a club since 1940, investing $10 a month. How has his club done? Consider this: One member died a few years ago and left an estate of $260,000 from the club. He had put in $8,500.

journal, published ten times a year, includes many interesting and timely articles that should be helpful in making your investment decisions. The individual investor who joins the AAII often joins an investment club as much to share ideas and research as to pool funds. A third reason for the clubs' popularity is that they help members share investment expenses, such as those incurred in buying magazines, market newsletters, and, particularly, computer software. Many investors now routinely use the computer in their investing activities. Software and data retrieval services are large expenses for a single individual to bear.

Organization and Operation Investment clubs are usually organized by people who have a common interest. They may work together, be members of the same church, or live in the same neighborhood. They typically meet monthly, and members pay monthly dues that can vary considerably. The average, though, is in the $20 to $25 range. Members are often given research assignments: they are expected to find securities to recommend for purchase. And the total membership reviews the club's portfolio each month to consider possible eliminations and new purchases and to decide the disposition of any interest or dividends received since the last meeting.

The club usually elects officers, and the position that should concern you most is the treasurer. While fraud is rare, it does exist, and instances have been reported in which club members lost as much as $10,000 to fraudulent operators.

Bonding the treasurer of an investment club seems a prudent move.

You might want the treasurer to be bonded; or, at the very least, avoid a club with a careless approach to handling cash or securities. It is also important to understand the club's policy of liquidating your interest, should you want to do so. Some clubs may hesitate to sell securities specifically for the purpose of redeeming a member's interest, which means there may be a waiting period until the club has sufficient cash.

Advantages/Disadvantages   Apart from the advantages of pooling and sharing resources and research efforts, an investment club offers fun and fellowship. These attributes should not be taken lightly; many members thoroughly enjoy the monthly meetings and the challenge of finding attractive investment opportunities. However, there are disadvantages to consider.

To begin with, too much fun often detracts from the main function, which is to invest. If a club worries more about entertainment during the meetings than investing, you may have a good time but a bad investment return. You must decide which is more important. Also, some clubs tend to be dominated by one or two strong-willed individuals who shape the club's investing activities. This situation can be fine, but only if they are good investors. Moreover, some clubs tend to degenerate into gambling operations. Their members grow impatient with conservative investments and look for more action. After a while, their portfolios consist mostly of options or futures contracts. Again, you must decide

Investment club returns are not tax-exempt.

if speculative investing of this sort appeals to you. Finally, investment clubs are not tax-exempt. You must keep a record of your share of all transactions having tax implications. This can be a real aggravation if the club engages in frequent trading or keeps poor records.

Money Manager Limited Partnerships

A **money manager limited partnership** is often created by a small group of investors who wish to place their investment funds with a professional money manager, but who lack sufficient funds to meet most managers' minimum investment requirements. These minimums usually start at $25,000 and frequently are $100,000.

Organization and Operation   The limited partnership is formed between the investors, who are the limited partners, and the money manager, who is the general partner. As a limited partner, you cannot lose more than the amount you have invested. Once formed, the limited partners usually allow the general partner to manage the portfolio, although they can place certain restrictions on securities to buy, the frequency of trading, and how interest or dividends are to be distributed. Joining an existing partnership might be difficult: they are not advertised and not often promoted by stockbrokerage houses. This means you probably must find some associates and form your own.

Advantages/Disadvantages The money manager limited partnership is a more formal arrangement than an investment club. The money manager should have more investment acumen than club members and show a better return, but don't take this for granted. If you are thinking of forming a deal, shop around for managers, asking for credentials and performance histories. Ideally, you should get a performance record compiled by an independent evaluation firm, not one that is prepared by the manager and is possibly unaudited. Assuming you find a good manager, another advantage is that most record-keeping chores are undertaken by the general manager or by an accountant the partnership hires. If you are a busy professional, this could be very helpful.

There are disadvantages to consider. First, unless you find a fairly large number of associates, you will face a heavy initial investment just to meet the manager's minimum requirement. Moreover, the annual expenses of running the partnership will be high, as a percent of your invested funds, if the partners raise only the minimum. A workable arrangement usually takes 20 to 30 partners, each investing $10,000 initially and, say, $2,000 each year. The annual expenses are the general manager's fee (in the range of 1% to 3% of assets) and an accountant's fee ($500 to $1,000, usually). Also, legal fees to set up the partnership are incurred. These can vary considerably, but you should figure at least $2,000 to $4,000. Finally, there may be restrictions on withdrawing from a partnership. A waiting period might be required, as it is in many investment clubs.

When all the expenses and other inconveniences are considered, you might wonder if this arrangement is worth it. Investing in a no-load mutual fund is surely much easier and less expensive. The answer, of course, rests squarely on the performance of the money manager. If he or she consistently does well, on a risk-adjusted basis, then these items are trivial in relation to your return; but, in the reverse case, it makes little sense to pay such costs and receive nothing extra in return.

> Investors are limited partners in the partnership; the investment manager is the general partner.

> Investing in a no-load mutual fund may be easier and more profitable than in a money manager limited partnership.

SUMMARY

A unit investment trust is a pooling arrangement that invests funds in certain types of securities, most often municipal bonds or GNMA passthrough certificates. Some trusts, though, invest in liquid assets, or in corporate bonds in an attempt to mimic a bond index. Real estate investment trusts (REITs) invest in tangible property (equity trusts) or mortgages (mortgage trusts). Some REITs have finite lives, and some invest in the property of a particular kind of business. The return from a REIT is similar to any stock return, and REITs' historical experience has been mixed. They did very poorly in the early and mid-1970s, but they have improved considerably since then.

A limited partnership is a unique business arrangement that combines features of a corporation and a general partnership. Prior to the 1986 Tax Reform Act, it was used to distribute tax losses to individual investors; however, that is no longer possible. Limited partnerships are active in real estate, energy resources, and other business areas. Without a tax advantage, though, they are no more appealing than other investments, and high start-up and operating costs put them at a disadvantage.

Investors often use self-directed pooling arrangements. An investment club is a somewhat informal arrangement with some advantages and disadvantages. While they offer social benefits along with investing, an excessive amount of entertainment defeats the purpose of the club. A money manager limited partnership is formed by a group of investors—limited partners—who use the investment skills of a money manager, who becomes the general partner. These partnerships can involve high fees, and a prerequisite for success is to find a competent manager, which might be a difficult task.

KEY TERMS

Select the alternative that best identifies the key term.

1. trust
2. unit investment trust (UIT)
3. municipal (muni) bond trust
4. GNMA trusts
5. liquid investment trusts
6. bond index trusts
7. real estate investment trust (REIT)
8. equity trust
9. mortgage trust
10. finite-life REIT (FREIT)
11. single-purpose REIT
12. CMO REIT
13. limited partnership
14. real estate limited partnerships
15. energy resources limited partnerships
16. investment club
17. money manager limited partnership

a. legally a trust, but often viewed as a closed-end mutual fund
b. most have finite lives
c. informal association of individual investors
d. invest in passthrough securities
e. a REIT that puts you in the commercial mortgage-lending business
f. a legal document involving the management of assets
g. public and private syndicates are examples
h. replaced by money market mutual funds
i. a REIT that invests in tangible, real property
j. exploratory, developmental, and income programs are examples
k. probably the most popular UIT
l. an investment here should match the overall bond market's performance

m. a hybrid between a corporation and a general partnership

n. its life is usually 10–15 years

o. you must find associates to be limited partners with you

p. might own a chain of Burger King restaurants

q. sells bondlike securities backed by mortgage passthroughs

---

1. Explain the differences between private and public trusts.
2. Describe the characteristics of a unit investment trust. How does one differ from a mutual fund?
3. Discuss advantages and disadvantages of investing in muni UITs as opposed to a no-load muni mutual fund and buying munis on your own.
4. Explain the "Double Play Trust" and the "Jefferson Trust."
5. Discuss the relative merits of investing in a bond index trust. Is one actually available?
6. Define a REIT, detailing the conditions it must meet to be exempt from federal income taxation.
7. Explain the following: equity trust, mortgage trust, finite-life REIT, single-purpose REIT, and CMO REIT.
8. Explain a REIT's EqPS and indicate the historical pattern of REIT discounts and premiums.
9. Discuss the investment potential of the six REITs highlighted in this chapter.
10. What is a limited partnership and how do its income tax implications differ from those of other investments?
11. Define the following terms: (*a*) public syndicate, (*b*) private syndicate, and (*c*) blind pool.
12. What three types of programs are available with energy resource limited partnerships? Explain each program, comparing it with another security having a similar return pattern.
13. Discuss the investment potential of limited partnerships.
14. Explain an investment club and discuss advantages and disadvantages of joining one.
15. What is a money manager limited partnership? Indicate advantages and disadvantages of such a partnership.

REVIEW
QUESTIONS

---

1. Assume that you have decided to allocate a portion of your portfolio (about $20,000) to municipal bonds; however, you are unsure whether to invest directly in them or to use UITs or mutual funds. The UIT you are considering will have a 20-year life, origination fees at 3% of amounts invested, and annual operating costs of 0.5% of net assets. The

PROBLEMS
AND PROJECTS

mutual fund is a no-load, but its annual operating costs will be 1.0% of net assets. A self-directed portfolio will involve commissions of around 1% on purchases or sales.

    a. Determine the amount of funds accumulated over a six-year period with each approach, assuming: (1) each earns an 8% rate on invested funds, (2) all annual earnings are withdrawn and reinvested at 6%, and (3) the self-directed portfolio is terminated at the end of the sixth year.

    b. Discuss how the following factors should be considered in reaching a decision: the quality of the securities selected, the need for insurance, management of the portfolio over time, and ability to lock in yields.

2. A certain REIT has assets of $226 million, liabilities of $3.2 million, and 20 million shares outstanding. Each share currently sells at a $2 discount. What is the market value of each share?

3. (*Student Project*)   Scan current and back issues of *The Wall Street Journal* looking for ads for limited partnership public syndications. (Or, you might call a large stockbrokerage firm for information.) If you locate one, call a member of the distribution syndicate and request a prospectus. Review it, paying very close attention to syndication costs and the discussion of risk factors. Express an opinion on how the offering appeals to you, discussing its advantages and disadvantages.

4. (*Student Project*)   Contact a stockbrokerage firm and ask if a prospectus or other information is available for any limited partnership offerings. If so, request a copy of one and scan it. Pay particular attention to sections describing potential returns and discussing potential risk factors.

CASE ANALYSES

**16.1
Nick Vlahos
Looks For Tax
Relief**

Nick Vlahos is employed by a major oil company as a petroleum engineer. Nick's salary is about $70,000 a year and he has no dependents. Nick has accumulated $25,000 and currently has it invested in a money market mutual fund. However, of the total, $20,000 is a temporary arrangement while Nick evaluates certain investment alternatives. He feels a major concern in selecting new vehicles should be his relatively high marginal tax rate of 40% (federal, state, and local taxes). Nick has not sought professional advice since he likes to make his own investment decisions. Nick feels he has a relatively high tolerance for risk.

    As he sees the picture, there are two alternatives: municipal bonds and limited partnerships. With respect to the former, he has seen an ad in the local newspaper indicating the bonds of a certain hospital in his area will be issued to provide investors with an 8% return free of all taxes. He also noted, though, in an investment magazine that a muni unit investment trust supposedly offers a guaranteed 8.5% return; however, this return would be subject to the combined state and local tax rate of 7%.

    As for limited partnerships, a friend of Nick's recommends a deal being offered by a large stockbrokerage firm. The partnership will invest in office buildings and shopping centers. Nick would be a limited partner and not active in managing the business. The annual return from the partnership is likely to be 15% before considering taxes. Another possible limited partnership is a small deal Nick has heard of in his home town. The partnership will acquire vacant land near a large university's sports center and develop it into a parking lot. Parking spaces then would be leased to football and basketball fans. The potential annual return here is 20%, although a tax loss of $2,000 (for each $5,000 investment) is expected in the first year of operation. Nick would be active in managing the business.

a. Which of the two municipal bond investments do you recommend for Nick? Give specific reasons for your selection.
b. Which of the two limited partnerships do you recommend for Nick? Give specific reasons for your selection.
c. Recommend a portfolio for Nick. Assume a minimum investment of $5,000 in each case.

Questions

Sue Markley is considering investing in REITs. She has read that their recent performances have been good and she thinks they will fit well within her portfolio, which now consists mostly of long-term corporate bonds and a money market mutual fund. She is looking for investments with characteristics different from those she already holds. Sue is not familiar with REITs, and she selected the four shown in the table simply because they appeared in a newspaper article about REITs. She would like you to advise her in this situation.

**16.2
Sue Markley
Evaluates REITs**

REIT	Type	Current Price	Equity Per Share	Current Yield	5-Year Annual Div. Growth
HO Properties	Equity	$22	$14	8%	10%
Van Atta	Mortgage	60	70	14	6
ZMC, Inc.	FREIT*	24	23	10	10
Delaney	CMO	16	43	23	2

*Terminates in five years.

The estimated market value of each REIT's assets varies considerably in relation to per-share equity. ZMC's and HO Properties' market value per share about equal per-share equity; Van Atta's is a bit lower while Delaney's is substantially lower.

a. Based on total return calculations, which is the most attractive REIT?
b. Indicate other important considerations, and then discuss the investment appeal and risks of each.
c. Which REIT(s) do you recommend for Sue? Explain your response.

Questions

**HELPFUL
READING**

Andresky, Jill. "Satanic Purses." *Financial World,* March 21, 1989, pp. 52–54.

Bettner, Jill. "Limited Partnership Investors Can Lose Sense of Worth." *The Wall Street Journal,* May 23, 1989, p. C1.

Bettner, Jill, and Neil Barsky. "In Partnerships, Who Shares Problems?" *The Wall Street Journal,* May 26, 1989, p. C1.

Gottschalk, Earl C., Jr. "Film Partnerships Are Often Star Crossed." *The Wall Street Journal,* July 12, 1989, p. C1.

Henriques, Diana. "Hopeful Sign: Interest Revives in Investment Clubs." *Barron's,* March 6, 1989, p. 16.

Kuntz, Mary. "A Realty Fund Primer." *Forbes,* March 9, 1987, pp. 162–64.

Monroe, Ann. "Pitfalls for Partnership Investors May Lurk In That Seemingly Insignificant Fine Print." *The Wall Street Journal,* February 13, 1987, p. 23.

White, James A. "How a Money Manager Can Pull a Rabbit Out of a Hat." *The Wall Street Journal,* March 17, 1989, p. C1.

PART SIX

Investing in Tangibles

Accelerating inflation rates during the 1970s and early 1980s increased investor awareness of tangibles. Traditionally, returns on tangibles increase with inflation, while returns on intangibles often decline. So, tangible investing not only improves portfolio return, it also tends to lower its risk. However, there are many tangibles to consider: some are added easily to the portfolio, while others require considerable skill to manage properly. Some, such as a personal residence or artworks, enrich our enjoyment of life.

Chapter 17 identifies and explains investment opportunities in real estate. An evaluation approach based on return analysis of cash flows is developed and applied to both the personal residence and the rental property. Advantages and disadvantages of a vacation home are also discussed, and various mortgage loans are explained.

Chapter 18 indicates advantages and disadvantages of investing in tangibles other than real estate. Specific tangibles discussed are gold and other precious metals, diamonds and other precious stones, artworks and antiques, and collectibles and hobbies.

CHAPTER SEVENTEEN

Real Estate

THE PERSONAL RESIDENCE

Investment Appeal

Housing Affordability

Kinds of Properties

Rent-Versus-Buy Decision

THE RENTAL PROPERTY

Residential Properties

Commercial and Industrial
Properties

The Vacation Home

Property Valuation

**FINANCING PROPERTY
INVESTMENT**

Fixed-Rate Mortgage

Fixed Rate-Fixed Payment Loans

Adjustable-Rate Mortgage

Sources of Mortgage Loans

BOXES

Risk Perspectives in Real Estate

Don't Forget: You Also Invest in the
Mortgage

After you finish this chapter, you
will be able to:

- understand why a personal residence has investment appeal and
  how to determine its profitability
  within a rent-versus-buy framework.

- recognize different forms of personal residences and determine
  the amount of mortgage funds
  available to purchase a home.

- identify different kinds of rental
  properties and determine a rental
  property's rate of return.

- understand why a vacation home
  has potential investment appeal
  and recognize the important role
  of income taxes with respect to
  renting a property or using it for
  personal pleasure.

- understand different methods of
  property valuation.

- evaluate the various types of
  mortgage loans available.

R egardless of how we measure the popularity of investments, real estate tops the list. Far more American families (about 6 out of 10) own homes than common stock (about 2 out of 10), and their investment is much greater. In addition, they often own other forms of real estate, such as apartment houses, or commercial and industrial properties. Moreover, millions of Americans now own a second home that is used partially for their own pleasure and partially to earn income. Owning a piece of America has been, and still is, the American dream. Unfortunately, this dream has sometimes stood in the way of sound economic decisions in real estate investing. The purpose of this chapter is to keep that from happening. It takes the view that all real estate—even the personal residence—should be evaluated as an investment, using traditional tools of analysis.

THE PERSONAL RESIDENCE

For the "average family," housing is an important investment decision made about every seven years.

The **personal residence** is any form of owned dwelling that provides a place in which to live. It obviously is different from all other investments in that you live in it, and a place to live is a necessity. A home typically has emotional appeal: many families enjoy their homes and would keep them even if they were terrible financial investments, and even if it meant changing jobs to avoid moving. Such families probably are not in the majority, however. Indeed, the average family probably stays in a house about seven years, rather than a lifetime, which means the housing investment decision is being made frequently. So, it is important to examine the investment appeal of the personal residence and to determine how much to invest in it.

Investment Appeal

A personal residence has three primary investment characteristics that enhance its appeal: price appreciation, tax sheltering of income, and a return variability that is relatively low. These three features are described below.

Housing prices have showed good appreciation over time and remarkable stability.

Price Appreciation   Many observers regard housing as an ideal investment. They point out that housing prices typically increase at least in step with the inflation rate, if not quicker. In addition, they note the return on the housing investment is often on a par with returns from other investments, such as stocks and bonds. Exhibit 17.1 shows evidence supporting this view. The median price of single-family homes jumped from $24,900 in 1971 to $89,200 in 1988, an average annual increase of 8.0% using the arithmetic mean and 7.9% with the geometric mean. These figures exceed the average annual increase of 6.6% in the CPI. The return on common stocks was somewhat better during this period, but the sizeable difference between the arithmetic and geometric means shows their greater return volatility. Comparing geometric means shows an edge (9.5% versus 7.9%) in favor of stocks.

(1)	(2) Median Price 1 Family Existing	(3) Annual Percentage	(4) Annual Percentage Increase	(5) Annual Rate of Return on the	**EXHIBIT 17.1** Investment characteristics of the personal residence
Year	Units	Increase	in the CPI	S&P 500
1988	$89,200	4.2%	4.1%	16.8%
1987	85,600	6.6	4.4	5.2
1986	80,300	6.5	4.4	18.5
1985	75,400	4.1	3.8	32.2
1984	72,400	3.0	4.0	6.3
1983	70,300	3.7	3.9	22.5
1982	67,800	2.1	8.9	21.4
1981	66,400	6.8	12.4	− 4.9
1980	62,200	11.7	13.3	3.2
1979	55,700	14.4	9.0	18.4
1978	48,700	13.5	6.8	6.6
1977	42,900	12.6	4.8	− 7.2
1976	38,100	6.4	7.0	23.8
1975	35,800	9.5	12.2	37.2
1974	32,700	10.9	8.8	−26.5
1973	29,500	5.7	3.4	−14.7
1972	27,900	12.1	3.4	18.9
1971	24,900	9.2	3.4	14.3
Averages:				
Arithmetic		8.0	6.6	10.7
Geometric		7.9	6.6	9.5
Housing beta (in relation to S&P 500) = −0.06				

Housing prices increased even during the recessionary periods of 1974–75 and 1980–82. However, the overall growth in housing prices often masks wide disparities among different regions of the country, as Exhibit 17.2 illustrates. The sharp decline in the Worcester, MA, market is interesting since the East Coast was one of the hotter markets several years earlier. Also interesting are the dramatic differences in housing prices from one region of the country to another; for example, from Oklahoma City to San Francisco.

Supply and Demand Influences. Exhibit 17.3 indicates the price of housing depends a great deal upon supply and demand influences. Family preferences for home ownership, population growth, income, and the *real* cost of mortgage funds are the primary demand factors. As preferences, population, and

EXHIBIT 17.2
Regional housing price
changes: First quarter
1988 to first quarter
1989 (existing units)

Location	Price Change (%)	Median Sales Price First Quarter, 1989
Hot Markets		
West Palm Beach/Boca Raton/Delray Beach, FL	+39.7	$127,800
San Francisco Bay Area, CA	+31.8	243,900
Orange County, CA	+30.2	237,800
Albuquerque, NM	+17.4	82,000
Raleigh/Durham, NC	+16.3	102,000
Cold Markets		
Fort Worth, TX	−10.9	75,300
Oklahoma City, Ok	−7.4	52,300
Baton Rouge, LA	−7.0	61,100
Worcester, MA	−5.9	139,100
Denver, CO	−3.5	80,800

SOURCE: *Home Sales: April 1989.* Economics and Research Division, National Association of Realtors ®, 777 14th Street NW, Washington DC 20005.

A strong demand for housing exerts upward pressure on housing prices.

income increase, or real mortgage rates fall, the demand for housing increases, thereby increasing the price of housing (all supply factors held constant). Reverse changes in these factors reduce price. It is important to see that real—not nominal—mortgage rates influence demand. During much of the 1970s, nominal mortgage rates appeared high (in a historical sense); yet, when adjusted for inflation, they actually were very low, and were negative in several years. As expected, the demand for residential housing was exceptionally strong in this period.

The level of construction technology, construction costs (wages, prices of materials, the price of land, and others—all again measured in real terms), and the rate at which existing homes are demolished determine the supply of housing. If technology declines, or construction costs or the demolition rate increase, the supply of housing falls. Reduction in the supply of housing, in turn, increases its price (all demand factors held constant). An improvement in technology, or a decrease in real construction costs or the demolition rate increase housing supply, thereby depressing price.

Construction costs, a key determinant of new-housing supply, are likely to continue their historical persistent increases.

While all supply and demand factors are important, the major price influences over the past 20 years seem to have been persistent increases in real construction costs and continually strong family preferences for home ownership. Will these conditions continue in the future? That is impossible to know. Perhaps the technology of manufacturing houses will improve, with greater emphasis on modular housing produced in the factory with production-line techniques. Perhaps family preferences for housing will change, moving away from ownership

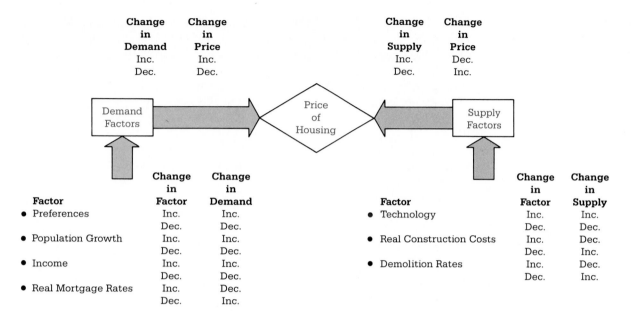

EXHIBIT 17.3
Supply, demand, and the price of housing

and towards renting. Few people now expect either of these changes, or any other, will take place, however, and most observers seem to believe housing prices at least will match inflation in the foreseeable future.

Local Influences. Supply and demand can be extended to include many local influences. Accessibility to highways or public transportation, good schools, places of employment, and shopping areas often increase demand, as do neighborhood aesthetics. Indeed, realtors are fond of citing the three most important factors to consider in buying a home: location, location, and location. While this quip might be an exaggeration, surely, the one feature of a home you cannot change is its location. Finally, characteristics of a house are important: one with a bad floor plan or structural defects, or one in run-down condition does not have a market value as high as another similarly situated but in good shape. As a potential investor, you need to evaluate the local situation carefully before investing. Of course, this takes time, as does maintaining a home after the purchase, which is another item to consider.

> Location is one characteristic of a home that cannot be changed; many realtors consider it the most important.

Tax-Sheltering Aspects The personal residence has important tax-sheltering aspects. First, you can defer any gain on the sale of a home by reinvesting (within two years of the sale) in another of equal or greater value. Second, you can avoid up to $125,000 of gains by selling your house at age 55 or older (if you meet several other conditions). This is unquestionably one of the best tax advantages available. Third, both interest on a home mortgage and state and local property taxes are deductible in determining taxable income.

> The $125,000 gain exclusion makes the personal residence a great tax shelter.

The tax deductibility of mortgage interest increases the attractiveness of the personal residence.

Under existing tax law the deductibility of interest creates another indirect advantage of owning a home with a mortgage. While the mortgage interest is deductible, interest on consumer loans is not. It makes sense, then, to use a mortgage loan as a source of consumer credit. This use is limited, however: you cannot deduct interest on borrowed amounts in excess of the cost of the property plus any improvements. In other words, you can't use any appreciation in value as a borrowing base. Exceptions are allowed, though, if the funds are used to meet medical or educational expenses.

Low Price Volatility   Exhibit 17.1 also indicates the low price volatility of houses. The figures are 12-month averages, which do not reveal volatility on a month-to-month basis, but even considering these data, volatility remains relatively low. Several studies have examined the risk characteristics of housing, using appropriate statistical methods. They have found, for instance, that housing has a low beta (a beta determined by the data in Exhibit 17.1 is −0.06), meaning its price volatility relative to the stock market is low. Low risk, of course, enhances its investment appeal. Other recent studies, though, contradict earlier findings. A segment of this research argues that it is not appropriate to consider the price of housing in relation to the market, but, rather, you should consider return in relation to the owners' equity, since a large portion of the housing investment is leveraged with mortgage debt. This return figure is far more volatile than housing prices, and, in fact, is about as risky as the overall stock market.

Unquestionably, housing is not a short-term investment, as we will see later in this chapter. There are high fixed costs in relation to obtaining a mortgage loan and paying a commission when a property is sold. It usually takes years of price appreciation to offset these costs and eventually show a gain.

Housing Affordability

An important investment decision is how much to invest in housing. Actually, if you apply for a mortgage loan, the lending institution will answer the question by applying their suitability rules to your case. For example, many follow a rule that your monthly housing expenses should not exceed some percentage of your monthly income. The Federal National Mortgage Corporation (which insures mortgage loans) recommends that monthly mortgage payments plus other consumer loan payments should not exceed 28% of monthly gross income. Assuming a monthly income of $2,500 and consumer loan monthly payments of $200 gives us the following example for Rita Winfrey, a potential buyer.

Lenders use specific rules to determine how much they will lend to borrowers.

Monthly income	$ 2,500
28% of monthly income	$ 700
Less consumer loan payments	200
Recommended monthly mortgage payment	$ 500
Affordable mortgage (see Exhibit 17.4)	$56,976
Plus the down payment	13,024
Affordable home	$70,000

Interest	Loan Maturities (Years)				
Rate	10	15	20	25	30
8%	$41,220	$52,301	$59,809	$64,767	$68,120
10	37,822	46,512	51,814	55,006	56,976
12	34,843	41,667	45,413	47,483	48,591
14	32,196	37,566	40,193	41,529	42,194
16	29,851	34,037	35,945	36,792	37,175

EXHIBIT 17.4
Amount of affordable mortgage for a $500 monthly payment: Various interest rates and loan maturities

In this case, Rita can afford a $500 monthly mortgage payment. She qualifies for a 30-year loan with a fixed 10% interest rate, which provides $56,976. This amount, along with her down payment of $13,024, means she can afford a $70,000 property.

Kinds of Properties

A number of options are available to home buyers. Your final decision should consider the amenities that appeal to you plus the potential financial return. The three popular forms of home ownership are the detached single-family home, the condominium, and the cooperative.

Detached Single-Family Homes The **detached single-family home** is still the number-one choice of most home buyers. Indeed, the demand for this form of housing has withstood the hippie, yuppie, and all other movements. When the suburbs were being assailed by sociologists and community planners as cultural wastelands during the 1960s, inner-city families were patiently saving their funds for a down payment on a three-bedroom ranch in the "slurbs." The trend seems equally strong today, judging by how young people respond to opinion polls asking them to rank their aspirations. At the top is usually the desire to own a detached, single-family home in a community with good schools and good police and fire protection.

A detached single-family residence still appears to be the home of choice for most buyers.

Condominiums **Condominium housing** is a blend of apartment living and home ownership. The condo complex includes common areas that unit owners share, both in use and expense. Keep in mind that you own your individual condo just as you would a detached house. You arrange your own financing and are responsible for its interior upkeep. Expenses of the common areas are met by charging individual owners a monthly maintenance fee, which can be quite high if the complex has a swimming pool, tennis courts, and other amenities. Clearly, a condo appeals to home buyers who do not want the maintenance demands of a detached house, yet want the tax advantages and price appreciation property ownership has to offer. While condominiums were slow to be accepted in certain parts of the country, buyer reluctance seems to have faded. You now can find very expensive condos being constructed in rather conservative areas. Their price

You arrange your own financing on a condominium.

appreciation relative to detached houses, however, may not be as good. Obviously, this generalization does not apply in all areas, but it makes sense to research your area if you are thinking of buying a condo and if price appreciation is important.

Cooperatives   A **cooperative** appears very similar to a condominium in that you own a unit that is part of a complex. However, the ownership form is different. A cooperative is a corporation, and you buy shares to it that entitle you to live in your unit. Again, you arrange your own financing to buy the shares and pay monthly maintenance fees. A possible disadvantage of a cooperative is that you must receive approval of the cooperative's board of directors before you can sell your shares. Cooperatives are popular on the East Coast, particularly in New York City, where many apartment complexes are actually cooperatives. Some of these apartments, such as those in the Trump Tower, cost in excess of $3 million for, perhaps, a unit with no more than 2,000 square feet of space. Your monthly maintenance fee might be about $5,000. Moreover, price appreciation on some of these has been spectacular, averaging 20% a year in some instances.

With a cooperative, you buy shares that entitle you to live in your unit.

The Rent-Versus-Buy Decision

Since everyone needs housing somewhere, the decision to buy is also a decision not to rent.

Since everyone must live somewhere, the decision to buy a home can be viewed as a decision not to rent. Let us ignore for the moment any nonfinancial motivation in the decision and concentrate strictly on the financial aspects. The steps involved in evaluating a rent-versus-buy decision are explained in the following sections. We will use the example of Rita Winfrey, whom we met earlier.

Cash Flows Before Taxes and Mortgage Payments   Renting or owning involves cash outflows. Exhibit 17.5 details these flows in Rita's case. Rita

EXHIBIT 17.5
Rita Winfrey's rent-versus-buy decision: Annual cash flows before taxes and mortgage payments

	(1) Rent	(2) Buy	(3) Difference (1) − (2)
Year 1:			
Rent payments	$6,000	$ -0-	$ 6,000
Utilities	1,200	2,400	− 1,200
Insurance	200	500	− 300
Maintenance	100	600	− 500
Property taxes	-0-	1,500	− 1,500
Totals	$7,500	$5,000	$ 2,500
Year 2: 1.05 × $2,500			2,685
Year 3: 1.05 × $2,685			2,879
Year 4: 1.05 × $2,879			3,083
Year 5: 1.05 × $3,083			3,297

currently pays $500 a month rent; she also must pay for some utilities, insurance, and small amounts of maintenance (mostly interior painting). As you see, she can save $6,000 a year in rentals by buying, but she will incur higher utilities, insurance, and maintenance, and also will pay property taxes of $1,500 each year. In total, buying saves her $2,500 in the first year. Assuming all items would increase each year by about the same rate (5% in this example), Rita's savings grow over time. For ease of presentation for now, we will extend the analysis only five years, but it is relatively easy to go out further.

Interest and Principal Payments on the Mortgage   Exhibit 17.6 details Rita's $6,000 annual mortgage payments ($500 a month, as determined above). As you see, practically all of the amounts are for interest. At the end of five years, Rita will have reduced her principal only to $55,024—$1,952 less than the beginning balance.

Income Tax Savings   From a tax point of view, paying interest on a mortgage is better than paying principal, because interest payments can be taken as an itemized deduction in computing taxable income. So can property tax payments, and combining the two gives Rita annual deductions as shown in column 4 of Exhibit 17.7. The value of these deductions depends on the taxpayer's marginal tax rate. Rita expects to pay a marginal rate of 28%; thus, the value of her deductions is shown in column 5. By purchasing a home, she will reduce her tax liabilities by the amounts indicated.

> Mortgage interest and property taxes, both income-tax deductible, favor the buy decision.

Annual Cash Flows   We now can determine the annual cash flows relevant to the rent-versus-buy decision. In Exhibit 17.8, the tax savings from Exhibit 17.7 and the cash flow savings before taxes from Exhibit 17.5 are combined, and the annual mortgage payment of $6,000 is deducted from the total. The resulting figures are the after-tax cash flows, and, as you see, they are negative. This means if she buys the home, Rita must pay additional amounts each year, starting at $1,489 and decreasing to $644 in the fifth year. Rita can view these amounts as additional investments in the property. The final step is to determine the

(1) Year	(2) Total Payments	(3) Interest	(4) Principal	(5) Ending Loan Balance*
Start	—	—	—	$56,976
1	$6,000	$5,683	$317	56,659
2	6,000	5,650	350	56,309
3	6,000	5,613	387	55,922
4	6,000	5,573	427	55,495
5	6,000	5,529	471	55,024

EXHIBIT 17.6
Rita Winfrey's rent-versus-buy decision: Mortgage payments

*Ending loan balance equals beginning loan balance minus principal payments; e.g.: 56,309 = 56,659 − 350.

(1)	(2)	(3)	(4)	(5)
		Property		
Year	Interest	Taxes*	Total	Total × 0.28
1	$5,683	$1,500	$7,183	$2,011
2	5,650	1,575	7,225	2,023
3	5,613	1,654	7,267	2,035
4	5,573	1,736	7,309	2,047
5	5,529	1,823	7,352	2,059

*Assumed to grow at a 5% annual rate.

profitability of these investments combined with the initial down payment of $13,024.

Profitability of the Investment   As it now stands, the investment has a negative return. However, an important factor—price appreciation—has yet to be considered. Suppose the property appreciates 5% a year. At the end of five years it will be worth $89,340. If Rita then decides to sell it, she will pay a realtor's commission of $6,254 (assuming a 7% commission rate), leaving her with $83,086. Her mortgage balance will be $55,024 (see Exhibit 17.6), and subtracting that from $83,086 leaves her with a final net of $28,062. Exhibit 17.9 illustrates these steps and presents the final cash-flow picture to be evaluated. Using internal rate of return (IRR) methods (see Chapter 3), Rita determines the investment has an IRR of 10.24%. This is an after-tax return that Rita should compare with other after-tax returns. At the time the analysis was made, it was a relatively attractive return.

> An internal rate of return (IRR) can be determined for the rent-versus-buy decision.

> The IRR is influenced considerably by the assumed increase in the home's price.

However, there are several items to keep in mind. First, it is assumed that no tax applies on the price appreciation. Second, the above analysis is very sensitive to the assumed annual price increase of the home. An excessively optimistic view will obviously favor the buy decision. Finally, it could be argued that your investment should not be limited to the down payment and annual cash

(1)	(2)	(3)	(4)	(5)	(6)
	Cash Flow	Income			Annual Cash
	Savings	Tax	Total	Mortgage	Flows
Year	Before Taxes	Savings	Savings	Payments	(4) − (5)
1	$2,500	$2,011	$4,411	$6,000	$ − 1,489
2	2,685	2,023	4,708	6,000	− 1,292
3	2,879	2,035	4,914	6,000	− 1,086
4	3,083	2,047	5,130	6,000	− 870
5	3,297	2,059	5,356	6,000	− 644

Cash Available at the End of 5 Years	
Market value of home at the end of 5 years	$89,340
Less realtor's commission (7% rate)	6,254
Net value	$83,086
Less mortgage balance	55,024
Net cash available	$28,062
Investment Cash Flows	
Year 0 (beginning investment)	$ – 13,024
Year 1	– 1,489
Year 2	– 1,292
Year 3	– 1,086
Year 4	– 870
Year 5 (– 644 + 28,062)	+ 27,418
IRR = + 10.24%	

EXHIBIT 17.9
Rita Winfrey's
rent-versus-buy
decision: IRR analysis

flows, but should consider also the annual build-up in equity resulting from price appreciation. This increases the size of the investment base and reduces the IRR, making the investment relatively less attractive. This perspective is appropriate if, in fact, the equity build-up could be withdrawn and invested elsewhere. However, that often is not the case.

THE RENTAL PROPERTY

A rental property is one that provides periodic income in the form of rentals or other types of revenues. These properties are available in many different forms, ranging from a single dwelling to something as huge as the Empire State Building. In a broad sense, they also include agricultural and mineral lands. Most of the larger property investments are owned by pooling arrangements, such as REITs or limited partnerships. Our present concern, though, is with a direct investment in real estate.

Residential Properties

An investment in a **residential rental property** is one that provides living space to others. A duplex or fourplex, for example, has appealed to many Americans. Some have used such an investment as a starting point from which to build an extensive and profitable portfolio of properties. Immigrants to the United States often are astounded at the relative ease of becoming a property owner here, since ownership is so difficult in many other countries where land is more scarce and incomes are generally lower.

The fact that residential real estate is relatively easy to own does not mean profiting from its ownership is equally easy. This distinction is often forgotten

While a potentially sound investment, real estate does not provide an easy way to wealth.

because of the number of "get-rich-quick-in-real-estate" hucksters who write books or appear on cable television. Some of their approaches are blatantly erroneous while others are more subtle; all, though, distort the risk and return characteristics of real estate. Clearly, you should evaluate a real estate investment as you would any other—using realistic assumptions and proper analytical methods that encompass both return and risk.

Evaluating an Investment   An evaluation of a rental property involves the same approach that was used to evaluate the personal residence. However, there are differences in determining the periodic cash flows. To illustrate these differences, we might assume that our hypothetical home buyer, Rita Winfrey, has decided to purchase the property she was considering, but rather than using it as her personal residence, she has decided to make it a rental property. Exhibit 17.10 shows annual cash flow data estimated for the next ten years. Because of the importance of the decision, Rita has decided to extend the analysis period from five years to ten, although she regards a holding period of six years to be the most realistic.

Rita feels she can rent the house for $800 a month, but she is allowing 10% of rentals for vacancies. The operating expenses are the same amounts estimated in Exhibit 17.5, except that she is adding $100 a year for miscellaneous expenses connected with renting: advertising, collecting rents, and so forth. Net rentals minus operating expenses is called net operating income (NOI); and, as you see, in Rita's case NOI is $3,540 in the first year and then assumed to grow at a 5% rate each year.

Depreciation is an allowable tax deduction for rental properties.

Depreciation and mortgage interest are deducted from NOI to determine taxable income. Depreciation is a noncash deduction the IRS allows to recover the cost of the property. However, it can be applied only to the building—not the land upon which the building sits—and must be estimated by dividing the building cost by 27.5, which is the current number of years of life the IRS requires you to use. Rita estimates the land's value at $10,000, leaving a value of $60,000 for the building. This gives an annual depreciation amount of $2,181. After deducting this amount and the annual mortgage interest from NOI, Rita determines the property will provide taxable losses in each of the ten years. Applying her estimated marginal tax rate of 28% to these losses indicates annual reductions in taxes as shown in line 15. Netting these tax reductions against Rita's taxable losses provides after-tax losses (line 16). Annual cash flows, then, are simply after-tax losses minus mortgage principal payments (observe that interest payments are deducted in determining NOI) plus annual depreciation, which was not a cash deduction. Rita's cash flows are negative in all but the last year. This means she must invest the amounts shown on line 18 to sustain the investment. (She can withdraw the $27 in year 10.)

Cash flow is a key concept in real estate evaluation.

Lines 19 through 26 provide data to determine cash flows arising from sale of the property. Taxes on gains are considered, since rental property does not enjoy any tax deferral or avoidance. A 5% annual appreciation in market value is assumed in line 19. The final cash flow resulting from sale of the property is shown on line 26.

EXHIBIT 17.10

Cash flows from Rita Winfrey's rental property

	Years									
	1	2	3	4	5	6	7	8	9	10
1. Rental income	$9,600									
2. Less: allowance for vacancies (10%)	960									
3. Net rentals	$8,640									
4. Less operating expenses:										
5. Utilities	2,400									
6. Insurance	500									
7. Maintenance	600									
8. Property tax	1,500									
9. Miscellaneous	100									
10. Total	5,100									
11. Net operating income	$3,540	$3,717	$3,903	$4,098	$4,303	$4,518	$4,744	$4,981	$5,230	$5,492
12. Less: depreciation [(70,000 − 10,000)/27.5]	2,181	2,181	2,181	2,181	2,181	2,181	2,181	2,181	2,181	2,181
13. Mortgage interest	5,683	5,650	5,613	5,573	5,529	5,478	5,425	5,364	5,297	5,224
14. Taxable income (loss)	($4,324)	($4,114)	($3,891)	($3,656)	($3,407)	($3,141)	($2,862)	($2,564)	($2,248)	($1,913)
15. Reduction in tax liability (t = .28)	1,211	1,152	1,090	1,024	954	879	801	718	629	536
16. After-tax income (loss)	($3,113)	($2,962)	($2,802)	($2,632)	($2,453)	($2,261)	($2,061)	($1,846)	($1,618)	($1,378)
17. Mortgage principal	317	350	387	427	471	522	575	636	703	776
18. Cash flow = 16 − 17 + 12	($1,249)	($1,131)	($1,008)	($878)	($743)	($602)	($455)	($301)	($140)	$27
19. Market value (year end)	73,500	77,175	81,034	85,085	89,340	93,807	98,497	103,422	108,593	114,023
20. Realtor's commission	5,145	5,402	5,672	5,956	6,254	6,566	6,895	7,240	7,602	7,982
21. Cumulative depreciation	2,181	4,362	6,543	8,724	10,905	13,086	15,267	17,448	19,629	21,810
22. Taxable gain on sale	536	6,135	11,904	17,853	23,991	30,326	36,869	43,630	50,620	57,851
23. Tax on gain (t = .28)	150	1,718	3,333	4,999	6,717	8,491	10,323	12,216	14,174	16,198
24. Cumulative principal payments	317	667	1,054	1,481	1,952	2,474	3,049	3,685	4,388	5,164
25. Mortgage balance due	56,659	56,309	55,922	55,495	55,024	54,502	53,927	53,291	52,588	51,812
26. Cash flow on sale	11,546	13,746	16,106	18,635	21,344	24,247	27,352	30,675	34,230	38,031

Single-Point Evaluation. Working with the data in Exhibit 17.10, Rita determines the investment has a return of +5.3% for a six-year holding period. Again, she must consider the after-tax nature of the return. Considering that long-term municipal bonds were also yielding about 7.5% at the time, Rita does not consider the 5.3% very attractive, given the possibly greater risk of the property investment and the fact that it would take more of her time to manage. However, she must balance these disadvantages against the advantage that the property might serve as a better hedge against increases in the inflation rate.

Multi-Point Evaluation. Since Rita has the data of Exhibit 17.10 on a spreadsheet computer program, she can make different assumptions and easily determine how they will influence cash flows. With new cash flows, she can equally easily determine rates of return. These data are shown in Exhibit 17.11.

Rita first wanted to know how IRR might change if her holding period was shorter or longer than six years. As you see, it declines appreciably to −6.3% if she sells at the end of two years, and it increases to +7.8% if she holds it ten years. Then, Rita assumed different price appreciation rates—3% and 7%—holding everything else constant. Her return falls to a −1.4% if price appreciates only 3% a year, but jumps to +10.8% if growth is 7%. Finally, Rita tested different annual rentals of $8,400 and $10,800; IRR falls to +0.3% in the first case and increases to +10.3% in the second.

EXHIBIT 17.11
Rita Winfrey's rental property sensitivity analysis: Cash flows and IRRs under different assumptions

A. Different holding periods: gross rentals and price appreciation held constant.

Year	Annual Price Appreciation 3%	7%		Annual Rentals $8,400	$10,800
0	$− 13,024	$− 13,024	$− 13,024	$− 13,024	$− 13,024
1	− 1,249	− 1,249	− 1,249	− 1,249	− 1,249
2	+ 12,615	− 1,131	− 1,131	− 1,131	− 1,131
3	—	− 1,008	− 1,008	− 1,008	− 1,008
4	—	+ 17,757	− 878	− 878	− 878
5	—	—	− 743	− 743	− 743
6	—	—	+ 23,645	− 602	− 602
7	—	—	—	− 455	− 455
8	—	—	—	+ 30,220	− 301
9	—	—	—	—	− 140
10	—	—	—	—	+ 38,058
IRR	− 6.3%	+ 2.2%	+ 5.3%	+ 6.8%	+ 7.8%

B. Six-year holding period: different rates of price appreciation and gross rentals.

Year	Holding Periods 2 years	4 years	6 years	8 years	10 years
0	$− 13,024	$− 13,024	$− 13,024		$− 13,024
1	− 1,249	− 1,249	− 2,027		− 472
2	− 1,131	− 1,131	− 1,948		− 315
3	− 1,008	− 1,008	− 1,865		− 150
4	− 878	− 878	− 1,778		+ 22
5	− 743	− 743	− 1,688		+ 202
6	+ 16,800	+ 31,174	+ 22,652		+ 24,637
IRR	− 1.4%	+ 10.8%	+ 0.3%		+ 10.3%

SOURCE: Exhibit 17.10 provides cash flows for Part *A* and the price appreciation columns of Part *B*. Cash flows for the annual rental columns of Part *B* were derived from simulations on Exhibit 17.10.

These simulations are no substitute for good data or sensible assumptions to begin with, but they do help Rita see what might happen under different circumstances. Rita is still unimpressed with the returns. She feels the odds are slim that 7% growth will take place, or that she can charge rentals of $10,800 a year; she is discouraged by the fact that return increases only to 10.8% and 10.3%, respectively, even if one or the other does happen.

Determining IRR under different sets of assumptions helps define potential profitability and risk.

Tax Limitations   Under the 1986 Tax Reform Act, allowable losses from real estate investing will be limited. If you are active in managing the property (such as Rita would be) and if your income is under $100,000, you will be allowed a maximum loss offset against other income of $25,000. As income exceeds $100,000, a portion of the maximum loss is taken away; specifically, the loss is reduced by 50% of income over $100,000 until the entire $25,000 is eliminated. For example, an income of $130,000 means $15,000 of the maximum deduction is taken away [0.5 × ($130,000 − $100,000)], and only $10,000 can offset other taxable income. This limitation applies to any business you own, not just real estate; and, to repeat, you must be active in the management of the business. Passive investors cannot use losses from any source to offset other taxable income, such as wages, interest, or dividends. However, they can offset losses from one business against profits of others; in effect, they cannot have *net* business losses.

Current Income Versus Price Appreciation   Rental properties are similar to common stock investing in that you can choose between those that provide good current cash flows (but poor price appreciation potential) and others that might appreciate in price (but have relatively poor current cash flows). In short, there are "income" properties and "growth" properties. Under the old tax law, growth properties enjoyed a tax avoidance advantage in the form of long-term capital gains. While that is no longer true, a growth property—such as the one evaluated above for Rita Winfrey—still provides better tax sheltering through tax deferral. For example, an income property might show smaller taxable losses than those of the growth property. As a result, less tax sheltering takes place each year. Of course, when the properties are sold, the growth property will show a larger gain, resulting in more taxes at that time. However, you have had the use of tax savings earlier with it, so that even if total taxes are the same, you are better off having the savings earlier.

Like common stocks, rental properties can provide good current income or good price appreciation.

Income properties tend to be found in sections of the community that are not developing or, perhaps, even declining. While rentals may not be as high as in the more affluent parts of the community, nevertheless, they may be fairly generous in relation to property prices. Growth properties, on the other hand, are often located in growing sections of town, usually the suburbs. While price appreciation may be better here, keep in mind that it must be sufficiently high to generate a decent return. The rental property evaluated for Rita Winfrey did not appreciate quickly enough to make the investment worthwhile.

Commercial and Industrial Properties

A **commercial or industrial property** differs from a residential property in that tenants are business firms rather than individuals or families. Of course, the properties might also be different, being designed or adapted for commercial or industrial use. Typical examples of such real estate that might be owned by an individual investor include small office buildings and warehouses, small shopping centers, and buildings used by restaurants and other retail or wholesale establishments. Rental periods tend to be longer, and long-term leases are fairly common. You evaluate an investment in such a property no differently than you evaluate a residential property. The objective again is to determine, as completely as possible, the risk and return on the investment.

Since long-term leases are so common with commercial and industrial properties, it is important to examine existing leasehold agreements very carefully before purchasing. Specifically, you should understand both your rights and obligations and those of the lessee under the lease agreement. Very often, lessors are expected to provide services for lessees. In the event these services are not provided, or are provided inadequately, lessees may be able to break their leases. Losing tenants could make the investment a disaster, since finding others may be exceptionally difficult if the property has very specialized uses. A related problem arises when costs of providing services increase rapidly while rentals are either fixed or rise only moderately. An example can be found in the energy crises in the 1970s. As energy prices soared, many lessors with fixed-lease rentals were caught in a profit bind, since their lease agreements required them to provide heat and other utilities to tenants. Ideally, contracts should be written to include escalator clauses or, better yet, to have tenants pay all expenses connected with using the property (except financing costs).

Moreover, with a property of this type, you may have only one, or few, tenants. This is an advantage if tenants are in sound financial shape and willing to pay the leasehold rental. But if they have financial difficulties or are irresponsible in paying rentals, you easily could experience a large negative cash flow that might exhaust your resources and keep you from making timely payments on your mortgage. In residential properties, you tend to spread the risk of losing collections among a larger number of tenants.

Considering that many commercial and industrial properties require a fairly large investment and are somewhat specialized in use, they often present a riskier situation than residential properties. The size of the investment means a greater use of leverage and, perhaps, less property diversification. Specialized use can lead to greater variations in operating income in response to vacancies or changes in costs. Of course, these are generalizations; it is possible to find a commercial or industrial property with strong contract protection that makes the investment risk very low. Finally, the same income tax provisions indicated above apply in the case of commercial and industrial properties.

Be careful of long-term leases with commercial and industrial properties.

The specialized uses and large required investments of many commercial and industrial properties often increase risk.

Risk Perspectives in Real Estate

To some people who have bought and sold homes over the years, almost always at substantial profits, the notion of risk in real estate seems remote. But it's there and it's a factor to reckon with if you plan on being a big-time real estate investor. Below are a few perspectives worth considering.

☐ Stacked up against stocks, real estate returns always appear far more stable. Some researchers argue, though, that the way values are measured creates the difference. Stock values reflect market-driven prices, while real estate values often are based upon appraisals, which are more stable. One study showed that if you substituted appraisal values for stocks (based upon earnings capitalization approaches), their risk declines significantly and is approximately the same as that of real estate.

☐ Most real estate investments are highly leveraged. If risk is measured by variations in appraisal value, the actual return volatility is understated since leverage magnifies both positive and negative returns. True, leverage is ignored also in measuring risk for financial assets, but they usually involve considerably less leverage than does real estate.

☐ Some important portfolio effects apply to real estate investment. For example, diversifying across property types—apartment units, industrial facilities, office buildings, retail outlets, and others—tends to reduce overall risk while not sacrificing return. Similar advantages are obtained by diversifying geographically, although not by following the traditional geographic divisions. The new perspective on geographical diversification focuses upon economic locations; for example, oil-sensitive regions, or coastal regions. While few individual investors have the means to achieve such extensive diversification, institutional investors often have them. Moreover, the portfolio approach should be considered by individuals in selecting real estate pooling arrangements, such as REITs or limited partnerships.

☐ Real estate often is viewed as a classic example of an inefficient market. Since property units differ so much in quality, location, financing terms, and in other ways, buyers and sellers find it difficult to measure economic value. Enter the opportunity for an ambitious, hard-working individual to exploit these market frictions and make a bundle. That's the good side of inefficiencies; the bad side—the risk side—is that you might be the victim, and not the victor. Inefficiencies create risk.

☐ While many people have never sold a home at a loss, that doesn't necessarily mean all their sales have been profitable. In weak markets, owners tend to hold on to their properties rather than lowering prices for quicker sales. But holding is expensive. If an appropriate opportunity interest rate is considered, a so-called profitable sale may actually have been a loss. Suppose you hold a $200,000 home a year longer than you anticipated. At 12%, you can knock $24,000 off of the profit as a holding cost. Naturally, this cost might be reduced if you continued living in the house for the year.

The Vacation Home

A **vacation home**—also called a *second home*—is a hybrid of a rental property and a personal residence. Some people buy such homes with the intent of using them part of the year as a vacation place and renting them the rest of the time. Other people purchase them strictly as an investment, or strictly as a vacation home. Whatever their intended uses, vacation homes have become exceptionally popular investments in the 1970s and 1980s. Areas such as Hilton Head and Kiawah islands along the East Coast, or practically anywhere on Florida's coasts, have seen rapid development of condominium complexes and detached housing projects. While many of these places have been purchased by permanent residents as first homes, many others represent vacation homes. These same patterns can be found in many other parts of the United States. Practically any part of the country with appealing physical features, such as shorelines, mountains, forests, or favorable climate, attract vacationers and vacation home buyers. Before purchasing a vacation home, though, buyers need to consider the income tax law.

Income Tax Considerations   The income tax law will influence the investment appeal of a vacation home. Indeed, it may well determine how you use the property. There are three possible situations, having to do with how often you use the property.

Situation 1: You rent the property for 14 days or fewer. In this case, the IRS is not concerned with your property as an investment. You need not report any rental income you might earn from renting it 14 or fewer days, but you cannot deduct any expenses other than mortgage interest and property taxes (assuming you file an itemized return).

Situation 2: You use the property for 14 days or fewer (or not more than 10% of the total days it is rented, whichever is greater). Now the property is considered an investment and is treated like any other real estate investment. This means you can deduct *all* business expenses, including depreciation, in determining the rental's profit or loss. However, the same loss limitation rules apply. If you are inactive in managing the property, you cannot deduct losses against other forms of income. If you are active, the maximum loss is $25,000 if your income is less than $100,000. As explained above, you then gradually lose this $25,000 as your income exceeds $100,000.

Situation 3: You use the property 15 days or more (or for more than 10% of the total days it is rented, whichever is greater). Now, the property is a combination of personal residence and investment, and its tax treatment is similar to that of hobbies. This means you must report any net income but cannot deduct any losses, even if you are active in managing the property. The IRS insists that you allocate all expenses on the basis of the property's use as a business and as a personal residence. An example is shown in Exhibit 17.12. Here, the taxpayer used the property 15 days and rented it 30 days, for a total of 45 days. The personal proportion then is one-third (15/45) and the business

| | Allocations | | |
	Personal 1/3	Business 2/3	Total
Rentals	$ —	$ 3,000	$ 3,000
Less: taxes and interest	(900)	(1,800)	(2,700)
operating expenses	(400)	(800)	(1,200)
depreciation	(300)	(600)	(900)
Net income (loss)	$(1,600)	$(200)	$(1,800)
Amount deductible for tax purposes	$ 900	$ -0-	$ 900

EXHIBIT 17.12
Allocating expenses of a vacation home for income-tax purposes

proportion is two-thirds (30/45). All expenses are allocated on the basis of these proportions. Notice the $200 business loss is not deductible. Moreover, the taxpayer can deduct only $900 of property taxes and mortgage interest, which is the personal allocation.

Notice in particular how much tax difference one day can make. Had the taxpayer stayed one fewer day, he or she would have been in situation 2 and total deductions would have been $1,800 (the total net loss), instead of $900! Obviously, you must become familiar with the tax law before buying a place or deciding how to use it after it has been purchased. Moreover, the law is currently being challenged in a number of court cases and may change if any of these are successful.

One additional personal-use day could lead to a substantial loss of tax deductions.

Investment Appeal of Vacation Homes   If the vacation home is used primarily for vacation purposes, it is questionable that it will ever offer a positive rate of return, unless annual price appreciation is very dramatic—probably in the range of 15% or more a year. Few properties consistently show increases of this magnitude. However, return is often not important, since the main reason for owning the property is enjoyment, not profit. Keep in mind that a first home may be profitable because of the saved rentals, but there are no similar savings here, unless you consider saved vacation expenses.

If the ownership intent is primarily business, then you should evaluate the property as you would any other investment, using the methods detailed previously and being careful again to make realistic assumptions. Despite what a rental agent might tell you, most properties have very high vacancy rates. This is due usually to the seasonal nature of vacationing but it might also reflect a large available supply of rental units. A thorough market research of the area and personal familiarity with it are often necessary to do a proper investment evaluation. Also, you must be concerned by the passive-owner aspect of the tax law. If you are completely inactive in managing the property, which is quite common with vacation homes, no losses will be deductible. This means you must be at least partially active to qualify for tax losses. The extent of this activity is a debatable issue, but it is understood by the IRS as being involved in finding

Return may not be crucial if a vacation home is purchased for pleasure; but it surely is if the home is purchased as a business.

renters, arranging for property upkeep, and performing many other routine chores, either directly or by hiring others. Sham activity, such as "visiting occasionally to make sure everything is OK" is clearly disallowed.

Property Valuation

Regardless of the type of real estate that interests you, a key question to consider as a buyer (or as an eventual seller) is, What is a property worth? It is a difficult question to answer for a variety of reasons. First, each property unit is unique to its owner in that it occupies a particular space unavailable to anyone else. In some instances this uniqueness of site is the sole source of value, while in others it amounts to very little since equally attractive space is available elsewhere. A property can also be unique in its construction, design, aesthetic appeal, neighborhood effects, or other factors. A second difficulty in evaluating the worth of a property is that it is often accompanied by other conditions, such as availability of owner financing or an assumable mortgage, fully occupied rental units, or a favorable property tax situation. Finally, a property's price may be negotiable, leading to good or bad buys depending upon an owner's disposition to sell. Clearly, valuing and then buying a property is quite different from buying 100 shares of IBM stock on the NYSE. The valuation isn't necessarily more difficult, but it is different. Three methods are used widely in the process: the cost approach, the comparative sales approach, and the capitalization of income approach.

Real estate valuation is a complex task because of the uniqueness of individual properties.

The Cost Approach   The **cost approach** bases the value of a property upon the cost of its replacement. If you are considering a duplex in a good neighborhood, you might estimate a cost of $200,000 to replace the unit. Adding, say, $50,000 for the value of the land, you estimate the property value at $250,000. If the unit is relatively new, this approach might work well; however, it is quite unrealistic for older properties. In some cases, you need to make large allowances for economic depreciation of the unit. For example, a newly constructed unit may have a 50-year life, while the existing one will last only 30 more years. The $200,000 replacement cost is then adjusted downwards to $120,000 (30/50 × $200,000).

The cost approach is usually appropriate only for relatively new properties.

While older properties tend to have less value than new ones, there are numerous exceptions arising from uniqueness. An existing unit may have a desirable site that allows its owner to charge rentals above competitive rates. This situation makes the older property worth more than a similar new one. While it is a starting point, replacement cost is seldom the final estimate of value.

The Comparative Sales Approach   The **comparative sales approach** determines a property's value by examining recent sales of similarly situated properties. This method is particularly important in owner-occupied residential property valuations since there are no cash flows or other profit indicators upon which to determine value. Anyone who has bought or sold a home appreciates the information provided by a comparative sales analysis. If several houses very

The comparative sales approach is particularly useful in valuing owner-occupied residential units.

similar to the one you are considering buying recently sold for $170,000, you might regard an asking price of $175,000 as realistic. Naturally, the key to this method's usefulness lies in being reasonably sure the target property is in fact similar to the recent sale units. If they are in mint condition while the target is in need of some repairs, a downward adjustment is warranted, at least by an amount equal to fix-up expenses, including an allowance for your own labor if you intend to provide it.

The Capitalization of Income Approach The **capitalization of income approach** finds the value of a property by capitalizing a stream of future cash flows. This is the method we have used to evaluate Rita Winfrey's target property in the previous examples. By determining the profitability of an investment *at a given price* we utilize the same present value techniques as if we discount cash flows at a required rate of return to *determine an intrinsic value*. You should recognize that this overall approach is very similar to the techniques used in determining the intrinsic value of common stock (review Chapter 8). Referring back to Exhibit 17.9, the IRR of 10.24% causes the cash flows in years zero through five to equal $0 exactly. If we discounted the cash flows at a lower rate, say 8%, there would be positive net present value indicating the purchase is attractive. Contrarily, discounting at a higher rate, say 12%, would lead to a negative net present value, and an unattractive investment.

> The capitalization of income approach involves discounting cash flows to determine an intrinsic value.

   While the discounting techniques apply to all property valuations with cash flows, simplified approaches are often used. One such method involves capitalizing net operating income (NOI) by some appropriate rate (r). The formula for this so-called **direct capitalization approach** is:

$$\text{value} = \text{NOI}/r$$

The approach essentially assumes NOI is a correct profit measurement and that it will continue forever (a perpetuity). Clearly, each assumption may be inappropriate in many situations. Moreover, the technique fails to address changes in NOI over time. Surely, a property with rising annual NOIs is worth more than one with static NOIs. A parallel example is the difference in valuing a common stock as opposed to a preferred stock.

> The direct capitalization approach, while easy to use, may have serious limitations.

   However, the method is used widely and we should illustrate it. To do so, let us return to the example in which Rita Winfrey is considering renting the house. Exhibit 17.10 shows NOI (line 11) in each of ten years. Working with the midpoint, assumed to be between years 5 and 6, NOI is estimated at $4,411 [($4,303 + $4,518)/2]. Assuming an appropriate capitalization rate is 8%, the property's value is $55,138 ($4,411/0.08). This amount is considerably below the asking price of $70,000, indicating it is excessive.

FINANCING PROPERTY INVESTMENT

Financing a property investment often involves as much time and effort as finding one. The number of financing options available today is considerably greater than in the past, and you should be familiar with the more common forms to decide

Don't Forget: You Also Invest in the Mortgage

To many real estate investors, financing an investment is often as difficult as finding the right property to buy. In today's credit environment, the choices are many, and making wrong ones can erode the profit you hope to make. Here are some of the more important factors to consider.

Fixed-Rate Versus Adjustable Rate Loan. Most people opt for a fixed-rate loan, but that isn't always the correct choice. A fixed-rate loan carries a higher interest rate, perhaps as much as two to three percentage points higher. By selecting the fixed-rate, you implicitly are betting that interest rates will rise in the future. Or you reason that

even if they decline you can always refinance the fixed-rate loan at a lower rate. Either way, you might be wrong: interest rates don't always go up and refinancing can be very expensive.

Focus on the most important factor in the decision—how long you believe you will own the property. If there is a reasonable chance you will own it less than four years, an adjustable-rate loan is likely to be more attractive. If you hold it longer than six years, the fixed-rate loan makes more sense; you might pay more interest, but the extra outlay is worth it as a hedge against rising interest rates.

Since loans differ so much, generalizations are difficult. The

best way to make the decision is to project annual interest and other costs each year for different holding lengths for each loan alternative. Then assume different interest-rate changes and see what happens. Does this take time and effort? Yes. Is there an easier way to do it? No.

One-Year Versus Three-Year Adjustment Periods. The same logic and analysis applies here as in deciding between a fixed-rate or adjustable-rate loan. Simply add another column to your worksheet, reflecting another adjustable-rate loan with a different adjustment period.

Which Adjustment Index? Adjustable-rate loans adjust on

---

what is best for your particular situation. The basic forms of mortgages are covered in the following sections, and Exhibit 17.13 provides an overview of the wide array of financing forms that are in frequent use.

Fixed-Rate Mortgage

Fixed-rate mortgages are still very popular with borrowers.

A **fixed-rate mortgage** has, as its name indicates, a fixed rate of interest over the loan's maturity. This is probably still the most popular loan from the investors' point of view, because a known rate of interest is locked in for the length of the loan. Not only does this make cash flow budgeting simpler, it represents an opportunity to profit from the investment if inflation accelerates after the loan is made. Many real estate buyers in the past negotiated low-interest loans with fixed payments, enabling them to acquire properties that subsequently increased considerably in value through inflation. Of course, their gains were the lenders'

the basis of changes in an interest rate index. Some use a Treasury bill index, while others are based upon mortgage or savings rates in various parts of the country, or nationally. A feature in *Money* (October, 1988, p. 80) indicated that for the period July 1, 1980, through June 30, 1988, interest on mortgages indexed to Treasury bills paid $2,814 less total interest than those tied to the average interest paid to depositors in the 11th Federal Home Loan Bank District (a widely used index). T-bill indexed loans also beat those tied to national mortgage rates by $1,144. So, they seem the best choice, although they showed greater variations from year to year.

15-Year Versus 30-Year Mortgage. Recently, many buyers seeking a fixed-rate loan have chosen a 15-year maturity rather than the traditionally sought longer ones of 25 or 30 years. The lure is a slightly lower rate and considerably less interest over the loan's life. For example, interest on a 10%, 15-year loan for $100,000 amounts to $93,429 over the loan life. While that seems a lot, consider that a 10%, 30-year loan for the same amount would total $139,627 in interest ($46,198 more) over 15 years and *still* leave you with an unpaid principal of $81,665.

However, the key to choosing one over the other rests solely on your marginal tax rate and what you might earn on the

monthly payment savings with the 30-year loan. For example, the monthly payment with the 15-year loan is $1,075; with the 30-year loan, it is $878 ($197 less). Assuming you have a 28% marginal tax rate, if you can invest the monthly savings to earn more than 7.2% (annual rate), you would be better off with the 30-year loan. The 7.2% rate represents the after-tax cost [10% $\times$ (1.0 $-$ 0.28)] of the mortgage; you also can view it as the opportunity earning rate of investing in the mortgage, which is what you do by choosing a 15-year maturity. So, if you can earn more than 7.2% (after taxes) in other 15-year investments, choose them, rather than the shorter mortgage.

losses, and these losses became so huge, they threatened the entire savings and loan industry in the 1980s. As a result, many institutions simply refused to make fixed-rate loans, or would make them only at very high rates of interest. The decline in interest rates in the mid-1980s brought renewed activity in fixed-rate lending, although variable-rate loans are still used frequently. Actually, there are now two types of fixed-rate loans: those with fixed payments and those with increasing payments.

Fixed Rate-Fixed Payment Loans

The so-called **conventional mortgage** has a fixed rate and fixed payments. Typically, it is not insured by the FHA or VA (both are explained later) and the borrower usually has a down payment of at least 20% of the property's appraised value. We have used a 10%, 30-year mortgage in our previous examples for Rita

EXHIBIT 17.13

Overview of mortgage financing options

Type	Description	Considerations
Fixed Rate Mortgage	Fixed interest rate, usually long-term; equal monthly payments of principal and interest until debt is paid in full.	Offers stability and long-term tax advantages; limited availability. Interest rates may be higher than other types of financing. New fixed rates are rarely assumable.
Flexible Rate Mortgage	Interest rate changes are based on a financial index, resulting in possible changes in your monthly payments, loan term, and/or principal. Some plans have rate or payment caps.	Readily available. Starting interest rate is slightly below market, but payments can increase sharply and frequently if index increases. Payment caps prevent wide fluctuations in payments but may cause negative amortization. Rate caps, while rare, limit amount total debt can expand.
Renegotiable Rate Mortgage (Rollover)	Interest rate and monthly payments are constant for several years; changes possible thereafter. Long-term mortgage.	Less frequent changes in interest rate offer some stability.
Balloon Mortgage	Monthly payments based on fixed interest rate; usually short-term; payments may cover interest only with principal due in full at term end.	Offers low monthly payments but possibly no equity until loan is fully paid. When due, loan must be paid off or refinanced. Refinancing poses high risk if rates climb.
Graduated Payment Mortgage	Lower monthly payments rise gradually (usually over 5-10 years), then level off for duration of term. With flexible interest rate, additional payment changes possible if index changes.	Easier to qualify for. Buyer's income must be able to keep pace with scheduled payment increases. With a flexible rate, payment increases beyond the graduated payments can result in additional negative amortization.
Shared Appreciation Mortgage	Below-market interest rate and lower monthly payments, in exchange for a share of profits when property is sold or on a specified date. Many variations.	If home appreciates greatly, total cost of loan jumps. If home fails to appreciate, projected increase in value may still be due, requiring refinancing at possibly higher rates.
Assumable Mortgage	Buyer takes over seller's original, below-market rate mortgage.	Lowers monthly payments. May be prohibited if "due on sale" clause is in original mortgage. Not permitted on most new fixed rate mortgages.
Seller Take-back	Seller provides all or part of financing with a first or second mortgage.	May offer a below-market interest rate, may have a balloon payment requiring full payment in a few years or refinancing at market rates, which could sharply increase debt.

EXHIBIT 17.13
Continued

Type	Description	Considerations
Wraparound	Seller keeps original low rate mortgage. Buyer makes payments to seller who forwards a portion to the lender holding original mortgage. Offers lower effective interest rate on total transaction.	Lender may call in old mortgage and require higher rate. If buyer defaults, seller must take legal action to collect debt.
Growing Equity Mortgage (Rapid Payoff Mortgage)	Fixed interest rate but monthly payments may vary according to agreed-upon schedule or index.	Permits rapid payoff of debt because payment increases reduce principal. Buyer's income must be able to keep up with payment increases.
Land Contract	Seller retains original mortgage. No transfer of title until loan is fully paid. Equal monthly payments based on below-market interest rate with unpaid principal due at loan end.	May offer no equity until loan is fully paid. Buyer has few protections if conflict arises during loan.
Buy-down	Developer (or third party) provides an interest subsidy which lowers monthly payments during the first few years of the loan. Can have fixed or flexible interest rate.	Offers a break from higher payments during early years. Enables buyer with lower income to qualify. With flexible rate mortgage, payments may jump substantially at end of subsidy. Developer may increase selling price.
Rent with Option	Renter pays "option fee" for right to purchase property at specified time and agreed-upon price. Rent may or may not be applied to sales price.	Enables renter to buy time to obtain down payment and decide whether to purchase. Locks in price during inflationary times. Failure to take option means loss of option fee and rental payments.
Reverse Annuity Mortgage (Equity Conversion)	Borrower owns mortgage-free property and needs income. Lender makes monthly payments to borrower, using property as collateral.	Can provide homeowners with needed cash. At end of term, borrower must have money available to avoid selling property or refinancing.
Zero Rate and Low Rate Mortgage	Appears to be completely or almost interest free. Large down payment and one-time finance charge, then loan is repaid in fixed monthly payments over short term.	Permits quick ownership. May not lower total cost (because of possibly increased sales price). Doesn't offer long-term tax deductions.

SOURCE: *The Mortgage Money Guide*, The Federal Trade Commission.

A conventional mort-
gage has a fixed rate
and fixed payments.

Winfrey. You should recall this loan had a monthly payment of $500, and you also might remember that Rita borrowed $56,976. You might not realize, though, that over 30 years Rita will repay $180,000 ($360 \times \$500$); since she borrowed $56,976, the difference—$123,024—represents total interest over the life of the loan. Of course, if the property increases 5% in value each year for the next 30 years, it eventually will be worth $302,535 [$\$70,000 \times (1.05)^{30}$]. As you see, the numbers become very large when compounding over a long period of time. Actually, they are more dramatically appealing than useful in decision making. As we saw, Rita did a return analysis that favored buying. This perspective is more appropriate than focusing on limited information such as how much interest you pay, or what the house is worth at some distant point in the future.

A growing equity mort-
gage is paid off more
quickly than a conven-
tional mortgage.

Growing Equity Mortgage   In response to borrowers' wishes for a fixed interest rate, but in an effort to cope with inflation uncertainty, some lenders developed what is known as the **growing equity mortgage**. This loan fixes the interest rate but requires the borrower to pay off the loan in a much shorter period of time. For example, you might negotiate a 15-year, 10% mortgage. Rather than paying a fixed monthly amount, however, your payments will be smaller at the beginning of the loan and gradually increase each year until they are much higher at the end. You might start at $500 a month if you borrowed $56,976, but in the fifteenth year the monthly payment might be twice that amount.

Of course, you pay considerably less total interest with this type of loan, but that does not necessarily make it a better loan. You must consider the income-tax impact and the opportunity investment rates available during the maturity of each loan. In effect, your monthly payments are less for the first 15 years with the fixed-payment loan and higher in the last 15 years (since the growing equity loan is then paid off). After considering these payment differentials and related tax effects, the important final question is: what rates can these differential amounts earn? It is a complex problem and you might ask the lending institution to help you evaluate it. At the very least, they should provide you with monthly payment information—principal and interest—for both types of mortgages. With these data, you then can apply an IRR or NPV analysis, after adjusting for the tax deductibility of interest.

Adjustable-Rate Mortgage

An adjustable-rate mort-
gage does not have a
fixed interest rate.

While the growing equity mortgage is one response to the inflation problem, the more popular response has been the **adjustable-rate mortgage (ARM)**. This loan does not have a fixed interest rate; instead, the rate varies in response to changes in market rates of interest. Clearly, this type of loan removes interest-rate risk from the lender and transfers it to the borrower. This is a decided disadvantage to you as an investor; however, there is a consolation in that the loan's initial interest rate is lower than the rate on a fixed-rate loan. For example, the latter might have a 10% rate while the former is only 8.5%. Of course, your monthly payments will vary over the life of the loan if interest rates vary. Investors with very high-interest ARMs were pleasantly surprised by the sharp decreases in monthly payments when interest rates fell in the mid-1980s. Before negotiating an adjustable rate loan, though, you should consider the following items.

The Frequency of the Adjustment   Some loans adjust annually, while others adjust less frequently (usually every three years). The more frequently an adjustment takes place, the more variable your monthly payments will be—for better or worse. This increased variability means greater risk, but also means you get a lower rate. For example, an annually adjusting loan might be offered at 8.5%, while a loan that adjusts every three years might call for a 9.0% rate. Choosing between the two requires a guess as to the future direction of interest rates.

> The more frequently a rate adjustment takes place, the greater the loan's risk.

Rate Cap or Minimum   Most ARMs have a rate maximum, or cap. This means the interest rate on the loan cannot exceed this figure. A cap can apply to an adjusting period—one or three years—and/or to the life of the loan. For example, a three-year ARM may have a rate cap of, say, 3 percentage points each adjustment period and a maximum rate of 16% over the life of the loan. So, if you took out a loan with an initial rate of 9%, its maximum value three years later would be 12%, and the most you would ever pay is 16%. Many ARMs also have minimums that favor lenders. For example, the rate may not decrease more than 3 percentage points in an adjustment period, or ever go lower than, say, 6%.

What Is the Adjustment Index?   ARMs use a variety of interest-rate indexes upon which to make loan interest adjustments. These vary from the three-month Treasury bill rate to the National Average FHLB Mortgage Contract Rate. The key question is, which are the more volatile rates? The Treasury bill rate has been the most volatile in the immediate past (past 10 years), while the FHLB rate has been the least volatile. However, these years have seen extraordinarily volatile short-term rates, and whether this pattern will continue is unclear. Probably the best advice is to avoid any index based on the so-called "cost of funds to the institution." Not only might this figure be difficult to measure, it also might be easy for the institution to manipulate. It is better to stick with a nationally derived index.

> Avoid rate indexes that relate to the institution's cost of funds.

Sources of Mortgage Loans

Mortgage loans are provided by a variety of lending institutions. Savings and loans do the most mortgage business, although commercial banks are increasing their share of the market very rapidly. You also will find mortgage companies active in the business. While most lending is still done on a local level, some observers believe that in the future you might negotiate a mortgage with many possible lenders located anywhere in the United States. This will be accomplished through computer networks integrating lenders with real estate salespeople. In other words, the person who helps you buy a property might also arrange for its financing under the most favorable terms to you. The lender might be your neighborhood bank, or it might be a mortgage company located 3,000 miles away.

One feature that increases the liquidity of a mortgage loan is insurance provided by the Federal Housing Administration (FHA) or the Veterans Administration (VA). Each establishes standards as to borrowers' suitability, maximum loan amounts, and down payments. If these standards are met, the agency insures the loan, which means it will compensate the lender in the event the borrower does not meet his or her obligations. This encourages lenders who might otherwise not be willing to make loans.

An advantage to the investor of an **FHA loan or VA loan** is a much smaller down payment, which can be as low as 5% of the property's purchase price. Another advantage is these loans are assumable by third parties. This means if you plan to sell your property, you can pass the mortgage to the buyer. Conventional loans have due-on-sale clauses that prevent such transfers. An FHA or VA loan with a low fixed rate could be a valuable asset in selling your home if interest rates rise above the contract rate. A disadvantage to the FHA loan is that .5% interest is added to the loan rate. (The VA loan does not add the differential; moreover, it attempts to establish a maximum rate on the loan for the veteran's benefit.)

SUMMARY

A personal residence has both emotional and investment appeal. The latter includes price appreciation and tax-sheltering aspects. Price appreciation is influenced by supply and demand factors at both the national and local levels, while the major tax shelter is the once-in-a-lifetime $125,000 exclusion of all gains resulting from personal residence sales. Housing affordability is determined by a person's income and level of consumer debt, along with the amount of down payment and mortgage interest rate. The most popular personal residence is the detached single-family home, although many people buy condominiums and cooperatives. An important decision for many investors is rent-versus-buy. The economics of the decision can be measured, using rate-of-return analysis.

Rental investment includes residential properties, commercial and industrial properties, and the vacation home. Each should be evaluated with rate-of-return analysis, paying particular attention to aspects of the tax law that might affect profitability. Property valuation utilizes four different methods—the cost approach, the comparative sales approach, the capitalization of income approach with discounting of cash flows, and the direct capitalization approach.

A property investment can be financed with a fixed-rate or adjustable-rate mortgage. If the latter is used, the borrower should determine how the adjustment process will work on a particular loan. Important questions deal with the frequency of adjustment, the existence of rate caps or minimums, and the specific adjustment index used. Mortgage loans are provided by many financial institutions. Some are insured by the Federal Housing Administration (FHA) or the Veterans Administration (VA).

Select the alternative that best identifies the key term.

1. personal residence
2. detached single-family home
3. condominium housing
4. cooperative
5. residential rental property
6. commercial or industrial property
7. vacation home
8. cost approach
9. comparative sales approach
10. capitalization of income approach
11. direct capitalization approach
12. fixed-rate mortgage
13. conventional mortgage
14. growing equity mortgage
15. adjustable-rate mortgage (ARM)
16. FHA loan or VA loan

a. offers a lower down payment than a conventional loan
b. your investment purchases shares of stock
c. has a fixed rate and fixed monthly payments
d. the only investment you live in
e. your tenants are business firms
f. desirable if you expect future interest rates to decline
g. has common areas you share with other owners
h. has a fixed interest rate but monthly payments increase
i. a duplex or fourplex are examples
j. the number-one choice of most home buyers
k. staying a fifteenth day could create a tax problem
l. desirable if you expect future interest rates to increase
m. valuation method based upon discounting cash flows
n. might be an appropriate approach for relatively new properties
o. represented by the formula, NOI/r = value
p. useful valuation method for owner-occupied residential units

1. Explain the following investment characteristics of a personal residence: price appreciation, tax-sheltering of income, low return variability. Explain whether recent data indicates the personal residence has been a good investment.
2. Identify factors that determine the demand for and supply of housing. Explain the impact each factor has upon demand or supply, and how demand and supply influence the price of new housing.
3. Identify local influences that might be important in determining the price of a specific property.

4. Explain the kinds of properties available to a home buyer. Which do you think will appeal to you? Indicate why.

5. Explain how the following factors are involved in the rent-versus-buy decision: mortgage payments versus rental payments, income-tax savings, and price appreciation.

6. Explain various types of rental properties that you might consider investing in; which appeals to you personally?

7. How does the evaluation of a rental property compare with a rent-versus-buy decision? Indicate similarities and differences.

8. Discuss tax limitations as they apply to rental properties.

9. How does a single-point evaluation differ from a multi-point evaluation? Does one input more data than the other? Discuss.

10. What is the investment appeal of a vacation home?

11. With respect to how frequently you rent or use a vacation home personally, explain three situations that influence your taxable income. Is it important to keep a good record of the number of rental and personal-use days? Explain.

12. Explain the following valuation methods: the cost approach and the comparative sales approach. Which method is more appropriate for valuing owner-occupied personal residences? In what type of situation would the cost approach make sense?

13. Explain the capitalization of income approach and the direct capitalization approach. Discuss limitations of the latter method.

14. Explain the following mortgages: fixed rate, conventional, growing equity, and adjustable rate. Which one appeals to you? Explain why.

15. Indicate what the following items mean with respect to an adjustable-rate mortgage: frequency of adjustment, rate cap, adjustment index.

16. What is an FHA or VA loan? Do they have any advantages over other loans? Explain.

PROBLEMS AND PROJECTS

1. Lena Klein expects to earn $36,000 next year. Her monthly installment debt payments will be $300. She would like to have a 30-year, 8% loan for the maximum allowable by her S&L. How much might she borrow? (Use Exhibit 17.4. If her monthly payment is more or less than $500, set up a proportion as follows: $X/\$500 = Y/\$68,120$. You will determine a value for X and then solve for Y.)

2. Lorraine French is thinking of buying the condominium she currently rents for $400 a month. Lorraine likes the place and feels its value should increase over time since it is situated in a very desirable neighborhood. If Lorraine goes ahead with the purchase she will pay $60,000 for the unit, putting down $3,024 and borrowing $56,976. (Her loan payments would be the same as those shown in Exhibit 17.6.) Property taxes are $600 a year and the condo association fees are $480 a year (nondeductible for income tax purposes). All other ownership expenses—utilities, insurance, telephone, etc.—are not relevant because Lorraine pays them now as a renter. Lorraine has a 28% marginal tax rate.

   a. Calculate the investment's IRR assuming the following: a five-year holding period, 4% annual inflation in property taxes, and annual price appreciation of 8% on the condo.

   b. Evaluate the investment for Lorraine.

3. Allison Zeitle will earn $140,000 in the upcoming year from consulting fees in her engineering firm. Allison also owns and actively manages a rental duplex that will show losses.
   a. Assuming the loss is $2,000, how much can she use to offset other income?
   b. Assume Allison's consulting fees are $80,000. How much can be deducted from rental losses of (a) $2,000 or (b) $30,000?
   c. Assume Allison is inactive in managing the property. How much can she deduct if the loss is $2,000?

4. Steve Grevey is considering purchasing a fourplex at 334 Shaw Avenue, a street near a local hospital. He plans to rent the units to nurses and other medical professionals. The building has been converted from a single residence, and it is located in a suburban area of a major city. His analysis of the property indicates a net operating income (NOI) of $16,000 which seems likely. The buyer is asking $180,000 for the property but will consider lower offers. Steve has talked with some of his friends who have shared financial information with him regarding properties they have recently purchased or sold. Details appear in the following table.

Property	Description	Recent Price	NOI
2100 Park Lane	Duplex in affluent neighborhood	$225,000	$20,000
76 Westbury	Fourplex close to a university in the central city	260,000	35,000
351 Shaw Ave.	Rented single family residence located a block away	70,000	4,000

   a. Assuming Steve uses the direct capitalization approach, discuss what you believe is the most appropriate capitalization rate. Given your estimate, determine the property's value.
   b. Discuss some limitations in this analysis.

5. (*Student Project*) The Sunday newspaper in most communities contains listings of both residential and commercial units. With a recent edition, consider personal residences first. Notice the wide variations in listed prices depending upon neighborhood. If you are familiar with the community, indicate the relationship of listed price to location, citing expensive and inexpensive areas. Of course, you should try to control for differences in types of homes. A large, well-appointed home in an expensive area might list for more than a small home in an expensive neighborhood.

6. (*Student Project*) Also contained in the Sunday newspaper are listings for rental units. You might consider contacting several realtors to gather financial data for rentals and expenses. Assuming you obtain adequate data for a property, evaluate it. Review credit conditions locally to determine available financing. In this effort, consider contacting a local bank or S&L, if available information is inadequate. With all data in hand, evaluate a possible purchase at the seller's asking price.

CASE ANALYSES

17.1
The Ryans' First
Home

Neil and Jeannie Ryan are a recently married couple with no dependents. Their combined incomes total $57,600 and they have no debts other than a car loan they are paying off at $300 a month. The Ryans are renting an apartment at present but hope to buy a home in the near future. They have located a place they like very much but are not sure they can afford it, or whether it represents a sound investment. The investment side of the purchase is important to them. They currently have the funds they would use for a down payment invested in a municipal bond fund that yields about 8%. The Ryans have a rather low tolerance for risk, so they have asked your advice in the matter. You anticipate they will have a 28% marginal tax rate indefinitely in the future.

   The home costs $120,000. The Ryans hope to finance the purchase with a 25-year, 10% mortgage for $111,000. Monthly mortgage payments would be $1,000. Expenses in the previous year related to the home and to their current apartment are shown in the following table. These expenses are expected to increase 5% each year. Home values in the neighborhood have been increasing about 6% annually, and this rate should continue in the future. While the Ryans hope to remain in the home for many years, either Neil's or Jeannie's career might require relocation to another city. In this event, the home would be sold and a realtor's commission of 7% (of the market value at the time of the sale) would be paid.

Expense Item	Apartment	New Home
Rent	$9,600	$ —
Utilities	1,400	3,000
Insurance	300	600
Maintenance	200	1,000
Property taxes	—	2,800

Questions

a. Can the Ryans afford the home? Explain.

b. Assume that interest on the mortgage loan is 98% of the annual payment in the first year and then declines by one percentage point in each of the next four years. Considering this information along with appropriate data above, determine a schedule of annual income tax savings associated with the home. Consider a 5-year horizon.

c. Considering your work to question *b* and above data, prepare a schedule of annual cash flows.

d. Evaluate the investment by determining an IRR or by calculating the present value of each future cash flow. The latter method is much easier if you do not have a suitable calculator or computer. If you use this approach, discount with an 8% rate and compare the sum of the present values with the down payment of $9,000. Consider a 5-year horizon.

e. Do you recommend that the Ryans buy the home? Give specific reasons for your decision.

The Rosens, Milt and Wanda, are thinking of buying a vacation condo at Hilton Head. They enjoy the area and believe that property values will grow about 5% annually in the future. The Rosens plan on retiring there, so by buying now they will avoid paying a higher price later. In the near future, they anticipate using the condo 20 days a year and hope to rent it another 80 days at $100 a day.

**17.2
The Rosens'
Vacation Home**

The condo has a cost of $82,500. If depreciation is allowable, it would be based upon the total cost and a write-off period of 27.5 years. The Rosens would put up $12,500 and finance $70,000 with a 10%, fixed-rate loan. First-year mortgage payments would total $7,633, of which about $7,000 is interest. Property taxes would be $1,500 annually and other operating expenses would total $2,000 a year. The Rosens would be active in managing the unit and their taxable income from other sources does not exceed $100,000. They will have a 28% marginal tax rate.

a. Given the above data, determine the total deductions available to the Rosens. What is the first-year cash flow from the property?

Questions

b. Suppose the Rosens decide to use the property for personal use only 14 days. What is their tax situation—income or loss—with this assumption? What is the cash flow with this situation?

c. Suppose the Rosens decide to rent the property only 14 days, and use it themselves for 36 days. What is their tax situation—income or loss—with this assumption? Estimate the cash flow in this situation.

d. Evaluate the condo purchase in terms of cash flow per personal-use day. Which is the best alternative?

Cole, Rebel, David Guilkey, Mike Miles, and Brian Webb. "More Scientific Diversification Strategies for Commercial Real Estate." *Real Estate Review,* Spring 1989, pp. 61–65.

Ficek, Edmund, Thomas B. Henderson, and Ross H. Johnson. *Real Estate Principles and Practices.* 5th ed. Columbus: Merrill Publishing Company, 1990.

Firstenberg, Paul B., and Charles H. Wurtzebach. "Managing Portfolio Risk and Reward." *Real Estate Review,* Winter 1989, pp. 61–65.

Hartzell, David J., et al. "A Look at Real Estate Duration." *The Journal of Portfolio Management,* Fall 1988, pp. 16–24.

Rickles, Roger. "This Old House May Not Be Worth Fixing These Days." *The Wall Street Journal,* April 13, 1989, p. B1.

Rudnitsky, Howard. "Landlord, Beware." *Forbes,* July 24, 1989, pp. 44–45.

Stern, Richard L., and Howard Rudnitsky. "Commercial Real Estate—The Worst Is Yet To Come." *Forbes,* January 26, 1987, pp. 64–68.

Vinocur, Barry. "Surprise: Equity REITs Are Top Performers." *Barron's,* June 12, 1989, p. 70.

**HELPFUL
READING**

CHAPTER EIGHTEEN

Gold and Other Tangibles

WHY TANGIBLES?

Tangibles' Advantages

Tangibles' Disadvantages

INVESTING IN GOLD

Gold's Price Volatility

Supply and Demand Factors

Ways to Own Gold

OTHER TANGIBLES

Silver and Other Precious Metals

Diamonds and Other Precious Gems

Artworks and Antiques

Collectibles and Hobbies

BOXES

What's in the Sotheby?

Trouble in Numismatics

After you finish this chapter, you will be able to:

- understand the use and investment characteristics of tangibles and the advantages they offer.

- understand how tangibles' disadvantages detract from their investment appeal.

- see why gold is considered an attractive tangible investment and learn the various ways of owning it.

- identify investment advantages and disadvantages in other tangibles: silver and precious metals, diamonds and other precious stones, artworks, and antiques.

- understand the risks and potential rewards from collectibles and hobbies.

U ntil recently, few investment advisors took tangible investing seriously. If you enjoyed owning art or jewelry, or collecting stamps or coins, and if you kept these activities within reasonable financial bounds, then little harm could be done; but few investors expected their collections to make them rich. As inflation accelerated during the 1970s, though, many investors found they were enjoying far greater price appreciation on the average stamp in their collection than they were on the average stock in their investment portfolio. If you were "into" the new rock and roll in the 1950s, and if you liked Elvis Presley and bought his 45 RPM single, "That's Alright (Mama)," in 1954 for $.69, you should be delighted to learn it is worth somewhere between $300 and $400 today.

Such successes certainly enhance everyone's interest in collectibles, including academicians, who—like investment advisors—often took a scornful view. The results of their search, though, have led them to consider tangibles more seriously. What they found is that price appreciation in many cases has indeed been excellent and, equally important, including tangibles in the investment portfolio can reduce its overall risk without sacrificing return. To be sure, there are many risks in tangibles and many factors you need to consider before you decide to invest in them.

WHY TANGIBLES?

To begin, let us define a **tangible** as any physical item that can be bought or sold in some market. This is a broad definition that allows us to consider virtually any item. Of course, the investment quality of the tangible will depend heavily upon how well its market functions. If you own gold in virtually any form, you can find a well-developed market for your sales, guaranteeing you a fair price. On the other hand, if your tangible normally trades through flea markets and garage sales, you may have a problem should you wish to sell. Along with marketability, you need to consider the intrinsic quality of a piece. You may own a coin that has a catalog price of $100; but this price usually presumes the coin is in mint condition, and if yours is not, its price will be far less than $100.

The investment quality of a tangible often depends upon the functioning of its resale markets.

There are advantages and disadvantages in investing in tangibles. The most important ones are explained in the following sections.

Tangibles' Advantages

To some, the primary appeal of a tangible is its beauty; any investment characteristics are secondary. In contrast, others have no concern for aesthetic attributes. Indeed, these are often seen as unnecessary complications. Gold held in a distant vault will do just fine for these investors, while the collector wants his or her gold in the form of jewelry to be worn and enjoyed. Exhibit 18.1 highlights the investment and use characteristics of tangibles.

Use Characteristics A tangible can be used in a number of ways. Broadly, we can say you enjoy the item for its own sake; or, you enjoy it because it reflects

EXHIBIT 18.1

Tangibles' characteristics

Use Characteristics	Investment Characteristics
☐ Direct enjoyment	☐ Hedge against political risks
☐ A display of wealth	☐ Hedge against inflation risk
☐ Item is needed anyway	☐ Portfolio diversification

your wealth to society; or, you must buy a noncollectible item to serve your needs, anyway.

Direct Enjoyment.   As mentioned above, many investors enjoy the items they collect. Indeed, perhaps one of life's true pleasures is enjoying the artistic expressions of human endeavor. Also, many people enjoy collections as hobbies. Coin and stamp collecting, for example, have challenged people for years, and other collections have become very popular recently.

A Display of Wealth.   Since tangibles can be seen, they serve as an excellent vehicle for displaying wealth. Our society frowns upon crass displays of wealth: you aren't likely to take out a newspaper ad announcing when you make your first million, but you might buy a Picasso oil painting. Each approach tells the world you have made it, but the latter also shows you are a connoisseur of fine art. It is socially acceptable, while the ad is in terrible taste. This display function should not be taken lightly. If we look closely, we are likely to find that most of us consider it in much of what we buy—our cars, for example. From an investment perspective, this behavioral pattern tends to support a market demand for certain tangibles.

A tangible displays your wealth—tactfully!

The Item Is Needed Anyway.   Apart from enjoyment or wealth display, you might consider investing in a tangible if a similar item must be purchased to meet some need. For example, if you are planning an engagement and future marriage, you will probably buy an engagement ring. Now, there are many from which to choose, and rather than just "buying a ring," you might devote extra time and spend a bit more to "invest in a stone." The same approach can be followed when you set up housekeeping and start buying furniture. A Shaker bench or chair purchased 30 years ago might not have cost more than a Formica alternative. Today, its value has increased at least tenfold while the Formica piece is most likely in the community dump.

Many engaged couples invest in a tangible—the diamond engagement ring.

Investment Characteristics   Most investors are interested in tangibles because of the potential returns they offer. However, there are other factors to consider. Since the value of many intangibles is independent of political boundaries, they serve as hedges against political risks. And, since tangibles' prices fluctuate, they offer potential investment advantages as inflation hedges or as components to a portfolio.

Tangibles' Returns.   Compared to intangibles, the returns on some tangibles have been excellent, as Exhibit 18.2 illustrates. As you see, for the

EXHIBIT 18.2
Returns on tangibles and intangibles (through June 1, 1989)

	20 Years	Rank	10 Years	Rank	5 Years	Rank	1 Year	Rank
Coins	16.6	1	12.9	2	14.5	4	30.2	3
Chinese ceramics[a]	13.3	2	8.7	6	12.2	5	40.3	2
Gold	11.5	3	2.8	10	−1.6	11	−20.5	13
Old masters[a]	10.9	4	9.6	5	18.4	2	50.7	1
Diamonds[b]	10.4	5	8.3	7	10.7	6	15.5	5
Stocks[c]	10.3	6	17.0	1	20.1	1	24.5	4
Treasury bills[c]	8.6	7	10.0	4	7.2	7	7.8	7
Bonds[c]	8.6	7	10.9	3	17.6	3	11.2	6
Oil	8.3	8	1.2	11	−10.7	13	3.2	11
Housing	7.6	9	5.5	9	5.1	9	6.6	8
CPI	**6.3**	**10**	**5.7**	**8**	**3.5**	**10**	**5.2**	**10**
U.S. farmland	6.0	11	−0.5	13	−5.3	12	5.9	9
Silver	5.5	12	−4.6	14	−11.2	14	−23.2	14
Foreign exchange	4.0	13	0.9	12	7.1	8	−13.3	12

[a]Source: Sotheby's.

[b]Source: The Diamond Registry.

[c]Stock returns assume quarterly reinvestment of dividends. Bond returns assume monthly reinvestment.

CPI = Consumer Price Index.

Note: All returns are for the period ended June 1, 1989, based on latest available data.

SOURCE: Salomon Brothers, Research Department, *Investment Policy*, June 5, 1989.

20-year period, tangibles take the top five slots, which is an impressive record. Bear in mind, though, that measuring a tangible's return within the context of an index is considerably more difficult than measuring one for an intangible. The problem is that prices paid for items at auction do not necessarily reflect the value of supposedly similar items not auctioned. For example, if a Van Gogh painting sells for $50 million (as one did recently), does that mean every Van Gogh painting is worth $50 million? Critics point out that often the most valuable pieces go to auction, while those less valuable are held. So, an upward bias in the index is created. While the index is far from perfect, it does provide some indication of tangibles' performances; and, even allowing for bias, the returns have been rather good.

Hedge Against Political Risks. As citizens of the United States, we often take for granted reasonable stability of our financial system and the intangible assets it creates. People in quite a few other countries face different situations. To them, holding your wealth in paper assets is foolish, because a weak government might allow their value to collapse. Along with real estate, tangibles represent a more sensible wealth-holding alternative. The price of gold, for example, is often thought to reflect world-wide peace or hostility, with the former leading to lower prices and the latter leading to higher.

Worldwide hostility often increases the demand for tangibles.

Hedge Against Inflation Risk. Since inflation is a form of political instability, intangibles' prices tend to change in step with inflation rates. Exhibit 18.2 shows that seven of the nine tangibles listed had a return greater than the CPI over the 20-year period. Of course, over shorter holding periods this is not the case. Gold, silver, and farmland were particularly poor performers for the 5-year and 1-year periods.

Portfolio Diversification. Tangibles can be used to achieve more efficient portfolio diversification than is possible by holding only intangibles. This is so because tangibles' returns are often poorly positively correlated—and sometimes negatively correlated—with intangibles' returns, particularly common stock returns. You should recall from Chapter 4 that such correlations, rather than strong positive correlations, are helpful in reducing risk without giving up return.

Exhibit 18.3 indicates correlations among five asset groups. As you see, the tangibles—paintings, gold, and housing—are moderately positively correlated with each other, with correlations ranging from +0.666 (paintings and gold) to +0.477 (gold and housing) to +0.321 (paintings and housing). Combining these assets in portfolio would have reduced risk only moderately. However, combining any one with, say, common stocks would have led to a reasonable reduction in risk. This reduction results from the poorer correlations: from +0.204 (with housing) to +0.003 (with paintings) to −0.213 (with gold). An interesting finding in this study is the correlation between stocks and bonds, which is −0.162. This means a portfolio of gold, stocks, and bonds would have been very efficient over the period indicated.

Tangibles' returns are often poorly correlated with intangibles' returns, enhancing their portfolio appeal.

A portfolio of gold, stocks, and bonds can be efficient.

Tangibles' Disadvantages

To this point in the discussion, tangibles seem almost too good to be true: high return, low risk (when held in portfolio), and enjoyment in use. Unfortunately, they have disadvantages that detract from their overall appeal.

EXHIBIT 18.3

Asset return correlations

	Paintings	Gold	Housing	Stocks	AAA Bonds
Paintings	1.000				
Gold	0.666	1.000			
Housing	0.321	0.477	1.000		
Stocks	0.003	−0.213	0.204	1.000	
AAA Bonds	0.336	0.243	0.307	−0.162	1.000

Perfect positive correlation = 1.000
Perfect negative correlation = −1.000
No correlation = 0.000

NOTE: Data apply to the period 1971–1984.

SOURCE: Michael F. Bryan, "Beauty and the Bulls: The Investment Characteristics of Paintings," Federal Reserve Bank of Cleveland, *Economic Review,* 1Q 1985, p. 3.

High Commissions and Holding Costs   Depending upon the tangible in question, you may pay commissions ranging from 1% to 2% (gold, for example) to as much as 30% (an art object, for example) on its purchase or sale, or both. As you move to the high end, it is obvious that trading tangibles on a frequent basis will enrich only the dealer, even if price appreciation is excellent.

Commissions of 30% and higher are common with some tangibles.

Holding costs with tangibles can also be high. All tangibles must be stored in safe places to prevent theft, and art objects and other collectibles might deteriorate in quality if they are not treated properly. Insurance and other guardian services, such as safe deposit boxes, home alarm systems, and storage companies, also add to costs. With respect to insurance, make sure your homeowner's policy has an endorsement to insure the market value of your items. If it doesn't, you will receive only the fair value to replace a lost item. Your Shaker chair, for example, will be valued at an amount no greater than that of the Formica alternative, rather than at its market value.

A Need for Specialized Knowledge   Anyone who has taken a serious attitude towards collecting knows that considerable time, effort, and skill are needed to develop a valuable collection. Serious collectors usually specialize in a narrow area, which they follow and study in depth, and most experts will probably tell you to do likewise. They also suggest that you should not begin collecting with the objective of making a profit; instead, you should concentrate on the aesthetic characteristics of your collectibles and understand them well. Don't buy something because you heard it is in fashion; rather, buy it because, in your experienced opinion, it is a good piece of work. Obviously, if you lack an experienced opinion, you must rely upon someone who has one. Expert opinion, though, is expensive, which also erodes any price appreciation.

Some tangibles should never be purchased without expert opinion.

Extremely Volatile Prices   Most tangibles' prices are very volatile. Gold, for example, went from $36 an ounce in 1970 to almost $900 an ounce in 1980, and down to $360 an ounce by mid-1990. A one-carat, D-flawless diamond could have been purchased for $4,300 in 1974; six years later it was worth $62,000, and one year after that it was down to $25,000. Such price volatility should serve as a warning not to hold an excessive proportion of your portfolio in tangibles.

No Current Return   Your only return from a tangible is price appreciation. Investing in tangibles means you must forego dividends, interest, or other regular cash flows that you could receive on alternative investments. In a sense, a tangible is similar to the common stock of an emerging growth company. It, too, usually pays no dividend and its future price appreciation is very uncertain. However, some tangibles investors might disagree with this analogy. In their view, certain tangibles are far less risky than most growth stocks; these investors would probably prefer to compare a tangible to a zero coupon bond, with its price appreciation only a little less certain.

Poor Resale Markets   We mentioned earlier that the investment quality of a tangible depends heavily upon the existence of an efficient resale market.

Efficient means there is a reasonable number of buyers so that price cannot be dictated by anyone. It also means trading takes place at reasonable cost; that is, commissions or other charges do not absorb a large portion of the item's resale value. Many tangibles fail to meet one or both of these criteria. Indeed, unless you limit your tangible investing to gold or other precious metals, you are likely to encounter difficulties. Naturally, there are varying degrees of difficulty depending upon the popularity of the tangible. Postage stamp and coin collecting are very popular hobbies, which means there is an active resale market that is reasonably efficient. On the other hand, if your collectibles are less popular you may be able to sell only at an annual show (usually held in a distant city) or through very limited mail-order operations where prices are set by buyers.

Rampant Fraud   A concern faced by all tangibles investors is the rampant fraud that exists in these markets. Many investors of both moderate and substantial means have been swindled in one way or another by unscrupulous operators. Keep in mind that virtually no regulation exists (other than the law in general) as it does with stocks, bonds, and many other intangibles. Anyone can call himself or herself an expert and set up shop as a coin dealer, an art importer, an antique auction house, or anything else. Moreover, placing a value on a collectible is often a highly subjective judgment, and dealers might overgrade items they sell while undergrading purchases. If you are not an expert in your collectibles area, then the best advice is to find one who is reputable and to follow his or her advice to the letter.

You should also be careful about participating in gold and other precious metal ownership plans. Several of these have gone into bankruptcy, leaving investors with virtually worthless certificates to claim gold coins or gold bullion that didn't exist. If you invest in any arrangement that you do not first check thoroughly, including asking for references and even seeking legal advice, you may be asking for trouble.

INVESTING IN GOLD

Gold is often called the perfect tangible. You can own it in many different ways, and over a long period of time its price has kept pace with inflation. Some years ago, a financial institution dealing in gold ran a clever advertisement that said: "Two hundred years ago a good suit of clothing cost 1 ounce of gold—it still does today." This ad appeared when inflation was accelerating and certainly drove home the inflation-protection quality of gold. As Exhibit 18.2 indicates, the 20-year return on gold of 11.5% is very good; better, in fact, than the return of 10.3% on common stocks.

Gold has other advantages. Because it is so valuable, a fairly large investment can be held in a small physical quantity. This facilitates storage and protection; for example, most investors can easily store their gold coins in a bank safe deposit box. Gold also can be purchased in standardized units, making it possible to invest precisely the amount you wish. Many other tangibles are not so

Other than the precious metals, tangibles often have very poor resale markets

The label "art expert" or "dealer" can be used by anyone; make sure the person you deal with really is one.

Gold has many advantages to justify its claim as the perfect tangible.

easily divisible—you either buy a whole painting or none at all. True, you can buy a lesser work if your funds are limited, but that may be difficult. Also, collecting gold requires no particular skill or effort, unless you choose gold jewelry or other gold artifacts. Finally, gold is exceptionally easy to buy and sell, and commissions are relatively inexpensive. Before you buy gold, though, you should understand its risks and the different forms of ownership.

Gold's Price Volatility

High price volatility with gold isn't necessarily bad.

Exhibit 18.4 indicates the absolute price volatility (the standard deviation) of gold and selected other household assets, along with the rate of return for each during the period indicated. Using the coefficient of variation (which compares risk to return) to measure risk in a relative sense shows that gold actually was less risky than common stocks and Chinese ceramics (a popular collectible). However, it was considerably more risky than housing, paintings, and corporate bonds.

However, volatility by itself is not necessarily undesirable. As we discussed earlier in this chapter, the important issue is whether or not gold's price volatility adds to, or reduces, an investor's overall portfolio volatility. The conclusion you can draw from the study cited in Exhibits 18.3 and 18.4 is that it reduces volatility significantly if it is held in portfolio with common stocks and bonds.

Supply and Demand Factors

As an economic commodity, gold's price is determined by factors of supply and demand. Advocates of gold like to point out that gold is a scarce commodity; there is only so much of it. Someone has determined that all the gold that has ever been mined occupies a space probably no greater than 18 cubic yards. Such references, of course, are intended to persuade you that gold's price must

Changes in supply and demand influence gold's price.

EXHIBIT 18.4
Return and risk measurements on selected household assets

	(1) Annual Rate of Return	(2) Standard Deviation of Returns	(3) Coefficient of Variation (2) ÷ (1)
Gold	16.2%	31.4%	1.94
Chinese ceramics	14.3	37.7	2.64
Paintings index	10.7	8.2	0.77
Stocks	8.4	19.4	2.31
Housing	6.4	4.3	0.67
AAA bonds	6.1	2.5	0.41

NOTE: Data apply to the period 1970–1984.

SOURCE: Michael F. Bryan, "Beauty and the Bulls: The Investment Characteristics of Paintings," The Federal Reserve Bank of Cleveland, *Economic Review* 1Q 1985, p. 5.

increase over time because of its scarcity. The truth is that the supply of gold is not absolutely fixed, but, rather, is responsive to gold's price: as that price increases, more gold is mined and brought to market. The main deterrent to gold production is the cost of extraction. As costs increase, mining gold becomes less profitable, and the amount supplied during any period of time tends to decrease. The typical mine is closed not because the gold "plays out," but because it is too expensive to extract.

One should therefore be cautious of claims exaggerating the importance of limited supply. However, there are supply factors that can be important at various times. Most of the world's gold is supplied by two countries: South Africa and the U.S.S.R. Needless to say, each represents a political risk in that their current gold supplies can be adjusted through government action. If the political turmoil continues in South Africa and threatens to close its gold mines, you can expect the price of gold to jump rapidly. Conversely, an easing of tensions will have the opposite effect. It should be noted that U.S. production of gold has increased sharply in recent years, due to new extraction methods using cyanide. Interestingly, most of the large new mining companies are foreign-owned.

Both supply and demand influences tend to increase gold's price volatility.

Looking at demand, the situation also suggests price volatility. This is so because gold is often seen as a world refuge for political instability. As indicated earlier in this chapter, investors shun financial assets during unstable times. This means many people increase their demand for gold simultaneously, which exerts upward pressure on gold's price. The ending of the Iranian hostage crisis probably contributed to the sharp decline in price from about $900 an ounce in 1980 to around $300 an ounce two years later.

Ways to Own Gold

Gold can be owned in a number of ways. Before choosing one, you should understand the advantages and disadvantages of each. If one of your reasons for owning gold is to enjoy its beauty, then some ownership methods will not be suitable because they involve holding your gold at a financial institution or owning claims to gold, rather than gold itself.

Gold Coins   A number of countries, including Canada, Mexico, the United States, and South Africa, mint **gold coins**. By far the most plentiful and popular is the South African Krugerrand, although the Canadian Maple Leaf is gaining rapidly in popularity because of the unsettled racial situation in South Africa. The most common size is one ounce, but smaller sizes are available. Coins can be purchased through many stockbrokers, coin dealers, and some banks.

Gold coins are easy to buy and store, and many people enjoy viewing them.

Owning gold in coin form has many advantages. The coins are a pleasure to view, conveniently small, and easily transferred to someone else should you care to sell them. Since the amount of gold embodied in them is known, you don't need to have them assayed upon transfer. Coins also have disadvantages. First, most states impose a sales tax on their purchase. Second, coins typically sell at premiums above their gold content. For example, if gold is quoted at $350 an ounce, you might pay $360 for a one-ounce coin. Third, you sell coins at a bid price less than the ask price you pay to buy them: if you sold the above coin, you might get only $356. (Also, prices vary among dealers, making it necessary to shop around for the best deal.) Finally, you will incur some expenses to safeguard your holdings.

Bullion and Certificates   **Gold bullion** comes in the form of bars, with the quantity of gold indicated by an assay report. You can buy a bar with as little as one ounce of gold, although most bars contain larger quantities. Brokers, banks, and gold dealers handle bullion and also offer certificate programs. A bar of gold has less aesthetic appeal than a coin, and when you consider both commissions and disposal costs (assaying and others), there is no advantage in owning bullion as opposed to coins, unless you are dealing in a large quantity.

Rather than owning bullion directly, you can participate in an ownership program. In this case, you buy gold and receive a **gold ownership certificate**. The gold is stored in a repository somewhere else, usually in a bank vault located in a state without a sales tax—Delaware, for example. You can make purchases over the phone, charging them to your credit card; however, you must present the certificate when you sell.

Certificate programs also have advantages and disadvantages. In most cases, you will buy gold at close to its market price—rather than paying a premium—and you eliminate the storage problem. However, you will pay a commission to buy the gold and a service fee for storage each year. Commissions are usually 3% (or less) of the amount purchased, and annual fees are typically one-quarter of one percent of cost, up to a maximum, such as $60 or $70.

Gold ownership pro-
grams should be re-
searched thoroughly for
safety.

Unquestionably, your chief concern with a certificate program is the integrity of the repository institution. As mentioned above, some nonbank firms have gone bankrupt, forcing huge losses on certificate holders. If you are a conservative person, you will sleep better if you choose coins or bullion bars over certificates.

Gold Jewelry and Works of Art   Gold is a principal element in many pieces of jewelry and works of art. Owning any of these items, then, is also an ownership of gold. However, all things considered, it is not an ideal way to own gold unless you are also enthusiastic about the creation. This is because the gold component of most pieces is quite small; in effect, you usually pay far more for the creative work than you do for the gold. There is quite a bit of bogus advertising about gold jewelry. The expression ''solid gold,'' for example, is virtually meaningless as a description of gold content; all it actually means is the piece is not hollow. Deal with a reputable jeweler and look for carat ratings: 18 carats indicates 75% gold, and 14 carats means 58% gold. So, if an 18-carat ring weighs one-half ounce and costs $500, you should see that you are buying 0.375 (0.5 × 0.75) of an ounce of gold; and if the current price of gold is $380 an ounce, your ring has $142.50 (0.375 × $380) worth of gold in it. You then judge if the creative component is worth $357.50 ($500 − $142.50).

In a gold work of art,
you probably pay more
for the art than for the
gold.

Gold Options and Futures Contracts Rather than owning gold directly, you can own a **claim on gold**. A call option allows you to buy gold at a set price for a given period of time. If gold's market price is above this set price, you exercise or sell the option at a gain; and if this gain is enough to offset the cost of the option, you will earn a profit on the investment. A futures contract is similar to an option except you pay nothing for it, but you will suffer losses if gold's price declines. Since options are discussed in Chapter 13 and futures contracts in Chapter 14, they will not be explained here. However, those chapters should be read thoroughly before you consider a gold option or futures contract. The risks with each are extremely high.

Gold Mining Stocks Another indirect ownership of gold is to purchase common stocks of gold mining companies, such as Campbell Red Lake, Newmont, or Giant Yellowknife. Studies have shown a high degree of correlation between changes in the price of gold and changes in the prices of mining company stocks. They also indicate that stock prices typically are more volatile; that is, if gold's price changes, say, 10%, mining stocks' prices might change 20%. Of course, this is desirable when prices increase, but not so welcome when they decline.

An advantage of this play on gold is that you probably will earn some dividends on the stocks, the amount depending upon the particular companies selected. The main disadvantage is the risk of investing in a company that might not do well, even if gold's price does increase. To overcome this obstacle, you should seek a diversified portfolio of gold mining stocks. Many investors choose mutual funds for this purpose; Exhibit 18.5 contains information from the prospectus of one such fund. Its performance, too, over time is highly correlated to changes in the price of gold.

A gold mining stock might give the advantages of gold ownership along with a dividend return.

OTHER TANGIBLES

Investors often consider other tangibles in addition to gold as part of their portfolios. Silver and other precious metals are popular investments and so are precious gems and artworks. Also, hobbies and collectibles intrigue many people, as much for entertainment as for profit.

Silver and Other Precious Metals

While gold is clearly the metal of choice to most investors, some are intrigued by other metals, particularly silver and platinum. Investing in these metals is at least as risky as investing in gold, and frequently more so. There are fewer market participants, which means prices can be manipulated by a particularly powerful buyer or seller. The legendary Hunt brothers from Texas—William and Nelson Bunker—supposedly intended to monopolize the supply of silver in the early 1980s in an effort to drive up its price for their own eventual gain. Whatever their intentions, we do know they were able to acquire over 200 million ounces of silver,

EXHIBIT 18.5

Investing in the stocks of precious metals and minerals mining companies. (Sources: Data for Fidelity's fund are from the *Prospectus* dated July 15, 1988, and the Semiannual Report of Select Portfolios dated December 23, 1988.)

Investing in a precious metals and minerals fund provides a diversified "play on gold."

The holdings of Fidelity's precious metals and minerals fund is shown at right, while data below show holding period returns since the fund's inception. As you see, returns are positively correlated over time, although year-to-year correlations are poor for small changes in the price of gold.

Holding Period Returns

Period	Fidelity Fund	Gold
7/14/81–4/30/82*	−40.9%	−28.9%*
Years ended:		
4/30/83	+122.6	+32.5*
4/30/84	+1.6	−5.0
4/30/85	+3.0	−13.0
4/30/86	+3.7	+4.0
4/30/87	+94.78	+21.5
4/30/88	−30.06	−5.5

*Returns are annualized

PRECIOUS METALS AND MINERALS

PORTFOLIO CONCENTRATIONS:
COMMON STOCKS   91.7%

AUSTRALIA	
Precious Metals	12.9%
UNITED STATES	
Precious Metals	4.5
Nonferrous Metals	0.9
CANADA	
Precious Metals	27.2
SOUTH AFRICA	
Precious Metals	42.8
UNITED KINGDOM	
Precious Metals	3.4
SHORT-TERM OBLIGATION	4.7%

Notice the magnified change in the fund's return in relation to the changes in gold's price. This is characteristic of such funds, which increases their relative risks.

a feat that most assuredly had some impact on silver's price. In addition to considering the possibility of thinly traded markets, you should consider other factors discussed below.

Gold and silver prices move together, but gold has shown the better return.

Silver   **Silver** is sometimes considered a good substitute tangible for gold. Its price variations over time tend to correlate in a strong, positive manner with those of gold, although silver is believed to be more volatile. When gold peaked at about $900 an ounce in 1980, silver reached its highest-ever price of around $50 an ounce. It subsequently fell to about $5 an ounce and has traded between $5 and $13 since then. The 20-year return on silver from Exhibit 18.2 is 5.5% which is far below gold's return of 11.5%.

Silver is in far greater supply than gold and it also has far more applications, since it is used in a number of industrial and commercial processes. Each of these factors explains silver's price volatility. For example, its industrial uses put it in competition with other metals or manufactured items such as plastic. When these items are substituted for silver, its demand falls, leading to lower prices; and, when silver is substituted for them, the reverse situation takes place.

Silver can be purchased in the same ways as gold. A popular form of silver investment is to hold silver coins. You can buy bags of silver coins through coin dealers. A bag of "junk" silver contains 715 ounces of 90% silver dimes, quarters, or half-dollars minted before 1965. "Clad" silver bags have 295 ounces in 40% silver Kennedy half-dollars minted between 1965 and 1970. A third bag consists of 755 ounces of 1878–1935, 90% silver dollars. You can buy fractional parts of bags and have them stored at a bank. Also, if the bag is unopened, you do not need an assay report if you decide to sell.

Silver is often sold in bags of coins with varying quality.

Other Precious Metals Other precious metals include platinum, cobalt, titanium, magnesium, and others, most of which are poorly understood by most investors. Various stockbrokerage firms occasionally issue research reports on platinum, since its industrial uses seem to be growing rapidly. When the news on cold fusion broke in early 1989, there was considerable speculation in palladium, which is used in the nuclear industry. Its price jumped around 30% in several weeks. As of this writing, the price is still rather high, historically speaking, although the verdict was still out on whether cold fusion would work. Prudence is necessary in investing in platinum, palladium, or any other precious metal. It is difficult to see why an investor should be attracted to an esoteric metal, other than on the strength of a recommendation, and that recommendation should be researched thoroughly. If you are considering a purchase, seek advice from several other sources, particularly those without a commission to earn.

Diamonds and Other Precious Gems

Diamonds are by far the most popular of all precious gems. Investing in diamonds is quite different from investing in gold. To begin with, judging quality is a serious problem, because each diamond has unique characteristics of size, clarity, and ability to refract light. To overcome the problem, the Gemological Institute of America has developed a grading standard that gemologists use to grade stones. More important, you receive a certificate indicating the grade. Obviously, grading adds considerably to the cost of an investment, and with commissions, sales and excise taxes, dealer markup, and possibly other expenses added, your total purchase costs could range from 30% to 100% of the amount invested.

Also, you cannot buy or sell diamonds as easily as gold. You must use a dealer who can provide a certificate, and it is important to select one who is reputable. Fraud has been extensive in the precious stone business, with dealers selling low-grade diamonds but charging high-grade prices. It is suggested that

What's in the Sotheby?

Not to be outdone by their counterparts who follow stocks and bonds by tracking the DJIA, the S&P 500, and countless other time series, aficionados of real wealth now have their very own scorecard—the Sotheby Index. Developed by Jeremy Eckstein, a statistician with Sotheby's in London, it consists of over 400 individual items grouped into 13 "market baskets."

The items have been hand-picked by Sotheby's experts to represent the types of items usually brought to market, instead of the infrequent super-sales that make the evening news. The index is quoted regularly in financial publications, and the 13 categories are shown below. Rates of return on most items are quite good in relation to returns on other investments. An interesting question, though, might be to ask how much you would have needed to afford an "average" piece in each category? A million dollars, maybe? You get the feeling there are very few people following the Sotheby as an aid to measure their own wealth. Perhaps it's a fantasy index.

Sotheby's Art Index®			
Category	Sept 1975	June 1987	June 1989
Old master paintings	100	346	610
19th century European paintings	100	303	536
Impressionist & post-impressionist paintings	100	521	1,266
Modern paintings (1900–1950)	100	544	1,264
Contemporary art	100	597	856
American paintings (1800–pre-WW II)	100	698	1,371
Continental ceramics	100	320	505
Chinese ceramics	100	550	815
English silver	100	343	388
Continental silver	100	201	315
American furniture	100	451	484
French & continental furniture	100	299	409
English furniture	100	594	822
Weighted Aggregate		435	798

September 1975 = 100.

SOURCE: © 1989 Sotheby's, Inc. Sotheby's Art Index reflects subjective analyses and opinions of Sotheby's art experts, based on auction sales and other information deemed relevant. Nothing in Sotheby's Art Index is intended or should be relied upon as investment advice or as a prediction or guarantee of future performance or otherwise.

you trade only with dealers in Chicago and New York, since they have experience with investment programs that your local jeweler cannot offer. The return on diamonds, though, has been fairly good, as Exhibit 18.2 indicated.

In addition to diamonds, you can invest in other precious gems, such as rubies, emeralds, sapphires, and others. You buy them in the same way you buy diamonds. However, they offer even greater risks because judging quality may be more difficult and they seem to be subject to fads in demand that come and go unpredictably.

> Judging a precious gem's quality is a difficult task.

Artworks and Antiques

Perhaps no tangible offers as much difficulty in collecting as do **artworks** and **antiques**. As Exhibit 18.2 indicated, the return on old masters over the 20-year period is a respectable 10.9%. Notice the large return of 50.7% for the year ended June 1, 1989. Returns like this lure many investors to the art market. Many people believe, though, that any original artwork by even some obscure artist might be worth something someday, if the artist is ever "discovered;" and, any piece of furniture over 100 years old automatically becomes a valuable antique. Of course, neither view is correct. Your chances of becoming rich by buying the works of an unknown artist are so slim that you would be better off panning for gold in one of your local streams. Most investors in art do not look for unrecognized artists; rather, they work through art dealers or other experts who guide their purchases in the direction of known artists. True, there are degrees of recognition, and you might prefer the risks of a lesser-known talent to the more assured value with an old master.

> Artwork returns have been exceptional in some years, but don't look for profit in the works of "undiscovered" geniuses.

As with diamonds and other precious gems, acquisition costs are extremely high, and resale is even more difficult. Small investors find entering the art market virtually impossible unless they settle for lithographic prints. However, extreme caution is needed here because of fraud, such as "limited editions" that are mass produced in virtually unlimited quantities. The situation became so bad that New York passed a law in 1981 regulating the sale of prints. The rule for an investor in art is quite simple: buy nothing unless you have it evaluated by an expert; and, if you can't afford the expert, buy nothing.

> The art market is fraught with fraud.

The same rule holds for the antique investor. While age can add to the value of a piece, it does not substitute for workmanship and quality. Indeed, much old, poorly constructed, and tasteless furniture will be worth nothing in normal times and with normal tastes. Admittedly, times and tastes are not always normal, and some outlandishly ugly pieces have had value because of a faddish appeal. You can guess the risks involved in this type of investing. Like the art investor, the antique investor typically does not scour the countryside looking in attics and barns for unrecognized masterworks; rather, he or she works with a dealer and limits investments to identified artists or pieces of work. And the right selection can be extremely profitable. For example, a Chippendale chair sold at auction recently for $2.5 million, which doubled the previous world record. The chair was strictly an investment, since it didn't even have upholstery!

Trouble in Numismatics

With rare coins topping asset return lists year after year, it's no wonder stock and bond investors are wondering if they are in the right game. Maybe it's time to cash in Big Blue and Ma Bell for an 1844 Seated Liberty, or a commemorative issue from the U.S. Mint. Before you take either step, think twice. The two following comments are food for thought.

The Rare Coin Market.
Supply and coin grading are the two keys here. Issues in short supply command the highest prices, but grading is equally important. Uncirculated coins are graded mint state (MS) with a scale from 60 to 70. An MS−69 is an almost perfect coin, while an MS−65 has far less quality and brings a far lower price. A few years ago, a push was made to develop and utilize uniform grading standards. These standards would be so strict that dealers would be willing to trade graded coins sight unseen. Such coins, then, would parallel stock or bond certificates—one just like the other.

The theory seemed good but the practice has left much to be desired. There are a number of grading firms, which apparently do not always assign the same grades to similar coins. Moreover, some of these firms are owned by coin dealers, who hardly can be considered impartial graders. Then, too, scamsters have been quick to seize upon profit opportunities. One scam is to have a common coin, worth maybe $5, graded, simply so that it can be listed on the grader's population report, which indicates the number of such coins graded. Once on the report, the coin becomes "rare" if few others of that type have been counted. All of a sudden the $5 coin is worth $500. Another scam has been outright counterfeiting of so-called "slabs," the supposedly tamperproof containers enclosing graded coins.

Will the industry truly clean up its act? Maybe, but in the meantime this is no place for the amateur.

U.S. Mint Commemorative Coins.
While some well-heeled investors have been attracted to the rare coin market, those of lesser means have tried to cash in on the coin craze by buying commemorative issues of the U.S. Mint. While this issuer's credentials are above reproach, it seems the mint has been the winner in these issues, with investors taking the losses. An article by R.W. Bradford in *Barron's* ("How to Lose a Mint," March 6, 1989) notes that of 61 issues from 1982 through 1987, only 13 have increased in value.

Investors drawn to both gold and coins are attracted by issues such as the American Eagle, which contains an ounce of gold. Unfortunately, the coin form adds about 25% to the cost above the gold content value. Apparently, this form has added little value in the marketplace, since prices on American Eagles have sunk in tandem with gold's falling price.

Collectibles and Hobbies

The profits in collectibles have often matched those in antiques.

The distinction between an antique and a collectible is quite tenuous. Historically, antiques referred to furniture and various other household items such as silver service sets. In recent years, though, practically everything found in the home, shop, or farm was sought after and referred to in general as **collectibles**. Semantics aside, the profits in collectibles have often matched those in antiques.

Almost any item you can imagine—depression jewelry, marbles, beer cans, paisley shawls, original battery-operated toys, 1930 watches, and many, many more—have been auctioned in recent years for very high prices. Baseball cards—rookie cards in particular—were big winners in the late 1980s. A 1952 Mickey Mantle rookie card was worth $6,000. Unfortunately, some of us are old enough to remember flipping many such cards into a trash can after we tired of them.

Rookie baseball cards were big winners in the late 1980s.

If the item is unique and relatively scarce in supply, a demand seems to develop for it eventually. With collectibles, there is hope for small investors. Do not discard items indiscriminately at housecleaning time, particularly in the case of a parent or grandparent's death. Some items may have value, although you should not expect to receive prices you might see in collector manuals. Quality is extremely important in determining price, and you will pay a heavy selling commission. Nevertheless, finding and investing in collectibles is one avenue open to you if you have background and experience with particular items.

You also have a chance of making a profit with your **hobbies:** rare coin collecting (numismatics) and stamp collecting (philately). Exhibit 18.2 showed that U.S. coins were the top-performing asset over the 20-year period, and stamp collections showed similar success.

The markets for rare coins and stamps are fairly efficient, although they also are quite fragmented, consisting of many dealers who trade either directly or through the mail. Quoted prices, markups, and commissions are high and vary among dealers, making comparative shopping important. If collecting is your hobby, and if you have skill at it, consider yourself fortunate that you enjoy doing something that might have value; on the other hand, if you know little or nothing about coins or stamps, but want to invest in them because you heard they are good inflation hedges, you are better advised to invest elsewhere—gold coins or gold certificates, for example. This investing requires little skill, involves far lower commissions, and you can check the value of your investment each day by finding gold's price in the morning newspaper.

Profits along with fun are often found in numismatics and philately.

SUMMARY

Tangibles are physical items that can be bought or sold. They have use advantages in direct enjoyment, or as a display of wealth, or they are items, such as an engagement ring, that are needed for some purpose other than investment. They also have investment advantages as hedges against political and inflation risks, and to achieve more thorough portfolio diversification. Tangibles' disadvantages include high commissions and holding costs, a need for specialized knowledge, extremely volatile prices, no current return, poor resale markets, and rampant fraud.

Gold is the most popular investment tangible. Its price is volatile, depending upon supply and demand factors. Gold can be owned directly in the form of coins, bullion, certificates, jewelry, and works of art; indirect ownership of gold includes gold options and futures contracts and gold mining stocks.

Silver and other precious metals are also popular investments. Diamonds and other precious gems appeal to some investors, as do artworks and antiques. Collecting the latter two items requires considerable experience and knowledge; moreover, transactions and holding costs are exceptionally high. Collectibles and hobbies have become popular in recent years. Many people enjoy these activities, apart from any monetary return. Engaging in them strictly for investment return could be a mistake, because substantial time is involved and market values vary considerably. Investors seeking them for investment advantages should find gold a simpler and equally effective alternative.

KEY TERMS

Select the alternative that best identifies the key term.

1. tangible
2. gold
3. gold coins
4. gold bullion
5. gold ownership certificate
6. claim on gold
7. silver
8. diamonds
9. artworks
10. antiques
11. collectibles
12. hobbies

a. being 100 years old doesn't necessarily make an item one
b. a Canadian Maple Leaf, for example
c. depression glass, for example
d. for investment purposes, these should have a quality grade provided by a gemologist
e. must be assayed if you sell it
f. called the "perfect" tangible
g. before owning one, make sure of the integrity of the issuer
h. often considered a substitute tangible for gold
i. any physical item with a market
j. when buying these, do not look for "undiscovered" geniuses
k. an option or futures contract
l. philately is one

REVIEW QUESTIONS

1. Provide a definition of a tangible and then discuss whether you would prefer investing in a diamond ring or gold bullion stored in a distant city.
2. Explain the use characteristics of tangibles. These are important to many investors. Which characteristic, in your view, is the most important? Discuss.
3. Have tangibles provided returns competitive with those of intangibles? Explain.
4. Is an index measuring a tangible's return likely to be as accurate as one that measures an intangible's return? Discuss.
5. Explain investment characteristics of tangibles other than return. Is there a reasonably strong investment rationale for including tangibles in your portfolio, or are tangibles too risky? Explain.
6. Discuss six potential disadvantages of investing in tangibles.
7. In what sense can gold be considered the "perfect" tangible?

8. Is gold production limited more by scarcity or by costs of extraction? Discuss.
9. Does the demand situation for gold tend to stabilize its price or enhance its volatility? Explain.
10. Indicate and briefly discuss various ways of owning gold. Explain which method you would select if you planned a gold investment.
11. Do you think buying a gold wedding ring is a good way to invest in gold? Explain.
12. Discuss silver as an investment. Explain whether you would prefer owning silver to owning gold.
13. What are bags of silver and how are they used in silver investing?
14. What factors are important to consider before investing in diamonds or other precious gems?
15. Discuss several precautions investors in artwork or antiques should take.
16. Would you advise numismatics or philately for an "average" investor? Explain.

<hr>

PROBLEMS AND PROJECTS

1. The correlation coefficient between gold and silver is +0.8 and the correlation coefficient between gold and stocks is −0.2. If the expected returns from each asset are the same, which two should be held in a portfolio? Explain why.
2. The following table shows return data for three assets:

	Gold	Art	Bonds
Rate of return	12%	15%	10%
Standard deviation of returns	26	47	4
Correlation coefficients: Gold	1.0	0.8	0.4
Art		1.0	−0.6
Bonds			1.0

 a. Which asset is the riskiest, if held by itself?
 b. If only two assets are to be held in a portfolio, which two do you recommend? Explain.
3. (*Student Project*)   Do a search to determine how you might invest in gold in your area. Contact commercial banks, inquiring if they sell gold coins or have gold certificate programs. If this search is not productive, try coin dealers or even pawn shops. Also, look under "gold" in the yellow pages.
4. (*Student Project*)   Determine if there are any coin or stamp collectors in your area. Also, see if there are others, such as baseball card collectors. If you locate one, visit the shop and attempt to discuss the economics of the market. What does he or she recommend if you want to become a serious collector?

CASE ANALYSES

**18.1
Are Tangibles
for the Berrys?**

Raymond and Alicia Berry are a young married couple who have no dependents and live in an apartment in San Francisco. Their combined incomes last year exceeded $100,000 and their investment net worth is approximately $40,000, represented mostly by common stocks and corporate bonds. Ray and

Ali also have excellent retirement plans provided by their employers. The Berrys enjoy visiting art museums but have no formal training in art appreciation. They also do not have hobbies, since their primary leisure activity is scuba diving.

The Berrys are concerned about the effects inflation might have on their investment portfolio. Discussing the problem with associates at work, Ali was told that tangibles are ideal investments to profit from inflation. One co-worker supposedly tripled her investment in rare coins over a two-year period. She said that investing in rare coins was easy since coin dealers frequently advertise in various financial publications.

Questions

a. In your view, should the Berrys consider adding tangibles to their investment portfolio? Explain your position.
b. Do you agree with Ali's friend that tangible investing is easy? Explain your position.
c. Evaluate the following potential investments and explain why you feel each item is or is not appropriate for the Berrys:.(a) an original oil by Paco Piblasso (an unknown artist toiling in Sausalito), (b) one of a limited number of copies of a Miro lithograph advertised on late-night TV, (c) a Van Gogh lithograph offered by an art dealer, (d) a sofa built in 1886, and (e) gold jewelry available from a reputable jeweler.
d. All things considered, which tangible do you recommend for the Berrys?

**18.2
Brad Toliver
Looks at the
Correlations**

Brad Toliver has decided to augment his existing portfolio with tangibles. He has narrowed potential investment alternatives to gold, silver, stamps, and diamonds. Brad has no particular preference for any of them; he is simply concerned with the manner in which they influence his portfolio return and risk. Brad was able to find return data for the tangibles, which he then correlated with historical returns from his portfolio. The correlation coefficients appear below.

Tangible (Return)	Gold	Silver	Stamps	Diamonds	Brad's Portfolio
Gold (10%)	1.0				
Silver (8%)	0.9	1.0			
Stamps (15%)	−0.5	−0.7	1.0		
Diamonds (11%)	0.8	0.5	0.9	1.0	
Brad's Portfolio (14%)	−0.3	−0.2	0.0	0.6	1.0

Questions

a. Brad seems indifferent as to which intangibles he invests in, but should he be? Is it as easy to invest in stamps as it is to invest in gold? Discuss.
b. Which alternative(s) do you recommend for Brad? Explain your choice(s).

Angrist, Stanley. "Precious Metal Lures Are Hooking Plenty of Suckers." *The Wall Street Journal,* April 24, 1989, p. C1.

Bradford, R. W. "How To Lose a Mint." *Barron's,* March 6, 1989, p. 54.

Brown, Christie. "Museum Pieces for Everyday Living." *Forbes,* August 21, 1989, p. 100.

Dorfman, John R. "Art of Investing May Mean Avoiding Art." *The Wall Street Journal,* June 6, 1989, p. C1.

Henriques, Diana. "Don't Take Any Wooden Nickels." *Barron's,* June 19, 1989, p. 16.

Kallen, Barbara. "Platinum's New Luster." *Forbes,* January 26, 1987, p. 85.

Peers, Alexandra. "Art Index of Sotheby's Is Really More Art Than Index, Some Say." *The Wall Street Journal,* March 23, 1989, p. C1.

Ritter, Lawrence S., and Thomas J. Urich. *The Role of Gold in Consumer Investment Portfolios.* New York: Salomon Brothers Center for the Study of Financial Institutions, New York University Graduate School of Business Administration, 1984.

Topolnicki, Denise M. "The Fine Art of Fraud." *Money,* September 1986, pp. 73–82.

HELPFUL
READING

PART SEVEN

The Overall Investment Plan

Investing often appears as disjointed activities: buying stocks, maintaining liquidity, insuring, and so on. The successful investor, though, takes a comprehensive look at his or her situation and attempts to place all the separate parts into a meaningful whole—the portfolio. A portfolio has a certain synergy, meaning that individual investments often complement each other to produce an end result that is more effective than the sum of their separate influences.

Chapter 19 deals with portfolio management. It emphasizes the importance of setting investment goals and selecting specific assets to achieve them. It also stresses the importance of diversification to reduce risk, and it explains how to measure and evaluate portfolio performance. Advantages and disadvantages of market timing are compared to those of a buy-and-hold strategy, with a discussion of how formula plans might be used to accomplish timing goals.

Chapter 20 indicates how the portfolio is extended by considering other, nontraditional investment opportunities. Internationalizing a portfolio is discussed, and methods to achieve an international posture are explained. Whole life insurance is evaluated as part of an investor's portfolio, and its advantages and disadvantages are compared to an approach of investing in term life insurance with premium savings invested in traditional investment vehicles. Finally, the techniques of retirement planning are explained.

CHAPTER NINETEEN

Portfolio Management

CONSTRUCTING THE
PORTFOLIO

Setting Goals

Forecasting the Investment
Environment

Selecting Specific Assets

MONITORING THE PORTFOLIO

Estimating Performance

Measuring Performance

Evaluating Performance

MODIFYING THE PORTFOLIO

Buy-and-Hold

Market Timing

Asset Allocation Models

Mechanical (Formula) Allocation
Plans

Defensive Techniques

BOXES

Asset Allocations of the Median
Household

If You Want Portfolio Insurance, Be
Your Own Underwriter

APPENDIX: MODERN
PORTFOLIO THEORY AND THE
CAPITAL ASSET PRICING
MODEL

The Efficient Frontier

Selecting a Portfolio

The Capital Asset Pricing Model

After you finish this chapter, you
will be able to:

- see the importance of goal setting
  and forecasting in constructing an
  investment portfolio.

- know how to select specific assets
  to meet your portfolio objectives
  and achieve adequate diversification.

- estimate portfolio performance by
  both measuring and evaluating it.

- understand advantages and disadvantages of both buy-and-hold
  and market-timing portfolio strategies.

- understand how mechanical timing plans work, and their advantages and disadvantages.

- identify strategic and tactical asset allocation models.

- understand how various defensive
  techniques are used to protect a
  portfolio's value.

M ost people realize intuitively that holding one, or even several, investments is risky. Of course, many still do it, recognizing the risks but hoping their luck will be favorable. Actually, some of the risks these investors take could be avoided by more thoughtful investment selection. The key is to design an effective portfolio—one that eliminates unnecessary risks while simultaneously meeting your investment objectives. In order to do this, the portfolio must be constructed properly to begin with, monitored closely over time, and modified as circumstances might warrant. This chapter discusses these important tasks.

CONSTRUCTING THE PORTFOLIO

A portfolio is any combination of assets.

A **portfolio** can be defined as any combination of assets held at the same time. All assets you own should be considered as parts of your portfolio. These would include typical investment assets such as stocks, bonds, mutual fund shares, and direct business interests, and personal assets such as your home, automobiles, jewelry, and other important items. As Exhibit 19.1 shows, for purposes of portfolio planning, you also should consider any equity you might have in retirement or profit-sharing plans, even though you may have no control over the manner in which these funds are invested. Constructing a portfolio involves three steps: first, you must set investment goals; second, you must anticipate the

EXHIBIT 19.1
Suggested portfolio composition in three different life stages

A. Couple in Early 30s:
- Family Income = $50,000
- Total Assets = $150,000
- Percentage of Total Assets Invested As Shown

Liquidity (8%)

Future Expenditures (5%)

Retirement:
- Employer plans (5%)
- Self-directed (5%)

Speculate (2%)

Real Estate: personal residence, vacation home, time share (60%)

Personal Assets (75%)

Personal Property: furniture, furnishings, jewelry, paintings, hobbies, collectibles, etc. (15%)

Investment Assets (25%) Include:
- Bank deposits
- Series EE Bonds
- Treasury securities
- Agency debt
- Stocks
- Corporate and municipal bonds
- Mutual fund shares
- Options
- Futures
- Direct business interests
- Investment properties
- Limited partnership interests

B. Couple in Early 50s:
- Family Income = $75,000
- Total Assets = $400,000
- Percentage of Total Assets Invested As Shown

EXHIBIT 19.1
Continued

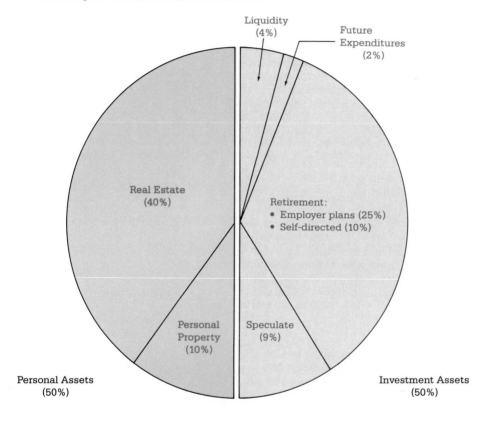

Liquidity (4%)

Future Expenditures (2%)

Real Estate (40%)

Retirement:
- Employer plans (25%)
- Self-directed (10%)

Personal Property (10%)

Speculate (9%)

Personal Assets (50%)

Investment Assets (50%)

investment environment for the upcoming planning period; and third, you must select specific investment vehicles to achieve your stated goals.

Setting Goals

Investment goals direct and shape the investment portfolio. Specific, tangible goals can guide the investor much more effectively than some nebulous criterion, such as "making as much as you can as fast as you can." Your goals might be to accumulate funds for a future important expenditure, to provide income during retirement years, to build an estate for your heirs, or simply to speculate. Whatever your goals are, they must be identified; otherwise it is impossible to know which investments are appropriate for the portfolio. Naturally, investors' goals differ considerably, which means a portfolio appropriate for one may not be appropriate for another. In setting goals, you establish priorities and define acceptable risk levels.

Portfolio management requires specific, tangible goals.

EXHIBIT 19.1
Continued

C. Couple in Retirement (Early 60s)
- Family Income = $50,000
- Total Assets = $600,000
- Percentage of Total Assets Invested As Shown

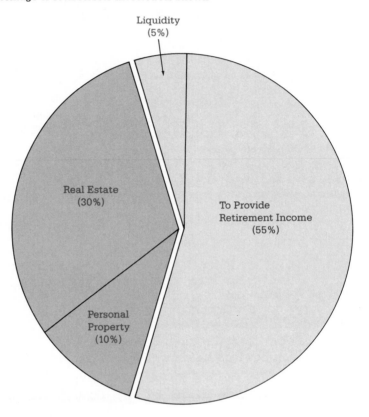

Investment Priorities   You can think of portfolio construction as analogous to moving through a cafeteria dinner line. In front of you are many offerings, each providing some enjoyment (return) at some cost (risk). In assembling your dinner, you balance the expected enjoyment an item provides with its cost; when you are finished, you hope to have the most enjoyable meal your limited funds can provide. The individual items before you reflect your eating priorities: if you enjoy sweets, you might include a piece of pie; if you are on a diet, the pie might be replaced by fresh fruit.

In the investment cafeteria, you follow the same procedure. If you wish to have considerable liquidity, you pick Treasury bills or a money market account; if your priority is inflation protection, you are drawn to real estate or perhaps gold; if you want high current return, you look at Treasury, agency, or corporate bonds; if you want growth over time and don't expect inflation, you move into common stocks; and, if you want maximum capital appreciation quickly, you venture into

Constructing a portfolio is like walking through a cafeteria line.

options, or warrants, or even futures contracts. And, if you, like most investors, have several priorities simultaneously, you hold a portfolio of several asset groups. Your portfolio, like the cafeteria tray, should represent your best effort to achieve your priorities, given your limited investment funds. A listing of investment objectives for Marita Hapner—an unmarried, young, professional person with no dependents—appears in Exhibit 19.2.

Setting Risk Levels   Your goals also establish tolerable risk levels. For example, if you are investing to accumulate a given sum of money at the end of a given period of time, and if it is absolutely essential to have that sum available (for a down payment on a house, for example), then you cannot tolerate any investment that might have some price risk. A zero coupon bond maturing on the needed

Investment goals often establish tolerable risk levels.

Investor Profile:	☐	Age 23; college graduate; business major.
	☐	Marital status: single, no dependents. No change in status is anticipated in the immediate future.
	☐	Annual income: $31,000 currently, expected to increase each year.
	☐	Investment funds: $18,000 (from inheritance and gifts).
	☐	Has adequate funds for liquidity.
	☐	Overall risk tolerance: moderate risk averter, although her lack of dependents permits some aggressive investing.

Goal	Discussion	Priority
1. Future expenditure	Must accumulate $10,000 in 10 years for down payment on house or condo	Highest
2. Self-directed retirement	Marita feels Social Security and employer plans may not be adequate	Moderately High
3. Cautious speculation: growth	Since funds are sufficient to meet goals 1 and 2, Marita is willing to take some risks with remaining funds; she wants to invest in common stocks for growth over time	Medium
4. Moderate speculation: inflation hedge	Marita is concerned over loss of purchasing power of her assets; she is willing to invest in assets that can hedge inflation	Low
5. Aggressive speculation	Marita is willing to commit 15% of her funds to very risky assets, even those that might be total losses	Very Low

EXHIBIT 19.2
Marita Hapner's investment goals

date would be ideal, while a coupon bond with a maturity much beyond that date is inappropriate. As another example, if one of your priorities is maximum capital appreciation, then the risk level you must accept is perhaps the total loss of funds allocated in this direction. If you feel such risk is too much to bear, then your goal is not really a priority, but a wish. But, wishes are of no help in effective investing. So, be realistic in establishing priorities and recognizing their related risks. Then, move to the next step.

Forecasting the Investment Environment

We can't avoid forecasting, even if we believe no one can do so accurately. To not forecast is actually forecasting by default. The choice, then, is to do it this way or to frame specific forecasts about the upcoming investment environment.

Forecasting by Default   Suppose you say that you have no idea what the investment environment will be next year: interest rates might go up or down; business activity might boom or bust; and the stock market might hit new highs or go into a tailspin. In short, anything is possible. However, would you say that every conceivable event has an equal chance of happening? Do you think inflation at a 100% rate is just as likely as it is at a 4% rate? When pressed this way, most people say that isn't what they mean by not being able to forecast. Rather, they view it as saying essentially that the immediate future will probably look very much like the immediate past, and our more distant future will reflect our long-run historical trends. For example, if inflation's rate over the past six months has been 6%, you might guess that is what it will be for the upcoming month, unless you had reasons to feel differently. And if you had to guess inflation's rate over the next ten years, you might use the very long historical U.S. rate of about 3.2%.

Forecasting by simple trend projection is a reasonable method.

Actually, there is nothing wrong in forecasting this way; in fact, it may make more sense than using unfounded specific projections. Perhaps the best advice is to realize that you are forecasting even when you might think you are not.

Specific Forecasts   With specific forecasts, you make projections for economic variables influencing your investments' returns. You say, for example, that the inflation rate next year will be 6.3%. It is not necessary that you personally develop these forecasts. You probably will choose instead to use those provided by professional forecasters. The key is to have forecasts and then to link them to expected returns from the investments you are considering. Suppose the 6.3% projected inflation rate is 2.3 percentage points higher than the current inflation rate, which is a fairly sharp increase. Given that projection, you should also project an eventual increase in interest rates, which implies a forecast of falling bond prices. Clearly, you should avoid buying long-term bonds at the present and perhaps consider selling any you currently hold.

In similar fashion, you make projections for the business cycle, the overall stock market, specific industries and firms, and the international situation.

However, keep in mind our discussions in previous chapters about the accuracy of professional forecasters, which has been poor. Simple trend projections, such as those discussed in projecting by default, might be just as accurate. Recognizing this inaccuracy is not the same as saying, "Why bother?" Our concern is with portfolio planning and not with getting rich on sharp forecasts. There is a distinction between planning and forecasting: forecasting has to do specifically with predicting future events while planning is concerned with preparing for them. A portfolio is a plan.

Forecasting predicts future events; planning prepares for them.

Selecting Specific Assets

The plan takes shape as specific assets are selected and as the proportion of the portfolio invested in them is decided. A hypothetical portfolio for Marita Hapner, who was introduced above, is illustrated in Exhibit 19.3. It serves as an aid in discussing the following topics that are important in actual asset selection.

Conformity to Goals It is important that assets selected conform to the investor's goals. If you are looking for a high current return, you must select income stocks or bonds, and not growth stocks. Marita has selected five assets that she hopes will achieve her goals. Since she must have $10,000 at the end of ten years, she is investing $6,000 in U.S. Series EE bonds. At the time she invested, they guaranteed an annual rate of 7.5% if held five years or longer (5.5% if held one year), which means they will be worth about $12,400 at the end of ten years. The extra $2,400 is necessary to pay income taxes when they are redeemed (she will choose to defer paying taxes each year).

The CATs are purchased to satisfy Marita's retirement fund objective. She purchased them using the IRA tax shelter. To participate in future economic growth, Marita wanted about a third of her portfolio in common stocks. To accomplish this, she purchased Adams Express and Lotus Development. Adams Express is a closed-end mutual fund that invests in blue chip common stocks. It has a beta of about 0.8 and has demonstrated an average annual growth rate of

	(1)	(2)	(3)		(4)
			Market Value		
	Assets	Units Held	Per Unit	Total	Percent
1.	U.S. Series EE bonds	—	$—	$ 6,000	34
2.	CATs maturing in 2011	12 bonds	162.50	1,950	11
3.	Adams Express	200 shares	19.50	3,900	22
4.	Lotus Development	100 shares	24.00	2,400	14
5.	Canadian Maple Leafs	10 coins	342.00	3,420	19
	Totals			$17,670	100

EXHIBIT 19.3
Marita Hapner's portfolio at January 1, 19X1

13% over the previous ten years. Lotus Development was an extremely successful developer of computer software programs with a very bright future. However, its beta of 1.8 indicates a high degree of risk. She realizes this is a speculative investment, but she is very much impressed with the company. The stock had traded as high as $39 a share in the past year and was selling at $24 when Marita purchased. Finally, to hedge inflation, Marita purchased ten Canadian Maple Leaf gold coins at a total investment of $3,420.

Adequate Diversification to Eliminate Random Risk   You should hold a sufficient number of securities to eliminate random risk. This usually means at least 15 different common stocks, selected somewhat randomly, and between 5 and 15 different bonds, depending upon quality rating. If your funds are not sufficient to acquire this many securities, you should consider mutual funds. Marita's choice of Adams Express makes sense, but investing as much as $2,400 in only one stock (Lotus) is very risky because of poor diversification. She might have been better off investing in a mutual fund seeking maximum capital appreciation.

To reduce risk, diversify among asset groups and among assets within a group.

Diversification Among Asset Groups   At various points in the previous chapters, but particularly in Chapters 4 and 18, we discussed the importance of examining asset correlations. We discovered that broad asset groups—stocks, bonds, and tangibles—have poorly correlated returns over time. This is fortunate in designing a portfolio, because it means that diversification across asset lines will reduce the portfolio's risk. In this regard, Marita's portfolio is fairly well diversified. The Series EE bonds are indexed to rates on other Treasury issues, giving her some protection against rising interest rates. Meanwhile, if interest rates fall, her CATs will increase substantially in market value. If inflation heats up, Marita's gold holdings should do well, although her stocks will probably do poorly; in contrast, if inflation remains moderate and the business cycle continues in the expansion phase, her stocks should do well, while gold may not.

MONITORING THE PORTFOLIO

Once the portfolio is constructed, the next activity is to monitor it. Monitoring involves three separate steps: estimating performance, measuring performance, and evaluating performance. Each of these is now discussed.

Estimating Performance

Many investors have false notions about investment returns.

At the beginning of each planning period, you should estimate the total return—current return and price appreciation—that you expect from each asset in the portfolio. These expectations should follow logically from your projections of the investment environment. Many investors have poorly conceived ideas of investment returns: some think you should get around 50% a year, while others

Asset Allocations of the Median Household

How does a typical household allocate its assets? This is a reasonably interesting question, so you might think there are reams of government data to answer it. Not true, at least not on an ongoing basis. However, an ambitious study that surveyed almost 87,000 households was undertaken by the Census Bureau and completed in 1984. The results shed light on asset priorities for many Americans, as the accompanying table indicates. While the dollar amounts have probably changed since the study was completed, the percentages are relevant since there is no evidence they have changed very much. Notice also the data are presented in terms of sources of net worth, which adjusts for debt—a particularly important adjustment in the case of real estate and vehicles.

As you probably expected, the largest source of net worth is the personal residence. Over 64% of all households own a home and it accounts for almost 40% of their net worth. Real estate is also an important investment asset, accounting for 13% of net worth, although only about 10% of all households invest in it. While many Americans make deposits at financial institutions, they are not avid stock or mutual fund investors:

only 20% invest and the two account for only 6.5% of net worth.

While the median amounts give us a picture of the so-called typical household, they reveal nothing about the upper or lower parts of the wealth distribution. If we profiled the

wealthy households, we would find the traditional financial investments—stocks, bonds, mutual fund shares—play a far greater role. Maybe owning them is how many of the wealthy households got that way.

SOURCES OF NET WORTH

Asset Type	Percent of Households That Own Asset Type	Source of Net Worth	
		$ Amount	%
Personal-Use Assets:			
Own home	64.3%	$13,036	39.9%
Vehicles	85.8	1,894	5.8
Total		$14,930	45.7%
Investment Assets:			
Interest-earning assets:			
At financial institutions	71.8	$ 4,541	13.9%
U.S. savings bonds	15.0	163	0.5
Other	8.5	979	3.0
Total		$ 5,683	17.4%
Real estate and business:			
Rental property	9.8	$ 2,841	8.7%
Other real estate	10.0	1,388	4.3
Business or profession	12.9	3,251	10.0
Total		$ 7,480	23.0%
Other			
Stocks and mutual funds	20.0	$ 2,141	6.5%
Other financial	6.9	1,547	4.7
IRA and Keogh accounts	19.5	694	2.1
Checking accounts	53.9	196	0.6
Total		$ 4,578	13.9%
Total investment assets		$17,741	54.3%
Grand totals		$32,671	100.0%

SOURCE: U.S. Department of Commerce, Bureau of the Census, *Household Wealth and Asset Ownership: 1984*, Current Population Reports, Household Economic Studies, Series No. 7, page 70.

believe 5% is good. Making estimates forces us to look realistically at performance, if we take the task seriously.

Marita Hapner's estimates for the upcoming year are shown in Exhibit 19.4. Marita felt inflation in 19X1 would be about the same as in the previous year, or down slightly. Thus, she thought interest rates might decline a bit. This projection affects the value of her CATs. Their yield to maturity at purchase was 7.54%. At the beginning of 19X2, there would be 24 years to maturity, and Marita sees a yield to maturity then of 7.0%; this means they should be worth $197.15 each. She would enjoy a 21.3% return on her investment, $416 in total.

Marita thought the economy would show moderate growth, and she felt the stock market would reflect this growth by not showing rapid increases or sharp declines. Adams Express, then, was thought to provide a 15% return, which is slightly better than its 10-year average. The stock pays dividends out of both current income and price appreciation, but Marita chose to reinvest all dividends to acquire additional shares. She expects her holding to be worth $4,485 at the end of the year. Marita was enthusiastic about Lotus, believing a 25% appreciation in price over the year was likely.

She was less enthusiastic about gold. A moderation of inflation and interest rates could lead to lower gold prices. Allowing for this possibility and to be consistent with her estimates for the CATs and Adams Express, she foresees only a 3% appreciation in gold's price. With all estimates made, Marita's portfolio is expected to increase 11.5% in value over the year. This is $2,034 of appreciation, which means its market value at 1/1/19X2 will be $19,704.

Measuring Performance

At the end of the planning period—a year in this case—it is necessary to gather data and measure performance. Data gathering consists mostly of finding year-end prices in the newspaper. In the case of mutual funds, you should have a report that shows either the value of your holdings or the number of shares that you hold. In the latter case (which applies to closed-end funds like Adams Express) you must find the market price in the newspaper or through your broker.

EXHIBIT 19.4
Marita Hapner's performance estimates for the year 19X1

(1)	(2) Expected Appreciation		(3)
Asset	$	%	Expected Market Value 1/1/19X2
1. U.S. Series EE bonds	$ 330	5.5%	$ 6,330
2. CATs maturing in 25 years	416	21.3	2,366
3. Adams Express	585	15.0	4,485
4. Lotus Development	600	25.0	3,000
5. Canadian Maple Leafs	103	3.0	3,523
Totals	$2,034	11.5%	$19,704

Performance measurement begins by calculating a **portfolio rate of return** (R_P). If new investments are not made during the year—either by depositing additional cash or by reinvesting earned dividends or interest—and if there are no withdrawals, the rate can be calculated as shown below:

$$R_P = \frac{(P_1 - P_0)}{P_0}$$

where P_1 = total portfolio value at the end of the period, and

P_0 = total portfolio value at the beginning of the period.

If activity takes place in the portfolio during the period, involving withdrawals (W) or new investments (I), the portfolio rate of return can be approximated with the following formula:

$$R_P = \frac{W + (P_1 - P_0)}{P_0 + I\,(n_1/12) - W(n_2/12)}$$

where I = new investments,

W = withdrawals,

n_1 = number of months I is in the portfolio, and

n_2 = number of months W is out of the portfolio.

Determining a portfolio's return is more complicated when deposits and withdrawals take place during the period.

Exhibit 19.5 illustrates this calculation for a hypothetical portfolio.

With this calculation, any dividends and interest reinvested in the portfolio are not considered as return items when received, but are considered as additional investments. So, the $100 dividend reinvested on 10/1/19X1 increases

EXHIBIT 19.5
Calculating a portfolio rate of return (R_P) with portfolio activity during the year

Item	Symbol	Amount
1. Portfolio value at 1/1/19X1	P_0	$10,000
2. Additional investment at 3/31/19X1	I	1,000
3. Sale of $2,000 of securities on 7/15/19X1	—	—
4. Withdrawal of funds at 7/31/19X1	W	2,000
5. Dividends received on 9/30/19X1	—	—
6. Reinvestment of dividends on 10/1/19X1	I	100
7. Portfolio value at 1/1/19X2	P_1	12,000

$$R_P = \frac{W + (P_1 - P_0)}{P_0 + I(n_1/12) - W(n_2/12)}$$

$$R_P = \frac{2,000 + (12,000 - 10,000)}{10,000 + 1,000(9/12) + 100(3/12) - 2,000(5/12)}$$

$$R_P = \frac{4,000}{10,000 + 750 + 25 - 833}$$

$$R_P = \frac{4,000}{9,942} = 0.4023, \text{ or } 40.23\%$$

the investment base (denominator) by $25, after adjusting for the fractional part of the year the funds are in the portfolio. Keep in mind that dividends and interest reinvested will increase the ending portfolio value (P_1) and will be included in return in this way. Any withdrawals taking place during the year can come from dividends and interest or sale of securities. In either case, the ending portfolio value will be lower by amounts withdrawn. Thus, withdrawals are included (in the numerator) as part of return. Also, the investment base is then reduced to allow for the part of the year funds are not in the portfolio.

Exhibit 19.6 shows what happened in Marita Hapner's case. The Series EE bonds' return was guaranteed. The CATs declined in value, rather than increasing as expected. Apparently, interest rates rose. While the loss was moderate in an absolute sense, it was considerably below her expectation (see Exhibit 19.4 to compare). Adams Express also performed below expectation, with a realized appreciation of only 12%, and the price of Lotus fell sharply, leading to a $500 loss. Fortunately, gold's price appreciated more than expected, leading to a gain of $180. In total, Marita's portfolio appreciated only $420, or 2.4%. Thus are the risks of investing; obviously, an evaluation is in order.

Evaluating Performance

Performance can be evaluated in two different ways. First, you can evaluate it in an absolute sense, which consists of comparing actual results to the estimates. Second, you can judge performance in a relative sense, which compares actual results to results you might have achieved had you invested differently.

Evaluating Performance in an Absolute Sense   If you took the time to make estimates at the beginning of the year, evaluating performance at year's end would consist primarily of asking "What went wrong—or right?" Marita misguessed the investment environment somewhat, but such errors are to be expected. Moreover, her asset diversification partially buffered the losses she might have taken had she invested most of her funds in only stocks or bonds. Although she is measuring performance annually and planning one year at a time,

> A simple evaluation of portfolio performance is determining whether the portfolio met expectations.

EXHIBIT 19.6
Marita Hapner's actual portfolio performance in 19X1

(1)	(2)	(3)	
	Realized Appreciation		Market Value at
Asset	$	%	1/1/19X2
1. U.S. Series EE bonds	$ 330	5.5%	$6,330
2. CATs maturing in 25 years	− 58	− 3.0	1,892
3. Adams Express	468	12.0	4,368
4. Lotus Development	− 500	− 20.8	1,900
5. Canadian Maple Leafs	180	5.3	3,600
Totals	$ 420	2.4%	$18,090

her investment horizons are actually much longer. Therefore, if 19X1 was not a particularly good year, she is not alarmed by the outcome, because there are many more years to follow.

Clearly, her biggest concern was investing 14% of her portfolio in one stock—Lotus. Originally convinced it could go no lower in price, Marita learned differently. While saying the investment was a mistake might be premature —after all, she was willing to speculate with a portion of her funds—her loss does indicate that she must consider carefully whether or not the stock should be held in the future.

Evaluating Performance in a Relative Sense   Evaluating performance in a relative sense requires a yardstick against which comparisons can be made. One yardstick could be the rate of return you might have earned investing on a completely risk-free basis. If you don't do this well over time, you should ask why you are taking any risks at all. Instead, why not invest everything in a risk-free asset, such as U.S. Treasury bills? Marita's 2.4% return was considerably below the risk-free rate of around 6.0% for the year.

Return yardsticks are needed to evaluate performance.

Another yardstick might be the return on a mutual fund that has characteristics similar to your portfolio. For example, Marita might review how well balanced funds (holding debt and equity instruments) performed during the year. If their returns were well above hers, she might consider investing exclusively with them, rather than relying upon her own skills. It should be repeated, though, that making a decision based on only one year's performance is premature.

A third approach could be to use the beta concept. This involves first determining a portfolio's beta weight and then deriving an expected return based on both the risk-free rate (R_F) and the rate of return on the market (R_M) over the investment period in question. For example, suppose Marita's portfolio had a beta of 0.5, while $R_F = 6\%$ and $R_M = 10\%$. Then, her portfolio return (R_P) should have been:

$$R_P = 6\% + 0.5(10\% - 6\%) = 6\% + 0.5(4\%) = 6\% + 2\% = 8\%$$

This return is far better than Marita's 2.4%. This method has the advantage of combining the risk-free rate and a rational allowance for risk in one return measurement. It has a very big disadvantage in that you must determine your portfolio's beta weight. If you have a computer and appropriate software, this is neither a complicated nor time-consuming task. Without these aids, though, it is unlikely you will make the effort.

Determining your portfolio's beta could be difficult.

Some finance academicians might urge you not to bother, particularly if you hold a portfolio diversified among many asset groups. They feel the market approach is too narrow in the sense that you derive a risk premium (2% in the above example) based solely on stock performance. Therefore, any comparison would be meaningless. To them, a better index would be one consisting of many assets, not stocks alone. Since this topic is still being debated, we will not pursue it.

MODIFYING THE PORTFOLIO

After the period's results are evaluated, the next step is to decide if the portfolio should be modified. Clearly, if your investment objectives change, so must the portfolio. If Marita decides that speculation is not appropriate for her, she will probably sell her Lotus shares and invest the funds elsewhere. We normally expect that most investors' goals will change over time. As retirement grows closer, for example, many investors give more priority to preservation of capital and less to its growth. Moving into a higher income tax bracket might also call for portfolio changes: municipal bonds will have greater appeal relative to taxable issues.

Apart from changing the portfolio in response to changing goals, investors also might wish to make changes for other reasons. They may hope to profit from their perceptions of a changing investment environment; or they may want to keep asset weights constant, assuming these have changed because of appreciation or depreciation during the previous period. The following discussion focuses on buy-and-hold as a strategy versus purposive portfolio changes.

Buy-and-Hold

Buy-and-hold is a simple approach. After you decide upon specific investments for the portfolio, you buy and hold them. You continue holding them (assuming no changes in your investment goals) despite changes in the investment environment. This approach has advantages and disadvantages.

Advantages   Surely the biggest advantage with a buy-and-hold approach is its simplicity. After the portfolio is constructed, it can be forgotten. Perhaps an equally big advantage is that you don't change investments needlessly or capriciously—a practice very common among first-time investors. As a result, commissions are much lower and investment results are usually better. Our discussion of market timing in Chapter 10 indicated that even so-called "professionals" cannot consistently forecast market changes, much less show profits from trading on such forecasts. Finally, by not trading frequently you avoid showing any taxable gains and thus avoid paying taxes on the gains.

With a buy-and-hold approach, you don't change investments needlessly or capriciously.

Disadvantages   While simple to follow, buy-and-hold does not address certain problems. First, and perhaps easiest to deal with, is the problem of reinvesting investment earnings, such as dividends and interest. You might choose to withdraw earnings, thereby eliminating the problem; or, you might reinvest them in the securities that paid them, if that can be done easily and inexpensively. (Mutual funds are ideal in this respect and so are individual companies with reinvestment plans.) You must make some decision, which means buy-and-hold is not completely free of portfolio management.

A more serious situation arises when asset weights are changed because of relative performance. Exhibit 19.7 illustrates the problem. The investor in this

EXHIBIT 19.7
Nate Bien's portfolio:
Constant ratio
investment objective

	(1)	(2)		(3)		(4)	(5)	
		At 1/1/19X1		At 1/1/19X2			Restored Desired Weights 1/1/19X2	
Asset		$	%	$	%	Adjustments	$	%
Common stocks		10,000	33.3	8,500	25.3	+ 2,667	11,167	33.3
Bonds		10,000	33.3	10,000	29.9	+ 1,166	11,166	33.3
Gold		10,000	33.3	15,000	44.8	− 3,833	11,167	33.3
Totals		30,000	100.0	33,500	100.0	− 0 −	33,500	100.0

case decided initially to invest an equal amount of funds in common stocks, bonds, and gold. However, during the year his stocks have declined somewhat in value, the bonds have remained the same, and gold has appreciated considerably. At year end, the asset weights are now quite different—about 45% gold, 25% stocks, and 30% bonds. What should the investor do? Under a strict buy-and-hold approach, the answer is to do nothing. However, the question can be raised whether buy-and-hold should apply to specific assets or to specific asset weights. In the latter case, the investor must take end-of-year action. Specifically, he would sell $3,833 of gold and invest $2,667 in common stocks and $1,166 in bonds, thereby restoring the equal proportional weights.

Another serious problem with buy-and-hold is that you do not take advantage of possible tax savings by selling assets with tax losses. Suppose, for example, that you hold AAA-rated bonds issued by GMAC, but because interest rates have risen sharply, the value of the bonds is down $2,000. If you are in a 33% tax bracket, you could sell the bonds and save $660 in taxes. Assuming any AAA-rated bonds are as good as the GMAC bonds, it would be foolish not to substitute for them and enjoy the tax savings. True, if the new bonds subsequently appreciate in value, you would have to pay a tax on any gain, assuming they are sold. But this might not happen for many years, and meanwhile you have had the use of current tax savings (less commissions to sell and buy the substitute). Even a hard-core buy-and-hold enthusiast would probably agree that tax swaps, such as the above, should be undertaken.

> A big disadvantage of buy-and-hold is not making tax swaps.

Market Timing

An alternative to buy-and-hold is to deliberately change the portfolio to accomplish some end. We saw above that deliberate changes are called for in the case of tax swaps, or to maintain asset weights. Another purposive change is in anticipation of a changing investment environment. If you feel strongly that stock prices will be rising, for example, or that interest rates will be falling, then it follows that you should adjust your portfolio to achieve the highest potential gain from your projections.

> Market timing presumes we can forecast changes in the investment environment.

While purposive portfolio changes can consist of substituting one individual security with another—sell GM and buy Ford, for instance—we are more concerned here with broad changes, such as selling stocks and moving into Treasury bills, or vice versa. Changes of this sort are referred to as **market timing.** Timing models can be simple, as in the above case, or complex, if they involve other asset groups such as bonds, gold, and even foreign securities or currencies. As with the buy-and-hold strategy, timing strategies involve advantages and disadvantages.

Potential Advantages and Disadvantages of Timing   Of course, timing's biggest potential advantage is a superior investment return. However, the key word is potential; clearly, a superior return is not guaranteed. Another advantage timers frequently cite is that you avoid the calamitous market decline. This sounds encouraging, but "riding the big loss" might not be as bad as taking many small losses that are possible with a timing approach. If you are in and out of the market frequently, your losses can easily grow to a figure as large as the one you would have had by simply holding.

For timing to improve returns, it must first overcome higher commission costs.

Perhaps the biggest disadvantages with timing are greater commissions and paying possible advisory fees. Moreover, a timing approach may keep you out of the market when it rebounds and starts to rise. Exhibit 19.8 illustrates this point. The investor in this case is taken through four investment periods. The choices are to buy and hold Treasury bills, buy and hold common stocks, or go back and forth between bills and stocks in an attempt to invest in the security offering the higher return. Column 4 shows return if the investor could guess correctly each period. As you see, the 26% average return is far better than the average return for holding either bills (9%) or stocks (15%). However, as Column 5 indicates, the average return is considerably worse (−2%) if incorrect guesses are made each period. Of course, actual return depends upon the investor's forecasting ability.

Empirical Analysis of Timing Methods   Numerous studies have been made to determine the effectiveness of timing techniques and the results of market

EXHIBIT 19.8
Illustration of risk with market timing

(1) Period	(2) Return on U.S. Treasury Bills	(3) Return on Common Stocks	(4) Return If You Guess Correctly Each Period	(5) Return If You Guess Incorrectly Each Period
1	+10%	+40%	+ 40%	+10%
2	+ 8	−20	+ 8	−20
3	+12	+50	+ 50	+12
4	+ 6	−10	+ 6	−10
Totals	+36%	+60%	+104%	− 8%
Average Return	+ 9%	+15%	+ 26%	− 2%

timers, when these are available. The results are mixed. Some timers apparently beat buy-and-hold strategies, but many do not. Exhibit 19.9 shows the results of a study that attempted to determine if persistent seasonal patterns could be identified and used to make timing decisions effectively. The investment choices in this case were: (1) buy and hold a portfolio of common stocks; (2) time purchases and sales of common stocks using seasonal indicators, holding Treasury bills when stocks are sold; (3) buy and sell stocks using a random method for making decisions, holding Treasury bills when stocks are sold; and (4) hold Treasury bills. The results are quite interesting: after allowing for transactions costs, the timing strategy shows a poorer return than buy-and-hold, but it also has somewhat less risk. There is no evidence giving a clear edge to either approach, so, you must decide between the two, trading off risk and return. Interestingly, the seasonal predictors did much better than the random method, both in increasing return and reducing risk. Perhaps this offers some hope to those who are looking for timing techniques.

Evidence of timing effectiveness is mixed: versus buy-and-hold, risk is sometimes lower, but so is return.

Asset Allocation Models

Market timing, as often practiced, essentially involves a decision to be either in or out of the market. In contrast, asset allocation models are designed to achieve investor goals by holding different kinds of assets at all times. The key decision with these models is the proportional weight each asset group should hold, and the following are popular approaches.

Strategic Asset Allocation Models A **strategic asset allocation (SAA) model** is a very broad plan that establishes a model portfolio designed to achieve

	(1) Buy and Hold Selected Securities[a]	(2) Timing with Seasonal Indicators	(3) Random Timing	(4) Buy and Hold Treasury Bills
Ten-year return[b]	206%	152%	43%	93%
Average monthly return	0.94%	0.77%	0.30%	0.55%
Average annual return	11.85%	9.69%	3.60%	6.79%
Standard deviation of monthly returns	5.18%	3.49%	3.54%	0.03%
Beta	0.941	0.554	0.518	—

EXHIBIT 19.9
Portfolio return and risk: Timing versus buy-and-hold (transaction costs included)

[a]Portfolio consisted of eighteen securities, selected on the basis of having demonstrated significant seasonal patterns in the period 1926–1971.
[b]Period was 1972–81.
SOURCE: Pettengill, Glenn N., "Persistent Seasonal Return Patterns," *The Financial Review*, November 1985, pp. 271–86.

an investor's long-run goals for return and risk. The major premise of such a plan is that, over the long run, a maximal target real return can be achieved, given the investor's risk tolerance, although this exact return may not be earned each year. A model portfolio is constructed, which calls for certain asset weights expressed as allowable ranges. For example, a portfolio equally weighted in gold, bonds, and common stocks might be appropriate, given an investor's return and risk objectives. However, these weights are only guidelines; and, as market conditions change, they may be modified to take advantage of certain opportunities. Expectations of a robust stock or gold market, for example, might lead the investor to tilt the portfolio weights in favor of these assets without seriously jeopardizing the long-run risk and return goals. Strategic asset allocation plans should not change frequently, however, unless the investor's risk tolerance changes.

Tactical Asset Allocation Models   A **tactical asset allocation (TAA) model** accompanies an SAA model. Essentially, it determines how the short-run asset tilts should be made. The key to tactical asset allocation is making sure funds are not over-invested in risky assets, which would threaten the plan. Tactical asset allocation clearly provides for considerable portfolio management as asset weights are tilted and retilted. However, the investor always maintains a position in each asset as determined by the strategic asset allocation plan. Considering the previous example, the guideline might be equal weights for stocks, bonds, and gold, but in no event should an asset's weight be less than 20%.

Most TAA models contrive asset-shifting schemes based upon a comparison of an asset's current performance to its historical long-run trend. Assets with current returns above their trends are invested in more heavily while those in the reverse situation are sold. Many of the models are computer-driven, with buy and sell signals determined by the computer. This supposedly is an advantage since it eliminates human emotion with its "follow-the-crowd" propensity. Mechanical allocation plans are discussed in the following section.

Mechanical (Formula) Allocation Plans

Realizing the difficulty of accurately forecasting future prices, some advisors recommend following mechanical investment plans, also called formula plans. The underlying premise of these approaches is that you should be a **market contrarian,** which usually means investing in assets that are out of favor. For example, if everybody is buying stocks, you should be selling, and vice versa. But, rather than allowing your judgment to decide when an asset is in or out of favor, it is better to establish a trading rule in advance, and then allow it to make decisions. Some popular formula plans are explained below.

Constant Ratio Plan   In a **constant ratio plan,** asset weights are determined in advance and a "trigger" is set up that calls for action to restore such weights if they are unbalanced by relative price appreciation or depreciation. Actually, the illustration in Exhibit 19.7 can serve as an example of a constant ratio plan. In this case, the investor wants one-third of his portfolio invested in common stocks, bonds, and gold. Suppose he sets the trigger at 45% for any of the assets; in other words, as gold's weight hits 45%, some gold is sold automatically and appropriate amounts are invested in the other two assets to restore the target weights. As you see, when you sell gold, you are selling the asset in favor; and when you buy common stocks and bonds, you are buying the assets out of favor. In the new TAA models, an out-of-favor asset is one whose price has fallen, thereby increasing its potential current return relative to its historical average.

A constant ratio plan restores a portfolio to its original asset weights.

Variable Ratio Plan A **variable ratio plan** allows the asset weights to vary, once action is triggered. In effect, you are increasing your "contrariness." For example, instead of restoring equal weights in the previous example, this plan might call for the most out-of-favor asset's weight to increase to, say, 40%; the next out-of-favor to increase to 35%; and the in-favor asset's weight to decline to 25%. Exhibit 19.10 shows the adjustments for the example illustrated in Exhibit 19.7.

A variable ratio plan replaces original asset weights with new ones, with heavier weights to out-of-favor assets.

Do mechanical allocation plans such as these two offer better risk-adjusted returns than those of professional managers using judgmental approaches? A number were effective in avoiding the October 1987 crash, which heightened their appeal. How well they will perform over longer periods of time remains to be seen.

Dollar Cost Averaging **Dollar cost averaging** is a mechanical method of investing initially in securities, rather than one that alters a portfolio's composition. Exhibit 19.11 shows how it works. As you see, the idea is quite simple. You establish an investment plan calling for equal dollar investments at regular intervals. By following the plan, you then buy securities at a wide range of prices, and over time you will have an average cost somewhere between the highs and lows. The mechanical nature of the plan keeps investors from using their own judgment to determine buying points, or from buying a given number of shares (rather than investing a given number of dollars) at regular intervals. Obviously, a supporter of this plan feels investors' judgments are usually wrong.

Dollar cost averaging has to do with how investments are made initially.

(1)	(2) At 1/1/19X2		(3)	(4)	(5)
Asset	$	%	Desired %	Adjustments	Restored Portfolio
Common stocks	8,500	25.3	40.0	+4,900	13,400
Bonds	10,000	29.9	35.0	+1,725	11,725
Gold	15,000	44.8	25.0	−6,625	8,375
Totals	33,500	100.0	100.0	−0−	33,500

EXHIBIT 19.10
Nate Bien's portfolio: Variable ratio investment objective

EXHIBIT 19.11

Illustration of dollar cost averaging, assuming $1,000 invested each month

(1) Date	(2) Shares Purchased	(3) Price per Share	(4) Total Shares Held	(5) Total Cost	(6) Average Cost (5)/(4)	(7) Cumulative Profit (Loss) [(3) × (4) − (5)]
1/1	100.00	$10	100.00	$1,000	$10.00	$ −0−
2/1	83.33	12	183.33	2,000	10.91	200
3/1	125.00	8	308.33	3,000	9.73	(533)
4/1	100.00	10	408.33	4,000	9.80	83*
5/1	166.67	6	575.00	5,000	8.70	(1,550)

*Investment hucksters often describe dollar cost averaging as a "can't miss" investment approach, and prove it with an example such as the one above. Notice that when price fell by $2 a share under the starting price (from $10 to $8), you automatically purchased proportionally more shares (25) than the number you cut back (16.67) when price increased by $2 (from $10 to $12). So, over time, the approach should guarantee a profit, such as the $83 above, even if price doesn't increase!

This argument is based on dollar—rather than percentage—changes. The decline from 10 to 8 is a larger percentage change than an increase from 10 to 12, which explains why more shares are purchased. In other words, the advantage is nothing more than a play on arithmetic. The method is a sensible way to invest in securities, since it eliminates emotional buying, or buying because we think we can forecast future prices accurately. But it is certainly no more than that.

Dollar cost averaging is a convenient and sensible way to invest. Many investors follow it by reinvesting earnings of their mutual funds and common stocks that allow dividend reinvestment. They also establish investment routines that are regular, rather than being dependent upon whether prices are high or low. However, it is a mistake to think dollar cost averaging can guarantee investment profits, as some promoters tout. Obviously, it cannot. If a security's price is in a long down trend, your average cost will always be higher than its current market price. Once the trend is reversed, the current price might jump above the average, but this result is not guaranteed. Be careful of salespersons who supposedly have a "sure thing" for beating the market. Very often their advice is nothing more than dollar cost averaging, in one form or another.

Dollar cost averaging does not guarantee investment profits.

Defensive Techniques

A defensive technique is designed to limit potential losses. As such, it reduces risk but also limits profits. The limitation on profit might arise because of less exposure to high-profit−high-risk assets, or because of costs related to specific strategies. A number of techniques are widely used as defensive strategies; among the more popular methods are portfolio insurance, buying puts or selling deep-in-the-money calls, competitive hedging, and using stop orders.

Portfolio Insurance   **Portfolio insurance,** currently the most popular approach by far, is an asset allocation technique that attempts to preserve a minimum gain or tolerate only a predetermined loss. Its starting point is the statement of a maximum loss an investor is willing to endure; for example, 10% of the portfolio value. The trick, then, is balancing investments in both a risky asset and a

Portfolio insurance establishes a maximum loss and then adjusts the weight of the risky asset to assure that losses never exceed the maximum.

If You Want Portfolio Insurance, Be Your Own Underwriter

We hear a lot these days about portfolio insurance. Many investors have portfolios bloated with profits from the seven-year bull market, and they aren't eager to see them vanish if and when prices head south. But is the Pru or the Met going to write a policy to lock in your profits? Not really; if it's insurance you want, you must do your own underwriting.

Actually, a number of strategies can buffer downside risk. These include buying put options or selling call options against stocks you own. Unfortunately, puts are expensive and writing calls does away with any future price increases. Another approach is to sell futures contracts on stock indexes; but, this too cuts off price appreciation and may not work well if changes in the stock index don't correlate closely with value changes in your portfolio.

If options, futures, and other esoteric securities scare you, take heart: there is a far simpler approach—a stop-loss strategy. Using stop-loss orders to protect profits is an old tune, but it is being played with new music. Today's theme is to parlay your money between a no-load mutual fund that invests in stocks and a money market fund. Since quite a few transfers might be called for, the no-load feature is practically a must, or commissions could take all the gains.

Many different approaches are used, one of them offered by Fischer Black of the famed Black-Scholes option pricing model and now a partner with Goldman, Sachs & Co. In an interview with *The Wall Street Journal* (Barbara Donnelly, ''Portfolio Insurance Strategies Can Limit Investor Losses, but Price May Be High,'' January 13, 1987, p. 35), Dr. Black described the plan: ''The version I like for individuals involves starting 100% invested, with an 80% floor. All you do is set trading points to sell half your stocks when the market declines halfway to your floor; sell half of what's left in stocks when the value of the portfolio drops another quarter of the way to the floor; again, half of what's left when it's one-eighth of the way from the floor, and so on. It's like a rabbit constantly jumping halfway to its hole—mathematically, it will never get there.''

While the rabbit never gets home, mathematically speaking, this approach could be mathematically hazardous to your wealth in volatile markets. Dr. Black's plan, in common with others, puts you back into stocks if the market subsequently increases; but, since you sold some off during the downturn, there is less to appreciate in value in the upturn. Given historical market volatility and assuming 5.5% return on cash assets, one version of the plan (reported in the *Journal* article) shows a portfolio loss of only about 13% when the market falls 30%; but you lose about 4% when the market is unchanged, and you gain around 12% if the market increases 20%. So, there is the inevitable return-risk trade-off.

Finally, if this plan's arithmetic seems too much bother to implement, consider investing in a mutual fund utilizing asset allocation approaches. The Vanguard Group has a rather large one. Make sure you get prospectuses to determine how frequently switching might take place and to make sure expenses are not exceptionally high in relation to assets.

risk-free asset to assure the loss never exceeds 10%. Assume you have $100,000 to invest, and you intend that the portfolio must never go below $90,000.

You might begin by putting half your funds in a risk-free asset—say, one-year T-bills—guaranteed to provide an 8% return. The other half goes into the risky asset—say, stocks—with an uncertain return. Then you resolve to sell 60% of the stocks whenever their loss reaches 10%. Suppose after three months, the return on stocks is a loss of 10%, or $5,000. Bills provide their expected 2%, or $1,000, so you are down $3,000 for the quarter. If the next three quarters were similar to the first, you would lose $12,000 for the year—an intolerable outcome. So, you sell $27,000 of the stocks (0.60 × $45,000), investing the proceeds in nine-month bills. Your position starting the second quarter is $18,000 ($45,000 − $27,000) in stocks and $78,000 in bills [$50,000 + $1,000 (interest) + $27,000 (the transfer)]. Suppose stocks then lose another 10%, or $1,800, requiring another transfer, this time of $9,720 [0.60 × ($18,000 − $1,800)]. Now, only $8,280 remains in stocks ($18,000 − $9,720). If then stocks began to increase in value, larger allocations would be made to them, keeping in mind the allocation cannot be so large that a loss of 10% would reduce the overall portfolio below $90,000.

We won't prolong the example, since the approach is relatively straightforward, although determining the initial asset weights and the trigger points for selling or buying stocks can be somewhat complicated. Also, if stocks initially increase in value, or subsequently increase the portfolio above $100,000, the target return is usually then increased as well. For example, if stocks increase initially by 10% to $55,000, you might rebalance to $52,500 each and now plan the portfolio never to be less than $94,500 (which is a 10% loss from $105,000).

While portfolio insurance limits your loss, its disadvantage is that since you reduce your position in stocks during a decline, you have less funds invested to increase in value when the market recovers. Over the course of a stock market cycle, your losses will exceed your gains even if the market ends the cycle unchanged.

Buying Puts or Selling Deep-in-the Money Calls   We discussed in Chapter 13 how each of these methods can be utilized to reduce or limit losses; a discussion will not be repeated here. We should note, though, that buying puts is the ultimate insurance since it guarantees no losses. Unfortunately, puts are expensive, which seriously reduces portfolio return over time. Also, while selling deep-in-the-money calls buffers any market losses, it also completely shuts out any price appreciation. Naturally, this defeats one of the main purposes of owning stocks—to realize growth.

Buying put options is expensive, and selling deep-in-the-money calls cuts off any price appreciation.

Competitive Hedging   **Competitive hedging** is a technique that allows the investor to invest in the stock of his or her choice, but then tempers the enthusiasm by short-selling another firm within the same industry. The company shorted is one that is expected to perform poorly in relation to the selected company. For example, you think NCR is a great selection. But suppose the market does poorly and drags NCR down with it? To overcome this obstacle, you decide to short-sell IBM, a company that you believe will lag the industry as a whole and surely lag NCR.

Of course, this approach is only as good as an investor's ability to identify industry leaders and laggards. If you guess wrong, you can lose on both ends: NCR decreases in value while IBM increases. This method takes the familiar difficulties of finding companies expected to overperform, and adds to them the difficulty of finding underperformers. Several large professional money management firms have employed the technique recently with supposedly good results. Again, a final verdict awaits its performance over a long period of time.

Using Stop Orders   As described in Chapter 2, a stop order is an order that is triggered by a market price. For example, you buy a stock at $50 a share; it subsequently rises to $60 a share and you think it will eventually reach $70 a share, but you don't want to lose your profit if it falls back to $50. The solution is to put a stop order (in this case, called a stop-loss) at, say, $58 a share. If the stock continues to rise, your order is never executed, but if price falls to $58, your order becomes a market order to sell the stock. You then take your profit, which as is often pointed out, you can never lose. Some years ago, a How-I-Made-a-Million-in-the-Market book was written that featured only one clever technique: the stop order. The author did indeed make a million—from the book. His profits from the market are less certain to us.

Clearly, using stop orders cannot guarantee a profit. To begin with, this strategy has nothing to say about which security to buy in the first place. Moreover, it often leads to excessive trading that absorbs most of your profits in commissions. As you know, many stock prices fluctuate over time. The stock that increased to $60 may show decreases for a while before it advances again. A stop-order takes the investor out of the stock and makes repurchase necessary if he or she wishes to hold it again. A double commission such as this is difficult to overcome with future price appreciation, but it probably explains why many stockbrokers favor stop orders.

An industry hedge requires selecting both an overperforming and an underperforming firm within the same industry.

Incorrect selections can lead to double losses.

Using stop orders often leads to excessive trading and reduced profits.

SUMMARY

In designing an investment portfolio, an important first step is setting goals. Goals establish priorities and indicate tolerable risk levels. Another portfolio activity is forecasting the investment environment. Forecasting by default implies the investor has no preconceived ideas about future prices, which contrasts with making specific forecasts. Assets are selected to conform to investor goals. There would be sufficient diversification to eliminate random risk and to take advantage of poorly correlated returns among broad investment groups, such as stocks, bonds, and tangibles.

After the portfolio is constructed, it must be monitored in three steps: (1) estimate performance in advance of the investment period, (2) measure performance after the period is over, and (3) evaluate performance. Evaluation can be in an absolute sense or relative to performances of other investments or market indicators.

Most portfolios are modified over time in response to changing investment goals or changed perceptions of future investment potentials. A buy-and-hold strategy would make portfolio changes only as investment goals change. Purposive portfolio changes are made in anticipation of changing investment potentials. Methods utilized to make portfolio changes include market timing, strategic asset allocation models, and tactical asset allocation models. Mechanical allocation plans establish investment purchases or sales using predetermined plans, which include constant and variable ratio plans and dollar cost averaging. To protect portfolio profits, investors use defensive strategies, which include portfolio insurance, buying puts or selling deep-in-the-money calls, industry hedges, and using stop orders.

KEY TERMS

Select the alternative that best identifies the key term.

1. portfolio
2. portfolio rate of return (R_P)
3. buy-and-hold
4. market timing
5. strategic asset allocation (SAA) model
6. tactical asset allocation (TAA) model
7. market contrarian
8. constant ratio plan
9. variable ratio plan
10. dollar cost averaging
11. portfolio insurance
12. competitive hedging

a. adjusts the portfolio to keep asset weights proportional
b. often does as well as strategies based on market timing
c. invests a constant dollar amount each period
d. buys out-of-favor assets
e. more difficult to calculate if activity takes place in the portfolio
f. this calls for "increased contrariness"
g. any combination of assets held at the same time
h. attempts to hold the asset offering the highest return in the upcoming period
i. takes a long position in one stock while short-selling another
j. directed towards determining asset tilts
k. a broad plan that establishes a model portfolio
l. operates within a predetermined tolerable portfolio loss

1. Define a portfolio and explain how goal setting establishes investment priorities and sets tolerable risk levels.
2. In what sense is constructing a portfolio similar to moving through a cafeteria line? Explain.
3. How do you forecast by default? Is it a big mistake to forecast this way? Explain thoroughly.
4. What guidelines should you follow in selecting specific assets for the portfolio? Explain.
5. Identify three separate activities associated with portfolio monitoring.
6. What advantage arises from estimating a portfolio performance? Explain.
7. How is portfolio performance evaluated in: *(a)* an absolute sense, and *(b)* a relative sense? Discuss several standards you might use with respect to the latter activity.
8. Explain advantages and disadvantages of a buy-and-hold investment strategy.
9. Explain what is meant by market timing and then discuss its advantages and disadvantages.
10. Explain a strategic asset allocation (SAA) model and a tactical asset allocation (TAA) model. Are they alternative or complementary methods?
11. In what sense do formula allocation plans take a contrarian view of the market? Explain several such methods.
12. What is dollar cost averaging and what goal does it accomplish?
13. Explain how portfolio insurance works. Is it true insurance in the sense it guarantees no losses? Discuss.
14. Explain the main shortcomings of buying puts or selling deep-in-the-money calls.
15. What is a competitive hedge and why would you use one?
16. Explain how stop orders are used in a defensive program.

1. Veronica Larue's portfolio was worth $60,000 at the beginning of the year and $75,000 at year end. She also received $5,000 in bond interest and $2,000 in dividends, and withdrew all interest and dividends when they were received. Given this information, calculate Veronica's portfolio rate of return.
2. Joel Tyler's portfolio had the following transactions last year:

Date	Activity	Amount
1/1	Beginning portfolio value	$50,000
5/31	Received dividends	2,000
6/1	Reinvested dividends	2,000
9/30	Sold securities and withdrew cash	10,000
9/30	Realized profit on securities sold	3,000
12/31	Ending portfolio value	45,000

Calculate Joel's portfolio rate of return.

3. You have decided to invest all your available funds equally weighted in stocks, corporate bonds, and 1-year Treasury bills. You will adjust the portfolio at the T-bills' maturity using a constant ratio plan. Assume you invested $60,000 initially and the following annual returns were earned: stocks, 20%; bonds, −12% price depreciation

and +8% coupon return; T-bills, 6%. Indicate the necessary adjustments at year end, assuming bond interest was withdrawn and T-bills were rolled over during the year. Indicate the adjustments if you rebalanced with a variable ratio plan that weights more heavily the poorest-performing asset and most lightly the best-performing asset. Assume weights of 44%, 33%, and 23%.

4. You have $100,000 to invest and have recently decided to utilize portfolio insurance as a defensive technique. Your initial allocation was 40% stocks and 60% Treasury bills. Suppose you set a loss limit of $10,000 and resolved to sell half the stocks when half the limit has been lost. Assume the T-bills earn a 12% annual return, and after three months stocks have declined to a point requiring an adjustment. Indicate the value of the stocks at that point and the adjustment that would take place.

5. Larry Ward plans to acquire shares of Exxon by dollar cost averaging with a stockbroker's monthly investment plan, and he has allocated $100 a month for this purpose. At the purchase date for the last five months, Exxon's price per share was $52, $48, $41, $43, and $45. For each period, determine Larry's cumulative total cost, average cost, and cumulative profit or loss.

6. *(Student Project)*   Contact an officer from the trust department of a local bank. Ask if the bank has any plans that utilize asset allocation models or portfolio insurance. If so, request information, if it is available.

7. *(Student Project)*   Contact a local stockbrokerage firm and ask if they sponsor any mutual fund that utilizes asset allocation or portfolio insurance techniques. Request a prospectus and a current financial report and use data contained within them to evaluate the fund. Also, contact the Vanguard Group of mutual funds and request similar information regarding the Vanguard Asset Allocation Fund. The telephone number is 1–800–SHIP.

CASE ANALYSES

19.1
The Walkers' Portfolio Plan

After several years of generally unsuccessful investing, Francine and Horace Walker have decided to simplify their future investment activities by holding only three assets: gold, Treasury bonds, and a mutual fund investing in growth stocks. While they have agreed that no portfolio adjustments will be made during a year, they disagree on how year-end adjustments should be made. Francine favors a constant ratio plan while Horace feels the ratios should be adjusted to favor the asset that performed most poorly in the previous year. As Horace sees it, buying the "relatively cheap" asset should enhance their return over time. Francine disagrees, arguing that his approach is the same as trying to pick winning stocks.

Initially, the Walkers will invest $8,000 in each asset and will adjust the portfolio at the end of one year. For the upcoming year, they expect to receive $800 interest on the bonds, which they will withdraw, but no dividends from the mutual fund. Based on their forecast of the investment environment, the Walkers feel the mutual fund shares will increase 20%, gold will increase 5%, and bonds will be unchanged.

a. Based on the above data, prepare a portfolio sheet, showing the initial investments, the expected appreciation, and the portfolio rate of return. Also indicate the necessary rebalancing with Francine's approach, assuming the expected returns are realized.

b. The year is now over for the Walkers. Their mutual fund declined 10% in value, the bonds fell 5% in value (but paid the same interest), and gold's price increased 20%. Treasury bills during the year yielded 8%, while the stock market was down 4%. Using research the Walkers conducted before investing, they believe their portfolio has a beta weight of about 0.8. Using the information provided, evaluate performance of the Walkers' portfolio.

c. Indicate how the portfolio will be rebalanced at year end using Francine's approach. Indicate rebalancing with Horace's approach, assuming his weighting scheme is 40%, 30%, and 30%.

d. Do the Walkers seem to have clearly defined investment goals? Discuss, indicating how a strategic asset allocation model might help the Walkers.

Terri Blair has accumulated $40,000 in a stock portfolio through successful investing over the past ten years. Terri was willing to take chances and she considers herself lucky. However, she will be married shortly and she wants to reduce her risk tolerance level. Terri's future husband suggests that she put her money in certificates of deposit as a safe haven. Terri, though, is reluctant to do so. For one thing, she is willing to take some risk, and for another, she wishes to stay invested in stocks.

19.2
Terri Blair
Considers
Portfolio
Insurance

Terri's broker has recommended a portfolio insurance plan consisting of two mutual funds—one that is indexed to the market and another that is a money market fund. The broker will manage the plan, and he suggests a maximum tolerable loss of 20% (a so-called 80% floor). All her funds will be invested initially in the index fund; if it declines halfway to the floor, half of the shares will be sold and funds transferred to the money market fund. Another drop of a quarter way to the floor calls for the sale of half the remaining shares, and so on. If the market declines initially and then rebounds, funds are transferred back into the index fund in the same fashion, only in reverse.

a. Suppose the overall market made two major moves during the year, first declining by 15%, and then advancing by 20%. Assuming Terri's stock fund tracked the market perfectly, what is the ending balance in the fund? (Assume for this question that no interest is earned on the money market fund.)

b. Suppose the 15% stock decline took place on March 31 (10%) and June 30 (5%), while the 20% recovery occurred on July 31 (5%), September 30 (10%), and October 31 (5%). For the purpose of evaluating portfolio insurance, assume that interest earned on money market deposits is withdrawn. Assuming the money market fund offered an 8% annual return while the stock fund paid no dividends, compare Terri's performance for three approaches: (1) buy and hold the stock fund, (2) invest totally in the money market fund, and (3) use portfolio insurance.

c. Will portfolio insurance reduce Terri's risk exposure? Is it likely to reduce her portfolio return? Discuss.

HELPFUL READING

Anders, George. "Portfolio 'Insurance' Helps Nervous Money Managers." *The Wall Street Journal,* June 16, 1986, p. 13.

Angrist, Stanley W. "Hedging by Industry Makes Smooth Ride." *The Wall Street Journal,* March 24, 1989, p. C1.

Bergeron, Woodrow. "The Benefits of Dividend Reinvestment." *Barron's,* September 16, 1985, p. 26.

Donnelly, Barbara. "Market Timing in New Form Gains Adherents." *The Wall Street Journal,* July 7, 1988, p. C1.

Droms, William G. "Market Timing as an Investment Policy." *Financial Analysts Journal,* January-February 1989, pp. 73–77.

Jeffrey, Robert H. "The Folly of Stock Market Timing." *Harvard Business Review,* July–August 1984.

Laderman, Jeffrey M. "Welcome to the New Money Game." *Business Week,* May 30, 1988, p. 88.

Liebowitz, M. "Horizon Analysis for Managed Portfolios." *Journal of Portfolio Management,* Spring 1975.

Michaud, Richard O. "The Markowitz Optimization Enigma: Is 'Optimized' Optimal?" *Financial Analysts Journal,* January-February 1989, pp. 31–42.

Speidell, Lawrence S., Deborah H. Miller, and James R. Ullman. "Portfolio Optimization: A Primer." *Financial Analysts Journal,* January-February 1989, pp. 22–30.

APPENDIX: MODERN PORTFOLIO THEORY AND THE CAPITAL ASSET PRICING MODEL

As a formal investment approach, modern portfolio theory (MPT) dates back to the early 1950s, when an academician, Harry Markowitz, first developed the theory. The term "modern" was applied to distinguish this new approach from conventional portfolio management, which focused most of its attention on the investor rather than on the behavior of assets when held in portfolio. Today, the professional portfolio manager blends the two approaches to meet client needs, much in the way we have just studied in this chapter. In fact, the tenets of MPT that involve asset correlations, the securities market line (SML), and the use of beta weights have been brought into the text at many points. These tools are widely accepted and often are key factors in making investment decisions. This appendix will explain the underlying rationale of MPT, although it will not go into formal proofs of its basic theorems.

The Efficient Frontier

An efficient frontier of investments represents all combinations of assets an investor can hold, when going from one combination to another *always* involves taking more risk to achieve a higher return. Although a simple concept, it does need some explanation.

An Example with Two Assets   Suppose you could invest in two assets—*A* and *B*—that have the following characteristics:

	A	*B*
Expected return, R_i	.10	.16
Expected standard deviation of returns, σ_i	.04	.12

If you could not hold the two together, then it would be necessary to choose between higher return (with *B*) or less risk (with *A*). Removing this restriction, though, opens new possibilities, their value depending upon the correlation of returns between *A* and *B*. We'll consider two possibilities: perfect positive correlation and perfect negative correlation. We also will look at only five combinations of *A* and *B*, since that is enough to illustrate the important points. The five combinations (portfolios) are: (1) 100% in *A*, 0% in *B*; (2) 75% in *A*, 25% in *B*; (3) 50% in *A*, 50% in *B*; (4) 25% in *A*, 75% in *B*; and (5) 0% in *A*, 100% in *B*.

Column 4 in Exhibit 19A.1 shows returns from the five portfolios just described. As you see, the portfolio return is simply the weighted average of the individual returns. For example, portfolio 3 is $(.5 \times .10) + (.5 \times .16) = .05 + .08 = .13$. The risk of each portfolio, though, depends upon correlation. Column 5 shows the standard deviation of the portfolios if *A*'s and *B*'s returns are perfectly positively correlated. As you see, there is no reduction in risk since σ_P is simply the weighted average of *A*'s and *B*'s individual σs. A diagram of σ_P is shown in Exhibit 19A.2.

EXHIBIT 19A.1
Return and risk
characteristics of five
portfolios constructed
from two securities

(1)	(2)	(3)	(4)	(5)	(6)
	Percent in:			Portfolio Risk (σ_P)	
	A	B	Portfolio	$r = +1.0$	
Portfolio	(2)	(3)	Return (R_P)		$r = -1.0$
1	100	0	0.100	0.040	0.040
2	75	25	0.115	0.060	0.000
3	50	50	0.130	0.080	0.040
4	25	75	0.145	0.100	0.080
5	0	100	0.160	0.120	0.120

Column 6 in Exhibit 19A.1 shows each portfolio's standard deviation when
A and B are perfectly negatively correlated. A quite different picture now
emerges. Risk not only can be reduced, it can be eliminated altogether with
portfolio 2. (Values for σ_P are determined by a formula not discussed in this text.)
A diagram of this situation is shown in Exhibit 19A.3.

The next step is to show a combination of portfolio returns and standard
deviations (σ_P). This is done in Exhibit 19A.4. Focus your attention on portfolio 1,
comparing it to portfolio 3. They are equally risky, but portfolio 3 offers a higher
return; it is said to dominate 1. A rational investor would never choose 1. So, we

EXHIBIT 19A.2
Portfolio risk (σ_P): Five
portfolios of securities A
and B with perfectly
positively correlated
returns ($r = +1.0$)

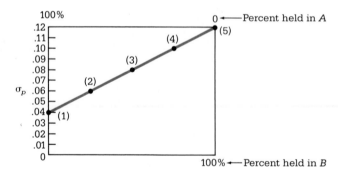

EXHIBIT 19A.3
Portfolio risk (σ_P): Five
portfolios of securities A
and B with perfectly
negatively correlated
returns ($r = -1.0$)

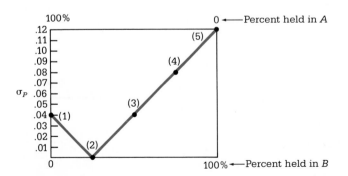

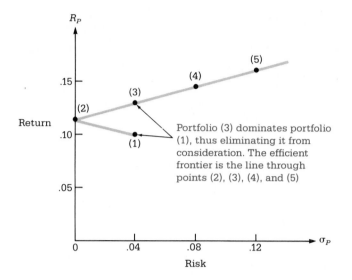

EXHIBIT 19A.4
The efficient frontier
constructed from
portfolios of securities *A*
and *B*

can exclude it from consideration. The efficient portfolios—those that involve trading off risk and return—are 2, 3, 4, and 5; and a line passed through these points is called the efficient frontier for the portfolios in question.

Generalizing from the Example Portfolio construction would be simple if we needed to consider only two assets with perfect correlation. Unfortunately, life is more difficult. But suppose you could analyze a large number of investments and derive an efficient frontier from your work. Exhibit 19A.5 shows an example of

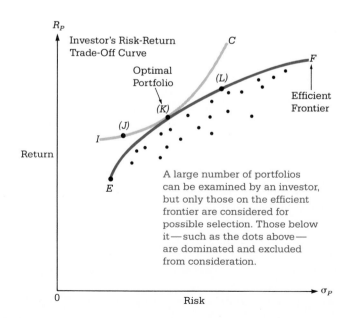

EXHIBIT 19A.5
Selecting an optimal
portfolio

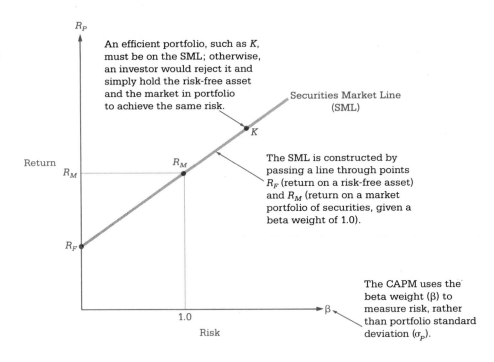

EXHIBIT 19A.6
The Capital Asset Pricing Model (CAPM) and portfolio construction

R_P

An efficient portfolio, such as K, must be on the SML; otherwise, an investor would reject it and simply hold the risk-free asset and the market in portfolio to achieve the same risk.

Securities Market Line (SML)

K

Return

R_M

R_M

The SML is constructed by passing a line through points R_F (return on a risk-free asset) and R_M (return on a market portfolio of securities, given a beta weight of 1.0).

R_F

β

1.0

Risk

The CAPM uses the beta weight (β) to measure risk, rather than portfolio standard deviation (σ_P).

how it might appear (temporarily ignore line *IC*). Again, only portfolios not dominated by others form the efficient frontier.

Selecting a Portfolio

You cannot select a portfolio only on the basis that it is on the efficient frontier. Many portfolios satisfy that criterion. In order to choose, you must first determine your willingness to trade off higher return for lower risk. Let's assume you can make such trade-offs; and, to see the process visually, let us further assume that you can describe the trade-offs in graphic form as the line *IC* in Exhibit 19A.5. Now we have a solution: the point where *IC* touches but does not intersect *EF* indicates the exact portfolio for you. It is portfolio *K*. Of course, you would like more return, but you would have to take more risk to get it. Your *IC* line shows that if you went to another portfolio (*L*, for example) to get a better return, you would be dissatisfied. The additional realized return from the *EF* line is less that what you have to earn, as indicated by the *IC* line. So, you would remain at *K* rather than going to *L*. By similar reasoning, you would also refuse portfolio *J*.

The Capital Asset Pricing Model

Applying MPT, in the form explained above, to examine an almost infinite number of portfolios that can be created from assets in the real world presents serious mathematical complexities. However, working with broad asset groups—stocks, bonds, gold, and so forth—reduces the problem. Moreover, it isn't necessary that you determine the exact optimal combination of assets to benefit from the lessons MPT has taught us. Even a rough approximation that recognizes asset correlations will provide a better portfolio than one derived without such recognition. In other words, an approximation of the *right* concept is far better than exact use of the *wrong* one.

Nevertheless, academicians and practitioners wanted an easier approach. One emerged from a body of ideas after Markowitz's original work, and it is referred to as the capital asset pricing model (CAPM). The major thrust of the CAPM is to measure the risk of each asset in terms of how its return varies in response to changes in the return of the overall market. This measurement statistic is called the asset's beta value. By determining every individual asset's beta, you can judge immediately its risk in relation to the market and in relation to other assets. It is no longer necessary to examine an infinite number of combinations of thousands of assets to derive an efficient frontier, since combinations of only two assets—one that is risk-free and one representing the overall market—will accomplish the same end, as Exhibit 19A.6 shows.

Actually, we have explained and used the CAPM at various points throughout the text, particularly Chapters 4, 8, and 9. Although certain fundamental propositions of the CAPM have been the subject of controversy, it nevertheless remains a useful investment approach that should be understood and used by individual investors.

CHAPTER TWENTY

Extending The Portfolio: International Investing, Life Insurance, and Retirement Planning

INTERNATIONALIZING THE PORTFOLIO

Advantages

Disadvantages

Ways to Internationalize

LIFE INSURANCE IN THE PORTFOLIO

Life Insurance and Your Estate

Popular Forms of Life Insurance

DESIGNING THE PORTFOLIO FOR RETIREMENT

Planning for Retirement

Using Self-Directed Investment Plans

Planning in Retirement

BOXES

Retirement Planning: How Much Will You Need and When Should You Start Saving?

Is There a Replacement for the IRA?

After you finish this chapter, you will be able to:

- understand the advantages and disadvantages of internationalizing a portfolio.

- identify different ways of achieving an international balance in the portfolio.

- recognize different types of life insurance and understand advantages and disadvantages of each.

- analyze the investment aspects of life insurance and decide whether to buy expensive whole life insurance or inexpensive term insurance, investing the saved premiums in other assets.

- understand the importance of retirement planning and how it shapes the investment portfolio prior to and after retirement.

- use appropriate techniques to determine a retirement portfolio requirement.

As we learn more about portfolio management, it becomes increasingly clear that there are advantages to holding a broad range of assets. We already have noted that combining tangible and intangible assets contributes to efficiency, and in this chapter we will see that further increases in efficiency are possible by holding securities issued in foreign countries. Also, a portfolio asset often overlooked is life insurance. This oversight is unfortunate because life insurance is often the single most important asset many investors hold. Its position in the portfolio is examined in this chapter. Finally, since so much of our investment activity is directed towards building a suitable retirement portfolio, the process of retirement planning is also explained.

INTERNATIONALIZING THE PORTFOLIO

As the value of the dollar, relative to other currencies, reached a peak in 1984 and then started to decline, internationalizing the portfolio became a popular investment theme. Many mutual funds specializing in foreign holdings were organized almost overnight, appealing to investors who wanted a convenient vehicle to play the theme. Actually, the advantages of international diversification had been noted long before this movement began. These advantages, as well as the risks, should be understood by all investors.

Advantages

There are two potential contributions any asset can make to a portfolio: it can increase portfolio return while leaving risk unchanged, or it can reduce portfolio risk, leaving return unchanged. There is evidence showing international investing offers such advantages.

Higher Returns   If you limit your investments to one country, then your return over time from a broadly diversified portfolio must be limited to that country's growth. For U.S. citizens, this restriction has often resulted in a relatively poor performance, compared to other countries. For example, Japan's average annual growth rate since the 1960s has been about twice as high as that of the United States. And in recent years, countries such as Hong Kong, South Korea, and Norway have shown much higher economic growth rates. International investing allows us to participate in these high growth areas and others.

> Higher economic growth rates abroad can lead to higher investment returns with foreign investments.

Lower Systematic Risk   As we discussed in Chapter 8, systematic risk cannot be eliminated by adding more securities to a portfolio, but considerable evidence shows that international diversification reduces such risk. This is so because of the relatively poor correlations between returns on U.S. and foreign securities. Exhibit 20.1 indicates correlations found in one study; others show similar results. While United Kingdom and U.S. returns are moderately correlated, in the other cases, correlations are weak. A U.S. investor, then, could have achieved risk

> Returns on foreign and U.S. securities are often poorly correlated, which reduces risk in a global portfolio.

United Kingdom	+0.50
Japan	+0.31
West Germany	+0.38

SOURCE: Gerald P. Dwyer, Jr., and R. W. Hafer, "Are National Stock Markets Linked?" *Review*, Federal Reserve Bank of St. Louis, November/December, 1988, pp. 3–14.

EXHIBIT 20.1
Return correlations between the U.S. and three other stock markets: 1957–1987

reduction by holding securities in any of the countries along with U.S. securities. This fact is highlighted in Exhibit 20.2, where the internationalized portfolio offers less risk for any given portfolio size.

Disadvantages

The advantage of lower systematic risk just discussed must be balanced against random risks associated with foreign securities. Some investment advisors believe these latter risks are too large to be eliminated through diversification of foreign holdings, and thus they could influence the internationalized portfolio. Indeed, these advisors doubt the effect shown in Exhibit 20.2 will hold over a long period of time, and believe that internationalizing your portfolio might actually increase its risk. Critics often single out exchange-rate risk and political risks as the most disturbing influences.

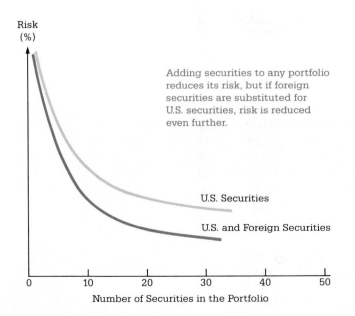

Risk (%)

Adding securities to any portfolio reduces its risk, but if foreign securities are substituted for U.S. securities, risk is reduced even further.

U.S. Securities

U.S. and Foreign Securities

Number of Securities in the Portfolio

EXHIBIT 20.2
Illustration of risk and portfolio size, holding return constant

Exchange-Rate Risk   When you invest in a foreign security, your investment return will be determined by two factors. The performance of the security in question is the first determinant. If you purchased bonds of a British firm paying 15% interest, then you will earn that rate, assuming interest is paid. It is paid, however, in pounds, not dollars. As Exhibit 20.3 shows, you must then convert pounds to dollars before the payout has any value to you. But suppose the dollar appreciated 10% against the pound during the year after purchase. (A currency appreciates when acquiring one of its units requires more units of a foreign currency. In the example, initially, 1 pound acquired 1.5 dollars, and later, 1 pound acquired only 1.35 dollars; at the new exchange rate it would take 1.111 [1.5 ÷ 1.35] pounds to acquire 1.5 dollars. Thus, the dollar has appreciated while the pound has depreciated.) Now, your return realized in dollars is only 13.5%. The adverse movement in the exchange rate—the dollar's *appreciation*—reduced your return.

> Appreciation in the dollar versus foreign currencies will reduce the return on foreign investments.

If exchange rates between the dollar and other currencies showed random movements over time, **exchange-rate risk** would be minimized, with any adverse movement against some currencies being offset by favorable movements against others. However, the historical pattern of rates suggests that most key currencies move together against the dollar, although there are important exceptions. Thus, the strengthening of the dollar in 1989 meant a general *appreciation,* with the implication that most foreign investment returns would be *reduced* (as they were). Exhibit 20.4 shows the dramatic impact changes in exchange rates can have upon investment returns. During most of the 1970s, the dollar depreciated relative to most other currencies. As you see, this had the effect of increasing annual rates of return in foreign countries. The rate of return in Switzerland, for example, was boosted from 2.0% to 11.3%.

Political Risks   Perhaps most U.S. investors are narrow in their view on world affairs, but the fact remains that many see foreign countries as considerably more risky than the U.S. This perception is clearly the biggest deterrent to investing abroad. In some cases, this fear is probably exaggerated; but in others, it may not

EXHIBIT 20.3
Foreign investment return and exchange-rate risk: Dollar appreciation reduces realized yield.

	Pounds	Exchange Rate: No. of Dollars to Acquire 1 Pound	Dollars
1/1/19X1: Purchase one British bond with a 15% coupon rate	600.0	1.50 to 1.0	900.0
12/31/19X1: Anticipate interest on bond	90.0	1.50 to 1.0	135.0
Anticipated yield	15%		15%
12/31/19X1: Interest on bond actually received	90.0	1.35 to 1.0	121.5
Realized yield	15%		13.5%

	In National Currency	In U.S. Dollars
United States	5.8%	5.8%
Australia	6.7	7.0
Canada	12.3	11.6
Japan	11.9	16.7
Switzerland	2.0	11.3
United Kingdom	10.1	9.8
West Germany	3.4	10.4

EXHIBIT 20.4
Annual returns in six foreign countries and the U.S.: 1970–1980

SOURCE: Richard K. Abrams and Donald V. Kimball, "U.S. Investment in Foreign Equity Markets," *Economic Review,* Federal Reserve Bank of Kansas City, April 1981.

be. Political instability can arise from a variety of causes, ranging from ineptness at managing internal fiscal affairs to outright confiscation of private property. Surely, diversifying among countries will reduce such risk; nevertheless, a massive change in the world socioeconomic structure could lead to substantial investment losses. (Of course, a movement this broad most likely would lead to sharp losses in the U.S. as well.)

Political instabilities range from a government's inability to control inflation to outright confiscation of property.

Unfortunately, with the exception of Japan, those countries with the highest expected growth also offer the highest **political risks**—South Korea, Taiwan, Hong Kong, and other countries in the Pacific basin being good examples. Hong Kong, for instance, becomes a part of mainland China in the 1990s. What then? No one knows for sure, but the risks of the situation were brought into clear focus during the student demonstrations in Beijing in 1989. The government's oppressive resistance led many investors to question whether a free-enterprise system can coexist with a totalitarian regime.

No one really knows the future in a broader perspective. We do know the past, however, and the record is mixed. Of course, many individual and institutional investors have done exceptionally well with foreign investments, but some have not. For example, massive investments have been made by commercial banks in Mexico and other South American countries, and the results so far border on disaster. The ultimate costs of these loans on bank stockholders and the public at large remain to be seen. Suffice it to say that internationalizing the portfolio in this manner has neither reduced portfolio risk nor increased its return.

Ways to Internationalize

A portfolio can be internationalized in a number of ways. While direct investment is possible, most individual investors prefer indirect methods.

Direct Investment Many large foreign companies, such as Volkswagenwerk (West Germany) or Telefonos de Mexico, S.A. (Mexico), have their shares

available in U.S. markets. In most cases, they do so through **American
depository receipts (ADRs).** The ADR process works like this: a foreign
company places shares in trust with an American bank, which in turn issues
depository receipts to U.S. investors. The ADRs, then, are claims to shares of
stock, and are, for all practical purposes, the same as shares. The trustee bank
performs all clerical functions — issuing annual reports, maintaining a stockholder
ledger, paying and keeping dividend records, and so on — allowing the ADRs to
trade in markets just as other securities trade. About 400 foreign companies trade
in this fashion, about a quarter of them on the New York and American stock
exchanges and the rest through the over-the-counter market.

You can invest in companies from all parts of the world using ADRs,
achieving a high degree of international diversification. However, doing your own
research to select companies may be difficult. There is, for one thing, a shortage
of data: the annual report may be all that is available, and its reliability is
questionable in some instances. With the exception of Australia, Canada, and the
United Kingdom, financial reporting and accounting standards are quite different
from those accepted in the U.S. While this isn't necessarily bad, it is different. If
you are thinking of finding an undiscovered growth company in Spain or
Singapore, for example, most advisors will probably tell you to forget it. Financial
reporting in each country is very poor and unreliable, making analysis difficult
even for people with extensive accounting training. On the other hand, if you limit
your selections to large, widely recognized companies, your risks are no greater
(other than exchange-rate and political risks) than they are with most U.S.
companies.

Investing in U.S. Multinationals   Actually, many investors achieve a reasonable degree of internationalization without recognizing it. This is so because

many U.S. companies have extensive multinational interests. Companies such as
IBM, Exxon, and ITT do a considerable portion of their business outside the U.S.,
as Exhibit 20.5 shows. Holding stocks such as these provides a high degree of
international balance to a portfolio. If you own U.S. stock you should review each
company's annual report to see the extent of its foreign operations; if these are
extensive, you already own an internationalized portfolio. If you are just beginning
to invest, you might adopt an international perspective.

Investing in International and Global Funds   As mentioned earlier, international and global mutual funds have become extremely popular. An **international
fund** holds only foreign securities, while a **global fund** holds both foreign and
U.S. securities. A relatively recent type of fund is a **world income fund,** which
invests in bonds issued in foreign countries. Most fund families, such as Fidelity,
Vanguard, and T. Rowe Price, have an international or global fund. Some are load
funds, while others are no-loads. Some hold widely diversified portfolios; others
target their investments in specific geographical regions, such as Merrill Lynch's
Pacific Fund. In addition, there are a number of international closed-end funds

Company	Primary Product Line	Percent of Total Sales Outside the U.S.
McDonald's	Restaurant operation	30%
Ford	Automobiles	23
Boeing	Aircraft manufacturing	46
Avon	Cosmetics and toiletries	51
Coca-Cola	Soft drinks	56
Black and Decker	Home appliances	48
IBM	Computers	58
Cray Research	Supercomputers	35
NCR	Computers	58
Gillette	Razors and grooming aids	50
Colgate-Palmolive	Household items	84
Exxon	International oil	61
International Flavors & Fragrances	Specialty chemicals	70
Schlumberger	Oil field equipment and services	70

EXHIBIT 20.5
U.S. corporations with extensive foreign operations

SOURCE: *Value Line Industry Reports,* various issues in 1989.

that invest exclusively in one country, such as Australia, Ireland, Brazil, Germany, India, Korea, Mexico, Thailand, and others.

In the mid-1980s, performances of the abroad funds were nothing short of spectacular. For example, the Merrill Lynch Pacific Fund showed a total return of 152.2% for the three-year period ended May 31, 1986. Practically any list of the top 10 or top 20 funds was dominated by the abroad funds. The weakening of the dollar was the major contributor to these successes, but relatively strong preconversion earnings also played a role. However, the strengthening of the dollar in the late 1980s reversed the situation, and the abroad funds did poorly. This reversal is indicated in Exhibit 20.6. Notice the 10- and 5-year returns do quite well versus the S&P 500. But the 1-year and 3-month performances are much poorer.

All things considered, investing through mutual funds is probably the best way for most investors to achieve international diversification, either on a broad basis or by targeting specific countries or geographical regions. The skills of the professional manager and the advantages of pooling are well worth the added costs of the pooling arrangement. Certain added risks should be considered, though. First, if you select a closed-end fund, be aware that they may be selling

Many closed-end funds invest in securities of only one country or area, such as Mexico or Malaysia.

Investing in international and global funds is often the best way to internationalize.

EXHIBIT 20.6
Returns on funds that
invest abroad

	Cumulative Returns for Periods Ended March 31, 1989			
	3 Months	1 Year	5 Years	10 Years
Global funds	3.7%	10.1%	122.5%	436.7
International funds	3.3	11.2	163.0	415.6
World income funds	−2.2	0.9	118.4	—
S&P 500 reinvested	7.1	18.1	123.7	354.1

SOURCE: Lipper Analytical Services, Inc., Summit, NJ

at rather high premiums to net asset value. If investor enthusiasm declines, these premiums might disappear. Second, if you select a fund that invests in a limited geographical area, you will have considerably more risk than if you pick a more cosmopolitan international fund or a global fund.

LIFE INSURANCE IN THE PORTFOLIO

You may not consider life insurance as part of your investment portfolio, but that would be a mistake if you are thinking of buying whole life or universal life policies. In either case, your annual premiums can be large and may well consume most of your funds that could be invested elsewhere. Many insurance agents now stress the investment aspects of their policies, so it makes sense for investors to evaluate them as investments. Moreover, you probably can invest in life insurance through the same person who handles your other investments, since many stockbrokerage firms are including life insurance as part of their product line.

Life Insurance and Your Estate

Not everyone needs life insurance; integrate its purchase within an estate plan.

Not everyone needs life insurance. Indeed, its primary purpose is to provide resources (an estate) for those who might need them in the event of your death. This observation raises two points: First, if you have no survivors who would be burdened by your untimely demise, then there is no need for an estate. This is why children and young adults have little need for life insurance. Second, if resources are available elsewhere, then life insurance is again not needed. For most younger investors, this situation is not likely.

Exhibit 20.7 shows how life insurance should be integrated within the overall estate plan. When a family is formed and then begins to develop, its needs soar, usually in response to desires for decent housing, medical care, and future education of the children. As these goals are gradually accomplished, family needs diminish over time and finally end with an amount a husband and wife

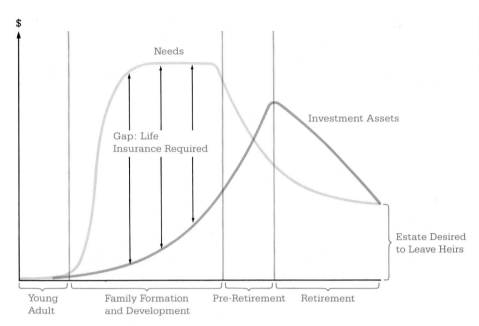

EXHIBIT 20.7
Needs, investment
assets, and life
insurance required

wish to leave to their heirs. Meanwhile, investment assets start to accumulate and increase in value. In the beginning, though, they are far less than the family's needs, thus creating a need for life insurance: it fills the gap between needs and available resources. At some point, the value of investment assets is enough to meet needs and life insurance is no longer necessary. Of course, Exhibit 20.7 represents a hypothetical—perhaps idealized—estate plan, but it is a useful guide to follow. Since life insurance is needed, the next question is: what kind?

Popular Forms of Life Insurance

A number of life insurance contracts are available, and the trend is to tailor policies to meet unique family needs. However, the most popular forms are term, whole life, universal life, and variable life. These are explained in the following sections.

Term Life Insurance **Term life insurance** provides protection for a given period of time—1, 5, 10, 20, or any number of years—without building any asset value. In other words, it is pure insurance: you pay premiums and you receive protection. In this regard, it is very similar to your auto or homeowner's insurance. Term is the simplest life insurance to understand, but there are policy variations. For example, constant term provides a constant level of protection over the policy's life, while decreasing term allows the face value of the policy to decline over time. Some policies allow you to convert to whole life insurance, if you wish, while others do not.

Term life insurance does
not build asset value.

Premiums on term insurance are very low for young people, but increase over time and eventually become prohibitively high for the elderly. If you are in your mid-20s, in good health and don't smoke, you should be able to buy $100,000 of insurance for a 5-year period for about $200 a year; if you are in your early 60s, the annual premium will be about $2,000—if you are insurable. (Premiums vary considerably among insurers, making comparative shopping important.)

Despite its low cost, term insurance is not very popular, accounting for less than 15% of new policies written. The lack of appeal might be explained by the buyers' fear of not being able to buy insurance later in life, but it also probably reflects the desire of most insureds to build an estate. Then, too, term insurance is not promoted very heartily by insurance salespeople.

Whole Life Insurance   **Whole life insurance** is the most popular form of life insurance. Approximately 55% of all new policies written are this type. Its popularity has grown in recent years because insurers have increased policy investment rates of return. Whole life insurance provides protection for the insured's entire life but, more importantly, it also builds up asset value over time, as Exhibit 20.8 shows. This latter feature makes whole life a hybrid of insurance and investment. The important question, then, is: how good an investment is it?

As you suspect, the annual premiums for whole life are considerably greater than for term insurance, for a given level of protection. You should view the additional premiums as you would any other investment you could make; in other words, if a term policy provides the same coverage at lower cost, then you should invest in a whole life policy only if the additional investment offers a satisfactory rate of return. Exhibit 20.9 presents an analysis of this decision for Megan Duffy. Megan has decided that her family will need $100,000 of additional protection over the next 10 years. She has obtained premium information for a whole life policy and a term policy, which are similar in all respects except for premiums and cash value at the end of 10 years.

Megan determines the amount she could save each year with term compared to whole life and assumes she will invest it to earn 8% each year until

Whole life insurance is more expensive than term, but it does build cash value.

EXHIBIT 20.8
Buildup of cash value of a typical $100,000 face value whole life policy with dividends applied to premiums

Year	Cash Value
1	$ -0-
2	-0-
3	2,748
4	5,278
5	7,962
6	10,648
7	13,332
8	16,017
9	18,872
10	21,728

the end of the 10 years. She then compares the future value of this series of investments with the cash value of the whole life policy at the end of 10 years. If the future value is greater, she will buy the term policy; if it is less, she will buy the whole life policy. As you see in Exhibit 20.9, the term insurance approach accumulates to $27,060, which is $5,332 more than the cash value of the whole life policy, making term the better alternative. Further analysis indicates the whole life policy offers about a 5% annual rate of return. If Megan can invest elsewhere at any rate better than this, she should choose the term insurance alternative. Since this decision is important, investors must consider the following factors:

Buying term and investing the difference is an appropriate way to evaluate the investment-insurance decision.

☐ Make sure the policies are almost identical. An important consideration is that the term policy must be renewable each year without a medical examination.

☐ Consider the impact of federal income taxes. The cash buildup with the whole life policy is tax-deferred; you pay no tax until your withdrawals from the policy exceed what you have invested in it. Megan's assumed 8% investment rate should not be a pre-tax rate; rather, it should also be a

EXHIBIT 20.9
Investment analysis of whole life versus term insurance

Insured: female, age 35
Term of insurance: 10 years
Dividends on whole life: applied to premiums

(1)	(2)	(3)	(4)
	Premiums		Savings
Year	Whole-Life	Term	with Term
1	$2,182	$253	$1,929
2	2,182	264	1,918
3	2,041	283	1,758
4	2,020	290	1,730
5	1,999	298	1,701
6	1,978	309	1,669
7	1,957	324	1,633
8	1,936	337	1,599
9	1,913	353	1,560
10	1,885	371	1,514

Compound value (CV) of column 4, assuming saving takes place at the beginning of each year and is invested to earn 8% each year until maturity:

$$CV = \$27,060$$

Cash value of whole life policy at the end of 10 years = <u>21,728</u> (from Exhibit 20.9)

Advantage of term insurance $ 5,332

tax-deferred rate. Using an IRA for the side investment would accomplish that end, although some differences might arise.

☐ You must, in fact, invest the premium savings. Agents who push whole life (and many do because their commissions are higher) stress the forced-savings element in whole life policies. They argue that if you buy term, you probably will spend your savings, rather than investing them. (You might find this argument insulting if you have discipline in managing your financial activities.)

☐ Whole life policies allow for borrowing. You can borrow easily and, perhaps, at an attractive fixed rate. This gives you immediate liquidity. Of course, you can also borrow with the term approach, using the side investments as collateral for a margin account, for instance. But, rates are volatile and may be much higher. At the very least, determine borrowing arrangements with whole life and then evaluate their importance in the decision.

Universal Life Insurance   As many consumers began evaluating their insurance needs in the manner just described, and as they concluded that term insurance was the more attractive alternative, insurance companies began to realize that unless they designed more attractive life insurance, their business would suffer. The answer was the **universal life policy.** Approximately 25% of life insurance sold today is this form, which didn't even exist until the early 1980s.

Actually, a universal life policy is nothing more than a combination of term insurance and an investment account on the side. In other words, the insurer is doing for you what you should be able to do for yourself. There might be some justification in this if the insurer could earn higher returns or save you a lot of time and aggravation, but that appears not to be true. Moreover, you will pay very high management fees, such as 7% to 10% on the annual premium plus 1% to 2% for annual maintenance. Very often, the side assets are nothing more than money market instruments, which means you are paying, say, a 7% load to invest in a money market fund. That is not effective investing. Review thoroughly any universal life policy being considered: Determine the fees, and then review the rates of return previously issued policies have earned in the past, comparing them to other market rates earned elsewhere during the same period. While considering returns, keep in mind that universal life policies also provide borrowing privileges, and income is earned on a tax-deferred basis.

Variable Life and Variable Annuities   **Variable life insurance** is similar to universal life in that typical insurance protection is combined with investment growth. Perhaps the major difference is in how premiums are paid. Many variable life policies are paid with a single premium at the time they are purchased, rather than with annual premiums. Variable annuities are actually not insurance policies, although they are often sold by insurance companies (along with many stockbrokerage firms). The most popular contract requires a single or several payments into the contract; then, the investor can make initial and periodic allocations among various mutual funds, such as stock, bond, or money market

Universal life is a combination of term insurance and an investment side account.

Retirement Planning: How Much Will You Need and When Should You Start Saving?

Let's consider the second question—When should you start saving?—first. The answer is, as soon as possible, even if you can afford only a modest amount and have only a hazy idea about how much will be needed in retirement. Starting early puts the power of compounding on your side, which never should be taken lightly. For example, suppose you are 25 and you want to accumulate $200,000 by age 65. Starting a savings program immediately and investing at, say, a 10% rate requires a monthly investment of a mere $31.63. But, waiting until you are age 45 to begin will then require $263.38 a month. That's almost nine times as much; true, your needs between ages 45 and 65 should be less than between 25 and 45, but it's doubtful they will be nine times less.

How much you will need in retirement depends upon how you want to live. If you are fairly typical, the budget information in the accompanying table (based on Census Bureau data) should be helpful. Most people need about 70% to 80% of their preretirement income, but don't rule out the possibility that you will have a different situation that could require more. Along this line, notice the sharp increase in health care costs. Clearly, these expenses can vary considerably from one family to another.

Retirement Living Expenses	How They Change in Retirement: Percent of Pre- Retirement Expenses	As a Percent of the Retiree's Budget
Housing	57%	32%
Food	59	17
Transportation	43	17
Health care	158	12
Clothing	41	4
Entertainment	38	4
Other (includes personal care, insurance, and contributions	43	15
Total	—	100%

funds. In contrast to variable life, which might offer death benefits at two to three times the amount of the initial investment, a variable annuity has no insurance protection.

As with universal life, variable life and variable annuities often have high annual maintenance fees and/or a high initial load. These have lowered the returns on most contracts in relation to returns you could have earned investing

Variable life and variable annuities have become popular because of their tax-deferring opportunities.

in similar assets on your own. Despite poor returns, these contracts have become exceptionally popular recently because they offer tax-deferring advantages. Such advantages will be explained later in this chapter.

DESIGNING THE PORTFOLIO FOR RETIREMENT

For many investors, their most important investment goal is to have sufficient funds to help them *enjoy* their retirement years. The word *enjoy* is emphasized for a reason: many people today no longer look upon retirement as a time to diminish their interests and activities in preparation for death. Indeed, today's elderly see retirement as an opportunity to accomplish goals previously unattainable because of work's demands. Retirees in the past might have been willing to accept whatever Social Security and the company pension provided them, and to scale down living standards if those amounts were inadequate to maintain them, but not so today. Living a comfortable and enriched life in retirement takes funds—and careful planning during the work years to make sure those funds are available.

Planning for Retirement

Planning for retirement involves three steps: First, you must estimate your living expenses in retirement; second, you must determine the proportion of those expenses that will be met by Social Security and employer-provided plans, and third, you must build a portfolio to provide additional retirement funds, if they are needed. These steps are explained below, using Martin and Francine Dixon as an example. The Dixons have prepared retirement plans recently, even though they are quite young. They recognize that investing for retirement is a long process and the sooner it is begun, the better are its chances for success.

Retirement Living Expenses   To estimate retirement living expenses, you first must decide how you wish to live in retirement. The Dixons have chosen to maintain a lifestyle similar to their current situation, which requires a budget of about $40,000 a year. However, because of certain savings, such as somewhat lower income taxes and the fact that their home mortgage will be paid off, they feel $30,000 a year will be adequate. This estimate is the first input on the worksheet shown in Exhibit 20.10.

> Consider inflation in determining the budget in the retirement years.

However, the Dixons are in their early 30s and won't start retirement for another 30 years. Clearly, any inflation over their working years will require a higher budget estimate. Column 5 shows the impact of an estimated annual rate of inflation of 4%. To maintain a $30,000 budget in current dollars will take $97,302 in future dollars. The 4% estimate seems realistic to the Dixons; of course, it could prove completely wrong, but at least it's a start and it provides a benchmark to reference portfolio returns that must be estimated later in the process.

Social Security and Employer-Provided Income   The next step is to estimate annual retirement income provided by Social Security and employer-provided

EXHIBIT 20.10

A retirement plan for Martin and Francine Dixon

Present ages: early 30s
Planned retirement date: 30 years in future

Item	(1)	(2) Current Amount	(3) Assumed Annual Growth Rate	(4) Compound Value Factor*	(5) Amount at Retirement (2) × (4)
1. Living expenses		$30,000	4%	3.2434	$ 97,302
Income					
2. Social Security		11,000	4%	3.2434	35,677
3. Employer-provided plans		9,000	6%	5.7434	51,691
					87,368
4. The "gap" = (1) − [(2) + (3)]		—	—	—	$ 9,934

5. Expected rate of return on assets held during retirement years	0.06
6. Retirement assets needed = (4) ÷ (5)	$165,567
7. Expected rate of return on assets held prior to retirement = 10%	
8. Future value annuity factor (ordinary annuity) at 10% for 30 years*	164.49
9. Annual investment required = (6) ÷ (8)	$ 1,007

*See Chapter 3 for a discussion of future value techniques.

retirement plans. As Exhibit 20.10 shows, the Dixons begin by determining how much would be available if retirement took place immediately; as you see, their estimates are $11,000 for Social Security and $9,000 for employer plans. Each of these must also consider future inflation.

Social Security benefit computations are indexed to the CPI and, so, will increase at the 4% inflation rate. The Dixons are less sure of their employer plans. These plans have beaten past inflation rates by an average of 2 percentage points, leading the Dixons to assume the same performance in the future. This means the annual retirement income from the two sources are $35,677 and $51,691, totalling $87,368. Subtracting this total from the required retirement income of $97,302 leaves an annual income shortage of $9,934. This is the retirement income gap the Dixons must provide for by themselves.

Social Security benefits are indexed to inflation.

Designing the Portfolio to Meet Retirement Needs The $9,934 gap must be closed either with income earned by holding retirement assets or by gradually liquidating the assets during retirement. This choice brings into focus another aspect of retirement planning: the amount you wish to leave your heirs at death. While not the most pleasant of topics, it nevertheless must be addressed or the retirement portfolio cannot be estimated. Some people hope to build a portfolio of sufficient size so they can live from its income in retirement and then pass it intact at death. Of course, there are many different wishes here, but this one makes planning convenient because you then do not have to consider depleting (or, possibly, increasing) the portfolio during the retirement years. The Dixons have made that assumption, as Exhibit 20.10 shows.

Beginning with the $9,934 requirement, they first estimate the rate of return they expect to earn on the retirement portfolio. As you see, this is 6%. Dividing $9,934 by 0.06 indicates the portfolio must have a value of $165,567. The Dixons have 30 years to achieve this target—this fact is certain. They are unsure, though, of what they will earn each year on their investments prior to retirement, so they must estimate a figure, and their estimate is 10%. Using the future value of an annuity approach (see Chapter 3, and assume an ordinary annuity OA), the annual investment the Dixons must make is $1,006.55 Their comprehensive investment plan, then, must allocate about $1,007 each year for retirement.

You must choose investment assets that will meet your return objective. If you select a return that is not guaranteed, then an element of risk enters the picture. For example, at the time the Dixons were planning, a 10% rate was not guaranteed, although it seemed realistic in light of their estimate of inflation. Specifically, they intended to invest in equity mutual funds, using any tax-sheltering or tax-deferring arrangements available. They are aware that a retirement plan requires periodic monitoring to determine if its assumptions are still appropriate or if they require revising. A change in the inflation rate or portfolio rate of return could lead to substantial changes in the annual required investment. A serious investor includes an annual retirement portfolio review as an important part of his or her investment approach.

Using Self-Directed Investment Plans

A key to successful self-directed investment plans is to use tax-favored arrangements. These can increase investment accumulations substantially over the years prior to retirement, as we will see below. The three most popular devices are IRAs, Keogh Plans, and 401(k) plans.

The IRA   The individual retirement account—IRA—has been called the perfect tax shelter. While this might be stretching it a bit, nevertheless, an IRA is a quick and effective way to save and invest for retirement. You set up an IRA by simply signing a form at the financial institution where you plan to invest—a bank, savings and loan, stockbrokerage firm, insurance company, or others—and your investment becomes an IRA; specifically, it allows up to $2,000 to be deducted in computing your taxable income. Notice that an IRA is not an investment itself, as some people mistakenly believe.

While IRAs are simple to start and maintain, they have several limitations. First, you can invest no more than $2,000 a year or the amount of your earned income (usually, wages or salaries), whichever is the smaller; also, you can invest up to $250 for a spouse with no earned income. Second, the maximum tax deduction is allowed only if income does not exceed $40,000 on a joint return or $25,000 for a single filer. You gradually lose the deduction as income exceeds these limits; however, you still can use IRAs for tax deferral.

Keogh Plans A Keogh plan is like an IRA except that it is based on self-employment income and allows far greater annual deductions. You also can borrow from a Keogh, which is a very useful way of getting money out of the account without paying a penalty. For these reasons, a Keogh is probably a better deal than the IRA, and if you have self-employment income you should investigate its possibilities. Many financial institutions will be helpful in providing information on establishing and maintaining a Keogh plan, and they also will serve as the plan's trustee.

Keoghs are available for people with self-employment income.

A 401(k) Plan In contrast to an IRA or Keogh, a 401(k) plan is made available, on an optional basis, by an employer. The amount you choose to invest is taken out of pre-tax dollars, so a 401(k) has the same tax advantages as the other two. Moreover, since many employers will match your contribution, either partially or fully, the 401(k) can become the best of the three. It also allows for annual contributions in excess of $2,000 and borrowing without penalty. By all means, determine if your employer has a 401(k) and, if so, obtain as much information as you can about the plan.

Employers frequently match employee contributions to 401(k) plans.

Investment Accumulations Choosing not to use a retirement plan could be a costly mistake, as Exhibit 20.11 shows. Column 6 indicates how much a $1,000 initial investment grows over time, assuming no retirement plan is used. As you see, the accumulation is $8,051 after 30 years, assuming a 10% pre-tax return and 7.2% after-tax, and all annual earnings reinvested at the latter rate.

Columns 2 and 3 indicate accumulations under the assumption that an investor uses a retirement technique that allows a deduction for the initial investment and further allows all annual earnings to be reinvested at the pre-tax rate. The plan could be a Keogh, 401(k) or IRA (assuming the maximum income limitation is not exceeded). Column 2 indicates accumulations before considering taxes that would apply when funds are withdrawn, while Column 3 allows for such taxes. As you see, even after making the allowance, the accumulation after 30 years is almost twice that of using no retirement plan.

Columns 4 and 5 show accumulations assuming a situation that allows reinvested earnings to be tax-deferred but does not allow a deduction for the initial investment. This situation describes the use of an IRA after income exceeds the maximum limitation for a deduction. Also, other tax-deferred annuities—not necessarily associated with retirement—would be applicable here. As you see, the 30-year accumulation in column 5 is less than in situation 1, but it still exceeds situation 3 by a considerable amount. Finally, you should note the long-term nature of retirement investing. Tax advantages become meaningful only after long periods of time. As Exhibit 20.11 indicates, even after a period as long as 10 years, the advantages are slight and probably not worth the illiquidity the tax shelters impose. However, after 20 or 30 years, the differences seem well worth the disadvantages.

Tax-deferral advantages are important, but only after many years do accumulations justify the poor interim liquidity.

EXHIBIT 20.11

Amounts accumulated from a $1,000 investment assuming three tax situations: (1) investment is deductible and earnings are deferred, (2) investment is not deductible but earnings are deferred, and (3) no deduction and no deferral

Assumptions:	Funds earn a pretax return of 10%.
	Marginal tax rate is 28%.
	Marginal tax rate does not change over time.

(1)	(2)	(3)	(4)	(5)	(6)
	Situation 1		Situation 2		
Year	Before Tax on Withdrawals	After Tax on Withdrawals	Before Tax on Withdrawals	After Tax on Withdrawals	Situation 3
0	$ 1,280	$ 922	$ 1,000	$ 1,000	$ 1,000
1	1,408	1,014	1,100	1,072	1,072
2	1,540	1,109	1,210	1,151	1,149
3	1,704	1,227	1,331	1,238	1,232
.					
.					
.					
10	3,320	2,390	2,594	2,147	2,004
.					
.					
.					
20	8,611	6,200	6,728	5,124	4,007
.					
.					
.					
30	22,335	16,081	17,449	12,843	8,051

Planning in Retirement

Portfolio planning *in* retirement involves a different set of considerations than planning *for* retirement. To begin with, the process of budgeting and living within one's means becomes a reality rather than a plan. Inflation still must be considered during the retirement years, particularly if it accelerates and strains the resources accumulated for retirement. Also, the portfolio is usually restructured, with riskier assets being replaced by those with less risk. Finally, estate planning becomes a more important factor, although, as we noted above, it must be considered very early in planning for retirement.

Budgeting in the Retirement Years As retirement begins, many retirees find that a relatively large portion of their income becomes fixed. The fixed income is a consideration among many employer-provided pensions, and it also arises when whole life insurance policies are converted to annuities. As long as inflation

Often, retirement income is fixed while living expenses escalate.

Is There a Replacement for the IRA?

It's just like the government to toss you an easy tax shelter, wait until everybody starts using it, then take it away. So it has been with the IRA, in the opinion of some critics. Actually, the IRA wasn't eliminated: All taxpayers can still use them to defer taxes, regardless of how much they make. But it has been put on an equal footing with other tax-favored investments for people whose incomes exceed the limits for deducting IRA contributions. This group of people must now weigh the advantages and disadvantages of the IRA in comparison with other choices.

What are the other choices? Investment advisors usually compare IRAs to variable annuities or municipal bonds. If you also want some life insurance protection, you can include universal and variable life policies in making comparisons.

From a tax point of view, a variable annuity has the same liquidity problem as an IRA, since withdrawals before age 59½ face a 10% penalty. An annuity's advantage is you can invest as much as you like, while an IRA has a $2,000 annual limit. However, you have far greater investment flexibility with an IRA, and it shouldn't be too hard to beat the performance record of most variable-annuity and variable-life funds.

The less-than-spectacular performance of annuity contracts leads many advisors to suggest municipal bonds as the better alternative to an IRA. Municipal bond interest is free of federal income tax; unfortunately, this means they offer relatively low returns to begin with. Still, even though tax deferring helps to accumulate asset value, taxes eventually must be paid at withdrawal time. It's almost impossible to determine which will have the better after-tax return—an IRA investment or municipals—since the investment-withdrawal period will encompass virtually an entire lifetime. But, you have perfect withdrawal flexibility with municipals—an advantage not to be taken lightly if there is a chance you may need the funds before age 59½.

Universal and variable life insurance policies also offer tax-deferring advantages and no limits on the amount you can invest. An advantage they offer over a variable annuity is ability to borrow on the policy. You can withdraw funds without penalty at low rates of interest; moreover, if insurance is in force at death, proceeds pass to heirs free of any income tax (although estate taxes may apply). Insurance policies, though, have higher annual expenses and other features that might not be important to you if you are not interested in the insurance part of the investment.

All things considered, finding an IRA substitute will not be easy. You should consider first the importance of liquidity and insurance protection, and then do comparative shopping among the many annuity products on the market. Like mutual funds, annuities present a wide array of investment features and return potential.

remains relatively tolerable (perhaps 3% a year or less), the loss of purchasing power is not dramatic, although it can be serious if the retiree has a long life. Naturally, at high inflation rates, you are forced either to reduce your living standards considerably or to deplete retirement assets, thereby reducing your estate. It is important to understand that the retirement planning discussed above and expressed in Exhibit 20.10 assumes no change in inflation during the retirement years. The inflation factor must be included in the analysis if inflation appears to be a serious problem. We will not rework the example to show inflation's impact, but the Dixons obviously could have a problem with their employer-provided income, forcing them either to accumulate more than $165,567 or to reduce the final estate they pass to their heirs.

The Portfolio in Retirement   There is no simple answer to the inflation problem. Perhaps being aware of it and then attempting to select assets that provide inflation-indexed income is the only solution. For example, you might choose to take the cash value of your life insurance policies, rather than converting them to annuities, and do your own investing. We saw in Chapter 3 that Treasury bills offered returns that about equalled the inflation rate over a long period of time. While there is no assurance this will continue—that is, the bill return is not contractually indexed to inflation—it is quite likely to do so. Or, U.S. Series EE bonds might be an appropriate choice for funds not needed immediately. These are indexed by contract to rates of return on Treasury securities. If you are willing to accept some default risk, you can consider adjustable-rate bonds.

Unfortunately, if you choose assets with variable returns, you often must forego the potentially higher returns with fixed-income assets. Moreover, your income will fluctuate—a situation many retirees wish to avoid. Clearly, investing in retirement is no different from investing at other times: we cannot have our cake and eat it too. If we want to protect against escalating inflation, we must accept both variable income and lower returns if the inflation rate diminishes.

At some point, we must consider arranging our portfolios for our heirs' conveniences, rather than for our own.

Investments and the Estate Plan   At some point, we must address the prospect of arranging our portfolios for our heirs' convenience rather than for our own. To meet this objective, we try to organize our assets in a fashion that makes transfer easy and minimizes the amount of estate tax. Doing so might call for another complete restructuring of the portfolio, with the above two factors being the primary considerations. **Estate planning** is a complex subject, involving both legal and tax factors. Therefore, generalization is difficult. However, there are usually advantages in beginning to distribute assets before death. These advantages derive from the tax law that allows credits to each spouse in determining the estate tax liability, and also allows deductions of annual gifts up to $20,000 (each spouse consenting) to children or other donees. These substantial estate tax savings should not be overlooked.

Distributing wealth before death offers important tax savings.

The larger the estate, perhaps the larger the potential savings. But even estates as small as $600,000 can benefit from effective planning. While this amount might seem large to you, actually it isn't. Inflation has elevated most investors' incomes and estates, and a home worth half the above amount is not uncommon today in some parts of the U.S. Even modest inflation rates over the next 20 or 30 years will put many families above the threshold level when estate taxes begin, although the government is likely to increase the estate tax credit to adjust for inflation.

SUMMARY

Internationalizing an investment portfolio offers the potential advantages of higher return and less risk. Higher return is possible because other parts of the world are growing more rapidly than the U.S. and less risk is possible because returns on foreign investments are often poorly correlated to returns on U.S. investments. Disadvantages of internationalization include exchange-rate and political risks. Internationalization can be achieved through direct investment in foreign securities (through ADRs), by investing in U.S. multinationals, and by investing in international, global, and world income funds.

Life insurance is often considered when investment choices are made, because it is part of an investor's total estate. Popular forms of life insurance are term life, whole life, universal life, and variable life. Choosing between term and whole life often involves an estimate of the results of buying term and investing the difference.

Considering retirement requires both planning for retirement and planning during retirement. In the case of the former, it is necessary to estimate retirement living expenses and income from Social Security and employer-provided plans. If such income is inadequate, the gap must be managed by the investor through self-directed plans. These investments should be made using the advantages of tax shelters such as IRAs, Keogh plans, and 401(k) plans. The portfolio during retirement is often adjusted to increase safety of principal and to plan for its eventual transfer to heirs. At this point, estate planning becomes important.

KEY TERMS

Select the alternative that best identifies the key terms.

1. exchange-rate risk
2. political risks
3. American depository receipts (ADRs)
4. international fund
5. global fund
6. world income fund
7. term life insurance
8. whole life insurance
9. universal life policy
10. variable life insurance
11. estate planning

a. the most inexpensive form of life insurance
b. unpleasant, complex topic important to your heirs
c. arises because values of currencies change
d. holds U.S. and foreign securities
e. what you own when you invest in most foreign companies
f. a hybrid of insurance and investment
g. arise because foreign countries lack the U.S.'s strength
h. holds only foreign securities
i. a policy that includes term insurance plus a side investment account
j. similar to universal life insurance
k. invests in bonds issued in foreign countries

REVIEW QUESTIONS

1. Explain and discuss two advantages of internationalizing a portfolio.
2. Discuss the various risks associated with an internationalized portfolio.
3. Explain three methods of internationalizing a portfolio. Which method do you favor? Give reasons for your choice.
4. Suppose you decide to invest in an international fund. How will its performance be influenced by: *(a)* strengthening of the dollar, and *(b)* weakening of the dollar?
5. What justifications are there for considering life insurance as an investment? Explain.
6. Discuss how your life insurance needs can change throughout your life. Discuss the "gap" as it applies to life insurance planning.
7. Compare and contrast: term life insurance, whole life insurance, universal life insurance, and variable life insurance.
8. Suppose you are considering either a whole life or a term policy. How should you analyze the decision? Discuss important factors that should be considered.
9. How does planning *for* retirement differ from planning *in* retirement? Also, what role does inflation play in each case? Discuss.
10. Discuss three steps in planning for retirement.
11. Explain the "gap" in retirement planning and how it is closed.
12. Explain IRAs, Keoghs, and 401(k) plans; and then discuss the advantages of accumulating funds with an IRA, investing in a tax-deferral plan, and investing with no deduction and no deferral.
13. Explain why and how you might restructure your portfolio, given considerations of estate planning.

PROBLEMS AND PROJECTS

1. Art Finkle is thinking of investing in German companies but he is concerned that the dollar will appreciate relative to the mark next year. Suppose the current exchange rate is 2 marks to the dollar, but Art thinks it will appreciate to 3 marks to the dollar. He expects to earn a 10% rate of return without considering the exchange rate shift. Determine his rate, assuming the shift takes place.
2. Flora Luckett is trying to decide if she should purchase term life insurance or a whole life policy. Each insurance would last five years. The annual premiums on the policies are: $200 for term and $1,500 for whole life. The cash value of the whole life policy at its maturity is $8,000.
   a. If Flora can earn 10% on her other investments (comparable in risk and tax treatment to the whole life policy), which is the better alternative? Show your calculations.
   b. What other factors should Flora consider before making a choice? Explain.
3. Assume you are 25 years old and plan to retire at age 65. Based on today's prices, you figure that you will need $40,000 annually to enjoy your retirement, and if you retired today, you could expect to receive $8,000 a year from Social Security and $5,000 a year from an employer-provided plan, which has shown an annual growth rate of 5% a year that you think will continue in the future. You also think inflation will be 3% annually until and during retirement.
   a. If $40,000 is adequate today, how much will you need at age 65?
   b. Determine the annual income from Social Security and the retirement plan when you retire.

c. Assuming your portfolio will match the inflation rate during the retirement years, and your portfolio held for retirement will earn 8%, determine how much you must invest each year to achieve your retirement goals. (Assume that you wish to pass your retirement portfolio intact to your heirs.)

4. Lars and Greta Oyen's parents are advancing in age but are in rather good health. The senior Oyenses have been very successful in farming and currently own an estate worth $2 million. The farm property is worth $1 million and the balance is invested in a portfolio of growth stocks and long-term bonds. Lars and Greta are concerned that their parents could die unexpectedly. A $2 million estate would be taxed very heavily and they lack sufficient funds to pay such taxes. However, there is a good chance the folks could live another 20 years. Both Lars and Greta have successful careers of their own and neither is interested in running the farm.

a. What step could the elder Oyenses take now to reduce the estate tax? Assuming each lives 20 years, how much of the estate could be passed to Lars and Greta?

b. What estate planning steps might be appropriate in the Oyens' situation?

5. *(Student Project)* Contact a local insurance agent and ask him or her to describe briefly a whole life policy and a universal life policy that could be written specifically for you. Assume you want $100,000 of protection. Then, ask for cost and other details of a term policy for the same amount. Assume you are interested in constant-level term and wish to maintain coverage until age 60.

CASE ANALYSES

**20.1
The Tiants
Consider Life
Insurance**

Leo and Maria Tiant are expecting their first child shortly. Maria will resign her position as a personnel director and devote full time to managing the household. Leo will continue his position as an agricultural economist with a large seed company where he earned $60,000 last year. The Tiants will need considerably more insurance on Leo's life when the baby arrives. They have been reviewing policies with an agent but are having difficulty making a decision. They regard themselves as having a very low tolerance for risk and preferring a high-consumption lifestyle. Their attempts at budgeting in the past have not been very successful.

The agent favors a whole life policy with a $300,000 face value (an amount paid to Maria, or other beneficiary, in the event of Leo's death). Annual premiums would be $5,000 and the policy would have a guaranteed cash value of $292,000 at the end of 25 years—the length of time the Tiants feel insurance is most needed. The agent also indicated that term insurance for $300,000 could be written with a level annual premium of $1,400.

Questions

a. Assume the Tiants have a 30% marginal tax rate and could earn 10% on their investments over the next 25 years; which form of insurance is the better investment? Show how you arrive at your answer.

b. Which form would you recommend for the Tiants? Explain your selection.

20.2
The Markleys
Plan for
Retirement

Delbert and Florence Markley have operated a motel on a major interstate highway for the past 15 years. The business has been quite successful, enabling the Markleys to enjoy a high standard of living while educating their three children. They have accumulated a modest amount of savings—$15,000—that is currently invested in certificates of deposit. However, Del and Flo, now in their early 40s, have not done any retirement planning. Because they are self-employed, their retirement years could be a disaster if they can't sell the motel at a reasonable price, or if their children intend to operate the business. Recognizing potential future problems, the Markleys have decided to draft a retirement plan and adhere to it over the next 20 years.

If they retired today, Del and Flo would need $40,000 a year to enjoy the lifestyle they desire. Of course, considerably more will be needed in 20 years if inflation averages 3% a year, as they anticipate. Flo called Social Security to determine the amount a retiring couple in a situation similar to theirs would receive if retirement occurred today. This amount was $12,000. The Markleys plan to live off the current income their retirement nest egg will provide, and they will pass the principal amount to their children as part of their will. Moreover, they intend to invest in securities that will match inflation, thereby covering rising living costs during the retirement years. Flo is somewhat familiar with time-value-of-money concepts, although she has not worked with them for many years. Neither she nor Del understands possible income tax implications of retirement planning. Flo had intended to "rough out" an amount they need to save and invest each year, based upon an assumption their investments would yield 15% before taxes and 10% after, since they estimate a marginal tax rate of 33%. They also believe their investments will yield 8% after taxes during their retirement years. The Markleys would like you to assist and advise them in drafting a retirement plan.

Questions

a. Determine the amount needed to meet annual living expenses in retirement. Also, determine the amount covered by Social Security and the "gap." Finally, indicate the retirement assets needed during the retirement years.

b. What portion of the "gap" will their current savings of $15,000 provide, assuming it is invested at the after-tax rate?

c. Considering your response to questions *a* and *b,* determine how much the Markleys must invest each year prior to retirement, again assuming the after-tax rate applies.

d. Suppose the Markleys can use a tax-sheltering arrangement that would allow them a $15,000 tax deduction immediately if the funds are invested under the shelter. How much would this accumulate over the 20-year period, also assuming reinvested earnings are tax deferred? How much would accumulate if a tax deduction could not be taken at the time of investing but all reinvestments are tax-deferred? Compare these amounts (after allowing for taxes on withdrawals) to your response to question *c.* (Point of concern: Tax-deferred investing involves certain complexities in the Markleys case since they do not anticipate reducing the principal accumulated at the time of retirement. This approach could lead to eventual problems since withdrawals are now required after a certain age, and it complicates any estate plan they may draw up later.)

Bettner, Jill. "Elderly Come Down with Tax Headaches." *The Wall Street Journal*, March 17, 1989, p. C1.

Eaton, Leslie. "If You're Bearish on Japan." *Barron's*, February 27, 1989, p. 13.

Giltenan, Edward. "The Tax Shelter That's Still Left." *Forbes*, February 6, 1989, pp. 132–33.

Herman, Tom, and Constance Mitchell. "Dollar's Rise Is Bad News for Holders of Foreign Bonds." *The Wall Street Journal*, May 19, 1989, p. C1.

"How to Get Financial Security the Rest of Your Life." *Money*, November 1986, pp. 70–110. (This is a series of seven articles dealing with retirement planning.)

"International Investing." *Forbes*, June 26, 1989, pp. 194–209. (This is a series of four articles dealing with foreign investing.)

Kallen, Barbara. "What's Under the Rock?" *Forbes*, February 23, 1987, pp. 134–35.

"The New World of Life Insurance." *Money*, March 1987, pp. 140–94. (This is a series of five articles discussing the investment quality of life insurance in light of the 1986 Tax Reform Act.)

Peers, Alexandra. "Currency Warrants May Be Sucker's Bet." *The Wall Street Journal*, July 11, 1989, p. C1.

Slater, Karen. "Whole Life Insurance Regains Pre-Eminent Position." *The Wall Street Journal*, June 22, 1989, p. C1.

Steptoe, Sonja. "Trusts with Insurance Find New Life." *The Wall Street Journal*, March 15, 1989.

Vertin, James. *International Equity Investing*. Charlottesville, VA: Institute of Chartered Financial Analysts, March 1984.

HELPFUL
READING

APPENDIX

Time Value of Money Tables

Period	1%	2%	3%	4%	5%	6%	7%	8%	9%	10%	12%	14%	15%	16%	18%	20%	24%	28%	32%	36%
1	1.0100	1.0200	1.0300	1.0400	1.0500	1.0600	1.0700	1.0800	1.0900	1.1000	1.1200	1.1400	1.1500	1.1600	1.1800	1.2000	1.2400	1.2800	1.3200	1.3600
2	1.0201	1.0404	1.0609	1.0816	1.1025	1.1236	1.1449	1.1664	1.1881	1.2100	1.2544	1.2996	1.3225	1.3456	1.3924	1.4400	1.5376	1.6384	1.7424	1.8496
3	1.0303	1.0612	1.0927	1.1249	1.1576	1.1910	1.2250	1.2597	1.2950	1.3310	1.4049	1.4815	1.5209	1.5609	1.6430	1.7280	1.9066	2.0972	2.3000	2.5155
4	1.0406	1.0824	1.1255	1.1699	1.2155	1.2625	1.3108	1.3605	1.4116	1.4641	1.5735	1.6890	1.7490	1.8106	1.9388	2.0736	2.3642	2.6844	3.0360	3.4210
5	1.0510	1.1041	1.1593	1.2167	1.2763	1.3382	1.4026	1.4693	1.5386	1.6105	1.7623	1.9254	2.0114	2.1003	2.2878	2.4883	2.9316	3.4360	4.0075	4.6526
6	1.0615	1.1262	1.1941	1.2653	1.3401	1.4185	1.5007	1.5869	1.6771	1.7716	1.9738	2.1950	2.3131	2.4364	2.6996	2.9860	3.6352	4.3980	5.2899	6.3275
7	1.0721	1.1487	1.2299	1.3159	1.4071	1.5036	1.6058	1.7138	1.8280	1.9487	2.2107	2.5023	2.6600	2.8262	3.1855	3.5832	4.5077	5.6295	6.9826	8.6054
8	1.0829	1.1717	1.2668	1.3686	1.4775	1.5938	1.7182	1.8509	1.9926	2.1436	2.4760	2.8526	3.0590	3.2784	3.7589	4.2998	5.5895	7.2058	9.2170	11.703
9	1.0937	1.1951	1.3048	1.4233	1.5513	1.6895	1.8385	1.9990	2.1719	2.3579	2.7731	3.2519	3.5179	3.8030	4.4355	5.1598	6.9310	9.2234	12.166	15.916
10	1.1046	1.2190	1.3439	1.4802	1.6289	1.7908	1.9672	2.1589	2.3674	2.5937	3.1058	3.7072	4.0456	4.4114	5.2338	6.1917	8.5944	11.805	16.059	21.646
11	1.1157	1.2434	1.3842	1.5395	1.7103	1.8983	2.1049	2.3316	2.5804	2.8531	3.4785	4.2262	4.6524	5.1173	6.1759	7.4301	10.657	15.111	21.198	29.439
12	1.1268	1.2682	1.4258	1.6010	1.7959	2.0122	2.2522	2.5182	2.8127	3.1384	3.8960	4.8179	5.3502	5.9360	7.2876	8.9161	13.214	19.342	27.982	40.037
13	1.1381	1.2936	1.4685	1.6651	1.8856	2.1329	2.4098	2.7196	3.0658	3.4523	4.3635	5.4924	6.1528	6.8858	8.5994	10.699	16.386	24.758	36.937	54.451
14	1.1495	1.3195	1.5126	1.7317	1.9799	2.2609	2.5785	2.9372	3.3417	3.7975	4.8871	6.2613	7.0757	7.9875	10.147	12.839	20.319	31.691	48.756	74.053
15	1.1610	1.3459	1.5580	1.8009	2.0789	2.3966	2.7590	3.1722	3.6425	4.1772	5.4736	7.1379	8.1371	9.2655	11.973	15.407	25.195	40.564	64.358	100.71
16	1.1726	1.3728	1.6047	1.8730	2.1829	2.5404	2.9522	3.4259	3.9703	4.5950	6.1304	8.1372	9.3576	10.748	14.129	18.488	31.242	51.923	84.953	136.96
17	1.1843	1.4002	1.6528	1.9479	2.2920	2.6928	3.1588	3.7000	4.3276	5.0545	6.8660	9.2765	10.761	12.467	16.672	22.186	38.740	66.461	112.13	186.27
18	1.1961	1.4282	1.7024	2.0258	2.4066	2.8543	3.3799	3.9960	4.7171	5.5599	7.6900	10.575	12.375	14.462	19.673	26.623	48.038	85.070	148.02	253.33
19	1.2081	1.4568	1.7535	2.1068	2.5270	3.0256	3.6165	4.3157	5.1417	6.1159	8.6128	12.055	14.231	16.776	23.214	31.948	59.567	108.89	195.39	344.53
20	1.2202	1.4859	1.8061	2.1911	2.6533	3.2071	3.8697	4.6610	5.6044	6.7275	9.6463	13.743	16.366	19.460	27.393	38.337	73.864	139.37	257.91	468.57
21	1.2324	1.5157	1.8603	2.2788	2.7860	3.3996	4.1406	5.0338	6.1088	7.4002	10.803	15.667	18.821	22.574	32.323	46.005	91.591	178.40	340.44	637.26
22	1.2447	1.5460	1.9161	2.3699	2.9253	3.6035	4.4304	5.4365	6.6586	8.1403	12.100	17.861	21.644	26.186	38.142	55.206	113.57	228.35	449.39	866.67
23	1.2572	1.5769	1.9736	2.4647	3.0715	3.8197	4.7405	5.8715	7.2579	8.9543	13.552	20.361	24.891	30.376	45.007	66.247	140.83	292.30	593.19	1178.6
24	1.2697	1.6084	2.0328	2.5633	3.2251	4.0489	5.0724	6.3412	7.9111	9.8497	15.178	23.212	28.625	35.236	53.108	79.496	174.63	374.14	783.02	1602.9
25	1.2824	1.6406	2.0938	2.6658	3.3864	4.2919	5.4274	6.8485	8.6231	10.834	17.000	26.461	32.918	40.874	62.668	95.396	216.54	478.90	1033.5	2180.0
26	1.2953	1.6734	2.1566	2.7725	3.5557	4.5494	5.8074	7.3964	9.3992	11.918	19.040	30.166	37.856	47.414	73.948	114.47	268.51	612.99	1364.3	2964.9
27	1.3082	1.7069	2.2213	2.8834	3.7335	4.8223	6.2139	7.9881	10.245	13.110	21.324	34.389	43.535	55.000	87.259	137.37	332.95	784.63	1800.9	4032.2
28	1.3213	1.7410	2.2879	2.9987	3.9201	5.1117	6.6488	8.6271	11.167	14.421	23.883	39.204	50.065	63.800	102.96	164.84	412.86	1004.3	2377.2	5483.8
29	1.3345	1.7758	2.3566	3.1187	4.1161	5.4184	7.1143	9.3173	12.172	15.863	26.749	44.693	57.575	74.008	121.50	197.81	511.95	1285.5	3137.9	7458.0
30	1.3478	1.8114	2.4273	3.2434	4.3219	5.7435	7.6123	10.062	13.267	17.449	29.959	50.950	66.211	85.849	143.37	237.37	634.81	1645.5	4142.0	10143.
40	1.4889	2.2080	3.2620	4.8010	7.0400	10.285	14.974	21.724	31.409	45.259	93.050	188.88	267.86	378.72	750.37	1469.7	5455.9	19426.	66520.	*
50	1.6446	2.6916	4.3839	7.1067	11.467	18.420	29.457	46.901	74.357	117.39	289.00	700.23	1083.6	1670.7	3927.3	9100.4	46890.	*	*	*
60	1.8167	3.2810	5.8916	10.519	18.679	32.987	57.946	101.25	176.03	304.48	897.59	2595.9	4383.9	7370.1	20555.	56347.	*	*	*	*

APPENDIX A.1

Future value of $1 at the end of n periods: $FV = (1.0 + i)^n$

Number of Periods	1%	2%	3%	4%	5%	6%	7%	8%	9%	10%	12%	14%	15%	16%	18%	20%	24%	28%	32%	36%
1	1.0000	1.0000	1.0000	1.0000	1.0000	1.0000	1.0000	1.0000	1.0000	1.0000	1.0000	1.0000	1.0000	1.0000	1.0000	1.0000	1.0000	1.0000	1.0000	1.0000
2	2.0100	2.0200	2.0300	2.0400	2.0500	2.0600	2.0700	2.0800	2.0900	2.1000	2.1200	2.1400	2.1500	2.1600	2.1800	2.2000	2.2400	2.2800	2.3200	2.3600
3	3.0301	3.0604	3.0909	3.1216	3.1525	3.1836	3.2149	3.2464	3.2781	3.3100	3.3744	3.4396	3.4725	3.5056	3.5724	3.6400	3.7776	3.9184	4.0624	4.2096
4	4.0604	4.1216	4.1836	4.2465	4.3101	4.3746	4.4399	4.5061	4.5731	4.6410	4.7793	4.9211	4.9934	5.0665	5.2154	5.3680	5.6842	6.0156	6.3624	6.7251
5	5.1010	5.2040	5.3091	5.4163	5.5256	5.6371	5.7507	5.8666	5.9847	6.1051	6.3528	6.6101	6.7424	6.8771	7.1542	7.4416	8.0484	8.6999	9.3983	10.146
6	6.1520	6.3081	6.4684	6.6330	6.8019	6.9753	7.1533	7.3359	7.5233	7.7156	8.1152	8.5355	8.7537	8.9775	9.4420	9.9299	10.980	12.135	13.405	14.798
7	7.2135	7.4343	7.6625	7.8983	8.1420	8.3938	8.6540	8.9228	9.2004	9.4872	10.089	10.730	11.066	11.413	12.141	12.915	14.615	16.533	18.695	21.126
8	8.2857	8.5830	8.8923	9.2142	9.5491	9.8975	10.259	10.636	11.028	11.435	12.299	13.232	13.726	14.240	15.327	16.499	19.122	22.163	25.678	29.731
9	9.3685	9.7546	10.159	10.582	11.026	11.491	11.978	12.487	13.021	13.579	14.775	16.085	16.785	17.518	19.085	20.798	24.712	29.369	34.895	41.435
10	10.462	10.949	11.463	12.006	12.577	13.180	13.816	14.486	15.192	15.937	17.548	19.337	20.303	21.321	23.521	25.958	31.643	38.592	47.061	57.351
11	11.566	12.168	12.807	13.486	14.206	14.971	15.783	16.645	17.560	18.531	20.654	23.044	24.349	25.732	28.755	32.150	40.237	50.398	63.121	78.998
12	12.682	13.412	14.192	15.025	15.917	16.869	17.888	18.977	20.140	21.384	24.133	27.270	29.001	30.850	34.931	39.580	50.894	65.510	84.320	108.43
13	13.809	14.680	15.617	16.626	17.713	18.882	20.140	21.495	22.953	24.522	28.029	32.088	34.351	36.786	42.218	48.496	64.109	84.852	112.30	148.47
14	14.947	15.973	17.086	18.291	19.598	21.015	22.550	24.214	26.019	27.975	32.392	37.581.	40.504	43.672	50.818	59.195	80.496	109.61	149.23	202.92
15	16.096	17.293	18.598	20.023	21.578	23.276	25.129	27.152	29.360	31.772	37.279	43.842	47.580	51.659	60.965	72.035	100.81	141.30	197.99	276.97
16	17.257	18.639	20.156	21.824	23.657	25.672	27.888	30.324	33.003	35.949	42.753	50.980	55.717	60.925	72.939	87.442	126.01	181.86	262.35	377.69
17	18.430	20.012	21.761	23.697	25.840	28.212	30.840	33.750	36.973	40.544	48.883	59.117	65.075	71.673	87.068	105.93	157.25	233.79	347.30	514.66
18	19.614	21.412	23.414	25.645	28.132	30.905	33.999	37.450	41.301	44.599	55.749	68.394	75.836	84.140	103.74	128.11	195.99	300.25	459.44	700.93
19	20.810	22.840	25.116	27.671	30.539	33.760	37.379	41.446	46.018	51.159	63.439	78.969	88.211	98.603	123.41	154.74	244.03	385.32	607.47	954.27
20	22.019	24.297	26.870	29.778	33.066	36.785	40.995	45.762	51.160	57.275	72.052	91.024	102.44	115.37	146.62	186.68	303.60	494.21	802.86	1298.8
21	23.239	25.783	28.676	31.969	35.719	39.992	44.865	50.422	56.764	64.002	81.698	104.76	118.81	134.84	174.02	225.02	377.46	633.59	1060.7	1767.3
22	24.471	27.299	30.536	34.248	38.505	43.392	49.005	55.456	62.873	71.402	92.502	120.43	137.63	157.41	206.34	271.03	469.05	811.99	1401.2	2404.6
23	25.716	28.845	32.452	36.617	41.430	46.995	53.436	60.893	69.531	79.543	104.60	138.29	159.27	183.60	244.48	326.23	582.62	1040.3	1850.6	3271.3
24	26.973	30.421	34.426	39.082	44.502	50.815	58.176	66.764	76.789	88.497	118.15	158.65	184.16	213.97	289.49	392.48	723.46	1332.6	2443.8	4449.9
25	28.243	32.030	36.459	41.645	47.727	54.864	63.249	73.105	84.700	98.347	133.33	181.87	212.79	249.21	342.60	471.98	898.09	1706.8	3226.8	6052.9
26	29.525	33.670	38.553	44.311	51.113	59.156	68.676	79.954	93.323	109.18	150.33	208.33	245.71	290.08	405.27	567.37	1114.6	2185.7	4260.4	8233.0
27	30.820	35.344	40.709	47.084	54.669	63.705	74.483	87.350	102.72	121.09	169.37	238.49	283.56	337.50	479.22	681.85	1383.1	2798.7	5624.7	11197.9
28	32.129	37.051	42.930	49.967	58.402	68.528	80.697	95.338	112.96	134.20	190.69	272.88	327.10	392.50	566.48	819.22	1716.0	3583.3	7425.6	15230.2
29	33.450	38.792	45.218	52.966	62.322	73.639	87.346	103.96	124.13	148.63	214.58	312.09	377.16	456.30	669.44	984.06	2128.9	4587.6	9802.9	20714.1
30	34.784	40.568	47.575	56.084	66.438	79.058	94.460	113.28	136.30	164.49	241.33	356.78	434.74	530.31	790.94	1181.8	2640.9	5873.2	12940.	28172.2
40	48.886	60.402	75.401	95.025	120.79	154.76	199.63	259.05	337.88	442.59	767.09	1342.0	1779.0	2360.7	4163.2	7343.8	22728.	69377.	*	*
50	64.463	84.579	112.79	152.66	209.34	290.33	406.52	573.76	815.08	1163.9	2400.0	4994.5	7217.7	10435.	21813.	45497.	*	*	*	*
60	81.669	114.05	163.05	237.99	353.58	533.12	813.52	1253.2	1944.7	3034.8	7471.6	18535.	29219.	46057.	*	*	*	*	*	*

APPENDIX A.2

Future value of $1 annuity: $\text{FV} = \left[\dfrac{(1.0 + i)^n - 1.0}{i} \right]$

Period	1%	2%	3%	4%	5%	6%	7%	8%	9%	10%	12%	14%	15%	16%	18%	20%	24%	28%	32%	36%
1	.9901	.9804	.9709	.9615	.9524	.9434	.9346	.9259	.9174	.9091	.8929	.8772	.8696	.8621	.8475	.8333	.8065	.7813	.7576	.7353
2	.9803	.9612	.9426	.9246	.9070	.8900	.8734	.8573	.8417	.8264	.7972	.7695	.7561	.7432	.7182	.6944	.6504	.6104	.5739	.5407
3	.9706	.9423	.9151	.8890	.8638	.8396	.8163	.7938	.7722	.7513	.7118	.6750	.6575	.6407	.6086	.5787	.5245	.4768	.4348	.3975
4	.9610	.9238	.8885	.8548	.8227	.7921	.7629	.7350	.7084	.6830	.6355	.5921	.5718	.5523	.5158	.4823	.4230	.3725	.3294	.2923
5	.9515	.9057	.8626	.8219	.7835	.7473	.7130	.6806	.6499	.6209	.5674	.5194	.4972	.4761	.4371	.4019	.3411	.2910	.2495	.2149
6	.9420	.8880	.8375	.7903	.7462	.7050	.6663	.6302	.5963	.5645	.5066	.4556	.4323	.4104	.3704	.3349	.2751	.2274	.1890	.1580
7	.9327	.8706	.8131	.7599	.7107	.6651	.6227	.5835	.5470	.5132	.4523	.3996	.3759	.3538	.3139	.2791	.2218	.1776	.1432	.1162
8	.9235	.8535	.7894	.7307	.6768	.6274	.5820	.5403	.5019	.4665	.4039	.3506	.3269	.3050	.2660	.2326	.1789	.1388	.1085	.0854
9	.9143	.8368	.7664	.7026	.6446	.5919	.5439	.5002	.4604	.4241	.3606	.3075	.2843	.2630	.2255	.1938	.1443	.1084	.0822	.0628
10	.9053	.8203	.7441	.6756	.6139	.5584	.5083	.4632	.4224	.3855	.3220	.2697	.2472	.2267	.1911	.1615	.1164	.0847	.0623	.0462
11	.8963	.8043	.7224	.6496	.5847	.5268	.4751	.4289	.3875	.3505	.2875	.2366	.2149	.1954	.1619	.1346	.0938	.0662	.0472	.0340
12	.8874	.7885	.7014	.6246	.5568	.4970	.4440	.3971	.3555	.3186	.2567	.2076	.1869	.1685	.1372	.1122	.0757	.0517	.0357	.0250
13	.8787	.7730	.6810	.6006	.5303	.4688	.4150	.3677	.3262	.2897	.2292	.1821	.1625	.1452	.1163	.0935	.0610	.0404	.0271	.0184
14	.8700	.7579	.6611	.5775	.5051	.4423	.3878	.3405	.2992	.2633	.2046	.1597	.1413	.1252	.0985	.0779	.0492	.0316	.0205	.0135
15	.8613	.7430	.6419	.5553	.4810	.4173	.3624	.3152	.2745	.2394	.1827	.1401	.1229	.1079	.0835	.0649	.0397	.0247	.0155	.0099
16	.8528	.7284	.6232	.5339	.4581	.3936	.3387	.2919	.2519	.2176	.1631	.1229	.1069	.0930	.0708	.0541	.0320	.0193	.0118	.0073
17	.8444	.7142	.6050	.5134	.4363	.3714	.3166	.2703	.2311	.1978	.1456	.1078	.0929	.0802	.0600	.0451	.0258	.0150	.0089	.0054
18	.8360	.7002	.5874	.4936	.4155	.3503	.2959	.2502	.2120	.1799	.1300	.0946	.0808	.0691	.0508	.0376	.0208	.0118	.0068	.0039
19	.8277	.6864	.5703	.4746	.3957	.3305	.2765	.2317	.1945	.1635	.1161	.0829	.0703	.0596	.0431	.0313	.0168	.0092	.0051	.0029
20	.8195	.6730	.5537	.4564	.3769	.3118	.2584	.2145	.1784	.1486	.1037	.0728	.0611	.0514	.0365	.0261	.0135	.0072	.0039	.0021
25	.7798	.6095	.4776	.3751	.2953	.2330	.1842	.1460	.1160	.0923	.0588	.0378	.0304	.0245	.0160	.0105	.0046	.0021	.0010	.0005
30	.7419	.5521	.4120	.3083	.2314	.1741	.1314	.0994	.0754	.0573	.0334	.0196	.0151	.0116	.0070	.0042	.0016	.0006	.0002	.0001
40	.6717	.4529	.3066	.2083	.1420	.0972	.0668	.0460	.0318	.0221	.0107	.0053	.0037	.0026	.0013	.0007	.0002	.0001	*	*
50	.6080	.3715	.2281	.1407	.0872	.0543	.0339	.0213	.0134	.0085	.0035	.0014	.0009	.0006	.0003	.0001	*	*	*	*
60	.5504	.3048	.1697	.0951	.0535	.0303	.0173	.0099	.0057	.0033	.0011	.0004	.0002	.0001	*	*	*	*	*	*

APPENDIX A.3

Present value of $1: $PV = \dfrac{1.0}{(1.0 + i)^n}$

Number of Periods	1%	2%	3%	4%	5%	6%	7%	8%	9%	10%	12%	14%	15%	16%	18%	20%	24%	28%	32%
1	0.9901	0.9804	0.9709	0.9615	0.9524	0.9434	0.9346	0.9259	0.9174	0.9091	0.8929	0.8772	0.8696	0.8621	0.8475	0.8333	0.8065	0.7813	0.7576
2	1.9704	1.9416	1.9135	1.8861	1.8594	1.8334	1.8080	1.7833	1.7591	1.7355	1.6901	1.6467	1.6257	1.6052	1.5656	1.5278	1.4568	1.3916	1.3315
3	2.9410	2.8839	2.8286	2.7751	2.7232	2.6730	2.6243	2.5771	2.5313	2.4869	2.4018	2.3216	2.2832	2.2459	2.1743	2.1065	1.9813	1.8684	1.7663
4	3.9020	3.8077	3.7171	3.6299	3.5460	3.4651	3.3872	3.3121	3.2397	3.1699	3.0373	2.9137	2.8550	2.7982	2.6901	2.5887	2.4043	2.2410	2.0957
5	4.8534	4.7135	4.5797	4.4518	4.3295	4.2124	4.1002	3.9927	3.8897	3.7908	3.6048	3.4331	3.3522	3.2743	3.1272	2.9906	2.7454	2.5320	2.3452
6	5.7955	5.6014	5.4172	5.2421	5.0757	4.9173	4.7665	4.6229	4.4859	4.3553	4.1114	3.8887	3.7845	3.6847	3.4976	3.3255	3.0205	2.7594	2.5342
7	6.7282	6.4720	6.2303	6.0021	5.7864	5.5824	5.3893	5.2064	5.0330	4.8684	4.5638	4.2883	4.1604	4.0386	3.8115	3.6046	3.2423	2.9370	2.6775
8	7.6517	7.3255	7.0197	6.7327	6.4632	6.2098	5.9713	5.7466	5.5348	5.3349	4.9676	4.6389	4.4873	4.3436	4.0776	3.8372	3.4212	3.0758	2.7860
9	8.5660	8.1622	7.7861	7.4353	7.1078	6.8017	6.5152	6.2469	5.9952	5.7590	5.3282	4.9464	4.7716	4.6065	4.3030	4.0310	3.5655	3.1842	2.8681
10	9.4713	8.9826	8.5302	8.1109	7.7217	7.3601	7.0236	6.7101	6.4177	6.1446	5.6502	5.2161	5.0188	4.8332	4.4941	4.1925	3.6819	3.2689	2.9304
11	10.3676	9.7868	9.2526	8.7605	8.3064	7.8869	7.4987	7.1390	6.8052	6.4951	5.9377	5.4527	5.2337	5.0286	4.6560	4.3271	3.7757	3.3351	2.9776
12	11.2551	10.5753	9.9540	9.3851	8.8633	8.3838	7.9427	7.5361	7.1607	6.8137	6.1944	5.6603	5.4206	5.1971	4.7932	4.4392	3.8514	3.3868	3.0133
13	12.1337	11.3484	10.6350	9.9856	9.3936	8.8527	8.3577	7.9038	7.4869	7.1034	6.4235	5.8424	5.5831	5.3423	4.9095	4.5327	3.9124	3.4272	3.0404
14	13.0037	12.1062	11.2961	10.5631	9.8986	9.2950	8.7455	8.2442	7.7862	7.3667	6.6282	6.0021	5.7245	5.4675	5.0081	4.6106	3.9616	3.4587	3.0609
15	13.8651	12.8493	11.9379	11.1184	10.3797	9.7122	9.1079	8.5595	8.0607	7.6061	6.8109	6.1422	5.8474	5.5755	5.0916	4.6755	4.0013	3.4834	3.0764
16	14.7179	13.5777	12.5611	11.6523	10.8378	10.1059	9.4466	8.8514	8.3126	7.8237	6.9740	6.2651	5.9542	5.6685	5.1624	4.7296	4.0333	3.5026	3.0882
17	15.5623	14.2919	13.1661	12.1657	11.2741	10.4773	9.7632	9.1216	8.5436	8.0216	7.1196	6.3729	6.0472	5.7487	5.2223	4.7746	4.0591	3.5177	3.0971
18	16.3983	14.9920	13.7535	12.6593	11.6896	10.8276	10.0591	9.3719	8.7556	8.2014	7.2497	6.4674	6.1280	5.8178	5.2732	4.8122	4.0799	3.5294	3.1039
19	17.2260	15.6785	14.3238	13.1339	12.0853	11.1581	10.3356	9.6036	8.9501	8.3649	7.3658	6.5504	6.1982	5.8775	5.3162	4.8435	4.0967	3.5386	3.1090
20	18.0456	16.3514	14.8775	13.5903	12.4622	11.4699	10.5940	9.8181	9.1285	8.5136	7.4694	6.6231	6.2593	5.9288	5.3527	4.8696	4.1103	3.5458	3.1129
25	22.0232	19.5235	17.4131	15.6221	14.0939	12.7834	11.6536	10.6748	9.8226	9.0770	7.8431	6.8729	6.4641	6.0971	5.4669	4.9476	4.1474	3.5640	3.1220
30	25.8077	22.3965	19.6004	17.2920	15.3725	13.7648	12.4090	11.2578	10.2737	9.4269	8.0552	7.0027	6.5660	6.1772	5.5168	4.9789	4.1601	3.5693	3.1242
40	32.8347	27.3555	23.1148	19.7928	17.1591	15.0463	13.3317	11.9246	10.7574	9.7791	8.2438	7.1050	6.6418	6.2335	5.5482	4.9966	4.1659	3.5712	3.1250
50	39.1961	31.4236	25.7298	21.4822	18.2559	15.7619	13.8007	12.2335	10.9617	9.9148	8.3045	7.1327	6.6605	6.2463	5.5541	4.9995	4.1666	3.5714	3.1250
60	44.9550	34.7609	27.6756	22.6235	18.9293	16.1614	14.0392	12.3766	11.0480	9.9672	8.3240	7.1401	6.6651	6.2492	5.5553	4.9999	4.1667	3.5714	3.1250

APPENDIX A.4

Present value of an annuity of \$1 per period for n period: $PV = \dfrac{1.0 - \dfrac{1.0}{(1.0 + i)^n}}{i}$

Index

Academic journals, investment
    information in, 56–57
Accounts, 44–46, 174–178
    cash, 44
    checking and NOW, 174–175
    in commodity futures trading,
        411–412
    discretionary, 46
    individual retirement accounts, 171,
        602
    margin, 44–46, 184–185
        bonds purchased with, 204
        in commodity futures trading, 412
        mechanics of, 45
    savings, 175–178
    of shareholders' equity, in business
        balance sheet, 262
Accumulation of funds
    calculated from historical rates of
        return, 90–92
    in retirement investments, 603–604
    in savings account, frequency of
        compounding affecting, 176
Adjustable-rate mortgages, 520–521
    based on adjustment index, 521
    frequency of adjustment in, 521
    maximum and minimum rates in, 521
Adjustable rate preferred stocks,
        339–341
    Dutch auction version of, 341
    performance of, 339–341
Adjustment index, adjustable-rate
        mortgages based on, 521
Advance/decline index, 302
Advice on investments
    expert opinions in, 534
    from full-service and limited-service
        firms, 40

Advice on investments, *continued*
    from investment advisory services, 51
Affordability of housing, 500–501
Agencies rating risks of debt
        instruments, 153–156
Aggressive management, compared to
        passive management, 4
Alpha values, 456–458
    of funds, 456–458
American Association of Individual
        Investors, 482
American Bond Exchange, 204
American depository receipts, 592
American Stock Exchange, 33
Analyst of securities, job of, 8
Analytical computer programs on
        investments, 54–56
Annual reports on common stocks,
        262–266
    sections of, 262–266
Annuity, 79
    annuity due type of
        future value of, 79–81
        present value of, 81–83
    calculation of, 83–84
    future value of, 79–81
    ordinary
        future value of, 79–81
        present value of, 81–83
    present value of, 81–83
    variable type of, 598–600
Antiques, as tangible investment, 543
Appreciation of price
    compared to income
        preference of investors concerning, 6
        from residential rental properties,
            509
    of personal residence, 496–499

Arbitrage
    with put and call options, 395–397
    with index futures, 428–429
Arbitrageurs, 396
Arbitration, binding, 43
Arrearage, dividend, investing in
        preferred stocks with, 344–345
Artworks, as tangible investment, 543
    Sotheby's Art Index on, 542
Asset allocation models, 569–570
    strategic models, 569–570
    tactical models, 570
Assets
    in balance sheet, 262–264
        current ratio to liabilities, 269
        and hidden assets, 265
        in total debt ratio, 270
    distributed to preferred stockholders in
        liquidation, 335
    key financial, historical returns from,
        86–90
    in portfolio, 559–560
        diversification of, 560
        selection of, 559–560
Attitudes of investors, 4–6
Average returns in holding period,
        75–77
Avoidance of income taxes, 23–24

Back-end loads of open-end funds,
        444–445
Balance sheet, 262–265, 268–271
    assets and liabilities in, 262–264
        current ratio of, 269
        hidden, 265
        in total debt ratio, 270
    debt/equity ratio in, 270
    function of, 262

Balance sheet, *continued*
  liquidity in, 268–270
  net working capital ratio to sales in, 268
  shareholders' equity account in, 262–263
  solvency in, 270–271
  strength of, 268–271
Balanced funds, 448
Bank(s)
  commercial, 171
  consumer, 172
  savings and loans or savings, 172
Banker, investment, job of, 9
Bankruptcy, recovery of bond investment in, 198
Barron's, investment information in, 53
Barron's Confidence Index, 302–304
Basis, in commodity futures trading, 417
Bear spreads
  in futures trading, 410
  in put and call options, 395
Bearer bonds, 200
Beating the market, 315
  in efficient market hypothesis, 315
  in insider trading, 316–317
Ben Graham NCAV rule, 263–264
Beneficiaries of trusts, 468
Best-effort basis, selling on, 19
Beta concept, 112–115
  calculation of values in, 112
  in estimation of returns on common stocks, 242–245
  in evaluation of portfolio performance, 565
  interpretation of values in, 112–113
  in management of market risk of common stocks, 242–248
  in measuring risk of funds, 456–458
  in modern portfolio theory, 584–585
  in portfolio design, 114
  problems with, 114–115
Binding arbitration, 43
Black-Scholes Model, in prediction of market values
  of convertible securities, 371
  of option securities, 360–361
Blind pool, in limited partnership, 479
Blue chip common stocks, 12, 234
Boesky, Ivan, 396
Bondholders of corporate bonds, rights of, 194–201
Bonds, 130–224
  agencies rating risks of, 153–156

Bonds, *continued*
  in bond index trusts, 472
  changes in price of, 144–148
  convertible, 13, 367–375
  corporate, 194–206. *see also* Corporate bonds
  default risk premium of, 92
  federal agency, 211–215
  indenture agreement of, 196
  long-term, historical returns on, 88–89
  maturity premium of, 92
  municipal, 215–218
  PIK
  tax laws on, compared to preferred stocks, 337–338
  Treasury, 178
    EE series, 179–180
    HH series, 180
  warrants attached with, 363
  yield of
    in Barron's Confidence Index, 302–304
    compared to preferred stocks, 337–338
  zero coupon, 135. *see also* Zero coupon bonds
Book value per share of common stocks, 264
Borrowing
  avoidance of, 183
  from credit cards, 187
  from life insurance policies, 185
  and liquidity management, 183–187
  loan sources in, 184–186
  in margin accounts, 184–185
  mortgage loans in, 516–522. *see also* Mortgage loans
  from retirement plans, 185
  from savings and loans banks, 172
  securities as collateral in, 185
Break-up value, 254
Breeding livestock, limited partnerships in, 480
Broker(s). *see* Stockbroker(s)
Brokerage firms. *see* Stockbrokerage firms
Bull spreads, in put and call options, 395
Bullion, gold, investment in, 538
Business Week, fund evaluation in, 460
Businesses
  balance sheet of, 262–265, 268–271
  economic cycles affecting, 279–286
  as market participants, 18
  risks of, related to security issuer, 119

Buy-and-hold approach to portfolio, 566–567
  advantages of, 566
  compared to timing methods, 566–567
  disadvantages of, 567
Buying
  of common stocks, by smart investors, 298–300
  of corporate bonds, mechanics of, 204–206
  in long position, 46
    of commodity futures, 410
  of odd lots, in purchases to sales ratio, 297
  of put and call options, 386–387
  right to, 384
  of Treasury securities, 208

Calculators, financial
  in future value calculations, 78, 80
  in present value calculations, 81, 82
  in rate of return calculations, 83–84
Call and put options, 13, 384–403. *see also* Put and call options
Capital, net working, 268
  ratio to sales, 268
Capital asset pricing model, 242–248, 581–585
Capital gains
  in maximum capital appreciation funds, 447
  in mutual funds, reinvestment of, 451
Capital losses, in income tax calculations, 23
Capital shares, in dual funds, 451
Capitalization of income approach in property valuation, 515
Careers in investments, 8–9
Cash account, 44
Cash dividends of common stocks, 232, 235
Cash flows, 134–137
  of business, in analysis of common stocks, 267–268
  from discount securities, 134–135
  discounted, in determination of expected returns from common stocks, 250–251
  from interest-bearing securities, 135–137
  from residential rental property, 503–504
Cash management, 168

Cash market, 408
    compared to futures market, 408
Cash position of investors, 298–299
Cash settlement, in option contracts,
        388
CATs (collateralized Treasury receipts),
        208–211
CD (certificate of deposit), 175
    negotiable, 181
Certificates
    of deposit, 175
        negotiable, 181
    equipment trust, 177
    of gold ownership, investment in, 438
Certification, for career in investments, 9
Certified Financial Planner, 9
Chartered Financial Analyst, 9
Chartered Financial Consultant, 9
Charts and graphs, on price of stocks,
        308–314
Checking accounts, 174
Chicago Board of Trade, changing
        structure of, 422–423
Claims
    on gold, investment in, 539
    residual, of stockholders, 232
Clearinghouse system in futures trading,
        413–414
Closed-end funds, 441–444
    discounts and premiums of, 443–444
    dual funds as, 451
    net asset value of, 441–442
Clubs, investment, 482–484
    advantages and disadvantages in,
        484
    organization and operation of, 483
    performance of, 482
    popularity of, 482
    tax laws on, 484
Coefficients
    of correlation, 153
    of covariance, 153
    of duration, 150–152
    of interest elasticity, 148–150
    of variation, in measuring investment
        risk, 104
Coins
    gold, investment in, 537–538
    rare collections of, as tangible
        investment, 544
Collateral
    in mortgage bonds of corporations,
        196–198
    securities used as, 185

Collateralized Treasury receipts (CATs),
        208–211
    creation of, 209
    popularity of, 210–211
    safety of, 209
    tax laws on, 211
Collectibles, as tangible investment,
        544–545
College education
    for career in investments, 9
Commercial banks, 171
Commercial paper, 181
Commercial real estate
    rental, investment in, 510
    vacancy rates for, 510
Commissions and fees
    in corporate bonds, 206
    in exercising rights, 366
    of full-service firms, 39
    of limited-service firms, 39
    in municipal bond trusts, 469
    in open-end funds, 444–445
        back-end loads in, 445
        front-end loads in, 445
        in 12b–1 plan, 445
    in put and call options, 344–345
    in tangible investments, 534
    in Treasury bills, 178
    in Treasury investment growth
        receipts, 210
Commodity futures, 414–419
    account for, 411–412
    advantages of, 417–418
    broker services in, 412–413
    buyers and sellers of, 410
    in Chicago Board of Trade, 422–
        423
    commodity funds in trading of,
        415–416
    contracts on, 13, 408–410
    deposit and margin requirement in,
        411–412
    disadvantages of, 417–418
    hedging in, 416–417
        basis changes affecting, 417
        mechanics of, 416
        perfect hedge in, 416
        problems in, 417
    investor protection in, 413
    losses in, 415
    margin calls in, 412
    marking to market in, 413–414
    money at risk in, 410
    in organized exchanges, 413–415

Commodity futures, continued
    quotations on, 409–410
    speculative trading of, 415–416
    trading of, 410–413
Common stocks, 12, 230–287
    advance/decline index on, 302
    annual reports on, 262–268
    balance sheet on, 262–265
    blue chip, 12, 234
    book value per share, 264
    buyers and sellers of, 296–300
    characteristics of, 230–237
    charts and graphs on price of,
        309–314
    convertible securities exchanged for
        shares of, 327–334
        conversion ratio in, 369
        conversion value in, 370
    cost control problems affecting,
        239–240
    cyclical, 235–236
    debt use of company affecting, 241
    defensive, 236
    dividends of, 233, 235
        per share, 250
        in stocks, 233
    earnings of company affecting,
        271–274
    earnings per share of, 249–251
    economic cycles affecting, 279–284
    in efficient markets, 314–320
    fundamental analysis of, 261–286
    growth, 234
    income, 234
    income statement on, 265–268
    industry analysis of, 284–286
    liquidity of, 238
    market activity in, interpretation of,
        300–304
    market position changes affecting,
        239
    new highs/new lows index on, 302
    odd-lot purchases ratio to odd-lot sales
        of, 297
    opportunities in, 234–236
    payout ratio of, 233
        estimation of, 250
    pressure indicators on, 296–308
    price/earnings ratio of, 250
    put and call options with, 385
    quotations on, 236–237
    returns on, 242–254
        beta concept applied to, 242,
        243–245

Common stocks, *continued*
    capital asset pricing model and
        securities market line on, 242–247
    current, 251
    dividend approach to, 251–253
    earnings approach to, 248–251
    expected, 248–254
    historical, 86–88
    minimum, 247–248
    reasonable estimates of, 243
    required, 242–248
    rights issued to, 366–367
    rights of stockholders of, 230–234
    risks of, 12, 238–242
        firm-specific and industry-specific,
            238–240
        high, 12
        inflation risk in, 238
        low and medium, 12
        market risk in, 241–242
    speculative, 236
    split of, 233–234
    technical analysis of, 295–320
    undervalued, 274–277
    warrants attached with, 363
Comparative sales approach in property
        valuation, 514–515
Compensation
    for assuming default risk, 143
    for giving up liquidity, 143
Compound interest, 79
    patterns of payment, and earnings of
        savings accounts, 176
Compound values, 79, 84–85
    and power of few extra years, 84–85
    and power of small additional yield, 84
Computer uses in investing, 54–56
Condominium housing, investment in,
        501–502
Confidence Index of Barron, 302–304
Consensus of experts, in forecasting
        economic cycles, 283–284
Constant ratio plan, 570–571
Consumer(s)
    credit card use of, 187
Consumer banks, 172
Consumer Price Index, 89–90
Continuous markets, definition of, 32
Contracts
    in commodity futures, 13, 408–409
        specifications of, 408
    in currency futures, 419–420
    gold claims in, 539
    in index futures, 427

Contracts, *continued*
    in interest rate futures, 420–421
    option, settlement of, 387–388
    in put and call options, 384–385
        settlement of, 387–388
Conventional mortgages, 459–462
Conversion ratio of convertible
        securities, 369
Conversion value of convertible
        securities, 370
Convertible securities, 13, 367–375
    Black-Scholes Model on, 370
    characteristics of, 368–369
    conversion ratio of, 369
    conversion value of, 370
    corporate bonds as, 201
    debt characteristics of, 368–369
    interest return on, 369
    investment opportunities in, 369–374
    option characteristics of, 369
    payback of, 372–373
    preferred stock as, 324
    sample of, 374–375
    value of, 370–372
        in conversion, 370
        as straight debt, 370
        theoretical market value, 372
Cooperative housing, investment in, 502
Corporate bonds, 194–206
    bearer, 200
    call option of, 203–204
    commissions and spreads in, 206
    convertible, 201
    floating rate, 202
    indenture of, 196
    interest payments of, 199–201
        on floating rate bonds, 202
    mechanics of buying, 204–206
    mortgage, 196–198
    put option of, 202–203
    quotations on, 205–206
    redemption of, 201
        serial, 201
    registered, 201
    rights of bondholders of, 195–201
    sinking fund of, 201
    special features of, 201–204
    trustee of, 196
    unsecured debenture, 198
Cost approach in property valuation, 514
Cost control problems, and risk of
        common stocks, 239–240
Covenants, restrictive, on preferred
        stocks, 234

Covered option writing, 387, 397–399
    example of, 397–399
    generalizations on, 398
Credit, for investments, sources of,
        184–187
Credit cards, borrowing from, 187
Credit unions, 172
Cross-sectional analysis of common
        stocks, 268
Cumulative dividends of preferred
        stocks, compared to
        noncumulative dividends, 331
Currency futures, 419–420
    contracts on, 419
    quotations on, 419
Current consumption, preference for, 143
Current ratio of assets and liabilities, 269
Current returns, 72–74
    on common stocks, 251
Current yield of debt instruments,
        137–138
Curve on yield, 157–160
    inverted, 158–160
    slope of, 304
Cycles
    of economy, 279–284
    of industry and business, 284–286
Cyclical common stocks, 235–236

Debentures, 198
    subordinated, 198–199
Debt/equity ratio, 270–271
Debt instruments, 11–12
    convertible securities as, 367–375
        value of, 370–372
    corporate bonds as, 194–206
    discount securities as, 134–135
    interest-bearing securities as,
        135–136
        forecasts on, 160–161
        historical analysis of, 157–161
        risks of, 144–154
    intermediate-term, 11–12
    liquidity of, 144–145
    long-term, 12, 157–160, 193–224
    maturity of
        and risk, 145–146
        yield to, 138–142
    municipal bonds as, 215–218
    rating of, 153–154, 218
    returns on, 134–144
        calculation of, 137–144
        cash flows in, 134–137
        interest rates in, 142–144

Debt instruments, *continued*
  and preference for current
      consumption, 143
  real and nominal, 143
  risks of, 144–154
    coupon rate affecting, 148
    default risk, 153–154
    maturity affecting, 148
    price and interest rate changes
        affecting, 148–153
    rating of, 154–155
    of zero coupon bonds, 148
  short-term, 11
  Treasury and agency issues as,
      207–215
  yield of, 137–142
    current, 137–138
    curve on, 157–160
    to maturity, 138–142
    and rating, 155–156
    from short- and long-term
        instruments, 156–160
    of Treasury bills, 138
Debt ratio, total, 270
Debt use of company, and risk of
      common stocks, 241
Default risk
  of bonds, premium paid for, 92
  compensation for, 153–154
  of debt instruments, 153, 153–155
    agencies rating, 153–155
  of municipal bonds, 217–218
    and municipal bond trusts, 468–470
  of preferred stocks, 344–345
Defensive common stocks, 236
Defensive techniques, 572–575
Deferring income taxes, 24
Deposits at financial institutions
  average national daily balances of, 175
  in checking and NOW accounts, 174
  in savings accounts, 175–178
Derivative instruments, 352
  option securities as, 356
Detached single-family homes,
      investments in, 501
Developmental programs, in energy
      resources limited partnership, 480
Deviation, standard, in risk
      measurement, 104
Diamonds
  as tangible investment, 541–543
  trust investment in, 472
Direct capitalization approach in
      property valuation, 515

Discount closed-end funds, 443–444
Discount securities
  cash flow from, 134–135
  yield to maturity, 138–140
Discretionary account, 46
Dispersion of returns, calculation of,
      103–104
  coefficient of variation in, 104
  standard deviation in, 104
  variance in, 103
Diversifiable risks, 110
  compared to nondiversifiable risks, 110
  elimination of, 560
Diversification of portfolio, 108–115
  eliminating random risks, 560
  international investments in, 118,
      588–594
  purposive, 110–111, 567–569
  random, 108–110
    number of securities to hold in,
        109–110
    returns in 108–109
  tangible investments in, 533
Dividends, 235
  of common stocks, 233–235
    in cash, 233
    dates in, 235
    in estimation of returns, 250
    liquidating, 235
    per share, 250
    ratio to earnings in payout ratio, 233
    reinvestment of, 235
    in stocks, 235
  as current return, 72
  growth of, and earnings of company,
      274
  importance of, 73
  of income stocks, 234
  of mutual funds, reinvestment of, 451
  of preferred stocks, 331
    agreement of, 334
    in arrears, 344
    cumulative and noncumulative, 331
    distribution of, 331
    in participating and
        nonparticipating stocks, 332
    rights of stockholders concerning, 331
    vote to pass, 331
Dollar cost averaging method, 571–572
"Double play trusts," 472
Dow Jones Averages, 63
  Industrial, 53, 63–64
    problems with, 64
  transportation, 63

Dow theory on market activity, 300
Dual funds, 450
  capital shares in, 450
  income shares in, 450
Duration coefficient, 150–152
  calculation of, 151–152
  interpretation and use of, 151–152
Duration concept of Macaulay, 150
Dutch auction rate preferred stock, 341

Earnings
  of common stocks, 249–251
    per share, 249–251
  and dividend growth, 274
  in price to earnings ratio
      compared to price to sales ratio, 276
  ratio to dividends in payout ratio, 233
  and returns on equity, 272–274
  and returns on investment, 272
  right of stockholders to share in,
      232–233
  strength measurement of, 271–274
    and risk of common stocks,
        271–274
  in times-interest-earned ratio, 272
Economic cycles, 279–284
  forecasting of, 280–286
    consensus of experts on, 283–284
    leading indicator series in, 281–283
  historical, 279–280
Education
  for career in investments, 9
EE series Treasury bonds, 179–180
Efficient frontier of investments,
      581–584
Efficient markets, 314–320
  definition of, 315
  hypothesis on, 315
  implications of, 319–20
  semistrong form of, 316–318
  strong form of, 318
  weak form of, 315–316
Elasticity coefficients, interest, 148–150
Emergency reserve of liquid assets, 169
Employer-provided income in retirement,
      600–601
Energy resources, limited partnerships
      in, 480
  developmental programs in, 480
  exploratory programs in, 480
  income programs in, 480
Enjoyment of tangible investments, 531
Equipment
  leasing of limited partnerships in, 480

Equipment, *continued*
trust certificates financing, 198
Equity investments, 226–345
common stocks as, 228–320
fundamental analysis of, 261–291
return and risk in, 230–255
preferred stocks as, 329–346
in real estate investment trusts,
421–422, 423
of shareholders
in business balance sheet, 262–263
in debt-equity ratio, 270–271
return on, 272–274
technical analysis of, 295–320
Estate planning, 606
life insurance in, 594–595
Estimating portfolio performance,
560–562
Exchange-rate risk, in international
investments, 590
Exchanges, organized, 32–34
American Stock Exchange, 33
in futures trading, 413–414
New York Stock Exchange, 33–35
Exercise price of option securities,
357–359
Expected return on investment, 102–103
Expert opinions
in forecasting economic cycles,
283–284
in tangible investments, 534
Exploratory programs, in energy
resources limited partnership, 480

Facilitation, financial
compared to financial intermediation,
16–18
definition of, 18
Farmerette Investment Club, 483
Federal agency bonds, 211–215
investment appeal of, 215
quotations on, 211
Federal Home Loan Mortgage
Corporation, 212
Federal Housing Administration
mortgages, 522
Federal Reserve banks
as source of investment information,
50–51
Treasury bills purchased in, 178
Treasury bonds purchased in, 208
Feeding livestock, limited partnerships
in, 480
FHA mortgages, 522

FIFO (first-in, first-out) calculation of
savings account balance, 177
Filters, 277
Financial calculators. *see* Calculators,
financial
Financial facilitation
compared to financial intermediation,
16–18
definition of, 18
Financial futures, 419–429
in Chicago Board of Trade, 422–423
in commodity funds, 419–429
in currency, 419–420
index, 427–429
interest rate, 420–427
Financial institutions, 171–174
accounts at, 174–178
checking and NOW, 174–175
savings, 175–178
types of, 171–174
Financial intermediation
compared to financial facilitation,
16–18
definition of, 17
Financial pages, quotations in. *see*
Quotations
Financial performance of company,
evaluation of, 268–279
cross-sectional, 268
historical, 268
Financial planner, job of, 8
Financial risk of security issuer, 119
Financial statements of common stocks,
262–268
balance sheet in, 262–265, 268–271
income statement in, 265–268
Financial World magazine, 55
Finite-life real estate investment trust,
474
Firms
common stock risks related to,
238–241
foreign, investments in, 591–594
industry analysis related to, 284–286
Fixed-rate mortgages, 516–520
and fixed payments in conventional
mortgages, 517–520
Floating rate bonds, 202
Floor brokers and floor traders, on New
York Stock Exchange, 35
Forbes magazine, 55
fund evaluation in, 460
Forecasting
charts and graphs in 309–314

Forecasting, *continued*
by default, 558
of economic cycles, 280–284
in estimating portfolio performance,
560–562
of interest rates, 160–161
of option security market value,
360–361
in portfolio construction, 558–559
pressure indicators in, 296–308
Super Bowl results in, 308
by trend projection, 558
Foreign investments, in international
diversification of portfolio,
591–594
Formula timing approach to portfolio
changes, 570–572
Formula value
of option securities, 356–357
of rights, 366–367
Fortune magazine, 55
401 (k) plan for retirement, 603
Fourth market, 38
Fraud, in tangible investments, 535, 543
Freddie Mac (Federal Home Loan
Mortgage Corporation), 211
Front-end loads of open-end funds,
444–445
Full-service stockbrokerage firms, 38–39
Fundamental analysis of common stocks,
261–286
Funds, 441, 444
alpha and beta values of, 456–458
balanced, 448
closed-end, 441–444
net asset value of, 441–442
dual, 450
family of, 444
growth, 447
income, 398, 447–448
index, 450
international and global, 592–594
junk, 447
managers of, performance of, 459–460
maximum capital appreciation, 447
money market, 449
objectives of, 446–450
open-end (mutual), 444–445
past performance summary on, 448
performance evaluation of, 452–460
on risk-adjusted basis, 456–458
popular press evaluations of, 460
returns on, 448
geometric average of, 454

Funds, *continued*
 in holding period for single year,
  452–453
 in holding period over time,
  454–456
 risk-adjusted rate of, 456–458
 risks of, 456–459
  in money market mutual funds, 182
  in sector funds, 449
 sector, 449
 selection of, 458–459
 specialized, 449–450
 Treynor Index on, 458
Future returns, 74–75
 of common stocks, 251
Future values, 77–81
 of annuity, 79–82
 compound, 79, 84–85, 154
 and power of few extra years, 84–85
 and power of small additional yield, 84
 of retirement investments, 601–602
 of single payment, 77–79
Futures, 408–433
 buyers and sellers of, 410
 characteristics of, 408–414
 in Chicago Board of Trade, 422–423
 clearinghouse system in, 413–414
 commodity, 414–419. *see also*
  Commodity futures
 contracts on, 13, 408–410, 419, 420,
  427
 financial, 419–429. *see also* Financial
  futures
 gold claims in, 539
 market traded in, 410–413
  compared to cash market, 408
 marking to market in, 413–414
 in organized exchanges, 413–414
 trading of, 410–413

Gems, precious
 as tangible investment, 541–543
 trust investment in, 472
General obligation municipal bonds,
 216
Geometric average of fund performance,
 454
Ginnie Maes (Government National
 Mortgage Association), 211, 213
 GNMA trusts investing in, 470–471
Global funds, investment in 592–594
GNMA trusts, 470–471
Goal setting, 6–7
 in portfolio construction, 555–558

Goal setting, *continued*
 and selection of specific assets,
  559–560
Gold, investment in, 535–539
 in bullion, 538
 in claim on gold, 539
 in coins, 537–538
 compared to other metals, 539–540
 in jewelry and artworks, 538
 in mining company stocks, 539
 in options and futures contracts, 539
 in ownership certificates, 538
 price volatility of, 536
 supply and demand affecting,
  536–537
Government
 federal agency bonds of, 211–215
 laws of, in regulation of securities
  markets, 41–44
 municipal bonds of, 215–218
 as source of investment information,
  49, 50
 Treasury securities of, 206–208
 units in, as market participants, 18
Government National Mortgage
  Association, 211–215
 GNMA trusts investing in, 470–471
Grantor of trusts, 468
Graphs and charts, on price of stocks,
  308–314
 evaluating use of, 313–314
 head and shoulders pattern in, 311
 interpretation of, 309–313
 point-and-figure, 309
 randomness in, 313–314
 support and resistance lines in,
  310–311
 time, 309
Growing equity mortgages, 520
Growth funds, 447
Growth stocks, 234
 and income, 234

Hardware of personal computers, for
  investing, 54–56
Head and shoulders pattern, in graphs
  on price of stocks, 311
Hedge ratios, 425–427
Hedging
 in commodity futures, 416–417
  basis changes affecting, 417
  mechanics of, 416
  perfect hedge in, 416

Hedging, *continued*
 problems in, 417
 in interest rate futures, 424–426
 in put and call options, 386, 390–
  392
 in tangible investments, 532–533
HH series of Treasury bonds, 180
Hidden asset, 265
Hidden asset plays, 265
High-risk common stocks, 12
Historical analysis
 of common stocks, 86–88, 268
 of economic cycles, 279–280
 of interest rates, 154–161
 of key financial assets, 86–88
 of real estate investment trusts, 476
 of returns on investments, 86–92
Hobbies, as tangible investment,
  544–545
Holding costs in tangible investments,
  534
Holding period return, 72
 average of, 75–77
 calculation of, 75–77
 of funds
  in single year, 452–453
  over time, 454–456
Home, investment in, 496–505. *see also*
  Housing, investment in
Households, as market participants, 18
Housing, investment in, 496–505
 affordability of, 500–501
 appeal of, 496–500
 in condominium, 501–502
 in cooperative housing, 502
 in detached single-family home, 501
 local influences on, 499
 mortgage payments on, 444–445
  compared to rent payments,
   502–505
  interest and principal in, 502
 in personal residence, 496–505
 price appreciation of, 496–499
 price volatility of, 500
 profitability of, 504–505
 rent-versus-buy decision concerning,
  502–505
 in rental property, 505–515
 supply and demand affecting,
  497–499
 tax laws on, 499–500, 509
 types of properties in, 501–502
 in vacation homes, 512–514
Hypothesis on efficient markets, 315

"In the money" call on option securities, 358

Income, compared to price appreciation
preference of investors concerning, 6
from residential rental properties, 506

Income funds, 447–448

Income programs, in energy resources
limited partnership, 480

Income shares, in dual funds, 450

Income statement on common stocks, 265–268
limitations of, 267–268
objective of, 267

Income stocks, 234
and growth, 234

Income tax, 21–24. see also Tax laws
avoidance of, 23
calculating liability for, 21
capital losses in calculation of, 23
deferring of, 23–24
marginal tax rate in, 22
progressive rate structure of, 22–23
savings in, as current return, 74

Indenture, bond, 196

Index(es), 63–65
adjustment index, as basis of
adjustable-rate mortgages, 520–521
advance/decline index, 302
Barron's Confidence Index, 302–304
Consumer Price Index, 89
market, 63–65
new highs/new lows index, 302
on-balance volume index, 301

Index funds, 450

Index futures, 427–429
arbitrage positions, 428–429
contracts on, 427
quotations on, 427
speculative trading in, 427–428

Indicators
leading, in forecasting economic
cycles, 281–282
pressure, 296–308
advance/decline index, 302
Barron's Confidence Index, 302–304
buyers and sellers, 296–300
cash position of institutions, 298
correct and false signals of, 306
Dow theory on, 300
evaluation of, 305–308
insider activity, 299
lead time of, 307
low-priced stock activity, 304

Indicators, continued
on market activity, 300–302
new highs/new lows index, 302
odd-lot ratio, 297
odd-lot short sales, 298
slope of yield curve, 304
volume of market activity, 301
of stock price, head and shoulders
graph pattern in, 311

Individual retirement accounts, 171, 602
alternatives to, 605

Industrial rental properties, investment
in, 510

Industry analysis of common stocks, 284–286
on industry and business cycles, 279–280
on new developments in industry, 285
related to individual firm, 285–286
on risks, 238–241

Inflation risk, 116
of common stocks, 238
tangible investments as hedge
against, 533

Information on investments
from computers, 54–56
expert opinions in, 283, 534
from full-service and limited-service
firms, 39–39
sources of, 49–56

Insider trading, 299
beating the market, 316–317

Insurance
as hedge position, 386
life insurance policies, 185, 595–600.
see also Life insurance
on municipal bonds, 218
in portfolio strategies, 594

Interest
compound, 79, 176
on convertible securities, 369
on corporate bonds, 199–201
in floating rate bonds, 202
as current return, 73
on debt instruments
expectations concerning, 142–144
forecasting of, 160–161
historical analysis of, 154–160
high real rate of, 146–147
on mortgage
in adjustable-rate mortgage, 520–521
in fixed rate mortgage, 516–517

Interest, continued
on municipal bonds, tax exempt, 215–216
on savings accounts, 176–178
frequency of compounding, 176
from day of deposit to day of
withdrawal, 176
on minimum balance, 177
securities bearing
cash flow from, 135–137
current yield of, 137
yield to maturity of, 138–142
in times-interest-earned ratio, 272
on Treasury securities, tax exempt, 207–208
and value of option securities, 360

Interest elasticity coefficients, 148–150

Interest rate futures, 420–427
contracts on, 421
hedging in, 420–422
quotations on, 421
trading of, 379–380, 420–427

Interest rate risk, 116–118
calculation of, 148–152
duration coefficients in, 150–152
interest elasticity coefficients in, 148–150
Macaulay's duration concept in, 150–152
of debt instruments, 148–152
of preferred stocks, 342–343

Intermediate-term debt instruments, 11–12

Intermediation, financial
compared to financial facilitation, 16–18
definition of, 17

International diversification of portfolio, 104–106, 588–594
advantages of, 588–589
direct investments in foreign
companies in, 591–592
disadvantages of, 589–591
international and global funds in, 592–594
methods of, 591–594
multinational corporations in, 592
returns on, 594
risks of, 118, 589–591

International funds, investments in, 592–594

Inverted yield curve, 158

Investment
concept of, 10
creation of, 15

Investment, *continued*
  definition of, 10
  steps in planning of, 14–15
Investment Advisors Act of 1940, 42
Investment advisory services, 51
Investment banker, job of, 9
Investment clubs, 482–484
Investment companies
  closed-end funds of, 441–444
  evaluating performance of, 452–460
  objectives and services of, 446–452
  open-end (mutual) funds of, 444–445
  pooling arrangements of, 436–490
Investment Company Act of 1940, 42
Investment professionals, 7–10
Investment strategies, 93–95
  long-term investing, 93
  short-term trading, 94
  exploiting economic cycles, 94
  defending against losses, 95
Investment trusts, 468–478. *see also*
      Trusts
Investors, 4–10
  aggressive and passive approaches of,
      4
  attitudes of, 5–7
  beginning, common mistakes of,
      16–17
  disposition towards risk, 5–7
  expectations concerning interest rates,
      159–160
  goals of, 6–7
    in portfolio construction, 555–558
  liquidity needs of, 6–7
  planning for retirement, 7, 600–602
  preference for current consumption,
      143
  preference for income versus price
      appreciation, 6
  professional, 7–10
    types of, 8–9
  protection of, 44
    in commodity futures trading,
      413
  psychological factors in decisions of,
      302–305
    Barron's Confidence Index on,
      302–304
  saving for large expenditure, 7
  smart
    cash position of, 298–299
    identification of, 296
    insiders as, 299–300
  speculating, 7

"Jefferson Trust," 472
Jewelry, gold, investment in, 538
Journals and magazines, investment
      information in, 49–56
Junk bonds, 199
Junk funds, 447

Keogh plans, 603

Laws, 41–44
  Investment Advisors Act of 1940, 42
  Investment Company Act of 1940,
      42
  Maloney Act of 1938, 42
  Securities Act of 1933, 41
  Securities Exchange Act of 1934,
      41–42
  Securities Investor Protection Act of
      1970, 44
  tax related, 21. *see also* Tax laws
  on time value of money, 85
  on truth in lending, 85
Lead time of pressure indicators, 307
Leading indicator series, in forecasting
      economic cycles, 281–283
Leasing
  of commercial and industrial rental
      properties, 510
  of equipment, limited partnerships in,
      480
Leverage-inherent investments, 11, 13,
      352–429
  commodity and financial futures in,
      13, 408–433
  convertible securities in, 13, 14–15,
      368–369
  margin accounts in, 184–185
  option securities in, 358–360
  put and call options in, 13, 384–403
  rights in, 366–367
  warrants in, 13, 363–366
Liabilities
  in business balance sheet, 262–264
    current ratio to assets, 269
    and hidden liabilities, 265
    in total debt ratio, 270
Life insurance, 594–600
  borrowing from, 185, 598
  determining need for, 594
  in estate plan, 594–595
  forms of, 595–600
  tax laws on, 597
  term, 595–596
    compared to whole, 596–598
  universal, 598

Life insurance, *continued*
  variable, 598–600
  whole, 596
    compared to term, 596–598
LIFO (last-in, first-out) calculation of
      savings account balance, 178
Limit order, 48–49
Limited partnerships, 478–481
  blind pool in, 479
  in energy resources, 480
  in equipment leasing, 480
  investment potential of, 481
  in livestock, 480
  money manager in, 484–485
  public and private syndicate, 479–480
  in real estate, 479–480
  tax laws on, 478, 481
Limited-service stockbrokerage firms,
      39–40
Liquid investment trusts, 472
Liquidating dividends, 235
Liquidity, 6–7, 168–191
  of accounts at financial institutions,
      174–176
  alternative types of, 174–176
  in balance sheet, 268–270
  borrowing and, 183–187
  of common stocks, 238
  compensation for loss of, 143
  emergency reserve of, 169–170
  of limited partnership interests, 481
  management of, 168–174
  of money market mutual funds,
      181–182
  of non-Treasury-issued securities, 181
  as store of value, 170
  of Treasury securities, 178–180
  for undertaking transactions, 168–169
  uses of, 168–170
  and yields on short-term investments,
      169
Livestock, limited partnerships in, 480
Living expenses in retirement
  budgeting of, 604–606
  planning for, 600
Loads in open-end funds
  front-end and back-end, 444–445
  and no-load funds, 444–445, 469
Loans, 183–187, 515–522. *see also*
      Borrowing
Long position, 46
  in commodity futures, 410
Long-term investments, 11, 194–218
  in corporate bonds, 194–206

Long-term investments, *continued*
historical returns on, 88–89
in municipal bonds, 215–218
in Treasury and agency issues,
206–215
Lorain Investment Club, 483
Losses, capital, in income tax
calculations, 23
Lottery winnings, time value of money
concept applied to, 85
Low-priced stocks, activity in, 304
Low-risk, common stocks, 12

Macaulay's duration concept, 150
Magazines and journals, investment
information in, 51–56, 460
Magnesium, as tangible investment,
541
Make delivery, in option contract
settlement, 387–388
Maloney Act of 1938, 42
Managers
of funds, performance of, 452–460
of money, in limited partnership,
484–485
of portfolio, job of, 8
Margin accounts, 44–46, 183–184
bonds purchased with, 204
in commodity futures trading
and margin calls, 412
requirements of, 412
mechanics of, 45
Marginal tax rate, 22, 24
Market(s)
and beating the market, 315
in efficient market hypothesis, 315
in insider trading, 316–317
cash, 408
continuous, definition of, 32
efficient, 315–320
fourth, 38
futures, 408
indexes on, 63–65
Dow Jones Industrial Average, 51,
63–64
Standard and Poor 500, 64–65
interpretation of activity in, 300–302
marking to, in futures trading,
413–414
over-the-counter, 35–38
participants in, 20–21
businesses, 20–21
government units, 20–21
households, 20–21

Market(s), *continued*
position changes in, and risk of
common stocks, 238
primary, 32
for resale of tangible investments,
534–535
secondary, 32
third, 38
volume of activity in, 300–302
Market contrarian, 570
Market order, 48
Market risks, 110
of common stocks, 241–242
causes of, 241
management of, 242
compared to random or diversifiable
risks, 110
premium for, 92
in put and call options, hedging of,
400–401
Market timing of portfolio changes,
567–569
Market value
of convertible securities, theoretical,
372
of option securities
determinants of, 359–361
minimum or formula, 356–357
prediction of, 360–361
Marketability risk, 120
Marking to market, in futures trading,
413–414
Maturity
of option securities, 359
and risk of debt instruments, 141
and spreads in put and call options,
393–394
Treasury securities with short
remaining maturities, 179
yield to, of debt instruments, 138–
142
Maximum capital appreciation funds,
447
Mechanical timing of portfolio changes,
570–572
Metals, precious, as tangible investment,
539–541
Minimum value of option securities,
356–357
Mining company stocks, gold,
investment in, 539
Modern portfolio theory, 581–585
Modification of portfolio, 566–575
Momentum of price, 312–313

Money magazine, 56
fund evaluations in, 460
Money managers in limited partnerships,
484–485
Money market deposit accounts, 175
Money market mutual funds, 181–182
characteristics of, 181–182
safety of, 182
varieties of, 182
Money at risk, in commodity futures,
410
Monitoring of portfolio, 560–565
Moody's
investment advisory service, 51
rating debt instruments, 154, 155
rating preferred stocks, 344
Mortgage bonds of corporations,
196–198
collateral in, 196–198
equipment trust certificates, 198
Mortgage loans, 516–522
adjustable-rate, 520–521
adjustment index in, 521
frequency of adjustment in, 521
rate maximum and minimum in,
521
affordable amount of, 500–501
compared to rent payments,
502–505
comparison of 15-year and 30-year
payments, 516–517
of Federal Housing Administration and
Veterans Administration, 522
for financing property investment,
515–522
fixed-rate, 516–517
fixed rate-fixed payment
(conventional), 517–520
growing equity, 520
interest and principal in, 501
sources of, 521–522
Mortgage trusts, 474
Moving average for odd-lot ratio,
297–298
Multinational corporations, investments
in, 592
Multiple growth rate, 252–253
Municipal bonds, 215–218
default risk of, 217–218
general obligation, 216
income tax advantage of, 215–216,
468–470
insured, 216
investment trusts in, 468–469

Municipal bonds, *continued*
    minimum investment in, 469
  put options on, 216–217
  rating of, 218
  revenue, 216
  types of, 216–217
  Washington Public Power Supply
    default on, 217
  zero coupon, 216
Mutual funds, 444–446
  back-end loads in, 445
  commissions and fees in, 444–445
  family of, 444
  front-end loads in, 444–445
  fund switching in, 451
  managers of, performance of, 459–460
  money market, 181–182, 449
  no-load, 444
  reinvestment of dividends and capital
    gains in, 451
  in retirement plans, 451–452
  services offered in, 450–452
  telephone transactions in, 451
  in 12b-1 plan, 445

Naked position, in put and call option,
    389–390
NASDAQ (National Association of
    Securities Dealers Automated
    Quotation), 36–37
  market indexes of, 65
National Association of Investment
    Clubs, 482
National Association of Securities
    Dealers Automated Quotation
    (NASDAQ), 36
  market indexes of, 65
Negotiable certificate of deposits, 181
Negotiated order of withdrawal (NOW)
    accounts, 174–175
Net asset value of closed-end funds,
    441–442
Net working capital, 268
  ratio to sales, 268–269
Net worth, in business balance sheet,
    262–264
Neutral spreads, in put and call options,
    394
New highs/new lows index, 302
New York Bond Exchange, 204
New York Stock Exchange, 34–35
  commission brokers in, 34–35
  floor brokers and floor traders in, 35

New York Stock Exchange, *continued*
  order execution on, 34–35
  seats on, 33
  specialists in, 35
    day in life of, 36–37
  as "The Big Board," 33
Newsletters, investment information in,
    49
Newspapers
  investment information in, 49–51
  quotations in. *see* Quotations
No-load funds, 444–445
Nominal returns, compared to real
    returns, 143
Noncumulative dividends of preferred
    stock, compared to cumulative
    dividends, 331
Nondiversifiable risks, 110. *see also*
    Market risks
Nonparticipating preferred stocks,
    compared to participating, 332
Notes, Treasury, with short remaining
    maturities, 179
NOW accounts, 174–175
Numismatics, 544–545

Odd lots, 297
  ratio of purchases to sales, 297–298
    moving average for, 298
  short sales of, 298
On-balance volume index, 301
Open-end funds, 444–445. *see also*
    Mutual funds
Open interest, in commodity futures, 409
Options, 356–361
  Black-Scholes Model on, 360–361
  contract settlement in, 387–388
  convertible, 367–375
  as derivative instrument, 356
  determinants of market value,
    359–361
  features of, 357
  gold claims in, 539
  "in the money" and "out of the
    money" calls concerning, 358
  interest rates affecting, 360
  as leverage-inherent investment,
    358–360
  maturity of, 359
  minimum or formula value of, 356–357
  number of shares controlled in, 359
  predicting market values of, 360–361
  premium paid for, 361

Options, *continued*
  price of underlying security affecting,
    359
  put and call, 11, 13, 383–405. *see also*
    Put and call options
  as right to buy, not obligation, 357
  strike or exercise price of, 357–359
Order execution, 48–49
  by full-service and limited-service
    firms, 40
  of limit order, 48–49
  of market order, 48
  on New York Stock Exchange, 34–35
  personal computers in, 55
  of stop order, 49
Organized exchanges, 32–33
  American Stock Exchange, 33
  in futures trading, 413–415
  New York Stock Exchange, 32–37
Originator of trusts, 468
"Out of the money" call on option
    securities, 358
Over-the-counter market, 35–38

Participants in market, 18
Participating preferred stocks, compared
    to nonparticipating, 332
Partnerships
  general, 478
  limited, 478–481
Passbook accounts, 175
Passing the dividend, 331
Passive management, compared to
    aggressive management, 4
Passthrough securities, 211–215, 470
Payback period of convertible securities,
    372–373
Payment-in-kind (PIK) preferred stock,
    332–333
Payout ratio of common stocks, 233
  estimation of, 250
Perpetuity, preferred stock issued in,
    336–337
  risks of, 342–345
Personal computers in investing, 54–56
Personal residence, investment in,
    496–505. *see also* Housing,
    investment in
Philately, 544–545
PIK bond, 200–201
Planner, financial, job of, 8–9
Planning investments, 14–15, 550–611
  construction of portfolio in, 554–560

Planning investments, *continued*
  internationalizing portfolio in, 588–594
  life insurance in, 594–600
  modern portfolio theory and capital
    asset pricing model on, 581–585
  modification of portfolio in, 566–575
  monitoring portfolio in, 560–566
  portfolio management in, 553–585
  for retirement needs, 600–606
  steps in, 14–15
Platinum, as tangible investment, 541
Play
  hidden asset, 265
  use of term, 265
Point and figure graph, on price of
  stocks, 309
Political risks of investment, 118
  in international diversification, 118,
    590–591
  tangible investments as hedge
    against, 532–533
Pooling arrangements, 14, 436–490
  blind pool in limited partnerships, 479
  funds in, 439–465
    money market mutual funds,
      181–182
  of investment companies, 439–465
  investment trusts in, 468–478
  limited partnerships in, 478–481
  self-directed, 481–485
    investment clubs in, 482–484
    money manager limited
      partnerships in, 484–485
Portfolios, 550–611
  buy-and-hold approach to, 566–567
  capital asset pricing model on,
    581–585
  in constant ratio plan, 570–571
  construction of, 554–560
    asset selection in, 559–560
    diversification in, 560
    forecasting investment environment
      in, 558–559
    goal-setting in, 555–560
    investment priorities in, 556–557
    setting risk levels in, 557–558
  definition of, 16, 554
  diversification of, 108–115. *see also*
    Diversification of portfolio
  in dollar cost averaging method,
    571–572
  efficient frontier of investments in
    581–584
  estimating performance of, 560–562

Portfolios, *continued*
  evaluating performance of, 562–565
    in absolute sense, 564–565
    in relative sense, 565
  insurance strategies for, 572–574
  international investments in, 118,
    588–594
  life insurance in, 594–600
  management of, 14, 553–585
    career in, 8
    computer programs on, 54–56
  of market contrarian, 570
  measuring performance of, 562–565
  modern portfolio theory on, 581–585
  modification of, 566–575
    stop orders in, 575
  monitoring of, 560–566
  option-bills in, 353–354
  purposive changes in, 110–111
  for retirement needs, 600–606
  returns on
    absolute and relative, 564–565
    expected, 560–562
    in international diversification, 588
    measurement of, 562–565
    in option-bills portfolio, 399–400
    in random diversification, 108–110
    rate of, 563–564
  risks in, 105–115, 554
    beta concept on, 112–115
    establishing tolerable level of, 557
    and insurance strategies, 594
    in international diversification, 118,
      588–594
    in purposive diversification,
      110–111
    in random diversification, 108–110
  tangible investments in, 472
  timing of changes in, 567–569
    advantages and disadvantages of,
      568
    difficulty of, 568
    empirical analysis of, 569
    market timing in, 568
    mechanical or formula plans in,
      570–572
    in variable ratio plan, 571
Positions, 46–48
  hedge, 390. *see also* Hedging
  long, 46
    in commodity futures, 410
  naked, in put and call options,
    389–390
  reversal of, 46

Positions, *continued*
  in option contract settlement, 387
  in put and call options, 387
  short, 46–48
    in commodity futures, 410
    in odd lot sales, 298
Precious gems, as tangible investment,
  541–543
Precious metals, as tangible investment,
  539–540
Predictions. *see* Forecasting
Pre-emptive right of stockholders of
  common stocks, 231–232
Preferred stocks, 12–13, 329–345
  adjustable rate, 339–341
    Dutch auction version of, 341
    performance of, 339–341
  assets distributed to stockholders of,
    in liquidation, 335
  call option of, 334, 337
    risks of, 337
  characteristics of, 330–335
  converted into common stocks, 334
  convertible securities exchanged for
    shares of, 367
  default risk of, 344–345
  dividends of, 331. *see also* Dividends,
    of preferred stocks
  interest rate risk of, 342–343
  issued in perpetuity, 336
    risks in, 337
  payment-in-kind (PIK), 332–333
  quotations of, 336
  rating of, 344–345
  restrictive covenants on, 334
  retirement of, 334
  returns on, 335–342
  rights of stockholders of, 331–334
  risks of, 342–345
  straight, 336–339
  tax laws on, 337–338
  yields of
    compared to bond yields, 337–
      339
    yield to call calculations in, 337
Premiums
  call, for right to call corporate bonds,
    203
  on closed-end funds, 443
  on life insurance, variable, 598
  on option securities, 361
  for risk, 92–93
Present value, 81–83
  of single payment, 81

Pressure indicators, 296–308. *see also* Indicators, pressure
Price
 appreciation of
  compared to income, 6, 509
  of personal residence, 496–499
  of residential rental properties, 506
  momentum, 312–313
 of bonds, changes in, 144–148
 to earnings ratio
  of common stocks, 250
  compared to price to sales ratio, 276
 of housing
  affordability of, 500–501
  local influences on, 499
  low volatility of, 500
  supply and demand affecting, 497–499
 of option securities, strike or exercise price, 357–359
 to sales ratio, compared to price to earnings ratio, 276
 of stocks
  activity in low-priced, 304
  graphs on, 309–314
  new highs/new lows index on, 302
  and volume of market activity, 301
 of tangible investments, volatility of, 534
 of gold, 536
Primary market, definition of, 31
Priorities in portfolio construction, 556–557
Private syndicate limited partnership, 479
Private trusts, 468
Probability estimates, in calculation of expected returns, 102–103
Professional investors, 7–10
Program trading, 429
Programs of personal computers, on investments, 54–56
Progressive rate structure of income tax, 22–23
Property investments, 14. *see also* Real estate
Property valuation methods, 514–515
 cost approach, 514
 comparative sales approach, 514–515
 capitalization of income approach, 515
 direct capitalization approach, 515
Prospectus, 41
Protection of investors, 41–44
 in commodity futures trading, 413

Psychological factors influencing investors, 106, 302–305
Public syndicate limited partnership, 479
Public trusts, 468
Purchase to sales ratio on odd lots, 297
Purposive modification of portfolio, 110–111
Put and call options, 13, 383–405
 arbitrage positions, 395–397
 brokerage commissions in, 384
 buyers and sellers of, 386–387
 cash settlement in, 388
 contracts on, 384
  settlement of, 387–388
 covered option writing in, 397–399
 definitions of, 384
 hedging in, 386, 390–392
 leverage quality of, 386
 making or taking delivery in, 387
 naked position in, 389–390
 in option-bills portfolio, 399–400
 quotations on, 385–386
 reversing position in, 387
 spreads in, 392–395
 and synthetic stocks, 392–393
 trading of, 384
  strategies in, 388–397

Quotations
 on commodity futures, 409–410
 on common stocks, 236–237
 on corporate bonds, 205–206
 on currency futures, 419
 on federal agency bonds, 211
 on index futures, 427
 on interest rate futures, 421
 on preferred stocks, 336
 on put and call options, 384–386
 on Treasury securities, 207–208

Random diversification of portfolio, 108–110
Random risks, 110
 compared to market risks, 110
 elimination of, 560
Random walk, 313
Randomness in price graphs, 313–314
Rate of return
 calculation of, 83–84
 from portfolio, 563
Rating agencies, 153–155, 344
Rating systems
 on debt instruments, 153–155
  municipal bonds, 218

Rating systems, *continued*
 on preferred stocks, 344
Ratios
 conversion, of convertible securities, 370
 current, of assets and liabilities, 269–270
 debt/equity, 270
 of dividends to earnings, in payout ratio, 233, 250
 of net working capital to sales, 268
 of odd lot purchases to sales, 297
 of price to earnings, 250
  compared to price to sales ratio, 276
 of price to sales, compared to price to earnings ratio, 276
 times-interest-earned ratio, 272
 total debt, 270–271
Real estate, 14
 investment trusts in, 474–477
  equity per share of, 476
  equity trusts in, 474
  finite-life, 474
  historical experiences with, 477
  mortgage trusts, 474
  regulations on, 474
  returns on, 476–477
  shares of, 468
  single-purpose, 475
  types of, 474–475
 limited partnership in, 479–480
 as tangible investment, 492–527
  financing of, 515–522
  in personal residence, 496–505
  in rental property, 505–515
  in vacation home, 512–514
Real returns, compared to nominal, 143
Receipts
 American depository, 592
 collateralized Treasury, 208–211
 Treasury investment growth, 208–211
Redemption of corporate bonds, 201
 put and call options concerning, 203–204
 serial, 201
Registered corporate bonds, 201
Reinvestment options
 in common stocks, 235
 in mutual funds, 451
Reinvestment risk, 153
Rental properties, investments in, 505–515
 in commercial or industrial properties, 510

Rental properties, investments in, *continued*
  lease agreements in, 510
  in residential properties, 496–505
    cash flow from, 502–503
    evaluation of, 506–509
    income compared to price appreciation in, 509
    tax laws on, 509
Reports, annual, on common stocks, 262–268
Resale markers, for tangible investments, 434–435
Research on investments
  by full-service and limited-service firms, 40
  with personal computer, 54–56
  sources of information in, 49–57
Reserve for emergencies, of liquid assets, 169
Residential properties, investments in, 496–509. *see also* Housing, investment in
Residual claim, of stockholders of common stocks, 232–233
Resistance and support lines, in price graphs, 310–311
Restrictive covenants on preferred stocks, 334–335
Retirement, 600–606
  designing portfolio for needs in, 600
  and estate planning, 606
  living expenses in, 604–605
    budgeting of, 600
  planning for, 7, 600–606
    accumulation of investments in, 603–604
    borrowing from funds in, 185
    401 (k) plan in, 603
    individual retirement accounts in, 171, 602, 605
    Keogh plans in, 603
    self-directed investment plans in, 601–602
    tax considerations in, 602–604
  portfolio management during, 606
  social security and employer-provided income in, 600–601
Retirement of preferred stocks, 334
Returns, 70–100
  in beating the market, 314–315
  on common stocks, 242–254. *see also* Common stocks, returns on
  in covered option writing, 397–399

Returns, *continued*
  current, 72–74
    on common stocks, 251
  on debt instruments, 134–144. *see also* Debt instruments, returns on
  dispersion of, 103–104
  from energy resources limited partnership, 480
  on equity, 272–274
  expected, 102–103
  on funds, 448
    risk-adjusted rate of, 458–459
  future, 74–75
    on common stocks, 251
  historical, 86–92
    and accumulation of wealth, 90–92
    on common stocks, 86–88
    on key financial assets, 86–92
    on long-term bonds, 88–89
    on Treasury bills and Consumer Price Index, 89–90
  in holding period, 72. *see also* Holding period returns
  on investment (ROI), 272
  nominal, compared to real returns, 143
  on personal residence investment, 504–505
  on portfolio. *see* Portfolio, returns on
  power of small additional yield and few extra years in, 84–85
  and preference for current consumption, 143
  on preferred stocks, 335–341
  and psychological factors affecting investment decisions, 106
  rate of
    calculation of, 83–84
    from portfolio, 563
  real, compared to nominal returns, 143
  on real estate investment trusts, 476–477
  and risk of investment, 102
  on tangible investments, 531–532
    compared to intangibles, 531–532
  and time value of money, 77–86
    determining future values, 77–81
    determining present values, 71–83
Revenue bonds, 216
Reversal of position, 46
  in option contract settlement, 387
  in put and call options, 387
Rights
  characteristics of, 366–367

Rights, *continued*
  commission fees in, 366
  creation of, 366
  failure to sell or exercise, 367
  formula value of, 366–367
  options as, 357
  trading of, 366
Rights of holders
  of bonds, 194–201
  of common stocks, 230–234
  of preferred stocks, 331–334
Risk(s), 100–120
  of collateralized treasury receipts and Treasury investment growth receipts, 208–211
  of common stocks, 238–246. *see also* Common stocks, risks of
  of debt instruments, 144–154. *see also* Debt instruments, risks of
  default. *see* Default risk
  and dispersion of returns, 103–105
  economic environment affecting, 115–116
  and expected returns, 102–103
  of funds, 182, 456–458
    of money market mutual funds, 182
    of sector funds, 449
  of futures trading
    in commodity funds, 415–416
    and investor protection, 413
    in spreads, 426
  of individual asset, measurement of, 102–105
  inflation, 116
    of common stocks, 238
    tangible investments as hedge against, 533
  interest rate, 116–118. *see also* Interest rate risk
  of international investments, 118, 589–591
  investor attitudes toward, 5–6
  of key financial assets, historical analysis of, 104–105
  market or nondiversifiable, 110. *see also* Market risks
  marketability, 120
  of maximum capital appreciation funds, 447
  of municipal bond trusts, 470
  political, 118
    in international investments, 589
    tangible investments as hedge against, 532–533

Risk(s) *continued*
  in portfolio, 105–115, 554. *see also*
    Portfolio, risks in
  of preferred stocks, 342–345
  premiums for, 92
    bond default risk premium, 92
    bond maturity premium, 92
    market risk premium, 92
  and psychological factors affecting
    investors, 106
  in put and call options
    in covered option writing, 397
    hedging of, 390–392
    in naked position, 389–390
    in spreads, 392–395
  random, 108–110
    elimination of, 560
  reinvestment risk, 153
  rollover risk, 153
  and returns on investment, 105
  security issuer affecting, 119
  sources of, 115–120
  tangible investments as hedge
    against, 533
  tax laws affecting, 120
Risk-adjusted rate of return, on funds,
  458–459
Risk averter investors, 5
Risk indifferent investors, 5
Risk return line, 5
Risk seeker investors, 5, 6
Rollover risk, 153

Sales. *see* Selling
Saving
  as investment objective, 7
  in life insurance policies, 596–598
  for retirement needs, 601–602
Savings accounts, 175–178
  first-in, first-out and last-in, first-out
    methods of balance calculation,
    177
  interest earnings of, 176–178
    compounding of, 176
    from day of deposit to day of
      withdrawal, 176–177
    on minimum balance, 177
Savings banks, 172
Savings bonds, 179–180
Savings and loans banks, 172
Screening with filters, 277
Seats on New York Stock Exchange,
  34

Second homes, investment in, 512–514
Secondary market, definition of, 32
Sector funds, 449
Securities
  convertible, 367–375
  discount, 134–135
  interest-bearing, 135–137
  leverage-inherent, 13, 353–433
  as loan collateral, 185
  non-Treasury-issued, 181
  option, 356–361
  in random diversification, number to
    hold, 109–110
  regulation of, 41–44
  rights to, 366–367
  of Treasury, 178, 206–208
  warrants to, 361–366
Securities Act of 1933, 41
Securities Exchange Act of 1934, 41–42
Securities and Exchange Commission,
  41–42
Securities Investor Protection Act of
  1970, 44
Securities Investor Protection
  Corporation, 44
Securities market line, 242–248, 516
  in evaluation of fund performance,
    457–458
  ex-ante, 457–458
  ex-post, 457–458
  shifts in, 246–247
  use of, 247–248
Security analyst, job of, 8
Security issuer, risks related to, 119
Self-directed investment plans
  pooling arrangements in, 481–485
    investment clubs, 482–484
    money manager limited
      partnerships, 484–485
  for retirement needs, 602–604
Selling
  on best-effort basis, 19
  of put and call options, 383–384
  and ratio of net working capital to
    sales, 268
  and ratio of odd lot sales to
    purchased, 297
  and ratio of price to sales, compared
    to price to earnings ratio, 276
  in short position, 46–48
  of commodity futures, 410
  of odd lots, 298
Semistrong form of efficient market
  hypothesis, 316–318

Serial redemption of corporate bonds,
  201
Series EE Treasury bonds, 179–180
Series HH Treasury bonds, 180
Settle price, in commodity futures,
  409–410
Share
  in earnings or asset distributions,
    right of stockholders to, 232–
    233
  of real estate investment trusts, 468
  and equity per share, 474
Shareholders, equity of
  in business balance sheet, 262
  in debt/equity ratio, 270–271
  in real estate investment trusts,
    474
  return on, 272–274
Short position, 46–48
  in commodity futures, 410
  mechanics of, 47
  in odd lots, 298
Short-term debt instruments, 10, 11
Silver, as tangible investment, 540–541
Single-family homes, investment in, 501
Single-purpose real estate investment
  trusts, 475
Sinking funds of corporate bonds, 201
Sleep insurance on municipal bonds, 218
Slope of yield curve, 304
Social Security benefits in retirement,
  600–601
Software of personal computers, on
  investments, 54–55
Solvency of company, 270–271
Sotheby's Art Index, 542
Specialists
  on New York Stock Exchange, 35
    day in life of, 36–37
  in tangible investments, 474
Specialized funds, 449–450
Speculation
  in commodity futures, 415–416
  in common stocks, 236
  in index futures, 427–429
  as investment objective, 7
Split of stocks, 233
Spreads
  in futures, 381
  in put and call options, 392–395
    bull and bear, 395
    maturity, 393–394
    neutral, 394
    volatile, 394–395

Stamp collections, as tangible investment, 544–545

Standard deviation, in risk measurement, 104

Standard and Poor
  debt instrument ratings, 154–155
  investment advisory service, 51
  preferred stock ratings, 344–345
  stock index, 64–65

Statement of income, 265–268

Stock(s)
  charts and graphs on, 309–314
  common, 11–12. *see* Common stocks
  convertible, 13
  dividends of, 233, 235
  Dow Jones Averages on, 53, 63–64
  in efficient markets, 315–320
  fundamental analysis of, 261–286
  of gold mining companies, investment in, 539
  market indexes on, 63–65
  preferred, 12–13. *see also* Preferred stocks
  price of. *see* Price, of stocks
  splits of, 233
  Standard and Poor index on, 64–65
  synthetic, 392–393
  technical analysis of, 295–320

Stockbroker (s)
  in commodity futures trading, 410–412
  factors in section of, 40–41
  of full-service firms, 38–39
  job of, 8
  of limited-service firms, 39–40
  in New York Stock Exchange, 34–35

Stockbrokerage firms
  liquid assets offered by, 174
  registered representatives of, 8
  types of, 38–39

Stockholders
  of common stocks, rights of, 230–233
  of preferred stocks, rights of, 331–334

Stop orders, 49, 575

Store of value, 170

Straight preferred stocks, 336–339

Strike price of option securities, 357
  and market price of underlying security, 359

Strong form of efficient market hypothesis, 318

Subordinated debentures, 198–199

Super Bowl results, and market activity, 308

Supply and demand factors
  in gold as tangible investment, 536–537
  in price of housing, 497–499

Support and resistance lines, in price graphs, 310–311

Syndication of limited partnerships, public and private, 479

Synthetic stocks, 392–393

Take delivery, in option contract settlement, 387–388

Tangible investments, 11, 14, 492–549
  advantages of, 530–533
  antiques as, 543
  artworks as, 543
  collectibles and hobbies as, 544–545
  commissions and holding costs in, 534
  definition of, 530
  diamonds and other precious gems as, 541–543
  direct enjoyment of, 531
  disadvantages of, 533–535
  as display of wealth, 531
  fraud in, 535
  gold as, 535–539
  as hedge, 532–533
  investment characteristics of, 531–533
  as needed item, 531
  in portfolio diversification, 533
  price volatility of, 534
    of gold, 536
  real estate as, 492–527
  resale markets in, 534–535
  returns on, 531–532
    compared to returns from intangibles, 532
  silver and other precious metals as, 539–541
  specialized knowledge in, 534
  use characteristics of, 530–531

Tax laws, 21
  on bonds
    compared to preferred stocks, 337–339
    municipal, 215–216
  on buy-and-hold approach to portfolio management, 506–507
  and CATs and TIGRs, 211
  changes in, and risk of investment, 120

Tax laws, *continued*
  on estate planning, 567
  income tax, 21–24, 65
  on individual retirement accounts, 171, 602–604
  on investment clubs, 484
  on life insurance, 597
  on limited partnerships, 478, 481
  on personal residence, 499–500
  on real estate investment trusts, 474
  on residential rental properties, 509
  Tax Reform Act of 1986, 23
  on Treasury securities, 207–208
  on vacation homes, 512–513

Technical analysis of stocks, 295–320
  charts and graphs in, 308–314
  pressure indicators in, 296–308

Telephone transactions, in mutual funds, 451

Term life insurance, 595–596
  compared to whole life insurance, 596–598

Third market, 38

TIGRs (Treasury investment growth receipts), 208–211

Time graphs on price of stock, 309

Time value of money, 77–86
  applied to lottery winnings, 85
  determining future values, 77–81
  determining present values, 81–83

Times-interest-earned ratio, 272

Timing of portfolio changes, 567–569
  advantages and disadvantages of, 568
  difficulty of, 568–569
  empirical analysis of, 568–569
  market timing in, 567
  mechanical (formula) plans in, 570–572

Titanium, as tangible investment, 541

Total debt ratio, 270–271

Trading
  of futures, 410–413
    buyers and sellers in, 410
    in organized exchanges, 413–415
    speculative, 415–416
  of mutual funds
    fund switching in, 451
    telephone transactions in, 451
  on New York Stock Exchange, 34
  of put and call options, 384–385
    buyers and sellers in, 386–387
    commissions in, 388
    covered option writing in, 397–399
    strategies in, 388–397

Trading, *continued*
  of rights, 366
  of warrants, 363
Transactions, with liquid assets,
    168–169
  from checking account, 174
Treasury investment growth receipts
    (TIGRs), 208–211
  commissions and fees in, 211
  popularity of, 210–211
  safety of, 210–211
  tax laws on, 211
Treasury securities, 178–180, 206–208
  bonds and notes with short remaining
    maturities, 179
  collateralized Treasury receipts
    (CATs), 208–211
  historical returns on, 89–90
  interest rate futures contracts on,
    420–421
  in option-bills portfolio, 399–400
  purchases of, 208
  quotations on, 207–208
  Series EE bonds, 179–180
  Series HH bonds, 180
  tax exempt interest paid on, 207–208
  yield of, 138
Treynor Index on funds, 458
Trustee
  of corporate bonds, 196
  of trusts, 468
Trusts, 468–478
  bond index trusts, 472
  "double play trusts," 473
  GNMA trusts, 470–472
  "Jefferson Trust," 472
  liquid investment trusts, 472
  municipal bond trusts, 468–470
  private, 468
  public, 468
  real estate investment trusts, 474–477
  unit investment trusts, 468–473
12b-1 plan, in open-end funds, 445

Underlying securities, 359
  convertible securities exchanged for,
    367–375
  options to, 356–361

Underlying securities, *continued*
  put and call options concerning,
    338–359
  rights to, 366–367
  warrants to, 363–366
Underwriting, 19
Unit (s), of unit investment trusts, 468
Unit investment trusts, 468–473
  bond index trusts, 472
  GNMA trusts, 470–472
  liquid investment trusts, 472
  municipal bond trusts, 468–470
  units of, 468
United States Treasury securities. *see*
    Treasury securities
Universal life insurance, 598
Uptick rule, 46

Vacation homes, investments in,
    512–514
  appeal of, 513–514
  tax laws on, 512–513
Value
  of common stocks, book value per
    share, 264–265
  compound, 79, 84–85
  of convertible securities, 370–372
  formula
    of option securities, 357
    of rights, 366–367
  future, 77–81
  market. *see* Market value
  present, 81–83
  and time value of money, 77–86
    applied to lottery winnings, 85
    determining future values, 77–81
    determining present values, 81–83
Value Line investment advisory service,
    51
Variable life insurance, 598
Variable ratio plan, 571
Variance, in risk measurement, 103
Variation coefficient, in risk
    measurement, 104
Veterans Administration mortgages, 522
Volatile price of tangible investments,
    534
  of gold, 536

Volatile spreads, in put and call options,
    394–395
Volume of market activity, 301–302
  in advance/decline index, 302
  in on-balance volume index, 301
  and price of stock, 301–302
Voting rights
  of common stockholders, 230–231
  of preferred stockholders, 331

Wall Street Journal, investment
    information in, 51
Wall Street Transcript, investment
    information in, 53
Warrants, 13, 361–366
  characteristics of, 363–366
  sample of, 365
  trading of, 363
Washington Public Power Supply
    System, default on municipal
    bonds, 217
Weak form of efficient market
    hypothesis, 315–316
Wealth, tangible investments as display
    of, 531
Weisenberger *Survey of Investment
    Companies,* 51
Whole life insurance, 596
  compared to term insurance, 596–598
Wilshire 5000 Equity Index, 65

Yield
  of bonds, compared to preferred
    stocks, 337
  curve on, 157–160
    inverted, 158
    slope of, 304
  of debt instruments. *see also* Debt
    instruments, yield of
  of preferred stocks
    compared to bonds, 337
    yield to call calculations in, 337

Zero coupon bonds, 135
  CATs and TIGRs as, 208
  municipal, 208–211
  risk of, 148
  yield to maturity of, 138